D0759399

Egalitarianism and the
Generation of Inequality

Egalitarianism and the Generation of Inequality

HENRY PHELPS BROWN

CLARENDON PRESS · OXFORD

1988

Oxford University Press, Walton Street, Oxford OX2 6DP
Oxford New York Toronto
Delhi Bombay Calcutta Madras Karachi
Petaling Jaya Singapore Hong Kong Tokyo
Nairobi Dar es Salaam Cape Town
Melbourne Auckland
and associated companies in
Berlin Ibadan

Oxford is a trade mark of Oxford University Press

Published in the United States
by Oxford University Press, New York

© Henry Phelps Brown 1988

All rights reserved. No part of this publication may be reproduced,
stored in a retrieval system, or transmitted, in any form or by any means,
electronic, mechanical, photocopying, recording, or otherwise, without
the prior permission of Oxford University Press

British Library Cataloguing in Publication Data
Brown, Harry Phelps
Egalitarianism and generation of inequality.
1. Income. Distribution. Theories
I. Title
339.2'01
ISBN 0-19-828648-1

Library of Congress Cataloging in Publication Data
Brown, Henry Phelps, Sir, 1906–
Egalitarianism and the generation of inequality.
Bibliography: p. Includes index.
1. Equality—History. 2. Income distribution—History. 3. Wealth—History. I. Title.
JC575.B74 1988 320'.01'1 88-9888
ISBN 0-19-828648-1

Printed and bound in Great Britain by
Biddles Ltd, Guildford and King's Lynn

UNIVERSITY LIBRARY
Lethbridge, Alberta
190526

ACKNOWLEDGEMENTS

I have been greatly helped by many friends and advisers. My knowledge of the relevant statistics, both the sources for them and their interpretation, was gained when I had the advantage of serving on the Royal Commission on the Distribution of Income and Wealth under the chairmanship of Lord Diamond, whose insistence on the highest standards of objectivity and professionalism made the output of the Commission as instructive as it was comprehensive. A number of economists who are specially equipped in mathematical analysis have been patient in commenting on ideas I have proposed to account for the formation of distributions, and I am glad to record my indebtedness if I may do so without implicating them in the notions with which I have persisted: David Champernowne, John Creedy, Peter Hart, Harold Lydall and David Worswick. Part II has gained greatly besides from the time and care that David Worswick has devoted to reading the whole text and enabling me to improve it at a number of points. Part I has gained likewise from the care with which it has been read, and commented upon in detail, by Kenneth Morgan, who has made me free of his own outstanding knowledge of the later history; and Jane Morgan has given me encouragement as well as guidance throughout a long undertaking. On the Tudor evidence I have been helped by the advice and comments of C. S. L. Davies and P. A. Slack. How heavily I have drawn on P. H. Lindert's recension of English statistics of income will be apparent, and I am grateful to him for making publications by himself and J. G. Williamson available to me. Other American scholars whom I want to thank for generously providing materials and discussion are H. M. Douty, David H. Fischer and Seymour Martin Lipset. I also owe a number of improvements to the comments of learned referees. The responsibility for the faults that remain in the text after all that these many experts have done to improve it remains my own. Throughout the four years and more in which this task has occupied me, the helpfulness and efficiency of my secretary Victoria Banbury have been unfailing.

Authors often conclude their acknowledgements with a tribute to the forbearance of their wives. If they are like me, they do so with good reason. Work on this book has for long been an absorbing preoccupation, in which I could not have indulged myself had it not been for my wife's toleration and support. What is offered to the reader here is in that sense a joint product.

H. P. B.

CONTENTS

ix

INTRODUCTION

The aspiration to greater equality has become widespread in contemporary societies. That governments should act 'to secure a fairer distribution of income and wealth in the community' (Royal Commission 1975: v) is not maintained by socialists alone, but is believed throughout the political spectrum from the centre leftwards. In the United Kingdom, the two most influential restatements of socialist or social democratic principles in the present century have both found their central and animating purpose in the pursuit of equality. Tawney's *Equality* (1931) was a humanist manifesto that found in material equality the necessary condition for a society of freely and fully developed individuals living in relations with one another unvitiated by the class divisions, the snobbery and the servility engendered by contrasts of wealth. 'The reason for equalizing, as means and opportunity allow, the externals of life is . . . to free the spirit of all' (pp. 289, 291). In his work on *The Future of Socialism*, Crosland (1956), found in 'the search for equality' the aim that, of all the basic socialist aspirations, emerged as foremost once the welfare state had been achieved:

'The socialist seeks a distribution of rewards, status and privileges egalitarian enough to minimise social resentment, to secure justice between individuals, and to equalise opportunities; and he seeks to weaken the existing deep-seated class stratification, with its concomitant feelings of envy and inferiority, and its barriers to uninhibited mingling between the classes. This belief in social equality, which has been the strongest ethical inspiration of virtually every socialist doctrine, still remains the most characteristic feature of socialist thought today. (Crosland 1956: 103, 113)

Crosland was following the leader of the Labour Party, Hugh Gaitskell, who had written early in the 1930s that

a Socialist party is different from other parties not because it offers a different mechanism for the same object, but because the object itself is different. Even economic planning, the institutional machinery of the Socialist State, is not a monopoly of Socialism and can exist without Socialism . . . But in the goal of equality, the determination to uproot the conditions of economic injustice, lies the true characteristic of a Socialist. (Durbin 1985: 128)

But the appeal of equality is not confined to socialists, or to the countries in which political parties are committed to explicitly egalitarian policies: a sense that existing inequalities are incompatible with humanitarian, democratic or religious principles is diffused more widely. A highly professional as well as judicious American economist, at one time chairman of the President's Council of Economic Advisers, Arthur Okun (1975: 68, 118), after noting that the top 1 per cent of families in the United States 'have as much after-tax income as nearly all the families in the bottom 20 per cent', exclaimed: 'That seems terrible to me': 'the society that stresses equality and mutual respect in the domain of rights must face up to the implications of these principles in the domain of dollars'. The Roman Catholic Bishops of the United States, in the first draft of their Pastoral Letter on *Catholic Social Teaching and the US Economy* (National Conference 1984), after setting out the complex criteria of distributive justice, beginning with 'the basic moral equality of all human beings', concluded that 'the level of inequality in income and wealth in our society and even more the inequality on the world scale today must be judged morally unacceptable according to these criteria' (pp. 97–100). 'In our judgement, the distribution of income and wealth in the United States is so inequitable that it violates [the] minimum standard of distributive justice' (p. 202). The text finally adopted, it is true, repudiates outright egalitarianism, but still finds that 'alleviating poverty will require fundamental changes in social and economic structures that perpetuate glaring inequalities'. The 'institutional relationships that distribute power and wealth inequitably must be examined and revised if we are to meet the demands of basic justice' (National Conference 1986: paras. 187, 76).

That existing inequalities should be reduced not only has come to be widely, and often deeply, believed, but also is tacitly accepted in practice by some who do not endorse it in principle. At least, measures designed to improve the lot of the poorest are accepted, even when they are paid for by graduated taxation of those who are comfortably off. A good many taxpayers, it is true, have come to think that redistribution has gone far enough. There have also always been some who have been opposed to egalitarian measures in principle. But seldom have they confronted it head on: they have found it easier to criticize particular measures. Equality itself seems inherently bound up with justice, and no one stands up to defend injustice. Those who defend inequality in things as they are do not commonly extol it as the shape of things to come.

Equality is sought in a number of fields—equality before the law and in citizenship come at once to mind. But the present work is concerned with the social equality that relates to the distribution of income and wealth, and to the differences of class, opportunity and amenity associated with them. In that application, the norm of equality can be applied in at least three ways, each of which appeals directly to our moral judgement.

One of these is the great initial judgement of fairness or justice, 'like for like'. We hold it wrong to treat two people differently when they are in like case. Justice demands that those guilty of offences of the same gravity shall receive the same penalty, and that the punishment shall fit the crime. No less do we hold that equal achievements should be equally rewarded. If two workers are to be paid differently, that can be only because of some corresponding difference in their product or performance; if women are employed alongside men, and doing the same work with the same efficiency, they must not be paid less because they are women. The whole movement against discrimination—by race, creed, colour or gender—rests upon this principle. To treat people equally in this way may well be to treat them unequally in another: if a number of workers are paid at the same piece-rate, the more industrious or skilful among them will earn more than the others. The principle accepts this outcome as not unfair: what would be unfair would be paying a higher piece-rate to men, say, than to women. The instance reminds us that 'like for like' needs careful formulation, for the payment of lower piece-rates to women has been defended in the past on the ground that the on-costs of employing them are higher—they need more support, or they have a higher rate of turnover. If this were accepted, then the principle of 'like for like' would allow a piece-rate that was reduced so as to offset the difference in cost. The general question this raises is, which differences are admissible grounds for treating people differently, and which not? It is wrong to pay a woman administrator less than her male colleague, but not to exempt women from military service, because in the first case the ground of discrimination, namely gender, is irrelevant to the purpose of the treatment, namely payment for work performed, whereas in the other case it is relevant to the purpose of making soldiers. Formally, the principle of 'like for like' requires that people shall be treated in the same way if they are in the same case in all respects that are relevant to the purpose of the treatment, but only on that condition. This principle of *equal treatment* is the principle of justice.

But egalitarians will feel that it does not take them nearly as far as they want to go. Everyone might be treated in strict accordance with the principle, yet inequalities would remain of a kind that egalitarians find repugnant, even if they could not hold them to be unjust in the strict sense of that term. They feel it unfair that some people should be able to earn so much more than others. They also resent the wealth that some people acquire without commensurate effort, especially what comes to them by inheritance. These outcomes seem unfair, because people do not have equal chances of attaining them. If a lawyer and a labourer are both paid in accordance with the principle of equal treatment, it may still be felt that life has not treated them equally. The lawyer is able to earn as much as he does because his parents sent him to a good school and supported him through lengthy training; the labourer had to turn his hand to whatever jobs he could find as soon as he could leave a crowded local school. How the two would rate relatively to one another if they had started level can only be conjectured. It is this level start that egalitarians want to arrange when they aim at *equality of opportunity*. However fairly the market works, the distribution of income that comes out of it will be unfair until life chances are equalized. If only equality of opportunity could be secured, it has been argued, the inequalities of income and wealth that remained would be acceptable, and would indeed serve a useful purpose, as incentives to exertion. This contention is supported by the general ready acceptance of the winning of a fortune in the football pools, when if the same sum had come into the same hands as a legacy from a rich uncle it would have seemed invidious. The difference is that everyone has the same chance of scooping the pool, whereas the possibility of inheriting a fortune is confined to a privileged few: the attitude taken up towards the fortune depends on the equality or inequality of the chance of receiving it, and not on the extent to which it is deserved or earned, for this is negligible in both cases. If everyone had the same initial chance of getting on in the world, those who got farther on than others would owe their greater income and wealth to their own greater energy and enterprise. They could not be criticized as privileged; on the contrary, their gains would appear as a fair reward for their efforts, and an incentive to others to go and do likewise. So at least the argument has run.

But not all egalitarians would agree. Equality of opportunity, evidently, will result in inequality of achievement; and for many egalitarians the fact that this inequality is between the more and the less able and vigorous, and no longer between the more and the less privileged, will be no sufficient justification. What is still missing is that sense of basic equality between one person and another, irrespective of what happen to be their capacities, for which egalitarians yearn. This dissatisfaction with equality of opportunity is deepened when the possibility of actually attaining it is examined. The difficulty is not only that, whereas equality of treatment can be attained by relatively minor changes in existing arrangements, those required by movement towards equality of opportunity are deep-going. It is rather that we do not know how far we ought to go. The very idea of opportunity implies that people's advancement depends in part on circumstances external to them and beyond their control; for the rest, then, it depends on what they have in them—on how hard they work, for example—and it seems fair enough for their gains to vary with that. But can we really sustain this distinction between the external and the internal, between what is beyond and what is within our control?

This question confronts us when we consider the justification of imposing handicaps to equalize chances. Apart from the sporting purpose of providing an exciting contest, the justification is that the persons handicapped are more proficient, and the others less so, through no merit or fault of their own. This comes out clearly in a race between children, where the younger ones are given a start: it is reckoned no merit of the older ones that their legs are longer, and the handicaps are imposed so as to give all competitors an equal chance of winning, by exerting the determination, energy and fitness that should be in the reach of all alike. The essential is that handicaps are felt to be fair if they offset differences in capability that arise from factors beyond the contestant's own control.

But which factors are and which are not within a person's own control is a question that divides thoroughgoing egalitarians from others, and egalitarians as a whole from their opponents. There will be general agreement that children cannot be held responsible for the amount of resources that their parents devote to their education; but what of their own use, keen or careless, of whatever schooling is provided for them? Some would say that this, clearly, is a matter of personal choice, and that those who decide whether to work hard or not must take the consequences of their decisions. Others, looking at the child who shows no aptitude for his schoolwork or interest in it, say, 'There but for the grace of God go I'; the child's abilities and character contain a large hereditary element, and for the rest, they have been formed by the home environment and treatment by parents and siblings. What is called laziness, on this view, is a defect like lameness, which may be present from birth, or inflicted by mishandling in the early years of life; a child has no responsibility for its capacity to take responsible decisions. In the same way, wrongdoers are seen not as evil but as sick or deformed. No line can ultimately be drawn between, on the one hand, those personal assets and shortcomings such as a hereditary defect or an injury sustained in infancy that are clearly not within a person's power to control, and, on the other, those sources of achievement or failure—that moral fibre—for which people are commonly given the credit or the blame.

If, then, all a person's capabilities, physical, mental and emotional, are regarded as the product of heredity and environment, the person himself or herself remains as a centre of consciousness without distinguishing characteristics. So envisaged, every human being, as such, deserves as much esteem as any and every other, because all share a common humanity, and indeed exist only as atoms of a common substance. This is the principle of *equality of consideration*. 'All souls are equal in the sight of God.' All that differentiates one man or woman from another, and justifies treating them differently, is extrinsic to the selves at their core between which no distinction of stronger and weaker, or better and worse, can be made. That one person is stupid and another clever appears as no more reason for assigning different incomes to them than that one suffered a crippling accident which the other escaped. If we implicitly retain the notion that one's income and wealth should be commensurate with one's output, but regard that output as dependent on personal attributes that in Robert Owen's words have been made 'for and not by' each person, then the question of justification of inequalities simply no longer arises. Attributions of income and wealth can no longer be regarded as capable of justification. The condition of everyone should be the same, for lack of any reason why it should be different.

Through most of the present century, and especially in the years 1908–14 and 1945–50, public policy in the United Kingdom has promoted all three kinds of equality. A change of government in 1979 brought with it a much greater reorientation than had previously accompanied such changes; the values of self-help and enterprise were raised over those of social welfare and community. But the egalitarian measures of earlier years had rested upon a wide consensus. There was dispute about how far they should go, but the dissidents who would rather have had nothing of the kind were not greatly influential, or persistent in their opposition. Nor were these tendencies confined to one country: the development of social policy in the twentieth century has had its striking similarities throughout the Western world.

But attitudes were not always thus. There have been many times and places in which thoughtful and responsible people saw no need for such measures, would indeed have regarded them as positively noxious. What many people now take for granted as a matter of common decency would have long seemed to many decent people unjust, dangerous, even outrageous. For two thousand years, through the epochs of Greece and Rome and the Middle Ages of Western Europe, the philosophers, pagan or Christian, found the basis of ordered society in the maintenance of inequality. That equality was in some way basic to the notion of justice was never disputed, and justice itself was paramount; but it was held to require the appropriately differentiated treatment of different kinds of people. Nor could there be equality of opportunity, or of consideration, when it was believed that the divine ordering of society had allotted each man his station, and breaking ranks would break society.

It is therefore natural to enquire how the change came about from that outlook to the egalitarianism of our attitudes today. Part I of this work is devoted to that enquiry. The processes of change began within the ancient world itself. Its philosophers' penetrating thought about society makes us more actively aware of our own attitudes and presuppositions, by confronting us with a reasoned case for inequality. But the impulses towards egalitarianism lie deep in human nature, and they broke surface early in men's thought about society. Among the philosophic principles of the ancient world there was one—that of the law of nature and of reason—in which the idea of equality lay compressed. In the great liberation of thought and feeling in the Renaissance and Reformation, this idea escaped and expanded. Other changes at the same time in man's attitude to himself and society made people more concerned with welfare in this world, more aware of their common humanity, more disturbed by the contrast of riches and poverty. But the immediate outcome of the great change of outlook between 1400 and 1600 was political liberalism, and we have to trace the transition from this to social egalitarianism. We have also to follow developments in both ideas and institutions that made possible the practical egalitarianism of the welfare state, as the qualitative concept of rank was supplemented or superseded by a quantitative measure of monetary income, and as government devised effective forms of tax on income and wealth. Always, our aim will be to seek the causes of the change whereby a policy that was once anathema to enlightened people has come to command the unquestioning support of many of their present counterparts. We seek the causes by looking more closely into the course of events, and trace observed changes back to other underlying changes.

This serves the purpose of all reasoned history, to enable us to understand the working of human affairs somewhat better. 'Social science', Marshall declared;

social science or the reasoned history of man, for the two things are the same, is working its way towards a fundamental unity; just as is being done by physical science, or, which is the same thing, by the reasoned history of natural phenomena. Physical science is seeking her hidden unity in the forces that govern molecular movement; social science is seeking her unity in the forces of human character. To that all history tends; from that proceeds all prediction, all guidance for the future. (Marshall 1897: 121).

However that analogy with physical science may appear after nearly a century of scientific advance, the stress on 'the forces of human character' has proved to hold good for social science. In tracing the history of ideas, we gain insights into human nature as a dynamic force—in its reaction to circumstances, its own persistent drives and its capacity for reasoning, speculation and action on principle. As yet, reasoned history is very far from yielding any unified theory or revealing any grand design; indeed, one of its uses is to save us from accepting any such notions prematurely. But we can trace particular connections—causal links here and there—and knowledge of these tells us what to look for in the situations with which we ourselves have to deal.

Tracing the course of change in attitudes also gives us a more detached view of our own ideas, whatever they may be: it removes the blinkers imposed by what we take for granted, and opens our eyes to the possibility of doing things differently. Ideas of equality gained their hold through a prevalent way of perceiving society. For those who do see society in this way, they seem self-evident; constituted as we are, it seems, we can make no other judgement if we judge at all, just as, when we look at a triangle, Euclid's propositions about it carry instant conviction. But we know that people have not in fact thought and felt like this at all times and places: for the greater part of recorded history, they have judged differently because they saw society differently. The category of 'fairness' may be given to us *a priori*, and as such be the same in all sentient human beings; but in itself it is empty. It has no meaning until we judge that these and these particular arrangements are fair or unfair. How we so judge depends upon our perception of the circumstances in question, and this perception changes with the times: do we see people, for instance, as by nature members of society, allotted a certain status and certain duties within it, or as individuals making their own ways in the world but entering at choice into relations with one another? The diffusion of egalitarian principles is to be understood as a part of social history in the widest sense.

This historical study is necessary also for an appraisal of egalitarianism as it stands today. Until we have entered into minds that saw human affairs so differently from ourselves, we cannot assess our own habits of thought. We need also to trace the process by which outlooks have changed; we cannot escape from our own unexamined presuppositions until we have drawn out some of the influences that have instilled them. We must not assume that this change was in the direction of enlightenment. Those to whom it seems palpably and monstrously unfair that the richest 5 per cent among us should hold half of all personal wealth will see a mounting will to change this as part of a general course of liberalization and humanization; they should make the acquaintance of people no less well disposed than ourselves who would not at all have approved what passes for humane and fair with us. But no less, those who see the advance of egalitarianism as insidious populism, sapping self-reliance and loosening the bonds of society, can at least see why so many people have come to think otherwise.

But not only is our field of view widened; we can also see particular issues more clearly. Ideas such as justice and equality can be formulated in general terms, and as such they lend themselves to discussion, but this too easily becomes a matter of semantics. A more definite object is provided by the meaning that particular people have attached to equality in particular times and places. That meaning is shown by their practice. It is brought out by the changes of content that are assignable to particular influences. Our assessment of a belief depends on our understanding of how it came to be held.

This is one aspect of the general principle that our perception of any position, material or intellectual, varies with our belief about its origins. An account, however careful, of things as they are does not of itself show us what to do about them. The study of the past is a way of diagnosing the present: it increases our powers of observation, and brings out the processes that drive on the film of which the current state of affairs is only one still. Those who doubt the significance of our view of the past for our understanding of the present should consider the concern of dictators to rewrite the history of their countries. In part, their aim may be simply to show how necessary and beneficial they are, how much improvement they have made. But they also find it necessary to account for past happenings in ways that agree with the theory that legitimizes their own power: otherwise, if people were free to interpret their past in whatever way seemed to them intelligible, the authority of the dictators would be undermined. The past, it is true, does not speak for itself—our understanding of it depends on the framework of ideas that we bring to it. But whatever interpretation we put upon it affects our assessment of the world about us.

That assessment also depends on our detailed knowledge of present circumstances. It might be held that this is unnecessary. Egalitarianism, it might be held, is a moral judgement, and as such is independent of the facts of particular cases. If concentration of wealth is unfair, its unfairness does not rise or fall with the percentage of all wealth that is held by the top 5 per cent, any more than the wickedness of cruelty to children varies with the number of children who suffer. But there are two reasons why the affirmation of a moral principle in general terms is no guide to policy. One is straightforward and will be generally agreed. This is simply that the effectiveness of any policy depends on its fitting the circumstances to which it is to be applied. It can hardly be designed to fit them without an understanding of the way in which they have come to be what they are. If governments are to take action with the object of making the distributions of income and wealth less unequal, they need to know at what points to intervene, and in what way. Their action, however successful in achieving its aim, will certainly have other effects as well, and what these may be can be foreseen or identified only out of knowledge of the processes that form the distributions. It is a commonplace that successful surgical intervention requires knowledge of anatomy and physiology. The purpose of the statistical studies that form Part II of this work is to provide some counterpart in respect of the distribution of income and wealth.

The second reason is another aspect of the first, but goes deeper. We have already contended that judgements of fairness, if they are to have content, must be judgements about particular arrangements. The judgements on which we act must be formed as we envisage actual circumstances. We cannot decide practical policy by invoking general principles, because we do not really know what those principles themselves import, until we have applied them to the facts of a case. If this were not so—if we could proceed simply by invoking principles that remained unaffected by our use of them—then there would be no such thing as case law. As each case arises, judges purport to apply to the facts of it an existing body of principles, but their decision may come to be cited as an addition to that body or a modification of it.

It is the same with egalitarian principles. Take that of equal treatment, in its application to the employees of a firm. Here we may take it to mean 'equal pay for equal work'; but what is this work? If it can be measured simply by a physical product, then the principle says only that all who turn this product out must be paid at the same piece-rate. But the work of a particular employee is not usually to be evaluated so impersonally: he or she may exert an influence on fellow-workers, or after long service may contribute experience—a contribution that it is desired to recompense even though physical output falls off with advancing years. It is not enough, then, to aim to be fair. Is it our aim to set an impersonal rate of pay for the job, or do we want to assign the individual employee a place appropriate to his or her capability and length of service, within a graded structure? Consider again the task of selecting applicants for a limited number of places. The principle of equal opportunity forbids giving preference to those of a certain ethnic or social type: so far, negatively, its meaning is clear. But suppose it is put to us that some of the applicants are less well qualified only because they have not enjoyed the same educational opportunities as the others: if we are really to avoid discriminating against them, must not we find some extra marks for them—though that will mean denying places to some other applicants who are better qualified as they stand? That is to say, does equal opportunity entail 'positive discrimination'? That one's principles can be assessed only as they are filled out in their application to particular situations becomes the more apparent when we consider how often a conflict of principle arises. If we find, for example, that the extension of education increases the inequality of earnings, how far do we wish to make opportunities more equal at the cost of greater inequality of condition?

There are also the effects of an intervention to be taken into account, and not only those at which it is aimed. Many egalitarians have allowed that discouraging vigorous people from getting rich, and subsidizing the less vigorous, would reduce incentives—and, if it did, that the average level of material welfare would be lowered. Is it then our aim to establish greater equality at whatever level? Do we hold it better that all be equally poor than that the average be higher, but some rise above and the rest fall below it? if we do not accept that, we have to judge whether each proposed intervention, in specified circumstances, will on balance make an improvement.

This means that we cannot treat the task of egalitarianism as if it were simply to redistribute a given total, as if we were rearranging piles of bricks. Its measures entail intervention in an organism that has laws of its own being, and will react in various ways. Existing inequalities are generated by the living economy. Its processes are persistent. They spring from the common propensities and the variety of human nature, impressed on the state of affairs by the unceasing activities of millions of persons seeking their own aims in their particular situations. Their actions can be channelled and deflected, but not shaped like inert matter. Prescription, or surgery, must be based on physiology.

For all these reasons, Part II is devoted to a study of the distributions of income and wealth in the living economy—of what they are like, and how they are formed. Only in the light of such a study can we proceed finally to an assessment of egalitarianism as a practical policy.

Such an assessment is attempted in Part III, which considers contemporary egalitarianism in its application to contemporary economies. This part rests upon the studies in the two preceding parts of the content and origins of egalitarianism, the extent of existing inequalities, and the process by which they have been and are generated. It asks how far change is desirable, and practicable. There is a case to show that the present state of affairs must be accepted as inevitable, or even upheld as the necessary condition for the fulfilment of other accepted purposes. But, recognizing that within egalitarianism there lies an unassailable core of values, we shall ask how they can be most fully realized.

Evidently, this account of the present undertaking is a commitment to a broad survey. It is naturally such, because its theme penetrates all the life of the community in all its aspects, social and political as well as economic. The view on which a judgement on equality is based is bound to be synoptic. But this requirement brings dangers with it. The survey can give only a few sentences to matters on which treatises have been amassed. The author, flying a high-level reconnaissance, is conscious of looking down on many fields, to each of which scholars have devoted a lifetime, only to feel at the last how much more there still is to do. He is bound to acquire a heightened respect for the work of others, and an increased awareness of the limitations of his own. He must recognize that the conspectus he has undertaken carries a liability to superficiality, and biased selection of particulars.

Yet nothing less than a comprehensive view will do. If we confine ourselves to intensive studies, we may miss insights that are yielded only to a wider perspective. The synoptic view not only offers the benefits of the comparative method, but presents to the eye those tendencies which, though general and persistent and therefore powerful, are inconspicuous in any one instance. It is the means of establishing the processes by which inequality has been generated in communities in many places and periods. It illuminates beliefs about equality by suggesting how changes in them have come about. There can be no doubt of its potential value.

PART 1

The Rise of Egalitarianism

1

Early principles of Equality and Inequality

Any survey of the ideas that people have held about equality must begin with the Greeks. Their city-states confronted them with the basic issues that still concern us. The democracy of Athens achieved an equality of citizenship that has remained an archetype and an inspiration ever since. But this equality obtained only in certain respects and within certain limits. The Greeks distinguished sharply between different types of person, and thought it only right and proper to treat them differently. This inequality of treatment they endorsed in the name of justice, an endorsement that with Aristotle included the justification of slavery. But they also saw a persistent source of disruption in the existence of wealth and poverty side by side within the state, and some proposals were made to limit the extent of inequality, or to ward off the clash of extremes by strengthening the middle ranks.

Opposed to the salient differences between one human being and another is the consideration that all are human. This was brought home to the Greeks by the value that they set upon individuality and their sense of the abilities that distinguished mankind from the rest of creation. In this recognition of the unique qualities common to the species lay a principle of egalitarianism that was to exert a hold on the minds of centuries to come. It was enunciated by the Stoics. From them, the Roman jurists derived and transmitted to posterity a faith in the entitlement of all human beings to equality of consideration, simply in virtue of their humanity. From the jurists, in turn, the doctrine reached the medieval Schoolmen.

But with them we come back to the endorsement of inequality, if on different grounds. What is seen to justify inequality of treatment now is not the difference of human capacity, but the need to maintain the appointed order of society. The different ranks of society are seen as the organs of one body, or as the levels of a structure of authority. On either way of looking at them, they are not to be tampered with, although the contrast of wealth and poverty should be softened by charity. An important task for us later will be to see what forces broke up this well-rounded conception of the function of inequality.

1.1. The Greek View of Inequality

The Greeks were very conscious of the difference between the ways of life that people led, and the types of personality that went with them. There followed corresponding differences in the way it was proper to treat people. A hierarchy of obligation was recognized, according to the degree of kindred and affinity. In his study of *Greek Popular Morality in the Time of Plato and Aristotle* Sir Kenneth Dover has shown how

> it may be said in broad terms . . . that an Athenian felt that his first duty was to his parents . . . his second to his kinsman, and his third to his friends and benefactors; after that, in descending order, to his fellow-citizens, to citizens of other Greek states, to *barbaroi* and to slaves. It may be observed that his wife and children cannot easily be fitted into his hierarchy . . . (Dover 1974: 273).

The scale of duties implied a corresponding scale of rights for different types of person. Yet there was an important sense in which equality of rights and treatment was observed among the citizens of Athens. It is true, they were a restricted class. Only those men were citizens who had certain qualifications. Beyond them — it was taken for granted — were all women, but also all farmers, labourers, mechanics, freedmen, slaves and aliens. Within the pale of citizenship, however, there was this basis of equality, that there was no clash of interests between employers and workers. The manual work was done by non-citizens; the citizen depended on no one other man for his livelihood. It was natural, therefore, for the citizens to enjoy equality — before the law, in the discussion of public affairs and in access to public office.

For both Plato and Aristotle, equality was a major issue. They differed in many respects, Plato a visionary philosopher vehemently critical of democracy and Aristotle a scientifically minded researcher into things as they are, whose views on human institutions were judicious and practical. But in what they had to say about equality, they largely agreed. Nor, it seems, did their views differ from what may be inferred about those of Athenian citizens generally (Dover 1974: 279).

A common starting point was that the differences between people are so fundamental and — this is the essential — so inherent, so innate, as almost to divide mankind into sub-species. These differences are found especially in the capacity to control oneself so as to lead a full and wholesome life. Education could do much to develop those powers of self-control, but only so far as the potential for development was there from the first.

Plato proposed two myths to bring home to people this priority of the genetic constitution. One, designed especially to convince them that all the 'nurture and education which we gave them was only something they seemed to experience as it were in a dream', told them that 'in reality they were the whole time down inside the earth, being moulded and fostered while their arms and all their equipment were being fashioned also; and at last, when they were complete, the earth sent them up from her womb in the light of day'. The other myth related 'that all of you in this land are brothers; but the god who fashioned you mixed gold in the composition of those among you who are fit to rule, so that they are of the most precious quality; and he put silver in the Auxiliaries, and iron and brass in the farmers and craftsmen'. Although children will usually be like their parents, sometimes it may happen that a golden parent has a silver child — or, we may take it, a child of iron or brass; and conversely, parents may have children of nobler metal than their own. But whatever the metal of the child turns out to be, he (there is no mention of daughters here) must be rigorously assigned to 'the station proper to his nature' (Plato's *Republic*, 1941 edn.: X, 414, 415).

The same belief in deep-going differences of nature underlies Aristotle's justification of slavery:

It is both natural and expedient for the body to be ruled by the soul, and for the emotional part of our natures to be ruled by the mind, the part which possesses reason. The reverse, or even parity, would be fatal all round. This is also true as between man and the other animals; for tame animals are by nature better than wild, and it is better for them all to be ruled by man, because it secures their safety. Again, as between male and female the former is by nature superior and ruler, the latter inferior and subject. And this must hold good of mankind in general. Therefore whenever there is the same wide discrepancy between human beings as there is between soul and body or between man and beast, then those whose condition is such that their function is the use of their bodies and nothing better can be expected of them, those, I say, are slaves by nature. It is better for them, just as in the cases mentioned, to be ruled thus. Aristotle's *Politics*, 1981 edn.: I, v, 1254, b2, b16)

Each person, on this view, was born with a particular, highly differentiated, constitution. This constitution provided that person with an aptitude for a certain kind of activity, to which he or she was also confined. Education was of the greatest importance, but it could only develop aptitudes implanted at birth: the notion of the *tabula rasa*, or even of a general endowment of ability that education can develop in various directions and degrees, was unknown to the Greeks. It is 'part of nature's intention to make the bodies of free men to differ from those of slaves—. . . Suppose that there were men whose bodily physique showed the same superiority as is shown by the statues of gods, then all would agree that the rest of mankind would deserve to be their slaves' (*Politics*, 1981 edn.: I, iv, 1254, b.32).

But the inequality of man is not only innate: it is also imprinted by education and occupation. It may happen, said Plato, that

the lion is brow-beaten and schooled from youth up to become an ape. Why, again, is mechanical toil discredited as debasing? . . . Is it not simply when the highest thing in a man's nature is naturally so weak that it cannot control the animal parts but can only learn how to pamper them? . . . Then, if we say that people of this sort ought to be subject to the highest type of man, we intend that the subject should be governed, not . . . to his own detriment, but on the same principle as his superior, who is himself governed by the divine element within him. (Plato's *Republic*, 1941 edn.: IX, 590)

Manual workers are types inherently incapable of subduing their own animal passions and leading their lives in the light of divinely instilled reason: better for everyone, themselves included, that they be subordinated to and ruled by those who are thus capable.

Aristotle's view was even more ruthless. He saw it as 'quite impossible, while living the life of mechanic or hireling, to occupy oneself as virtue demands'. Even 'the skilled mechanic is in a restricted sense in a condition of slavery'. For a master, so much as to know how to do a servant's work 'is simply slave-like' (Aristotle's *Politics*, 1981 edn.: III, v, 1278a; I, XIII, 1260 a36; III, iv, 1277 a33). All manual toil was debasing. The good citizen and free man was a man of leisure. Those who, in our eyes, formed the productive labour force were differentiated and degraded, by their occupations.

These views of the vast difference between people led to a particular conception of justice, that is, of what constituted fair dealing between one person and another. For both Plato and Aristotle, justice consisted of the meetings of those claims only that are proportionate to the virtue of the claimants.

Some of the political rights recognized in Athenian democracy disregarded that qualification, and Plato attacked them accordingly. In Book VIII of *The Republic*, it is observed by Vlastos (1981; 193–4),

Plato is saying that 'equality' (i.e. equal awards) should be given only to 'equals' (i.e. to those whose claims are equal). But since the democrats would be sure to retort, 'But all citizens do have equal claims', Plato also expects the reader . . . to understand him to be saying that the only relevant claims are those of merit (arete) — excellence at the job for which nature has fitted one. If Plato is right (and there is nothing on which he has greater confidence of being right), then the rule of distributive justice which he takes to govern the democratic state — 'equality for all be they equal or unequal in merit' — is viciously wrong.

This view Plato expanded in *The Laws* (1970 edn.: VI, 757). 'We use the same term for two concepts of "equality", which in most respects are virtual opposites.' One of these is a simple numerical equality, which would hand out the same to everybody, irrespective of differences in personal quality; but 'indiscriminate equality for all amount to *in*equality, and both fill a state with quarrels between its citizens'. The other concept needs the wisdom of Zeus to apply:

'the general method I mean is to grant much to the great and less to the less great, adjusting what you give to take account of the real nature of each — specifically, to confer high recognition on great virtue, but when you come to the poorly educated in this respect, to treat them as they deserve. We maintain, in fact, that statesmanship consists of essentially this — strict justice. (*Plato's Laws*, 1970 edn.: VI, 757)

Aristotle followed Plato here. 'It is thought', he said, 'that justice is equality; and so it is, but not for all persons, only for those that are equal. Inequality also is thought to be just; and so it is, but not for all, only for the unequal' (Aristotle's *Politics*, 1981 edn.: III, ix, 1280 a7).

So far, we have considered equality and inequality mainly with regard to status and citizenship: one of the most salient forms of inequality, that of wealth, remains to be considered. It came to notice because of its constant threat to divide the city-state by conflict between the rich and the poor. In Plato's *Republic*, Socrates was made to affirm that any state whose citizens were allowed to amass riches would be a state divided — 'not one state, but many: two at least, which are at war with one another, one of the rich, another of the poor . . . This state, then, is in the same precarious condition as a person so unhealthy that the least shock from outside will upset the balance—or, even without that, internal disorder will break out' (Plato's *Republic*, 1941; IV, 422; VIII, 556). He could only advise that his Guardians should exclude all riches from their ideal republic. The Plato of *The Laws*, coming down to earth and framing regulations for men 'born and bred and educated as ours are', set a ratio of four to one (or, according to Aristotle, five to one) between the wealth of the richest and that of the poorest. There would be four property classes, 'to ensure that offices and taxes and grants may be arranged on the basis of what a man is worth . . .'

The citizens must be esteemed and given office, so far as possible, on exactly equal terms of 'proportional inequality' so as to avoid ill-feeling. . . . The lower limit of poverty must be the value of the holding [the inalienable unit allotment of land] . . . The legislator will use the holding as his unit of measure and allow a man to possess twice, thrice, and up to four times its value. If anyone acquires more than this, . . . he should hand over the surplus to the state and its patron deities, thereby escaping punishment and getting a good name for himself. If a man breaks this law, anyone who wishes may lay information and be rewarded with half the amount involved, the other half being given to the gods; then besides this the guilty person must pay a fine equivalent to the surplus out of his own pocket. (Plato's *Laws*, 1970 edn.: V, 740, 744, 745)

Aristotle came even nearer the real world, with a practical and adaptive policy. He was in fact a distributist, as we should say today, and he put forward a proposal for what — if the public revenue were raised substantially from the rich — would be redistribution. The best constitution in his view was a mixed one, made up of democratic and oligarchic forces in balance. Such a constitution would rest upon an economy containing some rich and many relatively poor people, but it would be stable only if it held a broad middle section of modest property-owners. The presence of such a section would bring several advantages:

The state aims to consist as far as possible of those who are like and equal, a condition found chiefly among the middle people . . . It is the middle citizens in a state who are the most secure: they neither covet, like the poor, the possessions of others, nor do others covet theirs as the poor covet those of the rich . . . The addition of [the weight of the middle element] to either side will turn the balance and prevent excess at the opposing extremes. . . . The superiority of the middle constitution is clear also from the fact that it alone is free from fractions.

The very best form of middle people consisted of smallholders — 'an agrarian people is the best' — though this for the special reason that, being scattered over the land, these men would seldom attend the Assembly, and would be content to let offices be filled and business be transacted by wiser men than they.

It was therefore advisable to intervene and actively foster modest property-holding.

Since that is to the advantage of the rich as well as the poor, all that accrues from the revenue should be collected into a single fund and distributed in block grants to those in need, if possible in lump sums large enough for the acquisition of a small piece of land, but if not, enough to start a business, or work in agriculture. (Aristotle's *Politics*, 1981 edn.: IV, xi, 1295 b1, 28, 34; 1296 a7; VI, iv, 1318 b6, 27; VI, v, 1320 a35)

But Aristotle's approval of these capital grants in aid of smallholders and small businesses did not by any means carry with it any approval of redistribution at large. A certain Phaleas of Chalcedon, otherwise unknown, had proposed that the landholdings of all citizens should be made equal, as should be their education. At the base of Aristotle's comments is the belief that this would be contrary to human nature:

While there is certainly some advantage in equality of possessions for the citizens as a safeguard against faction, its efficacy is not really very great. In the first place discontent will arise among the more accomplished people, who will think they deserve something better than equality. . . . Secondly, the depravity of mankind is an insatiable thing. At first they are content with a dole of a mere two obols; then, when that is traditional, they go on asking for more and their demands become unlimited. For there is no natural limit to wants, and most people spend their lives trying to satisfy them. In such circumstances, therefore, a better point of departure than equalizing possessions would be to ensure that naturally reasonable people should not *wish* to get more than their share and that the inferior should not be *able* to; and that can be achieved if they are weaker but not treated unjustly.

When people get 'a free distribution of the surplus . . . they want the same again: this sort of assistance to the poor is like the proverbial jug with a hole in it'.

So Aristotle approved of redistribution only as a means to promote a sturdy independence. Although he thought disparities were dangerous, he was not a simple egalitarian — in a memorable phrase, he declared that 'it is more necessary to equalize appetites than possessions'. But he did put forward a practical plan for transferring resources towards a more equal distribution (*Politics*, 1981 edn.: II, vii, 1267 a37; VI, v 1320 a17; II, vii, 1266 b24).

This account of Greek thought about equality would be misleading if it brought out only the stress it laid on the inequality of man. That stress was the counterpart of the value set upon virtue, and the capacity to lead a good life to the full; it would be a betrayal of standards to accord an equal esteem to persons denied that capacity by nature or occupation. But attitudes were complex then as ever. Other and inconsistent valuations were present. These were of a kind commonly present in thought about human affairs; they were to recur, more distinctly and influentially, in centuries to come. We have seen how, within the bounds of Athenian citizenship, two political principles of equality held good: equality before the law, and equality of opportunity to attain office. That a man's abilities should be recognized by advancement, irrespective of his family connections or wealth, was a principle of limited application at the time, but one of great potential for the lowering of social barriers.

Besides this, the conception that each person was charged by nature with a function to perform might not simply imply disdain for those whose functions were menial: it might also carry approval for all those who faithfully performed an allotted task. They could not exhibit the highest virtue, but they had their place in the scheme of things. Labourer and mechanic, farmer and freedman, even the slave — each can be seen as a member of one corporate body, performing his function within it by doing his proper work. This was Plato's optimistic gloss on the inequality of man. In *The Republic*, he makes Socrates lay it down 'as a universal principle, that everyone ought to perform the one function in the community for which his nature best suited him . . . When each order . . . keeps to its own proper business in the commonwealth and does its own work, that is justice and what makes a just society' (Plato's *Republic*, 1941 edn.: IV, 432, 433).

There was another way in which the harshness of classification was mitigated. 'The categorization of people and the placing of different categories at different points on a scale of moral claims was counteracted . . . by the feeling that it was shameful, cowardly, arrogant or insensitive to exploit the strength of one's own position in order to triumph over the weak' (Dover 1974: 282).

Implicit in this feeling is respect for the weak as a fellow human being. It is not shameful for me to use my strength to kill a fly: it can be shameful to oppress weak men or women only if I ought to have a fellow feeling for them. That feeling was to find expression in the conception of the law of nature that put all persons on an equal footing with one another. The Greeks did not generally think of law in this way, as being one and universal. What struck them was how actual laws differed from place to place: laws meant local customs. But at the end of the line of philosophers, the Stoics did develop the idea of a law of nature, inherent in the very existence of humanity, and valid for all mankind. We go on to ask how the idea of such a law was conceived and transmitted.

1.2. Equality before the Law of Nature

The law of nature begins with the view held among the Greeks, that all things behaved according to the laws of their own being. Implanted in the acorn was the propensity to become an oak. Everything, animate or inanimate, performed its function, or grew and developed, according to a natural law inherent within it. If we rendered the last clause in present-day terms to read 'as it was programmed to do', the inadequacy of our word 'law' for the Greek conception would appear. For our word carries associations of statute law, and the prescription of boundary conditions, the enforcement of prohibitions, whereas what the Greeks meant was the direction of behaviour in a positive and creative sense. Even the concept of 'scientific law' does not convey the capacity for development and self-realization that the Greeks had in mind. The law of nature was the animating principle or soul of the universe. But more than this: it was revealed to man as a guide. Whereas in all objects and beings other than man it operated without the awareness or participation of the subject, man was able to perceive it, at least in part. He could do this because he was, uniquely, gifted with Reason. This gave him the capacity for self-direction. He had only to think for himself: Reason would then show him what was right, and in what direction he ought to move. It would reveal to him some part of the law of nature that was the law of his own being.

This view of the law of nature as revealed by Reason led to a belief in the the equality of man, in two ways. First, it was the distinguishing mark of man that he was gifted with Reason. This set him apart from all animals; but in this all men, as men, were alike, and equal. To be a man was by definition to be so endowed: no question arose of more or less, better or worse. Second, the use of Reason gave man a capacity for self-direction, through knowledge of the good, and the ability to choose. Every man experiences freedom to direct his own conduct under the guidance of Reason. But the same Reason tells him that he must allow the same freedom to others. He must not subordinate their wills to his, or act in such a way as to deny them the scope that he claims for himself. There can be no privilege of rank or status. Men must treat each other as equals.

Thought about the law of nature was linked with the conception of a state of nature. Just as the ability to scan the law of nature is innate in ourselves and anterior to any education or social regulation, so it was conjectured that there was a state of nature in which men lived before ever structured societies were formed. To see what life was like then, the Greeks thought away all the positive law and the customs and acquisitions that regulated human relations in the societies around them. They performed, as we should say, a thought experiment, until the men they were left with had only their innate endowment to direct them. Those men, it seemed, would then of necessity direct themselves by the light of Reason, which would mean, on the grounds we have seen already, that they would, one with another, be free and equal. It is this inference that concerns us here. If men were free and equal under the law of nature, that is where Reason was supreme, then how could the inequalities within existing societies be justified?

This basic challenge to inequality was transmitted to the Middle Ages through two channels: through the Christian Fathers and the Schoolmen, and through Roman law. In the first channel, however, the challenge was stifled as soon as it was posed. For the Christian Fathers, the law of nature became the law of God the Creator. This in itself was a change more of title than of conception. But when the Fathers identified the state of nature with mankind before the Fall, they drew a new inference: they concluded that the institutions of government and the hierarchy of ordered society were the necessary consequence of sin. We have seen that they held slavery to be justified, and this as a punishment for sin; but for the rest, all the weight of authority bearing down through differences in rank was held to be needed to repress and control the wicked propensities of fallen man. No egalitarian case could now be mounted on the contrast between contemporary society and the state of nature.

Nor could any be based on the way in which the Greek conception of natural law as a law of development reached the Schoolmen. This conception had been formulated by Aristotle. When he said that man was a political animal, he meant that it was in the nature of man to form and develop polities or structured societies. We have seen how this thought was absorbed by St Thomas Aquinas. In Aristotle's conception of the nature of man, St Thomas saw the working of that eternal law, in which

all things participate to some degree . . . ; in so far as they derive from it certain inclinations to those actions and aims which are proper to them. But, of all others, rational creatures are subject to divine providence in a very special way; being themselves made participators in providence itself, in that they control their own actions and the actions of others. (*Summa Theologica*, Prima Secundae Parties, qu. XCI, art. 2; in d'Entrèves 1948)

In this way, man as a political animal obeys the divinely ordered law of nature as he builds societies. There is no contrast between a state of nature where the law of nature rules and a manmade society whose inequalities conflict with that law:

The control of one over another who remains free, can take place when the former directs the latter to his own good or to the common good. And such dominion would have been found between man and man in the state of innocence for two reasons. First, because man is naturally a social animal; and in consequence man would have lived in society, even in the state of innocence. Now there could be no social life for people living together unless one of their number were set in authority to care for the common good . . . Secondly, if there were one man more wise and righteous than the rest, it would have been wrong if such gifts were not exercised on behalf of the rest . . . (*Summa Theologica*, Pars Prima, qu. XCVI, art. 4; in d'Entrèves 1948)

This, we now see, is to interpret the inequality of condition in society as the outcome of man's participation in divine providence through his use of the Reason with which he has been divinely endowed. The institutions of ordered society are seen not as having been imposed, but as having evolved, but their origin is no less divine; and there was inequality even before the Fall.

But there was also the second channel, that of Roman law; and here the challenge to inequality was sustained, and destined to resound down the centuries. Roman law from its first systematization was tinctured with belief in the law of nature. The jurists who began to codify Roman law in the later years of the Republic were pupils of the last great school of Greek philosophers, the Stoics, who taught that the revelation of the law of nature to mankind by the light of Reason prescribed to men everywhere a common code of duty. Part of the task of those jurists was to reduce to a single code the diverse rules prevailing in Rome itself and among the neighbouring tribes. They were the more ready to do this because their Stoic training had made them aware of a natural law which would be the same for all men everywhere.

The Stoic theory of the 'common law' was in fact the stimulus which enabled the Romans to transform their system of 'rights', gradually throwing over all that was in the nature of mechanical routine or caste privilege and harmonizing contradictions by the principle of fairness. (Arnold 1911: para. 428)

This was in the days of Cicero. In his treatise on the *Laws*, Cicero set out the Stoic belief in natural law and the equality of man as that was received by the Roman jurists. The case for equality stands on the unique endowment of Reason:

No single thing is so like another . . . as all of us are to one another. . . . And so, however we define man, a single definition will apply to us all . . . Reason, which alone raises us above the level of the beasts . . . is certainly common to us all, and, though varying in what it learns, at least in the capacity to learn it is invariable.

So the discussant Atticus sums up:

How can I help being convinced, when it has just been proved to us, first, that we have been provided and equipped with what we may call the gift of the gods; next, that there is only one principle by which men may live with one another, and that this is the same for all, and possessed equally by all; and, finally, that all men are bound together by a certain natural feeling of kindliness and good will, and also by a partnership in Justice? (*Laws*, XIII, 35; quoted here from Foster 1942: 185–6)

A. J. Carlyle (1903: 9) commented that we are here 'at the beginnings of a theory of human nature and society of which the "Liberty. Equality and Fraternity" of the French Revolution is only the present-day expression'. But this was the philosophy of human equality in which the early Roman jurists were schooled, and which imparted a distinctive unifying principle or axiomatic base to Roman law which it was to transmit to western posterity.

The same philosophy animated the jurists who undertook the great codification of Roman law under Justinian in the sixth century *after Christ*. They recognized the existence of a natural law (*jus naturale*) that was over and above all positive law, even over that of *jus gentium*, or the 'law of the tribes', which contained the rules applicable in common to many different peoples within the empire. The *jus gentium* recognized slavery: natural law did not. For, as Ulpian had written in his day (he died in AD 223), 'by natural law all were born free . . . people were once simply called by the one natural name of "man", and not divided into freemen, slaves, and freedmen' (*Digest of Justinian*, bk. I, tit. 1.4; see Monro 1904). Underlying the great written code was the thought of an unwritten law applicable to all men and at all times. This, moreover, was a higher law. The interpretation, adjustment and application of existing rules must therefore be guided by it. So this process was carried out in a spirit of equity; rights were granted even to the slave, who was allowed to enter as debtor or creditor into contracts.

The thought of a law applicable to all men everywhere had its counterpart in the citizenship of the Roman Empire. The most various people, spread throughout a vast area — for them their whole known world — had been brought into a single state, and shared a common status. It was in accordance with the wishes of the jurists that a great imperial edict of AD 212, the Constitutio Antoniniana, extended citizenship to almost all the inhabitants of the empire as it then stood, in its widest bounds. The universal rule of law was linked with equality of status before it.

That edict of AD 212 did but widen the coverage of the principle of equality that had been present in Roman law from early days. We shall not understand fully how Roman law later became an engine of political change in Europe unless we see how its role in Roman society was different from the role of law in the societies that grew out of the barbarian irruptions. Those societies were habituated to power exerted personally, by feudal lord or king: these high and mighty men held courts, and laws appeared as their will and pleasure. Even in the eighteenth century, Blackstone (1765, Introdn., sect. II) defined the law as a rule which is 'prescribed by some superior and which the inferior is bound to obey'. But Roman law was formulated first when Rome became a republic. 'One may infer', says Tony Honoré,

that the *XII Tables* and the legal profession were regarded as guarantors of the political revolution which was thought to have taken place when the Etruscan kings were expelled and the republic [was] established. In the private as in the public sphere there was a demand for laws public declared as the only techniques for securing limited, aristocratic government and, within the community of heads of families, a free and equal society.* (Honoré 1978: 83)

Honoré goes on to compare the role of law in Rome with its role in the United States, where, equally, a society that had thrown off an external power found its needed basis of authority in the law; and before this law all men—save for some excluded categories—were equal. Roman law became an engine of egalitarianism in a later epoch not only because of its spirit of equity, but also because its principles seemed part of the constitution of a free society.

It was not until a thousand years after Justinian's legal staff had compiled his Code that Roman law attained its widest influence. For the first half of that span it was submerged by the barbarian irruptions. At the end of the eleventh century it was rediscovered. Its principles were expounded and its text was studied minutely at Bologna. Throughout the following century, students repaired there from all over the West; another centre for its teaching arose in Paris; medieval jurists became well acquainted with its principles. When with the passing of feudalism the time came generally for the codification of law, the framework of Roman law was adopted by most European countries, and by Scotland. In England the common law held out, although the same influences were known here, not without some effect. Most important for our purposes, the principles and outlook of Roman law imbued the law schools of the Continent. This may help to explain what may surprise observers from common law countries, that on the Continent lawyers as a profession are by no means identified preponderantly with the political right: rather, the opposite. Their studies have trained them to think of law as finding its ultimate sanction not in the power of a sovereign but in the reason with which nature has endowed all mankind. This higher authority makes no distinction of rank, race or religion between one person and another; for, as Ulpian wrote, 'by natural law all were born free'—free, and in that sense equal.

1.3. The Medieval View of Inequality

The Schoolmen of the Middle Ages developed a positive view of inequality in two closely related ways: they saw society as an organism, and as an order of hierarchy.

The view of society as an organism was developed with care and subtlety by St Thomas Aquinas in the thirteenth century. The individual, he said, is not altogether submerged in the body corporate of the state, but is capable of doing things that the state cannot do; on the other hand, the state is much more than the sum of the individuals who make it up. The soldier can do what an army cannot do; but an army is much more than an aggregate of soldiers. 'There is . . . a whole which has not only a unity of order but also of composition . . . a unity which can be called absolute' (*Commentary on the Nichomachean Ethics*; see d'Entrèves 1948; Introdn. to bk. I, 191-3). In this conception of society, the function of each member was to fulfil an assigned role in co-operation with the other members. Although each member had individual existence, the health and welfare of each could be realized only through the harmony of all. When the analogy with members of a body was pushed further, not only their dependence on one another, but also the inherent differentiation of their function became apparent. A century earlier, John of Salisbury had pressed the analogy closely. The prince, he said, corresponds to the head, the senate to the heart, the exchequer to the belly, the husbandman to the feet and so on. Evidently no question of equality in any qualitative sense can arise between foot and heart; nor can we raise that question between husbandman and senator.

But the picture of differentiation of function is consistent with the notion of order. This was the second way in which society was viewed:

From the notion of an Organism, whose being involves a union of like with unlike, was derived the necessity of differences in rank, profession and estate. So that the individuals, who were the elements in ecclesiastical and political Bodies, were conceived, not as arithmetically equal units, but as socially grouped and differentiated from each other. (F. W. Maitland, in *Introduction* to Gierke 1900: 27-8)

There were different views about how the hierarchical order had been established. The Christian Fathers believed that men in a state of innocence before the Fall had been equal; but with the Fall had come sin and rapine, and God had had to set rulers over men to restrain their wickedness. St Thomas Aquinas also saw the social order as of divine institution; but he saw the ordering as having been a natural development, through the agency of the reason that God had planted in man. When man used his reason in order to find what he must do to promote his well-being, he found he could achieve nothing in a solitary life, for 'nature has destined him to live in society, so that dividing the labour with his fellows each may devote himself to some branch of the sciences, one following medicine, another some other science, and so forth' (*De Regimine Principum*, Litur Primus, Cap. 1; in d'Entrèves 1948: 3-4). Following Aristotle, St Thomas declared 'that Man is naturally a social and political animal, destined more than all other animals to live in community'. But when communities were in this way naturally formed for mutual support, they would as naturally generate their own form of government. The wisest and ablest members would take the lead (*Summa Theologica*, Pars Prima, qu. 96, art. 3, concl.; in d'Entrèves 1948). So there would have been inequality of some sort, even without the Fall.

The establishment of government was not only natural but essential. Without it, the community

would surely disintegrate unless there were one of its number to have a care for the common good: just as the body of a man or of any other animal would disintegrate were there not in the body itself a single controlling force, sustaining the general vitality of all the members . . . Whenever there is an ordered unit arising out of a diversity of elements there is to be found some such controlling influence. In the material universe, for example, there is a certain order of divine providence under which all bodies are controlled by the first or heavenly body. (*De Regimine Principum*, Libre Primus, Cap. 1; in d'Entrèves 1948: 3–4)

The same thought, that the ordering of society was essential to prevent confusion and violence, persisted in Shakespeare's day. He expressed it in the famous speech of Ulysses, in *Troilus and Cressida*. The case is made here not just for a supreme ruler, but for subordination in a gradation of ranks—what Ulysses calls degree—throughout society. No less than St Thomas Aquinas, he holds that the inequalities of society are the counterpart of the ordering of the cosmos:

> The heavens themselves, the planets, and this centre,
> Observe degree, priority, and place . . .
>   O! when degree is shak'd
> Which is the ladder to all high designs
> The enterprise is sick. How could communities
> Degrees in schools, and brotherhoods in cities,
> Peaceful commerce from dividable shores,
> The primogenitive and due of birth,
> Prerogative of age, crowns, sceptres, laurels,
> But by degree, stand in authentic place?
> Take but degree away, untune that string,
> And, hark! what discord follows. . . .
> Force should be right; or rather, right and wrong—
> Between whose endless jar justice resides—
> Should lose their names, and so should justice too.

Troilus and Cressida, I. iii

Such were the two views of society, the organic and the hierarchic. Both accepted, even endorsed, the inequality of man. On the one view, the different organs of the body have different functions: the question is not whether one is greater than another, but how they are to co-operate for the good of the whole body. On the other view, each rank in the hierarchy has its allotted duties and allegiance; correspondingly, it has respect due to it, and protection afforded it; in an ordered scheme it holds its rightful place, needing neither to envy those above, nor to oppress those below.

Neither view challenged the existing inequality of wealth and income. Was this not surprising, when the Schoolmen quoted the authority of the Gospels? For these made it plain that the rich as such were shut out from grace. 'It is easier for a camel to pass through the eye of a needle than for a rich man to enter the Kingdom of God' (Mark 10: 25; also Matthew 19. 24, and Luke 18. 25). 'The young man answered, "I have kept all these [commandments]. Where do I still fall short?" Jesus said to him, "If you wish to go the whole way, go, sell your possessions, and give to the poor, and then you will have riches in heaven; and come, follow me," When the young man heard this, he went away with a heavy heart; for he was a man of great wealth' (Matthew 19: 20-2). Then turning to his disciples he began to speak: How blest are you who are poor; the Kingdom of God is yours . . . But alas for you who are rich; you have had your time of happiness' (Luke 6: 20, 24). 'Next a word to you who have great possessions. Weep and wail over the miserable fate descending on you. Your riches have rotted; your fine clothes are moth-eaten; your silver and gold have rusted away, and their very rust will be evidence against you and consume your flesh like fire' (James 5; 1-3). Vermes (1981: 23) has remarked how, in preaching the immanence of the Kingdom of Heaven, Jesus drew likenesses from 'the landscapes, work-tools and inhabitants of the Galilean country and its lakeside life'. He likened the Kingdom of Heaven to a field, a vineyard, a mustard seed, the net and the catch, the leavening of dough. It was part of this exposition to declare that the Kingdom of Heaven belongs to the little children, and to those who resemble them, the humble and the trusting (Matthew 18: 3-4: Mark 10: 13 ff.). It belongs to the poor: the rich will find it more difficult to enter than the camel to pass through the needle's eye; i.e., they will find it impossible (Matthew 5: 3; Mark 10: 23 ff.; Luke 6: 20). de Ste. Croix (1981: vii, iv) has argued that Jesus was essentially a countryman, who kept out of the towns where he would have encountered the Greek view of life, which saw the poor as contemptible, whereas in the traditional attitude of the Jewish people among whom Jesus moved, poverty with its necessary abstention from self-indulgence was tinged with holiness.

However this may be, the Gospel teachings are the voices of primitive communism, and we are told that the early Christians did have all things in common. 'All those whose faith had drawn them together held everything in common; they would sell their property and possessions and make a general distribution as the needs of each required . . . Not a man of them claimed any of his possessions as his own, but everything was held in common' (Acts 2: 44, 45; 4: 32). Alexander Gray (1946: 53) remarked that 'for centuries one is almost tempted to say that these few verses in the Acts of the Apostles are quoted as frequently as any other passage in the New Testament'. But he also pointed out that the story of Ananias shows that the pooling of resources was not obligatory: those who joined the band of believers might give their all to it if they chose, and some did, but it was not a condition of membership. Gray also noticed the difference between the Beatitudes in St Matthew's gospel, where poverty and hunger are given spiritual meanings, and St Luke's, where they are economic; and, what is more, St Luke adds comminations, in which those who now are rich and well-fed are warned of a reversal of fortunes to come for them as painful as that promised in the Beatitudes for the poor and hungry will be joyful. As author of the Acts, St Luke may have been concerned to impart the same message there. 'His gospel', wrote Gray (1946: 42), 'reveals him as the leveller among the apostles; the passage in the fourth chapter of the Acts, after the manner of myths, served as a rallying cry of all the later egalitarian sects.'

But its influence was partial. Far greater was that of St Paul, and he was emphatic in his insistence that Christians should be no disturbers of the established order, but should submit to 'the powers that be'. 'Every person', he wrote, 'must submit to the supreme authorities. There is no authority but by act of God, and the existing authorities are instituted by Him; consequently anyone who rebels against authority is resisting a divine institution, and those who so resist have themselves to thank for the punishment they will receive' (Romans 13: 1.2; also 1 Peter 2: 13–17). The equality of Christians was within the Church, not within the world. They were all the children of God. By baptism in Christ they entered into a mystical unity. 'There is no such thing as Jew and Greek, slave and freeman, male and female; for you are all one person in Christ Jesus' (Galatians 3: 28; 1 Corinthians 12: 13). Being thus related within the Church, when they came out into the world they could take it as they found it. They not only could, but St Paul taught them that they ought to. 'Pay . . . reverence and respect', he had gone on to say, 'to those to whom they are due' (Romans 13: 7).

In the same way, St Augustine (Lakoff 1967: 126–7) taught that God had not intended that men should rule over men: it was as 'the result of sin' that he ordained inequalities. 'Slaves are, therefore, not to revolt but to remain in subjection, not in crafty fear but in faithful love, until all unrighteousness pass away, and all principality and every human power be brought to nothing, and God be all in all.'

St Paul had not only preached submission to temporal rulers, and the duty of workers to serve even harsh masters zealously: he had also lent his authority to the subordination of half the human race to the other half. There may have been nothing new about his treatment of women, unless in one way it showed more respect for them than was common in his time—'in Christ's fellowship woman is as essential to man as man to woman' (1 Corinthians 11: 11). But for ever after, those who heard the word of God spoken through him were left in no doubt that women stood lower than men in the divine scheme of things. 'Man did not originally spring from woman, but woman was made out of man; and man was not created for woman's sake, but woman for the sake of man' (1 Corinthians 11: 8, 9). That is why men do not cover their heads when they pray, but for women not to cover theirs is shameful. 'A man has no need to cover his head, because man is the image of God, and the mirror of his glory: whereas woman reflects the glory of man' (1 Corinthians 11: 7). Hence the duty of woman to respect their husbands. 'Wives, be subject to your husband as to the Lord; for the man is the head of the woman, just as Christ also is the head of the church'; 'the woman must see to it that she pays her husband all respect' (Ephesians 5: 22, 23, 33; Colossians 3: 18; Titus 2: 5). St Peter added his authority: women should not adorn themselves, as by braiding their hair, but be as 'it was among God's people in days of old: the women who fixed their hopes on Him adorned themselves by submission to their husbands. Such was Sarah, who obeyed Abraham and called him "my master" ' (1 Peter 3: 3–6). There was a reciprocal obligation on husbands to love their wives 'and not be harsh with them' (Colossians 3: 19); but that women were not entitled to equal consideration was made clear by a ban on their speaking in church. 'As in all congregations of God's people, woman should not address the meeting. They have no licence to speak, but should keep their place as the law directs. If there is something they want to know, they can ask their husbands at home. It is a shocking thing that a woman should address the congregation' (1 Corinthians 14: 34, 35). St Paul himself was of the kind that feels 'it is a good thing for a man to have nothing to do with women' (1 Corinthians 7: 1); but men of normal sexuality would continue to find in his teaching an agreeable assurance that their sense of superiority accorded with the intention of the Creator. The authority of the Bible would make it easier for a later generation to affirm the equality of man while taking it for granted that the great principle did not include women or slaves.

We have seen how the Christian Fathers accepted the existing differences of rank and status, from the highest constituted authority down to and even including slavery. These differences had become necessary to control the vicious propensities of human nature after the Fall. But they could not be maintained unless they were supported by corresponding differences of wealth and income. The Christian Fathers therefore held those differences to be just. What the Church came to teach about both property and wages was that their amount should be appropriate to a man's station in life.

As to property, the Christian Fathers, it is true, looked back to a Creation when a beneficent God had made the world for all men to enjoy. 'The only natural condition [was] that of common ownership and individual use' (A.J. Carlyle; quoted in McIlwain 1932: 162). But with the

Fall had come avarice, and the appropriation of private holdings. What sinful man had grasped in this way had to be regulated by positive law, but a good legal title to land did not mean exclusive entitlement in the eyes of God—or, as the Fathers said, according to natural law. For the wealthy to relieve the needy was not mercy but justice, because they were only enabling the needy to partake of what had been created to support them. No one was entitled to more property than would meet his needs and those of his family according to his station in life: anything more than that he held in trust for society, and he must hand its produce back.

But St Thomas Aquinas traversed that position. Instead of seeing private property as a usurpation, in conflict with the Creator's purpose, he argued that it helped to fulfil that purpose. 'Private property is not opposed to natural law, but is an addition to it, devised by the human reason' (*Summa Theologica*, Secunda Secundae Partis, LXVI, art. 2; in d'Entèves 1948). How private property works in this way St Thomas showed in an analysis like that of a modern market economist. The threefold case for it, he contended, is that it provides incentive, promotes the division of labour and ensures freedom from disputes. Under the natural order, material goods are provided for the satisfaction of human needs: and the institution of private property enables those goods to satisfy them more fully. But St Thomas is equally clear that this arrangement in no way removes the claim which every man has on the provision of the resources of the world for each and all that the Creator has made: those with superfluity must help those in need, and if those in desperate need help themselves forcibly, it is no crime.

The upshot is that property is considered as the endowment of a station in life. Its function and justification is that it enables the occupant of that station to perform properly the duties attaching to it. He must not hold more than he needs to that end. But in so far as what he holds does serve that end, he may hold it with a clear conscience: he is even warned not to give so much away in alms that he is left with less than enough to keep up the way of life appropriate to his station. That would be as much a misuse of property as to hold on to more than he needed. 'It would be excessive', said Aquinas, 'to take so much out of one's own means to give away to others that with what was left one could not very well keep up the way of life that accords with one's station, and meet contingencies as they arise; no one should live unbecomingly' (*Summa Theologica*, II-II, 32, a, b, c; in d'Entrèves 1948). The needs of one's station, moreover, are conventionally defined: they include the jewellery of the alderman's wife as much as the labourer's bench or bowl.

The notion of the station in life was equally basic to the Schoolmen's treatment of wages. The fair wage was the wage that would enable the worker to maintain the way of life traditionally associated with his occupation. That is the way in which it continues to be defined in the more recent teaching of the Church: it must be such as will enable the employee to keep himself and his family at the standard customary in and appropriate to their social class. A modern Catholic economist, following the Papal encyclicals Quad. Anno. 69 and Rerum Novarum 34, has defined it as 'an expression of employees' status in the social order' (Fogarty 1961: 268). Heinrich von Langenstein (1325-97) has often been cited for his statement that, if just prices are not fixed by the authorities, the producer must fix them himself so that 'the sales of his products will enable him to maintain his station' (de Roover 1958: 418-32).

But the Schoolmen also held two other views. One, which may have come to predominate, was that the just price—and with it the fair wage—was the market price, provided always that there was no collusion or emergency. This view saw the market price, in those circumstances, as being arrived at by a kind of popular vote—the Schoolmen said it was reached on a common estimation. The other view was not one of justice at all, but arose out of a theory of economic value developed later. This theory made value depend on the utility and scarcity of an article. The value of a man's work depended not merely on the number of hours he worked, but on his skill, and the quality of his product. The weight to be given to these latter factors was a matter for the judgement of those who hired the labour or bought its product: it is they who would decide what it was worth. Two consequences followed. One was that this valuation should be actually paid to the worker. Such was the requirement of commutative justice, or fairness in exchange: what is received by the worker must not be less than what he delivers. But second, the valuation is based on demand, and demand fluctuates. Here arose a conflict with the simple principle of the just wage as the means of maintaining the appropriate standard of living.

But no glaring conflict arose in practice, because standards of living had long since adjusted themselves to the earnings that each occupation could command as a fact of the market. If the authorities were concerned to fix a just wage for journeymen weavers, they might have regard equally well to the earnings the weavers had habitually been getting, or the outlay their households had been maintaining out of those earnings. The just wage thus appears as a rationalization of the existing state of affairs. But it had the active function, when demand fluctuated, of stabilizing the wage—although whether at the expense of greater variation of employment was not discussed; and it upheld the wage in particular cases against hard employers.

Thus, Christianity itself, and the views on wealth and income that came down from it, did not challenge the inequality of the secular world. They rather upheld it. In this they followed the main drift of the pagan philosophers. The inequality of human capacity was obvious, the need for subordination inescapable: how then could notions of egalitarianism so much as arise? But we have seen how Roman law brought one axiom of egalitarianism into the schools and chanceries of the Middle Ages.

2

The Transition to Liberalism

The potential effects of belief in the law of nature were powerful. They were destructive of hierarchy; they would substitute human contract for divine institution. But they could not be realized until men began to question the foundations of society, and to uncover the basis of authority. The Schoolmen had not really done that, for all their careful discussion. They had taken the existence of society for granted, as part of the natural creation. If with Aquinas they saw it as formed by a process of growth natural to a political animal, they still understood that process as designed by the Creator. Not for one moment did they consider man as himself the potential creator of his society, able to form and change its constitution, and to appoint and dismiss its rulers. Nor did they ask what right the rulers had to issue commands and inflict punishments: Chapter 13 of Romans was clear on that—all authority was held ultimately from God.

Contrasted with this outlook were certain habits of mind which grew in strength from the sixteenth century onwards and by the seventeenth had become prevalent. A child growing up in the house into which it has been born does not question its arrangements, still less its existence; but the traveller coming in the old days upon Stonehenge as it then stood on the open down will have asked himself, Who founded this structure, and how, and to what end? The Schoolmen did not pursue that kind of question, because they saw society, like all else about them, as the creation of the Heavenly Father: they were children in His house. But now a greater detachment prompted men to call into question the forms of government under which they grew up, and to ask how such forms were instituted and what was their justification. This change of outlook was linked with two other new approaches to society. One of these was a newly gained awareness of history: knowledge of the differences of past society, and how it had changed, was bound to carry with it reflections on the possibility of change continuing in present society, and on the mere contingency of some of its features that used to seem natural or inevitable. The other new approach was a growing capacity for realistic observation of human affairs as they are, and not as they may be categorized in some scheme of things *a priori*

These changes were stirring from the fourteenth century onwards. They were advanced by the breaking up of established authority, and by economic development, especially the growth of towns. These are the matters that we shall discuss in the first place. The concentration of the process of change in certain periods and places, known to us as Renaissance and Reformation, promoted egalitarianism through both its channels, and we go on to see how this was so. We look at the impact of the Renaissance on Sir Thomas More, and then examine individualism, as a product of both Renaissance and Reformation: egalitarian inferences were drawn from it at the time, and it persisted into the eighteenth century in the form of liberalism.

2.1. The Sources of Change: the Breaking Up of Authority

The visible sign of the divine ordering of human affairs, and of the unity of their governance, had been the papacy. In the Pope was vested the ultimate earthly source not only of all spiritual but of all temporal authority. But when for many years the Pope dwelt in Avignon, and when on the return to Rome in 1378 a schism broke out among the cardinals, and until 1414 there were two popes; when, moreover, thereafter the papacy became a principate fought for among the prowling heads of other Italian city states—then the reverence due to the Vicar of Christ was impaired most grievously. Meanwhile, the worldliness of the Church at many levels set up a revolt among the poor friars. And another revolt arose that went far deeper, because it challenged the ultimate and awful basis of the authority of the Church: its power, through control of access to its sacraments, to save from hell and admit to heaven. When Luther, like Wycliffe before him, proclaimed the priesthood of the individual believer, he denied the Church its ultimate sanction against disruption and secession.

The unity that was thus threatened had once seemed synonymous with Christendom: it was in the nature of the Creator's design for the world that all mankind should be under the one government, albeit with two arms, spiritual and temporal. But the authority of the Emperor had always been restricted and wavering. And although the Church was for long independent in practice as well as principle, local rulers increasingly asserted their administrative and financial control over it within their domains. By the end of the fifteenth century, the nation-state had affirmed itself—England; France, cleared of the English from all but Calais, though with Burgundy still an independent duchy; Spain, from which the Moors had been driven out; and the Hapsburgs, based on their possessions in Austria and south Germany. The nation-state not only broke up the conception of an ordered human society as part of an ordered universe: it also posed the problem of authority. For at the head was the king, or duke, or prince. In the principalities of Germany and the city-states of Italy, he appeared on a smaller scale but with the same autonomy. His salient attribute was that he acknowledged no superior. He could be fitted into the old cast of thought only by saying that he was overlord to himself. The question then arose, On what basis did his authority repose? Did he personally hold directly from God? Or was government of human institution, driving its authority from those who had set it up?

2.2. The Sources of Change: the Shaping of New Habits of Mind

While in these ways the established order ceased to appear as so wholly in the nature of things that no one thought of questioning it, other changes were shaping new habits of mind. It was in the population growth of the sixteenth century that towns first grew big in western Europe; but even in the previous century, the very high standard of living attained in the towns of Italy had brought a surge of political and economic as well as artistic energies there; and even during the English Wars of the Roses, the prosperous burghers could bar their gates against armed bands of retainers.

The growth of towns brought with it a new mental approach to political issues. One reason was that for the most part the town-dweller was engaged in manufactures or trade. His daily work typically required more rational thinking, that is, deliberate adjustment of means to end, than that of the countryman of the time. The countryman in his work was more like a churchman. He was guided by custom and ritual and authority; he did what was universally accepted as the right thing at the appointed time. There was little occasion for him to solve problems, or to innovate. But in the town, the trader on the large or small scale and the craftsman in his workshop did have at least some planning and estimating to do in the nature of his work, and from time to time those who were to survive did have to adapt their behaviour to changing circumstances. Custom, it is true, was still powerful. Change was unwelcome; merchants and craftsmen alike formed gilds to keep it down. None the less, they would see the arrangements of their trade or craft not as something to be taken as they found it and left reverently alone, but as made by man, and capable of being changed by him.

So we find Hobbes opening his treatise on the state in 1651 with an analogy that the medieval mind could never have entertained—an analogy between the watchmakers who give an 'artificial life' to the mechanisms they set ticking, and the founders of the state who create in it an 'artificial man'. 'For seeing life is but a motion of limbs,' he wrote,

the beginning whereof is in some principal part within; why may we not say, that all *automats* (engines that move themselves by springs and wheels as doth a watch) have an artificial life? . . . *Art* goes yet further, imitating that rational and most excellent work of nature, *man*. For by art is created that great LEVIATHAN called COMMONWEALTH, or STATE, in Latin CIVITAS, which is but an artificial man. (*Hobbes* 1651: Introduction)

The state is created by art, and the artificer is human. Hobbes's argument is that, given a realistic view of human nature, we can see how men must reasonably decide to form and maintain a state of a certain kind simply in the interest of self-preservation. There is much piety and citation of Holy Writ in his text, but the state no longer appears as of divine institution: men must have put it together, on a rational design of means to ends.

There was a second way in which the thinking of the town-dweller was stimulated to independence: his community within its walls attained a measure of self-government. Here the problems of the basis of authority, the choice of forms of government and the very maintenance of law and order were worked over and threshed about in gild and council, strife of factions, tumult of the people, seizures of power from within and without. Men became directly, sometimes forcibly, acquainted with change, experiment and the play of forces. In those crowded streets, the reality of human nature in politics broke through theological preconceptions about society. To weave his way, the merchant, the burgess, the syndic or doge or prince had to be able to see things as they were, unclouded by categories that, in purporting to order observations, would only obscure them. Such was the lesson of his experience in Florence that Machiavelli set down in *The Prince*:

Since it is my purpose to write what may be useful to those who heed it, I have thought it more fitting to concern myself with the effective reality of things than with speculation . . . . for there is such a difference between life as it is and life as it ought to be that he who neglects what is done for what ought to be done will ensure his ruin rather than his preservation. (Machiavelli 1961: C, xv)

That precept of realism carried the corollary that one should study history: the prince is not only to see clearly what sort of people he has to deal with, he has also to learn from experience what ploys succeed with them, and that experience need not be limited to his own life time. In his *Discourses*, Machiavelli devoted a long work to the drawing of lessons from the history of the Roman Republic. He saw states rising and thriving, weakening and falling, according as the morale of the citizens was high, sustained and periodically renewed; according as leaders and rulers came forward to take and enforce the right decisions; and, always, given the right turns of fortune's unpredictable wheel. Practical experience guided his reflection on history: he himself had seen how the fighting force of armies, and the setting that fixed the scope for effective political action, were alike determined by attitudes—that is, by settled forms of behaviour arising from deep-going feelings and opinions that may be held unconsciously.

Here Machiavelli was carrying out observations in the laboratory of the city-state, in quest of a science of politics. His work epitomizes the fresh look at the state that was stimulated by the growth of towns and the occupations of their inhabitants. The town-dweller, used to seeing equipment constructed, and to himself adapting means to ends, was ready to see the state itself as a device constructed to serve a purpose. He had practical experience of government, its ups and downs, and of human nature in politics, at his own door. The gild was an exercise in self-government. This realism carried with it a sense of history, of derivations, so that, when the question of origins was raised, the answer now given, though crude and conjectural, would be historical, not theological.

Other influences stimulated the town-dweller. One was the sheer effect of numbers, of the resonance and replication of opinion among people who were gathered together closely. 'There is something about towns', R. W. Southern has observed, 'which makes their inhabitants restive, rebellious, and above all, articulate . . .'

It is tempting to think that there is a critical size of population in towns which suddenly tilts the balance and creates a new climate of opinion. This point had been reached in Western Europe by the early years of the fourteenth century. For the first time for nearly a thousand years in Western Europe towns were the source of new thoughts and new modes of expression of general and lasting importance. *(Southern 1970: 21–2)

Another influence on the town-dweller was his higher standard of living. This gave him leisure, and some independence. He might take part in municipal government; or, if he lived under a dictator, he still enjoyed a measure of freedom in which to go about his business. He was less likely to be under the exclusive domination and direction of some immediate superior, lay or clerical. Burckhardt, in his *Civilisation of the Renaissance in Italy*, remarked on the stimulus of the setting. He pointed out that, even under despots like the Visconti, private persons forbidden political activity could still thrive, and added:

Wealth and culture, so far as display and rivalry were not forbidden to them, a municipal freedom which did not cease to be considerable, and a Church which, unlike that of the Byzantine or the Mohammedan world, was not identical with the State—all these conditions undoubtedly favoured the growth of individual thought. . . . (Burckhardt 1898: 131)

There is one facet of the egalitarianism of more recent years that was fashioned by the town-dweller's way of life, namely resentment not of all the rich but of the idle rich. That it was their idleness for which these were stigmatized is also a facet of what has been called 'the Protestant ethic', although many town-dwellers who were not Protestants held that ethic firmly. What Socrates has to say about drones in *The Republic* (Plato 1941 edn: ch. XXX, viii, 552, p. 276) is a case in point. As soon as the appetite for material acquisition is admitted, and oligarchy (or rule by the rich) arises, a man becomes able to sell his property and 'go on living in a community where he plays no part as tradesman or artisan or as a soldier capable of providing his own equipment: he is only what they call a pauper'. Machiavelli (1970: I, 55, 245-6) objected particularly to the landowners outside the city, the 'gentiluomini'. 'The term ''gentry'' ', he wrote, 'is used of those who live in idleness on the abundant revenue derived from their estates, without having anything to do either with their cultivation or with other forms of labour essential to life. Such men are a pest in any republic and in any province.' It was their lack of occupation that made them so objectionable. Riches gained by manufacture and commerce in the city were a different matter.

It was not only in the towns that economic change made for a change in attitudes and relations. It had always been a distinctive feature of the towns that people lived there by trade, and dealt with each other in the market and with money, whereas in the countryside transactions were regulated by custom and performed in kind. With the breaking down of customary services came a new flexibility and scope for individual differentiation. Money was a solvent of hierarchy. As contractual relations and cash transactions superseded feudal tenure, the opportunity was opened to some to improve their condition, while others fell back. Experience made people more aware of the differences in capacity and fortune among them. Especially after the Black Death had made labour scarce, some of them found it possible to get on in the world as never before outside the Church. When individual paths diverged more, the qualities of the individual became more conspicuous. It began to appear that society ought to afford scope to individual activity; and even that it had been formed by individuals to serve their purposes, instead of having been ordained to assign them to their stations.

A new habit of mind was also instilled by the rediscovery of history. The tradition of the Greek and Roman historians was lost to the Middle Ages, whose scholars did not see the world about them as the product of change through proceding centuries, or compare its institutions with those of other days and places. They described human nature in the light of religion, not of history. It was something new in its time when Machiavelli set out to draw lessons from the narrative of Livy. Great significance attaches to his procedure. Implicitly, it recognized that human propensities assert themselves in different forms in differnt circumstances, so that comparing these manifestations would help to distinguish persistent tendencies from the transient, and causal relations from contingency. It saw contemporary institutions and practices as only one set among many, and was able to assess them accordingly. They ceased to appear inevitable, unquestionable. They were seen, moreover, as the outcome of an antecedent course of change, during which they had been shaped by various forces; and as they had adapted themselves in the past, so they could be adapted in the future.

The change that the historical approach brought about in the way people thought about society was made very clear by one of the most influential works of the eighteenth century, Montesquieu's *De l'esprit des lois* (1748; see Carrithers 1977). His wide survey of institutions and practices proceeded on the assumption that they were to be understood and assessed through their relation to their environment. They had been formed by adaptation to physical and economic conditions; they were to be judged by the success of that adaptation, and not by principles of eternal verity and universal application. In his treatment of religion, for example, although Montesquieu was careful to set the one true faith apart from all the rest, he remarked that these others might be graded 'in relation only to the good they produce in civil society' XXIV, i). Slavery is abhorrent as a general rule, but

there are some countries where the heat enervates the body, and saps energy so much that men can be made to undertake a laborious task only by the fear of being chastised: slavery in such a setting is therefore less offensive to good sense: and the master there being as slack in the service of his prince as his slave is in his, civil slavery is accompanied there by political slavery (*De l'esprit des lois*, XV, vii).

Here a despotic political structure is explained by the organization of work—'the relations of production'—imposed by the climate. Equally, the possibility of maintaining a republic depends on the distribution of property. Following Aristotle, Montesquieu found the mainstay of a stable democracy in the preponderance of modest holdings. 'For a good democracy it is not enough that land holdings should be equal; they must be small, as they were among the Romans' (V, vi). It was among such smallholders that would be found the necessary condition of democracy which he called the spirit of frugality. This is essentially what was later to be called the 'Protestant ethic', though there is nothing exclusively Protestant about it. It could be maintained also in a trading republic like Athens, for 'the spirit of commerce carried with it that of frugality, thrift, moderation, hard work, practical wisdom, calm, good order, and disciplined bearing (V, vi).

Institutions that can be accounted for by their setting, climatic or economic, are evidently plastic, and capable of being remoulded by deliberate policy, but only within the limits set by human nature. Thus, when Montesquieu went on to ask how frugality could be promoted, he noted that an equal division of holdings, once made, would not last long unless transfers of all kinds were forbidden or strictly limited. But such constraints ask too much of human nature. In practice, we must accept a compromise.

Although in democracy real equality is the soul of the state, it is none the less so difficult to establish, that an extreme exactitude in this respect would not always be appropriate. It must suffice to establish a gradation that reduces or fixes differences to a certain extent; after which it is for particular laws to equalize—so to speak—the inequalities, by the levies which they will impose on the rich, and the benefits they will grant to the poor. (*De l'esprit des lois*, V, v)

Thus, in the hands of Montesquieu, the historical approach related institutions to their environments and compared that relationship as it appeared in different periods and places. Thereby it put society on the laboratory bench as the object of positive study. That study, in bringing out the ways in which societies had been shaped, indicated the possibility of further change.

2.3. The Impact of Change: Sir Thomas More's *Utopia*

The new ways of thinking about society that formed part of the Renaissance are illuminated by the work of Sir Thomas More. What stands out in them at first is the painful impact on a sensitive and complex personality of the abuses of society around him; but his thoughts on their origin reveal his view of human nature as the source of social structure, and of politics (to use modern language) as a branch of human relations. Some of the abuses that so grieved him were peculiar to England in the early sixteenth century; others were such as occur wherever people are greedy for their own gain. He tried to probe their basic causes: at least he found the conditions without which they could not exist. In his *Utopia* he pictured a society in which those conditions had been sedulously removed: the abuses were precluded, and the people were peaceful, orderly and relaxed. The same moral regimen made them egalitarian.

His account of *Utopia* was designed to instruct by amusing. The Jesuit scholar E. L. Surtz (1957: 9-10) has pointed out that the form of composition was a declamation—a literary exercise in which the author deploys his ingenuity and stylistic verve in the defence of some indefensible subject such as exile or ingratitude. Erasmus had used the form in his *Praise of Folly*. It enabled him to excoriate some tendencies of the times and put forward some unconventional thoughts without becoming deeply involved. In the hands of a master of learning and expression, this subtle medium fluttered lightly as a butterfly but could sting like a wasp; it amused the reader, to whom it could convey imperceptibly a message that he would have rejected if it had come straight at him; and the author avoided responsibility for having put about ideas whose direct utterance would have been shocking. Erasmus had written *The Praise of Folly* in 1509, in More's house. Six years later More had time on his hands, during a pause in the negotiations of a commercial treaty that he was conducting in the Low Countries. he drafted a script telling how he and a friend in Antwerp met 'an elderly foreigner with a sunburnt face, a long beard, and a cloak slung carelessly over one shoulder' (More 1965: edn. 38). This man returned from visiting countries beyond the Equator hitherto unknown, and most of the script consists of his account of them, and above all, of the arrangements of the one called Utopia.

We have said that the purpose of this account was to show how, when certain basic conditions of actual society were removed, many acknowledged evils would never arise. For the most part those evils were not named: what they were appeared by contrast with the good order of Utopia. But, as J. H. Hexter (1952: 26) has shown, when More returned to England he added a section in which he dealt specifically with two great present evils:- the enclosures for sheep pastures, and the violence of disbanded retainers. The addition suggests that More's purpose in devising the detailed account of Utopia was analytic. What purports to be a travelogue is really more like an economist's diagram, in which the working of certain forces is abstracted to be displayed in isolation. The account of Utopia, although it is carried into realistic detail, is not meant to be a design for a society to be set up by men and women, taking human nature as it is now. A modern counterpart might rather be found in some of the plays of George Bernard Shaw, in which principles very different from the orthodoxy of the time are given a working out in situations that are realistic in detail yet are all held within the framework of the stage. The result is a parable: the narrative follows a course natural enough to persuade us of the force of the underlying principle. As More contemplated society around him, his compassionate mind as a Christian humanist was filled and stirred by the thought of principles that would do so much, if men would only act upon them, to make their lives calmer and happier. In a time of enforced leisure, he turned to a form of composition that would endow those principles with an imaginative and appealing demonstration.

First among them was the principle that our lives will be filled with the only true happiness if we eschew the competitive pursuit of material gain and aggrandisement, and live modestly, co-operatively and communally. The necessary condition for this change is that the great objects of greed, namely private property and money, be available no longer. So long as private property exists, More argues through the mouth of the sailor Raphael returned from Utopia, the greedy and the ruthless get the greater part of it into their own hands, and most people will be propertyless, forced to labour long hours for a low wage.

I don't see how you can ever get any real justice or prosperity, so long as there's private property, and everything's judged in terms of money—unless you consider it just for the worst sort of people to have the best living conditions, or unless you're prepared to call a country prosperous, in which all the wealth is owned by a tiny minority—who aren't entirely happy even so, while everyone else is simply miserable. . . . I'm quite convinced that you'll never get a fair distribution of goods, or a satisfactory organization of human life, until you abolish private property altogether. So long as it exists, the vast majority of the human race, and the vastly superior part of it, will inevitably go on labouring under a burden of poverty, hardship, and worry. (More 1965 edn: 65–6)

The implied reference to land as the main form of property is clear, as is the consequent lack of prospect of more wealth for all through economic growth. Those unneighbourly and aggressive propensities of human nature for which private property provides a channel of exertion are actively fomented by money. This is not only a symbol and a lure, but a means of distorting demand, from just and beneficial objects to those that are selfish and socially destructive. Consider a recent year of bad harvest, when 'thousands of people died of starvation. Well, I bet if you'd inspected every rich man's barn at the end of that lean period you'd have found enough corn to have saved all the lives that were lost through malnutrition and disease. . . .' There follows a Shavian passage: 'Everyone could so easily get enough to eat, if it weren't for that blessed nuisance, money. There you have a brilliant invention which was designed to make food more readily available. Actually it's the only thing that makes it unobtainable' (More 1965 edn.: 130-1). Money loads the grasping hand of greed, where reason and nature alike would have prescribed the ordered distribution of fair shares. Money makes it possible for so many resources to be allocated to producing luxuries for the rich that even the basic needs of many other people cannot be met from the product of the resources remaining. Those thereby plunged into poverty are driven to crime. But on a rational arrangement of production and consumption there can be a modest sufficiency and comfort for all, and a great release from tension, social and personal:

Obviously the end of money means the end of all those types of criminal behaviour which daily punishments are powerless to check . . . And the moment money goes, you can also say goodbye to fear, tension, anxiety, overwork, and sleepless nights. Why, even poverty itself, the one problem that has always seemed to need money for its solution, could promptly disappear if money ceased to exist. (More 1965 edn.: 130)

The rational arrangement of the Utopian economy is described in some detail. The major problem of the efficient allocation of resources under socialism, as modern economists see it, did not arise in Utopia, because consumption was controlled and standardized. Households in groups of thirty dined at a common table. All people wore simple clothing of uniform colour and design. The standard housing units were assigned by lot, and every ten years they were reassigned. The maintenance of a modest but fully adequate standard of living was assured to every member of the community throughout life: no one was driven by anxiety to amass reserves against contingencies. It was therefore possible to dispense with a pricing system and with markets altogether. Every child was trained in a trade; More seems to have envisaged the adults working independently, like the self-employed craftsmen in the actual towns of his day, each in his own workshop. There was no question of anyone working for wages, or of any product being sold. Instead, the products were simply delivered to a warehouse, from which they were distributed to the 'shops'—if that misleading term may pass—specializing in particular types of product. 'When the head of a household needs anything for himself or his family, he just goes to one of these shops and asks for it. And whatever he asks for, he's allowed to take away without any sort of payment, either in money or in kind' (More 1965 edn.: 80). The problem still arose of how the output of such trades as the young people chose to enter would match the requirements of the prescribed standard of living. More's remark that sons would generally follow their fathers suggests that he was supposing production adjusted already to a pattern of consumption that was unchanging, in a population that he also supposed constant. There were special arrangements for agriculture. All schoolchildren were instructed in it. The whole population, normally resident in towns, had to spend two years in the country, the first working under the instruction of those who were in their second year, the second themselves acting as instructors while continuing to work.

This plan of communal and egalitarian consumption and 'production for use not profit' served several purposes, in More's view. It provided, in modern terms, a welfare state. In the terms of More's own day, it solved the problem of poverty that had begun to assert itself so painfully: if the corn were divided fairly, no one would lack bread, even in a year of bad harvest. Provision, too, could be made for the sick and disabled, the orphan, the widow and the aged. But More showed that the Utopians were relieved not only of anxiety, but of toil. There were slaves, it is true, some of them criminals and others imported to perform the heavier or more unpleasant tasks; but the great achievement of leisure for the citizen was simply the consequence of the labour power available—when everyone did his bit, and there were no idle rich, the output required to maintain the communal and egalitarian standard of living could be produced in a six-hour day. Egalitarianism not only gave the former working people a bigger share of the cake: it also obliged those who would formerly have eaten cake they had never helped to make to share the labour of making it.

But most of all, the plan of consumption and production served a moral purpose. Behind private property and money, More saw greed. The case for abolishing private property is that as long as it exists it will be amassed by the greedy. 'Wealth will tend to vary in inverse proportion to merit. The rich will be greedy, unscrupulous, and totally useless characters, while the poor will be simple, unassuming people...' (More 1965 edn.: 66). In the enclosures, 'a few greedy people have converted one of England's greatest natural advantages into a national disaster' (p. 48). The view of society that More's spokesman Raphael reaches at the last yields an outright Marxian analysis of the capitalist state:

When I consider any social system that prevails in the modern world, I can't, so help me God, see it as anything but a conspiracy of the rich to advance their own interests under the pretext of organizing society. They think up all sorts of tricks and dodges, first for keeping safe their ill-gotten gains, and then for exploiting the poor by buying their labour as cheaply as possible. Once the rich have decided that these tricks and dodges shall be officially recognised by society—which includes the poor as well as the rich—they acquire the force of law. Thus an unscrupulous minority is led by its insatiable greed to monopolize what would have been enough to supply the needs of the whole population. (More 1965 edn.: 130)

But granted that greed is an ugly and hurtful impulse, it is a trait of at least some people at most times: had it no part in the human nature of the Utopians? Did removing the object of desire remove the desire with it? In one passage (p. 130), More did write of 'the simultaneous abolition of money and the passion for money'; and one asks, if no woman is allowed to pass the monastery gate, does that simultaneously extinguish desire in the monks? But earlier (p. 80) More had argued that greed—such as 'the passion for money'—could arise only from two causes, both of which were ruled out in Utopia: one was fear of want, the other was pride, or 'vanity, the notion that you're better than people if you can display more superfluous property than they can'—'conspicuous consumption', as an unorthodox economist was to term it four centuries later.

We touch here on one of the basic drives towards egalitarianism. There is much in Utopia, so far as its arrangements have been sketched already, to remind us of a monastic rule. Detail might be added, such as the practice of beginning lunch and supper in the communal hall by reading aloud a piece of improving literature. The problems of incentives raised by the absence of stick or carrot for the worker More meets by instituting such pervasive and intrusive invigilation as again appears monastic. Each block of thirty households is supervised by a warden, whose chief business 'is to see that nobody sits around doing nothing, but that everyone gets on with his job' (More 1965 edn.: 75-6). A citizen can travel only with the permission of his superiors:

if you're caught without a passport outside your own district, you're brought home in disgrace and severely punished as a deserter . . . You see how it is—wherever you are, you always have to work. There's never any excuse for idleness. There are also no wine-taverns, no ale-houses, no brothels, no opportunities for seduction, no secret meeting-places. Everyone has his eye on you, so you're practically forced to get on with your job, and make some proper use of your spare time. (More 1965 edn.: 84).

As a young man, More had all but committed himself to the cloister; to the end of his life he practised the mortification of the hair shirt and flagellation. His natural capacity for abundant enjoyment brought him a sense of guilt; through his outgoing vitality there ran a streak of masochism. Only as an ascetic could he hold himself together. But ascetics, who have to deny themselves what they, like all of us, naturally enjoy, are angered by the sight of other people helping themselves liberally to the good things of this world, and still more by their glorying in their acquisitions. Greed and pride are faults in others very hard to bear by those who are holding in their own appetites. Those who determinedly refuse to indulge and aggrandize themselves are bound to have a keen eye for the harm that can come of self-seeking in others. The American scholar J. H. Hexter held that in this lay More's basic diagnosis of the disorders of the times:

> Once we recognize that More's analysis of sixteenth-century society led him to the conclusion that pride was the source of the greater part of its ills, the pattern of the Utopian Commonwealth becomes clear, consistent and intelligible. In its fundamental structure it is a great social instrument for the subjugation of pride. (Hexter 1952: 80)

On this view, More designed the almost Benedictine egalitarianism of Utopia, not as a society ideal in itself, but as one that would be free of the human propensities that vitiated actual societies. He was concerned with institutions only through their effect on personal conduct. But there were two other ways in which his intense moral purpose led him to egalitarianism not as a means but as an end.

One of these lay through his devotion to the teaching of Christ. In common with other Christian humanists, he turned away from the arid intricacy of the scholastic philosophy to the simplicity of the Gospel. This was part of the message of *The Praise of Folly* of Erasmus, which he wrote in More's house. The humanists' discovery in the classics of the romantic values of the heart turned them away from Aristotelian caution and practicality no less than from the logic-chopping that went on in Aristotle's name. 'The letter killeth but the spirit giveth life' (2 Corinthians 3: 6), and the spirit was that of charity—or, as we should say today, of love. 'Christ and Pythagoras and Plato', Surtz observes,

> are often linked together as religious teachers in the minds and works of many humanists. . . . In the Introduction to his *Adages*, Erasmus declares that, if one examines thoroughly the saying of Pythagoras on the community of all things among friends, one will find therein the whole of human happiness in a nutshell. Plato did nothing else than advocate this community and friendship among the founders of his republic. . . . Erasmus continues 'What else than this did Christ, the head of our religion, do? In fact, he gave to the world only a single commandment, that of charity, teaching that the whole of the law and the prophets depended upon it. Or what else does charity urge upon men but that all things must be common to all men? . . . Among Erasmus's reasons for denouncing Aristotle is Aristotle's defence of private property. 'From Aristotle we have learned that the commonwealth in which all things are common cannot flourish. We keep trying to amalgamate the principles of Aristotle with the doctrine of Christ, that is, to mix water and fire. (Surtz 1957: 170–1)

The Gospels made it clear that Christ required his own disciples to give up all private property, and keep only a common purse (Matthew 10: 9–10;

Mark 6: 8–9, 10: 21; Luke 9: 57–8, 10: 4, 12: 33; John 12: 6, 13: 29). The Acts of the Apostles related of the believers in the early days in Jerusalem that 'not a man of them claimed any of his possessions as his own, but everything was held in common' (Acts 4: 32; see also Acts 2: 44). More's own teacher, John Colet, had taught that God had created the world to be enjoyed in common by all, and the law 'of a defiled and corrupted nature' after the Fall had 'brought in ideas of *meum* and *tuum*—of property, that is to say, and deprivation; ideas clear contrary to a good and unsophisticated nature: for that would have a community in all things' (Surtz 1957, 165–6). Chrsit recalled His followers to God's purpose. It is understandable, then, that when More supposed the Utopians introduced to Christianity, a reason he found for their taking to it readily was that they were 'considerably affected by the information that Christ prescribed [to] His own disciples a communist way of life, which is still practised today in all the most truly Christian communities' (More 1965 edn.: 118). A marginal note shows that this last phrase refers to monasteries and convents.

The other path that led him to an egalitarian conclusion also began in Christian humanism. In the fifteenth century, certain humanists revived the philosophy of Epicurus, which treated pleasure as the great object of action and the Chief Good. Erasmus and More adopted it with this addition: that the greatest source of happiness lies in our knowledge of God and our prospect of heaven. The Utopians are credited with having arrived at the pleasure principle, which More justifies by a highly significant argument. Let us be clear, first, that 'pleasure' signifies only the higher type of physical and mental enjoyment, such as has no tendency to debase, or impair further enjoyment; and that one may have to undergo pain in order that pleasure may come of it. In *Utopia* More added the qualification, that we must not seek our own pleasure at the expense of other people's. With this understanding, we may take up the argument to show that it is pleasure and not virtue that is the Chief Good. The generally accepted view is that virtue consists in living according to the nature implanted in us by God, 'But this includes obeying the instinct to be reasonable in our likes and dislikes. And reason also teaches us . . . to get through life as comfortably and cheerfully as we can, and help all other members of our species to do so too' (More 1965 edn.: 91–2). The Creator has not only shown His approval of our seeking our own happiness, by implanting in us reason that tells us to do it; but has convinced even the ascetic who gives up his own pleasure that he should relieve the sufferings of others. That is to recognize pleasure as a natural object for them: why not for him too?

Two implications of this argument are to be noted. One appears in the confidence with which More appeals to common humanity: 'obviously nothing could be more humane,' he says, 'or more natural for a human being, than to relieve other people's sufferings. . . .' That is the positive side, the part of the Good Samaritan. But Nature also holds us back from exploitation. 'Nature also wants us to help one another to enjoy life, for the very good reason that no human being has a monopoly of her affections. She's equally anxious for the welfare of every member of the species (More 1965 edn.: 92). This sense that the poor deserve support by their neighbours in the nature of things because we are all human, forms one of the spontaneous and persistent impulses towards egalitarianism.

The other implication of the Epicurean argument was to be drawn out only much later, but we can see now how the Renaissance had let loose on the world another argument for egalitarianism. Once pleasure was accepted as the chief object of individual action, the road was open to the felicific calculus, and the demonstration that the total utility of a number of persons with similar needs would be maximized only if they had equal incomes.

Here are two of the basic impulses towards egalitarianism, or arguments for it:- our spontaneous sympathy for our fellow men, the solidarity of the species; and the recognition that, in transfers from the rich to the poor, the rich lose less than the poor gain. These can be added to the ascetic impulse noted previously; those who themselves exercise self-restraint prefer arrangements in which moderation is enforced equally on all.

Utopia also contains a fourth ground of egalitarianism: the conflict between our notion of justice as calling for a matching of rewards to efforts expended or contribution effected, and the actual state of affairs in which, as More saw it, the idle were rich and the workers poor. How hard the common people had to work More pointed out by contrast with Utopia. Under the six-hour day there, 'they don't wear people out . . . by keeping them hard at work from early morning till late at night, like cart-horses. That's just slavery—and yet that's what life is like for the working classes nearly everywhere else in the world.' 'They're not only ground down by unrewarding toil in the present, but also worried to death by the prospect of a poverty-stricken old age—since their daily wages aren't enough to support them for one day, let alone anything over to be saved up [for] when they're old (More 1965 edn.: 76, 129). Very different is the lot of the workers in Utopia, where they and all their families are assured of full support—it's just the same for everyone—throughout their lives.

Everyone gets a fair share, so there are never any poor men or beggars. Nobody owns anythings, but everyone is rich—for what greater wealth can there be than cheerfulness, peace of mind, and freedom from anxiety? . . . Now, will anyone venture to compare these fair arrangements in Utopia with the so-called justice of other countries?—in which I'm damned if I can see the slightest trace of justice or fairness. For what sort of justice do you call this? People like aristocrats, goldsmiths, or money-lenders, who either do no work at all, or do work that's really not essential, are rewarded for their laziness or their unnecessary activities by a splendid life of luxury. But labourers, coachmen, carpenters, and farmhands who never stop working like carthorses, at jobs so essential that, if they *did* stop working, they'd bring any country to a standstill within twelve months—what happens to them? They get so little to eat, and have such a wretched time, that they'd be almost better off if they *were* carthorses. (More 1965 ed.: 128-9)

The contrast has been noted—much more than noted, it has been called to attention very sharply—between the degree of toleration that was accorded to differences of religious opinion in Utopia (so long as there was no disturbance of the peace) and More's own strong stand against heresy. It is true that R. W. Chambers has shown that the figures of the London persecutions 'do not suggest that [they] had anything to do with More (Chambers 1935: 281). The toleration allowed in Utopia was only within so much religion as men could arrive at by the use of their reason, before they had received the truths of revelation. More wrote *Utopia* before heresy had assumed with Tyndale, and still more with Luther, the alarming potentialities that he saw in it by the time of his becoming Chancellor. None the less, he did by his own account have a boy of his own household tied to a tree and whipped for imparting heresy. He regarded heresy as a carbuncle that he was bound to cut out, 'not in reason only and good congruence, but also by plain ordinance and statute', as a law officer of the Crown. This does seem hard to reconcile with his treatment of toleration in *Utopia*.

It raises the question how far, even when he wrote, he stood by the ideas he floated there. Was he really an advocate of egalitarianism? That in two places in the discussion he puts objections to it into his own mouth need not hold us up. The first may be seen as a literary device: the standard objections are put up in advance, to be swept away by the subsequent discourse. The second—namely, that egalitarianism means the end of pomp and ceremony—can only have been satirical in purpose. To make his stance intelligible there remains his purpose of diagnosis, and of revealing the sources of present evils by displaying a contrasting society from which those sources had been removed. At the same time, he was displaying the great potentialities for good in human nature, given the right laws and constitution, which some wise Utopus, Lycurgus or Moses must first decree. Equality, then, was not an end in itself, but would follow, like relaxation, harmony and cultivation, as a natural outcome of conditions in which the virtues could operate and the vices were inhibited.

So far More the moralist. But More the lawyer and the counsellor had to work in a world where no such conditions obtained, and changes in prospect seemed to him to threaten the destruction of vital values. He had never hoped to order a new society, but he had hoped to make his readers more aware of what was most worth seeking in their own lives. In later years, and especially after the revolt of Luther, he came to see the aims of life as best served by the preservation of traditional faith and practice.

But the significance of *Utopia* can be found in the impact of the Renaissance on that faith. The humanists experienced through the classics a liberation of individuality; they discovered fresh possibilities of personal development and sheer enjoyment as an end of life. The Christian humanists re-interpreted their faith, and found a simpler, more direct and personal message in the teaching of Christ. Society appeared less as the ordered handiwork of the Creator, more as a human artefact, the object of positive study and possible reform. Into More's sensitive, deeply religious temperament, these new ideas poured as a current of excitement, dashing against the rocks of piety and obedience on which he had been raised. At a time of ease and confidence, he expressed in *Utopia* these ideas about the moral conditions of social betterment. But times changed. In the last resort, it was to the rock of authority that he himself had to cling; the stream of ideas poured on into the next two centuries.

2.4. Individualism

It is hard for those of us who have grown up in Western societies in recent years to understand what 'individualism' means; for in the sense that distinguishes modern from medieval society, it has been simply part of the air we have breathed from infancy onwards. Sometimes we use the term in opposition to 'collectivism', and then we have in mind different ways of organizing production or markets. Sometimes we contrast the individualist with the conformist. But neither of those meanings describes the new awareness of self that divided the modern from the medieval world. Consider the awareness on the farther side of that divide. It was above all an awareness of belonging. Medieval man had been brought into a world created of set purpose by a Heavenly Father, whose universal Church provided rules of conduct and means of grace; ordinary people were called upon only to accept its authority. In the temporal realm, no less, people were required to accept the authority of kings and emperors. This meant not only passivity, an absence of self-directed activity, but a dependence for one's personal confidence on sustained relations with one's fellows. For without them people were lost. They were not moved by internal drives or cogitations: they did as others did, or what they knew was expected of them. Their image of themselves had been imprinted by those around them, who had become an organic part of them; how much so children removed from home, and suffering all the miseries of homesickness, realize in the sudden cutting off of part of themselves. The children recover from homesickness as they learn to 'stand on their own feet'—attaining a power of initiative, and a sense of identity. This is individualism. Over against the passivity of an earlier type, it sets an active mind, holding itself responsible for directing conduct. Instead of the dovetailing of personality between the individual and the family or group, individualism forms persons who are more separable, even morally independent of their ties and dependencies.

They come to be thought of as having existed, on their own, before the formation of society. Instead of doing 'the thing' that everyone does without question, they set out to do what they themselves want to do, or are convinced in their own hearts and souls—no matter what other people think—that they ought to. The issue of 'human relations' arises. Instead of the relations of husband and wife, parent and child, master and man, seeming prescribed in the nature of things, like the motions of the sun and the stars, they become an object of concern for the reconciliation of different interests.

In some ways, the rise of individualism was like the transition from childhood to adult stature. Children often complain, but are not critical; they cannot be, when they know so little of other settings, other possibilities. Their dependence imposes the necessity of taking all things for granted, however painful, even hateful, they may be. With adolescence, and a growing capacity to look after oneself, comes detachment, and independence, and a more objective view of one's surroundings. Medieval man was a child in his father's house. God had created that house, not long before, had fitted it out and stocked it for the occupants whom He had likewise created and ordered. As He set 'the sun to rule by day, the moon and stars to rule by night', so He endowed with authority the spiritual and temporal rulers of His creatures. Although this was a matter of historical fact, people had little sense of history, which to us means a course of ongoing change. The world of the peasant is, as we say, limited. With greater knowledge comes a breaking of bonds. Awareness of a wider world brings with it a sense of one's own identity, and a capacity for choice. Adolescents assert themselves, their selfhood.

Medieval society may be likened to a corporation, whose officers and members have their appointed roles and relations with one another. To each person within it is assigned a station with its accepted functions, obligations and privileges. What people do and how they live depend not on their personalities and choice but on their place. That place is not fixed at birth: people can move up the hierarchy, and some move farther than others. But the hierarchy is not formed by them as they sort themselves out; they fit themselves into an order laid down at the foundation of the world. With the rise of individualism, on the other hand, society ceases to provide a framework anterior to individual exertions; instead, it is formed by them. It may then be likened to a frontier settlement, where people who have pushed out into unoccupied territory form such relations with one another as follow from each person's faculties and achievements. The settlers in all their variety come first, and society is what they form subsequently.

No doubt this analogy is over-simple. The acceptance of things as they are was never complete in the Middle Ages. Many traits of individualism existed within the regime of acceptance. In later years, equally, people continued to accept most of the features of the society into which they were born. But the analogy serves to portray a transition. Between the fourteenth and the seventeenth centuries, there was a shift in prevailing attitudes. The spectrum remained as wide as ever, but among the most active people—that is, those of whom we now know most—there had been a great change. It is apparent to us in the Renaissance and the Reformation.

In the classic work already quoted, Burckhardt contended that the Italian city-states not only fostered 'an *objective* treatment and consideration of the state and of all things of this world', in the way we have seen in Machiavelli, but that they also promoted individualism: 'The *subjective* side of the same time asserted itself with corresponding emphasis; man became a spiritual *individual*, and recognized himself as such. . . . It will not be difficult to show that this result was owing above all to the political circumstances of Italy.' One of these circumstances was freedom from domination by the teaching of the Church, and the requirement of conformity, when 'tyrants and free cities in the 14th century treated the clergy at times with such sovereign contempt. . . .' (Burckhardt 1898: pt. II, ch. i; pt. IV, ch. ii). Another circumstance was the looseness of social structure within the city walls, which left the way open to the rise of the talented and the enterprising as well as the ruthless: there could in any case be greater differentiation in personal development and attainment than in societies with more settled hierarchies. But a third powerful factor was one that became common to all countries that received the learning of the Renaissance: humanism gave men a heightened sense of unique personal identity and, especially, of potential.

Historially, the humanists were the scholars who rediscovered the Greeks. Thereby they came on a view of the world in which, although the gods are powerful, men are not their children or their creatures. No Greek could have said 'The Lord is my shepherd.' The Greek sees man as upstanding, bold in thought and deed, his features cut deeply by the strength of his will, capable of audacious achievements and tragic failures. The Chorus in Sophocles's *Antigone* celebrates man's amazing capabilities and powers:

Wonders are many, and none is more wonderful than man; the power that crosses the white sea, driven by the strong south-wind, making a path under surges that threaten to engulf him; and Earth, the eldest of the Gods, the immortal, the unwearied, doth he wear, turning the soil with the offspring of horses, as the ploughs go to and fro from year to year. . . .

And speech, and wind-swift thought, and all the moods that mould a state, hath he taught himself. and how to flee the arrows of the frost, when 'tis hard lodging under the clear sky, and the arrows of the rushing rain; yea, he hath resources for all; without resources he meets nothing that must come: only against Death shall he call for aid in vain; but from baffling maladies he hath devised escapes.

Cunning beyond fancy's dream is the fertile skill which brings him, now to evil, now to good. When he honours the laws of the land, and that justice which he hath sworn by the gods to uphold, proudly stands his city: no city hath he who, for his rashness, dwells with sin. (Jebb 1904: 138).

The double meaning of 'humanity' is significant. To this day, the word stands in the Scottish Universities for the study of classical language and literature; and Oxford has its 'literae humaniores' to the same effect. But in common usage, the term means respect and concern for the well-being of others, and in particular compassion for them, and the wish to spare them suffering. That a heightened sense of one's own identity and potential should bring with it an understanding of the like claims of selfhood in others, we can well understand. What is remarkable is that the same term should serve for this understanding as for the study of classical literature and art. The two go together because that study, and especially the discovery of the Greeks, was a main source of affective individualism.

In the rolling periods of his lectures on *Equality*, R. H. Tawney (1931) identified humanism with the awareness of personal potential. What was exciting and imperishable for him in the Greeks was the value they placed on the development of personality. It is by way of a hymn to humanism that his argument concerning equality and culture is advanced. Humanism in all its forms celebrates the dignity of man: it holds that all our economic resources and social institutions are only means to an end, and that 'this end is the growth towards perfection of individual human beings'. Then, if the potential of development is implanted in every breast, how can we justify denying the opportunity for development to some, when such opportunities are lavished on others?

It is not surprising that the temper which had as one of its manifestations humanism, or the perfecting of the individual, should have had as another manifestation an outlook on society which sympathized with the attempt to bring the means of a good life within the reach of all, and regarded the subordination of class to class, and the arrogance and servility which such subordination naturally produces, as barbarian or gothic, as the mark of peoples which were incompletely civilized. (Tawney 1931: 111, 114)

In this way we can see how the discovery of human sensitivity and creativity in the Renaissance stirred up resentment against privilege.

Individualism was manifested and stimulated not only by the Renaissance but also by the Reformation. The common element of all the reformed faiths was the stress they laid on the responsibility of the individual believer. For some, his salvation depended upon that exertion of his free will by which he accepted redeeming grace. Even those who in principle held each man's ultimate destiny to be predestined felt themselves personally bound none the less to direct their feet into the narrowest path of righteousness, and deemed their success in so doing an encouragement to believe in their own election. No longer could the cares of eternity be borne by the Church: an awful responsibility now rested on each person. But in this all were alike. Each could read the Scriptures, each could seek divine guidance in prayer and meditation: in these matters of ultimate and transcendent importance, no other person could claim authority—or so held those sectarians who carried the impulse of the Reformation farthest. Hence the equality of all believers, and the democracy of the meeting house, were signalled on one wing by the refusal of the Quakers to raise their hats to their social superiors. But the sects apart, the Reformation exalted individual judgement against authority, and individual action against collective conformity. The natural implication of such individualism is a demand for a field free of restrictions for one's own activity, so far as is consistent—this must be allowed—with like freedom for other people. Individualism leads to a demand for equality in the sense that it is against the obstacles to one person's advance set up by the privileges of another.

The Reformation thus promoted the principle of the equality of man, in two ways. Because the fate of every soul formed part of the divine plan, all people, it was said, were equal in the sight of God, and that cast doubt on the justification of the inequalities of this world. Because responsibility was shifted from the priesthood to the believer, the individual enjoyed a new sense of autonomy; but claiming freedom to exercise it obliged him to recognize the equal claim of others.

In this last respect, Protestant thinking was reinforced by the Stoic principles of Roman law. Stress on the autonomy of the individual raises the problem of how to reconcile it with political order; the consequent quest for the origin of lawful authority led to natural law. This might be and was held to legitimize more than one form of government. But for our present purpose what is significant is the principle of equality that emerged when Protestants invoked Roman law. The German jurist Pufendorf, whose work on 'The duty of man and of the citizen with regard to natural law' appeared in 1673, held that 'every man should recognise the "natural equality of man" by treating every other as his "equal by nature". By natural equality Pufendorf did not mean equality in capacity . . . but "equality of law (acqualitas juris)", based upon men's equal subjection to the natural law and consequently their equal obligations to one another' (Krieger 1965: 99). The reference to 'the citizen' in the title of Pufendorf's treatise is significant: it denoted a respect in which all men were equal, and differences of rank and wealth were irrelevant. Pufendorf is little read now, but he was studied by Locke and Rousseau, and by the American founding fathers. The title of 'citoyen' was to encapsulate the particular egalitarianism of the eighteenth-century revolutions.

Renaissance and Reformation thus combined to transform the way in which men thought about society. Instead of considering what was their own due place and role in its structure, they asked how it should be structured to serve their purposes. Instead of seeing the individual as formed by the society in which he grew up, they thought of society as formed by individuals who existed in independence before its formation. Aristotle, and Aquinas following him, had thought of man as naturally social, and of society as formed by the growth of family and tribe; but when, after the great transformation, Hobbes and Locke in the seventeenth century considered the same problem of the formation of government, they took it for granted that at the source they would find independent individuals, whether these were preying on one another or guarding each his own in isolation; and Rousseau, later, supposed even that there was no family unit, the sexes meeting for congress only occasionally and briefly, like dog fox and vixen. Nothing can illustrate the strength of individualism more powerfully than the spontaneity of assumptions that would have seemed as strange to medieval thinkers as they do to us. They were made naturally by men who were keenly and freshly aware of their own powers, responsibilities and freedom of choice. Such men saw the individual as preceding the community. In their mind's eye he existed fully formed and endowed before the state came into existence; he charged it with its functions, but derived none of his own capacity from it.

This individualism made for egalitarianism in politics. It is not to be equated with individuality, or with personal development each man in his own way: the individual was rather the unit man before ordered society was founded, and the representative citizen afterwards. Actual men differed widely in ability, conduct and wealth; the political thinkers who propounded the principle of equality had no doubt about such differences, or their legitimacy; but these were irrelevant to the common property of manhood. Under the law of Nature each had rights, equally with every other. This is the notion retained by later generations who spoke of all being equal before the law; and of 'one man, one vote'.

There is another manifestation of individualism that also fostered belief in equality. It goes deep into the psyche, and was to flower in romanticism. It may be called the discovery of the Innocent Self. Jean-Jacques Rousseau told how, as he walked one day in 1749 on the road to Varennes, and glanced through a newspaper as he walked, he came on the subject proposed for an essay contest by the Academy of Dijon—'Has the restoration of the sciences and arts helped to purify or corrupt social standards?' The theme fell on him as an inspiration. 'All of a sudden,' he said,

I felt my mind dazzled by a thousand lights, a host of vivid ideas presented themselves to it in such force and confusion as threw me into an inexpressible anxiety . . . No longer able to breathe as I walked, I let myself fall under one of the trees of the avenue, and there I passed half an hour in such agitation that when I got up I noticed that the front of my waistcoat was wet with my tears, that I had not known I had shed. (Rousseau 1959; I, 1135)

The discovery Rousseau had made was that the sciences and arts that he had regarded as man's supreme achievement had in fact only debilitated and debased society: natural man was inherently good, before his spontaneous impulses were warped by the contrived notions of culture. In this Rousseau was projecting upon civilization his own internal conflict between the simple ardours of his boyhood and the frustrations of his endeavours to establish himself in the Parisian world of letters. His discovery brought him horror at first, and then the tears of the joy of an immense relief. All the attainments in learning and eminence in the *beau monde* to which he had been striving unsuccessfully were a mistaken and a needless burden. Away with it—let him step forth again in the essential goodness and innocence of his pristine nature.

Many counterparts of that experience come to mind. The evangelists in their crusades, bringing men and women to the penitents' bench, and wrestling with them in the spirit, have reported often how the converts under conviction of sin groan in grief and guilt, until some assurance of redemption—most of all the reading of John 3: 16—suddenly dispels all their darkness and despair: they realize that their sins are all forgiven, and tears of joy and relief course down their cheeks. Bunyan's pilgrim, too, shed his burden with tears of joy.

He ran thus till he came at a place somewhat ascending; and upon that place stood a Cross, and a little below in the bottom, a sepulchre. So I saw in my dream, that just as Christian came up with the Cross, his burden loosed from off his shoulders, and fell from off his back; and began to tumble, and so continued to do till it came to the mouth of the sepulchre, where it fell in, and I saw it no more. Then was Christian glad and lightsome, and said with a merry heart, 'He hath given me rest, by his sorrow, and life, by his death.' Then he stood still a while, to look and wonder; for it was very surprising to him that the sight of the Cross should thus ease him of his burden. He looked therefore, and looked again, even till the springs that were in his head sent the waters down his cheeks. . . . Then Christian gave three leaps for joy, and went on singing. . . .

There is thus a sense in which the Innocent Self is revealed by the conversion of the sinner. Wordsworth made it explicit for his Peter Bell. The vicious tinker, haunted by the cries of the Highland girl he had destroyed, as he passed a Methodist conventicle heard the fervent preacher cry 'Repent! Repent!' and promise forgiveness of sins. In the common form of converts, Peter 'melted into tears':

> Each fibre of his frame was weak;
> Weak all the animal within:
> But, in its helplessness, grew mild
> And gentle as an infant child
> An infant that has known no sin.

All who had been saved entered into a fellowship of redemption. They were alike in this, that although their sins had been red as scarlet, now they were white as snow. The currents of evangelicalism and romanticism mingled. By their conversion, men and women were restored to the pristine equality of their Innocent Selves.

A secular counterpart to this casting off of accretions on the self was provided by Robert Owen. With him there had been no trauma or hour of revelation, but he did believe that a 'great secret' had been revealed to him 'by the gradual teaching of nature, through experience and reflection, forced upon one by the circumstances through which I had passed'. This secret was 'that the character of each of our race is formed by God or nature and by society; and that it is impossible that any human being could or can form his own qualities or character'. This discovery too brought its immense relief, a relief from responsibility, from the false notion 'that each one forms his own qualities, and therefore should be made responsible to his fellow-man and to God for them' (Owen 1920: 81). The self that is revealed when the false notion is stripped away is innocent in the sense that it is a *tabula rasa*. The right environment, upbringing and education can then act on this to form adults who will lead virtuous and happy lives in a harmonious and spontaneously ordered society.

There is another counterpart in Wordsworth's yearning for the freshness of impressions that in retrospect tinged his boyhood with the hues of heaven. His belief that 'training clouds of glory do we come' carried with it the faith that men, given freedom, would express their innate goodness, and a conviction that the potential for good, the Innocent Self in us all, demands the removal of oppressive restrictions on our liberty. Of his enthusiasm for the French Revolution, he wrote in later years:

> I had approached, like other youths, the shield
> Of human nature from the golden side,
> And would have fought, even to the death, to attest
> The quality of the metal which I saw.
>
> (*The Prelude*, XI, 79–82)

Belief in the pristine and innocent self was tantamount to belief in the equality of man. For that self was the essence of manhood, common to every man. The externals that differentiated one man from another were imposed arbitrarily by chance and circumstance: what constituted the man was a gift of God or nature with which all were endowed equally. So Rousseau opened his most influential work on government by naming this abstract species-type, man, as its leading concept—'Man is born free.' We have seen how differently Machiavelli viewed men in their variety when he too wrote about government: he saw them objectively, in their occupations and ranks and with their motives and passions, just as they were. What made the difference? Much is due to the contrast of personality between Machiavelli the man of action and Rousseau the introvert. But beyond that, we may conjecture a source of difference that brings out something more of the meaning of individualism, and its connection with equality—individualism, at least, in its Protestant form. This source was the tendency of individualism to introspection. The connection is as follows. Even where, as in Calvin's Geneva, Protestantism exerted its closest tutelage over personal conduct, it still laid on the individual the responsibility for right decisions. For guidance in those decisions he must study the Scriptures; he must pray; above all he must look within, and hearken to the still small voice. This intensified self-awareness was far from self-knowledge. It conveyed rather the notion of the soul, responsive to its Maker; or of natural man; or of a *tabula rasa*. These images of the self, revealed to introspection, display the common nature of mankind, in which all men share equally.

We have seen various ways in which individualism was implanted or deepened as part of the transition from the medieval outlook, and in which individualism in turn fostered the political principle of equality. The humanism of the Renaissance laid its stress on the qualities of the individual, their differentiation and their perfecting. The Reformation transferred the most awful and ultimate responsibilities from the priest to the individual, whom at the same time it elevated to a direct relation with God. If the power of government were regarded as a trust vested in it by the voluntary agreement of individuals, it could be reconciled with their enjoyment of their inherent freedom to order their own actions. The belief that beneath the mould imposed by a debased society lay a self whose untutored promptings were innocent and generous, or at least capable of being harmoniously developed, called for the removal of restraints on the individual whose potentialities were so constructive. Each of these ways in which stress was laid on the individual had its implication for equality. One person cannot claim freedom for self-development without recognizing the equal right of others to that freedom. Equality before God reinforced equality of citizenship. Just as the distinctive attribute of man had been found in reason, which all men alike possessed, so the notion of the Innocent Self that formed the core of every personality, without question of more or less, made all men equal in the essence of their humanity.

3

The Equality of Man in the Eighteenth Century

The two great revolutions of the century, the American and the French, both proclaimed at the outset the equality of man. 'That all men are created equal' was one of the truths held to be self-evident by the signatories of the Declaration of Independence in 1776. 'Men are born and remain free and equal in rights': so began the first Article of the Declaration of the Rights of Man adopted by the French National Assembly of 1789. There had been no proclamation of equality in the English Declaration of Rights in 1689. This had confined itself to matters like the levying of moneys and the upkeep of a standing army on which Parliament meant to secure its hold. But meanwhile, John Locke had been working out a philosophy of government the publication of which was to exercise an international influence throughout the following century and to lay the philosophic foundation for the American Revolution. Locke did deal with equality, at the very outset and basis of his argument.

The first questions to be raised in this chapter are, In what sense was the equality of man maintained by Locke and by the delegates who adopted the American and French Declarations? And, what other movements of thought and interest may have been stirring at these times, of a more actively egalitarian tendency?

3.1. Locke and Equality

Locke's affirmation of the original equality of man, in the state of nature, appears near the outset of his enquiry, not out of any egalitarian zeal on his part—we have no sign of that—but as a by-product of his argument. The object of that argument was to establish the basis of a government's right to govern. Its method was to discover the origins of government. This may well strike us today as strange: under the influence of utilitarianism, we leave origins to the historians, and concern ourselves only with present efficiency, considering the possibility of substituting a more efficient institution as justification for displacing an existing one. But Locke was concerned with origins because arbitrary authority had been seriously claimed for the existing institution of kingship, on the ground that it had been set up by God. In his *First Treatise* he dealt exhaustively with this belief in the divine right of kings. It remained possible to hold that all the rulers in the world owed their position to a seizure of office by brute force. Those who did not believe this 'must of necessity find out another rise of Government, another Original of Political Power . . .' (Locke 1690: I, 1). This he set out to do in the *Second Treatise*.

Locke believed that we must consider the state of nature:

> To understand Political Power aright, and derive it from its Original, we must consider, what State all Men are naturally in, and that is, a *State of perfect Freedom* to order their Actions, and dispose of their Possessions, and Persons as they think fit, within the bounds of the Law of Nature, without asking leave or depending upon the Will of any other Man. (Locke 1690: II, 4)

This reference to nature was ambiguous. On the one hand, Locke went back to 'the state of nature', as Rousseau was to do after him, in conformity with the ancient paradigm of creation. For centuries it had been assumed that the world had been brought into existence by an act of the Creator. As the scientific outlook grew, and the Garden of Eden became less credible as a statement of historical fact, the paradigm still held sway, and philosophers assumed that to understand society they must discover its origins. In this sense, the reference to nature was archaic. But it was the more likely to be made because any mention of nature conjured up the rule of reason, and carried the endorsement of the intellectual faith of recent times. 'The State of Nature has a Law of Nature to govern it, which obliges every one; And Reason, which is that Law, teaches all Mankind, who will but consult it . . .' (Locke 1690: II, 6). By thinking, by simply opening one's mind, one could realize what must necessarily be the case in the matter of the origin of government, with the same sort of necessity as the mind feels in the proof of a mathematical theorem. Here again, Locke was putting new wine in old bottles. In a paradigm coming down from past centuries, Revelation provided incontrovertible knowledge through God's Holy Word. Locke now found this God-given certainty in the apodeictic deliverances of the Reason that the Creator had implanted in human beings as the distinctive endowment of humanity.

But in reality, what was borne in upon the philosopher when he envisaged the state of nature was unconstrained by reason: it followed the mode of the times, or a personal bent. For Locke, that bent, strong and unquestioned, was to individualism. So it was as fully fledged individuals, living in independence of one another before ever they formed any association for common purposes, that men were termed equal by him. The 'State of Perfect Freedom' was 'a *State* also of *Equality*, wherein all the Power and Jurisdiction is reciprocal, no one having more than another' (Locke 1690: II,4). What 'Reason . . . teaches all Mankind' is 'that being all equal and independent, no one ought to harm another in his Life, Health, Liberty or Possessions' (II, 6). Equality is founded in freedom—'Man being born . . . with a Title to perfect Freedom, and an uncontrolled enjoyment of all the Rights and priviledges of the Law of Nature, equally with any other Man, or Number of men in the World . . .' (VII, 87). Locke combines the idea of men being put into the world by the Creator, and endowed with rights by Him, with the idea of the principles of human relations being revealed to reason as part of the structure of nature, in the same way as the principles of geometry.

The equality that Locke assigned to individuals in the state of nature was an equality in 'Power and Jurisdiction'. When these individuals found it in their interest to join in setting up a government, they delegated powers that were inherently incapable of being surrendered. As citizens, they were then on an equal footing in their relations to government, and to each other, and before the law.

Evidently this equality of man as Locke affirmed it, this equal footing, concerned civic and legal status only: it said nothing about what was or ought to be men's relative wealth or income. But this is a matter that Locke did take up, if not without embarrassment, in his discussion of property.

Superimposed on the state of nature as the scene of the 'rise of government', there was another view in Locke, a sketch of primitive man drawn by him from ancient history and contemporary travellers' reports. It was in the setting of this view that he developed his account of property. 'In the beginning all the World was *America*' (Locke 1690: v, 49). We are in effect invited to consider the pioneer clearing the bush, subduing the wilderness—the land itself is free—and making a farm for himself. Then, Locke said, his title to the farm lies in this: that no one can doubt his title to his own labour, and the farm consists of his share of the gifts of nature to all mankind with which he has now mixed his own labour. 'This *Labour* being the unquestionable Property of the Labourer, no Man but he can have a right to what that is once joined to, at least where there is enough, and as good left in common for others' (v, 27). That last proviso raised no difficulty on the American frontier in 1690: but how did Locke cope with its application to Europe, where every inch was already appropriated?

His only defence was to observe that the problem would never have arisen but for the invention of money. Before that, no one would want to enlarge his farm much beyond the acreage that would produce what his family could annually consume: if more were produced, the surplus could be exchanged only for other perishable consumables, which *ex hypothesi* were not wanted, or for such few durable valuables, such as jewels, that might be available. A rough equality of holdings was therefore ensured. But as soon as the possibility arose of selling for money output not wanted for home consumption, and piling the money up, the limit on output was removed. Inequality must be expected to follow.

This left Locke uneasy in his justification of private property in land, the gift of nature to all her children. He had no hesitation in repeating his argument from the labour content of the clearing, so long as there was land enough left for other pioneers to clear holdings for themselves, and there was no money for any one to amass by enlarging his holding and output:

there could be no reason of quarrelling about Title, nor any doubt about the largeness of Possession it gave. Right and conveniency went together; For as a Man had a Right to all he could imploy his Labour upon, so he had no temptation to labour for more than he could make use of. This left no room for Controversie about the Title, nor for incroachment on the Right of others . . . (Locke 1690: v, 51)

But where money had come in, and these conditions were removed, Locke still wished to justify the appropriation of natural resources, for all the resultant inequality. The paragraph is brief and tortuous, but there may be two arguments in it. First, the necessary condition is the use of money, and money 'has its value only from the consent of men'; the state of affairs it brings about is therefore subject to general consent, which evidently it receives, or money would not be usable. But second, that state of affairs is subject to consent more directly, and as a whole:

It is plain, that Men have agreed to disproportionate and unequal Possession of the Earth, they having by a tacit and voluntary consent found out a way, how a man may fairly possess more land than he himself can use the product of, by receiving in exchange for the overplus, Gold and Silver, which may be hoarded up without injury to any one, these metalls not spoiling or decaying in the hands of the possessor. (Locke 1690: v, 50)

There would be injury to others if the man who possessed more land than he himself could use the product of retained the overplus of consumables and allowed them to rot; but if he passed them on to those who were glad to consume them, and himself was ready to hold the durable precious metals instead, the produce of the earth was made available to others in as great amount as if the man's acreage were limited to supporting his own consumption. This fact, that no one can cultivate a big holding unless he makes the overplus of the produce available to his neighbours, is held by Locke to justify its bigness in their eyes—even, it seems, though they have to provide him with gold and silver in order to relieve him of the excess produce.

The fact is that Locke sees property from the first as part of the fortress of self, whose independence and liberty he affirms with apostolic fervour. He can no more allow private property to be invaded, than one man to be subordinated to another. Although often when he speaks of property the context allows that he means only material possessions, he really has in mind the whole of a free man's standing. Men unite in society, he says 'for the mutual *Preservation* of their Lives, Liberties and Estates, which I call by the general Name, *Property*'. It is to protect property in this broad sense that societies are founded: 'the great and *chief end* therefore, of Men's uniting into Commonwealths, and putting themselves under Government, is *the Preservation of their Property* . . .' (Locke 169: ix, 123, 124).

Government, having been instituted to that end, must be removed and replaced if it ceases to fulfil it. There must be no taxation, that is, no levy on property, without the consent of the proprietors. Most directly to our present purpose, there can be no public action to control or redistribute property, government having been set up

for this end, that Men might have and secure *their Properties*, the Prince or Senate, however it may have power to make Laws for the regulation of *Property* between the Subjects one amongst another, yet can never have a Power to take to themselves the whole or any part of the Subjects *Property*, without their own consent. For this would be in effect to leave them no *Property* at all. (Locke 1690: ix, 139)

There is no room for egalitarianism here.

No room, Locke would have said, in justice; but there is also charity to be considered. In the *First Treatise*, before he had affirmed the sanctity of property with the force of the *Second*, he accorded the needy not merely a claim on the benevolence of the affluent, but an actual title to part of their holdings. 'As *Justice* gives every Man a Title to the product of his honest Industry, and the fair Acquisitions of his Ancestors descended to him; so *Charity* gives every Man a Title to so much out of another's Plenty, as will keep him from extream want, when he has no means to subsist otherwise' (Locke 1690: iv, 42). This is dynamite. Marat was to make it an argument for communism. But it does not reappear to qualify the justification of the inequality of property that Locke offers in the *Second Treatise*. The impregnable premise there is the sanctity of property; whatever consequences follow from that must be accepted, be they the principle of no taxation without consent, the right to remove and replace an inefficient government, or the inequality of property and the division of society between penury and plenty.

3.2. The Declaration of Independence

The force of the Declaration was conveyed by an indictment of King George that set out his offences, clause after relentless clause. In the eyes of the signatories, this was more than enough to warrant their throwing off his rule. But in the eighteenth century it was not enough in the eyes of all the world.

When in the course of human events, it becomes necessary for one people to dissolve the political bands, which have connected them with another, and to assume, among the powers of the earth, the separate and equal station, to which the laws of nature and of nature's God entitle them, a decent respect to the opinions of mankind requires that they should declare the causes which impel them to the separation.

Thomas Jefferson drafted the preamble to the Declaration accordingly. So we read:

We hold these truths to be self-evident: that all men are created equal, that they are endowed by their Creator with certain unalienable rights; that among these are life, liberty and the pursuit of happiness; that to secure these rights governments are instituted among men, deriving their just powers from the consent of the governed; that whenever any form of government becomes destructive of these ends, it is the right of the people to alter or abolish it, and to institute new government, laying its foundation on such principles and organizing its powers in such form, as to them shall seem most likely to effect their safety and happiness.

What did Jefferson mean, and what did his fellow-signatories understand, by the proposition 'that all men are created equal'? If it was self-evident, like the proposition that the sum of the angles in a triangle is equal to two right angles, why put it at the outset of the Declaration? Jefferson's own view was that he was only setting down what was in the air. 'I knew only that I turned to neither book nor pamphlet while writing it. . . .' His aim had been

to place before mankind the common sense of the subject, in terms so plain and firm as to command their assent . . . neither aiming at originality of principles or sentiments, nor yet copied from any particular or previous writing, it was intended to be an expression of the American mind . . . All its authority rests on its harmonizing sentiments of the day, whether expressed in conversation, in letters, printed essays, or the elementary books of public right, as Aristotle, Cicero, Locke, Sidney, etc. (Becker 1922: 24, 25)

'The common sense of the subject', 'the American mind'—this is how we must interpret the proposition 'that all men are created equal'. In that light it appears as part of the Whig tradition in the eighteenth century—as one of its assumptions, so widely accepted as to rest unexamined. In the radical tradition of English politics coming down from the Commonwealth men, the *Cato's Letters* of John Trenchard and Thomas Gordon, first published in England in the 1720s, were widely reprinted in America, and as widely influential (Bailyn 1967: 35; Nash 1979: 348). A letter of 1721 (no. 45), 'Of the equality and inequality of man', makes it clear enough what Jefferson meant half a century later. 'Men are naturally equal . . .', we are told at the outset. 'Nature is a kind and benevolent parent; she constitutes no particular favourites with endowments and privileges above the rest; but for the most part sends all her offspring into the world furnished with the elements of understanding and strength to provide for themselves' (Trenchard and Gordon 1754). This is the common stock of eighteenth-century political philosophy. Montesquieu was to say the same, in 1748. In the course of the discussion of slavery in his *De l'esprit des lois* (XV, 7 (4)), he observed that, 'as all men are born equal, slavery must be accounted unnatural'; the reference to equality is made incidentally, as to an accepted principle that needs no argument. Again, in the *Wealth of Nations*, in 1776, we meet Adam Smith's belief, taken to be a matter of fact, that the future philosopher and street porter are indistinguishable in their early years. It rests on the psychology of sense impressions. All photographic plates are the same, so to speak, when they leave the factory, but they come to bear different images as they are exposed to different objects. The same *Cato's Letter* points out that men endowed with equal abilities are—strangely—unequal in their ability to use them; and in any case are variously circumstanced. 'According to the use that they make of their faculties, and of the opportunities that they find, degrees of power and of names of distinction grow amongst them, and their natural equality is lost.' Much more than this, fortune 'acts wantonly and capriciously, often cruelly . . . counterplotting justice as well as nature'. But 'it is evident to common sense, that there ought to be no inequality in society, but for the sake of society. . . .' 'Whoever pretends to be naturally superior to other men, claims from nature what she never gave to any man.' This was the common stock of ideas on which Jefferson drew. We come back to Nature, and Nature's God.

Thereby we come back to Locke. Jefferson would not have prefixed a statement of the Colonists' grievances against King George with a statement so philosophically rarified if he had not been laying the basis for a philosophic defence of the right of the free men to change their government. 'So far as the "Fathers" were, before 1776, directly influenced by particular writers,' said Carl Becker (1922: 27), 'the writers were English, and notably Locke. Most Americans had absorbed Locke's work as a kind of political gospel; and the Declaration, in its form, in its phraseology, follows closely certain sentences in Locke's second treatise on government.' The equality of man meant to Jefferson what Locke meant when he said that the 'state all men are naturally in' was 'a state of perfect freedom to order their actions . . . without asking leave or depending upon the will of any other man'. Men were equal in that each and every man had a right to that freedom; and all men, therefore, stood on an equal footing in ordering their actions. No man's will was to be subjected to another's: those who served in the office of magistrate could exert only such powers over their fellow citizens as these had entrusted to them, and—this is the essential—could withdraw from them.

But this is an equality only in citizenship. Nothing is affirmed or claimed in respect of any personal attributes or conditions: let men be as like or unlike one another as you will in these respects, that is wholly irrelevant to the one claim of right staked by the affirmation that 'all men are created equal'. The immediate relevance of that affirmation was that it showed the authority of kings and magistrates to be delegated, and subject therefore to withdrawal if it were not exercised conformably with the terms of delegation. In its practical application the affirmation bore a meaning that was forcible and even revolutionary; but if human affairs can be divided into the political, the economic and the social, then its impact did not spread far beyond the political.

Yet Jefferson felt that he was expressing the *American* mind: was there not a distinctive dynamic in it, a faith in men's hearts that this was no mere change in allegiance and forms of government that they were about, but the creation of a new society? And in that society would not equality bear a wider, fuller meaning? Did not the equality of man mean more to the American mind than to the European liberals?

Certainly there were some Americans, very likely many, who believed that on those shores they were creating such a free and equal society as the world had not yet seen. The Revolution would establish it in yet greater strength and beneficence. 'The liberties of mankind and the glory of human nature is in their keeping,' John Adams of Massachusetts had written in 1765. 'America was designed by Providence for the theatre in which man was to make his true figure, on which science, virtue, liberty, happiness, and glory were to exist in peace!' (Bailyn 1967: 20). In New England, moreover, there was a Puritan faith in God's special purpose in leading his people thither—a purpose not for them alone, but for all the world. Like the chosen people of old, the American people had a unique role to play in God's plan for all mankind.

Observers fresh from Europe were very conscious of a different sort of society already formed around them, and of manners, J. R. Pole (1978: 56) has said, that 'may after Cromwell be called "russet-coated" egalitarianism'. de Crèvecoeur was a cadet in Montcalm's army, wounded when Wolfe took Quebec, and subsequently discharged, who moved down into the colony of New York and farmed there for many happy years—until at the Revolution he refused to take sides and was driven out by his Loyalist neighbours. Later, in his *Letters from an American Farmer* of 1782, he painted a picture of the society he remembered:

We are all animated with the spirit of an industry which is unfettered and unrestrained, because each person works for himself . . . A pleasing uniformity of decent competence appears throughout our habitations. The meanest of our log houses is a dry and comfortable habitation. Lawyer or merchant are all the fairest titles our towns afford; that of farmer is the only appellation of the rural inhabitants of our country . . . There, on a Sunday [the traveller through our rural districts] sees a congregation of respectable farmers and their wives, all clad in neat homespun, well mounted, or riding in their own humble waggons. There is not among them as esquire, saving the unlettered magistrate. There he sees a parson as simple as his flock, a farmer who does not riot on the labour of others. We have no princes for whom we toil, starve, and bleed; we are the most perfect society now existing in the world. Here man is free as he ought to be, nor is this pleasing equality so transitory as many others are. Many ages will not see the shores of our great lakes replenished with inland nations, nor the unknown bounds of North America entirely peopled. . . . (Bourden *et al.* 1925: ch. iv)

de Crèvecoeur knew that his society of equals depended upon access to the land, but the account he gave of the wildness and degradation of the back-settlers who were actually winning land on the frontier—'the most hideous parts of our society'—was appalling. Even in the settled districts, only a minority of the Irish made good.

The number of debts which one part of the country owes to another would greatly astonish you. The younger a country is the more it is oppressed, for new settlements are always made by people who do not possess much. They are obliged to borrow; and if any accidents intervene, they are not enabled to repay that money in many years. . . . Many never surmount these difficulties. The land is sold, their labour is lost, and they are obliged to begin the world anew. (Bourden *et al.* 1925: 56, 57)

There was rural poverty, then. The country folk of Virginia were in any case made up very differently from the society of small and independent farmers in upper New York whose churchgoing was so pleasantly depicted: about a quarter of the white males were labourers owning no land and with few personal possessions of any kind. Even in Massachusetts, up to a quarter of the population—or, if we include indentured servants, a third—owned little property beyond their personal belongings (Main 1965: 57, 41-2). A fifth of the whole population of the colonies were slaves.

Land ownership was at its most equal in the settlements that were still engaged in subsistence farming. In his study of *The Social Structure of Revolutionary America*, Jackson Turner Main has given us a picture of Goshen, Connecticut, 'just emerging from the pioneer stage' in 1741. There were forty-nine taxpayers. The wealthiest five—virtually the top 10 per cent—paid 22 per cent of the tax, excluding poll tax. Judging by the ownership of cattle, about forty of the men were landowners, but since none owned more than thirteen cattle, none was in a big way (Main 1965: 14). But as development went on, and farming became commercial, the distribution of property became more concentrated in the hands of the enterprising and the fortunate. In the rural areas of Massachusetts cited in Table 3.1, the proportion of wealth owned by the top 10 per cent was over 40 per cent. In the towns the proportion was still higher: the same table cites estimates of 45 per cent for New York, 56 per cent for Boston and two figures of around 70 per cent for Philadelphia. This partly marks the effect of the towns having attracted numbers of propertyless young people looking for work; partly it marks the possibility of amassing mercantile fortunes there. A comprehensive estimate of distribution in the Middle Colonies is cited in Table 3.2, where it may be compared with the distribution estimated for a fairly recent year in the United Kingdom. The more significant comparison is with the B series for the United Kingdom, as it is

TABLE 3.1 *Concentration of Wealth in American Colonies*

Proportion of total wealth held by the top 10 per cent of free adult potential wealth-holders, according to the evidence of tax lists or probate, in rural areas and towns of the North-Eastern and Middle Colonies, about the time of the Revolution*

	Year(s)	Rural areas/towns	%
(1)	1782–8	Boston, probate wealth	56.0
(2)	1777–8	Suffolk County (incl. Boston), Massachusetts, probate wealth	41.4
		Massachusetts rural areas:	
(3)	1760–9	Rural Suffolk (excl. Boston), probate wealth	42.4
(4)	1779	Hingham, tax lists	46.5
(5)	1782–8	Worcester, probate wealth	43.0
(6)	1770–4	Hartford, Connecticut, incl. real property	49.4
(7)	1789	New York City, tax lists	45.0
(8)	1774	Philadelphia, tax lists	72.3
(9)	1766–75	Philadelphia, probate wealth	69.9
(10)	1782	Chester, Pennsylvania, tax lists	33.6
(11)	1782–8	Maryland, probate wealth	60.0

* Row (6) is age-adjusted, to estimate the distribution of estates among living adult males with property; row (4) is the only estimate adjusted for the propertyless.

Sources: All these estimates are cited here from Appendix A of Williamson and Lindert (1980).

this that brings into reckoning the whole population, and not merely those whose estates are reported for probate: on this comparison it appears that property in the Middle Colonies about the time of the Revolution was much more equally distributed than it is in the United Kingdom at the present time—and still more so, we have reason to believe, than in the England of 1776. But even so, the American distributions reveal a substantial concentration of wealth, and it had been growing. Beyond the colonies reported in these tables, moreover, lay the great plantations of Virginia and the Carolinas, with their landless labourers, white as well as slave. The dominant influence on men's outlook, as on their individual fortunes, was still that America remained the land of opportunity, and 'a good poor man's country'; but it was not a land of economic equality. Williamson and Lindert (1980: 37) observe that 'the 1774 colonial wealth distribution has a close resemblance to the [revised] distribution implied by the Federal Reserve survey for 1962'.

Despite the broad belt of farmers, lawyers and merchants in the Middle and Northern Colonies, then; despite the consciousness of the plenty if not the full equality of opportunity, and the freedom of mobility; and despite the absence of hereditary privilege and status: despite all this, the society of revolutionary America had arrived at some outright inequalities, of a kind familiar in the Old World, in the distribution of income and wealth. The attitudes of the revolutionary leaders towards those inequalities were conflicting, by our standards, but not by theirs. They held that the ownership of property was essential to responsible citizenship, and they despised, or dreaded, the labourer without land or capital. Yet they also feared the divisive force of economic interests, and the over-mighty power of riches. It is apparent how closely their outlook in these respects resembled that of the Greeks, at least as expressed by Plato and still more by Aristotle.

TABLE 3.2   *Distribution of personal wealth in Mainland Colonies and the United Kingdom*

American Mainland Colonies and Philadelphia County, 1774: distribution of net worth among free adult potential wealth holders; United Kingdom, 1975: percentage shares of estimated total personal wealth (A) in the population included in Inland Revenue estimates using estates passing at death; (B) in the total adult population aged 18 and over, assuming that persons not covered by the Inland Revenue estimates have no wealth.

| | 1774 (%) | | 1975 (%) | |
	Middle Colonies	Philadelphia County	United Kingdom A	B
Top 10%	41	55	47	62
Next 10%	18	15	16	19
Lowest 80%	41	31	37	18

Sources: Colonies: Jones (1971: tables 13 and 17); cited here from Henretta (1973: table 3.2); *UK*: Royal Commission (1977; table 28).

Under the first of these heads, the problem of the propertyless. we must remind ourselves that belief in men having been created equal, as a principle of political philosophy, could be held together with a very realistic view of the inequality of their abilities, or an unyielding view of their rightful ordering in society. Because nothing but tumult and uproar could result when power was vested in the common people, 'democracy' was a pejorative term, until Tom Paine exerted himself to put a better face on it. With part of his mind, or in a certain sense, Jefferson had proclaimed that all men were created equal, but when he set up his scheme of further education for Virginia, he spoke of his scholarship boys being raked out of the rubbish (Pole 1978: 120). The authors of *Cato's Letters* held a view of the threat to the social order from overweening wealth that will be cited here shortly, but even the politics of the radical Whig bore no tincture of social egalitarianism. One of the Letters assails charity schools for disturbing the social and economic order:

[They] tear the lowest dregs of the people from the plough and labour, to make them tradesmen, and by consequence drive the children of tradesmen to the plough, to beg, to rob, or to starve . . . No education ought to be more discountenanced by a state, than putting chimeras and airy notions into the hands of those who ought to have pickaxes in their hands. . . . What benefit can accrue to the public by taking the dregs of the people out of the kennels, and throwing their betters into them? (Letter no. 133, 1723: Trenchard and Gorden 1754)

This was to whip up indignation against the High Church by which the charity schools were promoted, and we do not know that the Americans, who liked Cato's attacks on tyranny so much, were partial to his views on the need to keep labourers illiterate; but it is to be remembered, when we think of equality in the eighteenth century, that the two sorts of view could keep company in the Whig mind.

The Founding Fathers had no doubt that the franchise must be restricted to men of property. Men without it could not be entrusted with the vote—for the same reason that it could not be given to women and children: all these lacked the essentials of independence and responsibility that only the possession of property could safeguard. John Adams went farther. 'Such is the frailty of the human heart,' he declared, 'that very few men who have no property, have any judgement of their own. Generally speaking,' even women, whom nature had 'made . . . fittest for domestic cares', and children, who had 'no judgement or will of their own', had 'as good judgements, and as independent minds, as those men who are wholly destitute of property' (Greene 1976: 26–7).

On the other hand, the self-interest that led to the accumulation of property, and the consequent inequality, was a danger to the republic. The 'divisive force of economic interests' dispelled the original hope of the republicans that in devotion to the state men would be of one mind. Virtue consisted in devotion to the public good, and this was inconsistent with the pursuit of self-interest. But money-making concentrated man's passions in self-interest. Hence the doctrine that commerce corrupts. The money-maker loses his virtue. As he amasses wealth he becomes over-mighty. James Harrington, whose *Oceana* was widely read in America, had bequeathed the principle that 'where there is inequality of estates there must be inequality of power'.

Recognition of the impact of economic inequality, and consequent divergence of interests, on the politics of the republic led to two kinds of policy. There were some reformers, Evangelicals for the most part, and middle-class intellectuals, as we should say today, who drew the conclusion that the state must intervene to redistribute property—at least, to reduce the greatest contrasts of wealth and poverty (Nash 1979: 13). In principle, they were Levellers. They could have drawn strong drafts from *Cato's Letters*.

As Liberty can never subsist without Equality, nor Equality be long preserved without an *Agrarian Law*, or something like it: so when Men's Riches are become immeasurably or surprizingly great, a People, who regard their own Security, ought to make a strict Enquiry how they came by them, and oblige them to take down their own Size, for fear of terrifying the Community or mastering it. (Letter no. 35, 1721: Trenchard and Gordon 1754)

It proceeds from a consummate ignorance in politics, to think that a number of men agreeing together can make and hold a common-wealth, before nature has prepared the way: for she alone must do it. An equality of estate will give an equality of power; and an equality of power is a common-wealth, or democracy: an *Agrarian* law, or something equivalent to it, must make or find a suitable disposition of property, and when that comes to be the case, there is no hindering a popular form of government, unless sudden violence takes away all liberty, and, to preserve itself, alters the distribution of property again. (Letter no. 85, 1722: Trenchard and Gordon 1754)

But when the great issue of the day became the active struggle with the British, and the reformers needed to form a common front with the prosperous merchants and the men of landed estates, they could not persist in, still less brandish, proposals so unwelcome to their comrades in arms. Enough had been heard of the alarming prospect of an Agrarian Law, however, for Tom Paine later on to apply his ingenuity to showing how to steer round it.

The artisans of Philadelphia, among whom Tom Paine had found himself at home, had drawn the same conclusion as Cato. In 1776 they tried to insert in the new constitution of their state a clause declaring 'That an enormous Proportion of Property vested in a few Individuals is dangerous to the Rights, and destructive of the Common Happiness of Mankind; and therefore any free State hath a Right by its Laws to discourage the Possession of such Property' (Foner 1976: 133). James Madison was to advise a like policy later on:

In one of a series of articles published in 1792, Madison advanced the view that new laws should be enacted to withold '*unnecessary* opportunities from the few to increase the inequality of property by an immoderate, and especially unmerited, accumulation of riches'. Moreover, laws should be passed so as silently to 'reduce extreme wealth towards a state of mediocrity, and raise indigence towards a state of comfort'. (Pole 1978: 122)

But Madison's earlier and major remedy for the threat levelled at the republic by economic inequality was political. He recognized that differences of personal ability, the exercise of which it was the role of government to protect, must result in unequal acquisitions of property; that these inequalities must create divergences of interest; and these conflicting interests in turn must form factions:

From the protection of different and unequal faculties of acquiring property, the possession of different degrees and kinds of property immediately results; and from the influence of these on the sentiments and views of the respective proprietors, ensues a division of the society into different interests and parties. The most common and durable source of factions has been the various and unequal distribution of property. Those who hold and those who are without property have ever formed distinct interests in society. Those who are creditors, and those who are debtors, fall under a like discrimination. A landed interest, a manufacturing interest, a mercantile interest, a moneyed interest, with many lesser interests, grow up of necessity in civilized nations, and divide them into different classes, actuated by different sentiments and views. The regulation of these various and interfering interests forms the principal task of modern legislation, and involves the spirit of party and faction in the necessary and ordinary operations of the government. (Hamilton *et al.* 1941: 55, 56)

Economic inequality, then, was inevitable. It could not be checked at the source, because the state must protect the exercise of individual powers of acquisition, out of whose diversity it arose. 'A rage . . . for an equal division of property' Madison referred to as 'an improper or wicked project'. But inequality caused faction, and if that was unchecked it would disrupt the republic. Madison found the remedy in the representative principle. When representatives, put forward by the different interests, met to take counsel together, and they themselves had been chosen as men of experience and sound sense in the first place, the common interest would prevail. The effect of the representative principle was 'to refine and enlarge the public views, by passing them through the medium of a chosen body of citizens, whose wisdom may best discern the true interest of their country . . .' (Hamilton *et al.* 1941: 62, 59). The President was to be elected not by the people to whom candidates might appeal directly, but by the considered opinion of a college of electors, chosen as men of judgement by the knowledge of their neighbours. The claims of the multitude were to be met not by a heady populism, but (as we might see it now) by Mr Attlee's kind of government, in which working people eager for change put in office highly educated middle-class politicians, and trade union leaders of a pragmatic, deliberate and socially integrative tendency.

So economic inequality did concern the Founding Fathers, but more for its effects on the republic than on personal welfare: the rich would be too powerful, the poor would be unruly, and every man might push his own interests too hard. But in the North at least, there was some sensitivity to the personal issue, in the matter of differences in pay. There is evidence of egalitarian sentiment there. When, after the Revolution, Congress came to fix the pay of its soldiers, the Southern delegates thought it only fitting that the differentials between ranks should be wide, and they got their way; but that was not how it would have been in New England. 'Those ideas of equality,' John Adams commented, 'which are so agreeable to us nations of New England, are very disagreeable to many gentlemen in other colonies . . . They think the Massachusetts establishment too high for the privates, and too low for the officers, and they would have their own way' (Pole 1978: 31).

The tincture of egalitarianism in New England owed something to the Puritan and evangelical traditions. Puritanism itself in its early days had formed a stern theocracy, cruelly repressive of those who tried to go their own way, in faith or manners. Far from inhibiting the pursuit of wealth, its code was conducive to zealous attention to business, and to thrift; and this made for inequality. But there was a leaven in Puritanism also, which worked against subordination. Its emphasis was laid on moral qualities that the humblest person could evince as much as the most substantial. It proclaimed the supreme importance of the soul, and its direct relation with God: in this respect all persons were alike, all were equal in the sight of God. This equality transcended the things of this world, but belief in it reduced the respect accorded to the wealthy; even more, it called into question the justification of great differences in the material condition of persons who in the supreme issues of this world and the next were equal.

The economic circumstances of the region, moreover, provided a setting retentive of this outlook: although Boston saw fortunes made in commerce beside growing numbers in destitution, the countryside had not been settled by large estates; nor did the farming that the terrain permitted tend to large units each worked by numerous labourers. The outlook on human relations was naturally more egalitarian in communities with relatively few indentured servants and slaves.

We began by asking whether the principle that all men were created equal was more than the first step in a strictly political argument. Most of our discussion has shown how closely it was restricted to that purpose. Liberal minds even drew back in horror from the thought of laying levelling hands on other men's property. But some tincture of equality was diffused from its political application, to colour social life and even personal relations. Contemporaries noted a democratization of manners at the time of the Revolution. At the outset, as the states made their own constitutions, the question arose of who should have the vote. The franchise in the colonies had generally followed the property qualifications usual in England, and we have seen that there was no question of waiving these altogether at the Revolution. But, except in Massachusetts and Virginia, they were generally reduced; and before long manhood suffrage followed. Pennsylvania gave the vote to all adult men in 1790, Massachusetts followed in 1820 and New York in 1822. That was a state of civic equality—for males—not reached in Great Britain in practice until 1918.

Another way in which the setting of one group of men apart from and above the others was found incompatible with the spirit of the Revolution lay in establishing religious freedom. Jefferson regarded his Bill for that purpose 'as one of his greatest contributions to humanity. In its assertion that the mind is not subject to coercion, that civil rights have no dependence on religious opinion, and that the opinions of men are not the concern of civil government, it is indeed one of the great American charters of freedom' (Malone 1933: 20). It was the equality of all citizens in the enjoyment of this freedom that was now established.

But the greatest, the most problematic, divisive and powerful diffusion of the idea of equality, was over slavery. In the rhetoric of the day, the tyranny under which the colonists groaned had been reducing them to slavery: when they threw off its shackles, how could they in all conscience continue to inflict it on others? Their theoretical answer was Aristotle's: those others were so different, by nature, that arguments concerning the rights of man could not be extended to them. The practical case in the plantation colonies was that the economies could not operate without them. In the Middle Colonies and the North it was different. A movement against slavery arose there about the mid-eighteenth century. In Philadelphia, where in the 1770s seven of the ten richest citizens were Quakers, as early as 1758 the Quakers' yearly meeting had resolved to exclude all members who traded in Negroes, and subsequently many Quakers set their slaves free (Pole 1978: 33). The legislative of Massachusetts made several attempts before the Revolution to abolish the slave trade, but the Governor vetoed them. When the Continental Congress had assembled, in 1774, it pledged itself to abolish the slave trade throughout the thirteen colonies, and in 1776 it voted that no slaves be imported into any of them (Bailyn 1967: 245). Jefferson, himself at all times the benevolent owner of some two hundred slaves, was unhappy with the institution. He did try to include a clause in the Declaration that would have held the British Crown 'responsible and censurable for American slavery', but if the Declaration were to be adopted unanimously, it had to say nothing about slavery at all (Smith 1927: 45-6). In his report on the government of the Western Territory, he was able to recommend that slavery be forbidden throughout it. This was in accordance with the spirit of the Revolution in the North, where it had brought forth many abolitionist societies; but the South held its ground. There was a long road still to be trod, and a bloody one.

None the less, the principle that all men are created equal, once proclaimed, would continue to fret men's minds. For those who appended their signatures to that original document of 1776, there were well understood interpretations, reservations, limitations; but the simple words rang out. A genie had escaped from the bottle. Robert Frost's minister, thinking of the widow who had lost her husband in the Civil War—'he fell at Gettysburg or Fredericksburg'—felt it so:

> Her giving somehow touched the principle
> That all men are created free and equal.
>   . . .
> That's a hard mystery of Jefferson's.

What did he mean? Of course the easy way
Is to decide it simply isn't true.
It may not be. I heard a fellow say so.
But never mind, the Welshman got it planted
Where it will trouble us a thousand years.
Each age will have to reconsider it.

'The Black Cottage'

'I have a dream', proclaimed Martin Luther King in Washington in 1963, a dream of what those simple words of the Declaration might yet mean for the raising up of his children, the black people.

3.3. The Declaration of the Rights of Men and Citizens

When the breakdown of the French King's finances obliged him to summon the States General, in the mid-summer of 1789, the Third Estate went ahead on its own, in what was called 'the revolution of the lawyers'. As the National and Constituent Assembly, it charged itself with drawing up a new constitution. On 26 August Lafayette read to the Assembly a Declaration of the Rights of Men and Citizens.

The Preamble maintained that 'the sole cause of disorders in the body public, and of the corruption of government, is that the rights of men are unknown, forgotten, or held in contempt'. A right is an entitlement: it lays a corresponding duty on another person. The rights possessed by every man, therefore, can be found only in the body of civil law regulating relations between persons at large. The rights of men that the Declaration proclaimed were legal and civic rights, and it was with those alone that the only kind of equality it envisaged was concerned.

FIRST ARTICLE
Men are born and remain free and equal in their rights; social distinctions can be based only on services to the public.

II
The end of all political association is the preservation of the natural and imprescriptible rights of man; these rights are liberty, property, security, and resistance to oppression.

. . .

IV
Law is the expression of the general will; all citizens have the right to take part personally, or through their representatives, in forming it; it should be the same for all, both when it protects, and when it punishes. All citizens, being equal in its eyes, are equally admissible to all honours, appointments and public offices, according to their capacity, and without other grounds of differentiation than their character and talents. (reproduced from plate at p. 128 of Lavisse 1920)

'Men are born . . . equal in their rights'; and this principle is opposed to conventional social distinctions. A first step in assessing its egalitarianism is to consider the minds of its authors. The Declaration 'reflected the views of men like Lafayette, Mounier, Talleyrand, Lally-Tollendal and Alexandre de Lameth who contributed most of the work of drafting' (Goodwin 1970: 74).

It was as a young captain in garrison at Metz that Lafayette had been carried away by reading the American Declaration of Independence: he decided to leave at once to help the Americans in their struggle, and although the disclosure of his project led to threats to imprison him in the Bastille, he slipped away. How he was received with high honours by Washington, shared the hardships of campaign with him, commanded in the field and received the capitulation of Cornwallis at Yorktown is a familiar but still amazing story. When he returned to America in 1784, after the conclusion of peace, it was, he said, in order to help 'establish the temple of liberty there on a firm base' (in Robert *et al.* 1891). His special interests in 1787–9 were in the disabilities of Protestants and Negroes, and generally the establishment of equality of civil rights, the abolition of hereditary titles and the introduction of juries on the English pattern.

Alexandre de Lameth was a colonel of the Household Cavalry who like Lafayette had fought in the War of American Independence; he voted with the left of the Assembly; but, like Lafayette again, he later went over to the Austrian forces, and was held by them as a prisoner.

Mounier was a lawyer of Grenoble, who came to the fore on the morning when the King locked the Assembly out: Sieyès would have carried it off to Paris and the mob, but Mounier saved it by proposing the Oath of the Tennis Court. He had earlier gathered the three Estates of the Dauphiné in the tennis court of a castle there, with the Third Estate given double weight, and they had elected him secretary by acclamation. But on the great night of 4 August in the National Assembly, when successive speakers vied with one another in surrendering their feudal privileges, he spoke in defence of the rights of private property. Later he introduced the report of the constitutional committee. A great admirer of the English constitution, he stressed the division of powers, the importance of a permanent second chamber and the royal veto. The Assembly would have none of them, and he had to go. As the Revolution proceeded, he removed to Switzerland.

The Marquis de Lally-Tolendal had stood out on the side of reform by reason of the long battle he had fought for the rehabilitation of his father, a governor of the French Indies who had been disgraced and executed in consequence of his defeat by Sir Eyre Coote at Wandewash and Pondicherry. The son in his ultimately successful struggle had been helped by Voltaire. Elected a representative of the nobility of Paris, he served as a member of the committee appointed to draft the constitution, but left it at the same time as Mounier. The irruption into Versailles on 5 and 6

October 1789 that hailed the royal family back to Paris made an *émigré* of him.

By 1789 Talleyrand, Bishop of Autun, at the age of thirty-five, was a man of wide reading, administrative experience and knowledge of the world. The scion of an old noble family, he would have followed his father in the army but for an accident in boyhood that left him lame. Instead, in five years as a seminarist he read the *philosophes*, and then he spent some time at the Sorbonne. For some eight years, as *agent-general* of the clergy of France, he showed himself singularly resolute and unyielding in defending each and every privilege of the clergy. Now, a deputy of the clergy to the Estates General, he joined the Third Estate; putting the helm hard over, he proposed the abolition of tithe, and the sale of church property to pay off national debt. A man without fixed stars in his firmament, without values deeply cherished or aims sustained, but with a supple genius for arranging, contriving and executing, he applied himself to the requirements imposed by the dominant forces of the day. In 1789 these included the work of the Committee of the Constitution. But later, as the Revolution moved into Terror, even his indifference to principle would not have satisfied the inquisitors, and he found it advisable to withdraw to the United States until their flames had consumed themselves.

Such were the personalities who now proclaimed that 'men are born and remain free and equal in their rights'. They were aristocrats, all save Mounier, and he was a lawyer of the upper middle class. But they joined with the Third Estate, and drafted the Declaration, because they were men of cultivation, their minds kindled by the adventurous, illuminating and liberating thought of the century. Those who themselves held positions of comfort and privilege in a society that they knew to be oppressive, but had no means of changing, found their frustrated zeal for reform ascending into visions of a happier, more brotherly community; in moving terms, they affirmed the principles on which it would rest. At the same time, they remained the creatures of their own upbringing, with its inculcated expectations and assumptions about the world around them. These were bound to conflict with the principles they had received from the philosophic light and teaching of the time. So long as no political action was stirring in France, they could indulge their liberalism. In America Lafayette and de Lameth had fought to aid its application where the texture of another society and the authority of another king were at stake. But when, in France, itself, the conflict between upbringing and principles was forced into the open by the advance of the Revolution, it was the attitudes inculcated by upbringing that prevailed. All five of these draftsmen became *émigrés*.

Meanwhile, the meaning of their affirmation of equality may be brought out if we consider what are likely to have been the two sources of their philosophy, namely Rousseau, and the Enlightenment.

Conflicting influences made up the ideas that strove together in the turmoil of Rousseau's mind. In his childhood he had absorbed the puritanism of Geneva, and the resentment of the lower town for the wealth of the upper. His own passionate, sensitive nature was taut with the need for acceptance by others whom he suspected of a conspiracy to reject him. In his reading as an adolescent he entered into the minds of the *philosophes*. Evidently Locke was not the least of those who influenced him then. His thought about society began along customary lines. He set out to discover by a thought experiment what Locke had called the original of government. For a whole week, he tells us, he walked in the forest of St Germain—'There I sought, there I found, the image of the earliest times' (*Confessions*, 381; in Green 1955: 120). He was engaged, he would have said, not in viewing the actual past through some mental telescope that enabled him to see down the vistas of time, but in examining 'a state of affairs which no longer exists, which perhaps never has existed, which probably never will exist, but of which it is necessary to form an accurate conception, in order to judge our present state correctly'. (in Vauphan 1962: I, 136).

But in his second *Discours*, *On the Origin and Basis of Inequality among Men* (see Vaughan 1962), he mingled the analytic use of the notion of a state of nature with information arriving from missionaries and explorers about primitive peoples discovered overseas. The Caribs he accepted as 'of all living peoples those who so far have departed least from the state of nature' (in Vaughan 1962: I, 164). He was even fascinated by the orangutang, and thought that they might be 'actually truly wild men, whose race dispersed at some early date in the woods, did not have occasion to develop any of its potential faculties, did not acquire any degree of perfection, and found itself still in the primitive state of nature' (in Vaughan 1962: I, 208). But these reports and conjectures did nothing to modify his persuasion that in the state of nature each person had roamed alone. There were not even family units: men and women met briefly for sexual intercourse, but no more; and as soon as the child could fend for itself, the mother drove it away. The state of nature thus established was one of substantial equality. Much of the inequality of capability that we see about us in the world of today and are apt to regard as natural is not really so, he held, but is due to upbringing. In the state of nature, moreover, the strong have no opportunity to exploit the weak—no one depends on anyone else. He believed that he had 'proved that inequality in the state of nature is inconsiderable, and its influence is practically nil' (Vaughan 1962: I, 168). This is the familiar language and lore of the *philosophes*.

The same outlook appeared in the article on political economy which he wrote for the *Encyclopédie* and which was published in the same year as the second *Discours*, 1755. It contained strong words about the sacredness of property—'the most sacred of all the rights of citizens, more important in some respects than liberty itself . . .' (Rousseau 1755: V). Hence the terrible paradox of taxation, that, when the state has been set up in order to protect property, it must then invade property by imposing taxation in order to maintain itself. The sacred rights were recognized by an Article in the Declaration:

XVII

The rights of property being inviolable and sacred, no one can be deprived of his property, except when public necessity, established by due process of law, clearly requires it, and subject to the previous payment of fair compensation. (Lavisse 1920: 128)

The earlier Rousseau had also been opposed to social mobility, and the diffusion of property that went with it—that is, to what was to be Condorcet's liberal path towards reduced inequality. Rousseau held that property should be kept within the family as much as possible, not only because this was only fair to the children who had helped to accumulate it, but even more because continual changes in the status and fortune of citizens were extremely harmful to the morale of the community: confusion arose when those who had been brought up for one station in life found themselves in another, and neither those who rose nor those who came down in the world could adapt themselves to their new station or carry its duties out.

This appreciation of the propriety of the social order may go back to the days when, as a young man in his late twenties, Rousseau was first introduced at Lyons to the society of affluent merchants, manufacturers and professional people: he found them intelligent, cultivated and receptive to himself. In the rhymed epistle that he wrote afterwards to one of them, he told how he had given up the utopian notions of his youth, and come to see that

> Twould not be good, within society,
> To have between its ranks less inequality.

(letter to M. Parisot, 1742; quoted here from Green 1955: 72-3)

Rousseau followed Locke in his conception of the self-sufficient individual in the state of nature, but not in his account of the origins of inequality. With Locke, we saw, the essential condition for the rise of unequal properties was the use of money. As Rousseau pictured it, inequality came in two stages.

In the first, a number of causes, vaguely indicated, brought the solitary wanderers together in groups and tribes, each with its own tongue, its way of life and its unwritten laws. Inequality made its appearance here in prestige of achievement.

Each person began to cast an eye over the others, and want to be an object of attention himself, and public esteem was highly prized. The man who was the best dancer or singer, the most handsome, the strongest, the most adroit, or the most eloquent, became the most admired; and that was the first step towards inequality, and at the same time towards vice. (Vaughan 1962: I, 174)

But the state of society so attained was a happy one. Rousseau identified it with the condition in which 'the savages of various countries of the world' were living in his own day, and he remarked that, whereas many missionaries had paid tribute to the restfulness of their years among the savages, no savage had yet been moved to adopt the civilized way of life (Vaughan 1962: I, 217-19). Here is the world of the Noble Savage. Adam Smith examined it, among other contemporary productions, in a letter to the *Edinburgh Review* in 1755 (Lindgren 1967: 24-5). He saw in it an inversion, or an embellishment, of Mandeville's *Fable of the Bees*, a change made by substituting for the wretched and miserable primitive state of mankind in the *Fable* a state, 'the happiest and most suitable' to human nature. The appeal of this romantic fantasy (if we may read between the lines of his appreciation) lay solely in its style:

M. Rousseau, intending to paint the savage life as the happiest of any, presents only the indolent side of it to view, which he exhibits indeed with the most beautiful and agreeable colours, in a style, which, though laboured and studiously elegant, is everywhere sufficiently nervous, and sometimes even sublime and pathetic. It is by the help of this style, together with a little philosophical chemistry, that the principle and ideas of the profligate Mandeville seem in him to have all the purity and sublimity of the morals of Plato, and to be only the true spirit of a republican carried a little too far. (Lindgren 1967: 24-5)

But this state of innocence, so happy despite its pangs of emulation in the performance of dancing and singing, was ending by an economic Fall. Men discovered metallurgy and agriculture. With these came the division of labour and the subordination of the labourer; the appreciation of land as private property and the formulation of rules of positive law, other than those of the law of nature; and differences of individual output and earnings responding to differences of energy, ability and circumstances. The possessions of the wealthy would then have been open to attack by the poor, and would in any case have been the object of jealousy: in such a state of insecurity, the rich must have proposed setting up by common consent a supreme power to keep order. 'It is reasonable to believe that something has been devised by those to whom it is useful, rather than by those whom it harms' (Vaughan 1962: I, 182). 'Such was, or surely must have been, the origin of society and of the laws that fixed new shackles on the weak and brought new power to the rich, irrevocably destroyed natural liberty, and laid down in perpetuity the law of property and inequality. . . . .' (Vaughan 1962: I, 181).

This imaginative account of the origins of inequality led Rousseau into a thundering attack on private property as the origin of all social evil—and this he published in the same year as his declaration in the *Encyclopédie* that the rights of property were sacred, and 'more important in some respects than liberty itself'. What he maintained in the second *Discours* was that private property 'brought death into the world, and all our woe':

The first man who having enclosed a piece of ground took it into his head to say 'This is mine' and found people simple-minded enough to believe it, was the true founder of civil society. Oh how many crimes, and wars, and murders, what miseries and horrors mankind would have been spared by the man who, pulling the fence down or filling up the ditch, called to his fellows, 'Look out, don't listen to this impostor, you'll be lost if you forget that the fruits of the earth belong to everyone, the earth itself belongs to no one'.

Voltaire noted on his copy here: 'What! the man who has planted, sown and enclosed has no right to the fruit of his efforts. What! this dishonest man, this thief, is to be the benefactor of mankind! There you have the philosophy of a beggar who would like to have the rich robbed by the poor' (Rousseau 1964: 164)

'This is mine.' Rousseau had been fascinated by the fatal, poisoned phrase some years before, when he was defending his thesis that the growth of luxury and the arts corrupted the innocent self. 'Before those frightful words *thine* and *mine* were invented,' he cried, 'before private property appeared, and the division of master and servant, and of the wealthy and the needy: before the Fall, how could men possibly have been wicked?' (from the *Dernière Réponse,* 1752: Rousseau 1964: 80). He is in a tradition of the Church. We saw (p. 47) how, around 1500, John Colet had used the same terms *meum* and *tuum* to epitomize the positive law 'of a defiled and corrupted nature' which had succeeded the principles of the 'good and unsophisticated nature' that had ruled until the Fall. The terms appear again, in the latter part of the seventeenth century, in Bossuet's *Panegyric on St Francis of Assisi*. Here, in a passage that anticipated what Montesquieu was to write about equality, and affirmed the Church's view that the needy had not merely a claim on the charity of the rich but a title to their superfluity, Bossuet traced 'those cold words' back to the Fathers.

Nature, or to speak in a more Christian way, God, the Father of all men, has given all his children from the first an equal right to all they need for the preservation of their lives. None of us can pride himself on being more favoured than the others by nature: but the insatiable desire to acquire more has not allowed this fine fraternity to last for long in the world. A dividing up had to come about, with private property which has given rise to all our disputes and litigation: thence has come this word of *mine* and *thine*, so cold a word, as the admirable St John Chrysostom said.

(Panégyrique de saint Francois d'Assise, IV, 434 of 1846, edn.; quoted here from Gray 1946: 56, 17.1)

The image of a Fall prompts the thought of a Redemption. Rousseau, we have seen (p. 00), had undergone the experience of conversion: on the road to Varennes he had recovered his innocent self. An internal conflict he could never resolve was waged between his desires for independence and for acceptance and approval. While he was writing his account of the origins of inequality, which left men alienated from one another by it, his mind was turning to the possibility of transcending it. As far back as 1750 or 1751, he took up the idea that was to form a mainstay of *The Social Contract* in 1762. He had supposed, as we have seen, that the state was formed when the man of substance reached an agreement to adopt certain laws. 'Let me now forget', we can suppose him to have said to himself, 'what I put into my *Discourse* about all this being done and the state being instituted in order to protect property—I got this from Locke. Instead, let me think of the general agreement as the voluntary surrender by each man of his own faulty self, with all its anti-social propensities, in order that it may be restrained and guided by the laws that the collective self now adopts and enforces.' It has it mystical interpretation: but its application to human equality is straightforward. Men as physical beings retain all their bodily and mental inequalities, but as citizens they are made equal: in the very nature of the state—at least, of the state as it ought to be—the citizen as such enjoys civic and legal rights that are the same for all. Thus Rousseau sums up, at the end of the first Book of the *Social Contract*, in an observation which, he said,

'ought to serve as basis for the whole social system: it is that instead of destroying natural equality, on the contrary the fundamental agreement' (we may take this to mean the social contract) 'substitutes equality in the domains of morality and law for the extent of physical inequality that nature would introduce between men; and that, though they may well be unequal in strength and ability, they all become equal by agreement and as of right.' (Rousseau 1947: I, ix)

He has solved his problem of reconciling the independence and freedom of the individual with the integration and union of each man with his fellows.

The distinctive influence of Rousseau is to be seen in the Fourth Article of the Declaration, quoted above, beginning 'Law is the expression of the general will.' How his mystical conception of the fusion of the individual and the general will could be realized, in a country of 28 million inhabitants, was not considered: what his eloquence had won in practice was the case for manhood suffrage, albeit with a property qualification. With this went the abolition of privilege, that is, the positive principle that, as the Fourth Article stated, all citizens were equal in the eyes of the law. This civic and legal equality was as much as Rousseau himself had seemed to think possible.

But in another way, the impact of Rousseau made for egalitarianism in a wider sense. What he had done, be it unconsciously, in attacking the problem of the validation of government was to change the target from government itself to society. If his ideas were acted upon, not only would the form of government and the process of legislation be changed, but the relations between one person and another would be transformed. It may be that he was working out the conflict in his own personality between the withdrawal, the loneliness, of the seer and his passionate need for acceptance and support. Be that as it may, he was certainly concerned with political theory as a field not of law but of what we have come to call human relations. His doctrine of the general will concerned the integration of the individual with the group. That could be effected only on terms of equality that extended beyond civic rights to social status, wealth and income. The egalitarianism of his later writings was a development of the earlier motions of his thought, and not a departure from them.

At all times, moreover, he had broken out in tirades against the contrasts of rags and riches. The radicalism of his father's workshop, and his own resentment of his makeshift penurious existence, had sunk deep into a proud and touchy nature. In one of his earliest writings, in 1752, he had called it abominable that some men should possess a superfluity while others died of hunger: the more so, because the luxuries of the rich were made possible only by the deprivations of the poor:

Luxury supports a hundred poor persons in our cities, and is the death of a hundred thousand in the countryside . . . The waste of foodstuffs is alone enough to make luxury hateful to humanity . . . Our cuisines must have stock: that is why our sick can have no soup. There must be liqueurs on our tables: that is why the peasant has nothing but water to drink. Our wigs must have powder: that is why so many poor people have no bread. (Dernière Réponse: Rousseau 1964: 79, fn.)

Even in the article in the *Encyclopédie* in which he declared property sacrosanct, he castigated the arrogance of riches. In the course of justifying a progressive tax on the rich, he assailed them for being above the law and treating the lower orders with contempt—assault and battery, even murder, commited by the man of substance being hushed up, and heard of no more after six months. Later, in a fragment on 'Luxury, Commerce and the Arts', having reverted to Locke's notion that it was the use of money—not metallurgy and agriculture—that brought on inequality, he saw the development as natural; given the variety of men's capacity for hard work, and human covetousness, it was virtually inevitable. None the less, he railed against it in tones of passionate moral indignation.

A poor wretch who, to get bread, takes a crown from a hard man who is dripping with money, is a rogue who is led off to the gallows; while honoured citizens batten peacefully on the blood of the artisan and the labourer. . . . the fortunes of the millionaires increase the misery of the citizens. For in this monstrous and enforced inequality, it comes about necessarily that the sensuality of the rich devours for its delicacies the subsistence of the people, and barely sells them a dry black bread in exchange for the sweat of their brow and at the price of servitude. (*Sur la luxe, le commerce et les arts*: Vaughan 1962: I, 347–8)

So much egalitarian revulsion leads us to expect an egalitarian policy: but how could this be reconciled with the sanctity of property? The *Encyclopedie* article in which Rousseau proclaimed that sanctity did contain the suggestion that large estates should be, not cut down after they had been formed, but prevented from arising; there followed stirring precepts for maintaining an economy of virtuous husbandmen and craftsman. Here Rousseau was following Montesquieu—and Aristotle. Elsewhere, in his essay 'Sur le luxe, le commerce et les arts' (Vaughan, 1962: I, 347–8), he held that an equal distribution was inconceivable; for, so long as individual energies and appetites were free to strive after money, inequalities of accumulation were bound to ensue. The nearest one could approach to equality he indicated in *The Social Contract*, in a passage whose rapid and confident style wings its way above all practical problems, like a bird catching the light on its plumage as it flickers over a thicket. Legislation, he held, has two main objects, liberty and equality; and liberty cannot subsist without equality. But what are we to understand by equality?

[Not] that the extent of power and of wealth shall be absolutely the same; but that, as to power, it shall stop short of all violence, and never be used except in virtue of position and the law; and, as to wealth, that no citizen shall be rich enough to buy another, and none so poor that he must needs sell himself: which implies, on the part of the great men, moderation in their possessions and credit, and, on the part of the little men, moderation in their avarice and cupidity. This equality, it will be said, is a speculative fantasy that cannot exist in practice. But if abuse is inevitable, does it follow that one should not at least regulate it? It is precisely because the force of circumstances is always tending to destroy equality, that the force of law ought always to tend to maintain it. (Rousseau 1947: II, xi)

In the end, however, Rousseau turned against private property. His *Project for Corsica* (1765) would make the public sector on that island as big, and the private sector as small, as possible. Indeed, the state would be regarded as the owner of all property, and each person would be allowed a holding only in proportion to his services. So long as the acquisition of private property was unrestricted, inequality must arise, and increase, through the working of men's acquisitive drives, and the variety of their capacities for work: the only preventative was the reduction of the sector of private property to the smallest practicable extent (Vaughan 1962: II, 337).

This collectivist solution set no mark on the Déclaration, nor did Rousseau's passionate denunciation of economic inequality affect the direction of the Revolution as it flowed on. His influence could be effective only where it was concerned with the same issues as the Revolution; these were political, and not economic. What Rousseau had to say about the general will was exciting and relevant, but his indictment of the exploitation of the poor by the rich was not.

To this there is a partial exception. During the dominance of the Mountain, in the terrible year 1793, a constitution was adopted that was preceded by a revised Declaration of Rights. In its first Article, this proclaimed that 'the aim of society is the social welfare' (Hardman 1973: II, 81). It went on to affirm the right of the weaker brethren to relief, and generally to amend the principles of 1789 somewhat in the interests of social solidarity. The support of public assistance and education were now declared to be obligations laid on society. The relation between employer and employee was declared to be strictly contractual, and no loss of status for the employee was permissible; the statement in the relevant Article that no man might sell himself or be sold echoed a phrase in the *Social Contract*. The 'inviolable and sacred' rights appeared no more, but a new Article defined the right of property as that 'which every citizen possesses to enjoy and utilise as he chooses his goods, his income, the produce of his labour and of his industry'. 'Equality' was now added to the opening list of natural and imprescriptible rights; but what still remains most striking is the merely political significance that even the Mountain attached to it. Robespierre might adopt a stance of socialist tendency, so long as he was opposed to the Girondins, but the rights of property were never at risk. On 17 March 1793 the Convention imposed the death penalty on whoever so much as proposed the 'agrarian law' for the redistribution of landed properties.

The light that gave its name to the Enlightenment was the light of reason. As travellers who have been immobilized by darkness are set free by sunrise to view the landscape, take their bearings and plan their way forward, so in the age of Newton could the philosophers scan the laws of nature and discern the principles of the right ordering of human affairs. They had great confidence. The word they used again and again was 'lumières'—illumination by knowledge and understanding. They were sure that the solution to many a human problem lay in the laws of nature, and would be revealed to reason with the same certainty as the theorems of geometry.

But why was it that the principles they found were liberal? Why should they have discovered in the landscape of the state of nature the imprescriptible rights of man? There was nothing in the method of their inquiry, nor in the faith that inspired it, to dictate the content of their findings. The reason must be that, when they opened their minds to consider a possible state of nature—to perform a thought experiment, remove the institutions of society and leave men standing by themselves—the prevailing individualism of the times dominated their conception. Like Locke, they posited the individual, fully fledged, independent, indeed insular, leading a tolerable life on his own before the formation of any government. They followed Locke likewise in seeing the equality of rights thus originally vested in each man by the law of nature as establishing a basis for the legal and political structure of society.

Those rights were affirmed positively in abstract terms, but in 1789 their great practical appeal was to the upper middle class of lawyers, bankers, merchants and manufacturers, who were determined to break down the obstacles to their own rise and growth; and by them the doctrine was applied negatively. Especially did they mean to abolish the privileges of the nobility. To that extent they stood for equality. For most of them the policy had well understood limits. The illiterate mass of the people they despised as rabble. There was no question of laying hands on the estates of the rich: property was sacred—again, as with Locke. But there was a belief that a removal of barriers to enterprise, a policy of liberalism in the economic and market sense, would result not only in a general advance in prosperity, but also in a substantial reduction of inequality.

This liberal prescription for breaking down inequality was carried further than most of the Assembly of 1789 would have wished to go by one of the most remarkable of the *philosophes*, Condorcet. He was a mathematician whose liberalism began as a gospel of freedom for the individual unhampered by monopoly, gild or state. The release of that activity would result in greater equality: competition would break down the big fortunes, enterprise would build up the small ones, and poverty would be alleviated as the whole community became more prosperous. These changes would reveal the harmony of interests that natural laws would produce if they were not stupidly obstructed. Such effects would be welcome, but they would not be ends in themselves. The supreme end was the liberation of the individual and the enlargement of his personality. So far, he was tacitly identified with the people of substance, education and enterprise—the *philosophes* themselves, and their patrons; the liberal aristocrats; the rising bourgeoisie. Property was sacred. Only men of property could be entrusted with the vote, for only they could form an independent judgement: a state with universal suffrage would only be dominated by the rich, upon whom the propertyless voters would be in practice dependent.

But Condorcet's sympathies widened. As he looked back later, it seemed to him natural that concern for the rights of man should generate a loving care for all humanity. 'Humanitarianism, that is to say, a tender and active compassion for all the ills that afflict the human race, and a horror of everything in political institutions and the actions of governments or private persons that added fresh sufferings to the inevitable afflictions of nature—this humanitarianism was a natural consequence of the general acceptance of the liberal principles of the Enlightenment' (Condorcet 1970: 161–5). Condorcet took up the question of slavery in the colonies; with Lafayette and Mirabeau, he founded a Society of Friends of the Blacks. By 1790 he advanced to votes for women, with a pamphlet on 'The Admission of Women to Civic Rights'. The next year he was criticizing the new constitution for the property qualifications it set for voters and representatives. Hunted by the Terror, he went into hiding: and there, a supreme feat of courage and faith, he wrote his 'Sketch of a Historical Tabulation of the Progress of the Human Moral and Intellectual Faculties'—if those last words may stand for the untranslatable 'Esprit'.

When he came to the tenth and last epoch in his presentation, and looked ahead, Condorcet went on from the civic and legal equality based on the rights of man to consider social inequality in its substantial and interpersonal reality. The great prevailing differences between political equality and the inequality between individuals had three main causes. One was the inequality of wealth; a second was the difference of status between those persons who were able to transmit the means of livelihood to their families and those whose means were cut off with their own working lives; the third source lay in the inequality of education. The working of natural laws would always tend to reduce inequality, were it not for man-made obstructions—laws that prevent free enterprise from competing with existing accumulations, governments that create privileged offices, red tape that stops small businesses from growing; marriages made for money; and sheer hoarding. But although the liberalism of the Enlightenment thus held out hopes of a more equal society, the three named sources of social differences would never disappear, for they had natural and necessary causes, and one could not seek to be rid of their effects altogether without opening up more copious sources of inequality, and at the same time impairing the rights of man. It was therefore necessary to counteract them by adopting more positive measures.

Condorcet advised accordingly. First, credit should be made more accessible to the small man by the setting up of co-operative banks, with state banking. Second, the plight of the mass of the working population who have no means of support once the working life of the head of the family is ended should be remedied by developing contributory insurance on an actuarial basis. This would provide old-age pensions for the workers themselves, together with widows' and orphans' pensions. Third, education should be widely diffused. By a judicious choice of curriculum and method of teaching, all men and women could learn enough to look after their households, follow their trades, know and defend their rights, think for themselves and see through errors.

When that was so, the inhabitants of the same country would no longer be separated by speaking the same language in coarser or more refined accents. They would be equally capable of directing themselves by their own instructed intelligence. They would no longer be limited to a mechanical acquaintance with the processes of a trade or the routine of an occupation. They would depend no longer . . . on the men of ability who rule them in virtue of their evident superiority. A real equality should ensue . . . (Condorcet 1970: 215).

Not many of the members of the Assembly will have gone as far as

Condorcet towards humanitarianism. For them, it was enough to proclaim 'the natural and imprescriptible rights of man', and these were essentially individualist—'liberty, property, security, and resistance to oppression'. When the Second Article of the Declaration affirmed that the preservation of these rights was the end of all political association, it was echoing the doctrine of Locke, who—as we saw—declared that societies were founded for the preservation of their property, by which he meant 'their lives, liberties and estates'. This was the main tenet of the Enlightenment that united the *philosophes*, and the liberal aristocrats, with the rising bourgeoisie. It was individualist in its tendency rather than egalitarian.

But the affirmation with which the Declaration opens, that 'men are born and remain free and equal in their rights', did also spring from the Enlightenment—at least, from the whole habit of the philosophic mind in the eighteenth century. This followed Locke in affirming that men were *born* free because it so envisaged them in the *state* of nature; they *remained* free because the world around them was governed by the *law* of nature. Montesquieu's conception of the forces governing the development of societies and their culture was to revolutionize the study of them; yet even in *De l'esprit des lois* the doctrine of nature lingered. 'Men certainly are born equal in the state of nature,' he wrote; 'but it is not for them to remain so. Society makes them lose their equality, and they regain it only by virtue of law.' Again, 'as all men are born equal, slavery must be accounted unnatural'. The intuition is simply that of Locke: we are to be guided by the purposes shown in the framing of the laws of nature, and we can find no purpose in nature to make men unequal, or to place them in this world in subordination one to another—'there being nothing more evident, than that Creatures of the same species and rank promiscuously born to all the same advantages of Nature, and the use of the same faculties, should also be equal one amongst another without Subordination or Subjection' (Locke 1690: *Second Treatise*, II, 4).

The argument from birth was thus in one way a negative argument: indeed, Locke brought this out when he went on to say that we can infer equality in the absence of any divine declaration to the contrary. But the law of nature also conferred positive rights. In the state of nature, all individuals stand on an equal footing; they have the imprescriptible right so to continue in whatever association they chose subsequently to form. The social distinctions not based on public service, which the First Article goes on to condemn, are wrong because they place some persons from the outset on a different footing from others.

In sum, in proclaiming the indefeasibility of individual rights, the sponsors of the Declaration were drawing on teaching of the Enlightenment that came down from Locke. The law of nature established the indefeasibility of individual rights. It was of the nature of these rights that they put every man on an equal footing with every other; but this equality was confined to political and legal relations. The contrast between it and social and economic inequality led some *philosophes* to humanitarianism; but these appeared only latterly and on the flank of a main body, which remained tenacious of individualism and the sanctity of property.

There was much egalitarianism in France in the eighteenth century, as a foam on the tide of liberalism, catching the light, but with no weight of interests behind it. Rousseau's own egalitarianism was very like that of l'abbé Mably, and he complained of having been plagiarized by him; in fact, Mably's copious publications drew directly on Plato and the noble institutions supposedly designed for Sparta by Lycurgus (Janet 1883: 122). From these he derived the principles that the task of the state was to make men virtuous; and that private property was the source of all evils. 'Nature says to us in a hundred different ways: You are all my children, and I love you all equally . . . the whole earth is the patrimony of each of you; you were equal when you left my hands' (Gray 1946: 87). The institution of property thus found no warrant in the intentions of nature. Mably offered two explanations of why it arose none the less, and, paradoxically, both were that it arose out of human nature. One was that there were 'free-riders' around, people who were prepared to consume without producing, so the rule had to be enforced that each must have and keep so much only as he produced. The other explanation was that, when magistrates were appointed, they helped themselves or their friends and relatives to more than their fair share of the earth's produce. But however private property was set up in the first place, once it was established, all the ills and vices of society followed from it; and—again, a charge levied by Rousseau—the indulgences of the rich are made possible only by the deprivations of the poor. Fortunately, however, 'property finds no support in the laws of nature; its sanction is to be found solely in convention; and what convention has made, convention may unmake' (Gray 1946: 89). Admittedly, incentives are necessary, but in a society of equals, without private property, they could be provided by immaterial awards, 'distinctions'.

It is amazing to find how far these ideas concerning property were accepted, as part of the intellectual patois of the time, by those who would have been very much alarmed by any serious proposal to act upon them. Thus, how shall we understand it when we find Necker, the Genevan banker who twice was Louis XVI's minister of finances, bringing up Mably's artillery in his own controversy with Turgot, and arguing that the title to property is merely conventional? 'Have you brought your land in from a neighbouring planet? No, you benefit from the effects of a convention.' Hereditary property is a privilege established by human laws, by which the strong are enabled to oppress the weak, by reason of 'the power that the owners of property enjoy of not giving in exchange for labour more than the lowest wage possible (quoted here from Janet 1883:

106). All the inference Necker drew immediately was that the state had a duty to support the needy, and, as he said, to moderate their unfair treatment by property. His language implies that he shared the view that the luxury of the rich was obtained directly by deprivation of the poor. He is likely, therefore, to have looked with favour, in his personal judgement, on such a scheme for the reduction of the inequality of wealth as Mably had put forward. The reduction was to be brought about gradually, by laws concerning bequests, inheritances, dowries and gifts *inter vivos*.

Property has been brought under more severe indictment by a *philosophe* who, for his empyrean egalitarianism, is linked with Mably, namely Morelly. In the same year that Rousseau published his *Discourse on the Origins of Human Inequality* (1755), Morelly's *Code de la nature* set out his faith in both the bounty of nature and the good nature of men. 'The world is a table spread with enough for all the invited guests, and all the dishes on it belong sometimes to all, because all are hungry, sometimes only to some, because the others have been satisfied, so that no one is wholly the master or has the right to pretend to be so' (Morelly, *Le Code de nature*: see Rose 1958: 140). When Malthus wrote, in the second edition of his *Essay on Population*, of 'a man born into a world already possessed', that 'at nature's mighty feast there is no vacant cover for him', and developed that metaphor into a whole paragraph of argument against the notion of providing for unlimited numbers—had Morelly put it in his mind? As to human good nature, Morelly reached it in a single leap from self-interest: each of us surely must see that, if he wants others to be helpful to him, he must be helpful to them. But, despite the clarity of moral vision thus attributed to us all, there was still a basic vice to ward off, and this was avarice: the needed safeguard was that there should be 'no private property, apart from the things of which a man is making actual use, whether for his needs, his pleasure, or his daily work (Gray 1946, 98). There followed the arrangements for a Utopia singularly like Sir Thomas More's.

The same readiness to abolish property by a stroke of the pen appeared in the *Philosophic Inquiries into Property and Theft* of Brissot de Warville, in 1778 or 1780. Brissot contended that need alone conferred the right to take and to use. In the animal kingdom, each living being had the right to destroy any other, in order to satisfy its own needs. In the state of nature, 'it is the rich man who is the thief. Exclusive property is theft' (Warville, *Recherches philosophiques sur la propriété et sur le vol*; in Janet 1883: 93–5). Paul Janet, in his *Origins of Contemporary Socialism*, posed but could not answer the question, whether Proudhon took his famous axiom from Brissot, or devised it anew.

Brissot, who thus swung his axe against the base of the whole fabric of society, was to become a moderate deputy to the Convention, and to vote against the execution of the King. This was typical. The pens of the intellectuals moved so easily across the paper because the writers were far removed from action. They had no ballast of experience. No burden of responsibility held their thoughts to the ground. The immediate effect of their root-and-branch destruction of contemporary society was no more than titillation for their readers. The Revolution itself affirmed the rights of property unmistakably, and the affirmation was made by people who meant what they said. The most that came at the time out of these philosophic underminings of society was that softening of the individualism of the Enlightenment into humanitarianism, and its direction into practicable measures of social welfare, which was evident in Condorcet.

While the Revolution was going on, there were some voices raised for egalitarian principles and action. There was one group, linked with the Girondins and known as the Cercle Social, whose attention was concentrated upon the division of society between the rich and the poor. Here was a blend, said Paul Janet, of the Enlightenment, Christianity and freemasonry: a vague doctrine of benevolence and brotherhood. One thinks of Pierre Bezúkhov in *War and Peace*. In the well attended lectures of l'Abbé Fauchet, and the pages of its journal *La Bouche de fer*, the 'infernal régime' was indicted in which millions who were not certain of getting enough to eat must ask for work at the hands of a few 'riches insolents' who themselves had everything they wanted without working (Rose 1958: 146–7). Society must ensure a minimum of subsistence for all. The land should be divided into smallholdings of equal size. But a proposal for an inheritance tax that came nearest to practical politics aroused fierce opposition, and Fauchet had to defend himself against the charge brought by some of the Jacobins that he was advocating the outrageous Agrarian Law. No, he explained, he had only suggested a law to forbid the future formation of estates in excess of 50,000 livres annual rental, all inherited estates being so limited. He died with the Girondins. If his group left any legacy to the Revolution, it was the word 'fraternité'.

Marat has been celebrated as the first revolutionary to have proclaimed, in effect, 'all power to the Soviets', and 'the dictatorship of the proletariat'. During the Revolution his paranoia made him see the hosts of Midian prowling around wherever he looked, and he did in fact detect and expose some counter-revolutionary affairs. But when, in 1779, a decade before the Revolution, he completed his *Plan de législation criminelle* (Hamiche 1974), he carried the common stock of Enlightenment ideas no further towards egalitarianism than advocating some measures of the welfare state. What he had to say about the formation of society, the institution of property and the sufferings of the poor followed the lines of much thought of the Enlightenment. Where he was unusual, and outran his times, was in the account he gave of how 'money makes money', and of the self-perpetuating potential of class. Of the rich, he observes:

It doesn't matter to them if they lack talent, merit, and character—the way is always cleared for them, to let them get at what they want. It's to the rich that the great undertakings are reserved, the fitting out of fleets, the provisioning of armies, the administration of the public revenues, the exclusive privilege of plundering the State; it is to the rich that the lucrative businesses are reserved, the establishment of manufactures, shipbuilding, commercial speculations. You must have money to make money; if you haven't got it, there is nothing that takes its place. Even in the less exalted classes, it is for the man in easy circumstances that the respectable occupations, the fine arts, and the liberal arts are reserved; but it is for the poor to take up the contemptible, the dangerous, the repulsive occupations: such is the repugnance heaped upon poverty. (Hamiche 1974, 62)

If we read later thinking back into this, here we have an analysis of class structure, more pregnant with future development than the radicals' concern with property: but did Marat realize that he was calling into question the basic structure of society? The conclusion he drew for policy was only that the poor had a claim on society for maintenance and welfare, to be paid for by the rich. Instead of alms-giving, there should be public workshops, in which beggars and paupers would be taught a trade. The estates of the Church should be cut down to so much only as would maintain incumbents at a modest level: the rest should be divided among the poor in small portions. Free schooling for the poor should be financed by taxation of the well-to-do.

In a Project and Plan,[1] which he published when the Revolution was under way, in August 1789, Marat went a little but not very much further. Nature implants needs, and these needs confer rights to satisfaction. If these rights are denied, men will take forcible, it may even be murderous, action to assert them. To avoid that, the law must prevent great inequalities of wealth from arising in the first place; and part at least of the property of the rich should be confiscated and used to lighten the lot of the poor.

This was more directly egalitarian than with most of the Revolutionaries. Yet we need to remind ourselves that the Revolution was political, and concerned with civic equality, in a world where the well-being of the poor, although a proper matter of concern for the benevolent, was not yet seen at all generally as bound up with the structure of the state or the business of government. Marat, moreover, knew his Rousseau. So in the work just cited, which legitimized the raiding of large fortunes, he declared that the rights of private property were essential to the maintenance of civil liberty. The Bolsheviks were to name a cruiser after him.

Gracchus Babeuf, with his Conspiracy of the Equals, is the other Revolutionary who has been canonized by the communists: more properly

---

[1] 'La Constitution, ou Projet de déclaration des Droits de l'homme et du citoyen, suivi d'un Plan de constitution juste, sage et libre': contents cited from Gottschalk (1927: 45-8).

than Marat, for although he began with an attack upon a rural problem, he did advance to the conception of the communist organization of a whole economy in its modern extent. The landowners of Picardy, where he grew up, were suffering like many elsewhere in France from rising prices and the social competition of commercial capital. One way out was to revise and enforce their feudal and other rights, and Babeuf himself found employment as one of the 'feudists' who searched the records to bring lapsed rights to light. Another way was to copy the English, consolidate holdings and abolish the three-field system with its year of fallow. But this meant breaking up the communal way of life of the villages, and in particular it meant denying access to the fallow to the fringe of landless families. With ever-growing population, these were becoming much more than a fringe. Access to the land was the central issue. As an autodidact reading the works of the *philosophes*, Babeuf was acquainted with the argument that private property was the root of all evil. What he feared for Picardy was what came about at that time in some English villages—a few big farms, each with its staff, and a large number of landless labourers for whom there was no work of any kind. His ultimate remedy was communal: let the land be taken into public ownership, and let each farm be worked collectively by from twenty to fifty men.

But in a work he published called the *Cadastre perpetuel*, or *Perpetual Register*, he put forward a scheme of practical egalitarianism by progressive taxation to support social benefits. All existing taxes should be superseded by a single graduated tax on land and income. From the proceeds there should be financed the personal services of the Church such as baptism and burial, a basic subsistence allowance, a national health service, free education for all, and courts in which justice would be dispensed without charge by salaried magistrates (Rose 1978: 49–51).

The problem of population pressure, and of the landless, jobless labourer which concerned Babeuf in Picardy, was the same as confronted the younger Pitt in those same years in the villages of southern England. With his income tax, and that draft Poor Law of his in 1796, who knows how far Pitt's thinking might not have taken him, but for the war, along that same road as Babeuf laid out towards a national minimum of sustenance and welfare financed by national taxation. The same setting and source of the great suffering of the times brought comparable responses from widely contrasted men.

When Babeuf went on from the egalitarianism of his first phase to his fully fledged communism, it was on different experience that he drew. After some seven years of revolution running into war economy, he must have come to see the collective farm as a distraction: he let it drop. He had been engaged in 'l'administration des subsistances', the food control, the maintenance of supplies generally and the rationing for the half-million inhabitants of Paris. He had seen the effectiveness, during the Terror and the war on the frontiers, of central organization in making distribution regular and equitable and harnessing the enthusiasm of the people in the war effort. In modern terms, he came to believe in central economic planning. We could think no longer as the *philosophes* had done of societies being based on law and subject to transformation by proclamation of law: there must be a pervasive control of economic activity. But equally, this control must be exercised with the active participation of the people. Such was the communism for which he formed a conspiracy against the Directory, and paid with his life.

When we look back on these years, we cannot rid our minds of knowledge of what was to follow. When economic issues are raised, they stand out as prologues to the omen coming on. There is much in these last pages to mark a rise of egalitarianism or the dawn of socialism, and in a sense that is undeniably what it is: we cannot mistake its continuity with later developments. Yet equally, it is unhistorical to overlook how peripheral it seemed to contemporaries. The effect of these manifestations on the actual course of the Revolution was negligible. Humanitarianism took some effect—we may even include the provision of the guillotine itself; but egalitarianism, none at all. The intense and passionate interests of the revolutionaries were concentrated upon other objects. The Loi le Chapelier, passed almost without debate by the Assembly in June 1791 to prohibit all associations of capital and labour, has been represented as an anti-union law, and indeed, it did serve as such in later years; but its immediate purposes were to implement the proposal to abolish gilds that had been adopted on the night of 4 August 1789 as part of 'the abolition of feudalism', and to ward off the threat apprehended by Rousseau, that factions would obstruct the cohesion of the general will. Egalitarianism did not yet have a head of public pressure behind it. The people in 1789 wanted relief from oppressive taxation and dues, and they meant to abolish privilege, but farther than that they were not oriented to advance. After the fall of the Jacobins, not until 1830 did the base of French society shake.

There is a way, however, in which the Revolution did promote egalitarianism. For it marked a first great attempt to change not merely the government, but the whole structure of society. It is true that the changes to be made in that structure were largely conceived in political and legal terms alone; but the aim and justification of this liberalism was the welfare of all. Locke's liberalism had been narrower. His problem had been to constitute not a just society, but a legitimate government. What government might do to improve the life of its citizens—and even improve those people themselves—he was not concerned to enquire: evidently it must maintain law and order, but, given this, individuals would mind their own business. It was the great object of law and order to enable them to do so. Each of them knew what he wanted, and government was instituted to enable him to strive for it freely, subject to the like freedom of his neighbour. Adam Smith went beyond this when he found in 'the obvious and simple system of natural liberty' the arrangement that would give the greatest general satisfaction because every man would be pursuing his own interests, not at the expense of his neighbours, but to their positive advantage. But the Constitution of 1793 had meant more than this again when it declared that 'the aim of society is the social welfare'. What was in view there was the extent to which 'we are every one members one of another' (Romans 12:5), and at the same time the possibility of reforming that fabric of relations on which the quality of individual life depended. For a brief time, the possibility emerged of remoulding not government alone but the social structure, and designing in equity and reason not only constitutions, but the way of life of a whole people. As Wordsworth said, reformers of all kinds found 'stuff at hand, plastic as they could wish' (*The Prelude*, XI, 138). Rousseau had moved on, from the notion of an original state of nature in which each person roamed alone, to an appreciation of our mutual dependence, and the possibility of so ordering it that it would be more fruitful and fair. In his later thought the individual no longer stands self-sufficient in the sanctity of his private property, but depends for the quality of his life on his relations with his fellows. They in turn have their claims on him. The task of the philosopher is to show how those relations can be regulated and enriched. The object of enquiry has shifted from the legitimization of power to the design of social fabric.

If for the time being that design was conceived primarily in terms legal and political, it could not continue to leave poverty and riches out of account. When the young Wordsworth was walking beside the Loire in 1792 with the officer Michel Beaupuy, they came on 'a hunger-bitten girl', leading a browsing heifer by a cord over her arm, as she plied her knitting needles in pallid hands. 'Tis against *that* that we are fighting,' cried Beaupuy. 'I with him believed', wrote Wordsworth,

> That a benignant spirit was abroad
> Which might not be withstood, that poverty
> Abject as this would in a little time
> Be found no more, that we should see the earth
> Unthwarted in her wish to recompense
> The meek, the lowly, patient child of toil,
> All institutes for ever blotted out
> That legalised exclusion. . . . .

The Prelude, IX, 519–26

If the Revolution itself contained little egalitarianism, it opened the way for it.

3.4. Social Inequality as the British Eighteenth Century Saw It

The eighteenth century brought no British Declaration of the Rights of Man; no statements about human equality were pronounced to be self-evident. The men of substance, thoughtfulness and initiative such as made such affirmations in other lands felt no need to make them in Great Britain. Here they had scope enough, and all the freedom they needed, to make their own way in an expansive economy. The gradations of rank represented to them not the exclusive and oppressive barriers of caste and privilege, but the necessary structure of any stable society, and at the same time the rungs of a ladder on which they themselves might ascend.

Richard Watson was a Westmoreland lad who in the 1750s was admitted a sizar of Trinity College, Cambridge, in 'blue worsted stockings and coarse mottled coat'; he went on to become Professor of Chemistry and FRS; being then elected to the Regius Chair of Divinity, he stood out as notably liberal and outspoken in matters of church and state. But in 1793, as Bishop of Llandaff, he was moved to publish a sermon on the text, 'The rich and the poor meet together, the Lord is the maker of them all' (Prov. 22: 2), and to attach to it an appendix entitled 'Strictures on the French Revolution and the British Constitution'. Here he drew in bold lines the picture of British liberty, equality before the law, and the career open to talents. By 1793 there were many ardent or burdened spirits who would have scanned this at best with a wry smile. The young Wordsworth, his head full of Tom Paine and the speeches he had heard in the Convention, drafted an indignant rejoinder. But the Bishop's contrasting account of British society expressed what one man who had found a career open to his talents, and had been able to express radical opinions freely, did genuinely feel, and what made many of his fellow countrymen, when they looked abroad, thankful that they themselves lived in a free country. 'The equality of man in a state of civil society', he wrote,

does not consist in an equality of wisdom, honesty, ingenuity, industry, nor in an equality of property resulting from a due exertion of these talents; but in being equally subject to, equally protected by, the same laws. And who knows not that every individual in this great nation is, in this respect, equal to every other? There is not one law for the nobles, another for the commons of the land—one for the clergy, another for the laity—one for the rich, another for the poor. The nobility, it is true, have some privileges annexed to their birth; the judges, and other magistrates, have some annexed to their office; and professional men have some annexed to their professions:—but these privileges are neither injurious to the liberty or property of other men. And you might as reasonably contend that the bramble ought to be equal with the oak, the lamb to the lion, as that no distinctions should take place between the members of the same society. The burdens of the State are distributed through the whole community, with as much impartiality as the complex nature of taxation will admit; every man sustains a part in proportion to his strength; no order is exempted from the payment of taxes. Nor is any order of men exclusively entitled to the enjoyment of the lucrative offices of the State. All cannot enjoy them, but all enjoy a capacity of acquiring them. The son of the meanest man in the nation may become a general or an admiral, a lord chancellor or an archbishop. If any persons have been as simple as to suppose that even the French ever intended, by the term equality, an equality of property, they have been quite mistaken in their ideas. The French never understood by it anything materially different from what we and our ancestors have been in full possession of for many ages. (Grosart 1876: 26–7)

'Georgian England', R. H. Tawney observed (1926: ch. IV), 'was to astonish foreign observers, like Voltaire and Montesquieu,[2] as the Paradise of the *bourgeoisie*, in which the prosperous merchant shouldered easily aside the impoverished bearers of aristocratic names.'

Much that was still being contended for on the Continent, or would not be so much as claimed yet for years to come, was taken for granted in Britain. England and Wales owed much to the extension of the King's courts over all other jurisdictions: the privileges of clergy and nobility, and the arrogance of local tyrants, were swept away. Squire Western was a tyrant by English standards, but he was twice pulled up for exceeding his authority as a magistrate. Sir Thomas Bertram and Lady Catherine de Burgh likewise had their formidable aspect as local grandees: but compare them with those other local grandees, Don Juan and Count Almaviva, types who swaggered not only in opera.

Men who felt that the society in which they grew up and its form of government gave them all the scope they asked for were not thrown back to take their stand on first principles. Since they did not find authority oppressive, they did not need to question its basis. Nor were they set upon devising radically new forms of government. They were free to look around them, and see things as they were: that things were as they were seemed readily intelligible. Society appeared as part of nature.

This was the habit of mind of the century. The achievement of Newton had seemed far greater even than it was: the whole universe was reduced to a single rational plan, of which Nature was the manifestation, and to which revealed religion could attach itself only as a supplement. What was 'natural' now came to have a double meaning. It meant proceeding necessarily, according to a sequence of cause and effect. It also meant existing rightly, as being in agreement with the dispositions of the Great Architect of the universe. The Scottish philosopher Adam Ferguson, lecturing on moral philosophy around 1770 to students in the college of Edinburgh, said quite simply that 'any general rule, expressing what is fact, or what is right, is termed a law of nature' (1773, Introd no. 2). We

---

[2] Tawney gives references to Voltaire, *Lettres Philosophiques*, no. x, and Montesquieu, *De l'esprit des lois*, xix, 27, and xx, 22.

maintain the double meaning at the present time when we say of some action, 'It's only natural', thereby extenuating if not justifying it. With this preconception, men would see contemporary society as the product of forces in the course of natural history; they would be more disposed to show in what ways its arrangements were effective than to devise plans of their own for improving on them.

There was a particular way in which society appeared as a product of natural forces. The immense influence of Montesquieu's *De l'esprit des lois* (1748): flowed from its treatment of the forms of government, the institutions of society, even sacrosanct religion, as moulded by local soil and climate, so that customs and practices that would be condemned as foolish or even immoral in one country became intelligible and even demonstrably beneficial in the circumstances of another. The adaptation to environment, moreover, was seen as an historical process: institutions were to be approached as the products of evolution.

Montesquieu's relativism revealed the underlying unity of mankind. He showed that the manifold variations of outward seeming and behaviour were imprinted by environment on a common stock of humanity. 'As all men are born equal,' he observed in 1748, 'it has to be said that slavery is contrary to nature, even though in some (tropical) countries, there is a natural reason for it' (*De l'esprit des lois*, XV, vii (4))

Here were three principles to guide the study of society: the assumption that the social no less than the material world was subject to natural law; the discovery of mankind as a species, the variety of whose behaviour could be explained by adaptation to environment; and the view of this adaptation as a process of historical evolution. It was on these assumptions implicitly that the great Scots social philosophers proceeded. Social philosophers they may be called in the broadest sense of the term, for it was the bent for scientific observation that distinguished them. The impetus of scientific investigation that had been so powerful in England in the later seventeenth century was not maintained far into the eighteenth, but in Scotland there arose a group of scholars of great originality, steady judgement and wide international learning. Scotland had retained and renewed its links with the schools of the Continent, because for several reasons it had been shut out of the English universities, and because its young men needed to study Roman law. Here, around the middle of the eighteenth century, as nowhere else in Great Britain, were scholars trained as of old in the classics, but in touch no less with the French savants of the day, and as students of society avid readers of the reports of primitive peoples that were coming back from the Caribbean and North America; they approached the past and the present day alike on the presumption that all were part of the natural order. We are concerned with the works of Adam Smith, professor of moral philosophy at Glasgow and immortal author of *The Wealth of Nations*; Adam Ferguson, already mentioned, who as chaplain of the Black

Watch had been present—and, it is said, wielded a broad sword—at Fontenoy, and survived to become professor of pneumatics and moral philosophy at Edinburgh (pneumatics was 'the physical history of mind'); John Millar, a pupil of Adam Smith, himself professor of law at Glasgow; and, in so far as he wrote on society, another immortal, the philosopher David Hume.

Their outstanding characteristic, as students of society, was precisely that they were students. Their role was to observe, to trace and to understand. History they saw not as a struggle between good and evil, or the working out of a beneficient purpose, or a theatre dominated from time to time by some personality of heroic build, but as a sequence of cause and effect, or a cumulation of contingencies. In the course of praising Machiavelli above all other modern historians for his impartiality, Adam Smith (1963: 110-11) gave it as 'the chief purpose of history, to relate events and connect them with their causes'. Adam Ferguson's conception of the way in which developments come about in the blind course of history implied that the historian could record the sequence of past events, but could derive no principles from them to impose on the ceaselessly working leaven of individual endeavour. 'Mankind,' he wrote,

in following the present course of their minds, in striving to remove inconveniences, or to gain apparent and contiguous advantages, arrive at ends which even their imagination could not anticipate, and pass on, like other animals, in the track of their nature, without perceiving its end. Men, in general, are sufficiently disposed to occupy themselves in forming projects and schemes. But he who would scheme and project for others, will find an opponent in every person who is disposed to scheme for himself. Like the winds, that come we know not whence, and blow withersoever they list, the forms of society are derived from an obscure and distant origin; they arise, long before the date of philosophy, from the instincts, not from the speculations, of men. The crowd of mankind are directed in their establishments and measures by the circumstances in which they are placed; and seldom are turned from their way, to follow the plan of any single projector. Every step and every movement of the multitude, even in what are termed enlightened ages, are made with equal blindness to the future; and nations stumble upon establishments, which are indeed the result of human action, but not the execution of any human design. (Ferguson 1767: III, 2)

Gathering the facts about the actual course of human affairs past and present made the spinning of theory about the foundation of authority seem needless if not positively foolish. Asked about the condition of the earliest stages of society on which much political theory was based, the Scots philosophers for their part could only infer it from what we can learn of the actual earliest conditions, from Holy Writ and the classical authors, and especially from the reports coming in of primitive peoples in North America, the Caribbean, Siberia and the Cape of Good Hope. With a flick of the wrist, Adam Ferguson dismissed the social contract theorists at the outset:

The desire of laying the foundation of a favourite system, or a fond expectation, perhaps, that we may be able to penetrate the secrets of nature, to the very source of existence, have, on this subject, led to many fruitless inquiries, and given rise to many wild suppositions. Among the various qualities which mankind possess, we select one or a few particulars on which to establish a theory; and in framing our account of what man was in some imaginary state of nature we overlook what he had always appeared within the reach of our own observations, and in the records of history. (Ferguson 1767: I, 1)

It was not by philosophic argument but by a straightforward appeal to 'what has always appeared within the reach of our own observations' that David Hume (1875 1, II, XII) dismissed those philosophers who held that the authority of the sovereign is granted to him conditionally upon his observance of the terms of a contract with his subjects.

Would these reasoners look abroad into the world, they would meet with nothing that, in the least, corresponds to their ideas, or can warrant so refined and philosophical a system. On the contrary, we find everywhere, princes, who claim their subjects as their property, and assert their independent rights of sovereignty, from conquest or succession. We find also, everywhere, subjects, who acknowledge this right in their prince, and suppose themselves born under obligations of obedience to a certain sovereign, as much as under the ties of reverence and duty to certain parents. These connexions are always conceived to be equally independent of our consent, in PERSIA and CHINA; in FRANCE and SPAIN; and even in HOLLAND and ENGLAND, wherever the doctrines above-mentioned have not been carefully inculcated. Or, if curiosity ever move them, as soon as they learn that they themselves and their ancestors have, for several ages, or from time immemorial, been subject to such a form of government or to such a family, they immediately acquiesce, and acknowledge their obligation to allegiance. (Hume 1875: 1, II, III)

But if the realism of the Scots philosophers kept them away from theorizing about the origins of society, it did not prevent them from tracing a pattern of growth. In the records of history, and the reports of contemporary travellers, they found evidence that mankind from the earliest times had been 'assembled in troops and companies', and that the subsequent course of development had been one in which a number of processes were intertwined—the enlargement of the political unit; the progress of the economy and change of its technique; and the growth of inequality, or of subordination as they would say, through the differentiation of ranks by wealth, status, and income.

Adam Ferguson gave three grounds for what a sociologist of our own time might call differences of class. The first was that, in the transition from the earliest state of society, 'the members of any community, being distinguished among themselves by unequal shares in the distribution of property, the ground of a permanent and palpable subordination is laid' (1767: 111, 2). It is the distribution of property, moreover, that locates effective power in the community, whatever the constitutional form:

In every society there is a casual subordination, independent of its formal establishment, and frequently adverse to its constitution. While the administration and the people speak the language of a particular form, and seem to admit no pretensions to power, without a legal nomination in one instance, or without the advantage of hereditary honour in another, this casual subordination, possibly arising from the distribution of property, or from some other circumstance that bestows unequal degress of influence, gives the state its tone, and fixes its character. (Ferguson 1767: III, 2)

The second ground of subordination was 'the difference of natural talents and dispositions'; the third, 'the habits which are acquired by the practice of different arts'. This last implies that a country which has attained an industrial development, so that much of its working population is engaged in mechanical and repetitive labour, cannot form a healthy democracy. For those workers will have minds that are stunted and narrowed by their employment, and at the same time filled with envy:

The principal objections to democratical or popular government, are taken from the inequalities which arise among men in the result of commercial arts. And it must be confessed, that popular assemblies, when composed of men whose dispositions are sordid, and whose ordinary applications are illiberal, however they may be intrusted with the choice of their masters and leaders, are certainly, in their own persons, unfit to command. (Ferguson 1767: IV, 2)

The subtitle of John Millar's work on *The Origin of the Distinction of Ranks* (1771) described it as 'an Inquiry into the circumstances which given rise to influence and authority, in the different members of society'. Millar worked, in his day, as a social anthropologist, his subject being the development of manners, knowledge, law and customs. Montesquieu, he says, had attributed too much of that development to the influence of climate and region, which cannot explain the differences between Athens and Sparta, or between the mild Chinese and the rough Japanese, or between the successive phases of the history of one region, as in ancient Rome and contemporary Italy. Nor can particular characteristics be imprinted in a whole people by one strong personality: a Lycurgus or a Solon must already have embodied in himself the dominant traits of the people to whom he gave laws. But when we look for Millar's own account of development, we find that he has no theory, no hypothesis or approach in which his work can be summed up. What he does is to describe the gradual formation of larger and larger groups, with more formal structures, requiring greater differentiation of rank and function. But he does not make much of this, except as a narrative, for although his subject is rank, he has little conception of it. In a retrospect at the beginning of his last chapter, he names the distinctions of rank as attaching to the husband, the father and the civil magistrate—that is all.

Yet disappointing though his failure is to keep hold of his subject, he did make a remarkable start on it when he devoted his first chapter to 'the rank and condition of Women in different ages'—from a condition of slavery, to the effects of pastoral economy, then to 'the consequences of the introduction of agriculture', and 'changes in the condition of women, arising from the improvement of useful arts and manufactures'. In these successive economic stages, Millar was following his teacher Adam Smith. What is significant is that he thought first about how those stages affected 'the condition of women'. How different, then, his view of society was from that of Rousseau, for whom the man who figures as its persona is certainly and solely a male—in the state of nature, he said, 'his desires are limited by his physical needs; the only goods he knows in all the world are food, a female, and rest . . .' (Rousseau, in Vaughan 1962: I, 151). Millar's was a realistic view of society, in all the variety of the membership of its households, the stages of its development and its regional environment.

Adam Smith's own account of development was the most systematic. Smith taught that development had passed through four stages: those in which the main source of livelihood was, successively, hunting, the keeping of flocks and herds, agriculture and—as he termed it—commerce. Each change of predominant form of economic activity brought changes with it in the social and political structure. 'Civil government supposes a certain subordination. But as the necessity of civil government gradually grows up with the acquisition of valuable property, so the principal causes which naturally introduce subordination gradually grow up with the growth of that valuable property' (Smith 1776: V, i, pt II). In fact, there are four sources of subordination, or its converse the superiority of some men 'over the greater part of their brethren', and the possession of valuable property is only one of these. The others are: superiority of personal qualifications in body and mind, superiority of age (short of dotage) and superiority of birth. In the stage of hunting, there is no accumulation and transmission of property, 'and the superiority either of age or of personal qualities, are the feeble but the sole, foundations of authority and subordination'. But outstanding pastoralists can accumulate great herds and flocks, and hand them on to their heirs. 'Birth and fortune are evidently the two circumstances which principally set one man above another . . . among nations of shepherds both those causes operate with their full force.' At this stage, moreover, 'the inequality of fortune . . . introduces some degree of that civil government which is indispensably necessary for its own preservation: and it seems to do this naturally . . .' 'Civil government, so far as it is instituted for the security of property, is in reality instituted for the defence of the rich against the poor, or of those who have some property against those who have none at all' (Smith 1776; v, i, pt. II). The stage of agriculture brings property in land. That of commerce brings a differentiation of occupation, associated with the division of labour, which sets the ranks of society at a greater distance from one another than ever before.

In this last observation, Adam Smith developed relentlessly a social psychology of great sadness. Men differ much less in their abilities than they appear to, he said: their apparent differences have been imposed on them by their occupations.

The difference between the most dissimilar characters, between a philosopher and a common street porter, for example, seems to arise not so much from nature, as from habit, custom, and education. When they came into the world, and for the first six or eight years of their existence, they were perhaps very much alike, and neither their parents nor playfellows could perceive any remarkable difference. About that age, or soon after, they come to be employed in very different occupations. The difference of talents comes then to be taken notice of, and widens by degrees, till at last the vanity of the philosopher is willing to acknowledge scarce any resemblance. (Smith 1776: I, ii)

The effect, moreover, of repetitive and mindless work on those who are condemned to it is appalling:

The man whose whole life is spent in performing a few simple operations . . . generally becomes as stupid and ignorant as it is possible for a human creature to become. Hence that drowsy stupidity which, in a civilised society, seems to benumb the understanding of almost all the inferior ranks of people. (Smith 1776: V, i, iii, art, II)

The subordination of the lower orders of society was seen to be imposed by the narrowness of outlook and incapacity for office inflicted on them by their daily toil.

This view was social dynamite: it called for drastic changes in the constitution of society. We find it hard to understand how it could have been propounded, as it was, without a call to equalize opportunity; hard, too, to realize how unquestioningly it was held. We have to think away the awareness of the genetic part in the formation of personal characteristics, which has been diffused since Darwin's time. Even today, there are many people by whom the notion of innate differences in potential IQ is repudiated passionately. In their equation of human dignity with human identity, we see something of the explosive force of Adam Smith's belief. But their own holding of it owes much to the will to believe; with Adam Smith; the belief was a matter of fact.

As a social psychologist, Smith made another contribution to the explanation of inequality in society when he pointed to the human propensity to admire riches, and crave for them. There is, he said, an 'irregularity', or as we might say, an asymmetry, in human nature, in that we sympathize with joy more readily than with sorrow, and admire the rich more wholeheartedly than we pity the poor. 'Upon this disposition of mankind, to go along with all the passions of the rich and the powerful, is founded the distinction of ranks, and the order of society' (Smith 1759: I, iii, 2-3). This order, it must be allowed, however, is also disturbed by constant elbowing for status—to use a more recent term. 'Place, that great object which divides the wives of aldermen, is the end of half the labours of human life; and is the cause of all the tumult and bustle, all the rapine and injustice, which avarice and ambition have introduced into this world' (Smith 1759: I, iii, 2, 8).[3] The major consideration, however, is that the distinction of ranks, which is marked by a difference of riches, is upheld by the spontaneous admiration of riches among those who have none, and by their own desire to obtain riches for themselves. Yet Adam Smith's insights vary with the subject in hand, and elsewhere he speaks of a very different attitude of the lower orders. 'The affluence of the rich excites the indignation of the poor, who are often both driven by want and prompted by envy to invade his possessions.' Hence the necessity for civil government, and its origin. 'It is only under the shelter of the civil magistrate that the owner of that valuable property, which is acquired by the labour of many years, or perhaps of many successive generations, can sleep a single night in security' (Smith 1776: v, i, Pt. II).

Such was the main account that the Scots philosophers gave of inequality. They saw it as arising from proclivities of human nature in society. As soon as the gathering of flocks and herds provided the possibility of accumulating property and handing it down to heirs, the differences of energy, ability and luck between different people resulted in the differentiation of rank between families; hence subordination, which was supported by the human tendency to admire riches. But since those who have no property and may suffer want for lack of it will always be tempted to take it away by force from those who possess it, civil government grows up together with property, in order to protect it. On this, Smith follows Locke, and is even more eloquent than Rousseau.

In this account of the adaptation of the social and political structure to the economic base, there was much that Marx was to take over. Even more, Adam Smith provided a theory of value and distribution which in one of its different forms was a straightforward account of the exploitation of the worker by the landlord and capitalist, who robbed him of much of the produce of his labour. Sometimes, it is true, Smith allowed that land and capital made their own contributions to output: in agriculture, 'nature labours along with man' (1776: II, v, 12), and when a machine is erected, productive capacity is built into it (I, x, b6). On these specific contributions, presumably, a fair return would be due to the owners of land and capital. But elsewhere, Smith contrasts the 'original state of things', in which the labourer was able to enjoy the whole product of his labour, with the advanced state of society, in which he could use land only on paying rent to a landlord, and gain employment only on obtaining advances from

---

[3] I am indebted for guidance here to A. S. Skinner's essay, 'Moral Philosophy and Civil Society', in his *A System of Social Science* (Skinner 1979).

the stock of masters who require profits in return. 'The landlords, like all other men, love to reap where they never sowed' (I, vi, 8). His most outright statement of exploitation comes when he is discussing the 'Causes of the Prosperity of new Colonies'. 'In other countries, rent and profit eat up wages . . . but in new colonies, the interest of the two superior orders, obliges them to treat the inferior one with more generosity and humanity; at least where that inferior one is not in a state of slavery' (IV, vii, b3).

The wages that were thus subject to exploitation were also, Smith observed, kept down by the bargaining power of the masters. If it came to a bargain about the rate for the job, the individual workman was in no position to hold out for a higher rate than the master was willing to pay; 'in the long run the workman may be as necessary to the master as his master is to him; but the necessity is not so immediate' (1776: I, viii, 12). Should workmen seek a remedy in combination, they would only get into trouble with the magistrates, and the end would be 'the punishment or ruin of the ringleaders' (I, viii, 13). The masters, on the other hand, were 'always and everywhere in a sort of tacit, but constant and uniform combination, not to raise the wages of labour above their actual rate (I, viii, 13); they sometimes even combined to lower wages. There were spurts of expansion, when funds outstanding for the maintenance of labour overflowed for a while, and wages were raised by the bidding of the masters for labour. But the response of labour to that higher standard of living would be an increase in supply—perhaps through earlier marriages—which would bring wages down again. In the long run, they could only fluctuate about the subsistence level.

This was a prospect of inescapable inequality amid growing prosperity. The aggregate wealth of the nation might continue to rise as the liberation of individual energies in a free country advanced manufactures and commerce. There would (we must infer) be room for more wealthy households, or for some households of greater wealth, than before; but so long as the great mass of the labouring population responded to a rise in their own standard of living by an increase in population, and in the numbers seeking employment, for so long must their standard of living be brought down again to the level at which their numbers were no more than maintained—the level of subsistence.

An account of inequality which analytically rests upon exploitation and descriptively is unflinching in its harshness leads us today to expect at least a declamation, if not a call to reform: but there is none. How can this be? The explanation is not that the philosophers viewed the scene with any active approbation. Adam Smith certainly did not claim that the inequality of income represented any just apportionment to ability or moral worth. On the contrary, as we have seen, he is very clear that the poor personal quality of the labouring people is only a deformation imposed by their lack of education, or else a kind of industrial disease caught during their working life. We have noted this belief that, were it not for their being incarcerated in brutalizing work from an early age, they would be capable of as full a personal development as their most cultivated neighbours. Nor do differences of earnings compensate differences of effort:

the opulence of the merchant is greater than that of all his clerks, though he works less; and they again have six times more than an equal number of artisans, who are more employed. The artisan who works at his ease within doors has far more than the poor labourer who trudges up and down without intermission. (Smith 1896; II, ii, 3)

Far from attempting to justify the distribution of income, Smith emphasized its contrasts. 'There is no equal division, for there are a good many who work, none at all. The division of opulence is not according to the work. . . .' (1896: II, ii, 4). Many who 'do not labour at all . . . consume the produce of ten times, frequently of a hundred times, more labour than the greater part of those who work' (Smith 1776: Introdn., 2, 4). In stating the case for high wages, he observed that 'it is but equity . . . that they who feed, clothe, and lodge the whole body of the people, should have such a share of the produce of their own labour as to be themselves tolerably well fed, clothed, and lodged' (1776; I, iii). What, then, is the explanation of the Scots philosophers' tacit acceptance of a social structure whose painful contrasts they saw so clearly?

The first and foremost part of the explanation is negative. It lies in the absence of the indispensable machinery of the welfare state: on the one hand, an expansive and flexible system for collecting revenue; on the other, an expansive and flexible system for diffusing benefits. There was no machinery for transfer. Any people in the eighteenth century who were disposed to reduce inequality had no means at hand with which to set about it. They were much like those in the West today who are moved by the sufferings of the undernourished in the Third World; no system exists that includes both themselves and the sufferers and can be either utilized or recast to enable resources to be pooled and reallocated. All that the humanitarian can do is to make gifts through relief agencies, and that seems like bailing out the ocean with a bucket. So it was in the eighteenth century: protest against inequality did not arise, because there was so patently no practical action open to reduce it.

But there were also positive reasons for the placidity of the social philosophers. One of these was that the state of society had come to be seen, like all else, as the outcome of a natural development. The laws of nature were supreme overall. Whatever existed was part of the Great Design—and this, not only in an original act of creation, but in a course of change.

'Development' was itself a word of recent introduction, marking the coming of a new approach to society. On this approach, human affairs must take their course according to their natural tendencies. There was a presumption that what was natural bore the approval of the Great Author of all things.

Human nature, moreover, whether or not the hand of the Great Architect could be seen in it, must on a realistic view be allowed to be persistent and powerful in its propensities. Thus, David Hume disposed of the possibility of an equal division of the product, on the grounds—his words were prophetic—that it would run so contrary to human nature that by removing incentives it would strifle output, and its continued enforcement would ultimately demand a pervasively tyrannical administration. 'Render possessions ever so equal,' he wrote, in his essay 'Of Justice',

man's different degrees of art, care and industry will immediately break that equality. Or if you check these virtues, you reduce society to the most extreme indigence; and, instead of preventing want and beggary in a few, render it unavoidable to the whole community. The most rigorous inquisition too is requisite to watch every inequality on its final appearance; and the most severe jurisdiction, to punish and redress it. But besides, that so much authority must soon degenerate into tyranny, and be exerted with partialities; who can possibly be possessed of it, in such a situation as is here supposed? (Hume 1875: II, 188-9)

Adam Smith was to echo that reference to 'man's different degrees of art, care and industry'. 'Law and government', he declared, '. . . maintain the rich in the possession of their wealth against the violence and rapacity of the poor, and by that means preserve that usefull inequality in the fortunes of mankind which naturally and necessarily arises from the various degrees of capacity, industry and diligence in different individuals' (1978, Report of 1762-3, vi, 19). Here (in his lectures on jurisprudence in 1762–3) it will be seen that inequality is treated as a source not of revolt but of order-keeping. Elsewhere in the same lecture he has another argument for it: those who amass riches provide society with a contingency reserve. 'Tho an agrarian law would render all on an equality, which has indeed something very agreable in it, yet a people who are all on an equality will necessarily be very poor and unable to defend themselves in any pressing occasion. They have nothing saved which can give them relief in time of need' (1978, Report of 1762–3, iii, 138).

On the positive side, again, there were reasons for satisfaction in the contemporary outlook. The Scots philosophers themselves enjoyed freedom of thought, discussion and publication: they were not under the pressure of the persecuted academic, to align himself with the oppressed and discontented elements of the population in a radical movement. They were conscious that they were living in an advancing society, which owed its prosperity to its political stability and freedom, and had within itself the means of further progress. 'Great Britain', said Adam Smith, 'is certainly one of the richest countries in Europe' (1776: iv, iii, pt. II). In his Glasgow lectures he had declared that in Britain the day labourer had 'more luxury in his way of living than an Indian sovereign' (Smith 1895: II, ii, 3). John Millar observed how the contemporary advance in the standard of living was changing attitudes:

The farther the nation advances in opulence and refinement, it has occasion to employ a greater number of merchants, of tradesmen and artificers; and as the lower people, in general, become thereby more independent in their circumstances, they begin to exert those sentiments of liberty which are natural to the mind of man, and which necessity alone is able to subdue . . . The long attention and perseverance by which they became expert and skilful in their business, render them ignorant of those decorums and of that politeness which arises from the intercourse of society; and that vanity which was formerly discovered in magnifying the power of a chief, is now equally displayed in sullen indifference, or in contemptuous or insolent behaviour to persons of superior rank and station. (Millar 1771: 284 in 3rd edn.)

The growth of commerce and industry that had brought these changes about was itself due to the freedom and security which the people of Great Britain enjoyed, in happy contrast to the countries of the Continent. Although that freedom was still impeded here and there by some absurd survivals of an older system, no more was required for a further advance than to sweep these away. In the passage already quoted in which Adam Smith affirms the outstanding wealth of Britain, he attributes it to the freedom of its people.

That security which the laws in Great Britain give to every man that he shall enjoy the fruits of his own labour, is alone sufficient to make any country flourish. . . .; and this security was perfected by the Revolution. . . . The natural thought of every individual to better his own condition, when suffered to exert itself with freedom and security, is so powerful a principle, that it is alone, and without any assistance, not only capable of carrying on the society to wealth and prosperity, but of surmounting a hundred impertinent obstructions with which the folly of human laws too often encumbers its operations. (Smith 1776: IV, iii, pt. II)

The best possible state of affairs was freedom of enterprise, and the country was already within sight of it: 'in Great Britain industry is perfectly secure; and though far from being perfectly free, it is as free or freer than in any other part of Europe' (1776: IV, iii, pt. II).

The underlying belief that the pursuit of self-interest worked out to the common good was prevalent in the eighteenth century. It was taken to be the moral of Mandeville's *Fable of the Bees*. In Pope's *Essay on Man* it was interwoven with the other quietest belief, that all the affairs of the world formed part of a divine design for Nature, which it was not for man in his intellectual pride to presume to question. Pope trusted he might be found to have directed his verse.

From sounds to things, from fancy to the heart;
For Wit's false mirror held up Nature's light;
Shew'd erring Pride, WHATEVER IS, IS RIGHT;
That REASON, PASSION, answer one great aim;
That true SELF-LOVE and SOCIAL are the same . . .

Essay on Man, 4, 392-6

Adam Smith's epigram is well known: that 'it is not from the benevolence of the butcher, the brewer, or the baker, that we expect our dinner, but from their regard to their own interest' (1776: I, ii, 2). In his *Theory of Moral Sentiments* he had gone further, with an argument to show that, because the rich are obliged to spend largely on personal services, they effectively redistribute income at the level of consumption. The rich, he said,

consume little more than the poor, and in spite of their natural selfishness and rapacity, though they mean only their own conveniency, though the sole end which they propose from the labour of all the thousands whom they employ, be the gratification of their own vain and insatiable desires, they divide with the poor the produce of all their improvements. They are led by an invisible hand to make nearly the same distribution of the necessaries of life, which would have been made, had the earth been divided into equal portions among all its inhabitants. . .

When Providence divided the earth among a few lordly masters, it neither forgot nor abandoned those who seemed to have been left out in the partition. (Smith 1759: IV, i, I, 10)

In all these considerations that account for the complacency of the Scots philosophers in the face of the contrasts of riches and poverty, a powerful factor has been their individualism, and their belief in letting individual energies continue their work of general improvement in freedom. This might naturally be expected to be linked with a democratic tendency in politics. But that would be moving too fast. There remained in their minds unshaken vestiges of the older notion, that hierarchy and subordination were essential to the survival of any society. When David Hume had contended that the attempt to suppress inequality in its every appearance would lead to tyranny, he forthwith maintained—for good measure, it would seem, although not consistently—that equality of possessions if achieved would lead to anarchy. For 'destroying all subordination, [it] weakens extremely the authority of magistracy, and must reduce all power, nearly to a level, as well as property (Hume 1875: II 189).

Political democracy was not yet a practical issue. 'One man, one vote' was plainly impracticable: for illiterate and ignorant people to make responsible use of the vote was out of the question. And much more than that: if the state had been formed to protect property, its powers could never be entrusted to those by whom property would be plundered.

There was one other reason for accepting the present order of society without denying its inequality—the rise of utilitarianism. If that order could no longer be ascribed to divine institution, a new basis must be sought for it. One was found in the balance of advantage in retaining it. The survival, if not the origin, of social institutions was ascribed to their usefulness. Their anomalies could be freely recognized: but plainly, if they were destroyed, the resultant plight of humanity would be still worse.

Archdeacon Paley's *Principles of Moral and Political Philosophy* (1785) was adopted as a textbook for the young men at Cambridge as soon as it appeared, and it ran through fifteen editions. Paley himself was described by Leslie Stephen (1909) as having 'inherited the qualities of a long line of sturdy north-country yeomen. He was the incarnation of strong common-sense.' Like Adam Smith, Paley fully recognized the great inequality of wealth in his day; and, more even than Smith, he found it shocking, and said so in language positively inflammatory. This was in the parable that gained him the name of 'Pigeon Paley'. 'If you should see a flock of pigeons in a field of corn,' he wrote,

and if (instead of each pecking where, and what it liked, taking just as much as it wanted, and no more) you should see ninety-nine of them gathering all they got into a heap; reserving nothing for themselves, but the chaff and refuse; keeping this heap for one, and that the weakest perhaps and worst pigeon of the flock; sitting round, and looking on, all the winter, while this one was devouring, throwing about and wasting it; and, if a pigeon more hardy or hungry than the rest, touched a grain of the hoard, all the others instantly flying upon it, and tearing it to pieces; if you should see this, you would see nothing more, than what is every day practised and established among men. Among men you see the ninety and nine, toiling and scraping together a heap of superfluities for one; getting nothing for themselves all the while, but a little of the coarsest of the provision, which their own labour produces; and this one too, often the feeblest and worst of the whole set, a child, a woman, a madman, or a fool; looking quietly on, while they see the fruits of all their labour spent or spoiled; and if one of them take or touch a particle of it, the others join against him, and hang him for the theft. (Paley 1785: III, pt. I, ch. I)

Must not the author of this manifesto go on to justify the masses in rising up to take that superfluous wealth away from the child, woman, madman or fool who was squandering it? At the outset of the next chapter, Paley allowed that 'there must be some very important advantages to account for an institution, in one view of it so paradoxical and unnatural.' These advantages he found. The chapter is headed, 'The Use of the Institution of Property'. The term 'use', and the appeal to an audit of advantage in order to decide what is right, are significant. When Bentham's *Moral Philosophy* appeared, he was told that his principles had been anticipated by Paley. The advantages of the institution of property, Paley now argued, were that 'it increases the produce of the earth; it preserves the produce of the earth tò maturity; it prevents contests; it improves the conveniency of living'. As a result, the poorest folk in lands where the institution is upheld are better off

than *any* are, in places where most things remain in common. The balance, therefore, upon the whole, must preponderate in favour of property with a great excess. Inequality of property, in the degree in which it exists in most countries of Europe, abstractly considered, is an evil; but it is an evil, which flows from those rules concerning the acquisition and disposal of property, by which men are incited to industry, and by which the object of their industry is rendered secure and valuable. If there be any great inequality unconnected with this origin, it ought to be corrected. (Paley 1785: III, pt. I, ch. II)

It was significant of the tendencies of enlightened English thought at the time that a cleric who was not an original thinker but an expositor of what was generally accepted should have shown so much sensitivity to the inequality of wealth and should have accepted a criterion by which to assess social institutions that was capable in other hands of warranting so much change in them.

3.5. The English Tradition of Revolt and Levelling

It is remarkable that no advocacy of equality broke the surface of society in England in the eighteenth century until the time of the celebration of the centenary of the Glorious Revolution. There were 'Real Whigs' who passed for Commonwealth men it is true, and were acquainted with the pamphlets of the Levellers of the 1640s; but their own egalitarianism did not go beyond proposals to remove rotten boroughs, extend the franchise to leaseholders, widen religious toleration and improve education. A few did renew the proposal, coming down from the days of the New Model Army, for an agrarian law that would limit the size of individual holdings. But these 'Real Whigs' were like those other liberals who were later to subscribe to Declarations of human rights in America and France: they took it for granted that only men of some substance were qualified to vote. In a work that is said to have suggested to Bentham the wording of 'the greatest happiness of the greatest number', Joseph Priestley was later to maintain that only people of considerable fortune should hold the highest offices of state, and that

those who are extremely dependent should not be allowed to have votes in the nomination of the chief magistrates . . .; but if . . . we suppose a gradation of elected officers, and if we likewise suppose the lowest classes of the people to have votes in the nomination of the lowest officers and, as they increase in wealth and importance, to have a share in the choice of persons to fill the higher posts, till they themselves be admitted candidates for places of public trust; we shall, perhaps, form an idea of as much political liberty as is consistent with the state of mankind. (Priestley 1768: 17–18 in 2nd edn.)

It does not seem, either, that any stream of revolutionary or egalitarian thought, fed from Commonwealth springs, continued to flow underground. Riots did break out from time to time. In years of bad harvest there were bread riots. Labour disputes moved from strikes that were only a withdrawal of labour to battles on the picket line, slashing of cloth on the loom, breaking of machinery and attacks on employers' houses. But these uprisings had no objects beyond the removal of the grievances that prompted them. Even where a city mob could be raised readily, it seems to have responded more to the lure of loot than to any whirling of ideas or visions of a new order. Neither in town nor in country does any common purpose appear, or any tradition of revolutionary betterment.

This is surprising, when under the Commonwealth there had been so great an outpouring of egalitarian argument, carried even as far as projects for Christian and agrarian communism. That time was not so far past—it lay within the lifetime of the grandparents of people in their own prime at the mid-eighteenth century. For some five years, from 1644 onwards, the Levellers had stood forth as advocates of the equality of man. The name originally was given to the villagers who levelled the hedges and ditches that were formed when the common fields were enclosed; Charles I transferred the epithet to the advocates of equal rights for all.

There were, in fact, two sorts of Levellers. The greater part were concerned with equality only as the American colonists and the French Deputies were to be in their Declarations. Lilburne among them anticipated Locke. In two of his pamphlets, he stated the gist of his doctrine of human equality in a sentence of which a simplified version runs:

'God . . . gave Man . . . a rational soul or understanding and thereby created him after His own image . . . Every particular and individual man and woman that ever breathed in the world since [Adam and Eve] are and were by nature all equal and alike in power, dignity, authority and majesty, none of them having (by nature) any authority, dominion or magisterial power, one over . . . another. Neither have they or can they exercise any, but merely by institution or donation, that is to say . . . by mutual consent and agreement for the good . . . and comfort each of other . . . (Brailsford 1961: 118–19)

The practical programme of these political Levellers was much like that of the Chartists two hundred years later. Their aims were primarily constitutional—biennial parliaments, equal constituencies, manhood suffrage, religious toleration for all except Roman Catholics and the reform of legal procedure. In claiming manhood suffrage, they were divided between those in the army, led by Colonel Rainborow, who claimed it for every man, without any property qualification, and the civilian Levellers, who would not have given the vote to dependants such as paupers and servants. But although these political Levellers had their economic demands, such as the abolition of the tithe held by lay impropriators, and particularly the breaking up of enclosures and the return of common lands to the people, they were very far from having any radical or egalitarian programme of social change. If they were tarred with the brush of Levelling, it was because of their advocacy of manhood suffrage, with what seemed to its critics its inescapable consequences. There was a famous exchange between Rainborow and Ireton in the Putney Debate. 'I do think', said Rainborow, 'that the poorest man in England is not at all bound in a strict sense to that government that he hath not had a voice to put himself under.' Ireton replied, 'If you admit any man that hath a breath and being . . . this will destroy property . . . Why may not those men vote against all property?' (Brailsford 1961: 274–5).

Behind the political principle there certainly did lie the conviction that landowners had too much power, and the ancient tradition of the peasantry that this had been forcibly and wrongfully seized in the Norman Conquest. Although Rainboro agreed 'that the law of God recognised property', he went on to observe that

gentlemen with three or four Lordships (God knows how they got them) can always get into Parliament and evict the poor from their homes. I would feign know whether the potency of rich men do not this, and so keep them under the greatest tyranny that ever was thought of in the world. . . . The first thing I am unsatisfied about is how it comes about that there is such a propriety in some freeborn Englishmen and not in others. (Brailsford 1961: 282–3)

It was this theme of access to the land that formed a major motive of the second sort of Leveller, the 'true Levellers'. The mounting population pressure of the sixteenth century had greatly increased the resentment felt against enclosures. It was the poorest members of the village community who suffered most from them, and it was their sufferings for which the 'true Levellers' spoke. But beyond the immediate remedy of undoing the enclosures and giving back the commons to the villagers, the 'true Levellers' looked forward to an egalitarian society. William Walwyn was moved by what the fourth chapter of the Acts of the Apostles reports, that the early Christians 'had all things common', to conceive of a society of Christian communism. The anonymous tract *Tyranipocrit Discovered* (1649), having denounced the prevailing universal tyranny of the rich over the poor, declared that

to give unto every man with discretion so neere as may bee an equall share of earthly goods, is consonant to the Law of God and nature, and agreeable to the rule of Christ . . . If you should make and maintain an equality of goods and lands, . . . as God and nature would have, as justice and reason doth crave, . . . then mankind might live in love and concord as brethen should doe . . . (Schenk 1948: 149–52)

The greatest visionary was Winstanley, the prophet of the Diggers, who gathered to form brotherly colonies on the commons where they squatted. As Lilburne anticipated Locke, so Winstanley, with his raking fire on property, came uncannily close to sallies of Rousseau and Proudhon. 'In the beginning of Time, the great Creator Reason made the Earth to be a common treasury . . .' But then came the Fall, through covetousness, which induced men 'to lock up the treasures of the Earth in Chests and Houses'. 'This particular propriety of Mine and Thine hath brought in all misery upon people. For, first it hath occasioned people to steal from one another. Secondly it hath made laws to hang those who did steal.' Private property, once instituted, is maintained by the sword, which 'sets up one part of Mankinde, to rule over another; . . . by murder and theft, treading others under foot . . . Indeed, this Government may well be called the Government of highwaymen (Schenk 1948: 100). Winstanley's *Law of Freedom in a Platform* (1652) sets out a constitution for so pure a communist society that the death penalty would be inflicted for buying and selling.

This was far out, even for those wide-ranging days. The Diggers were soon dispersed. Yet the 'true Levellers' for the most part were not speaking only as zealots on the fringe of society. In two respects they were expressing a popular tradition coming down from the later Middle Ages: these were the resentment of rural oppression, and the cherishing of vague egalitarian ideals. We have evidence for the continuous flow among the common people of a current of egalitarianism, crude, hasty and ruthless. When agrarian tensions or taxation brought a rising, these ideals inflated the fantasies of the rebels and fired their audacity.

Shakespeare knew of these things, as appears from the notions he puts into the mouths of the rebels in Jack Cade's revolt. Cade himself he makes declaim: 'Be brave, then; for your captain is brave, and vows reformation. There shall be in England seven half-penny loaves sold for a penny; the three-hooped pot shall have ten hoops; and I will make it felony to drink small beer. All the realms shall be in common, and in Cheapside shall my palfrey go to grass.' That was satirical, the more so as the actual demands of those rebels had been realistically concerned with particulars of the current administration; but very likely, Shakespeare was reporting ranting that he had heard, or that some chronicler had put in an agitator's mouth. As he went on, moreover, he was only following the actual course of peasants' revolts. 'The first thing to do,' says Dick the Butcher, 'let's kill all the lawyers,' and Cade replies: 'Nay, that I mean to do. Is not this a lamentable thing, that of the skin of an innocent lamb should be made parchment! That parchment, being scribbled o'er, should undo a man?' (2 *Henry VI*, IV, ii). In the Peasants' Revolt of 1381 it had been particularly lawyers who had been slain at sight, and the records of the Courts that had been destroyed.

In Spenser's *Faerie Queene* (see Hill 1972, 92), again, a Giant appears with a great balance in his hand, and a passion for weighing everything in the world and apportioning it all in equal parts. ('Leasings' in the second line are 'lyings'.)

> Therefore the vulgar did about him flocke,
> And cluster thicke unto his leasings vaine,
> Like foolish flies about on hony crocke,
> In hope by him great benefit to gaine.
> And uncontrolled freedome to obtaine.

He had a programme not only of levelling the mountains with the plains, but of ironing out the distinctions of rank and the inequalities of wealth:

> Tyrants that make men subject to their law,
> I will supresse, that they no more may raine;
> And Lordings curbe, that commons over-aw;
> And all the wealth of rich men to the poor will draw.

> (Book V, Canto II, xxx–iv)

But The Giant was confounded by argument expressed in verse after verse paraphrasing the Scriptures, which proclaim the governance of all nature by the will of God, and the subordination of all human affairs to the authority that he delegates to the temporal powers. The Giant's inability to use his balance in pursuit of equality in practice was then glaringly exposed: he and the balance were tumbled down a cliff into the sea, the balance was shattered and the Giant drowned. That led to the armed revolt of the people, for 'losse of so great expectation':

> Thus as he spoke, loe with outragious cry
> A thousand villeins round about them swarmd
> Out of the rockes and caves adjoyning nye,
> Vile caytive wretches, ragged, rude, deformd,
> All threatening death, all in straunge manner armd,
> Some with unwieldy clubs, some with long speares,
> Some rusty knives, some staves in fire warmd.
> Sterne was their looke, like wild amazed steares,
> Staring with hollow eyes, and stiff upstanding heares.

> (Book II, Canto ix, xiii)

But in the story of the Giant, the 'lawless multitude' and 'rascall crew' were scattered quickly by the charge of a knight laying about him with his flail.

Spenser may have had Irish peasants in mind when he wrote those lines; but in England the tradition of revolt, armed 'with unwieldy clubs', and driven on also by levelling impulses, came down from the Middle Ages. A great, sudden and still unexplained revelation of the strength of popular resentments and aspirations, at least in certain regions, came in the Peasants' Revolt (but it was the revolt also of many townsmen) in 1381. The immediate provocation was certainly taxation, and the provision for the efficient collection of a third round of direct taxation, in support of an unpopular war, in certain counties enjoying a rising standard of living. But resistance to the tax collector detonated an economic and social struggle of longer duration. Thirty years before, the Black Death, by killing off a third of the population, had given labour a scarcity value on the land: wages rose, labour services in kind became harder to enforce, the stigma of servile status appeared increasingly intolerable. Landlords reacted by trying to hold labour down to the wages and customs that obtained before the Plague. They enacted laws to that effect in Parliament, and in the village they appealed to the records of the manorial court. The peasantry, who had been wont to use custom as a defence against landlords trying to squeeze more rent or services out of them, now found the landlords using custom against them; and lawyers keeping the records baffled an illiterate peasantry, who in any case did not understand the lingo even when it was spoken. So the peasants decided that the lawyers were cheating them. When they rose in arms, their first object was to burn the records of the courts, and often enough, as Dick the Butcher advised, to kill the lawyers too. But, like the 'true Levellers', they went beyond protest against oppression, and thought they were fighting to bring about a new reign of brotherhood.

In this, they drew on a vein of the teaching, if not of the Church, at least of the poor priests and friars. 'Sermons in denunciation of the rich', R. H. Hilton (1973: 211) has observed, '. . . were not exclusive to heretics or other conscious rebels . . . They were a commonplace of clerical moralists who selected the characteristic crimes of every estate in the social order for castigation.' The Bible has many indictments of riches. In the Magnificat itself, Our Lady glorifies the Lord for that 'He hath put down the mighty from their seat: and hath exalted the humble and meek. He hath filled the hungry with good things: and the rich He hath sent empty away.' There was authority in Scripture, and ammunition, for the unbeneficed clerk to use against the sleek and well-lined authorities of the Church; and in using it he went on readily, despite St Paul's injunction, to attack the temporal authorities and landlords too. He might himself have risen from among the peasantry; at least he well understood their grievances. They did not have the Bible to read, but they were taught the Bible story, and when they learned that all—lords and serfs alike—were the children of Adam and Eve, they took the point that all were by rights equal inheritors of the earth:

> When Adam dalf and Eve span
> wo was thanne a gentilmann?

was a couplet that ran current in Germany as well as England. The belief in an ancestral equality of rights was accompanied by the trust that, when oppression had been swept away, some sort of community or fellowship of equals would be left, in the nature of things. This was supported by the lingering chiliastic or millenarist expectation of the coming of a new reign on earth.

The egalitarianism compounded of the teaching of the Church and the economic conflicts of decaying feudalism found forcible expression in the sermons attributed by the chronicler Froissart to John Ball, an agitator in the revolt of 1381. Froissart is quoted here in Lord Berners's translation of 1523-5:

Of this imagination was a foolish priest in the country of Kent called John Ball, for the which foolish words he had been three times in the bishop of Canterbury's prison: for this priest used oftentimes on the Sundays after mass, when the people were going out of the minster, to go into the cloister and preach, and made the people to assemble about him, and would say thus: 'Ah, ye good people, the matters goeth not well to pass in England, nor shall do till everything be common, and that there be no villeins nor gentlemen, but that we may be all united together, and that the lords be no greater masters than we be. What have we deserved, or why should we be kept thus in servage? We be all come from one father and one mother, Adam and Eve: whereby can they say or shew that they be greater lords than we be, saving by that they cause us to win and labour for that they dispend? They are clothed in velvet and camlet furred with grise, and we be vestured with poor cloth; they have their wines, spices and good bread, and we have the drawing out of the chaff and drink water: they dwell in fair houses, and we have the pain and travail, rain and wind in the fields; and by that that cometh of our labours they keep and maintain their estates: we be called their bondmen and without we readily do them service, we be beaten; and we have no sovereign to whom we may complain, nor that will hear us nor do us right. Let us go to the King, he is young, and shew him what servage we be in, and shew him how we will have it otherwise, or else we will provide us of some remedy; and if we go together, all manner of people that be now in any bondage will follow us to the intent to be made free; and when the King seeth us, we shall have some remedy, either by fairness or otherwise. (Macaulay 1895: 250-1; Dobson 1970: 371)

The Reformation added a new element to these inherent levelling tendencies within the Church. Already in the first manifestation among the Lollards, the stress that John Wycliffe laid on the experience of grace in each human heart, and the access of each person to the means of grace, put all persons on an equal footing before God. He taught that 'a man cannot be sav'd without grace, which must be conferred directly by God'. His poor priests, in their 'long russet gowns of one pattern', went out from Oxford to bear a simple message that would be intelligible to everyman. The Bible, too, was to be open to all: Wycliffe arranged for its translation into the language of the common people. It does not appear that the Peasants' Revolt of 1381 was directly stimulated by his teaching: Hastings Rashdall allows only that 'the way for the movement was in places apparently prepared by vague socialistic or communistic teaching akin to Wycliffe's tenets about lordship and grace' (Rashdall 1909). But his religious thought was working towards a great change in political outlook in the longer run, because of its appeal to the individual conscience and judgement. This was seen to be undermining temporal as well as spiritual authority. As Archbishop Arundel, with his ripe experience of Lollard methods, asked William Thorpe in 1407 (according to the latter's account): 'Why loseell! Wilt not those and others that are confederated with thee, seeke out of holie Scripture and of the sence of doctours, all sharpe authorities against lords, knights and squiers, and against other secular men, as thou doest against priests.' (Pratt 1877: iii, 272; Aston 1960: 11). The trouble was not so much what the Lollards were thinking, as that they were thinking for themselves. Individualism would prove incompatible with hierarchy; the equal and direct relationship of all souls with God would imply the equality of all men here below. Especially, moreover, as the Reformation came to proclaim redemption by faith, believers insisted that the sacrifice of Christ on the cross had been made for all, without distinction of rank or wealth. That argument was advanced, probably by a Swabian tanner, in one of the Articles of Menningen, drafted early in the German Peasants' War of 1524-6. Writing on the peasants' behalf, the draftsman declared:

It has been the custom hitherto for men to hold us as their own property, which is pitiable enough considering that Christ has redeemed and purchased us without exception, by the shedding of His precious blood, the lowly as well as the great. Accordingly, it is consistent with the Scripture that we should be free and we wish to be so. (Dobson 1970: 348)

Just the same argument, that Christ's redeeming blood was shed for all, was advanced on Mousehold Heath near Norwich in 1549 by Robert Kett and his followers in their rebellion. 'We pray', said their petition, 'that all bonde men may be made ffre for God made all ffre wt his precious blode sheddyng' (Russell 1859: 51; Hilton 1973: 8).

Men of property were well aware of the egalitarian tendency—the necessary implications, even—of popular religion. They had reason to know how, when some twist of circumstance raised discontent past breaking point, the rebels could be inflamed by a resentment that they deemed righteous, and sanctioned by Holy Writ, against inequality and subordination. Lured by a chimera of brotherhood, they would subvert the existing order. That part of the Christian tradition which makes for equality and came down from the unbeneficed clerks of the Middle Ages, joined with the individualism of the gospel of salvation in the Reformation, had come by the seventeenth century to form a doctrine of wide and direct appeal to the propertyless. So it was seen in a petition from the gentry of Cheshire, in 1641. In entering a remonstrance against Presbyterianism as a form of self-government in the Church, they maintained that it 'must necessarily produce an extermination of nobility, gentry and order, if not of religion'. It would be dangerous doctrine if once grounded on vulgar apprehensions . . . The old seditious argument will be obvious to them, that we are all the sons of Adam, born free; some of them say the Gospel hath made them free. And law once subverted, it will appear good equity to such Chancellors to share the earth equally. They will plead Scripture for it, that we should all live by the sweat of our brows. (Hill 1974: 191–2)

Within a few years there were indeed Levellers and Diggers abroad in the land, ready to share the earth equally. The current that we have traced from the fourteenth century broke out in spate. But then, suddenly as it seems, it disappeared. Were there no successors to the radicals and visionaries of the Commonwealth? At first glance it might seem as if the countrymen of Devon and Dorset and Somerset who joined the Duke of Monmouth, some of them bearing the blades of scythes lashed to poles, belonged to the tradition of the Peasants' Revolt of three hundred years before. But Peter Earle (1977), in his study of the provenance of Monmouth's five thousand, shows that this was not so at all. Few of that army were husbandmen or farmers. 'The rebels were overwhelmingly concentrated in the middle ranks of society. There were very few gentlemen and very few labourers or paupers. The typical rebel was a weaver or a shoemaker, a tailor or a woolcomber. But all occupations were represented' (p. 17). Out of more than five hundred recorded as rebels by the parish constables, more than half were clothworkers. Responsible and married men for the most part, in the middle years of life, the rebels were not of the levelling kind. What moved them was resentment at religious persecution, and a fear of popery heightened by the accession of James II. In their region, the Civil War had brought not only more local fighting but also more division between neighbours than many other parts of the country suffered. At the Restoration the Royalists and Anglicans took their revenge on the Parliamentarians and Dissenters. Their meeting houses were pulled down, and a bonfire was made of the pews; they took to the fields, to worship by night. Behind the arm of the vindictive justices they saw the advancing power of Rome. The old dread, coming down from Mary's time, of popery, the Inquisition and the stake was stirred up. The Book of Remembrance of the Independent Congregation of Axminster recorded their fear, when they learned of James's accession, that 'as his brother had chastised them with whips, so he would now chastise them with scorpions' (Earle 1977: 16) When Monmouth landed, they rallied to the Good Old Cause. Their aim was to restore their freedom to worship God in their own way, and to recover the standing in the local community that they had lost at the Restoration. Once again, the children of light would overthrow the sons of Belial. But no change in the structure of society, or in the relations of rich and poor as such, seems to have entered their minds.

Nor did that issue of inequality stir people up again for another hundred years. Times had changed, as we say—meaning that, for reasons we can only conjecture, issues that had long filled the mind receded, without having been the object of decisive action. 'Reasons we can only conjecture': some may be put forward. The mounting population pressure that had forced down the standard of living of the labourer domestically in the course of the sixteenth century was ended, by disease and misery, early in the next century. Some modest but progressive recovery in living standards then became possible, subject to the interruption of the Civil War. It was advanced by agricultural improvements. There was a pause in enclosures between the Tudor movement and the renewed general movement towards the end of the eighteenth century. In all, these were times of betterment for the villager. Meanwhile, politically, there was a general desire to avoid a return to civil war, and consequently an atmosphere of 'live and let live', with a realization, quite alien to the minds of authority a hundred years before, that toleration of diversity of doctrine or forms of worship was compatible with the preservation of an orderly society. The settlement of 1689 was felt to have secured the liberty of the subject, whether or not he was enfranchised.

These considerations may go some way to explain the hundred years of calm. Those years ended in the last quarter of the eighteenth century, when a fearful growth of population in the villages revived the agrarian problem of inequality, and the dramatic examples of the American and French revolutions combined with the growth of commerce and industry to arouse the political awareness of the urban worker.

3.6. The Limits of Eighteenth-century Liberalism

All that has been written in this chapter has gone to show the limits of the doctrine of the equality of man in the eighteenth century. As a plan for action it was primarily negative: it meant the sweeping away of arbitrary power and the preserves of privilege. The beneficiaries were limited: they were the men of substance, standing and enterprise, who had a stake in the country, and were fitted by mind and character to assume the responsibilities of citizenship. The rights of man did not extend to the rest—to women, or Negroes, or even to the mass of the labouring population. This was long accepted with little notice. The social philosophers saw the sorry state of the labourer as an aspect of an indispensable social structure. The sociologists of the Scots enlightenment saw it as having been formed in the course of a natural development: the structure of society was in the nature of things. Meanwhile, the outcry of rural oppression and popular protest that had broken cover under the Commonwealth was seldom heard in years of greater ease and rising standards.

The proposition that adult white males with adequate resources should enjoy equal civic and legal rights is far removed from the egalitarianism that requires the extinction or at least the reduction of all differences of wealth or income between the persons within its purview. Yet it did mark a move in that direction. In comparison with an antecedent world of arbitrary authority or privileges or conflicting jurisdictions, eighteenth-century liberalism did represent a step towards egalitarianism. For within a certain category, and quite a broad one, everyone had an equal claim to consideration. Each person, moreover, was seen as endowed with certain rights, which in the American Declaration included the right to pursue happiness; this concept could be broadened into a right to welfare, and there the case would follow for increasing welfare in the aggregate by transfers from the rich to the poor. But more developments than these, in thought and practice, were needed before egalitarianism could affect policy; and some of them did come about in the eighteenth century, as we shall now see.

4

Eighteenth-century Developments Propitious to Egalitarianism

Much more is required than faith in the equality of man before egalitarianism can offer itself even as a notion of policy. At least three conditions may be specified. For one thing, personal resources must be reduced to and summed up in a common unit, such as money. If one person has great beauty and another is short of breath, how shall we set about equalizing them? And the task is no simpler if their difference is in status. The same difficulty appears in some degree when we compare incomes that accrue some in kind, directly from the produce of the land their owners cultivate, and some in visible payments for work or property. Only when an economy has been thoroughly monetized can the resources of all its members be readily compared with one another. A second condition for putting egalitarianism into practice is that administrative means should exist with which to transfer resources—taxation that can cream off the higher incomes, forms of social benefit to raise the lower. Each of these must be capable of adjustment to the circumstances of the individual taxpayer or beneficiary. Third, there must be fellow feeling. This goes beyond recognizing that different persons have equal rights under the law, or deploring the contrast between riches and poverty as a division within the community: it means accepting an identity of interest and concern between each and all, such that no one can claim a pleasure for himself with a clear mind if it is purchased at the cost of a deprivation to another. At the limit, this means that I must not enjoy something that is mine by common consent if a poorer person would enjoy it more.

In the following pages we shall see how these three conditions came closer to realization in the course of the eighteenth century.

4.1. Monetization and Political Arithmetick

Before the onset of the economic development that has marked out the last five or six centuries in the western world, most production was within the household, for the household. It so remains for much of the less developed world today. The very word 'economy' meant originally 'the law of the household'. It is true that there were always markets which were indispensable for those needs that they met, and in the markets money changed hands. There were also 'cash crops'. But few if any people could reckon their incomes in money. The members of the humble household were clothed and fed by the produce of their own labour. Those who lived more at ease, drawing revenue from their tenants, drew it largely in kind. The tithe barn was built to hold the share of the Church. Even the King found it convenient to travel round the royal estates with his court, eating his way. Feudalism was in one of its aspects a way of providing for the raising of an army without financing it.

When the incomes of different classes are not expressed in money, the possibility of adjusting as distinct from seizing them does not present itself. Indeed, the very notion of income is as yet only latent. What is apparent is the difference of rank and power and of outward seeming, of possessions, dress and ease. Here are ways of life so different that at the extreme they sever all ties of common humanity. Where they diverge less from one another, in intermediate gradations, they still appear as set apart, each in its own role. But measurable inequalities can exist only between quantities expressed in common terms. Differences between knights and villeins, burgesses and labourers, were hierarchical, not numerical. The underdog might resent them and rise up violently against them. The mob might burst in the gates of the château, or string up the lawyers who documented labour services; but the possibility of orderly transfer of resources from the wealthy to the poor had to wait upon the monetization of incomes.

This came about gradually. One step was the commutation of labour services for money wages, a change driven on fast when the Black Death made labour scarce, and gave it the whip hand in the bargain. But the most general factor was the increasing division of labour, in all its forms. This implied more exchanges and greater use of markets, for labour itself, for the materials it worked on and for its products; and these exchanges used money. The practice of working and reckoning in money must have been facilitated by the inflation of the sixteenth century. When a carpenter earned 3 pence a day and meat cost a farthing a pound—rates typical of the thirteenth century—pricing small quantities must have been much more difficult than when, by 1600, the wage had risen to 12 pence, and the prices of foodstuffs had been much more than quadrupled. The reckoning of income in money was also promoted by the advance of account-keeping: the farmer, trader and self-employed craftsman became more likely, as time went on, to keep books of a sort and to make a reckoning of their net gains. In the eighteenth century the basic process of the extension of the division of labour and the widening of markets was carried further by the growth of commerce and industry and the improvement of agriculture. It was assisted by the expansion of domestic banking.

But already, by the end of the preceding century, incomes had come to be so generally paid out or reckoned in money, that tables could be drawn up in which the incomes of different ranks and occupations were set out more or less comprehensively, on a national plan.

Towards the end of his life, the great French military engineer, Vauban, turned his mind towards the problems of public finance. His travels, in pursuance of the work of fortification, through the length and breadth of the realm had impressed him with the condition of the people. He found it appalling. A tenth of them were beggars; of the remaining nine parts, five were little better (Vauban 1933: 7). Much of their misery he attributed to taxation—to its harsh exactions from them directly, and to its strangulation of all initiative that would have raised their productivity. Accordingly, he sought to sweep away the existing patchwork of taxes, with their grossly inequitable exemptions and capricious incidence, and to substitute a single tax to be paid by everyone without exception in proportion to his capacity to pay. In 1694 he drew up a 'Project for a Capitation' of that kind, but only as a supplementary and temporary source of revenue, for the duration of the current war. Four years later he began to develop the idea to provide the main and permanent source of the revenue of the Crown as the 'Dixme Royale', the Royal Tithe.

To substantiate his claim that there was a sufficient basis for the Capitation, Vauban set out a list of the principal offices and paid employments that would bear the tax, together with an inventory of the lands and other fixed or moveable possessions that might be taxed as indications of the taxable capacity of their occupiers or owners. For the Dixme Royale he estimated the taxable basis in the same way. The intention was always to take income as the measure of taxable capacity, but many substantial people were not assigned and did not record an income in money, so the tax collector had to fall back on the value of their real estate and moveables as surrogates for their income. We shall see how, repeatedly in British taxation, what was intended to be an income tax became in this way a tax on property. Vauban will have felt no inconsistency in interpolating his list of occupations and employments with such entries as 'more than 80 000 flour mills, which one can put at a return of 200 livres each on the average'; or '2.4 million houses at an average annual value of 20 livres'; or 'at least 15 000 fulling-mills, oil-mills, flax-mills, paper-mills, cork factories, saw-mills and other factories of the kind' (Vauban 1933: 263, 265, 266). It was only through taxing such properties that he could hope to reach the incomes of most of the middle class outside agriculture, in their self-employment as professional men, traders and manufacturers. The greatest interpolation of all was for agriculture itself—he reckoned the whole realm to contain more than 124 million arpens of land, of which two-thirds were cultivable (Vauban 1933: 264). But the particulars he gave of the occupations themselves enabled a few big incomes to be compared numerically with those of working people—only a few; for all the clergy are grouped, and although all the offices of the state are listed, the salaries of only two are given separately. These are:

4 Intendants de l'Armée, each with 240 000 livres
140 Commissaires de Guerres, each with 5100 livres.

At the other end of the scale are the male and female servants, whose numbers, and wages in money and kind, Vauban estimated very differently in the Project and the Dixme Royale. In the Project his estimate was of 800 000 servants with wages ranging from 6 to 114 livres, average 60 livres. In the Dixme Royale he raised the total to 1.5 million, but put the average wage down to 20 livres (Vauban 1933: 261, 266).

Above the servants were the artisans; Vauban showed a detailed knowledge of their working life, as well as a humane concern, in reckoning their taxable capacity. You must take not only their daily output when they are at work, he says, but the expenses they must incur if they are masters: how many journeymen and apprentices they employ, and, especially, how many days are commonly not available for work in their occupation. For example, a typical weaver can weave six ells of cloth in a day, and at 2 sols per ell that makes 12 sols; but he does not work on Sundays, or feast days, or during frost, or when he is delivering his cloth, or when he has to go to the fair or the market to get supplies; he will also lose some days from illness. In all, Vauban concluded, he will have only 180 working days in the year. (If the 2 sols per ell was a return clear of outgoings, and we can take 20 sols to the livre, his annual earnings would be 108 livres.) Vauban showed an equal concern for the irregular employment of the unskilled labourers, whose earnings over the whole year might, on an investigation of individual cases, prove to be so low that they must be exempted from all contribution:

These people may very well find the kind of work they can do for part of the year, and it is true that during haymaking, corn harvest, and grape-harvest they usually earn good money; but it's not like that for the rest of the year. And this again is what we must go into with much care and patience, to be sure of separating the strong from the weak, always in that spirit of justice and charity which is so necessary in such a case if one is not to bring about the ruin of poor folk, who are so near the edge already, that the smallest charge over and above what they can bear would be enough to overwhelm them. (Vauban 1933: 78).

The labourers, then, should be entered at a lower income than the servants.

These are fragmentary estimates, but they are also bold. What is significant is that the estimating should have gone so far, in such a form. The principle was proclaimed that equity and efficiency in taxation alike depended upon a sound statistical knowledge of taxable capacity. As yet, that knowledge was largely lacking. Vauban, a trained surveyor, knew that it could be provided by fieldwork. He set an outstanding example by his social survey of the district of Vézelay, tabulating the details of its lands, woods and animals under thirty-six headings for each of its fifty-six parishes, but also providing a careful and systematic, if necessarily harrowing, verbal description of the wretched conditions of the inhabitants, an analysis of the causes of their lethargy and a number of practical proposals for raising the level of production.

There were two Englishmen of Vauban's time, Sir William Petty and Gregory King, whose abilities and achievements had much in common with his. Petty was like him in his early training, his genius for surveying and his adaptation of both techniques to social problems. As a bright lad from Hampshire, serving in a vessel trading with France, he had been marooned with a broken leg on the coast of Normandy: eventually he entered the Jesuit College at Caen. There he obtained, he said, 'the Latin, Greek and French tongues; the whole body of common arithmetic, the practical geometry and astronomy conducing to navigation, dialling etc; with the knowledge of several mathematical trades' (Fitzmaurice 1895: 5). He went on to Paris, where he helped Hobbes with drawings for his treatise on Optics and was in touch with much of the scientific and philosophic speculation so active there at the time. Later, after he had become Professor of Anatomy at Oxford, he was attached as Physician to the Commonwealth forces in Ireland. There he established his reputation by carrying out a great survey of the Irish lands—a survey remarkable not only for its immediate application, but for its method. After the Restoration he published a number of works on economic policy, and here again he was a pioneer in bringing systematic quantitative thinking to bear. He was held to be the founder of what was called Political Arithmetick. 'By political arithmetick,' said Sir Charles Davenant (1771: i, 128–9), we mean the art of reasoning by figures upon things relating to Government. The art itself is undoubtedly very ancient, but the application of it to the broad objects of trade and revenue is what Sir William Petty first began.'

Just when Vauban was moving on from his Project to the Dixme Royale, and in the very year (1696) in which he published his survey of Vézelay, Gregory King drew up his 'Scheme of the Income of the Several Families of England'. Although he had made his career in the College of Heralds, as the son of an accomplished mathematician he had at one time supported himself by teaching arithmetic; he was a competent map-maker and surveyor; like Vauban at Vézelay, he carried out a detailed local survey of 395 households, at Sevenoaks in Kent. Like Vauban, also, he was a cartographer. His use of the Bills of Mortality to estimate population movements showed a statistical flair that has continued to compel the admiration of later demographers. Under an Act of 1692 he was appointed Secretary of the Commissioners for Stating the Public Accounts. Colin Clark has remarked that 'the duties of this post apparently corresponded in a primitive form, to those of the Secretary of the Treasury and Chairman of the Board of Inland Revenue at the present day' (Clark 1937: 214). During his tenure, in 1696, he drew up the 'Scheme of the Income of the Several Families of England, Calculated for the Year 1688', which is reproduced in Table 4.1. Later on (c. 11.1) we shall examine his estimates on their statistical merits, and compare the picture they afford of the distribution of income in his day with other estimates available at various dates down to a recent year. We shall there see reason to believe that, although his own estimates call for some amendment, they are by no means to be discarded as unfounded guesses.

Peter Laslett (1973) has argued that this was a state paper, worked up with materials made available by officials, and designed to inform the government of the taxable capacity of the country, and the effect of the war on it. G. S. Holmes (1977) has strong grounds for contending that King, as a Tory, thought that the government had been taking the country downhill since 1688, and that, if Petty's estimates had not made this clear, it was because they were overblown. King's own bias was therefore the other way. In particular, he understated the numbers and incomes of the well-to-do.

The materials available to him, Holmes has also shown, were fragmentary. He did not use the hearth tax or poll tax records, although he did have figures of the total yields of two recent polls. But he had a firm basis in the number of inhabited houses; and so, from household sizes, and estimates of various base for the average income of each type of household, he built up his estimate of the whole national income. Holmes says that he built it 'by the most convoluted and questionable means' (1977: 60), but those of us who have ourselves engaged in this kind of estimating may take a kinder view; when one has a framework of some strength, as King had in his estimate of the number of houses and the total population, one can use slight and scattered evidence, and even suppositions based on everyday knowledge, to fit pieces into place within it.

King made a division, to our eyes a strange one, between the last four classes in his table and all the rest. These last were the Common Seamen, the Labouring People and Out-servants, the Cottagers and Paupers, and the Common Soldiers. In all, they contained half the total population of the country. King marked them off because, he said, they 'decreased the wealth of the Kingdom'. The remaining ranks and occupations increased it. His thought may have been that as a body the people in those four classes were not self-supporting: although the head of the family might keep his family while he was fit for work, he and his dependents would be 'a charge on the parish' for some part of their lives. The other classes, he may have thought, achieved some net saving, or paid the poor rate. His strange formulation calls our attention forcibly to the extent of poverty—half the population partially dependent on transfer payments—before the agricultural and industrial revolutions.

TABLE 4.1 Gregory King's scheme of the income of the several families of England, calculated for the year 1688

No. of families	Ranks, degrees, titles and qualifications	Heads per family	No. of persons	Yearly income per family (£)	Total of the estate or income* (£000)	Yearly income per head (£)
160	Temporal lords	40	6 400	2 800	448	70
26	Spiritual lords	20	520	1 300	33.8	65
800	Baronets	16	12 800	880	704	55
600	Knights	13	7 800	650	390	50
3 000	Esquires	10	30 000	450	1 200	45
					(1 350)	
12 000	Gentlemen	8	96 000	280	2 880	35
					(3 360)	
5 000	Persons in offices	8	40 000	240	1 200	30
5 000	Persons in offices	6	30 000	120	600	20
2 000	Merchants & traders by sea	8	16 000	400	800	50
8 000	Merchants & traders by land	6	48 000	200	1 600	33
10 000	Persons in the law	7	70 000	140	1 400	20
2 000	Clergymen	6	12 000	60	120	10
8 000	Clergymen	5	40 000	45	360	9
40 000	Freeholders	7	280 000	84	3 360	12
140 000	Freeholders	5	700 000	50	7 000	10
150 000	Farmers	5	750 000	44	6 600	8.15s.
16 000	Persons in sciences & liberal arts	5	80 000	60	960	12
40 000	Shopkeepers & tradesmen	4½	180 000	45	1 800	10
60 000	Artisans & handicrafts	4	240 000	40	2 400	10
5 000	Naval officers	4	20 000	80	400	20
4 000	Military officers	4	16 000	60	240	15
50 000	Common seamen	3	150 000	20	1 000	7

364 000	Labouring people and out-servants	3½	1 275 000	15	5 460	4.10s. (4.6s.)
400 000	Cottagers & paupers	3¼	1 300 000	6.10s.	2 000 (2 600)	2
35 000	Common soldiers	2	70 000	14	490	7
	Vagrants	—	30 000	—	60	2
			5 500 520		43 505 800	

* Figures in brackets are interpolated corrections. It is assumed that the basic estimates are the number of families and the yearly income per family, and when the product of these two figures does not (subject to rounding) appear as the 'Total of the estate or income', the product as now calculated has been inserted.

Source: Gregory King, *Natural & Political Observations and Conclusions upon the State and Condition of England*, 1696; the table reproduced here from Laslett (1973).

When King's estimates were compiled, they were probably intended immediately only for the eyes of the government, and they were never published in their entirety before 1802, although Sir Charles Davenant quoted them largely in his essay, *Upon the Probable Methods of Making a People Gainers in the Balance of Trade*, in 1698. It is still significant that so systematic a tabulation was possible in the 1690s. By this time income had become so largely monetized as to lend itself to enquiries that served the purposes not only of national finance, but also of those numerical comparisons that open a clearer way to practical egalitarianism than does the mere awareness of differences in rank.

In Gregory King, as in Vauban and Petty, we see how the advance of mathematics during the seventeenth century into the field of public administration combined with the increasing monetization of income to display the inequalities of society in a quantitative form for the first time. No longer did these inequalities appear simply as a contrast of poverty and riches. The gradations could now be marked and measured. What is more, the taxable capacity at different social levels was now apparent, and with this, the possibilities of reducing inequality by transfers through the public accounts.

4.2. Taxation as an Instrument of Redistribution

If money incomes are to be made more equal, one obvious instrument is taxation. From early times, taxation did in fact reduce the absolute difference between the rich and the poor, because it was felt that 'the broad back should bear the burden', and more was taken from those who could afford it. An income tax could in principle be fairly proportioned to individual capacity to pay. But where income, as we have seen, was seldom wholly paid or reckoned in money, the difficulty was to assess it; and several times what began as an income tax, in intent and even in a rough and ready way in practice, slid back into a property tax. The adoption of a viable income tax had to wait upon William Pitt's introduction of an effective method of assessment.

A first direct tax intended to be proportional to the capacity to pay had been introduced by Henry II on the occasion of the Saledin tithe—so called because it was raised in 1188 for the Second Crusade. There were two features, often relied upon in later measures. One was that the value of the taxpayers' moveables was taken as an indication of what a later age would have called his taxable income. What may be termed the operational equipment of the knights and the clergy was exempt; but otherwise all the cattle, farming stock and stored produce of the landowner, and all the tools, stock-in-trade and furniture of the burgher, were valued, and the owner was required to pay a tax levied from time to time, at some fraction such as a tenth or fifteenth of that value together with his rent. The second feature was that a method of assessment, under local commissioners, was provided from the first. The original ordinance of 1188 began with self-assessment, in the tradition of the contribution to good causes at the church door that was voluntary but was performed under the eyes of priest and neighbours. 'And if any one shall, in the opinion of those presiding at the collection, have given less than he ought, let there be chosen from the parish four or six freemen, who, on oath, shall state the amount which he ought to have given; and then he shall add the amount which before was wanting (Dowell 1884: I, 46). Here was the germ of the younger Pitt's great constructive development when he designed the procedure of self-assessment in 1799. But in the thirteenth century the provision for assessment became very different. At some times and in some places, at least, the assessment of moveables was carried out by inspectors with penetrating thoroughness. Schedules for the borough of Colchester, one for the seventh of 1295 and the other for the fifteenth of 1301, record

every beast of the plough, ox, cow, calf, sheep, lamb, pig, and horse and cart; every quarter of wheat, barley and oats, haystack and woodstack; all the little stock-in-trade of the local sea-coal dealer, pepperer, mustarder, spicer, butcher, fisherman, brewer, and wine seller, tanner, skinner, shoemaker, fuller, weaver, glazier (verrer), carpenter, cooper, ironmonger, smith, potter, and bowyer . . . The money of the taxpayers of which they seem to have had very little, their valuables, in the shape of silver buckles, spoons and cups, their suits of clothing, linen, beds, table cloths and towels, brass pots and pans, basons and andirons or fire dogs, are put down and valued. (Dowell 1884; I, 80)

Assessments like that must have been resented as intrusive. Certainly they were laborious. Year by year, in strictness they required to be revised and renewed, as personal fortunes waxed and waned, and the population turned over. Small wonder that the collectors fell back upon a more permanent and less disputable basis of taxation—the value of land and houses. Instead of being freshly assessed from time to time, moreover, and yielding amounts that varied according to what income was revealed, from 1334 the fifteenth and the tenth became fixed amounts, which in each district were broken down into fixed rates borne by particular pieces of property.

Yet one or two particular taxes were imposed, in which much care was taken to adjust the rate to each man's taxable capacity. All that we know suggests that in the poll tax of 1379 the intention was to take about the same proportion from each man's net income, which was reckoned after deducting from his gross income the necessary expenses of his station or office. We have two national schedules, one for the clergy, the other for the laity. The lay schedule began with the two dukes, who were each to pay 10 marks (£6. 13s. 4d.), and the earls, who would pay £4. It went on through the barons, knights and esquires, with rates from £2 down to ¼ mark (3s.

4*d*.), to specify many others, such as the mayors of the great towns, at £2 each, and the smaller merchants and artificers, paying 2*s*., 1*s*. or 6*d*. according to their estate, with finally the married couples and single men and women, each paying 4*d*. Here is a spread of 240 or 400 to 1 from the highest to the lowest, or 120 to 1 between the mayor of a great town and the working man: did this fairly represent the ratio of their incomes? We have no means of telling, but the spread does seem wide—perhaps the tax was progressive. In the tax that was hurriedly imposed in the following year to meet the demands of the war with France, a much narrower spread was stipulated. A lump sum laid on each district and township was to be allocated within it, 'the rich helping the poor', provided that no one should pay more than 60 groats, that is £1, and no married couple less than 1 groat, that is 4*d*. So the permissible spread within the locality was no more than 60 to 1.

In the next century two taxes were enacted which do seem to have been progressive in the modern sense, at least in so far as lower rates were charged on lower incomes. That of 1435 was based upon a clear notion of net annual income received from property, annuities or offices after allowance for expenses. The first £50 of net annual income was exempt. At that point a charge of 2*s*. 6*d*. was incurred, and from there up to £100 a year each additional £1 bore a tax of 6*d*. Between £100 and £400, the tax was 8*d*. in the pound. Over £400 a year, the tax jumped to 2*s*. in the pound—'probably none but Dukes and Earls would come under the last category', the historian Sir James Ramsay observed (Ramsay 1892: I, 478-9). Parliament had been moved by violent hostility against the 'false foresworn' Duke of Burgundy, and took a number of measures for the prosecution of the war against him, even down to the issue of a free pardon to an outlaw from Winchelsea, then at sea with a pirate crew, who might attack his Fleming subjects. It was as a further war measure that Parliament granted, in addition to a subsidy spread over two years, the graduated income tax. The point of this tax was that it would have to be paid by all recipients of income, whereas the incidence of the subsidy was capricious, and peers did not contribute to it at all; the graduation of the income tax ensured that the peers would contribute to it fully, and Ramsay says, they 'might be supposed to belong to the war party' (Ramsay 1892: I, 478).

The second graduated tax is recorded for 1450. By this, income from £1 to £20 a year bore tax at the rate of 6*d*. in the pound. From £20 to £200 the rate was 1*s*. in the pound. Over £200, the rate was 2*s*. in the pound (Dowell 1884: I, 123-4, 127-8). This seems to have arisen from a compromise between the Commons and the Crown, at a crisis of the Crown's finances. The Commons told the King that he could pay his way if he would only resume the many grants that he had so freely made of 'lands, rents, franchises, pensions, or hereditary offices'. He was willing to do this only if he could reserve the grants he had made to a list of recipients who proved to be the principal magnates and the Court party, as well as his charitable foundations. The Commons accepted this, but reciprocated by witholding a subsidy and granting instead an income tax, which would fall on the Lords, the types who had kept their grants. They took care to include in the Act a clause to make it clear that peers would not be exempt as they were from the subsidy. One chronicler records a joyful popular belief at the time that the fifteenths and tenths were to be abolished in favour of this more equitable form of tax.

But these were exceptional measures, in a particular political setting. When later a fresh start was made with the aim once again of taxing persons, not things, according to the capacity of each person, the outcome in each case was that the tax came to rest upon particular pieces of property. The Tudor subsidies, which began in 1514 and were supposed to be originally a grant of a certain rate in the pound on the value of the moveables of every person and corporation, had become by the later years of Queen Elizabeth a fixed total sum; and the amount allocated to each county or borough was collected from the estates of a limited number of 'subsidy men', or a subsidiary class of 'bearers', according to certain accepted and unchanging valuations. The new tax, again, that was instituted after the Glorious Revolution was meant to rest on income drawn from every sort of personal possession. In the words of the Land Tax Act, it was to be assessed on the annual value of 'any estate in ready money, or in any debts whatsoever, or . . . any estate in goods, wares, merchandises, or other chattels or personal estate whatsoever'. 'So ran the Act, but in practice personal property, which had long before this slipped out of assessment, continued to be free from the tax, which was collected solely from land' (Dowell 1884: II, 119).

But the most striking example of this slide down from income tax to property tax was the poor rate—the most striking, because the original intent to bring income under contribution was clearest when the contributions were to be pooled for neighbourly aid. The statutory poor rate of 1572 had its origin in the collections for the relief of the poor taken up at the church door. These may well have been like the 'neighbourhood drives', by which many American communities raised funds for the relief of the local unemployed in the Depression of 1930–2; contributions were voluntary, but there was strong social pressure to participate, and to give according to one's means, as the neighbourhood judged them. But with ever rising population, the problems of the poor mounted faster than social sanctions could extract donations, and some local authorities at least resorted to compulsion. We know that London did so in 1547, and Norwich in 1570 (Leonard 1900: 29, 104 n. 1). When Parliament legislated in 1572 to make compulsory contribution general, it did not specify the basis of assessment, but said only that the authorities 'shall by their good discretions tax and assess all and every the inhabitants . . . to such weekly charge as they and every of them shall weekly contribute (Bland *et al.* 1914: pt. II, iv, 4). The great Poor Law Act of 1601 was no more explicit: it only authorized the overseers of the poor 'to raise weekly or otherwise, by taxation of every inhabitant parson, vicar and other, and of every occupier of lands, houses, tithes impropriate or propriations of tythes, coal mines or saleable underwoods, in the said parish, in such competent sum and sums of money as they shall think fit, a convenient stock, etc. (Bland *et al.* 1914: pt. II, iv, 8). How this was to be done must have been well enough understood: the local authorities would be expected to follow the customary course of assessment for the taxes they had to collect already. As one Act put it—an Act settling a dispute between Cardiff and Glamorgan about the maintenance of a bridge at Cardiff—the rate should be levied 'in due and proportionable manner, according as rates, taxes and tallages have been before this time used to be there rated and levied, or as near thereunto as they can (Cannan 1896: 33). This meant that the amount to be paid by each contributor was at the discretion of the local authorities, but they would be guided by a valuation of his property. Because the intention was to tax him personally according to his capacity, the valuation would cover his property in all its forms. But manifold difficulties soon appeared. There were the problems already noticed of making and revising the valuation of moveables. Even more, where the parish was the accounting unit, there was the difficulty that land within the parish might be occupied by people who were not parishioners; by Jeffery's case in 1589, the courts decided that such land should pay the parish poor rate none the less. This was part of the twofold process by which the valuation, which had been meant only as a guide to personal capacity, became itself the object of taxation; and within that valuation, moveables dropped out, and the rate came to be levied on the value of houses and land alone. But outside farming, the second part of the process went on to various extents in different places. Local authorities were still able to act at their discretion. As late as 1840, Parliament was legislating against the rating of stock in trade. Not until the Rating Act of 1874 did the poor rate finally come to apply to all houses and land and no moveables.

In the eighteenth century the issues of progression and regression were raised by force of circumstance: the discussion of principle held to proportionality. The justification of taxation, it was maintained, was that all persons, rich and poor alike, were equally dependent for life and livelihood on the protection of the state: all, therefore, should contribute equally to its necessary expenses. By a step in reasoning that is not altogether clear, this last 'equally' was taken to mean 'by the same proportions of their ability to pay'. As an intuitive justification of this position, it was observed that a proportionate tax would leave all persons undisturbed, in the same relative positions as before. But it was recognized that this would not really be so: it would not hold in terms of welfare even if it held in units of money—if the smaller incomes were now so reduced that they no longer afforded a bare livelihood. 'Ability to pay' could fairly be reckoned only after setting aside the amount needed to provide for sustenance—for the essentials of existence, to impair which would be to destroy labour and industry. But with that important reservation, the principle of proportionality generally held. To depart from it by graduating taxes would be to infringe the rights of property and discourage thrift and enterprise. To spare the poor was one thing, to despoil the rich quite another. It is true that the thought that a pound sterling does not mean as much to a rich man as to one of modest means did receive passing mention. Adam Smith, holding that the higher a person's income, the greater the proportion of it that he spends on his house, concluded that:

a tax upon house rents . . . would in general fall heaviest upon the rich; and in this sort of inequality there would not, perhaps, be anything very unreasonable. It is not very unreasonable that the rich should contribute to the public expense, not only in proportion to their revenue, but something more than in that proportion. (Smith 1776: V, ii, pt. II, art. I).

But this was only an incidental remark.

It might seem that the case for graduation was made out by Archdeacon Paley in his *Moral and Political Philosophy* (1785), to which we have already referred (pp. 110–11). Paley called in question the customary opinion 'that a tax to be just, ought to be accurately proportional to the circumstances of the persons who pay it'. If our concern is to minimize loss of welfare, the tax should be steeply progressive:

the point to be regarded is not what men *have*, but what they can *spare*; and it is evident that a man who possesses a thousand pounds a year can more easily give up a hundred pounds than a man with a hundred pounds can part with ten pounds; that is, those habits of life which are reasonable and innocent, and upon the ability to continue which the formation of families depends, will be much less affected by the one deduction than by the other. It is still more evident that a man of a hundred pounds a year would not be so much distressed in his subsistence by a demand from him of ten pounds, as a man of ten pounds a year would be by a loss of one pound. (Paley 1785: bk. VI, ch. xi (iv))

But although Paley had declared at the outset that 'the final view of all national policies is, to produce the greatest quantity of happiness in a given tract of country', he was far from any application of the felicific calculus. His case was that the sum of happiness would generally grow in proportion to population; the sound growth of population depended on the marriage rate; and people would not marry unless they were assured of the level of subsistence that they were accustomed to look for. Nothing, therefore, should be done to deny that assurance to the labouring classes who make up the bulk of society: 'the population of every country being replenished by the marriages of the lowest ranks of the society, their accommodation and relief become of more importance to the State, than the conveniency of any higher but less numerous order of its citizens' (1785, VI, xi (iv)).

The case for sparing the poor, then, was accepted without its utilitarian counterpart, demanding more from the rich. The prevailing view agreed with Adam Smith's first maxim:

> The subjects of every state ought to contribute towards the support of the government, as nearly as possible in proportion to their respective abilities; that is, in proportion to the revenue which they respectively enjoy under the protection of the state. The expense of government to the individuals of a great nation, is like the expense of management to the joint tenants of a great estate, who are all obliged to contribute in proportion to their respective interests in the estate. (Smith 1776: V, ii, pt. ii)

An equal proportionate contribution is required from rent, profit and wages. The call is clearly for an income tax. But this seemed so plainly impracticable to Adam Smith that, in all he wrote on taxes in the *Wealth of Nations*, he did not discuss it. By implication, he dismissed it when he considered taxes upon the revenue arising from stock:

> The proprietor of stock is properly a citizen of the world, and is not necessarily attached to any particular country. He would be apt to abandon the country in which he was exposed to a vexatious inquisition, in order to be assessed to a burdensome tax, and would remove his stock to some other country where he could either carry on his business, or enjoy his fortune more at his ease. . . . In all countries a severe inquisition into the circumstances of private persons has been carefully avoided. (Smith 1776: V, ii, pt. II, art. II)

The only kinds of tax he discusses that were intended to fall on incomes of all kinds were the old capitation taxes, and taxes on consumable commodities.

But while proportionality held the field of discourse, the exigencies of public finance were bringing in the practice of progression and differentiation. Successive wars and the interest on mounting debt made it essential to revenue. The staples of the revenue were customs and excise. But raising the duty on articles of general consumption was barred by a reluctance to increase the burden on the labouring classes, by a fear of their forcible expression of their resentment that was heightened by memories of the reaction to Walpole's Excise, and by the prospect of only improving the market for the already vigorous smuggling industry. It was necessary, then, to resort to some form of direct taxation. But since income itself was considered impossible to assess, the most that could be done was to seize on various outward signs of ability to pay. Some of these by their nature lent themselves to graduation. The window tax brought in by Pelham, who became Chancellor of the Exchequer in 1743, was graduated, in that the tax was levied at a higher rate per window in houses with more windows. There was graduation by one step also in Lord North's house tax of 1778;

this was levied at 2½ per cent on the rent up to £50, but at 5 per cent above that. There were other forms of direct taxation which were not graduated in themselves, but which provided graduation as part of the whole system of taxation, because effectively they rested solely on the well-to-do. These began with Pelham's carriage tax; many were added by William Pitt the Younger. They came to include men and women servants; gun-dogs and gamekeepers; carriage horses, saddle horses and racehorses; men's hats; perfumery and hair powder; ribbons and gauzes; silver and gold plate; painted linens and calicoes; playhouses and operas; and bachelors, in proportion to the number of servants they kept. The younger Pitt recognized the specific incidence of these taxes, and the principle of progression, when he had to raise taxation steeply during the French wars: by his 'Triple Assessment' in 1798, he separated those taxes that rested on the general taxpayer, mainly the house duty and window tax, from those linked with signs of affluence, such as men servants, carriages and horses, and provided an exemption limit for the first class alone.

The multiplication of these many taxes marked a pressing need to raise more revenue, when the extension of the old staple source of custom and excise was forbidden alike by popular resistance and considerations of equity, and by the vigour of the 'gentlemen' of the smuggling trade, while an income tax was beyond the bounds of administrative possibility. The Chancellor had to go for the money where he could get it, even in penny packets. But at the same time—this was certainly true of the younger Pitt—if he was pushed into equity, he went willingly. He felt the need to establish a tax system that was fairly balanced as a whole. 'In Great Britain,' said Adam Smith in 1776, 'ten millions sterling are annually levied upon less than eight millions of people, without its being possible to say that any particular order is oppressed' (Smith 1776: V, ii, pt. II, art. IV). In 1784 Pitt dealt the smugglers a blow, and cheapened what had now become a cherished comfort of working people, by bringing the duty on tea down from an average of 119 per cent to, in the end, 25 per cent *ad valorem*. To make good the loss of revenue, he raised the window tax sharply, and houses with ten windows and more had to pay 2.5 s. per window, as against the 1s. per window in smaller houses. But he still needed more, and he resorted to some of those small taxes that would rest mainly on the well-to-do. Altogether, then, this Commutation Act redistributed the fiscal burden. In his most famous Budget, that of 1792, he took the opportunity of rising prosperity to remit the window tax on houses with less than seven windows and the additional half-penny in the pound (just over a fifth of 1 per cent) that had been imposed on candles eight years before—this, he said, 'pressed more, perhaps, than any other tax on consumption upon the poorer classes'. The assessed taxes, just mentioned, he graduated steeply. He trebled the tax bill for both classes of tax at assessments of £25, and the multiplier then rose by four steps to reach 5 on assessments of £50 and over.

That Triple Assessment was widely evaded; its yield was small. It had been Pitt's last attempt to avoid the desperate experiment of an income tax. To this he now came, perforce. Naturally, he graduated it, but only in the old sense, in that he provided exemption for the lowest and relief for the smaller incomes. Those of less than £60 a year paid no tax; between £60 and £200 the rate of tax rose from less than 1 per cent to 10 per cent, at which rate it was levied on all incomes from £200 upwards. Thus there was no progression beyond £200.

Yet here, at the beginning of 1799, the wheels of the great engine of progressive taxation and redistribution began for the first time to turn in Great Britain. There had been voices calling for an income tax; there were merchants who wanted to be quit of the complexity as well as the charge of the customs duties. But Pitt had always thought the administrative difficulties insuperable. On the other hand, his genius for taking pains had already proved itself in mastering the detail of administrative procedure and reconstructing it. The arrangements by which he and his advisers now made the income tax administratively robust form a turning point in our social as well as our fiscal history. A tax introduced at a dark hour of the war, as a measure 'for the duration' only—and in fact withdrawn at the end of the war—was to be brought back by Peel in 1842, again as a temporary and emergency measure, but this time to stay. The tax itself was never in danger of breakdown. The vital element of Pitt's design was his provision for assessment. The collection of the tax would be supervised by Commissioners who would be persons of substance and impartiality. They would be assisted by an official called a 'surveyor'. The taxpayer would assess himself, that is, make out his own return of income. Should it appear to the surveyor that the taxpayer's assessment was inadequate, the Commissioners might examine him upon oath. They had no right of search, but he could refuse to open his books to them only under penalty of accepting whatever assessment they chose to make. Here were two basic principles: self-assessment, subject to the scrutiny of professional and experienced officials, the taxpayer having the right of appeal to Commissioners; and the right of the taxing authority, in the absence of an adequate self-assessment by the taxpayer, to impose an assessment, and place the onus of disproof on him. This was a social invention. In the twentieth century, through the taxation it made effective, it was to operate powerfully on the structure of society.

The financial genius of Pitt developed another form of taxation, which also was to form a powerful instrument of social change in later years. During the wars against Louis XIV, the British government had followed Dutch practice in imposing stamp duties on the probate of a will. Lord North graduated the duty, according to the amount of property under the will. Pitt now extended the graduation, until estates of £500 000 and more paid £6 000 in duty. He added a duty on legacies, the rate of which varied inversely with the closeness of its legatee's relationship—Lord North had introduced the duty, but it was Pitt who for the first time made if effective. Thus were the death duties founded. It remained for Gladstone's succession duty in 1853 to cover what the legacy duty left out—in particular, landed estates, and property passing under settlements. The road was constructed on which Goschen was to advance in 1889 to a progressive duty—an extra 1 per cent on all estates over £10 000.

By the end of the eighteenth century, then, an effective income tax had been devised in embryo, if not yet fully fashioned. It had long been desired, in point of equity as well as for the sake of the revenue, but hitherto it had proved impracticable. Now the administrative difficulties had been shown to be not insuperable. A substantial beginning had also been made with the taxation of property passing at death. Both these forms of taxation were adjusted to the circumstances of the individual taxpayer. They could be used, and were in fact going to be used, to change the relative wealth and income left with different groups in the community after tax.

Those potentialities were brilliantly illuminated in England and the United States by the financial acumen of Tom Paine. In the Second Part of *The Rights of Man* (1792; see Paine 1937), Paine set out a detailed programme of social security and welfare. The poor rate was to go. In its place there were to be child allowances, conditional upon the child being certified to be in receipt of adequate schooling, and old age pensions for all persons who needed them, at a lower rate from the age of fifty, and a higher rate from sixty onwards. There would be grants-in-aid of the education of children in families not eligible for relief but not able to keep their children in school without support. Maternity benefit, and a grant for every newly married couple, would be available on demand. Paine was concerned to show that these proposals were practical: he supported them with estimates of the total numbers eligible for them, hence of their total cost. From these provisions of social benefit and security, he proceeded to set out a scheme for (again, in modern terms) a progressive income tax: a 'tax on estates', as he called it. Table 4.2 reproduces his proposal. At £23 000 the tax becomes confiscatory: its total take is then £10 631. The income recipient is left with £12 369, and no one can have a greater income than that.

Putting benefits and finance together, in these few pages we seem not only to have rushed already into the welfare state, but to have a thoroughgoing scheme of redistribution. That impression would be mistaken. Paine did not think of the benefits as being financed out of the tax. This tax is devised for particular purposes quite other than reducing inequality or transferring resources. He conceived of betterment for working people as coming not through redistribution, but through political revolution, from which bread-and-butter benefits would follow. He had himself taken part in the American Revolution, and in the last three years

TABLE 4.2   *Thomas Paine's proposal for 'a tax on all estates of the clear yearly value of £50, after deducting the land tax, and up'*

	Tax rate per £	
	s.	*d.*
To £500	0	3
£500–£1000	0	6
On the second £1000	0	9
On the third £1000	1	0
On the fourth £1000	1	6
On the fifth £1000	2	0
On the sixth £1000	3	0
and so on by rises of 1 *s.* on		
each successive thousand, to		
On the twenty-third £1000	20	0

Source: Paine (1937: 232).

he had seen revolution in France. If a British revolution could follow, the potentialities of the British public finance would be transformed. For not only were the revenues of the royal house devoted mainly to stag-hunting, but the existence of monarchy was the cause of the maintenance in all countries of costly armed forces and their engagement in wars. Let monarchy be swept away, and England, France and America could form an alliance that would make a great disarmament possible. There would remain only 'the honest purposes of government', and a million and a half would suffice for that: 'there will remain a surplus of upwards of six millions'.

It was to dispose of this surplus, the by-product of his great political aim, that Paine drew up his list of social benefits. The purpose of his progressive tax was also mainly political. The first object he gave, it is true, was to tax according to capacity to pay. But he was thinking only of income from landed estates, not of income in general, and his main object was to break up the great estates. This the steep progression of his tax would have some tendency to do; for, whereas the nett income of the estate of £23 000 could not exceed £12 369 if the estate were kept intact in the hands of the eldest son, it would amount in the aggregate to £18 688 if it were divided between two heirs, and to £20 607 if it were divided between three. Paine gave his objects as:

First, That of removing the burden to where it can best be borne. Secondly, Restoring justice among families by a distribution of property. Thirdly, extirpating the overgrown influence arising from the unnatural law of primogeniture, and which is one of the principal sources of corruption at elections. (Paine 1937: 217, 230)

So far, the Paine of *The Rights of Man*. Although his concern was with the wrongs that working people suffered, he believed that these would never be righted until the commons of England gained control of the legislature. This concentration upon the franchise was to mark the leadership of the working-class movements that arose towards the end of the eighteenth century and in this respect culminated in Chartism. But the ownership of the land was an issue in itself; we need a great effort of the imagination to realize how large it bulked in those days. The moral case, too, for common beneficiary enjoyment seemed so clear. When Paine took it up, he did aim at redistribution and work out a practical plan for it.

This was in his *Agrarian Justice* (Paine 1796), a pamphlet printed in Philadelphia. The subtitle proclaims 'Agrarian Justice Opposed to Agrarian Law and to Agrarian Monopoly'. For American readers, the reference to 'agrarian law' would have carried them back to the Roman history in which their republican ardour was kindled. We have seen (p. 71) how one widely influential source of the English radical tradition, the *Cato's Letters* of John Trenchard and Thomas Gordon, referred to it when it declared that 'Liberty can never subsist without Equality, nor Equality be long preserved without an *Agrarian Law*, or something like it.' In France, where Paine's pamphlet was first printed, the term 'agrarian law' carried a clear reference to Baboeuf and his Conspiracy of the Equals. The proposal to divide property equally 'had been a nightmare of both Girondins and Jacobins; its advocacy had been made a capital offence in 1792' (Paine 1796: 251). But on the other side, we have already seen Paine's determination to break up the great landed estates. He had to find a middle way. It offered itself in the distinction between appropriating what nature intended to be free to all, and what a man had fashioned by his own labour; on the prevailing theory of property (that is, implicitly, Locke's) the second kind of appropriation could be defended, but not the first. The problem was to 'restore the right of every man to a share in the natural endowment of all mankind, naturally his' (p. 6). The proprietor of land was entitled to the benefit of improvements made by cultivation, and private property might properly embrace these, but not the earth itself. 'Every proprietor therefore of cultivated land, owes to the community a *ground-rent*; for I know no better term to express the idea by, for the land which he holds; and it is from this ground-rent that the fund proposed in this plan is to issue' (p. 8). Paine works the plan out with a statistical boldness, if not a sureness of aim, that puts one in mind of the young Josiah Stamp—even though he has to say that 'my state of health prevents my making sufficient enquiries with respect to the doctrine of probabilities, whereon to found calculations with such degrees of certainty as they are capable of' (p. 14). The 'ground-rent' takes the form of a 10 per cent duty on all property—not land alone—passing at death to next of kin, with twice that rate on what passes to more remote recipients. The laying of the duty on property of all kinds is justified because 'personal property is the *effect of*

Society; and it is as impossible for an individual to acquire personal property without the aid of Society, as it is for him to make land originally' (p. 25). Mr Pitt in his Budget statement of 1796 put the national capital 'of England' at £1 300 million. Assume this all held by persons aged not less than twenty-one, with an expectation of life of thirty years, so that one-thirtieth becomes dutiable annually, say

£30.0 m @ 10%	£3.0 m	
£13.3 m @ 20%	2.6 m	
	£5.6 m	annually

This revenue can now be used to provide a bounty of £15 for each person reaching the age of twenty-one, and a pension of £10 per year for each person aged fifty and over. For the total population 'of England' being not more than $7\frac{1}{2}$ million, 'the number of persons above the age of fifty will in that case be about 400 000'. In that population the annual deaths will be about 220 000, but more than half will be of persons under the age of twenty-one, so only about 100 000 will be reaching the age of twenty-one annually, to replace the population. Of these, again perhaps a tenth will refuse the bounty. So we have:

400 000 pensioners @ £10	£4 000 000
90 000 bounties @ £15	1 350 000
	£5 350 000

'It is not charity,' said Paine, 'but a right':

not bounty but justice, that I am pleading for . . . The contrast of affluence and wretchedness continually meeting and offending the eye, is like dead and living bodies chained together. Though I care as little about riches as any man, I am a friend to riches because they are capable of good. I care not how affluent some may be provided that none be miserable in consequence of it. But it is impossible to enjoy affluence with the felicity it is capable of being enjoyed, whilst so much misery is mingled with the same.

There is also a prudential consideration:

The superstitious awe, the enduring reverence, that formerly surrounded affluence, is passing away in all countries, and leaving the possessor of property to the convulsion of accidents. When wealth and splendour, instead of fascinating the multitude, excite emotions of disgust; when, instead of drawing forth admiration, it is beheld as an insult upon wretchedness; when the ostentatious appearance it makes serves to call the right of it in question, the case of property becomes critical, and it is only in a system of justice that the possessor can contemplate security.

There was one way in which redistribution was actually being carried out. We have looked at the poor rate as an income tax, and a graduated, at least a proportional, tax in intent. The relief of the poor from the early sixteenth century onwards is to be seen also as a means of transferring resources from households well provided with them to people who lacked them. What stands out here is the positive element, the provision of benefit—the 'relief and sustentation' provided for the poor people by the justices and mayors under the Act of 1572, and the 'competent sums of money for and towards the necessary relief of the lame, impotent, old, blind and such other among them being poor and not able to work, and also for the putting out of such children to be apprentices', disbursed by the overseers of the poor in pursuance of the duties of their office as that was established by the Act of 1601 (Bland *et al.* 1914: pt. II, sec. IV, 4, 8). These statutory requirements took the place of voluntary and charitable donations. But in some towns the administration of these donations had already been organized thoroughly: the law only generalized existing good practice. For within the locality there was enough sense of community to warrant the obligatory transfer of resources: strangers who came in hoping to draw a dole would be expelled, and whipped if they returned, but the poor who had a settlement had a recognized claim on their more prosperous neighbours.

This obligation of neighbourhood was not limited to the parish: an Act of 1555, before the poor rate was compulsory, laid it down that, if the mayor of a town containing a number of parishes found that any parish had no poor, or had more than enough resources to relieve what poor it had, then, 'with the assent of two of the most honest and substantial inhabitants of every such wealthy parish', he would 'move, induce, or persuade the parishioners of the wealthy parish charitably to contribute somewhat according to their ability towards the weekly relief of the poor in the neighbouring parishes' (Cannan 1896: 61).

Records have been preserved which show the relief of the poor being administered with what seems a zealous attention to detail, in some places at least. The Privy Council was warm in its chiding of neglectful local authorities. The system had to cope with a rapid growth of population in the sixteenth century, an increased pressure on the supply of food and a great lowering in the real standard of living of working people. That there was so little disorder and, so far as we know, so little starvation, may be put to the credit of this first experiment in redistribution and the finance of social welfare.

From 1760, the relentless pressure of population set in again. Overseers of the poor in the villages, who had been levying a trifling rate—to support a few pensioners, equip a widow with a spinning wheel and now and then apprentice an orphan—found themselves beset by able-bodied men and women, without work or prospect of it, increasing in number year by year. In the 1790s bad harvests and the cutting off of supplies by the war drove up the price of bread; the ever rising numbers seeking work kept wages down; the propertied classes feared Jacobinism. The benefits paid out of the poor rate expanded in amount and type. The practice had grown up in the course of the century of giving out-relief to the unemployed—although they might be required to carry out some task, such as road-mending, or as roundsmen to perform the ritual of going to farm after farm, asking for work. When the price of bread rose sharply relatively to the prevailing wage, some parishes began to supplement the wage. The supplement might take the form of a family allowance—so much a week for each child beyond the third. The decision of the Berkshire justices at Speenhamland to enjoin the supplementation of wages according to a sliding scale that would assure the labourer a constant purchasing power in terms of bread was far from being innovative or influential, as it has been taken to be: Mark Neuman has shown that

the decision to promote a uniform, country-wide, scale of relief for the able-bodied was not an unusual one in the troubled year 1795. Other Quarter Sessions, confronted with shortages, high prices and the possibility of Jacobin-inspired tumults, adopted similar though sometimes less elaborate schemes, in some cases before the Speenhamland decision in May. (Neuman 1972: 89–90)

The decision attracted little notice at the time, and became widely known only when Sir George Nicholls stigmatized it as the type of systematic out-relief for the able-bodied, in his *History of the English Poor Law* (Nicholls 1854). What the Justices did was accepted as lying within the habitual scope of their own discretion or that of the overseers to whom they recommended the scale of relief. But it is doubtful whether there was any statutory authority for it. The basic Act of 1601 explicitly authorized the raising and use of the poor rate only for 'the necessary relief of the lame, impotent, old, blind and such other among them being poor and not able to work', and for apprenticing poor children. But the Tudor poor laws had only generalized practices developed locally; the Justices of the Peace to whom the supervision of local administration was entrusted were quite capable of extending it as they thought necessary in an emergency, without legal misgivings.

On the other hand, although Quarter Sessions could make its own rules, it could not make the parishes follow them. Mark Neuman (1972: 100, 102) has shown that, although by 1795, when the sliding scale was promulgated at Speenhamland, 'the practice of supporting the able-bodied from the parish was commonplace in Berkshire', in not one of the sixteen parishes that he studied in the county was that scale definitely adopted at any time from 1795 to 1834. The overseers of the poor went their own way, parish by parish. On such evidence at least as is available for Petty Sessions, they took no more notice of their own local Justices than they did of the general directions of Quarter Sessions. 'It is probably true that at one time or another more Berkshire parishes adopted some sort of bread scale as a general guide for relieving their able-bodied poor . . . But the point is this: The parishes gave this relief precisely as often, widely and generously as they chose' (Neuman 1972: 107–8).

This helps to answer the question, How far did the poor law redistribute income? The poor rates were levied on the *occupiers* of land and houses, not on the landlords. After the rates had gone up, the occupiers might be able to pass the rise on to the landlords by way of a rent rebate, if they could establish their immediate embarrassment, or a lower rent on the renewal of the lease. But these were painful adjustments: unless the landlord was benevolent, they were likely to come about only in the presence of widespread and acknowledged hardship for tenants. Now the overseers of the poor were drawn chiefly from the class of tenant farmers and small freeholders, the Justices from the larger landholders. It was thus the element of the community from which the poor rate was collected that provided its local administrators, and these had an interest in keeping down disbursements, and the poor rate that must cover them. When these figures went up, it was the overseers themselves and their likes who had to take the strain. The Justices, on the other hand, generally stood at some remove: they did not pay the poor rate themselves on the lands they leased out, and when the rate went up, although their rent-rolls might suffer eventually, the effect was not immediate or definite. They could indulge their benevolence, and discharge their duty to prevent disorder, by ordaining the provision of full maintenance for all. But what was actually done depended, parish by parish, on the decisions of those who had to foot the bill. So long as the war lasted and corn prices kept high, the overseers were able to combine subsistence for the unemployed with rates that were tolerable, given current profits. Rents were raised as new leases were negotiated, or even put up to auction; but meanwhile, tenants did well. Some of the windfall profits that would otherwise have accrued to the occupants of the land, until eventually they were pulled in as higher rents by the landlord, were transferred to the poor. But when, after Waterloo, the prices of farm products collapsed, and tenants' incomes with them, the poor rate became a burden hard to bear, even though the cost of relief also fell. Leases might be renegotiated, but bankruptcy could come first. The effect on redistribution can be interpreted as follows. In principle, a tax laid on land and houses for the maintenance of certain poor persons represents a transfer to them of part of the beneficial title to the property. But the tax being collected from the occupiers in the first place was a transfer from the incomes of those persons until such time as the terms of their own rent payments were revised. To the extent that changes in rents lagged behind those in the prices of farm products, in both the rising and the falling phases, the poor rates transferred income from the tenant farmers to the poor. To the extent that rents were adjusted to current profitability, and also in so far as the rates fell on owner-occupiers, they transferred income to the poor from proprietors great and small. The most important consideration in the years when the rates were rising, because of both a growing real burden and inflation during the French wars, was that a rise shifted incidence downwards, from landlord to tenant.

If the proposals of Pitt's Poor Law Bill had been adopted, they would have carried the redistribution of income much further. Pitt offered these proposals in December 1796, in lieu of a minimum wage in agriculture. They arose, he said, from 'an extensive survey of the opinions of others' (Ehrman 1983: 471–6). They provided for family allowances; they stipulated that possession of property was not to disqualify a person for relief; parishes were to set up superannuation funds providing old-age pensions; an advance was to be made available, it seems to each and every respectable applicant, for the purchase of a cow. What was perhaps no less significant, every Guardian of the Poor was required to transmit to the Privy Council at least once a year a full account of all his transactions, and the Council would prepare a general abstract for the whole country, to be laid annually before both Houses of Parliament. Thus, in Pitt's words, 'there should be an Annual Budget opened, containing the details of the whole system of Poor Laws, by which the legislature would show, that they had a constant and a watchful eye upon the interests of the poorest and most neglected part of the community' (Eden 1797: III, Appendix XI, ccxii). One wonders whether that central inspection of the fulfilment of centrally imposed requirements, of varying local incidence, could have been maintained without acceptance of some central financial responsibility—that is, without grants-in-aid. What was done forty years later, in the new Poor Law, does not show what Pitt might have moved towards. But the question was never posed; for his proposals—or those of his advisers—were shot down as impracticable as soon as they appeared, and his Bill died in committee.

It still remains significant, however, as evidence of Pitt's concern for poverty. No doubt it was the bad harvest of 1795, and the threat of riot, that brought this to a head. But when he brought his Bill in, those pressures had abated; and the reliefs he proposed were remarkably far-reaching. If they were acceptable to a statesman of financial genius, that must have been because there was now enough egalitarianism in the air for them to seem fair to him. The possibility does at least present itself, as we look back, that the country might have stumbled into some practical application of egalitarianism, under the pressure of the growing needs of the times. Rising expenditure in the localities, with ever greater numbers to care for, and an enlarged conception of the objects and scale of support; the obligation to report to the centre, with the annual 'Budget' marking a national sense of responsibility—might not these together have led to grants-in-aid of the local ratepayer? And might not the revenue have been found by graduating the income tax?

Thus, at the end of the eighteenth century, the spirit of egalitarianism was troubling the waters; at least, there was a lively sense in some quarters of the need to act to reduce inequality. Yet no action was taken. In Chapter 5 we ask why.

4.3. The Bond of Common Humanity

The preceding sections have shown how two conditions for egalitarianism were developed: personal incomes came to be expressed in terms of money; and income tax provided a means of adjusting each person's contribution to the size of his or her income and personal circumstances. A third condition noted at the outset was that the members of society should feel themselves united by a bond of common humanity. If any two men, whatever their stations in life, were cast adrift in a ship's boat with one pack of rations between them, they could hardly do other than divide it equally: in that predicament, this sharing of the common lot of humanity would transcend all differences on which entitlement might otherwise be based. Where all the differences of rank and income are removed, the likeness—the identity, even—of manhood dominates the relationship. In all the piled-up circumstances of actual affairs, the likeness recedes under hierarchies and classes, but in the nation-state, even in a country of many millions, there must still be some fellow feeling and sense of obligation between its members. That sense may be latent, except in times of national crisis, but the state itself is threatened with collapse if it is altogether absent, or is witheld between major groups.

So at least we think today; but this has not always been so. On the practical issue of the relations between the well-to-do and the poor, in the early years of the eighteenth century the relief of suffering was commended as the Christian virtue of charity, but the labouring poor stood at such a remove that the well-to-do could not think of them as exerting a claim as members, however distant, of their own family. They were regarded instead as part of the necessary equipment of the state. They were objects, seen from without; their proper treatment was a question of efficient working, not of their feelings. Here, for example, was the opinion on whether the labourers should be taught to read and write, of a Welshman with a mathematical and mechanical bent, who, from his first employment as a blacksmith in his uncle's forge in Breconshire, had made his way up to become assay master of the Mint. In his *Essay upon Money and Coins* (1757), Joseph Harris gave an account of the real wages of the labourer which showed that he must be allowed enough margin to bring up a family and that, given the constant competition for employment, he was unlikely ever to get more. Thereupon Harris observed:

It seems then to be no good policy in the rich to deal too hardly with the poor. . . . But the benevolence here hinted at, is to be tempered with discretion: the children of the poor should be brought up and inured, as early as may be, to some useful labor; and be taught with due care, the great principles of religion and morality. But all are not agreed that reading and writing, are qualifications necessary for the obtaining of those ends; some think, that these accomplishments are useful only in higher stations; and to instruct at a public expense the youth of the lower class in reading, writing, etc. is a kind of intrusion upon the class next above them; that these qualifications, instead of being advantageous to the poor who possess them, serve only to render their state more irksome, and to inspire them with notions subversive of society. There must be labourers; and that most useful class of men should be duly cherished and taken care of: But books and pens will not alleviate the weight of the spade, or at all contribute to dry the sweat off the labourer's brow. (Harris 1757: 11)

Equally, a good farmer's horses would be 'duly cherished and taken care of'. His labourers were considered in the same light. If they would work all the better and the more contentedly if they were kept in the darkness of an ignorance in which not for one moment would he consider keeping his own children, so be it: that was what they were there for. This stirred no misgivings: it was in the nature of things.

But about the middle of the century, around the time when Joseph Harris was writing, the prevailing outlook was changing. The labouring poor began to be seen as men and women entitled as such to respect, and in some sense to parity of esteem, for all their limitations. They became integrated into society, no longer as its servitors merely and part of its stock, but as members. The difference between their incomes and those of the propertied classes began to be subject to the scrutiny that arises naturally between people who rest upon a common humanity.

Among the forces that combined to bring this change about, the foremost was the rise of humanitarianism. At the time the word was *humanité*, or, as in Hume, humanity. This may be taken as equivalent to benevolence, provided that we understand this to mean a social attitude of much further-reaching consequence than a charitable disposition. It is true that, in so far as humanitarians felt a compassionate concern for suffering, and took action to relieve it, they did but follow the tradition of the Christian church. They extended it as they entered into the wrongs of oppressed minorities, such as the Protestants and the Jews in France. They cared for those who suffered from mindless or malevolent cruelty, or parsimony, or neglect—children, paupers, prisoners in the noisome gaols. Especially they attacked the slave trade, and in both France and England they worked for the abolition of slavery in the colonies. But they were not only concerned to relieve distress: they were also concerned with its causes, and with institutions; they wanted to get new legislation enacted and to set up more efficient arrangements. This was their distinctive characteristic—that they were so moved because their view of society accorded a more equal weight to the feelings of every member. This was the essence of humanitarianism.

Its sources are to be found in the heightened attention to the inward life brought about in different ways by both Renaissance and Reformation.

There followed a discovery of mankind, both intensive and extensive. Intensively, there came the beginning of the systematic study of human nature. Hobbes devoted the first eight chapters of his *Leviathan* to human psychology; Locke propounded his 'sensational psychology'; some philosophers held that man was distinguished from the brute creation by the possession of Reason; others, that he was uniquely endowed with a faculty of moral judgement. These studies were all implicitly concerned with man as a species. It was thus he increasingly appeared, also extensively, in the accounts of primitive man sent back by missionaries and explorers, and eagerly studied by French *philosophes* and Scots professors. There might be sub-species, but, as report after report came in of peoples hitherto unknown, what stood out was the unity in diversity of the species 'man'. There was a 'human race'. To be a member of it was, in a certain sense, to be in fellowship with every other human being. The force of the old tag from Terence was rediscovered; 'Homo sum: humani nil a me alienum puto'—'I am a man: I deem naught of humankind a stranger to me.' Any and every human being has a claim of kinship on me.

A natural consequence of this concern with human feelings, and this realization of our common humanity, would be sensitivity to the sufferings of fellow men, and endeavours to bring relief—that is, humanitarianism in practice. But the change took a long time to work through. Locke could quite well place some of his capital in the profitable slave trade: it was a hundred years later that Condorcet joined with Mirabeau and Lafayette in La Société des Amis des Noirs, and Wilberforce became the leader of the English movement for the abolition of slavery. Various factors operated to delay the development. Old attitudes persisted. The 'lower orders of society' had been seen as a rough lot, plainly incapable—taking them as they were—of absorption within any orderly and civilized body of citizens. The French *philosophes* regarded them with contempt, and called them *canaille*. They were not only uncouth, moreover, but dangerous, liable to riot—and this was always a thought at the back of the minds of the men of property, even in the stable England of the eighteenth century.

But even if the poor had been objects of sympathy, there were not many people with the capacity to sympathize. Compassion is an indulgence of the comfortable: those to whom life gives no quarter, for whom each day is a struggle through a raw and rough existence, have no reserves of emotion out of which to grieve for others. The great rise in population in the sixteenth century had made life very hard for many people in England. It remained so for most of a hundred years after the Civil War. Then, about the mid-eighteenth century, the consciousness of unprecedented and rising prosperity set off a continuing discussion of luxury. The word became a challenge to the politician and the pamphleteers: would luxury once again, as so often in the empires of the past, portend downfall? In a pamphlet of 1767 on the *Causes and Consequences of the Present High Price of Provisions*,

Soame Jenyns gave an impression of what we should call the economic growth of recent years. The liveliness of that impression may owe something to his being not only Member for Cambridgeshire for many years, and a commissioner of the Board of Trade, but a minor poet; it still indicates the powerful impact of recent development on attitudes and the way of life, not in the great new Georgian mansions alone:

That our riches are in fact amazingly increased within a few years, no one, who is in the least acquainted with this country, can entertain a doubt: whoever will cast an eye on our public works, our roads, our bridges, our pavements, and our hospitals, the prodigious extension of our capital, and in some proportion that of every considerable town in Great Britain; whoever will look into the possessions and expenses of individuals, their houses, furniture, tables, equipages, parks, gardens, cloaths, plates, and jewels, will find everywhere round him sufficient marks to testify to the truth of this proposition . . . . The consumption of everything is also amazingly increased from the increase of wealth in our metropolis, and indeed in every corner of this Kingdom; and the manner of living, throughout all ranks and conditions of men, is no less amazingly altered: the merchant who formerly thought himself fortunate, if in a course of thirty or forty years, by a large trade and strict economy, he amassed together as many thousand pounds, now acquires in a quarter of that time double that sum, or breaks for a greater, and vies all the while with the first of our nobility, in his houses, table, furniture, and equipage: the shopkeeper, who used to be well contented with one dish of meat, one fire, and one maid, has now two or three times as many of each; his wife has her tea, her card-parties, and her dressing-room; and his prentice has climbed from the kitchen-fire to the front-boxes at the play-house. (Jenyns 1767: 6–7, 11–12)

The higher standard of living achieved by the middle and upper levels of society worked on their humanitarianism in two ways. It heightened the contrast between their condition and that of the poor who remained at, or at times below, the level of subsistence; and it increased their ability to help: as the saying goes, they could afford to be generous. We expect, moreover, from our knowledge of the working of economic processes generally, that, so far as working men were assured of employment, they would have shared in the rise in standards of living, so that the barrier to humanitarianism and the sense of identity raised by the uncouthness of the labouring poor would have been lowered somewhat.

David Hume was clear that economic development fostered 'humanity'. The advance of the mechanical arts, he said, could be relied on to bring an advance of the liberal and refined arts with it. 'We cannot reasonably expect, that a piece of woollen cloth will be brought to perfection in a nation, which is ignorant of astronomy, or where ethics are neglected.' And

the more these refined arts advance, the more sociable men become . . . Both sexes meet in an easy and sociable manner: and the tempers of men, as well as their behaviour, refine apace. So that, beside the improvements which they receive from knowledge and the liberal arts, it is impossible but they must feel an encrease of humanity, from the very habit of conversing together, and contribute to each other's pleasure and entertainment. Thus *industry, knowledge,* and *humanity,* are linked together by an indissoluble chain, and are found, from experience as well as reason, to be peculiar to the more polished, and what are commonly denominated, the more luxurious ages. (Hume 1955: 22)

Hume was thinking of 'humanity' in the polished sense of what Voltaire called the 'spirit of society'; but certainly, the eighteenth century also saw a great growth of benevolence and philanthropy. This was a time when charity schools proliferated, a number of hospitals were founded and—in the later years—all manner of societies were set up for bettering the state of mankind at large or the poor of the home country in particular.' ''The Age of Benevolence'', Hannah More later called it . . .' (Himmelfarb 1984: 36).

The concern with economic growth that is central to *The Wealth of Nations* (Smith 1776) is linked with a basic change of attitude towards 'the labouring poor'. In Adam Smith's outlook, these folk became integrated with society. More than once, he reminds us that they are 'the great body of the people'. The substantial rise achieved in recent years in the workers' standard of living, having set up 'the common complaint that luxury extends itself even to the lowest ranks of the people', raised the question whether wages must not be kept low to prevent idleness. Adam Smith objected to the very formulation of that question:

Is this improvement in the circumstances of the lower ranks of the people to be regarded as an advantage or as an inconveniency to the society? The answer seems at first sight abundantly plain. Servants, labourers, and workmen of different kinds, make up the far greater part of every great political society. But what improves the circumstances of the greater part can never be regarded as an inconveniency to the whole. No society can surely be flourishing and happy, of which the far greater part of the members are poor and miserable. (Smith 1776: I, viii)

Smith assumes that the minority consisting of the propertied and the well-to-do will care about the well-being of 'the far greater part', whom they will regard as their fellow citizens, and not as helots. There are passages in which he laments the narrowing of mind and cramping of body by repetitive work, but generally he says nothing of the workers to portray them as a race apart. On the contrary, he credits them potentially with the qualities of the middle class. Far from being sunk in fecklessness and idleness unless spurred by hunger, they are responsive to encouragement, ready to work hard for their present advancement and to save for the future. Part of his case against the old belief that wages must be kept low to maintain industry was, in effect, that human nature is the same among 'the common people' as among the industrious and mercantile classes:

The liberal reward of labour . . . increases the industry of the common people. The wages of labour are the encouragement of industry, which, like every other human quality, improves in proportion to the encouragement it receives. A plentiful subsistence increases the bodily strength of the labourer, and the comfortable hope of bettering his condition, and of ending his days perhaps in ease and plenty, animates him to exert that strength to the utmost. Where wages are high, accordingly, we shall always find the workmen more active, diligent, and expeditious, than where they are low . . . (Smith 1776: I, viii)

But the most striking instance of Adam Smith's integration of 'the common people' in society appears in his treatment of education. That he advocated universal compulsory elementary education, subsidized from the public purse, has long been noted as one of the exceptions to his supposedly predominant principle of non-intervention. What is to our purpose here is his reason for this advocacy. When we compare his stance with the case that Joseph Harris stated for keeping 'the poor' illiterate, the change appears revolutionary. The labourers are now no longer instruments: they are considered in their own right. Smith's basic reason for wanting 'the whole body of the people' to acquire the 'most essential parts of education' was just that without it they would be less than men:

A man without the proper use of the intellectual faculties of a man is, if possible, more contemptible than even a coward, and seems to be mutilated and deformed in a still more essential part of the character of human nature. Though the state was to derive no advantage from the instruction of the inferior ranks of people, it would still deserve its attention that they should not be altogether uninstructed.

In fact, the state would derive great political advantages, which Adam Smith set out: 'the inferior ranks' when instructed would be more orderly; they would live in relations of mutual respect with 'their lawful superiors', they would be 'more capable of seeing through the interested complaints of faction and sedition'. But these advantages were incidental. The case for combating ignorance was like that for preventing 'a leprosy, or any other loathsome and offensive disease', from spreading through the great body of the people. Ignorance is like cowardice, in that it involves a 'sort of mental mutilation, deformity, and wretchedness', which it is painful and shocking to see in one's fellow man. Education, on the other hand, permits the healthy development of the natural faculties—the same, we remember, at birth, in the future street porter and philosopher. Every man as such can claim it in his own right. And great prospects open out that suggest how economic growth was shortening the distance between 'the inferior ranks' and 'their lawful superiors':

There is scarce a common trade which does not afford some opportunities of applying to it the principles of geometry and mechanics, and which would not therefore gradually exercise and improve the common people in those principles, the necessary introduction to the most sublime as well as to the most useful sciences. (Smith 1776: V, i, pt. III, Art. II)

Already, a quarter of a century before, Thomas Gray, in his 'Elegy in a Country Churchyard', had dwelt on the belief that only lack of education had held many a humble labourer back from filling the highest offices in the land, for which nature had endowed him with all the needed abilities:

> Perhaps in this neglected spot is laid
> Some heart once pregnant with celestial fire;
> Hands, that the rod of empire might have sway'd
> Or wak'd to extasy the living lyre:
>
> But knowledge to their eyes her ample page
> Rich with the spoils of time did ne'er unroll;
> Chill penury repress'd their noble rage,
> And froze the genial current of the soul.

That the Elegy, of all Gray's poems, was immediately and widely received with admiration has been attributed to its pathetic power, but it could not have been so welcome if its view of human nature had been unfamiliar and unacceptable. If the poor—or not a few of them—were lowly by force of circumstance, not of their nature; if they were deprived, not debased: then the case for extending to them some of the opportunities for development enjoyed by their more fortunate neighbours was bound to work its way into men's minds.

The heightened attention to the inner life, as has been said, coming down from Renaissance and Reformation, will be expected to have had its impact on the modes of literature and religion. This did in fact come about during the eighteenth century. Initially, the free play of feeling was inhibited by the authority of Reason. As that authority waned, a many-sided impulse was released: from classicism to romanticism, from sense to sensibility, from deism to evangelicalism and from liberalism to socialism. From these flowed fresh or renewed currents of egalitarianism.

But Reason itself had already contributed in its own ways to the rise of egalitarianism. Its authority derived from the extraordinary achievements of the astronomers and mathematicians, Newton most of all. These had exalted man's reasoning powers to dazzling heights: all the profusion of the universe, it was believed, had been shown to obey a few principles of elegant simplicity. At the same time, the development of experimental inquiries in natural science was beginning to find the answers to some old questions. In all this lay the notion—it was a new one—of problem-solving. Its method was the application of reason to observed facts. In so far as the reasoning was mathematical, the conclusions were indisputable. When the ills of society came to be regarded as problems to be tackled in this way, a fundamental change had come about in modes of thought. The Church had found the cause of human suffering in sin, and the Fall: this new approach considered it as a problem in social pathology. The prescriptions to which these enquiries would lead would be for the reform not of human nature, but of social structure. The aim would now be not a rightful government, but a fairer society.

The same end was approached by Reason in another way. Applied to theology, Reason led to 'natural religion', or deism. This saw man as part of Nature. In earlier centuries most people would never have thought of mankind in this way, any more than a farmer would include himself and his family in his inventory of livestock: God had created man in His own image, and given him dominion over all creatures in sea and air and on the earth (Genesis 1: 26). But when man appeared as one species among others, the common features that distinguish and unite 'the human race' stood out. Natural religion fostered a sense of the brotherhood of man.

Both of these approaches to human betterment—the way of applied science and that of natural religion—appeared in Joseph Priestley, the discoverer of oxygen. In his self-assurance and the facility with which he designed reforms, he reminds us of the mathematical philosopher Betrand Russell in our own day. Man, he wrote in his *Essay on the First Principles of Government*, in 1768, is capable of 'unbounded improvement':

a man at this time, who has been tolerably well educated, in an improved Christian country, is a being possessed of much greater power, to be, and to make happy, than a person of the same age, in the same, or any other country, some centuries ago. . . . It requires but a few years to comprehend the whole preceding progress of any one art or science; and the rest of a man's life . . . may be given to the extension of it. . . . Whatever was the beginning of this world, the end will be glorious and paradisaical, beyond what our imaginations can now conceive. (Priestley 1771 edn: 2, 4, 5)

Priestley was a Unitarian, and the sect's doctrine arose out of the pruning by Reason of the convolutions of accepted theology. There was actually no overt egalitarianism in his prescriptions: on the contrary, he was against giving poor men the vote. But natural religion, or deism, of which Unitarianism may be regarded as one manifestation, did tend to egalitarianism, because the respects in which all men are alike were more conspicuous in its eyes than the differences between the godly and the sinful.

Thus, egalitarianism was fostered by the reign of Reason. But it was also fostered by the modes of thought and feeling that rose against that reign. The Age of Reason had been calm, orderly and contained. It sought to discover and abide by those laws and propensities upon which the Great Architect had built the universe; as Pope said,

> Those RULES of old discover'd, not devis'd,
> Are Nature still, but Nature methodiz'd;
> Nature, like Liberty, is but restrain'd
> By the same laws which first herself ordain'd.

Essay on Criticism, 88–91

On that view of nature—human nature included—there was little to ponder over in the tears and laughter of which the peasant girl knows as much as the philosopher, or more. But the principle of natural order gave way to the always present awareness of natural vitality. The romantic movement in the arts was a revolt against 'Nature methodiz'd', and a return to a free, pulsating Nature—to human nature with its unaffected joys and sorrows, and the surrounding natural world, whose exquisite flowers and towering mountain tops aroused deep feelings of delight and awe. These feelings became a religious experience: the presence and purpose of the Creator were revealed in his creation. The William Wordsworth of 1798 communed in his pantheism with 'the blessed power that rolls, about, below, above'; he felt 'the sense sublime of something far more deeply interfused'. The purpose he divined in the very song of the linnet was that the whole creation should be joyful: why then were men stricken with woe? It was not the Creator that had made them so: their wounds were self-inflicted:

> If this belief from heaven be sent,
> If such be Nature's holy plan,
> Have I not reason to lament
> What man has made of man?

> *Lines written in Early Spring* (1798)

The inference is plain: that what men have marred they can mend; that society can be refashioned, so as to bring humanity into harmony with Nature. Wordsworth's enthusiasm for the French Revolution in its early days had been kindled by the prospect of liberating an essentially virtuous human nature from the distorting trammels of oppression:

> Nature, as in her prime, her virgin reign
> Begins, and Love and Truth compose her train.

> *Descriptive Sketches* (1793), ll. 784-5

When those hopes had been overthrown, he kept his faith, at least for a while, in the power of Nature to ennoble everyone, so that a fairer society might be formed by the diffusion of that love for humanity that filled his own heart when he opened it to the influences of natural beauty. He and Coleridge were entrusted with a mission:

> Though men return to servitude as fast
> As the tide ebbs, to ignominy and shame
> By nations sink together, we shall still
> Find solace . . .
>   joint labourers in the work
> Of their deliverance, surely yet to come.
> Prophets of Nature, we to them will speak
> A lasting inspiration, sanctified

> By reason, blest by faith; what we have loved,
> Others will love, and we will teach them how. . . .
>
> *The Prelude* (1805), bk. xiv, ll. 435–47

The same romantic faith in the essential goodness of human nature animated Shelley. All the 'hate, disdain, or fear, self-love or self-contempt' that ruled mankind in the world of everyday around him he likened to a mask concealing the lineaments of love and beauty. He envisaged a world from which the tyrannical institutions that distorted humanity were banished:

> The loathsome mask has fallen, the man remains
> Sceptreless, free, uncircumscribed, but man
> Equal, unclassed, tribeless and nationless,
> Exempt from awe, worship, degree, the king
> Over himself; just, gentle, wise; but man
> Passionless?—no, yet free from guilt or pain . . .
>
> *Prometheus Unbound,* III, iv

The divisions of mankind are impositions upon its essential unity. Beneath the hierarchy of class and power, men and women possess the inherent equality of their common humanity.

The poets' faith had some counterpart in the changes wrought by Romanticism in attitudes elsewhere. If it was feelings that mattered most of all, the cultivated could no longer despise the peasantry and labouring folk as illiterate and unsophisticated: rather, they were to be admired because their spontaneous feelings flowed in a deeper, purer stream than those of the more self-conscious upper classes, whose manners were artificial and insincere, and whose responses were conventional. Hence, in part, cults of Arcadia, of shepherds and shepherdesses, and, at a more thoughtful level, of the Noble Savage. These cults were artificial, or fantastic, but they expressed a prediliction for the capacity to experience the primary emotions of humanity. The emphasis on the heritage of joy and sorrow that was common to all alike, exalted or lowly, prepared the way for a more equal esteem and consideration.

In England, an influence working in the same direction was the rise of evangelicalism. The term is used here in a broad sense, to cover not only one tendency within the Church of England, but all those believers who stressed salvation through faith in the redeeming sacrifice of the Cross, whether they were Anglicans, or Wesleyans or other Nonconformists. It is true that there was no necessary connection between this faith and a particular social attitude. Those who believed that rich and poor alike were guilty sinners might and often did remain convinced of the need to maintain the existing social order. They could continue to see authority in church and state as resting upon divine institution and not upon the consent of the people. In practical issues they might be less benevolent than the paternal High Churchman. Prospects of glory in the next world, moreover, might be used to palliate squalor in this one. Yet willy nilly, the evangelical fervour had an egalitarian germ in it. Although in issues of national politics the Wesleyans were conservative, their concern for the souls of the rough and outcast and despised extended naturally to the debasing conditions in which those folk were living. 'Christianity is essentially a social religion', Wesley declared. 'And he acted upon this principle,' Himmelfarb has observed, 'when he established, among other things, a poor house, a soup kitchen and dispensary for the poor, and a "contingent fund"—the latter made up of contributions by the employed for the relief of the unemployed.' He reminded those of his followers who had amassed wealth 'of their obligation to share their good fortune with the poor' (Himmelfarb 1968: 280). To many evangelicals later in the century the message was clear that, as followers of One who had gone about doing good, especially to the poor and the afflicted, they in their own day must mitigate the sufferings of prisoners, provide schools for the illiterate and try to liberate the slaves. Their theology might make the path of the soul through all eternity depend solely on the convulsive act by which it accepted salvation and gave itself to Christ; but the trauma of conversion generally brought a quickening of the social conscience, a deepening of compassion and a widening of sympathies.

But the impulse of compassion was by no means solely dependent upon religious fervour: it permeated the Enlightenment. We have seen liberalism as the self-regarding creed of men of substance, and have noted the narrow boundary around the Rights of Man. Yet by the end of the century it was possible for one of the great *philosophes* to see liberalism as proceeding directly and naturally into heartfelt humanitarianism. We have already referred (p. 87) to Condorcet's 'tabulation of human progress'. In its ninth and latest Epoch, it was distinguished by the increasing acceptance of liberal principles:

a general knowledge of the natural rights of man; the belief no less that these rights are inalienable and imprescriptible; a deeply held desire for freedom of thought and publication, for that of commerce and industry, for the relief of the people, for the repeal of all penal laws against religious dissidents . . . (Prior 1970: 164–5)

and so on. In some countries, Condorcet held, these principles had already been accepted by the bulk of public opinion. But now comes, as we see it, a turn and development in the thought; it can have seemed to him only a gloss on what had gone before. 'The feeling for humanity,' he concludes,

a tender and active compassion for all the ills that afflict the human race, and revulsion against everything in political institutions, acts of government or private actions that add new sufferings to the inevitable sufferings of nature; this feeling for humanity is a natural consequence of these principles . . . (Prior 1970: 164–5)

No explanation of the transition seemed called for. And indeed, when Jefferson made his amendment, and every man was held entitled not to Life, Liberty and Property, but to Life, Liberty and the Pursuit of Happiness, he put the meanest and poorest on an equal footing of consideration with the most substantial. Once the feelings of the individual were accepted as an object of his own life, and of public policy in aid of him, humanitarianism had been implicitly endorsed, and with it the bond of common humanity.

If religious fervour led to humanitarianism, so also did secularism. This brought about a shift in the focus of attention that is hard for us to appreciate, because we have always been on this side of the shift. The great issue of welfare used to lie in the next world: in purgatory, and in an eternity of bliss or of torture. However literally or symbolically the Book of Revelation was interpreted, the pains and pleasures of this world appeared insignificant in comparison with the awful judgement that awaited the soul in the next. But in the course of the eighteenth century the vividness of that apprehension declined: attention moved towards welfare in this world.

Montesquieu exerted a significant influence in this, through his relativism. His treatment of religion was very cautious. Explicitly, he was punctilious in distinguishing between the one true faith and all the others that were lost in darkness; but then he held himself free to judge them all by the same criterion of their practical effects:

As amid several degrees of darkness we may form a judgement of those which are the least thick, and among precipices, which are the least deep; so we may search among false religions for those that are most conformable to the welfare of society; for those which, though they have not the effect of leading man to the felicity of another life, may contribute most to their happiness in this. I shall examine therefore the several religions of the world in relation only to the good they produce in civil society; whether I speak of that which has its root in Heaven, or of those which spring from the earth. (*De l'esprit des lois,* XXIV, i, 2; quoted here from Carrithers 1977).

How directly humanitarianism followed upon the switch to welfare in this world appears from Hume's Essay *Of Justice* (1753). The overriding object of all policy was human welfare. A generation that had discovered mankind, the species man, must specify that object as the sum total of the welfares of all persons comprised. Evidently we can increase this total, in a particular instance, by taking £1 away from a rich man, which he can easily spare, and giving it to a poor man, who will use it to get something he needs greatly. Pressing this argument to its limit, and assuming that each person's capacity for enjoyment is the same as every other's, we reach equality of income as the condition for maximizing the sum of welfare. This is the point that Hume makes. On an equal division of the product, he says, 'Every individual would enjoy all the necessaries, and even most of the comforts of life'; whereas, 'wherever we depart from this equality, we rob the poor of more satisfaction than we add to the rich' (Hume 1875). It is true that Hume goes on to set out concisely most of our contemporary objections to an attempted thoroughgoing equalization of incomes; but at the outset he has put in a nutshell the basic case for at least some transfer of resources from those who have plenty to those who are going short, that is, the case for egalitarianism in its modern and practical sense.

In a passage of his *Principles of the Civil Code*, which followed Hume's argument closely in both its stages, Bentham provided a Euclidean demonstration that 'the more nearly the actual proportion [between two masses of wealth] approaches to equality, the greater will be the total mass of happiness'; but he also showed why, 'if all the property were to be equally divided, the certain and immediate consequence would be that there would be nothing more to divide'. 'The establishment of equality', he concluded, 'is a chimera: the only thing which can be done is to diminish inequality' (Bowring 1843: I, 305, 311).

It was probably the combination of rising standards of living relieving pressures in the household and the increase of sympathy and respect for personality irrespective of status that brought about one of the greatest social changes of the century—the raised status of women. Wives became more the companions and less the servants of their husbands. Correspondingly, daughters came to be allowed more say in the choice of husband. In families where the boys were educated, the girls had been getting little schooling at the opening of the century, but they got much more as it went on. In the later years it had come to cover

a broad sweep of subjects, including history, geography, literature and current affairs; and some women were now boasting, with reason, of the positive superiority of their education over the narrow classical linguistic training of their brothers. In 1790 *The Ladies Monthly Magazine* claimed that 'many women have received a much better education than Shakespeare enjoyed'. (Stone 1977: 358)

The bluestocking appeared, and also the hostess whose salon was frequented by men of letters and politicians. In France, the possibility of women playing an active part in the formation of political policy was demonstrated among the Girondins.

These were the achievements of an outstanding minority, but the increased respect paid to women, and the greater opportunities and influence accorded them, had spread through the middle ranks of society. This diffusion of women's outlook and values, and the force and freedom with which they could be expressed, is significant for the rise of humanitarianism, whose own spirit of compassion is itself akin to maternal care. Not only were some women prominent in the humanitarian movement, but the very terms in which humanitarian measures began to be advocated had echoes of maternal solicitude. A diffusion over the ranks of society of womanly care for children may then be added to the forces strengthening the bond of common humanity in the course of the eighteenth century.

It is probable that, besides the maternal instinct, a general altruistic impulse towards other members of one's own species has been selected for by evolution among mankind as among other animals. Such at least is an inference to be drawn from the study of altruistic behaviour by social biologists. In the light of this study, we see people in modern society drawn to help their fellows in trouble by a propensity genetically transmitted from their forebears engaged as hunter-gatherers for 2 million years before the Neolithic Revolution, and maintaining their animal existence for how many years before that. But this impulse is activated only by the distress of those who are recognized as of one's own kind—of the same flock or herd in the narrower sense, of the same species in the wider. From this comes the application to that growth of humanitarianism, or broadening of sympathies, that has been noticed in the eighteenth century. So long as the poor, or the labouring classes, were seen by their betters as squalid and uncouth, they seemed to belong to a different nation: how they should be treated was a question, like how horses should be treated, of how the master could get the most out of them. Probably, it is true, the social distance was never as great in England as in France: in the English countryside, at least, before population overflowed there was in part a habit of neighbourliness, of mutual respect and a shared enjoyment of sport. But so long as the labouring classes remained desperately poor, with all the visible disabilities of their poverty, the well-to-do must have seen them as so far removed from themselves that they had small claim upon them. We might—pushing the comparison to an extreme—liken the position of the well-to-do to that of the white settlers in a colony among a native population in their huts. But now, in the course of the eighteenth century, as standards of living rose, the social distance lessened and the poor became more respectable in the literal meaning of that word: they appeared to the well-to-do as members of the same society. The historian observes a new sensitivity of the social conscience. On the line of explanation developed here, we should say that the poor, being now more assimilated to membership of the substantial classes, became the objects of the genetically transmitted propensity to help distressed members of one's group.

There is thus a paradox. So long as the poor desperately needed help, they were denied it by their very need: the extremity of their poverty shut them off. To the extent that their need lessened and their lot improved, they received consideration, and the prospect of further improvement.

5

Action Delayed

By the time of the revolutions in America and France and of rapid development in the economy of Great Britain, changes of outlook had been brought about that prepared influential sectors of society for some measures of practical egalitarianism. But that application was not to come for another hundred years. The purpose of this chapter is to consider the forces that supervened to delay action on egalitarian principles when it seemed that these had gained sufficient acceptance.

5.1. The Obstacles to Redistribution

If nothing was done for so long to apply principles that were so much in the air, the reasons can be found in the presence of obstacles in both practice and theory.

Foremost of the practical obstacles was the lack of financial and administrative resources. For many years the war was preoccupying, and financially overwhelming. The income tax itself was a war measure, seen as a burden that must be lifted as soon as war ceased. But, that apart, the administrative machinery was lacking. If more was to be spent in poor relief, more revenue would have had to be raised; the income tax would have had to be kept on, but what Peel could do in 1842 would hardly have been practicable at the end of the war. Even, moreover, if it had been, there were still no means for administering benefits, no offices, national or local, through which they could have been disbursed and controlled. We know now how the Poor Law Act of 1834 centralized the administration of relief, and together with the new system created a new type of administrator; and how the Municipal Reform Act of 1836 regularized the administration of local government, with its duty of protecting welfare. But the Poor Law Act was passed only after a Commission had found that the Elizabethan arrangements for relief, which had been imposing a mounting charge on the ratepayer, were often inefficient as means of helping the needy; the Municipal Corporations Act was passed only after a cholera epidemic had revealed the chaotic state of local government; and both measures were adopted only by a reformed House of Commons. It would be unfair to blame the men of the 1790s for not having found their way to such creative solutions at the time. The development

of post offices in the towns and many of the villages throughout the country was a gradual process following the adoption of the
penny post in 1840. When old-age pensions were instituted in 1909, the
post office counters were there for them to be paid over. The social benefits
that followed in the next three years had the experience of the friendly
societies and the trade unions to draw upon: they partly absorbed the
administrative machinery of those bodies, partly had to create their own. A
century and more earlier, with the best will in the world, what could
administrators have done? Pitt attached importance to the provision in his
Bill for a new order of Visitors, to assist the Justices in the choice and
supervision of the guardians; and every Guardian was to transmit annually
to the Privy Council 'copies of all schedules, representations, certificates,
answers and reports made by or to him from time to time, to any petty
sessions of the peace . . .' and much else. Then one turns to what the
records tell of the various doings of Overseers and Guardians and Justices,
place by place: no wonder that Pitt's Bill was dismissed for its utter
impracticability. Any policy of redistribution had to wait upon, or begin
with, the creation of administrative machinery. But we see a morning
star—the beginning of the villagers' own mutual insurance, which Pitt's
Bill would have encouraged and subsidized by its provision for 'Parochial
Funds for Superannuation'.

Beyond the administrative gap, the path of benevolence was blocked by a
still greater obstacle, the menacing growth of the population. In the
eighteenth century British statesmen were constantly aware how small the
population of the country was in comparison with that of France, and when
Pitt introduced his Poor Law Bill he had still been able to speak of 'those
who, after having enriched their country with a number of children, have a
claim upon its assistance for support'. But not long afterwards it became
widely recognized that much of the suffering of the poor was due to the
growth of population. Nothing that the government could do, it seemed,
would check it. Relief to its hungry victims would only foster it.

How the growth of population overwhelmed the social system is
illustrated by some records of the Overseers of the Poor. At Tysoe in
Warwickshire in the 1730s, the Overseers were found 'on a rough rota of
persons of known capacity' chosen by general agreement in a meeting of
neighbours who addressed each other by their Christian names (Ashby
1961: 273–8). Spending £3 or £4 a year, they were able to meet the known
needs of the villagers for help in sickness as well as for poor relief. In 1750
the ailing widow Claridge believed that the waters of a spring seventeen
miles away would do her good, and the Overseers paid 3 s. to Isaac Clark to
ride over to Leamington and fetch some for her. In 1758 they provided half
the cost of finding substitutes for those drawn for military service. To those
suffering lengthy illness, they supplied wine as well as nursing. These
things were possible because claims of the destitute were so few; but now

they mounted. In 1752 one workless man was helped. In 1774 four or five men without work during the winter months were set to trenching in the common fields, or roadmending. Before long, the village had its troop of 'roundsmen', obliged to tramp daily from farm to farm, asking for work that everyone knew was not available. Already by 1750 the annual outlay had risen to £87; by 1800 it was near £3 000. In the Somerset village of Leigh on Mendip, where once the Overseers had even met bills for beer, bread and cheese at laying-outs, the poor rates rose from £165 in 1754 to £518 in 1800 and £743 in 1820.[1] Over the same span, the cost of living had little more than doubled.

We know now that the growth of population from the mid-eighteenth century onwards was common to much of western Europe. The researches of the Cambridge Population Group have indicated that in England at least it came about mainly as the cumulative effect of reductions in the age of women at marriage, and in the proportion of women who remained unmarried (Wrigley and Schofield 1981: 265-9). Very likely, this was the effect of rising prosperity; comparison of cohort gross reproduction rates with a twenty-five-year moving average of real wages suggests that the rise in those rates from the end of the Civil War until about 1780 was a response to the improvement in real wages, whose moving average rose persistently if gently for the 120 years from 1631 to 1751. But of course, all this was utterly unknown to the observers of 1820. They attached importance to factors that were salient because they were shocking, as they appeared among the labouring classes. As the poor laws were then administered, every year more children were being born into pauperdom, through early and improvident marriages or outright bastardy, in the confident expectation of maintenance by the parish. This was a mounting menace. So long as a shilling or two for every child brought into this world would be paid every week across the Overseer's table, and the parents asked no more of life than the miserable subsistence such money afforded, there was no prudential check on the indefinite growth of a destitute and demoralized population.

The key word there is 'prudential'. Investigators searching for a remedial policy could find it only in the restoration of prudence and foresight in the labouring classes. What was wrong with the poor law as then administered was not that it relieved suffering, which was a proper object in so far as misfortunes could not be provided against; but that the doles it gave to the able-bodied removed the incentives to prudence and foresight. The great objection to government action designed to protect the weak, or to give benefits to the needy at the expense of their neighbours, became the fact that it would reward the feckless equally with the prudent.

---

[1] From a pamphlet on the history of the village, prepared by Rev John Fisher. Ten volumes of the Overseers' accounts have survived.

'A labourer who marries without being able to support a family may in some respects be considered as an enemy to all his fellow-labourers', Malthus said in his first edition (Malthus 1960: 33–4); he held the poor law to blame for removing the threat of starvation, which alone would induce labourers to restrain themselves from procreation. But in his second edition Malthus did allow hope that the inculcation of 'moral restraint' would prove a practicable means of bettering the labourers' lot. Later he went on even to envisage 'an increase in the happiness of the mass of human society' through a reduction in the number of labourers—at least

of those employed in severe toil. If the lowest classes of society were thus diminished, and the middle classes increased, each labourer might indulge a more rational hope of rising by diligence and exertion into a better station . . .; the lottery of human society would appear to consist of fewer blanks and more prizes. (Malthus 1803: 594–5; see also Himmelfarb 1968)

But all this was to be attained by self-control on the part of more enlightened labourers, without benefit of social support. Ricardo in the same way based his hope of betterment on a change in the attitude of the labourers, but more realistically he hoped for this to be effected by a rise in their subjective standard of living. He followed Adam Smith in holding that the standard of living actually realized by the labouring classes depended on the balance between the accumulation of capital, in the sense of 'the funds destined for the maintenance of labour', and the rate of increase of the labouring population. If the rate of accumulation took the lead, the state of society was cheerful, but population would grow; and when it grew faster than capital, the mood would become melancholy, as hunger and disease reined population back again.

With a population pressing against the means of subsistence, the only remedies are either a reduction of people, or a more rapid accumulation of capital. But in countries where the land was already fully cultivated, more capital could not be applied without running into rapidly decreasing returns: the only remedy was the reduction of the growth of population. So 'the friends of humanity' cannot but wish that in all countries the labouring classes should have a taste for comforts and enjoyments, and that they should be stimulated by all legal means in their exertions to procure them. There cannot be a better security against a superabundant population. (Ricardo 1817: ch. v).

The importance that Ricardo attached to the subjective standard of living is borne out by the observations of a doctor, closely acquainted with the labourers of Edinburgh and Manchester, on how Irish immigrants had lowered the English standard. In his terrible factual account of 'The Moral and Physical Condition of the Working Classes of Manchester in 1832', Dr Kay observed:

The paucity of the amount of means and comforts *necessary for the mere support* of life, is not known by a more civilised population, and this secret has been taught the labourers of this country by the Irish. As competition and the restrictions and burdens of trade diminished the profits of capital, and consequently reduced the price of labour, the contagious example of ignorance and a barbarous disregard of forethought and economy, exhibited by the Irish, spread. (Kay 1862)

The great source of ever-impending poverty, then, was to be countered by prudential restraint that the labourers would exert on a view of their own interests; but what action could be taken to promote that view was not clear. All that did seem clear was that improvements in relief would work in the opposite direction. The force of that difficulty appears in the reasons given by Nassau Senior for rejecting the proposal to make poor relief a national charge.

Senior, a lawyer who absorbed the economic thought of the time through his membership of the Political Economy Club, and became professor of that subject at Oxford, may be reckoned the first outstanding economic adviser to government. Chief of the problems of the day on which he reported was the poor law. He had been ready enough, in his report on the handloom weavers, to make elementary education a charge on the taxpayer nationally and the ratepayer locally; but when he came to the poor law, although he recognized the advantages of a system financed out of national revenue, he rejected it. His reasons are instructive. They make clear what practical considerations were holding back well-informed and judicious men from egalitarian measures at this time.

The case for a national charge was a strong one, and Senior did justice to it. As long as each parish relieved its own poor, and found the money by its own rate, it had a strong incentive to prevent anyone coming in from another parish who might sooner or later need relief. Under the Act of Settlement, a parish had the right to return any such immigrant who 'fell on the rates' to the parish of his birth, or to claim a repayment from that parish: hence much hardship and litigation, and the penning up of labourers in the parishes of their birth from which they dared not move. These appalling and, as it seems now, absurd difficulties would disappear if relief were financed nationally instead of parochially. Another anomaly would go at the same time—the great differences in the burden of poverty between one district and another, not necessarily matched at all by the differences, also great, in the ratepayers' capacity to pay. More could be said also of the advantages of a unified administration.

'Still admitting the force of all these arguments in favour of a national charge,' wrote Senior, 'we do not recommend one.' He had three arguments. Two of them concerned administrative practicability. A national system was liable to become lax, and political pressure would be exerted to loosen it further; the floodgates would be opened again. 'In this case, as in many others, what was beneficial as a remedy might become fatal as a regimen' (Poor Law Commissioners 1834: 99–100). There was also a problem of finance. If a national system were set up, the local rates must be superseded by a national property tax, in England and Wales alone; but this could not be levied equitably. Senior's first and main objection, however, concerned population and morale. To make poor relief a national charge was 'objectionable in principle':

> To promise, on the part of the government, subsistence to all, to make the government the general insurer against misfortune, idleness, improvidence and vice, is a plan better perhaps than the parochial system, as at present administered; but still a proposal which nothing but the certainty that a parochial system is unsusceptible of real improvement, and that a national system is the only alternative against immediate ruin, the only plank in the shipwreck, could induce us to embrace. (Poor Law Commissioners 1834: 99–100)

There must be no indiscriminate handing out of doles, no subsidization of improvidence and, implicitly, no discouragement of thrift and prudential self-restraint.

This was an apprehension that Ricardo had expressed some years before with exceptional force:

> If by law every human being wanting support could be sure to obtain it, and obtain it in such a degree as to make life tolerably comfortable, theory would lead us to expect that all other taxes together would be light compared with the single one of the poor rates. The principal of gravitation is not more certain than the tendency of such laws to change wealth and power into misery and weakness; to call away the exertions of labour from every object, except that of providing more subsistence; to confound all intellectual distinction; to busy the mind continually in supplying the body's wants; until at last all classes should be infected with the plague of universal poverty. (Ricardo 1817: ch. v)

In one way, these arguments keep close to the circumstances of the case and the possibilities of practical policy; but they also rest on presuppositions about the proper role of individual responsibility and the limits of intervention by government. In fact, the principles of currently influential political theory agreed with the lessons that observers of the labouring classes were drawing from their behaviour and propensities. The constraints on benevolence and the reluctance to extend relief more widely, which were prompted by acquaintance with the state of the poor, were reinforced by doctrine coming down from the rationalists and philosophers.

The stress laid in the eighteenth century on reason as the unique but universal and distinctive attribute of man led in more than one way to the belief that government should not intervene. First, although the workings of social sympathy were recognized, 'society' was commonly taken to denote only an aggregate of individuals. This was not merely an extravagance of the *philosophes*: Paley (1785: VI, xi) with his common sense observed: 'although we speak of communities as of sentient beings . . . nothing really exists or feels but *individuals* . . .' Bentham followed a beaten path when he declared that 'individual interests are the only real interests' (Bowring 1843: i, 321). When society was envisaged in this way, it did not exist at all as we commonly understand it: there was no common interest, over and above the self-interests of individuals, for government to protect or promote. Government, it is true, had been instituted by individuals for the purpose of enabling them to pursue their own ends in security; law and order was an end that they could best attain by combination. But there were no ends not sought by individuals that government should itself pursue. To this rule there was one exception, although this was in conformity with the purpose of the rule. If it was only too apparent, as one looked around, that some people's pursuit of their self-chosen ends would lead only to trouble for themselves and their neighbours, that was because they had not received the education that would enable them to choose wisely. It was therefore proper that governments should provide education. Its function was to enlighten self-direction, not to fashion or supplement it. But in advocating *Schools for All* as James Mill did, the Philosophical Radicals were not moved by any desire to create a fairer or healthier society. They envisaged no such target.

If the concept of society as an entity with its own needs was absent, still less was society envisaged as an organism that would grow and develop. Visions of perfectibility there had always been; the great Scots scholars had depicted what today it would seem natural to describe as the stages in the evolution of society; but there was no general presumption that institutions and procedures were normally subject to change that might be for the better. On the contrary, change was more likely to present itself as the loss of strength brought by advancing years, and a falling away from standards formerly upheld 'Change and decay in all around I see', wrote Henry Lyte. Before Darwin, in particular, there was little realization that change in the body politic might be adaptive. Thoughtful people conscious of the pressing problems of the time sought to make existing institutions work better, but not to devise new ones.

The belief that governments should not intervene was strengthened, in the second place, because the individualist view of society provided an account of its working as a self-regulating mechanism. Each man sought his own interests, and the rational pursuit of these, it was believed, involved no conflict. In part this provided an explanation of the actual ills of society—men were not all rational. But there is a familiar transition of belief, from grasping how things work in principle to thinking that this is how they work in practice—or would easily do, if only some frictions were removed, and some scales fell from men's eyes. Here, in effect, was a mechanism well designed to run unattended: there is no need for governments to be pushing it here and braking it there. Men are in fact always and everywhere engaged in advancing their own interests; and in doing this, so far from clashing, they help one another.

Third, and here we come nearest the overshadowing problem of the day, for the system to work men must act in accordance with reason. So they must be held responsible for their actions, if only to discourage irrational conduct. If a man is impulsive, careless or short-sighted, he must bear the consequences: to relieve him of them is only to encourage disorder. The school of experience taught the lesson of rationality. Nothing should be done in the name of benevolence to make that lesson less effective.

The doctrine which in these various ways strengthened the judgement of practical men against intervention might be summarized in the phrase *laissez-faire*. True, that actual phrase was little used before John Stuart Mill declared in 1848 that '*Laisser-faire* . . . should be the general practice: every departure from it, unless required by some great good, is a certain evil' (Mill 1848: V, xi, 7; Robbins 1952: 43, fn. 2). But there was an understanding that the teaching of the political economists and the utilitarians agreed in denying the usefulness of governmental intervention, and disapproving of all extensions of social over individual responsibility. There are some phrases that are destined to take off like rockets and dazzle the eyes of beholders who never saw the page of argument in which they began. It was in this way that many people came to know of Adam Smith's 'invisible hand' and of his 'obvious and simple system of natural liberty'. Each individual, in seeking the highest return on his own capital, 'generally, indeed, neither intends to promote the public interest, nor knows how much he is promoting it. . . . he intends only his own gain, and he is in this, as in many other cases, led by an invisible hand to promote an end which was no part of his intention.'

Every system which endeavours, either, by extraordinary encouragements, to draw towards a particular species of industry a greater share of the capital of the society than what would naturally go to it; or, by extraordinary restraints, to force from a particular species of industry some share of the capital which would otherwise be employed in it; is in reality subversive of the great purpose which it means to promote. It retards, instead of accelerating, the progress of the society towards real wealth and greatness; and diminishes, instead of increasing, the real value of the annual produce of its land and labour. All systems either of preference or of restraint, therefore, being thus completely taken away, the obvious and simple system of natural liberty establishes itself of its own accord. Every man, as long as he does not violate the laws of justice, is left perfectly free to pursue his own interest his own way, and to bring both his industry and capital into competition with those of any other man, or order of men. The sovereign is completely discharged from a duty, in the attempting to perform which, he must always be exposed to innumerable delusions, and for the proper performance of which no human wisdom or knowledge could ever be sufficient: the duty of superintending the industry of private people, and of directing it towards the employments most suitable to the interest of the society. (Smith 1776: IV, ii, ix)

These passages, taken by themselves, seemed to provide the authority of political economy for what many active people were ready to believe, that the state should let well alone while they themselves pursued their own ends. That certainly was the impression left by Bentham's winged phrases. They stood out of the text of his *Political Economy* (1798):

With the view of causing an increase to take place in the mass of national wealth, or with a view to increase of the means either of subsistence or enjoyment, without some special reason, the general rule is, that nothing ought to be done or attempted by government. The motto, or watchword of government, on these occasions, ought to be—Be quiet. . . . The request which agriculture, manufactures, and commerce present to governments is modest and reasonable as that which Diogenes made to Alexander: 'Stand out of my sunshine.' We have no need of favour—we require only a secure and open path. (Bowring 1843: iii, 33)

But principles set out in a few simple and striking sentences gave no adequate account of the ideas behind them. Neither in Adam Smith nor in Bentham did those ideas confine the state to the functions of defence and the maintenance of law and order, or preclude all restraint on the activities of private enterprise. Adam Smith's 'invisible hand' was part of his attack on the notion that government could single out some industries as more beneficial to the community than others, and should favour them accordingly while it held back the others. His 'obvious and simple system of natural liberty' left government with a potentially wide agenda: besides defence and law and order, it was charged with all those works and services that were of use to the community but which it was not in the interest of any individual to supply—Smith himself proposed that local government bear part of the cost of schools. In any case, what he girded against was 'the wretched spirit of monopoly'. If he objected to governmental activity, it was because he thought governments would be nobbled by interest groups, or, however disinterested, would lack the necessary knowledge. It was not that he was a hard and rigid individualist. On the contrary, he held an evolutionary and organic view of society, and his sympathies, as we have seen, were actively engaged with its poorer members. As for Bentham, what seemed the most abstract of doctrines provided the most flexible and pragmatic of codes to live by: the test of every proposed arrangement was not whether it was right by the book, but whether the state of affairs resulting from it seemed on the whole likely to be preferable to the present—in terms of human welfare as conceived by the observer. Many forms of governmental activity and intervention passed this test, and were in fact approved by Bentham himself.

But if the founding fathers of political economy and Utilitarianism never propounded a narrow and prohibitive doctrine of *laissez-faire*, the impression certainly spread abroad that they had established a presumption against any extension of the activities of government. This distillation of their teaching commanded widespread attention and assent after the Napoleonic wars, because it bore directly on the foremost social problem of the day, the rapid growth of population. It was this that made people listen to the stern voices of 'the gods of the copybook headings', and held them back from those developments of social welfare that had seemed so near not long before, and would have taken them a step towards redistribution.

Besides the obstacles formed by these practical and theoretical considerations against egalitarian measures, there was a singular absence of popular demand for them. The eyes of the activists and spokesmen among the workers, such as Place, remained fixed on parliamentary reform. This was a cause that united creeds and interests of diverse tendencies. It was by a sad conjuncture that a growing indigenous working-class movement had encountered a reaction and resistance driven by loathing and dread of the Jacobins. From the British point of view, it was irrelevant that, just when the hopes stirred by the American Revolution, and the French Revolution in its beginnings, had combined with the growing pressures of industrial change and population growth at home to stimulate organization and agitation among working men, revulsion at the Reign of Terror, and fear of contagion, led to an era of at least a threatened and imminent repression of combination and publication. The anti-Jacobin reaction taught most forward-looking British labour that it could not move until it had parliamentary clearance; the repeal of the Combination Laws in 1824—although it was let through by inadvertence—showed what could be done even in an unreformed Parliament. It seemed clear that the democratization of Parliament was the most promising measure, indeed the essential prerequisite, for the relief of working people. Their leaders generally believed with Tom Paine that, so great would be the change in their condition when they obtained control of the legislature, they need not look beyond it.

In any case, what measures could they have looked to? The belief that suffering can be alleviated by public policy has been brought home only by the experiments and advances of more recent years. In those times, provisions that would seem obvious today simply did not present themselves within people's field of vision. Adam Smith had remarked on the strange absence of 'popular clamour' against the law of settlement that effectively prevented people from moving from overcrowded villages to places where jobs were available:

There is scarce a poor man in England of forty years of age, I will venture to say, who has not in some part of his life felt himself most cruelly oppressed by this ill-contrived law . . . The common people of England, however, so jealous of their liberty, but like the common people of most other countries never rightly

understanding wherein it consists, have now for more than a century together
suffered themselves to be exposed to this oppression without a remedy. (Smith
1776: I, x)

The difficulty may have been the lack not so much of realization of the
oppression, as of any known remedy. Simple repeal would not have been
enough.

The concentration upon political reform culminated in Chartism.
Carlyle said in 1839 that 'Chartism means the bitter discontent grown
fierce and mad, the wrong condition therefore, or the wrong disposition, of
the Working Classes of England . . . The matter of Chartism is weighty,
deep-rooted, far-extending; did not begin yesterday; will by no means end
this day or tomorrow . . .' Yet the then five points of the Charter were all
concerned with elections to Parliament. 'The English people are used to
suffrage; it is their panacea for all that goes wrong with them; they have a
fixed-idea of suffrage' (Carlyle 1915: i, 165–6; ix, 223). So long as that
panacea dominated the minds of the workers, they would not throw their
weight behind the egalitarian tendencies coming down from the eighteenth
century but now long obstructed.

5.2. Early Socialism—Not Primarily Egalitarian

The conclusion of the last section, that the British workers gave political
equality priority over economic, may seem a strange observation to make
about the age of early socialism. The aim of equality has guided the central
thrust of the socialism of later years, but the main concern of the early
socialists was not with the distribution of income but with the conditions of
production. The industrial revolution had overrun them, carrying old
customs away, increasing their insecurity, setting brother against brother,
denying them satisfaction in their work. 'The huge demon of Mechanism',
said Carlyle

smokes and thunders, panting at his great task, in all sections of English land;
changing his *shape* like a very Proteus; and infallibly, at every change of shape,
oversetting whole multitudes of workmen, and as if with the waving of his shadow
from afar, hurling them asumder, this way and that, in their crowded march and
course of work or traffic; so that the wisest no longer knows his whereabouts.
(Carlyle 1915: 185).

Against this upheaval, the early socialists offered the protection of
autonomous and co-operative associations of producers. Against 'wage
slavery' they advanced workers' control. Envisaging those workers as alike
in their present suffering, they were little concerned with the differences
among them in earning capacity. The changes that socialists proposed
would provide all workers with an equal status. That would be so great an

achievement that relative earnings presented no problem. Only in the French tradition coming down from Babeuf was there an explicit commitment to equal earnings or an equal meeting of needs. Elsewhere, the attention of socialists was fixed on the worker in production and the conditions of his working life, not on the worker as consumer, and his relative income.

That this was so explains the contemporary appeal of writings that, as we see them now, contained much fantasy. They were read widely none the less, and were taken seriously, as the puffs for patent medicine used to be, because they began by describing the ills they set out to remedy in a way that showed a real understanding of where and how much they hurt. There were three sorts of those ills in the main, and the reaction to each of them formed a particular type of socialism.

One was inflicted by the opposition between employer and wage-earner. Year by year, a rising proportion of a growing working population was brought under that relationship. Formerly, much work was done by self-employed people, or by craftsmen who, although they were sometimes hired by the day, had their own workshop and perhaps a plot of land; but now, with population growing, machinery coming in and transport opening markets, more and more workpeople had to find employment as wage-earners. This meant the bargain at the yard gate about the rate to be paid. It meant attendance at stated times, and submission to the employer himself or his foreman within the workshop, instead of the freedom of the self-employed man to work in his own way at his own time. An unaccustomed discipline took the place of independence. Instead of taking his chance of what he could earn in the market, but at least standing on his own feet, the worker must depend for his livelihood on another man—who would take him on and turn him away as suited him for his own profit. In all, by contrast with an idealized past, the relation was stigmatized as wage-slavery.

One practical reaction was of course to form trade unions. But we are concerned here with the reaction that took the form of socialism, and this centred upon workers' control and the self-governing workshop. Let the employer be eliminated; let producers' co-operatives be set up, and let them exchange their surplus products with one another. Robert Owen's co-operative villages were of this kind, even though he himself saw them primarily as a means to the moral regeneration of their inhabitants, whom he would have kept under paternal control, at least until he had seen them well advanced on the right lines. Louis Blanc, in his widely read *L'Organisation du travail* (published in 1839), proposed that the state should set up 'national workshops' which would become self-governing, the managers being elected by the workers. The workshops within each industry would be subordinate to a central workshop, and so would form a guild. The desire for self-government, or industrial democracy, that found expression in these early projects has remained a persistent element in socialist thought.

Closely associated with the pressure that gave rise to that element was the second kind of conflict, and stimulus to early socialism: the class conflict between labour and capital. The self-employed worker might make a poor living, but if he was not a domestic worker under the thumb of a particular merchant, he could not blame his troubles on any other person. For the worker who could earn a living only if he could gain access to the use of land or machinery, the case was different. The owner of that land or machinery would charge him a toll. From the product of his labour, a margin would be deducted for rent and profits. What margin was reasonable? Or, what decided the level of wages, and thereby how wide the margin should be? Early socialism took two lines from this point. One was to assert for the workers their right to the whole product of labour. Rent was the toll levied by the natural monopoly of land; but God, or Nature, intended the land for the use of us all. Capital was stored-up labour; workers should not have to pay now for the use of the product of their labour wrongfully withheld from them in the past. Under socialism, therefore, all land and capital would be owned collectively, and there would be no attribution of rent or profits to any landowner or capitalist. How relative incomes would then take shape was not a matter that needed much thought in advance:

While every individual would be permitted to accumulate the fruits of his own labour, the prohibition of interest and inheritance would make it impossible to accumulate large amounts of property . . . 'every man might start fair, in the field of competition or co-operation as they thought fit, and be in full condition to receive the full equivalent for their services to society'. (Himmelfarb 1984: 240; the quotation is from *The Poor Man's Guardian, 28 March 1835*.)

The other line of reaction against exploitation by landlord and capitalist was to proclaim the existence of the class war. The workers were seen as a body with a common interest, which was necessarily a political interest, because they were ranged over against the men of property by whom the state was controlled. The programme of socialism must therefore be revolutionary. What arrangements would be made for the economy after the workers had seized power could be left to be worked out in the event.

The third kind of conflict was set up by competition. Machines competed with handicrafts. New and improved forms of transport broke into once sheltered markets. Employers operated under a pressure to keep prices down, which they transmitted as a drive to get ever more output from their machines and workpeople. As employers competed for markets, so workers competed for jobs. The socialism that was formed, particularly in reaction to these wounds inflicted by increased competition, was in part of a kind already noticed: it stressed co-operation, and looked to the setting up of communities in which production for use would be undertaken by teams made up of volunteers of high morale. But the main reaction took a distinctive form. Its stress was laid on the disorder and inefficiency that it alleged to be necessarily linked with competition. There was not merely the dislocation due to the impact of new men and new methods, but also the continuing wastefulness of the overlap between would-be suppliers of the same product. In addition, there was the inherent clash of interest between different sections of the community, so that good prices for farmers meant dear food for industrial workers. The remedy lay in planning. The associations of producers were to undertake programmes of output, or to exchange the surpluses of their output over their own consumption, according to a rational plan drawn up by a central authority. The great potentialities inherent in science and technology could be released if experts organized and directed production for the common good. Instead of men obstructing one another or duplicating each other's efforts, under socialism they would help one another, and their tasks would be co-ordinated. The planners must have authority, the experts must have status and ample means; it is in the interests of the whole community that the élite should be rewarded.

There was one respect, however, in which the early socialists were concerned with equality—the equality of women. It was sympathy for them that moved John Stuart Mill in his revision of his *Principles of Political Economy*:

In proclaiming the perfect equality of men and women [he wrote in the first draft of his *Autobiography*], and an entirely new order of things in regard to their relation with one another, the Saint-Simonians in common with Owen and Fourier have entitled themselves to the grateful remembrance of all future generations. (Himmelfarb 1974: 201)

Thus, among many of the early socialists, equality of income received scant attention, as being of small account in comparison with the radical improvement to be made in the whole way of life of every worker; it was treated as subordinate to the imperatives of production. But we have noted a French tradition in which it was made the primary aim. One of Baboeuf's fellow conspirators, Buonarrotti, survived to bring his countrymen back to the principles of the later Rousseau. Every man had an equal right to a share in the property with which Nature had endowed mankind; society was formed not to protect property, but to curb inequality. There must be no inheritance; no one must be allowed to sell his products for money; instead of different pay for different occupations, the principle of distribution should be 'to each according to his needs' (Halévy 1948, 61). This programme of thoroughgoing communism was largely taken over by Blanqui, who in 1839 led a rising that seized the *hotel de ville* and the police headquarters in Paris, and held them for a time. The same concern for equality of income appeared two years later in the otherwise very different programme put forward in his *L'Organisation du travail* by Louis Blanc. As the title of his book suggested, he was mostly concerned with the disorders of the economy arising from unrestricted competition, and he advocated various measures of planning; but when he came to distribution, he rejected differentials for skill, and propounded the principle, 'From each according to his ability, to each according to his needs.' He is remembered chiefly for the 'national workshops' that were set up on his motion by the revolutionary government of 1848. With the collapse of that government and the coming of Napoleon III, the current of revolutionary socialism went underground in France for fifteen years; but it had given to the world an idealism of equality that went far beyond the conceptions of the eighteenth century, and had powered it with slogans.

6

The Movement into Redistribution

Between the Reform Act of 1832 and the Great Exhibition of 1851, Great Britain was transformed. The principles of the people who brought the change about had mostly been developed and received in the eighteenth century. A new thrust towards equality was to be exerted after 1880, but the reformers' achievement in those two earlier decades was to find means of applying principles to practice as never before. Obstacles that had seemed insuperable declined, gradually at first, but in the end enough to brighten all the prospects of social betterment. New institutions were designed and established. They were manned by a new type of administrator.

The machinery of redistribution that was mounted in those years continued to be developed in the three decades following. The course of social and economic change pushed the process on through all the ins and outs of government, and against all fear of innovation and centralization. Meanwhile, a new view of mankind and of society was fostering attitudes that were to renew egalitarianism.

6.1. The Rise of Administration

We may take it for granted today that if principles are to take effect they must be equipped with 'administrative machinery', and that there is room for ingenuity and innovation in its design. To provide it even seems to be the main task and test of the reformer. But this has not always been so: the possibilities of administration in the modern sense had to be discovered. It is true that governments have long been referred to as administrations. It is also true that Pope wrote

> For forms of government let fools contest;
> What'er is best administered is best

as far back as 1733. But this is a use of 'administration' with a connotation very different from our present usage. If anyone concerned with social questions today returned to the Great Britain of 1830, he or she would be struck by the difficulty that Parliament encountered in giving its legislation on those questions any force beyond that of exhortation, and by the slenderness of the provision that sufficed for all the functions of local government as we see them now.

The filling of these gaps owed much to Bentham. For a time his work took a firm hold on many spirits ardent for reform, because it provided them with a complete do-it-yourself kit. This it did in two ways: it showed how to decide what was the right course in all manner of circumstances, and it opened up the possibilities of social engineering by the design of administrative devices.

To find the right course, the Benthamite as Utilitarian used the 'felicific calculus': what outcome would yield the greatest utility in the aggregate, and do so for the greatest number? The 'happiness philosophy' that provided the terms in which this principle was expressed soon proved itself vulnerable to criticism: the axiom that all actions aim at happiness was either the identity that what we choose to do is what we want to do, or an assertion about human nature and behaviour that simply is not true. But although the formulation of Utilitarianism was objectionable, there lay within it a fruitful observation concerning the human faculty of choice—namely, that we are capable of weighing the various consequences of an action against one another, and deciding what is the best thing to do 'on the whole'. Utilitarianism became a liberating force because it told people that they were free to do this. The alternative was to find the right rule or commandment with which to comply. This rule may have been prescribed by revelation, or may have been transmitted by tradition that preserved the wisdom that earlier generations had accumulated by experience. The difficulty was to find any rule that would not, in some readily conceivable circumstance, do more harm than good. Utilitarianism said, in effect, look not at the action but at the consequences. It also said that the harm and good among the consequences were not particular values, but different quantities of the common stuff of human happiness. This last assertion is arbitrary; no one has devised a thermometer for measuring the warmth of feelings; but we can treat the quantification as heuristic—as shorthand for the proposition that the many different components of the human condition enter together into our judgements, under which they are commensurable, so that we can, for instance, balance moral elevation against physical gratification. Given two alternative courses of action, each with a variety of consequences, we can decide which is the better, 'all things considered'.

The essence of Utilitarianism in this first respect, then, was reliance on the intuitive moral judgement. This faculty of ours enables us to find the right course because it is capable of taking all the consequences of each course into consideration, and deciding which course will do most on the whole to promote the welfare of all concerned. The evaluation of different consequences in a common scale in this way presupposes a judgement of what sorts of consequence are harmful, and what beneficial, in the first place, and this the moral judgement also determines: it decides what is good and bad as well as what actions will do most good or least harm.

This sovereignty of intuition made an adaptable instrument for the reformer. When he used it, he was no longer constrained by authority, however derived; he could make up his own mind about what was best to do, with the assurance that, if only he proceeded on a careful examination of the relevant facts, and with equal care assessed the various consequences of different actions, he would do the most possible for the benefit of humanity. He could proceed in this way, moreover, in all manner of circumstances: he need not be constrained by the principles traditionally applied to regulate this or that sector of society or form of activity. Pragmatic solutions were canonized.

But this trust in individual judgement implies an enlightenment, and an altruism, that common observation often finds lacking. Fixing the overriding end of all activity in 'the greatest happiness of the greatest number' exposes the Utilitarian to familiar difficulties. If he is saying that we *ought* to make this our end, he is only repeating the old injunction to love your neighbour as yourself. If he is saying that we *do* in fact make this our end, then he has to explain how it is that, if people each pursue the end of their own happiness, they do not continually collide with one another. Shall I not choose the course that will maximize my own happiness, never mind what effect it has on other people's? Instead of a harmonious social order, we are confronted with jarring atoms, conflicting self-interests, a war of all against all.

Three ways were found of meeting this difficulty (Halévy 1928). One rested on introspection, and on recognition as a matter of everyday observation that we do have a moral sense that requires us to take other people's interests into account. We do so, Adam Smith had held (following his teacher Hutcheson), because we put ourselves in their place: we are moved by spontaneous sympathy, in the sense not of pity but of fellow-feeling and identification. The happiness we of our nature seek to maximize includes theirs as well as ours. The second way, which is also found in Adam Smith, invoked the invisible hand, which designed and maintained an unforced harmony of interests: each in pursuing his own interests would, whether he intended it or not, promote those of others. This view evidently held good for many economic transactions: in a deal between a willing seller and a willing buyer, each gains something he wants by providing what the other wants. But even in the market-place, some relations are suspect of being exploitative, of profiting one party at the expense of the other; and elsewhere, the exertion of power is clearly capable of disregarding the precepts of altruism. The third solution accepts the second one as having seized on the predominant tendency, but allows that at a number of points conflicts of interest do arise; these, however, can be removed by regulations. 'Hume . . . concluded that the art of politics consists in governing individuals through their own interests, in creating artifices of such a kind that in spite of their avarice and their ambition they shall co-operate for the public good' (Halèvy 1928: 19).

It is here that utilitarianism proceeds from the right choice of ends to that of means, and that Benthamism made its distinctive contribution. This was based on that view of society as the outcome of the actions of autonomous individuals, which dominated the political thought of the eighteenth century. On this view, society appeared as a largely self-acting mechanism, whose working could be improved by the removal of frictions and the building in of devices here and there; but, subject to that, it could be left to tick away like a clock. We have seen how the analogy of clockwork went back to Hobbes. It marked a great change in the conception of society; instead of its institutions being believed to have been designed by some great law-giver, or sculpted by the experience and wisdom of the ages, they were seen as the outcome of propensities installed by nature in each individual. In the widely influential thought of Locke, the notion of sense impressions being combined by memory and reflection in each person's mind reinforced that of individual autonomy. The activity of individuals, and the social arrangements that emerged from it, appeared as part of the order of nature.

If, then, it was desired to change those arrangements, the proper course was not to exhort people, or try to order them about, but to devise arrangements that would deflect or canalize the currents of their self-directed energies. Sometimes those arrangements might be physical; Bentham himself devoted a large part of his energies to the advocacy of his Panopticon, a form of prison whose layout would be both sparing of custodial manpower and conducive to the reform of the convicts. In the same way, his disciples were to propose the provision of workhouses in the form of four separate buildings, one each for the male and female able-bodied adults, a third as a hospital for the old and infirm, the fourth, including a school, for the children. The function of these arrangements was to set bounds to individual actions, and define the terms on which permitted actions might be performed: they induced actions that people would not have taken without them, but still took of their own volition. To use a modern analogy, they provided the traffic lights and roundabouts and highway code that enable the traffic to flow more smoothly, as the drivers proceed on journeys of their own choosing. They came to be called 'the machinery'—appropriately, for it was to be designed by 'social engineers'.

Administration in this form needed administrators; the machinery needed managers. The expansion and development of this type of public servant was to make an essential contribution to the formation of the social structure after 1830. Servants of the central government there always had been. In the localities a few functionaries—the lord lieutenant, the sheriff, the justice of the peace—received the central government's orders, which it was their responsibility to see carried out within their jurisdictions. Under th Tudor poor law, the justices in particular had been charged with initiating action, setting up houses of industry and providing stocks of materials on which the unemployed could be set to work. It was this function of management that was developed in the age of reform. Instead of orders requiring particular actions at particular times, the central government made regulations, the administration of which was much more than a matter of police: it required initiative and decision-taking; it also required the qualities of the expert, who now makes his appearances on the national scene. Experts are characterized by knowledge, both wide and detailed, of the issues with which they deal; they are in some sense disinterested; their influence depends on the information they command and their professional equipment. Some administrators, among them some of the greatest, have combined these qualities with a sustained drive towards the attainment of certain ends, but their zeal has been productive because it was harnessed to a due detachment.

In considering the social construction that was to make possible the movement into redistribution later on, we must notice the new institutions together with the experts who designed and administered them. We have already met a leading figure in the person of Nassau Senior (p. 165). Petty had been an expert in his day, but it is in Senior's time that the expert began to appear in numbers on the national stage, to carry out inquiries into the problems of the day. One much used medium of inquiry was the royal commission. This was 'a device hardly met with before 1832' but once devised it was found indispensable: 'every major piece of social legislation between 1832–1871 was ushered in by this type of investigation' (Finer 1952: 39). Senior's judicious and constructive turn of mind, and power of vigorous expression, were well suited to that form of inquiry. In the last chapter we noticed his characteristic approach; we were concerned especially with the considerations that held him back from committing the national Exchequer to the cause of benevolence. Here we shall take up his constructive proposals. We shall notice especially his proposals for initiatives to be taken by government at the centre, and given effect in the localities by new forms of administration. He was asked to inquire into and report upon three major problems.

The first was that of the Irish poor. He found that virtually a whole peasantry was in poverty by reason of low productivity. The remedy lay not in poor relief, but in a programme of public investment in roads, canals, docks, drainage and reclamation. These he advocated not as relief works but as a means of increasing output, and so enlarging the fund, as it was called, available for the support of the labouring population. The aim was always to enable them to support themselves; but to do this, government and its administrators should go into business.

Senior's treatment of the second problem, that of the poor law, we have already noted. We have seen his reasons for not making poor relief a national charge. But it was still necessary to improve on the existing system, in which the relief of the able-bodied was relaxed partly by the benevolence of the local gentry, and partly by the connivance of the larger arable farmers, who were able to pass on rises in their own rates to their landlords, through abatements of rent, and could pay low wages that were subsidized by their humbler neighbours. The effect was to degrade the labourers—not only those who had no work, but those who were employed and would have been self-respecting, responsible and thrifty but for a vicious system. A new system must be devised. Thanks to Edwin Chadwick, Senior found its essential device in the principle of 'less eligibility': relief should be given to the able-bodied only on conditions that made it less attractive than earning a full week's wage. the able-bodied who still required relief must go into the workhouse and carry out the tasks assigned to them within those forbidding walls. Evidently it was assumed that the alternative of employment was open to the claimant. The moral fibre of the labourer was to be restored not by preachment, nor, as some proposed, by simply withdrawing relief from the able-bodied men altogether, but by creating a situation in which he would find his own advantage in supporting his household himself. To make this device effective, there must be a new administration, both locally and at the centre. It was in providing a central control that the plan made its constructive innovation. A commission was set up at the national level, and its staff of assistant commissioners were to ensure that the directives it issued under statutory authority were complied with in the localities. Two social inventions appeared here: the virtual use of what came to be called delegated legislation, and the posting of civil servants to stimulate, advise, check and inspect in the localities. There was innovation too in the formation of a new administrative area, the union, transcending the parish and in the provision for the election of the Board of Guardians.

The third problem was that of the handloom weavers, some 100 000 of them, who had prospered during the War but now were beaten down by the competition of machinery, and who cheapened their work even more by the long hours they worked in a desperate endeavour to keep their earnings up. Here again, Senior invoked the administrative capability of the national government to enable these people to improve their own lot—which meant, for most of them, finding and taking up other occupations. What they needed to give them this mobility was education. This must be paid for by the public purse. He also felt it necessary for the state to intervene to improve the sanitary condition of working-class housing. 'We believe that both the ground landlord and the speculating builder ought to be compelled by law, though it should cost them a percentage of their rent and profit, to take measures which will prevent the towns which they create from being the centre of disease' (Bowley 1937:

261). Such legislation would have required local enforcement by inspectors: once again, administration is developed for the purpose of improving the capacity of the labourer to help himself.

Where Nassau Senior was the type of academic called into public life as an adviser, Edwin Chadwick was strenuously engaged in administration both as designer and practitioner throughout most of his working life. His training had been in the law; he knew the slums around his Inn; he associated in his early years with the doctors who were concerned to make known the appalling filth of the growing towns; and he was a disciple of Bentham, whom he tended in his last hours. Tireless and single-minded, he pursued his own enquiries into the problems of the day with extraordinary pertinacity, and devised solutions to them which he pressed, assiduously and relentlessly, on wavering politicians. Two great Reports, and two great works of institutional construction, stand to his credit. In its essentials, the *Poor Law Report* of 1834 was his work, and the institutions that the ensuing Act was intended to set up were of his design. Even more distinctively was the momentous report on *The Sanitary Condition of the Labouring Classes*, 1842, his creation; indeed, it was published over his name. As an administrator he exerted himself—as far as he was allowed to—as Secretary of the Poor Law Commission, and he was variously employed in the activities instigated by his Sanitary Report—as unofficial Secretary to the Health of Towns Committee, and as a Commissioner of Sewers in London and on the General Board of Health. But these were only the chief among his many interventions in the social problems of the day.

As an administrator, Chadwick had every merit except that of being able to get on with other people, whether those he worked under or those he sought to direct. He had all the qualities that give bureaucracy a bad name—he knew best, because he had investigated the subjects with which he dealt, as others had not; when people resisted the rational principles that it was his clear duty to apply, they did but stiffen his determination to overcome their ignorance, inertia or vested interests. Concessions were worse than weakness: they were a betrayal. Early on he had written, 'The law must be made to conform to public opinion *or* the public opinion must, by means of public instruction be made to conform to the law' (Finer 1952: 477). Only the second course was open to one who saw clearly the benefits to be won by his policy, and that alone; nor was it in his impatient temperament to proceed so slowly as 'public instruction' would require.

But these faults, which brought him so much trouble as an administrator, were only the other side of his faith in administration and his capacity to design it. 'He was supremely confident of what administration could achieve', Finer (1952: 195) observed: 'he looked on it as a machine from which one might expect the utmost exactitude; and he hoped all things from it.' His Sanitary Report was designed to prevent 'the disease *that results from the neglect of proper administrative measures*' (p. 218). It may be said that the Benthamites conceptualized administration; they saw its necessary place in the social structure, and seized on its potentialities as an organ of government and engine of progress.

The administrative structures designed by Chadwick to deal with poor relief and public health were based on a number of principles. A first requirement was that plans should be based on detailed knowledge of the facts, obtained by inquiry in the field—abroad as well as at home. Chadwick himself devoted two years of incessant inquiry to the preparation of the Sanitary Report:

He had gone to every foreign source he could lay hands on, from the French statisticians . . . to the German authorities on medical police . . . He had grasped the meaning of Liebig's revolutionary work *The Chemistry of the Soil* and incorporated its doctrine as an integral part of his solution of the sanitary problem. Omitting any reference at all to his countless secondary authorities in English and the innumerable private correspondents to whom he turned in his insatiable quest for facts, the official data alone must have equalled *nine* folio volumes . . . (Finer 1952; 209–10)

Chadwick laid particular stress on the value of statistics. With these he showed, for instance, that Malthus was mistaken in thinking that poor relief made population rise faster. The task of planning was one for experts, and this was the way to equip them. Quite late in life, he proposed a 'think tank': legislation should be prepared by a standing committee of the Privy Council, aided for each particular Bill by a committee of experts assisted by a number of commissioners charged with enquiries.

But next, the function of administration was to bring this expert knowledge to bear. Those who were thoroughly well informed must stimulate and check those who lacked their clear sight. They must be given the scope that their technical task required. The old muddle of partial or overlapping bodies—corporations, courts leet, vestries, improvement commissions—must be swept away. The new poor law unions were conceived 'as units in a national local government system, to undertake singly such duties as registration, vaccination, and the upkeep of highways, and in combination the upkeep of district schools, auditors, officials and contractors' (Finer 1952: 93). The local health authority must cover the area dictated as a matter of engineering by a unitary plan for water supply and sewage disposal. Local administration must be professional. This it could be only if some members at least were appointed from the centre.

Even more closely, it followed that the national centre must maintain control. It should do so by inspection and audit. Chadwick's distinctive contribution to the Factory Act of 1833 had been the provision of a Board of Inspectors. His proposals in the Poor Law Report, says Finer, (1952: 88), 'have proved the source of nearly all the important developments in English local government, viz., central supervision, central inspection, central audit, a professional local government service controlled by local elective bodies, and the adjustment of areas to administrative exigencies'.

James Kay (he took the name of Kay-Shuttleworth later in life) had been deeply moved as a young doctor by the state of the poor in the slums around the dispensaries where he worked in Edinburgh and Manchester. It was not only the squalor and filth of the overcrowded housing that appalled him, but the brutality and ignorance of the people. His strong sense of social responsibility led him first to gather information systematically about the conditions he was intent on seeing changed. Manchester prepared for the coming of cholera in 1832 by a survey and house-to-house visitation of the districts likely to be worst affected. 'The facts collected by the visitors', he wrote afterwards, 'were subsequently carefully tabulated, and formed a basis on which all humane and thoughtful men could found their efforts to secure for the municipality whatever powers were needed for the sanitary improvement of the Town' (Kay-Shuttleworth 1964: 8). There followed his pamphlet on 'The Moral and Physical Condition of the Working Classes employed in the Cotton Manufacture in Manchester'. This in turn led to the foundation of the Manchester Statistical Society in 1833; the London Society was founded on its pattern the following year. Poulett Thomson, elected Member for Manchester in 1832, was later, as President of the Board of Trade, to set up a statistical department in the Board.

The salient finding of the Manchester inquiry was the need for better housing and sanitation, but even before these Kay put education. In his pamphlet, he listed the causes of evil as

the sanitary condition of the factories, excessive hours of labour, the influence of the discomfort of the homes in promoting intemperance, the influence of the corn laws and bad fiscal legislation in increasing the cost of living and generating social discontent, the causes of infant mortality, the mal-administration of the poor laws, the abuse of private and public charity, and, over and above all, the ignorance and barbarism of a large part of the population, to remove which there was no adequate provision of schools. (Smith 1923: 24).

The Statistical Society carried out a survey of the provision for elementary education in Manchester itself and other towns of Lancashire. But it was when Nassau Senior called Kay into the Poor Law Commission in 1835, and Chadwick directed him to report on pauper education in East Anglia, that his interests became concentrated on education. When in 1838 he reported on the training of pauper children, he put forward the recommendation, which Chadwick was then to take up, that unions of unions should be formed to maintain efficient schools. To the Select Committee on the Education of the Poorer Classes, in that year, he recommended that schools should everywhere be supported from the local rates, at least until parents were enlightened enough to pay fees. In 1839 he was appointed secretary of the newly formed Committee of the Privy Council on Education.

Through the ten arduous years that followed, Kay's zeal for education was sustained by two convictions. One was that the ultimate cause of the terrible ill-health of the poor was their ignorance. 'Was this degradation and suffering inevitable?' he asked; '. . . Might not this calamity be traced to its source and all the resources of a Christian nation [be] devoted, through whatever time, to the moral and physical regeneration of this wretched population?' (Kay-Shuttleworth 1964: 5). The other driving force was the fear of wild disorder. 'Government,' he wrote in his Manchester pamphlet,

unsupported by public opinion . . . can only retain its power by the hateful expedients of despotism. But ignorance . . . makes the people the victims of those ill-founded panics which convulse society, or reduces them to those tumults which disgrace the movements of a deluded population. . . . That good government may be stable, the people must be so instructed that they may love that *which they know to be right*. (Kay 1862; 61–2)

His years with the Privy Council saw government take the first hesitant but ultimately decisive steps towards the public provision of elementary education throughout England and Wales. He went abroad, to study the schools of the Low Countries, France, the Rhineland and Switzerland, with special reference to the training of teachers. At home, he helped to found and maintain a teachers' training college in London. In 1839 the first HMIs—school inspectors—were appointed. The pupil-teacher system, first tried in the workhouse schools, was extended widely. In 1846 the national government moved on from making grants of fixed amount to the voluntary societies maintaining schools, to accepting financial responsibility for all schools throughout England and Wales, albeit only so far as its grants were matched by voluntary contributions. When he retired, exhausted, he had earned the title of the founder of popular education south of the Border.

These three—Senior, Chadwick and Kay-Shuttleworth—illustrate the type of person and the type of thinking that laid the administrative foundations of the welfare state. They gave it a form that is not to be regarded as inevitable. If it is once decided that certain services shall be provided collectively, qualified staff will have to be appointed; but the question remains whether the functions of control and initiative shall lie with laypersons holding political office at the centre or in local government, or shall be vested in the staff themselves. Generally the answer will be, in some measure with all three, but that leaves room for variation in the allocation. In the formative years that we have been viewing, the decision was taken implicitly to rely most upon the national government and its civil servants, that is, to establish a centralized bureaucracy. This may not have done most in the long run for the life of the community; it did not draw on and develop the neighbourly initiative that has contributed so much to some American communities. But it was the quickest way of meeting the menacing need of the hour—when the population of London was doubling, and that of some northern cities much more than doubling, in the first four decades of the century. A model was found, studied and admired in the logical, unified and authoritarian system that Napoleon had given to France. The adoption of some such measures in Great Britain was facilitated by the technical advances of the time. The railways, and with them the telegraph, made the island smaller. Administration from the centre became possible as never before. Campaigns for social betterment that had once been practicable only here and there, locally, could now be conducted throughout the country. The machinery for a measure of redistribution, and the understanding of its purpose, which had obtained only parish by parish under the old poor law, could now be created on the national scale. But only by degrees—the tradition of local autonomy was too powerful. To the reformers dedicated to stemming a rising flood of ignorance and disease, local resistance seemed merely obstructive.

This was the more so, because those reformers were not moved by benevolence. True, it was horror at the condition of the poor that stirred them to action in the first place; but they had no fellow feeling for creatures so lost to decency that they could not be their fellows. The only way to help them was to change them—to raise them in understanding, responsibility and self-respect. The improvements to be made in their housing or education were not packages of welfare to be handed out to them, but changes in their circumstances that would enable them to do better for themselves. They must submit, like children, to a regimen of improvement.

This was not alien to the Benthamite outlook. Its initial individualism rested on the assumption that individuals were well informed and well able to calculate their own advantage. Where that assumption did not hold, the enlightened must exercise a *tutelle*, as the French said—a guardianship. The further assumption that the reformers were themselves among the most enlightened was one to which we are all prone. But a glimpse of the possibilities of social engineering may go to the head of the social engineers. The *tutelle* may easily become authoritarian. The Benthamites held that each man was the best judge of his own happiness, but only when he was as enlightened as they were; until then, they would have to make him happier whether he liked it or not. It is not surprising that some of the leading Fabians, who maintained the tradition at the end of the century, were sympathetic to imperialism. The Benthamite ethic was calculated to inspire a dedicated colonial administration: it has been said of its exponents that 'their most spectacular successes were gained in British India' (Harvie

1984: 437). The justification of its application to the British people in 1830–50 was that so many of them then, in the manufacturing towns and the South Country villages, stood in desperate need of the help it could certainly give them; and they were not able to help themselves. In the matters of health, housing and education, moreover, the reformers were not forcing an alien culture on the working class: they were bringing relief from misery, in ways whose efficacy could not be doubted, and if the objects of their authoritarian benevolence did not welcome the means, they desperately needed the end. When compulsory vaccination came, many working people resisted it; but one and all wanted to be freed from the threat of disfigurement and death from smallpox. If those endowed with knowledge had not been armed with compulsory powers, how many families would have broken out of the cycle of disease, ignorance and squalor?

6.2. The Later Development of Administration

The impetus towards administration persisted after its breakthrough in the 1830s, and gathered strength as it went. By the 1880s it had laid the foundations of a welfare state. The work went on both locally and at the centre. The Justices of the Peace lost many of their functions; their place was taken and new tasks were performed by functional Boards. These acted under direction of the central government, and sometimes received grants from it. The towns, which had maintained their own forms of government outside the purview of the justices, received their own new form of government by the Municipal Reform Act of 1836, and obtained special powers by private Act. At the centre, there was a transition from the setting up of commissions *ad hoc* to the formation of new departments and the allocation of responsibility to a minister. Central government, which itself used to have little to administer outside the armed forces, was now in the business of management. That business came to comprise not only poor relief but health, housing and education.

These developments were promoted not so much by any vision of future well-being as by the continuing rapid growth of population, and the even more rapid growth of the towns. The most crusted adherent of the good old ways, or the most indoctrinated believer in *laissez faire*, could not stop his ears to 'the crying need of the times'. Those who had been slow to hear were shaken into awareness by appalling visitations of cholera. This new malady, killing quickly but horribly, the more alarming because the means of transmission were long mysterious, struck first in 1831, and returned in epidemics of 1848–9 and 1866. Although it raged the most violently where housing was worst, it was no respector of persons: householders in the substantial streets could no longer ignore the slums around the corner.

'One visible Blessing', wrote Dorothy Wordsworth on 1 December 1831, 'seems already to be coming upon us through the alarm of the Cholera. Every rich man is now obliged to look into the miserable bye-lanes and corners inhabited by the poor, and many crying abuses are even in our little town of Ambleside about to be remedied' (Morley 1927: 225; Bruce 1968: 64). But cholera only made the problems created by the growth of population more conspicuous as it aggravated them.

The traditional method of administration outside the towns was that Parliament laid requirements on the justices, but how far they met them in practice lay within the wide limits of their discretion. They might do less than the law required, as in the first provision for inspection of factories, or more, as when they subsidized wages in the villages. Their responsibility for relief was now transferred to the Boards of Guardians, elected locally, but like the justices subject to direction from the centre, and—what is more—to inspection. Inspectors appeared too for the enforcement of the factory laws, and for education. Such changes were not made without much local resistance. The substantial proprietors in each locality had long been accustomed to a wide autonomy, which they held justified by their interest in and personal knowledge of their neighbours. In two matters they retained it in great measure. Schools continued to be provided only by voluntary associations or local subscription, until the many remaining gaps were filled by the Act of 1870, which provided for the setting up of schools, chargeable to the rates and administered by locally elected Boards. But even here, a central control was exerted early on, for the grants to the voluntary associations, begun in 1833 and growing in size, had to be monitored. The other subject of effective resistance was the police force—to use an anachronism, for the village constables and the town watch of early years had no common authority. When the local police were organized, and came to receive grants from the centre, then here as in schooling the government set and monitored standards of efficiency. But attempts to extend Peel's new London model to the whole country came to nothing. Only for prisons could responsibility be remitted to the Home Secretary. In policing, as in education, an unstable and contentious balance between central and local finance and control has persisted down to our own day. Centralization made for the enforcement of standards, and for ensuring that each district made its due contribution to meeting a national need; it also brought the national taxpayer to the help of the local ratepayer. But it brought a remote authority into what the freeborn Englishman had been proud to hold as a no-go area: it was regarded as a Napoleonic or Prussian device, out of place in a free country.

Centralization was needed to stir up the local administrators, to set aims before them and require them to observe rules. In the new system, which began to provide grants to local agencies from the national Exchequer, centralization was also needed to monitor expenditure. It was called for, further, to secure uniformity in the name of justice. A Whig committee of 1835 concluded that the needed uniformity of treatment in prisons everywhere 'was possible only under a system of state inspection and the enforcement of regulations by a central authority' (Woodward 1962: 469). Direction from above also suited the temperament and outlook of the reformers. They thought they knew best, and with reason; for they knew more than most about 'the condition of England question' in local detail and in the statistical aggregate. Driven by a strong sense of responsibility for meeting the often appalling needs that they uncovered, they were naturally authoritarian; it was as though they were already taking up 'the white man's burden' at home. They were businesslike, moreover; if the Reform Act of 1832 brought no 'bourgeois revolution' in Parliament, the Whigs did give the businesslike impulse its head. Once set up, the system tended to grow—not on principle, or through bureaucratic empire-building, but pragmatically. Getting to grips with one problem not only revealed its own extent more fully, but opened up another: poverty led to health, and that in turn to housing and education. The railway network, promoting the growth and efficiency of the system pervasively from the mid-century onwards, removed the remoteness and comparative isolation of the regions, to make centralization possible as never before.

It came about in any case only by stages. The initial Benthamite stage of inquiry, often by royal commission, would reveal the nature and extent of a problem, and by doing so would often indicate lines of action. The Registrar-General's office was set up in 1837, and before long statistics of local mortality rates began to display objectively the appalling state of sanitation, housing and health in the poorer parts of the towns. By 1848 it was possible for an Act of Parliament to require local Boards of Health to be set up in districts whose death rate exceeded 23 per 1,000. If inquiry indicated the need for stimulus and regulation by the centre, and Parliament agreed, some limited powers were delegated to a body—the Poor Law Commissioners, or the Educational Committee of the Privy Council. But as business increases, the government became involved more directly. The powers of the Poor Law Commissioners, transferred to a Poor Law Board in 1847, were taken over in 1871 by the Local Government Board under a Minister. There had been no Board of Education because too many of the Lords would have opposed such a further invasion of the jurisdiction of squire and parson; but in 1856 the committee that had been set up was superseded by a Department of Education, again under a Minister. The functions of the Board of Health set up in 1848 were assigned, some years later, to several departments. In all, fourteen new departments were formed between 1833 and 1854 (Roberts 1979: 206).

The very idea of a civil servant was fixed at this time. In 1853 a royal commission, led significantly by a distinguished Indian civilian, Sir Charles Trevelyan, recommended that the higher grades of the home civil service should be filled through an examination covering the field of studies of university graduates. The examination was at first only for qualification, not selection; but before long it was made competitive, and in 1870 it was opened to all applicants. Whitehall itself became more businesslike. The Committee on Public Accounts was set up in 1861 to monitor departmental expenditure, and an Act of 1866 provided for the audit of all use of public money, centrally and locally. Control by the centre was also made effective by the work of inspectors of various types—inspectors of factories, schools, police, railways, weights and measures; while locally the sanitary inspectors, school attendance officers and the like brought the care of government down to the street and the household.

The new local agencies, working under central control and initiating improvements, were even more conspicuous in the towns than in the former jurisdictions of the justices. Already in the eighteenth century some towns had transcended the limited powers of their traditional government by obtaining private Acts of Parliament to set up Improvement Commissions. After civic government elected by the ratepayers had been established in 1836, the more vigorous municipalities continued to obtain statutory powers to improve housing and sanitation, to take over or instal water and gas supply and generally to abate nuisances and provide amenities. These changes were later to be hailed as 'municipal socialism'. In so far as they did not pay for themselves, they required the ratepayers to pay for improvements of which they felt some benefit themselves, but which were even more helpful to their poorer neighbours. Conspicuous among the constructive municipal leaders was Joseph Chamberlain in Birmingham. His achievement, and stock of ideas, present the contemporary tendency towards redistribution in high relief.

Chamberlain became Mayor of Birmingham in 1874, twenty years after he had come there from his father's cordwaining (shoemaking) business in the City of London. As a boy in the City, he had been steeped in Unitarianism with its social conscience, and had taught in a school for the children of the slums near his home. His own schooling had begun in a Quaker dame school; he went on to University College School, which had been founded by the philosophic radicals, and whose headmaster was a former professor of mathematics in the University of Virginia who had sympathized warmly with the cause of reform in the years down to Chamberlain's entry to the school in 1850. In Birmingham Chamberlain devoted himself for many years to the screw manufacture of his relative, Nettlefold; he worked long hours with unflagging energy, imagination and initiative, and advanced the firm's fortunes greatly. But the agitation for reform of the franchise that arose in 1866 stirred the sense of responsibility he had already shown for the condition of his own workpeople, to improve that of the teeming city around them and of their like throughout the land. He entered politics, first locally and then nationally. The men given the vote in 1867 must be educated: he threw himself into a campaign for the advancement of state education. This was to be universal, compulsory, unsectarian and free. In 1869, at the age of thirty-three, he was elected a Councillor; five years later he became Mayor.

In the two and a half years in which he held the mayoral office, Chamberlain drove through a programme that provided a signal demonstration of the potentialities of municipal socialism. In carrying the ratepayers with him, he was powerfully assisted by a group of gifted and influential Nonconformist ministers. His work was founded on the conviction that the two great causes of misery and crime were the lack of education and the lack of decent housing, and he saw and proved that much of the remedy lay in the hands of civic administration. 'I believe', he said, soon after he became Mayor,

we hardly ever find misery or poverty without finding that intemperance is one of the factors in such conditions. But at the same time I believe intemperance itself is only an effect produced by causes that lie deeper still. I should say these causes, in the first place, are the gross ignorance of the masses; and, in the second place, the horrible, shameful homes in which many of the poor are forced to live. (Boyd 1914; 43–4)

Ignorance Chamberlain would tackle through the national campaign for education that he launched; housing, through statutory powers granted to the town council. He obtained private Acts empowering the council to take over the two gas companies, and to acquire the water supply by compulsory purchase. But for slum clearance, his opportunity came when the Home Secretary and the President of the newly created Local Government Board were drafting the Bill that became the Artisans' Dwelling Act of 1875. It was an opportunity he seized with 'sagacious audacity'. In interviews with the two Ministers, he persuaded them to insert a provision by which local authorities could submit to the Local Government Board plans for the development of sites after slum clearance. He submitted his plan accordingly, and when it was approved obtained a third private Act. There followed the purchase and complete clearance of forty closely packed acres of property in the centre of the city, the laying out of a broad avenue and the erection of new buildings throughout by the purchasers of seventy-five-year ground leases.

His aim in all this was the aim of Chadwick and Kay-Shuttleworth: the removal of the menace of crime and contagious disease and of the degradation of humanity, by securing for all an education and a home, through which they would become self-reliant and self-respecting. There was no intent to redistribute income for the sake of greater equality: nor was the mood one predominantly of compassion and charity. Cholera and typhoid, and the threat of riot, gave those who would have to pay for the new measures a direct interest in them: they were not being asked to contribute to charity. 'I believe no better advertisement [? investment] could be made,' said Chamberlain in a speech already quoted,

than to pay parents to send their children to school instead of demanding a tax from them or charging them for doing it . . . I am told that the rates would go up. Suppose the rates do go up—for, of course, education must be paid for in one way or another. One friend of mine thinks it hard that I, your Mayor, should be called upon to pay for the education of the poor people who live in the Inkleys. I do not think it hard at all. I think it right and just that I should pay for what I demand in the interests of the whole community. I believe that I have a direct interest and gain a clear advantage from the education of every one of my fellow citizens. (Boyd 1914: 45)

In another sense, again, Chamberlain's municipal socialism was not egalitarian. It could improve the lot of all, because it gave power to good managers, and enabled them to administer the affairs of the community on a plan of their rational devising. When Chamberlain laid down municipal office, on becoming President of the Board of Trade, he compared his achievements in Birmingham with those of the empire-builders. In the light of his later career, his choice of comparison was ironical. But that it arose in his mind as it did is significant: municipal socialism and colonial administration had much in common. 'I look with greater satisfaction', he said,

to our annexation of the gas and water, to our scientific frontier in the improvement area, than I do to the results of that Imperial policy which has given us Cyprus and the Transvaal; and I am prouder of having been engaged with you in warring against ignorance and disease and crime in Birmingham, than if I had been the author of the Zulu war, or had instigated the invasion of Afghanistan. (Boyd 1914: 77)

The new administration had its egalitarian potential and effect, but redistribution was its means and not its end. Its socialism was an aspect of efficient urban management. That it arose to tackle the problems of the rapidly growing towns is a statement that gains significance when we consider what it excludes. Municipal socialism was not created in opposition to capitalism, or to industrialism as such; it left the social structure alone, and it did not apply where industry was growing up in the countryside. It responded not to the factory system but to the cholera epidemic, not to the exploitation of the workers but to their ignorance, not to the contrast of riches and poverty but to the menace of disorder. Egalitarianism was to emerge later; but meanwhile, this type of socialism was more akin to a businesslike form of household management in the cities.

That said, it must be added that Chamberlain's municipal socialism also sprang from the humanitarian belief that it was the slums that made their denizens bad, and not bad people who made the slums. There was no difference in human nature dividing the respectable middle classes from the drunk and disorderly. This was one strand of egalitarianism coming down from Locke and Robert Owen: the child, like a photographic negative, receives the imprint of the images to which it is exposed. When Chamberlain presented his Improvement Scheme to the city council, he appealed to the Councillors to put themselves in the slum-dwellers' place. 'We bring up a population', he said,

in the dark, dreary, filthy courts, and alleys . . . we surround them with noxious influences of every kind, and place them under conditions in which the observance of even ordinary decency is impossible; and what is the result? . . . Their fault! Yes, it is legally their fault, and when they steal we send them to gaol and when they commit murder we hang them. But if the members of the Council had been placed under similar conditions—if from infancy we had grown up in the same way—does any one of us believe that he should have run no risk of the gaol or the hangman? . . . It is no more the fault of these people that they are vicious or intemperate than it is their fault that they are stunted, deformed, debilitated and diseased. (Garvin 1932: 195–6)

Chamberlain's expressed willingness to pay higher rates in order to maintain free schools for his poorer neighbours' children was an outspoken form of a more general if tacit acceptance of the need to finance the country's growing equipment for social betterment in ways that involved redistribution. In one way, as we have seen, redistribution had long been accepted. The poor law had laid the relief of the poor on their more substantial neighbours, and as the population continued to increase the charge grew, even after the reform of 1834: in the county of Sussex, it seems, in the 1840s 'the landlords and farmers . . . did pay out for the care of the poor roughly 10 per cent of the assessed value of their property' (Roberts 1979: 124). But the willingness of taxpayers to pay for social benefits was to be gradually tested more widely. At the same time the question was opened whether the well-to-do should not contribute in greater proportion than their less prosperous neighbours. This edging towards redistribution by fiscal means was possible only because of the contemporary expansion of national resources as a whole, which we shall now examine.

6.3. The Expansion of Resources

The pressure of ever-growing population, which had long made all attempts to relieve the poor seem futile or mischievous, by the mid-century was relaxed. The expansion of economic activity and the national product had been so powerful as to exceed the still rapid growth of numbers, and to make possible a great rise in the real pay of the working population. No longer need kind-hearted people be warned that their impulses would only increase the number of children who took their seats at nature's board only to find that there was no cover laid for them.

It may seem strange to claim this advance as achieved by 1850. The 'hungry forties' have borne a bad name. The depression of 1841-2 was the deepest of the three cyclical troughs experienced since the postwar contraction. Ireland was stricken by a famine, the deaths from which, together with the ensuing emigration, were to reduce its population by nearly a third in twenty years. In England there was a run of bad harvests. That Chartism subsided so completely after 1848 has been attributed to the contrasting leap forward of the economy in the next two decades. But although it is true that those were years of rapid economic progress, they marked no contrast with the twenty years before. When in the third chapter of his *History of England* Macaulay had surveyed all the ways in which the condition of the country and the welfare of its people had been improved, even transformed, since 1685, he went on to reflect that

we, too, shall in our time, be outstripped, and in our turn be envied. It may well be, in the twentieth century, that the peasant of Dorsetshire may think himself miserably paid with twenty shillings a week; that the carpenter at Greenwich may receive ten shillings a day; that labouring men may be as little used to dine without meat as they now are to eat rye bread; that sanitary police and medical discoveries may have added several more years to the average length of human life; that numerous comforts and luxuries which are now unknown, or confined to a few, may be within the reach of every diligent and thrifty working man. (Macaulay 1848; I, iii)

Macaulay's expectations were only a projection, and a cautious one at that, of the progress he had seen in his own lifetime. The wages he foresaw, say, sixty years ahead were about double those being paid at the time of his writing; and we know now that real wages and salaries had about doubled in the thirty years down to that time (Lindert and Williamson 1983, Table 5). In the villages, it is true, the pressure of population remained severe. Where cultivable land is an indispensable factor of production, more jobs are hard to find beyond a certain point; if more children are growing up than suffice to fill the places vacated by their elders, they must take themselves off to the towns, where the factor giving and limiting employment is not land but capital, which can be increased indefinitely. In much of the North of England there were industrial towns within reach, and we have seen how they grew; not so in the South, save for London. In Lindert and Williamson's estimates, the real wages of farm labourers rose over the same thirty years by only a third. The North is fairly sampled in this series (Lindert and Williamson 1983: 6, n. 17); probably wages rose more there, and less in the South, than the series indicates for the country as a whole. But even in the overcrowded South real wages did rise somewhat; and in the country as a whole, they rose even through the years of southern rick-burning. Away from the villages, moreover, the advance of industry, the accumulation of capital embodying new techniques, perhaps most of all the cheapening of transport by the new railways, raised the productivity of the labour so much that real wages and salaries could double although the population had become half as great again.

Awareness of this—not of the statistics, but of the change visible all round—must have removed that dread of stimulating the growth of population which had once worked so strongly even on benevolent minds. It removed another barrier at the same time, the sense that remedial measures were more than the country could afford. The public purse was longer now. Taxable capacity, nationally and locally, had risen, and was expected to go on rising.

When Peel brought the income tax back in 1842, his immediate aims were to extinguish the deficit that had persisted through the previous five years, and to find revenue to take the place of duties on commodities. He genuinely hoped—indeed, as Gladstone did in his turn—that a tax that was first resorted to in wartime and was now activated again to cover the rehabilitation of outmoded finances might be put back into reserve when that job had been done. But once the national course had been set towards free trade, and national expenditure continued to mount, the income tax remained indispensable as a main source of revenue, and a flexible one. To influential opinion, it seemed the least objectionable form of the necessary evil of taxation.

That it was much more than this—that, potentially, it was a powerful engine of redistribution—was hardly thought of at the time. In one sense, it is true, it did effect a substantial redistribution by the very fact that its introduction made possible a reduction of duties, chief among which, before long, was the duty on imported corn. This brought a transfer of income from the protected interests, especially the landlords, to the consumers of the product concerned, the labourer's loaf most of all. But it was not in the outlook of the times to see the aim as a reduction of inequality.

What discussion there was of equality concerned the sacrifice borne by the taxpayer and not the income he was left with after tax. The principle that all taxpayers should bear an equal sacrifice was taken to imply that income tax should be proportionate to taxable income at all levels. This was qualified by recognition that a tax which cut into 'the necessaries of subsistence' would impose a heavy sacrifice indeed; therefore the smallest incomes, less than say £150 per annum, should not be taxed at all. But all above that should contribute the same proportion of their income. At the end of the century, Edgeworth (1925; ii, 103) was to show that proportional taxation would impose equal sacrifices only if Bernouilli's belief was warranted, that the utility yielded by income declined in inverse proportion to the increase of income; thus, a tax of 5 per cent would impose equal sacrifices on persons with taxable incomes of £500 and £1,000 if a doubling of income brought a halving of the marginal utility of money: the £50 of tax paid out of the income of £1,000 would, if retained, have brought utility at half the rate per £ applicable to the £25 paid out of the income of £500. But there is reason to believe that the marginal utility of income falls off more rapidly than that. This had long been recongnized. Archdeacon Paley had put the case with his usual good plain sense:

The point to be regarded is not what men *have* , but what they can *spare*; and it is evident that a man who possesses £1000 a year can more easily give up £100 than a man with £100 can part with £10; that is, those habits of life which are reasonable and innocent, and upon the ability to continue which the formation of families depends, will be much less affected by the one deduction than by the other. (Paley 1785: Bk. V, xi, 26)

Bentham had made the same point in his chapter on 'Propositions of Pathology upon which the Advantage of Equality is Founded' in his *Principles of the Civil Code* (Bowring 1843; 305).

On this view, it followed that to impose equal sacrifices the rate of tax must rise more than in proportion to taxable income: there must be graduation. The principle, moreover, was known to have been applied in the Netherlands and Austria, and, in a way, in France during the Revolution—here, a 'tax on income and property' was levied at 5 per cent throughout on income assessed as a multiple of house rent, but this multiple rose with rent, from 2 to $12\frac{1}{2}$. This was copied in an American federal tax of 1798, but here it was the selling value of the house that was assessed, and the rate of tax that was varied (Seligman 1908; 29). There were British radicals in 1842 who advocated graduation, but the French and American examples may have been deterrent. In any case, there were objections to graduation on principle. John Stuart Mill was deterred from accepting it by the difficulty of ascertaining the degree of utility that their incomes yielded to different people; he could not be as sure as Paley. It seems likely also that Mill's approval of proportionate taxation was reinforced by his belief that it would minimize the loss of utility in the aggregate of taxpayers, and so meet the basic utilitarian criterion:

As a government ought to make no distinction of persons or classes in the strength of their claims on it, whatever sacrifices it requires from them should be made to bear as nearly as possible with the same pressure upon all, which, it must be observed, is the mode by which least sacrifice is occasioned on the whole. If any one bears less than his fair share of the burthen, some other person must suffer more than his share, and the alleviation to the one is not, *ceteris paribus*, so great a good to him, as the increased pressure upon the other is an evil. (Mill 1848; V, ii, 2)

This is mistaken. To minimize the total sacrifice imposed by the raising of a certain sum, we must tax away the £s that can be most easily spared. We must begin by taxing the biggest income until what remains is no greater than the next income in order of size. We must then take equal amounts from those two incomes until they are no bigger than the third in order of size; and so on, until the required sum has been obtained. A large number of incomes after tax will have been equalized, by taking much more from those persons whose incomes before tax were biggest to start with. Some incomes may remain untaxed altogether. There is no question of equality of sacrifice.

But this argument from least total sacrifice was only a reinforcement of the principle of proportionate taxation, which needed support, because it could hardly be held to bring equality of sacrifice. Paley's case for graduation was a matter of common sense. Here, for example, is Gladstone's disciple Robert Lowe examining a witness before the Parliamentary Committee on the income tax in 1861:

Do you think that the sacrifice of a washerwoman, upon her pound of tea, if 1 *s.* a pound duty is imposed upon it, is the same sacrifice as the case of a millionaire when a pound of tea is consumed by him?

Do you think . . . that a shilling taken from a poor man is no greater sacrifice than a shilling taken from a rich man? (in Shehab 1953: 152)

Why, then, did the proportionate principle prevail for so long? The answer is partly that every citizen with an income above the subsistence level was thought obliged to share the cost of common services. 'For what reason ought equality to be the rule in matters of taxation?' John Stuart Mill asked (1848; V, ii, 2): 'For the reason that it ought to be so in all affairs of government.' But there were also reasons against progressive taxation, that is, against graduation. One was the absence of all objective justification for one scale rather than another. 'Whether the person with 10 000*l.* a year cares less for 1000*l.* than the person with only 1000*l.* a year cares for 100*l.*, and if so, how much less, does not appear to me capable of being decided with the degrees of certainty on which a legislator or a financier ought to act'—thus John Stuart Mill again, making his reason clear in the third edition of his *Principles* (V, ii, 3). Gladstone was to express the same misgiving when in 1889 a Conservative Chancellor led the way into graduation by an extra 1 per cent duty on estates over £10 000: he saw 'no injustice in the principle', but what rule was there by which 'that gradation is to be kept within bounds'? (*Parl. Papers*, 335, 2 May 1889, 1001). Once admit that the relative contributions of different taxpayers might be fixed by the fiat of a parliamentary majority, and what was there to prevent graduation from running away into outright confiscation? In the early days of the discussion, the economist McCulloch had opposed graduation 'not only because of its redistributional effects, which would subvert the order of society, but because it would also lead, if carried to its logical conclusion, to total confiscation' (Shehab 1953; 89). The Chairman of the Committee of 1861 called graduation 'an approach to socialism'.

There was the further objection that 'to tax the larger incomes at a higher percentage than the smaller is to lay a tax on industry and economy (Mill 1848; V, ii, 2).

These considerations were widely accepted, especially the last. The only form of graduation that was acceptable was the complete exemption from tax of incomes at or below a reasonable level of subsistence, together with some abatement of the rate at which tax was levied on incomes not far above that level. Peel exempted incomes of not more than £150 altogether, but an income of just £1 more than that paid tax on all £151. Gladstone in 1853 substituted a tax-free deduction of £100 from incomes of all sizes, with a lower rate on income between £100 and £150. This was as far as public opinion expressed in Parliament was willing to go before the 1880s. The matter could in any case hardly be one of urgency, when income tax was so light. In 1853 Gladstone planned its disappearance in seven years. It did in fact come down to a low point of 2 $d.$ in the pound, or well under 1 per cent, in 1874/5. After that it rose again, but it can never have presented itself to contemporaries as an instrument of social change; nor were Chancellors as yet drawn into graduation as the most practicable way of raising much needed additional revenue.

There were radicals, however, at home and abroad, who did advocate the use of graduation for the sake of greater equality of income and wealth as an end in itself. This did not agree with the prevailing view that existing inequality arose for the most part from differences in the ability, industry and thrift of those concerned. But that view was qualified by a distinction between 'producers' and 'non-producers': big incomes seemed less defensible when they were simply drawn from financial assets. This was felt especially when property was acquired by inheritance. The beneficiary could not claim that the legacy was the reward of effort and abstinence, least of all when what was transmitted was land that had been accumulated by no one but was the gift of nature. Whatever form it took, property passing at death could be taxed without such a deterrent to work and saving as high marginal rates of income tax might be expected to impose. For these reasons, it was recognized that the objections to graduation of income tax did not apply to estate duties. These were to be the postern gate through which, from 1889 onwards, graduation crept in.

Meanwhile, one measure was being canvassed that did raise the issue of equity between large and small incomes. This was discrimination between earned and unearned incomes—to use a more recent shorthand: at that time the terms in use were 'precarious' and 'permanent'. or 'transitory' and 'realized'. It was generally recognized that a lawyer earning £1000 a year was not as well off as a rentier with £1000 in interest; the lawyer's earnings would cease with his working life, and while they continued he must put savings aside to provide for his own old age and for his dependents after his death. As much as a third of professional earnings were believed to be commonly absorbed in this way. These savings were taxed twice: tax was levied first on the income out of which they were made, and then on the interest they earned. The rentier's income, on the other hand, would continue through his own old age, and after his death would still be available to his dependents. It seemed fair, therefore, to tax earned incomes at a lower rate, or at the least to allow contributions to life insurance and terminable annuities as a deductible expense. The issue here was not really about the appropriate rate of tax, but about the proper definition of income, or the basis of taxation—whether the equitable basis was not income but expenditure. In the course of the discussion, however, another issue of equity arose. If differentiation took the form of a lower rate for earned income, then there would be cases in plenty of wealthy businessmen paying that lower rate while small rentiers and landlords with very modest incomes had to pay a higher rate. If this was found anomalous, as it was, the implication was that the rate of tax should vary with the size of income—at least, should not vary inversely. Lowe's questions quoted above were put to a witness who advocated differentiation. The case for it was regarded as made out. Disraeli's abortive budget would have provided different rates of tax of income assessed under different schedules. Gladstone provided exemption for contributions to life assurances and deferred annuities, up to one-sixth of income. But to satisfy one requirement of equity was to raise another. Since differentiation between transitory and permanent incomes sometimes involved higher tax rates for small than large incomes, it kept the case for graduation before the public.

The growth of taxable capacity was a necessary condition for the growing willingness to consider measures of redistributive effect, but that willingness would not have grown as it did had not prevailing views of society come to foster it. We shall now consider the ways in which the sense of community was deepened.

6.4. A new view of society

The growth of social administration was promoted by a change in attitudes towards society. There was a growing sense of social responsibility. The obligation, long accepted, to relieve the indigent broadened into a sense of neighbourly or civic duty to improve the lot of the poor. The extension was promoted by a fuller knowledge and appreciation of how hard that lot could be, and by the increased possibility of alleviating it by measures more effective than charity. With these things went a deepening of sympathy: the differences of condition between the ranks of society were taken less for granted; the poor appeared less as a different order of being, and more as disadvantaged members of the same human family. The natural obligation to help family and friends in need extended with the enlargement of the perceived bonds of kindred and affinity.

There came about also some shift in the object as well as in the scope of responsibility. As what was in common between the different social orders loomed larger, society appeared increasingly as a single whole, and then as an entity, a being with an existence over and above that of the people it contained at any one time. By application of the biological habit of thought, it appeared also as an evolving organism. Its progress and improvement appeared as something more than a means to benefit its individual members. This conception of it might take the form of nationalism, or a mystique of 'the race', but in practice it served as vehicle for a principle of altruism: it regarded the relations between persons not only as a matter of free exchanges between self-interested individuals, but also as requiring each person to contribute to others without reckoning how much he or she received from them. It might be said that people owed this to to the family or the society of which they were members. Certainly, the extension of altruism from a radius of close proximity in family or parish to more remote beneficiaries was promoted by the sense that all concerned, as members of one body, owed a duty to it.

One powerful influence on the formation of these attitudes was the growth of the towns. Where once the ways of life of the British people, and their perception of neighbourhood and community, had been predominantly rural, now they became urban. By 1851 half the population of England and Wales had come to live in towns; by 1901 the proportion was to pass three-quarters. The problems of habitation and health that urbanization created far exceeded the capacity of the old methods of local administration: they could be dealt with only by new measures that must perforce be paid for by the ratepayer and taxpayer, that is, predominantly by people who were better off than the beneficiaries. The obligation of the ratepayer to relieve the destitute was extended to cover provision for housing, health, schooling and amenities. Urban necessities enforced some transfer of resources from higher to lower incomes; principle then followed upon practice. It became accepted that, at least within a certain range, people might reasonably be called upon to bear the cost of measures that, primarily and directly, would benefit only their poorer fellow citizens. The reduction of inequality was not in itself the aim, but it was the outcome of urban betterment, and it was capable of extension on the national scale.

The growth of the towns was associated with that of the middle class. Its members brought their businesslike or academic habits of mind to bear on the state of the people. Their awareness was fed by a fount of activity—in dispensaries, hospitals, Sunday schools and night schools where reading was taught, and in the initiatives of local government. This combination of information and responsibility was found especially in the expanding professions. Their members combined an investigative habit of mind with some detachment from the dominant economic interests within the present system: they were relatively free to envisage change, and qualified to devise and administer it in practical form. 'The essential fact', Woodward observed,

lay in the control of technical knowledge by the professional members of the middle class; there was no longer any need of aristocratic direction and, unless they joined the professional classes, the upper class had little or nothing to contribute to the management of the common affairs of a highly organised society .
. . . The problems of society, reflected as always in literary and artistic movements, were problems more familiar to the professional than to the upper class. (Woodward 1962: 622-3)

The British Association for the Advancement of Science, founded in 1831, soon 'found itself discussing the state of education in Bolton, Manchester, Liverpool and York; the housing and domestic condition of six cotton towns and Bristol; wages in Nottingham during the depression; the causes, progress and cost of the Preston strike; the relation between literacy and crime; the extent of juvenile delinquency' (Young 1962: 28-9).

In the literary movement of the times lay another source of greater awareness of 'how the other half lived', and of responsibility towards all members of the one social body. A wide gap appeared between the comedy and romance of the British novelists down to the death of Scott in 1832, and the social concern of the novelists of the 1840s and 1850s—Dickens, Disraeli, Mrs Gaskell, Kingsley. To show what conditions other people are living under, and to do this so vividly that the audience is moved to help as if those unhappy people were members of their own family, has been a function of television in our own day, and Kingsley and Dickens were the television of theirs. Their message was, 'put yourself in his place'. This was explicit in Kingsley:

> When packed in one reeking chamber,
> Man, maid, mother and little ones lay;
> When the rain pattered in on the rotting bride-bed
> And the walls let in the day;
>
> We quarrelled like brutes, and who wonders?
> What self-respect could we keep,
> Worse housed than your hacks and your pointers,
> Worse fed than your hogs and your sheep?
>
> Our daughters with base-born babies
> Have wandered away in their shame;
> If your misses had slept, squire, where they did,
> Your misses might do the same.
>
> Kingsley, 1848: ch. XI

Dickens depicted the scene so unsparingly that he did not need to draw the political moral explicitly, though this he did in his Postscript to *Our Mutual Friend* (1864–5):

That my view of the Poor Law may not be mistaken or misrepresented, I will state it. I believe there has been in England, since the days of the Stuarts, no law so often openly violated, no law habitually so ill-supervised. In the majority of the shameful cases of disease and death from destitution, that shock the Public and disgrace the country, the illegality is quite equal to the inhumanity—and known language could say no more of this lawlessness.

This literature of social concern marked not only the coming of a new type of author, but the rise of a new type of reader. Dr Thomas Arnold in 1832 had found it

an enormous evil . . . that the rich and poor in England have each what is almost a distinct language; the language of the rich, which is of course that of books also, being so full of French words derived from their Norman ancestors, while that of the poor still retains the pure Saxon character inherited from their Saxon forefathers. (Arnold 832: 2)

The new reading class, and the newspapers, journals and novels they read, helped to bridge this gap. The information the readers acquired was to be combined with the value they set on the rational ordering of affairs to renew egalitarianism in the form of benevolent administration.

While social ties had been extended in these ways, the hold on people's minds of the notion of society itself had been strengthened from another quarter. Lyell published his *Principles of Geology* in 1830–3, and his *Geological Evidences of the Antiquity of Man* in 1863. Darwin's *Origin of Species* appeared in 1859 and his *Descent of Man* in 1871. These works were foremost in the advance of science that radically changed people's understanding of their own status in the universe. It was a second Copernican revolution. By that first revolution, people who had thought of themselves as made by God in His image, and placed by Him in the centre of the universe, came to see themselves as travellers on one planet among others, circling a sun that itself was only one of a myriad such. Now, the geologists and biologists reduced mankind again, this time to the ranks of the animal kingdom. The negative effect, in dispelling belief in a Creator and traversing the argument from design, for many people was shattering. But except for those who closed their minds to this new view of mankind and its place in nature, it brought with it a new view also of society. In particular, it instilled a new conception of change, and of society as the vehicle of evolution.

It was the achievement of Lyell and Darwin to provide accounts of how the ordinary laws of nature could be made to yield sufficient causes of even the greatest changes, given a sufficient time scale. They freed the 'historical' natural sciences from finalism and providentialism as physics and chemistry had been freed in the seventeenth century. The similarity to evolutionary social theory is obvious. (Burrow 1966: 111)

Instead of change being seen as like the alteration of a building, it was understood as a process of growth, or of decay; and the changing society itself was regarded as an organism, developing according to the laws of its own nature and the constraints or stimuli of its environment.

But the theory of evolution also inspired a faith that the course of change was for the better. The notion of progress gained a fresh hold. If, as the popular notion ran, men were descended from monkeys, what they had actually done was evidently to *ascend*. Evolution provided not only an account of how change came about, but reason to believe that change was guided towards the survival of ever more complex organisms—'higher forms of life'. This misunderstanding of natural selection was promoted by the ambiguity of the English world 'fit'. In common usage, to be fit is to be healthy, strong, capable of vigorous exertion. In 'the survival of the fittest', to be fit is only to be well adapted to a particular environment: fat people may be the fittest to survive an Arctic winter, thin people to escape a predator. But the confusion was ineradicable. People got it into their heads that evolution created types that were ever more admirable when judged by current standards of excellence—types of society as well as of men and women. There was a presumption in favour of change, at least of the kind of change that 'progressive' people desired.

Nor was it necessary to have any clear view of the goal towards which society was moving. The realization of the vast changes that had come about already was thrilling. From the primeval slime there had evolved higher and ever higher forms of life; there was no halt to a process inherent in all nature. As a pupil-teacher, Ramsay MacDonald had studied geology, and when he came to his first post in the South he wrote an account of the geology of the region of Bristol (Marquand 1977; 12, 17). We can understand that his vision of socialism was of a far better society to be attained by posterity; how exactly it would evolve, and just what form it would take, he had no need to think out.

In the popular acceptance of Darwinism, two opposite views followed about the way in which progress was made, and two oposite inferences were drawn for policy. On the one hand, it appeared that there was a struggle for survival between individuals: those who survived were the stronger, the cleverer. This process, making for the transmission and enhancement of desirable characteristics, should be helped on by policy that favoured the reproduction of the strong and clever, and checked that of the weak and stupid. This Social Darwinism, as it was called, offended humanitarian feelings. It rested in any case on a very imperfect understanding of Darwin's essential hypothesis of selection by adaptation to a changing environment. The alternative view came nearer to Darwin, although it still endowed a mindless, normless process with propensity to improve. It considered not the struggle for survival, but the modification of species, even the emergence of new species, by successive adaptations. It was the species that advanced or became differentiated in various parts of the world. 'Race' or 'society' were alternatives to 'species' in that context: the sub-title of *The Origin of Species* was 'The Preservation of Favoured Races'. The focus of attention became *Homo sapiens*, not the individual member of the species; or, we might say, the individual was seen again as 'a social animal'. Even though it was in the better lives of individuals that progress would be realized, the vehicle of progress was, in the terms of later years, the gene pool.

This view of the advance of society took a powerful effect on political thought: instead of thinking of society as a human artefact that, implicitly or historically, had been created, people saw it as an organism that had evolved. Those who desired to change it took heart, for they thought they had reason to believe that change was for the better. The term 'progressive' came to denote the believers. There was a ready link with the Whig or meliorist view of history. But there was a possible affinity too with a conservative tradition, coming down from Burke, with his view of a society as a partnership between the past, the present and posterity, and from Coleridge—a tradition in which society was regarded as an organism, whose members were parts of one body, dependent on it for their own life, and finding their purpose in the role and function assigned to them in it.

Social evolution combined this tradition with the new ideas of biology, and with the desire of the Positivists for a science of society. Hitherto, Comte taught, thought about society had proceeded on theological or metaphysical assumptions; the origins of society had been ascribed to divine institution, or its proper constitution had been derived from natural law. What was needed now was knowledge of society, based like all scientific knowledge on patient observation, and made up of 'propositions about the regular connection between phenomena . . . propositions that can be tested' (Fletcher 1966: 10). What is presently significant here is that the object of study is not the individual but society itself; and under the influence of Condorcet, Comte saw society as evolving through successive stages. Because he held that only a limited number of first-class minds were fit to be charged with the responsibility of forming social policy, he was far from egalitarian; but his followers in practice were concerned with devising or fostering institutions that would help the less advantaged. The assumption that society was an organism subject to physiological laws, the understanding of which would enable us to improve its functioning, attracted men and women who were drawn to reform in an age of scientific ascendancy. The approach created the object: in the faith that social phenomena could be studied as animal bodies are, the student arranged the facts in a conceptual system appropriate to an organism, and the system was then treated as an entity with its own capacity for experience and development.

We find this outcome in the two prophets of the new Liberalism. J. A. Hobson, says Freeden (1978; 111), 'envisaged a society which, by its concerted action, encouraged and engendered the development of individual capabilities. But society did not exist for this purpose, as some old liberals would have maintained. Society encouraged individual development because society itself was the beneficiary.' L. T. Hobhouse justified the advance towards equality through a raising of the condition of the working class as an improvement of the community as a whole. 'The true aim of social progress', he wrote in 1899, 'is not so much to make one class richer, as to purify and brighten the life of the whole community by seizing on the best conceptions of social order that are afloat within it and translating them into political or economic institutions' (quoted by Freeden 1978: 127).

In these ways, Darwinsm deepened social awareness, and the concern of each for all; but there was also one way in which, as time went on, it was to work against egalitarianism. By emphasizing the genetic transmission of characteristics, it brought out the irreducibility of personal differences, and the unlikelihood of reaching equality of condition between persons differently constituted from the moment of conception. We have seen how little this was realized in the eighteenth century. An effort of the imagination is required today to recover the frame of mind to which it came as a new, still questionable, idea. Although the great change that selective breeding could make in livestock was becoming apparent as the eighteenth century wore on, humanity still stood far above the beasts of the field, and the inference for human heredity was not taken. That very word, 'heredity', used to have only legal usage: the first genetic use of it is recorded in 1863. But as humanity was brought into the animal kingdom, and the degree of each person's dependence on genetic makeup came to be appreciated more widely, the potentialities of egalitarianism were narrowed, as were those of improved environment and education for the poorly equipped families.

6.5. Marx and Equality

Although Marx was working in London during most of the years that this chapter covers, his thought took little effect on those around him—indeed was not known at all to most of them. But it falls to be noticed here as it grew in those years, out of his study of earlier thinkers and his observation of the circumstances of the time. We are concerned with his views on egalitarianism.

Equality was no ideal for Marx. As a theorist of social evolution, he saw attachment to equality as part of the system of rights corresponding to the capitalist phase of the relations of production: as that phase gave way to a succeeding order, equality would be transcended by self-fulfilment. Meanwhile, as a romantic in the school of Rousseau, he condemned the hard and narrow bourgeois outlook, which set so much store by the acquisition of property that the sight of others with more than oneself became painful.

It was this atrophy of the human personality through the cult of property that Marx stressed first. In his early writings he stigmatizes property as disruptive of personality, because it is the objectivization of selfishness and exclusiveness. So long as property continues to be seen in that way, communal property is as bad as private.

He attacks 'crude communism', which would establish 'general private property' as opposed to individual:

By systematically denying the personality of man, this communism is merely the consistent expression of private property which is just this negation. Universal envy setting itself up as a power is the concealed form of greed which merely asserts itself and satisfies itself in another way. The thoughts of every private property owner as such are at least turned against those richer than they as an envious desire to level down. This envious desire is precisely the essence of competition. Crude communism is only the completion of the envy and levelling down to a pre-conceived minimum. (McLellan 1977: 88)

Here the desire for equality is represented as a negative and stultifying drive, connected with the love of possessions, with envy, greed and pride. In *Private Property and Communism*, Marx held that the mere equalization of wealth would only 'universalize greed and materialism'. 'Since it completely negates the *personality* of man, this type of communism is only the logical expression of private property, which is just this negation' (quoted here from Lakoff 1964: 231). Marx was following in the footsteps of the Christian moralists. We have seen (pp. 47, 81) how possessiveness and greed were condemned by John Colet and More, and by Bossuet; and we have heard Rousseau cry out against 'these frightful words *thine* and *mine*'. Human nature was openhearted and generous until property corrupted it. But, whereas Colet thought that 'a good and unsophisticated nature . . . would have a community in all things', Marx held that to make property a communal possession was no remedy—it would only generalize possessiveness. If there was equality when property was so held, it was equality in the self-impoverishment of acquisitiveness.

Much later, on a more practical political level, Marx expressed his objection to a policy that came near to asserting the right to the whole produce of labour, that claimed at least 'a fair distribution of the produce of labour'. This was in his *Critique of the Gotha Programme*, of 1875. He considers here 'a communist society . . . just as it emerges from capitalist society: which is thus in every respect, economically, morally, and intellectually, still stamped with the birthmarks of the old society from whose womb it emerges'. Here the worker 'receives a certificate from society that he has furnished such and such an amount of labour (after deducting his labour for the common funds), and with this certificate he draws from the social stock of means of consumption as much as costs the same amount of labour'. In this system, Marx points out, there is equal right, but no substantial equality. 'Equal right here is still in principle—bourgeois right.' One man is stronger or abler than another, 'and labour to serve as a measure, must be defined by its duration or intensity, otherwise it ceases to be a standard of measurement': so one man will receive more than another. The rule of equality 'tacitly recognises unequal individual endowment and thus productive capacity as natural privileges'. Further, since men have different family responsibilities and other needs, even equal returns would make some better off than others. 'But these defects are inevitable in the first phase of communist society as it is when it has just emerged after prolonged birth pangs from capitalist society. Right can never be higher than the economic structure of society and its cultural development conditioned thereby' (McLellan 1977; 568, 569). For practical purposes, although property incomes will be extinguished in the emrgent socialist state, earned incomes will retain the range of differences that they held in capitalist society.

In the Marxian prospect there was no place for equality save in a visionary and romantic future state of bliss, where indeed it takes on a very different significance. In the *Critique of the Gotha Programme* Marx moved on into fantasy, into a realm where scarcity would be unknown, and where there would be no more question of equality in the distribution of material produce than there need be now in the distribution of the air we breathe. Mankind would 'leap from necessity to freedom'.

In a higher phase of communist society, after the enslaving subordination of the individual to the division of labour, and therewith also the antithesis between mental and physical labour, has vanished; after labour has become not only a means of life but life's prime want; after the productive forces have also increased with the all-round development of the individual, and all the springs of co-operative wealth flow more abundantly—only then can the narrow horizon of bourgeois right be crossed in its entirety and society inscribe on its banners: from each according to his ability, to each according to his needs! (McLellan 1977: 569)

This is a world of heavenly plentitude, in which the productive powers so far surpass anything as yet conceived of, that everybody can be what he likes when he likes and there will still be plenty for all. This was a vision retained from Marx's early writings. In *The German Ideology* (*c.* 1845), he had envisaged a

communist society, where nobody has one exclusive sphere of activity but each can become accomplished in any branch he wishes, society regulates the general production and thus makes it possible for me to do one thing today and another tomorrow, to hunt in the morning, fish in the afternoon, rear cattle in the evening, criticize after dinner, just as I have a mind, without ever becoming hunter, fisherman, cowherd, or critic. (McLellan 1977: 169)

Here Marx at the age of twenty-seven appears as a humanitarian. His basic objection to capitalism is that of Shelley—it denies mankind self-realization. The aim of change is not to make people equal, but to set their spirits free to realize their humanity.

7

The Formation of Modern Egalitarianism

Helen Lynd began her study of *England in the Eighteen-Eighties* with a quotation from Winston Churchill's life of his father (1906: I, 268–9):

It was the end of an epoch. The long dominion of the middle classes, which had begun in 1832, had come to its close and with it the almost equal reign of Liberalism. The great victories had been won. All sorts of lumbering tyrannies had been toppled over. Authority was everywhere broken. Slaves were free. Conscience was free. Trade was free. But hunger and squalor and cold were also free and the people demanded something more than liberty . . . How to fill the void was the riddle that split the Liberal party. (in Lynd 1945: 3)

Today we may draw back from that view of the ending of 'the long dominion of the middle classes' in years during which landowners continued to predominate in both Houses of Parliament and in the Cabinet. But the rhetoric of the passage lights up the distinctive character of the 1880s. Principles that had served to guide reform, and to adapt the institutions of the country in some measure to its evergrowing population and its new ways of life, were now proving unequal to the challenge of social disorders that had been worsened by a depression of unprecedented length and severity, and thrown into prominence by the increased political weight of the working man who suffered from them most. These were the years of the crucible. New political alignments were being propelled by ideas which, although long present in some people's minds, impinged on the present times with a force drawn from their applicability to increasingly insistent problems. Thereby they tempered or displaced the prevailing orthodoxy, and a new cast of liberal countenance took shape. In one form or another it was to dominate social policy for most of the next ninety years. These were to be years of application rather than origination. They were to add something to the content of egalitarianism, and to see changes that greatly affected its acceptance; but the lineaments of egalitarianism down to 1970 were apparent already in the pressures on social policy that rose in the 1880s, and the ideas that were shaped or propagated then.

7.1. Changes in the Setting

When the great boom after the Franco-Prussian war broke in 1873, a depression set in of exceptional initial severity and, as it proved, exceptional duration. The trough was not reached until 1879, when unemployment among skilled men in the heavy industries was over 15 per cent. The shock to opinion was very great, the more so because arable farming suffered a catastrophic fall in prices at the same time, and in the 1880s the prices of livestock followed. The sense of depression was to persist until the 1890s. There were in fact two rounds of the trade cycle, bringing good times as well as bad, through those years; and, for those who kept their jobs in the towns, a falling cost of living mediated a substantial rise in real wages. But at the time, it seemed to many that the whole prospects of the country had changed for the worse. After a Royal Commission on Trade Depression in 1885–6 came one on Agricultural Depression in 1894–7. The principles in which the progress of earlier years had inspired so much confidence were called in question. When free enterprise and free trade were found to be consistent with falling profit and high unemployment, the minds of many people entertained new possibilities.

There was fresh thinking about what government could and should do. The current change of prospects was made the more threatening by awareness of the advances that Germany and the United States were making under protection: intervention by government in the market could not be dismissed as merely wasteful, restrictive or invidious. Unemployment, once seen as the problem of relief for the able-bodied pauper, now asserted itself as a problem of maladjustment of the market mechanism.

A distinction was made formerly between intervention to protect the weak and unfortunate, and interference with the pursuit of their own interests by competent adults; but it was hard now to draw the line between relief subject to tasks in the labour yard, providing jobs in relief works, and varying the volume of public works so as to offset fluctuations in private activity. The presumption against intervention, if not reversed, was greatly weakened. Suggestions of what government might do to put it right could not be dismissed on the ground that they conflicted with a harmonious natural order. They could be discussed on their merits, and they might be put aside in consequence, but no longer could they be rejected *a priori*. Evidently, moreover, the principle that government could act in pursuance of social values, even when that meant intervening in the market, could be extended to aims other than the reduction of unemployment. Those who wanted to use forms of government to reduce inequality, whether by helping the poor or taxing the rich, would now encounter less resistance.

The depression of agriculture affected attitudes towards inequality more directly, because it revived the old animosity against the big landholders, the idle recipients of unearned riches. So long as agricultural improvements and good prices went together, the tenant farmer could afford to pay a higher rent and still do increasingly well for himself; but when prices collapsed, the charge levied on access to the gifts of nature appeared unwarranted. The landlords did give abatements, sometimes large ones, but tenants in the arable counties were still throwing their leases up in large numbers. Bad weather followed bad prices.

Two years after that disastrous year 1879, an extraordinarily influential work reached Great Britain from the United States. Henry George's *Progress and Poverty* traced the persistence of poverty despite economic growth to the absorption of the fruits of growth by the rising rents of increasingly scarce land. His remedy was to take this unearned surplus value out of private appropriation into the service of the community, by raising the whole public revenue from a single tax on land:

The simple yet sovereign remedy which will raise wages, increase the earnings of capital, extirpate pauperism, abolish poverty, give remunerative employment to whoever wishes it, afford free scope to human powers, lesson crime, elevate morals, and taste, and intelligence, purify government and carry civilization to yet nobler heights, is—*to appropriate rent by taxation*. (George 1880: VIII, ii)

The power of ideas depends on the time of their introduction; no one gets a better hearing than the speaker who voices the thoughts already forming all around. When Henry George toured Great Britain in person in the early 1880s, his message from the platform aroused a warm response among thoughtful working men, and gave some of his hearers their induction to socialism. The lack of all statistical proportion in his diagnosis and prescription did not deter those whom recent troubles had caused to reflect on the anomaly of such great incomes being drawn by so few people merely because their ancestors had appropriated what should be a common heritage. That appropriation was effected originally, as the Levellers held under the Commonwealth, simply by force of arms; in later years lesser men had been deprived of their rights by the transformation of customary tenure, and enclosure of the commons. Thereby a persistent sense of deprivation in a recently and unwillingly urbanized people was stimulated. It was to this that Joseph Chamberlain had appealed by his doctrine of ransom. In a working men's demonstration at Birmingham in 1885, he declared that in the beginnings 'of our social system . . . every man was born into the world with natural rights, with a right to share in the great inheritance of the community, with a right to a part in the land of his birth'. But now 'private ownership has taken the place of these communal rights, and it has become so much a part of the social fabric that it can hardly be reversed. But then I ask what ransom will property pay for the security which it enjoys?' (Garvin 1932: 549)

At a dinner two years before, Beatrice Webb had found herself with 'a Whig Peer on one side of me—Joseph Chamberlain on the other. Whig Peer talked of his own possessions; Chamberlain passionately of getting hold of other people's—*for the masses* (1926: 123). He would do it by fiscal means—by the graduated taxation of income, new death duties and the taxation of unearned increment. This was the crux. Chamberlain did not propose that his own fortune should be distributed to the masses, and this in all good faith; for had he not acquired it, himself created it, by hard work and enterprise? But when the searchlight that agricultural depression turned upon the landowners lit up unearned income, it called attention to all income from property, industrial and financial capital as well as land. There was a special and traditional case for a more equal distribution of land; it could not be stimulated as it was now without imparting an impulse to egalitarianism at large.

There was another way in which Henry George stimulated egalitarianism, so far as it was directed against the private ownership of capital. His thought had been formed by the experience of the settling of the American West. He saw that if the state had retained ownership of the land, instead of putting it up for grabs, no one person could have grown rich by the accretion of site value, or drawn rents from land he did not work; instead, a great revenue would have accrued to the public exchequer, to be used for the benefit of all the people. This established a presumption in favour of the public ownership of the means of production. It appeared that the way in which income was distributed between persons was not determined by the impersonal working of the market, but depended on what action the state took. The idea floated by the later John Stuart Mill, that although production was governed by immutable natural laws, the processes of distribution were malleable, was given wider currency, at least in the practical form—that rent could be taxed heavily, even to the point of confiscation, without loss of output. The economists, moreover, were now broadening the notion of rent, to cover all payments to factors of production over and above what was necessary to secure the participation of each particular unit: so that there were elements of rent in the returns to labour and capital as well as land. These elements were thought to make up a large part of the highest incomes, which were vulnerable to taxation accordingly.

7.2. The Growing Awareness of Social Need

Willingness to redistribute income in order to relieve hardships was heightened by increased knowledge of how harrowing those hardships were. This knowledge was in great part the product of the scientific habit of mind, and the application to social affairs of the detailed, patient and objective investigation that it inculcated. In the disillusionment brought later by the First World War, it was hard, Beatrice Webb wrote, 'to understand the naive belief of the most original and vigorous minds of the 'seventies and 'eighties that it was by science, and science alone, that all human misery would be ultimately swept away' (1926: 130). The belief may have been naive, but it inspired thoroughgoing studies like those of Beatrice herself, when she selected 'the chronic destitution of whole sections of the people, whether illustrated by overcrowded homes, by the demoralised casual labour at the docks, or by the low wages, long hours and insanitary conditions of the sweated industries, as the first subject for enquiry' (p. 149). There were other investigators in the same field, notably Charles Booth in East London, and Seebohm Rowntree in York. The same work of fact-gathering on social conditions was performed by the royal commissions in which the 1880s and 1890s abounded. These surveys transcended the reportage that could be dismissed as impressionistic or dramatized: with painstaking objectivity and statistical measurement, they demonstrated the breadth of the contrast between the conditions of the middle and the working classes. The narrow and harsh circumstances of the working classes, moreover, were seen to constrict the lives of all except the skilled tradesmen; they harassed the sober and industrious equally with the demoralized. A special problem of a minority of unemployables was isolated, but no longer could it be believed that poverty was due largely to the defects of character of the poor. It was seen instead as arising in various ways out of existing institutions and the functioning, or malfunctioning, of the economy. The very act of compiling the statistical record implied the approach of the scientist rather than the moralist: it proceeded on the assumption that phenomena arose from causes within the same material realm, and could be controlled by changing objective conditions. At the same time, the record was a guide to action. In particular, it showed how the difficulty of making ends meet impinged at different phases of life—when there was a young family to clothe and feed, in old age and in spells of sickness or unemployment. The remedy lay in family or child allowances and in social insurance.

The compilation of statistics also laid the distribution of the national income on the public conscience in a new form. This flow of information was used to show 'the Progress of the Nation', but it was becoming available at a time when pride in achievement and confidence in the inherent primacy of the British had been hit hard. It appeared that the great rise of the national product had left more than half the population in straitened circumstances, and a third in poverty without the means that, on the most austere reckoning, were needed for a physically and socially healthy existence. The contrast of riches and poverty that had long been denounced rhetorically was now defined statistically. The question was raised, whether the standard of living of working people was held down not, as used to be believed, by the inability of production to meet the needs of a growing population, but by a faulty distribution of the product. In 1885 an Industrial Remuneration Conference was convened under the auspices of numerous public figures to consider the questions, 'Is the present system or manner whereby the products of industry are distributed between the various persons and classes of the community satisfactory? Or, if not, are there any means by which that system could be improved?' The conference found no clear answers, but its questions would not go away.

They were kept before Parliament and the middle class by the increased ability of wage-earners to make their voices heard. The extensions of the franchise in 1867 and 1884 were bound to affect social policy powerfully. 'Today,' said Joseph Chamberlain in January 1885,

Parliament is elected by three millions of electors, of whom, perhaps, one-third are of the working classes. Next year a new House will come to Westminster elected by five millions of men, of whom three-fifths belong to the labouring population. It is a revolution which has been peacefully and silently accomplished. The centre of power has been shifted, and the old order is giving place to the new . . . (Boyd 1914: 131)

It was not that the working men who now got the vote, in town and country, felt a common interest in promoting their own policy. Some retained traditional and deferential attitudes, and those who did not were more likely to choose between the prospects held out by the two existing parties than to originate a drive of their own. But the very fact that they were free to choose was bound to take its effect on the candidates already in the field. There were too many constituencies in which the wage-earners' vote could decide the result. In the preface to the 1872 edition of his *English Constitution*, Walter Bagehot wrote:

'In plain English, what I fear is that both our political parties will bid for the support of the working man; that both of them will promise to do as he likes if he will only tell them what it is; that as he now holds the casting vote in our affairs, both parties will beg and pray him to give that vote to them. (Bagehot 1872:)

'It seems to me', Sidney Webb told the Royal Commission on Labour in 1892,

that if you allow the tramway conductor a vote he will not for ever be satisfied with exercising that vote over such matters as the appointment of the Ambassador to Paris, or even the position of the franchise. He will realize that the forces which keep him at work for sixteen hours a day for 3 s. a day are not the forces of hostile kings, or nobles, or priests; but whatever forces they are, he will, it seems to me, seek so far as possible to control them by his vote. (Royal Commission on Labour, Minutes of Evidence, 17 November 1892, Q. 3935)

But few working men were moved by any thoroughgoing intent to recast the economy. What trade unionists wanted was expressed by the Parliamentary Committee of the Trades Union Congress. The Congress itself had been gathered first in 1868, when trade unionism was threatened with legal constriction if not repression. In the event, Parliament gave the unions a legal status by which, it was believed at the time, they would be free to perform their functions, including the peaceable conduct of disputes, without constraint. That this was effected by legislation, first under Gladstone and then under Disraeli, is a mark of the influence that the extension of the franchise in 1867 had conferred on the urban artisan. What he wanted was put to government when the Parliamentary Committee represented to Ministers the demands adopted by the Trades Union Congress. These were for the extension to all workers of the kind of benefit and protection that many of them had already secured through friendly societies. The trade unions themselves had grown out of the natural tendency of brethren of the craft to meet together sociably and to keep a purse from which help could be given to members in trouble, be it through loss of tools, sickness, unemployment or old age. The same mutual insurance, except against unemployment, was provided for a wider membership by the friendly societies, like the Oddfellows, the Foresters and the Hearts of Oak, which extended on a national scale; a Registrar had been set over them in 1846, and a royal commission was appointed to examine them in the 1870s. There was a growth also of collecting societies, in which local agents called each week to collect a premium at the door; and of industrial insurance—the Prudential was founded in 1848 (Bruce 1968: 112). The benefits thus provided identified the needs that pressed hardest on working people. At the national level the leaders of the trade unions were concerned mostly with issues arising at the place of work—safety legislation, limitation of hours, minimum wages and control of sweating, employers' liability, old-age pensions and the reform of the poor law, which meant relief of the unemployed without the stigma of pauperism. Themselves often models of self-help, the leaders sought to protect their members within a social and industrial structure that they accepted much as did their employers. In the 1890s socialism gained ground among trade unionists, but most of them continued to keep their politics apart from the issues that concerned them in their working lives.

The measures they called for, however, did make for redistribution. In so far as those measures required increased public expenditure, the trade unionists would have taken it for granted that it must be covered by direct taxation, not by a higher duty on the working man's beer. The ideas of Henry George and the taxation of land values were well received by thoughtful working men. Both political parties were being nudged towards the welfare state, whose main function was to provide for everyone the benefits, mostly by insurance, that the craft unions were already providing for their own members.

The representatives of the Trades Union Congress were reinforced by new manifestations of resentment, unity and bargaining power. In 1886 London saw the first great demonstration since the Chartists gathered in 1848. This time it was the unemployed who gathered in Trafalgar Square; as they marched off along Pall Mall they responded to mockery by breaking the windows of the Carlton Club. Three years later the London dockers revealed a disciplined unity, under leaders from their own ranks, of which unskilled workers had been thought incapable; in a dispute about pay they held out for six weeks, gained much public support and won their 'tanner'. Not only the dockers, but all manner of unskilled workeres were now swept—at least for a time—into militant unionism.

This was only one part of a wave of unionization that rose at this time in several countries of western Europe. Whether it came about by force of example and contagion of ideas, or by the operation of some common cause, we do not know. But it marked a basic change in the forces converging on governments. The impact on the British government was manifest in 1893, when the Miners' Federation, resisting a cut, was able to stop enough pits to threaten to halt the daily life of the country, in the workshops and the home, as winter drew on; and for the first time, a government found itself forced to intervene in an industrial dispute, and obtain a settlement, largely in the men's favour. In 1897 the engineers engaged in a struggle to maintain custom and practice against new machines and methods imposed by management—a struggle that proved to be the most extensive and protracted that the country had yet seen. Meanwhile, the miners in some fields were showing that, policies apart, what they required first and foremost of the Member they sent to Parliament was that he should be one of themselves. In this preference lay a basic reason for the rise of a separate Labour Party. But that rise apart, no government after the formation of the TUC and the extension of the franchise in principle to manhood suffrage could neglect the existence of a labour movement, and the pressure it exerted towards measures that involved redistribution.

We shall now see how the effect of increased awareness of the conditions of the lives of wage-earners, and their own increased ability to exert political pressure, was heightened by contemporary changes of outlook on social questions. These changes affected particularly the middle-class sense of duty, the relation of the individual to society and the justification of unearned incomes.

7.3. Changes of Outlook

The vastly lengthened perspective of the time span of the natural world, and the displacement of man from the lordship of creation to cousinship with the apes, which had been brought home by Lyell and Darwin, affected thought about mankind increasingly as the years went by. In a letter of 1887, the historian Lord Acton wrote that 'unbelief in the shape of doubt is yielding to unbelief in the shape of certain conviction' (Himmelfarb 1952: 164). 'The impregnable rock of Holy Scripture' was shattered, and active minds could no longer accept dogma that few of their predecessors had questioned. But if revealed religion had lost its hold on people's minds, it kept it on their conscience. 'The revolt of 1885 to 1910,' John Galsworthy wrote, 'turned on a passionate or ironic perception of inequalities, injustices, call them what you will, on the emergence of the introspective social conscience, and the sympathies and compassion which belong thereto' (Galsworthy 1923: xii–xiii). Yet it was not so much that a social conscience emerged as that the sense of guilt inculcated by evangelicalism for one's own sinfulness became aroused by the thought of one's own comfort in the presence of want and misery. In place of redemption by the sacrifice of the Cross, people sought relief in a self-sacrificing devotion to social service. Faith in a better ordered society took the place of trust in the promise of religion. Beatrice Webb (1926: 154), asking why 'a generation reared amid rapidly rising riches and disciplined in the school of philsophic radicalism and orthodox political economy' was demanding state intervention, found the answer in

a new consciousness of sin among men of intellect and men of property . . . a collective or class consciousness; a growing uneasiness, amounting to conviction, that the industrial organisation, which had yielded rent, interest and profits on a stupendous scale, had failed to provide a decent livelihood and tolerable conditions for a majority of the inhabitants of Great Britain . . . This class-consciousness of sin was usually accompanied by devoted personal service, sometimes by open confession and a deliberate dedication of means and strength to the reorganisation of society on a more equalitarian basis. (Webb 1926: 154–7)

It was to this guilt-laden movement of thought, this substitution of a religion of politics for the religion of salvation, that Beatrice Webb attributed the fact, so shocking to the upholders of the old order, that 'each successive administration, whether Whig or Tory, indeed every new session of Parliament, led to further state regulation of private enterprise, to fresh developments of central and municipal administration, and, worst of all, to the steadily increasing taxation of the rich for the benefit of the poor'. For

it was neither in Parliament nor in the Cabinet that the battle of the empirical Socialists with the philosophic Radicals was fought and won. Though the slow but continuous retreat of the individual forces was signalised by annual increments of Socialistic legislation and administration, the controversy was carried out in periodicals, pamphlets, books, and in the evidence and reports of Royal Commissions and Government committees of enquiry. (Webb 1926: 158–9)

Beatrice Webb could have defended her view of the power of published fact and argument out of her own and her husband's achievement of propaganda and persuasion. But instead of people's actions being directed by their acceptance of a social philosophy, they may arrive at their philosophy as a rationalization of actions to which they are moved in any case. Those who propounded collectivism as the means to a less unequal society were moved by their awareness of the hardships around them and the record of what intervention had achieved already for social betterment. That awareness was not merely a matter of information. It sprang from a moral sensitivity, a nagging consciousness that one does not deserve the good things of life that have come one's way, a need to expiate one's privileges by acts of self-denial and altruism. The profession of egalitarianism, it is true, may be only an opiate. It is always open to those who deplore inequality to reduce it as far as they themselves are able, by giving away most of what they have to those who need it more, and themselves subsisting in Franciscan poverty. Few egalitarians have done this. It is easier to live as comfortably as the rest of the monied world, while easing one's conscience by a wholehearted advocacy of a more just society, and an outspoken contempt for reactionaries. But evangelicalism went deeper than this. It drove its adherents hard. The Puritan, evangelical and Nonconformist tradition was one of self-control, self-sacrifice and duty—'stern daughter of the voice of God'. The sins that should have been washed away in the experience of conversion continued to gnaw the conscience, and could be expiated only by good works. It is remarkable how many of the devoted Fabians had been brought up in evangelical homes (Mackenzie and Mackenzie 1977: 16–17, 46, 57–9). Affection had not been easy to come by there: they had learnt that they must seek approval by making great efforts to be good. They had been taught that they must serve God, and they went on to serve society.

In a number of ways, society itself came to be seen as an object of policy distinct from the aggregated interests of the individuals it comprised. Once the human species had been brought within the purview of biology, it became an object of study as such. The method of study created its object; when the concepts of evolution were applied to mankind 'species' became 'society', which continued to evolve as its individual members came and went. The positivism of Auguste Comte had prescribed an objective study of human affairs that would look for cause and effect, and not assess arrangements as good or bad, or seek to establish the moral basis of authority. This exerted a powerful influence in Great Britain in the 1840s and 1850s. Its mental discipline and its religion of humanity relieved the anxiety caused by the crumbling of settled faith. Sociology and social anthropology took their rise at that time; in the quarter-century after 1850 they 'began to establish themselves . . . as recognizable or at least partially recognised disciplines', and in the 1860s 'a systematic, well-documented social anthropology was born' (Burrow 1966: 80). This approach did more than rediscover man as a social animal: it envisaged society as an organism whose structure was subject to natural selection, and would grow, or decay, like the body of an animal. Understanding of the organism, like medical knowledge, would enable the professional expert to make it healthier.

The organic conception of society brought a changed view of the obligation of the individual. On the one hand, the sense of common membership laid on each person the responsibility for mutual support attaching to members of a family. On the other, individuals were relieved of responsibility to the extent that they were seen to have been made what they were by society and not by themselves. Much of what was being urged to help the needy was an extension to a wider society, be it the municipality or the whole nation, of the obligations commonly felt and fulfilled within the family. Old-age pensions were seen not as organized charity, the fruit of benevolence, but as the entitlement of the old folk resting by the family hearth among children they had brought up. The knowledge that children were coming to school too hungry to learn moved the taxpayer to provide meals for them as he would if they were his own. These family ties had formerly been extended in some measure through the parish; they had been swamped by the growth of population and its migration into the towns, but there they found a new application. The heightened sense of social solidarity that has been noticed in the later years of the nineteenth century marks the advance of a principle of community to take the place of a lost order. The term 'collectivism', which came into use in the 1880s, stood for the assumption of some responsibility by all for each. But this extension of family ties implied that those who received help, especially the children, were dependent, and that their growth, morally as well as physically, was shaped, as Robert Owen had said, not by but for them. Drunkenness was traced to bad housing; the criminal was seen as the victim of society. The Oxford philosopher D. G. Ritchie, in a work significantly entitled *The Moral Function of the State* (1887), criticized those who distinguished the undeserving from the deserving poor, and would not help those who failed to help themselves; it was not those poor wretches who were responsible for their own plight, but society, which had tolerated the conditions that made moral cripples of them. The old objection to social benefits, that they would sap independence and discourage self-help, although it persisted, was disregarded by those who believed that the recipients of benefits could not be expected to look after themselves in any case. The aid they received would not weaken their characters but would improve the circumstances by which those characters were formed.

A strong influence on the movement towards collectivism in the 1880s was the economic achievement of the previous fifty years. This was widely recognized despite current discouragement. Consciousness of it worked on people's minds in more than one way. That the national product had been raised so much, yet the poor seemed more numerous than ever, indicated that poverty and squalor would not be banished by the forces of the market alone: the community must intervene. On the other hand, those forces of individual energy and enterprise had proved far more able to cope with the insistent pressure of mounting population than had once seemed possible; the greater part of a people whose numbers more than doubled in the sixty years after 1831 were now fed and clothed far better than they had been then. The fears that shortsighted benevolence would demoralize workers, and bureaucratic intervention shackle industry, were proved groundless. The need to assure a growing multitude of at least a subsistence, and to avoid the fate of Ireland, no longer took priority. It became possible to attend to ethical and aesthetic considerations. It was only through the achievement of the industrialism they criticized that Ruskin and Morris could find an audience; their teaching, that production should be so organized that the workers might realize and fulfil themselves in their work, appealed to those who themselves had some margin of means, some leisure. It called on them to realize, and reduce, the contrast between the amenities of their own lives and the lot of the labourer. By its standards of the good life, it threw a fresh light on the inequalities of society.

There were changes too in the prevailing outlook on matters of political economy. In several ways, the views of the economists became more favourable to measures of redistribution, even to the pursuit of greater equality for its own sake.

We have seen (pp. 195-9) how graduated taxation was found reasonable in principle but was distrusted in practice; in the absence of any means of deciding what rate of graduation was appropriate, there was no evident limit to it short of complete expropriation of all income above a certain level. All that we could be sure of, in the view of John Stuart Mill (1848: V, ii, 3), was that a tax that cuts into the essentials of subsistence 'in ever so small a degree' would cause more suffering than any that deprived the taxpayer only of luxuries. This judgement was accepted, and was applied through abatements, by which, for instance, Gladstone in 1865 exempted the first £100 of income altogether, and allowed £60 off the next £100. But the argument that, throughout the range of incomes, the loss of a given percentage of income imposed a smaller sacrifice the higher the income remained in circulation, as it was bound to do, when the only reason for not taking some action on an obvious disparity was that it could not be measured. The case for action, moreover, received support from another quarter: when people thought about high incomes, in the circumstances of the times they were most likely to think of the incomes of the landowners, and we have seen that there was a special case for taxing these; the rent of land was seen as a surplus that could be tapped without checking production, and the increment of land values enabled the owner to draw on the growth of the economy, to which he himself might have contributed nothing.

This moral vulnerability exposed high property incomes to discriminatory taxation—discriminatory in that they were unearned, and large. The Chancellor of the Exchequer's recurrent need for more revenue was deflected towards them by the objection to raising indirect taxes, that is, in practice, raising the prices of articles of popular consumption. This would have been objectionable to many people as plainly unfair—'let the broad back bear the burden', not the bowed backs of working men. In Ireland especially, indirect taxation currently bore a high ratio in the aggregate to direct, and laid too heavy a burden on the poor. Now that most working men had the vote, even politicians who had no compassionate scruples would have fought shy of alienating so many voters. A Conservative Chancellor, looking back in 1903, 'remembered years ago that the principle of taxation in this country was that direct taxation should only be half of indirect taxation, but as years had gone on that proportion had been reversed' (Emy 1973: 196). (There had in fact been no *reversal*, but direct taxation was beginning to draw level with indirect.) At the time to which the Chancellor looked back, a third of the national revenue came from duties on alcohol. It was coming to seem unjust to raise the cost of the worker's beer; it was certainly impracticable politically. The needed extra revenue must be found from direct taxation. Equity and expediency alike directed Chancellors towards graduation as well as raising the standard rate. It was a landmark when, in his Budget of 1894, Sir William Harcourt imposed an estate duty that was graduated from 1 to 8 per cent according to the size of the estate. But graduation of the income tax, although much discussed, continued to be regarded as impracticable, because two-thirds of it was deducted at the source, where only the standard rate could be applied.

Meanwhile, the development of what may now be called economic theory had greatly strengthened the case for graduation as an equitable form of taxation, and even for the deliberate reduction of inequalities of income. It seems strange now that the original utilitarians, whose theory rested upon the possibility of quantifying satisfaction, never developed a systematic treatment of the quantities. The political economists of the time remained entangled in a labour theory of value, which they were able to make acceptable only by importing the influence of demand into the measurement of the quantity of 'homogeneous socially necessary labour time' contained in the hour of any one person's work. It followed that discussion of the effects of economic policies concentrated upon production, not consumption. The concept of economic welfare remained to be discovered. The way to it was opened in Great Britain by Jevons and Marshall, who brought into the theory of value an analysis of demand based on marginal utility as a function of the quantity of an article consumed. Attention was now directed to the total utility that a person would derive from laying out his or her income, the arrangement of outlay that would maximize that utility and the dispositions of production that would enable consumers to get the most out of the available resources.

But the maximization of economic welfare was now seen to depend not on the allocation of resources alone, but also on the distribution of income. Instead of John Stuart Mill's black and white distinction between expenditure on essentials and on luxuries, successive units of expenditure were now envisaged, whatever they were spent on, as bringing in utility in a gradation that declined continuously as total expenditure grew. It followed, if all human beings were to be credited with much the same sensibility, that taking £1 from a person with £1000 a year would deprive him or her of less utility than would be gained by a person with £100, or indeed anything less than £1000 a year, to whom it might be transferred; and that to maximize the total utility derived by a group of persons from a given sum of income, it must be divided among them equally. Archdeacon Paley's plain man's observation was now given a theoretical development that strengthened and extended its claim on the policy-maker.

Of course, this was not the end of the argument: the old case against reducing the rewards of effort, skill and enterprise remained. But there were some radicals who went on to regard the use of taxation not merely as an evil necessary to provide revenue, but as a means of reducing the inequality of wealth and income. In this they went beyond those who had long approved taxation, implicitly of the better off, to pay for benefits for the poor. The target now was not poverty but inequality in itself: it would be found objectionable, as reducing the sum of welfare, even in a society where there were no poor. John Stuart Mill had said that 'the true idea of distributive justice . . . consists not in imitating but in redressing the inequalities and wrongs of nature'. Haldane said the same, in an article on 'The Liberal Creed' in 1888 (quoted here from Freeden 1978: 121): the state must be supplied 'with the means of in some measure modifying the advantages of fortune which one man gets over another, and the inequalities of fortune that must always arise from diversity of natural capacity'. The Cambridge philosopher Sidgwick, in his *Principles of Political Economy* (1883), also followed Mill in distinguishing the policies appropriate to production and distribution: for production, *laissez-faire* remained the general rule, but in distribution, interventior to reduce inequality was permissible so long as it did not impair self-help. Before long, the argument from economic analysis could be formulated academically without reserve. In his treatise on public finance published at Leipzig in 1890, Adolph Wagner declared that it was

wrong to conclude, as a general principle, that the distribution of income and property and the relative order of private income and property are sacrosanct and that taxation must not interfere with them. It is legitimate, nay essential, to establish a second criterion of taxation beside the purely financial one: a criterion of social welfare, by virtue of which taxation is not merely a means of raising revenue, but at the same time intervenes to improve the distribution of income and wealth resulting from free competition. (quoted here from Musgrave and Peacock 1967: 13–14)

Some went farther. Those who had broadened the attack on the unearned increment of land values to an attainder of all forms of private wealth found in taxation a means of taking property back into communal ownership without storming the chateaux. In his Fabian Essay on 'Property under Socialism' (1889), Graham Wallas declared that 'the progressive socialization of land and capital must proceed by direct transference of them to the community through taxation of rent and interest . . .' (Shaw 1920: 140). 'In this way,' the sociologist L. T. Hobhouse (1893: 78) remarked, 'we should make Rent and Interest pay for their own extinction.' Thus, the single tax led on, not so much to egalitarianism as to socialism.

From the early days of reform in Great Britain, the example of other countries had been a stimulus and support to the reformers. The country that was leading the world in mechanical invention was backward in the design of social structure. This was especially the case in education. We have seen (p. 185) how Kay-Shuttleworth, when appointed Secretary of the newly created Committee on Education of the Privy Council, travelled widely in Europe to study especially the training of schoolteachers; he was impressed by Pestalozzi's principles. The victory of the North in the American Civil War made a profound impression, ascribed as it was in part to the superior education of the Northerners, and it was followed shortly by a national campaign for popular education. The campaigners were fortified again by the victories of Prussia: 'the overthrow of Austria and the union of North Germany were as much the triumph of Prussia's schoolmasters as of their drillmasters' (Garvin 1932: 89). The technical college of Charlottenburg was used to demonstrate the deficiencies of the British system.

Foreign example was particularly instructive when it extended to the provision of benefits, which so many British people thought likely to do more harm than good. It is rarely possible to try out novel institutions on some test-bed, especially when they are necessarily wide in their application. All we can do is to envisage their operation and possible consequences. But these will always be various; it is hard to attach degrees of probability to them, and people who foresee insuperable difficulties always have a case. Institutions have to be set up first and proved practicable afterwards. A notable instance was to be social insurance. Its British advocates in 1910 could point to its having worked for nearly a quarter of a century without sapping the energies of the country's greatest naval and industrial rival. Between 1883 and 1889, Bismarck had introduced sickness insurance, workers' compensation for industrial injury, health insurance, and old-age pensions. At the same time, he proposed to the Reichstag that income tax be graduated according to the size of income, and differentiated according to its source. In December 1908 Winston

Churchill wrote to Asquith, 'The Minister who will apply to this country the successful experiments of Germany in social organisation may or may not be supported at the polls, but he will at least have left a memorial which time will not deface of his Administration' (Pelling 1968: 45); his aim, Churchill said, was to 'thrust a big slice of Bismarckian tissue over the whole underside of our industrial system' (Emy 1973: 177-8). In the summer of that same year, Lloyd George had visited Germany to study the working there of the kind of institution he had in mind for the United Kingdom. When the legal enforcement of minimum wages was contemplated, a leap in the dark as it seemed to many, and in a dangerous direction at that, an investigator sent out to Australia reported that the wage boards that fixed minimum rates in Victoria were 'greatly valued and widely believed in', and were regarded moreover as a natural extension of the Factory Acts (Aves 1908). Those who doubted the usefulness of labour exchanges could be confronted with their actual working in half a dozen European countries.

In all, the movement in Great Britain towards state intervention, with the measure of redistribution that this implied, was only part of an international movement from the 1880s onwards. The simultaneity of similar developments in a number of countries, most of whose inhabitants knew little of what was going on elsewhere, remains mysterious. But some influential people did have such knowledge, and were strengthened in their own purpose by the concurrence of the others.

The change of outlook that we have been considering contained little that was properly egalitarian. The changes in society that the rising Radicals wanted to see would, it is true, narrow the gap between rich and poor, but they would do this by improving the lot of the poor rather than by cutting the great incomes down. It was this improvement that constituted their end; as the means, they would impose graduated taxation. This they justified not only as the most accessible source of revenue, but as fairer than taxing the working man's purchases; but if they had not had to find more revenue somewhere, not many of them would have advocated it for the sake of cutting down the tallest poppies. There were reasons for laying imposts on the great landed estates, other than the size of the incomes they supported. The fiscal system should be equitable, but equal sacrifice was consistent with wide differences in incomes after tax. Fresh imposts on the rich should be linked with the particular benefits those taxes were required to pay for.

This general willingness to leave the large fortunes alone admitted of one conspicuous exception. In the eyes of a people only recently urbanized, the land was different from other forms of property. Here was a gift of nature in which all should share. Its appropriation by the few denied the majority their birthright. The great estates appeared particularly anomalous. The cries of 'Back to the land' and 'Three acres and a cow' made a powerful appeal. The growth of population had long made them delusory, but they stirred up folk memories, and revived a long tradition of resentment. The single tax, if pushed far enough, would have virtually transferred the ownership of land to the community; but what arrangements the community should then make for occupancy was far from clear. Chamberlain's Unauthorized Programme of 1885 went straight to that issue by giving government compulsory powers for the purchase of estates which it would then parcel out as smallholdings and allotments. We might think that this way of making property holdings more equal might well have been extended to industrial capital; but the device of limited liability was still too little adopted for the idea of a diffusion of shareholding to have any appeal. The division of a landed estate into a number of small tenancies could at least be envisaged, as the division of a family business could not be. So land remained distinguished as a target for egalitarians—paradoxically, for the notion of resettling city dwellers in a countryside of smallholders was chimerical.

In the various ways surveyed in this and the preceding sections, changes in thought and circumstance propitious to egalitarianism had come about by the 1880s. It remains for us to notice how these tendencies took shape in practice.

7.4. The Years of Application

In the sixty years after the end of the 1880s, the tenets of social policy that had gained prominence in that decade were applied in political practice. The changes of circumstance and the movements of thought that moulded radical opinion account for the constructive measures of British domestic policy, from Harcourt's graduation of the estate duty in 1894 to the consolidation of the welfare state in the 1950s. The timing of particular applications depended, it is true, on the contingencies of current affairs. There was an interval between the wars when changes were fewer. The importance attached to particular measures, and the extent of public acceptance or demand for them, was strongly influenced by the course of events, notably by two world wars, and the great depression of the 1930s. But little was added to the stock of ideas about social betterment that had been evolved by the 1880s: there were changes of emphasis, but not of principle.

The first great burst of application, from 1908 to 1914, laid down the lines on which further steps were taken down to 1950. This was in three fields.

First, there were outright transfers from the National Exchequer. The

issue of non-contributory old-age pensions, beginning with the first week of
the new year 1909, was a matter of much more significance than the relief
from dread of the poorhouse that it brought to many old people, great
though that was: a Rubicon of principle had been crossed in public policy.
When a system of national insurance against sickness and, in a limited
group of trades, against unemployment was set up in 1911, although it was
contributory, and intended to be self-financing, the Treasury added its 3 d.
to the 6 d. paid between them by workers and employers. A remission of
taxation may be considered under this same head—the allowance of £10 for
each child, in the assessment of incomes under £500, in Lloyd George's
budget of 1909.

Second, under the heading of insurance, a number of benefits such as
had been provided to their members by friendly societies and trade unions
were now provided nationally, made universal and compulsory within
certain limits and—as we have seen—subsidized by the Exchequer. The
contributory principle, which had to be given up if the immediate needs of
old-age pensioners were to be met, was retained here. It provided an
answer to those who feared 'bread and circuses', it upheld the self-respect
of claimants and it eased the load on the Exchequer. But another Rubicon
was crossed when insurance was made compulsory. It was this feature of
Bismarck's measures that had long prevented their adoption in the United
Kingdom. Now, as with the regulation of wages, that objection was
overridden, at least in application to a limited field of employment.

Third, at a time of rising expenditure in other respects, the costs of the
above measures required more revenue, and this was raised in ways that
increased the redistributive effect. In his first budget, in 1906, Asquith
noted that the high rate of income tax—it was 5 per cent—raised the
questions of differentiation and graduation. The next year he introduced
differentiation, by taxing earned income up to a certain limit at only three-
quarters of the standard rate, and allowing certain abatements to earned
income exclusively. Graduation followed, when Lloyd George in 1909
overcame the impossibility of deducting tax at the source at anything but
the standard rate, by imposing a super tax on the higher incomes, assessed
by personal declaration.

The effect was a substantial redistribution. The charge for benefits
accruing to those of lower incomes was met by heavier taxation of the
higher incomes. It was significant that Asquith made good the loss of
revenue through his concession to earned incomes, by raising the estate
duty and imposing an extra duty, a kind of super-tax, on the greatest
estates. Whereas in 1906 direct taxation had been raising no more revenue
than indirect, by 1914 it was yielding twice as much (Matthew 1973: 256).
The direction in which the new fiscal course was heading was brought out
by Colin Clark (1937: 147–8) when he estimated that 'in 1913 . . . the
working classes contributed more than the cost of the services from which

they were the direct beneficiaries, leaving a surplus contribution to general revenue. In 1925 working-class taxation contributed 85 per cent of the cost of these specified beneficial expenditures; in 1935, 79 per cent.'

The measures of 1908–14 were adopted because, for one thing, many Liberals had become convinced, in the ways we have discussed, that such provision for their poor or unfortunate neighbours was not only fair, but urgently called for. So far from being held back by the old fear of sapping self-help by the public provision of benefits, they saw in this provision the indispensable means to remove crying evils, and the way forward to a more just and healthy community. But had this outlook not prevailed, the politicians who had stood on the hustings in 1906 were aware of the expectations of a widened electorate. What people wanted was the relief and prevention of hardship. It was only fair that those who were comfortably off should at least help the workers to help themselves. But the possibility of a deliberate redistribution of income had not yet been envisaged at all widely. What was gaining hold was the idea of a national minimum below which no one should be allowed to fall. When money had to be found to maintain it, then it seemed fair, and politically was the only practicable way, to call on the well-to-do for a more than proportionate contribution. But the Liberals did not see redistribution as a main object. If their measures did in fact bring about some redistribution, that was because the taxes that would encounter least resistance were those laid out differentially on the highest incomes. At the same time, it was true that to contemporary opinion the size of those incomes had come to seem anomalous.

These considerations were blended in a Treasury minute of 1907. An inexorable rise in public expenditure (for defence as well as social benefits) demanded more revenue. But 'the time has gone by when it was possible to look to indirect taxes . . . to supply the want of funds. The country refuses any longer to drink itself out of its financial straits. Unless the whole system of our taxation is to be recast, the solution must be found in the increase of direct taxation.' This should take the form of a graduated super-tax. 'It is the existence of so much income in the shape of incomes far above the average level that makes the incidence of a uniform rate of tax inequitable, and calls for redress by means of a super-tax' (Cab. 37/87, no. 22, 26 Feb. 1907; quoted here from Emy 1973: 201). There is a hint of egalitarian sentiment here, but the main consideration is practicability. Whatever the motive, the outcome was a fiscal revolution. We shall see that in recent years graduated direct taxation has done no more than offset the regressive incidence of indirect taxation, so as to yield near proportionality overall; but that this should be so is a measure of the redistributive effect of the increased use of direct taxation since 1906.

The tendencies implicit in the measures of Asquith's government were projected powerfully by the First World War. This transformed accepted notions of taxable capacity: the standard rate of income tax was raised to heights that had been inconceivable a year or two before. That was possible only as part of the war effort, and was tolerable because it was expected to be temporary; but probably it did permanently raise the threshold of revolt—the level at which, in the general judgement, what had been borne as an unavoidable if heavy burden became rejected as an outrage. The social solidarity, moreover, which had made high taxation acceptable during the war was not all lost when the war was over: some greater sense of mutual responsibility remained, and when unemployment rose, the thought of it gnawed the social conscience of many who stood in no fear of it themselves. The experience of state control during the war weakened presumptions in favour of *laissez-faire*, and encouraged the benevolent to take up schemes of social reconstruction. One salient intervention—the rent control that was begun during the war and continued afterwards—had as its unintended consequence the requirement that governments themselves provide or subsidize housing.

These impacts of the war would of themselves have strengthened the tendencies of 1908–14. That effect did appear in the provision of contributory pensions for widows, orphans and old people in 1925. At the same time, economic depression worked to curtail public expenditure. Yet that same depression, bringing unemployment unprecedented in persistence and depth, was decisive in forcing the extension of benefits and the reconstruction of their administration. How the unemployment of those years would have been dealt with had there been no scheme of insurance already in place is hard to say. As it was, what was done was to extend the coverage of that scheme, enlarge its benefits by extending them to dependants and lengthening their duration, and thereby transform self-financing insurance for a limited number of contributors into a system of national assistance largely financed by the taxpayer—although contributions remained, as a matter of principle. Unemployment overwhelmed the poor law as well. The unemployed who had exhausted their benefit or were not covered at all by existing schemes were falling on the Board of Guardians and the local rates in numbers far too great for some localities to support. Neville Chamberlain's Local Government Act of 1929 abolished the Board of Guardians, and transferred their functions to committees of the counties, which received grants-in-aid from the National Exchequer. In 1934 an Unemployment Assistance Board was set up to maintain all those who had exhausted their benefit. Nearly a hundred years after the first great reform of local government and construction of new administrative areas and machinery, a second major reform carried centralization further, and with it the redistribution of income.

The unemployment that had darkened all the 1920s, even after recovery from the trough of 1921–2, was gravely worsened by the world economic depression that set in from the end of 1929. The years that followed were like those since 1973 in this, at least: that severe and persistent unemployment, and the contraction of certain industries, was accompanied by rising standards of living for the majority who kept their jobs. The effect in the 1930s was to combine a faith in the possibility of material progress with the belief that this could be achieved only if the waste and confusion of uncoordinated enterprise were superseded by planning. A main aim of this was to prevent unemployment; it would also preclude the accumulation of large private fortunes. But it was not egalitarian in its inspiration.

None the less, it expressed the widely held belief that the structure of society could be changed for the better. This belief was strengthened when the unemployment that had persisted through the interwar years came to be contrasted with the full employment reached in 1941. War itself in 1939-45 had the same influence as in 1914-18, in deepening the sense of social solidarity, increasing governmental intervention and controls and imposing a regime of uniform austerity. That regime was lightened by an active concern for social welfare, especially for young children, whose health was promoted by a national milk scheme and the provision of school meals. The relief that people found from the sufferings of wartime, in looking forward to the day 'when they sound the last All Clear', and envisaging a better country for everyone, was supported by the publication of the Beveridge plan, which showed how every citizen could be secured from want, 'from the cradle to the grave'. It was 'a method of redistributing income, so as to put the first and more urgent needs first'. The disillusionment and disarray that had followed the First World War were still fresh in people's memories: they were determined that they should not happen again. In 1945 the Labour Party offered the electors the credible prospect of an alternative government, as it had not done in 1918. Its return to office is understandable.

But it did not form a government of innovation. With the exception of planning and nationalization, the stock of ideas of the new government was largely that of the radicals of 1908-14. The welfare state was created by pushing further along the three lines that had been followed then—transfers, insurance and taxation. Children's allowances for income taxpayers were succeeded by family allowances for all, payable to the mother. Outright transfers and insurance schemes were combined in a system assuring every citizen of a minimum of subsistence at all times, and support in the contingencies of life. A national health service, including hospitals as well as the local practitioner, uncovered a great popular demand and need, hitherto unmet. Benefits that had first been provided to particular groups by a contributory system designed to be self-supporting were now provided by a public service available to all, and chargeable to the general revenue as well as to specific contributions; these came to be regarded not so much as earmarked for particular accounts as part of general revenue. The varied needs not covered by national insurance were met by a network of national assistance designed to maintain a minimum of subsistence, which was in practice to rise together with the standard of living of the population generally. The charges laid in these ways on the Exchequer were met by taxation maintained at high basic and particularly high marginal rates. This was the third of the redistributive channels of policy in 1908–14. The formerly regressive incidence of taxation was offset. When we go on to take account of the allocation of benefits, we find a substantial reduction in the inequality of household resources. But this was a by-product, albeit a welcome one, of a policy whose drive was to relieve and prevent hardship, and to establish a minimum standard not merely of subsistence but of well-being. Such an enterprise could only be collective. Although the benefits were accessible to everyone, there had to be a transfer of resources from those who had more than enough for essential needs to those who had less.

The distinctive element of the post-1945 policy—nationalization—was not egalitarian either in origins or in tendency. It had several sources. The oldest was the tradition that 'God gave the land to the people'—the belief that natural resources should not be appropriated by particular persons, who made them the means of exploiting other men's labour. This belief could be extended readily to all private ownership of industrial and commercial capital, for this equally was seen as enabling the owners to exploit the propertyless workers who could not find work except with them. The remedy seemed to be that all land and capital should be owned by the community. The question then arose, when the existing capitalist employers were displaced, how should production be directed? Here another source of faith in nationalization took effect—the Benthamite tradition of management by the disinterested and authoritarian expert. The tradition had found its practical expression in municipal socialism. This was government of the people, by the middle class, for the people. Administration in the public interest, inspired by the morale of efficient bureaucracy and not the quest for private profit, was a leading principle of Fabian or evolutionary socialism. Beatrice Webb's quip, that she and Sidney belonged to 'the B's of the world—bourgeois, bureaucratic, and benevolent' (Cole 1945: 65–6), encapsulates the spirit of a movement whose aim was to do good to the workers, but was bound to do it at arm's length. Nationalization should bring a more orderly and public-spirited administration of industry, not a transformation of society, or even of organizational hierarchies. This conception received increasing support when the world economic depression of the 1930s dominated the thinking of reformers as the great Victorian depression had done in the 1880s, and their eyes turned to planning as the preventive of boom and slump and unemployment. Stalin's four-year plan appeared as the full development of 'gasworks socialism' or London Transport. The same conception of nationalization as the unified and disinterested, or joint-interested, administration of industry was to commend itself to trade unionists by their experience of the corporatist organization of industry in which they had participated during the war.

There was one way, however, in which nationalization was associated with egalitarianism. We have seen how one source of it was the good old cause of 'the land for the people'. That cause derived some of its force from the identification of the landowners as a class with great riches. Even down to the First World War, this was natural: most of the wealthiest people in the country were landowners, and fortunes made in the city or industry were often put into land. The landowners did not only typify the rich: unlike the capitalists in business, they were also conspicuous as 'the idle rich'. In claiming to share in what should be the common heritage, the advocates of land nationalization were therefore standing for the redistribution of the greatest fortunes, and their policy appealed to many who had no thought of going back to the land themselves. That those great incomes should be drawn from rent, moreover, often simply of sites, made them the more objectionable; for Henry George had driven home to a wide audience what Ricardo had demonstrated to students of political economy, that rent was a surplus which the expansion of output conferred upon the inert landlord. As a policy taken up by Labour after the First World War, 'the nationalisation of the means of production, distribution and exchange' may have been only municipal socialism writ large, but those who widened it thus far were bringing all rent and interest under the same condemnation as the rent of land itself—'God's gift to sleeping men'.

We said at the outset that, although little was added after 1945 to the principles that had become prominent in the 1880s, the emphasis of the reformers did shift. This change sprang from a greater sensitivity to differences of culture between classes. The term 'class' is not to be taken here in a Marxian sense, as meaning a number of persons who are aware of their common economic interest which marks them off from, and opposes them to, other groups: here the term refers to those who, whether or not they are aware of one another or have a common economic interest to pursue, are alike in their way of life. They resemble one another, and differ from other groups, in the range of their interests and information, their speech and manners, and their activities outside work. These differences flow from upbringing and education, and from the margin of means that allows the acquisition of amenities. The differences of culture are linked with those of income, but not wholly so: there have been 'gentlemen in reduced circumstances' and 'nouveaux riches'. Much more than differences of income, those of culture provide the signals by which people are 'placed' as belonging to 'us' or 'them'. Much more than money, they cause resentment.

Yet it is remarkable how little of the egalitarianism that such resentment inspires used to be found among the British. It was rather the opposite that was apparent. 'Every Englishman loves a lord,' John Stuart Mill wrote in 1858:

The English, of all ranks and class, are at bottom, in all their feelings, aristocrats. They have some conception of liberty, and set some value on it, but the very idea of equality is strange and offensive to them. They do not dislike to have many people above them as long as they have some below them. (Mineka and Lindley 1972: 553)

de Tocqueville said much the same when, during his travels in England in 1835, he noted that:

the French wish not to have superiors. The English wish to have inferiors. The Frenchman constantly raises his eyes above him with anxiety. The Englishman lowers his beneath him with satisfaction . . . Does this effect not arise from the fact that the Englishman was used to the idea that he could advance himself, but the Frenchman could not? (de Tocqueville 1958: 75)

Gladstone recorded a similar impression:

The love of freedom itself is hardly stronger in England than the love of aristocracy . . . Call this love of inequality by what name you please, — the complement of the love of freedom, or its negative pole, or the shadow which the love of freedom casts, or the reverberation of its voice in the halls of the constitution,—it is an active, living, and life-giving power, which forms an inseparable essential element in our political habits of mind, and asserts itself at every step in the processes of our system. (quoted by Matthew Arnold 1879: 51)

But this acceptance of inequality contained elements opposed to itself. For such sensitivity to social status goes with resentment of privilege and exclusiveness. The superiority of the upper classes may be both admired and resented at the same time, because it is attained more by birth than by effort. The realization that the grandees are not a superior race but ordinary people who have enjoyed superior advantages changes attitudes towards them. The very different life-chances of children born into homes at different social levels are felt to be particularly unfair. Those who do better at school and at work are suspect of owing their achievements to their parents' status and means, not to higher personal potential. These tensions set up an inchoate drive towards social equality for which redistribution of wealth and income is only a means—a drive for society no longer divided by culture. Engels (1878) noted this, in his way (his definition of class differs from that implicit here), when he said that, while the bourgeoisie demanded the abolition of class privileges, the proletariat demanded the abolition of the classes themselves. It is hard to write a programme for that, but one practical outcome is the demand for greater equality of opportunity. Politically, in the division between 'us' and 'them', the working people who were becoming increasingly influential from the 1880s onwards required to be represented by 'one of us'. Few of them held a vision of an egalitarian society, but they increasingly resented the gap between classes in education and amenity.

That resentment rose as the gap narrowed. The provision of the board schools had begun to ensure that almost every child would receive at least some elementary education. In 1891 the proportion of the people of London within the ages of twenty-five to fifty-five who had passed through an efficient school was still less than a quarter; by 1921 it had become 90 per cent (*New Survey*, 1930: ch. viii, table II). Those for whom that schooling half-opened a window on the world wanted more. Ernest Bevin, who himself had left school at the age of eleven, put this clearly in the address to a Court of Inquiry that earned him the title of 'the dockers' KC':

If you, my Lord, say in spite of all this that we have not established our claim, you have one alternative: you must go to the Prime Minister, you must go to the Minister of Education, and tell him to close our schools, tell him that industry can only be run by artisan labour on the pure fodder or animal basis, teach us nothing, let us learn nothing; because to create aspirations in our minds, to create the love of the beautiful, and then at the same time to deny us the wherewithal to obtain it, is a false policy and a wrong method to adopt. Better keep us in dark ignorance, never to know anything, if you are going to refuse us the wherewithal to give expression to those aspirations which have thus been created (House of Commons Papers 1920: 3rd day, p. 9)

Greater literacy not only set up a demand for wages that would provide middle-class amenities, it created more resentment of the privilege of being born to enjoy them. What they were became increasingly known, as newspapers and magazines and the cinema reached the people who used to have little view of the world outside their own daily round.

At the same time, as the middle classes looked at workers now much less removed and set apart from them than they used to be, they began to see people who would have been like themselves if they had enjoyed the same advantages. There was a time when there had indeed been two nations, when the ignorance and squalor of the poor might attract the pity and philanthropy of the middle classes, but hardly their fellow feeling. Even the good servant belonged to a different race: the duties of the master towards him were not very different from those he felt towards his horses. Like colonial administrators in some backward province, the middle classes followed their own way of life without feeling guilty of being so much better off. In the countryside rank was marked, but each person had his or her accepted place in the hierarchy, and was entitled to respect within it. In the towns there was more fluidity but less neighbourliness: those who were plainly not of the kind a respectable person would wish to consort with had little claim on his or her regard. But when those poorer townsfolk themselves became respectable, it was no longer so easy to ignore their afflictions. Some middle-class people felt threatened by their advance; but others came to see them as those children at the family table whose helpings were small because of favouritism for others seated beside them.

Meanwhile, middle-class people became better informed about the condition of their neighbours. The statistical reports prepared by William Farr in the office of the Registrar-General made clear the great difference in mortality rates, or their correlation with the expectation of life, between different occupations and localities. These were systematic differences, not a matter of 'black spots': the lottery of birth assigned some people to much greater hazards of health than others. The Report of the Registrar-General for 1911 showed that the infant mortality rate in the homes of 'unskilled workmen' was almost exactly double that in the 'upper and middle classes'. This evidence was supplemented by social surveys in the Benthamite tradition of inquiry; and the collection of household budgets, displaying 'life on a pound a week'. Measurements of Oxford and Cambridge undergraduates aged twenty, in 1908–10, found average heights and weights for them which proved to be greater by $3\frac{1}{2}$ inches and more than 30 pounds than those of lads of eighteen conscripted in 1918 in the West Midlands and the North-west of England (Martin 1949). The appalling physical condition evidenced by the high rejection rate of recruits during the Boer War brought this stunting of the national stock home to the notice of the middle classes, at a time when it already had reason to be concerned about the ability of the British people to match their rising competitors abroad. The slogan of 'national efficiency' took hold for a time. Many of its proponents were concerned primarily with the military potential of an imperial race, and the threat to a pallid, under-sized, town-bred people posed by the rise of vigorous and envious nations. Some sought a remedy in eugenics. But the diagnosis of poor diet, cramped housing, scant training and too little exercise pointed to more practical measures: what could be done to give young people a better start in life? Once again, the attention of the middle class was directed to the conditions that debilitated the physique of their poorer neighbours and impoverished their lives.

Realization of the hardships and disabilities of the working classes disturbed especially those whose own minds had been fired and prospects enlarged by higher education. The progressive reform of Oxford and Cambridge brought forth a new race of young scholars to join graduates in the great Scots tradition. They were uncommitted to traditional roles and values. The philosophic and scientific issues of their day exercised their minds; its social questions stung their consciences. As the civic universities rose, and secondary education extended to provide new routes to the university, the number grew of those who could not but contrast the resources of interest and prospects of achievement that their education had afforded them with the lot of those not inherently different from themselves, to whom the light of learning had been denied. Arnold Toynbee, son of a cultivated middle-class home and a student and teacher in Oxford at a stirring time, poured out his sense of guilt at the end of an address to a meeting of middle-class folk and workmen in 1883:

Now I turn to the workmen. We—the middle classes, I mean, not merely the very rich—we have neglected you; instead of justice we have offered you charity, and instead of sympathy, we have offered you hard and unreal advice; but I think we are changing. If you would only believe it and trust us, I think that many of us would spend our lives in your service. You have—I say it clearly and advisedly—you have to forgive us, for we have wronged you; we have sinned against you grievously—not knowingly always, but still we have sinned, and let us confess it; but if you will forgive us—nay, whether you will forgive us or not—we will serve you, we will devote our lives to your service, and we cannot do more. (Toynbee 1894; 318)

That passage was delivered extempore and, as Alfred Milner recorded, 'in the extremity of physical weakness': two months later Toynbee was dead, at the age of thirty-one. But the high tension of his message only reveals the strain that increased knowledge of the workers' condition imposed on the members of the middle class who themselves were entering an ever more exciting, even enchanting, world of thought and feeling.

For another Balliol man, of a later generation, the case against inequality was essentially that it vitiated relations between people of unequal education, between those entering upon fulness of life and those whose attainments were constricted. In his *Equality* (1931), Tawney recognized two objects of egalitarianism: to give more to the poor, and to improve human relations. The second had priority:

an improvement in relations, such as would be fostered, it is generally agreed, by a diminution of sharp contrasts of economic conditions, is not to be desired primarily as a means of putting more money into the pockets of those who have too little, though that result is, doubtless, to be welcomed; on the contrary, if it is desirable to put more money into their pockets, the reason is primarily that such a course may be one means, among others, to a much-needed improvement in human relations. (Tawney 1931: 46)

'The tradition of inequality . . . a cluster of ideas at the back of men's minds', results among the British in 'a paralysis, which is the natural result of a divided will'; this 'is less noticeable in nations where classes are less sharply divided' (pp. 38–40). This division is one of education and manners much more than of money.

Tawney spoke from experience: he had served in the ranks of the Manchester Regiment in the First World War; he became a pillar of the Workers' Educational Association. Sometimes he held that the cultural divide of which he had become so conscious was the outcome of human nature-'the injustices survive, not so much because the rich exploit the poor, as because the poor, in their hearts, admire the rich (Tawney 1931, 38). Elsewhere he found the cause in social convention, which men had made and men could change (p. 280); or at least he thought that the reverence for riches could be abolished if riches themselves were swept away (p. 114). But always his aim was to end the alienation of classes, by bringing to those whose mental and emotional lives were at present constricted and impoverished the enlargement and enrichment enjoyed by the well educated.

Some part of the present vitiation of human relations he found in snobbery. A snob is defined in the *Concise Oxford Dictionary* as 'a person with exaggerated respect for social position or wealth and a disposition to be ashamed of socially inferior connections, behave with servility to social superiors, and judge of merit by externals'. It is hard for those who do not remember the way of the world before 1914 to realize how pervasive was that attitude: it constituted not a weakness then, but a code of correct behaviour. Those who failed to show a proper respect for their betters, or who dressed above their station, were made painfully aware of their impertinence. Manuals of etiquette were studied by those fearful of betraying their low origins. Decorum required a due appreciation of one's position in the social order; it prescribed how one should address those above or below one in it; they could be readily identified by their clothes, speech and manners. Self-respect depended on knowing one's place: if this required deference as one looked upwards, it conferred a gratifying sense of superiority as one contemplated the stigmata of those below. These distinctions made a powerful impression on visitors from countries of more democratic manners: Americans in particular were apt to suppose that economic inequality was much greater in Great Britain than in their own country (which it was not), because differences of speech and bearing made so strong and disagreeable an impression.

Since 1914 those differences have greatly diminished; at the same time, what remains of them has become more prominent as an object of discussion, and a source of embarrassment to those still privileged. The change has been brought about partly by the general rise in the standard of living that has elided the visible marks of class: people can no longer be 'placed' at a glance by their dress, or even by their possessions such as their cars. In the 1920s ready made clothing of good quality became available for both men and women as never before: the once very evident class distinction between the smartly dressed and the shabby was no longer apparent. But an even deeper-going change was brought about in another way by the two world wars. For many men who served as officers in the armed forces, war brought closer contact than ever before with the men in the ranks; it instilled respect, and a sense of responsibility. High morale was attained by a form of consensus, and those who had experienced it wanted to carry it into civilian life. At the same time, war cut down the patrician families with their great estates and houses, which had for so long stood at the summit of the British social structure. Since 1760 the country had seen a growth of industry, but no industrial revolution, no supersession of the political ascendancy, the prestige and the values of the great landowners by a new order based on industry. It was war that overthrew the old order at last. The rise in estate duties during and after the First World War, and the lag of income behind the costs of upkeep, made it increasingly difficult to maintain the great country houses. A differential casualty rate cut down their sons—the proportion killed in the army during the First World War was 15.8 per cent among officers, and 12.8 per cent among other ranks (Winter 1985: table 3.10); in the infantry the disparity was probably greater.

Under conditions of trench warfare, junior officers almost always led from the front, whether reconnoitring, raiding, or just holding the line. Few contemporaries had the slightest doubt that they were in a particularly vulnerable and frequently exposed position; hence the high death rates among the subaltern class . . . (Winter 1985: 90).

Meanwhile, at home, people who had been used to keeping their distance from one another were drawn together to share the sufferings and efforts of wartime. In both wars rationing imposed a rigorous egalitarianism; in the Second World War the bombs fell on rich and poor alike. These were all impacts on the old class structure. They helped to transform the exercise of benevolence into the pursuit of reciprocity in human relations—a term that now came into vogue.

Both wars had a powerful effect on the role of women. In doing so they carried forward a course of social change that had set in with the rise of humanism. We have seen (pp. 159–60) its manifestations in the eighteenth century. The major source of inequality in the difference between the ways of life traditionally assigned to the two genders was in part the natural outcome of differences in bodily size and function, but these led easily to subordination of the women to the man and exploitation by him. A more humane conception assigned to each gender its distinct sphere and function, with equality of esteem for due performance in each, or even special respect by men for the qualities that women displayed. But in practice, their role imposed restrictions far beyond those of biological function. The assigned sphere was narrow; it meant a denial of opportunity. The change of attitudes, however, that was brought in by Renaissance and Reformation gained increasing hold as the nineteenth century wore on. For this there were several causes.

One was the diffusion of the influence of humanism itself, and especially its intensification in romanticism. The 'religion of humanity' was concerned with those aspects of human experience that are common to men and women. Romanticism with its stress on feelings, and the capacity to feel, found as much to admire in women as in men, perhaps more, In so far as it made women an object of adoration, and still more of sexual pursuit and conquest, it denied them personality; but its delight in the unfolding of youthful sensibility and the flowering of the lyrical and creative faculties valued aspects of personality as marked among women as among men. Where romanticism joined religion, in evangelicalism, where there were souls to be saved, no distinction of gender was made between sinners, or in their access to the means of grace.

The movement of the population into towns worked in its own way to the same effect. In the countryside the division of labour between the genders followed naturally the difference of physique between them; there were few jobs in which women could be regularly occupied outside the home—with its spinning wheel—and the dairy. Urbanization increased the number of such jobs, partly by providing machine-tending tasks in factories, more generally by the growth of shops and offices. The possibility grew of single women supporting themselves otherwise than in domestic service.

This was the more so because of the extension of the education of women. When attendance at an elementary school was made compulsory, the obligation applied to girls no less than boys; that this came as a matter of course by 1870 shows how far opinion had already moved since the days when the benefactors who endowed grammar schools had boys alone in mind. The new schools made more difference to girls than boys: more brides than grooms had had to sign the register with an X. Equally, in the middle class, although the girls were not left illiterate, they lacked the opportunities for learning and training that were accessible to many boys. But now there followed an extension of secondary schools for girls, under voluntary auspices until the Act of 1902 provided a national system. When girls were taught alongside boys, they showed just as much ability to learn—a finding that was reinforced when IQs came to be taken. Those who today still hold that 'women don't have as much brains as men' are relics of days when that was believed by most people, including many women; the limitations imposed by upbringing were mistaken for an innate lack of potential. It now became clear that to deny girls as good an education as boys were getting was to discriminate between equally eligible recipients. As women became better educated they became fitted for more jobs, better able to meet men on equal terms in their working lives, better equipped to go out into the world and make their way in it independently.

The presumptions about the natural relation between the sexes on which people proceeded were radically changed in the last third of the nineteenth century as religion shifted its ground, or with some influential thinkers lost its hold altogether. Notions of evolution, and some knowledge of genetics, took the place of a literal belief in Adam and Eve. No longer did the woman appear as derivative from and ancillary to man, or—even more demeaning—as the temptress, offering

> fruit
> Of that forbidden tree, whose mortal taste
> Brought death into the world and all our woe.

As the authority of the Bible slowly waned, so did its teaching, in the New Testament (pp. 30–1) as well as the Old, of the ordained inferior status of women.

As some women, often pioneers who had to endure ridicule as well as overcome resistance, broke through customary barriers in education and occupation, their performance showed how unreasonable the opposition had been, and made it easier for others to follow them. The breaking down of barriers and the demonstration effect that followed were to be quickened and enhanced by the First World War. All manner of male doubt about women's capability, intellectual and temperamental, to do 'a man's job' were disposed of as women took up war work. No longer could it be alleged, for instance, that women would never be able to drive cars—even to swinging the starting handle on a cold morning.

One reason for keeping women apart from the world in a Western kind of purdah, and requiring a Muslim kind of modesty in dress, had been the fear of sexuality, whether of exciting desire in the male, or exposing the female to molestation. As contraceptives became known and available, the risk of conception that was a rational base for these restraints was greatly reduced. Women began to enjoy more freedom of movement, without chaperonage or surveillance, more choice of company, more independence. If one outcome has been the more frequent breakup of marriage, this may indicate the extent to which women had been held in subjection within marriage before.

The inequality of women had depended on attitudes and unquestioning assumptions. To many people it must have seemed as much part of the natural order of things as the week of seven days. The sources of change that have been noted here show how far it was only conventional. Gradually, a number of factors came to bear on people's outlook on their own species: they came not so much to judge the rightful position of women differently, as simply to *see* women differently. Given that new view, a more equal status and a wider scope followed naturally. The old status had followed from the Aristotelian maxim, that justice consists in treating unequal people unequally; but now women ceased to appear unequal in themselves, or in some relevant respects even different. A change in prevailing attitudes comes about only slowly; and, like other changes in fashion and convention, it is apt to move down the social scale, and to encounter more conservatism as it gets lower. But the changes that did in fact occur in the hundred years after Mary Wollstonecraft wrote her 'Vindication of the Rights of Women' effected a great reduction in the sum total of human inequality, a sum we underestimate altogether if we reckon it only in money.

In the course of the preceding discussion, we have noticed a number of factors that have shifted the thrust and content of egalitarianism. This effect was brought out by Crosland's influential review of 'the basic socialist aspirations', in his *Future of Socialism* (1956: 103). The achievements of economic growth, full employment and the welfare state had left comparatively little more to be done, he thought, for the realization of three of those aspirations: the removal of 'material poverty and physical squalor', the provision of social welfare and correction of 'the inefficiencies of capitalism as an economic system, and notably its tendency to mass unemployment'. We had come also to realize that human nature did not really lend itself to the attainment of that 'ideal of fraternity and co-operation' by which some socialists had aspired to replace 'competitive antagonism'. The full force of contemporary socialism must therefore, he held, be directed towards the realization of the remaining aspiration that he noted. 'a belief in equality and the "classless society"', and especially a desire to give the worker his "just" rights and a responsible status at work'. The immediate identification here of 'equality' with 'the classless society'—not one from which the inequalities of income and wealth have been banished—is significant. When in Part Four of his work Crosland addressed himself to 'The Search for Equality', he went straight to 'The Determinants of Class'. The 'interacting triad, at the top of the social scale, of education, style of life, and occupational status is unquestionably a more important cause of social inequality than income . . .' (Crossland 1956: 178). In his survey of the aims of socialism, his stress was laid not on differences of income and wealth in themselves, but on their effect on human relations. The keyword was *social* equality. 'The socialist', he had said earlier,

seeks a distribution of rewards, status and privileges egalitarian enough to minimise social resentment, to secure justice between individuals, and to equalise opportunities; and he seeks to weaken the existing deep-seated class stratification, with its concomitant feeling of envy and inferiority, and its barriers to uninhibited mingling between the classes. This belief in social equality, which has been the strongest ethical inspiration of virtually every socialist doctrine, still remains the most characteristic feature of socialist thought today. (Crosland 1956: 113)

It followed that the main thrust of socialism must be against social distancing by education. 'The ideal of social equality requires the first priority to be given to educational reform', to reducing 'the prestige-distinction between different types of school. If socialism is taken to mean a "classless society", this is the front on which the main attack should now be mounted' (p. 518).

Crosland spoke for many of his provenance and generation. Those who themselves had felt all the excitement of realizing the potentialities of their own development, and seeing a world of thought and feeling opening up to them as they passed through school and college, felt their experience unwarranted unless others could enjoy it too. Their own life-chances should be made available to all. At this point egalitarianism encounters a familiar dilemma, for equal opportunities will be used by different people to very different effect. The evidence that this is due in part to differences of IQ, and that these are largely innate, has consequently been disputed passionately by those who would rather believe that the right arrangements can secure a rewarding development for every child. Such controversies show how far the content of egalitarianism has changed. The bones of contention used to be the amounts of income and wealth; egalitarians are concerned with them now as means to personal development and fulness of life, and as the source of social distance.

7.5. The Difference of Attitudes in the United States

The course of development that we have traced in Great Britain in the last hundred years has depended upon the wide acceptance of greater equality as an aim of public policy. This attitude has never been general in the United States: on the contrary, its manifestations have been commonly dismissed as un-American. In 1906 Sombart asked why there was no socialism in the United States. Today, it is true, we could not pose the question in such a sweeping form. There have been socialist candidates for high office. From the New Deal to the Great Society, successive administrations have adopted programmes designed to help the underdog and charge the public revenue with the cost. Straw polls have continued to show some support for socialist principles. The Roman Catholic church has upheld the principles and practice of social justice. But the predominant difference of attitude is unmistakable. Over against 'the more just society' sought by Europeans is set 'the American way of life'.

This attitude precludes the deliberate transfer of resources from the rich to the poor, except in so far as is necessary to relieve destitution. It does not look to governments to bring about greater equality, because the American people enjoy equality, as none else, already. That equality is marked by manners, with none of the courtesy made up of patronage and servility that impresses the American visitor to Great Britain so painfully with the extent of class difference there. With manners go dress, and styles of life generally; paradoxically, as it seems to the European visitor, the individualism of the American goes with a compulsive conformity. This contrasts with the freedom to go his own way in his own manner enjoyed by those who do not care about what people will say. But the American does care about this, precisely because he and they are on the same footing—not social betters and inferiors, but equals. The immigrant to the United States left class differences behind him; nowhere in the American scene, whether in the cities or on the frontier, did he find those trappings of the *ancien régime* that betokened the subordination of the lower orders of society. Instead, the avenues of achievement were open to all. 'It is by the maintenance of equality of opportunity', President Hoover said in 1932,

and therefore of a society absolutely fluid in the movement of its human particles, that our individualism departs from the individualism of Europe. We resent class distinction because there can be no rise for the individual through the frozen strata of classes, and no stratification of classes can take place in a mass livened by the free rise of its particles. (Quoted here from Samson 1974: 435)

Equality of opportunity is an article of American faith held so unquestioningly that it has come to be experienced as a fact. Education is not directed towards the upholding of academic standards that are, in practice, congenial to only a minority of pupils, but is designed to provide pupils of all sorts with what interests them and will help them get a job. The need to avail oneself of opportunity is enforced by the absence of acknowledged rank: one's standing depends not on one's birth but on acceptance by one's neighbours, and that in turn depends on achievement. The substitution of success for status as the basis of respect puts people under pressure to succeed; but it is linked with an exhilarating sense of liberation from the fetters of class-ridden societies. If the outcome is that some get on much further than others, they are to be not envied but admired. Policies that would change the arrangements of society so as to benefit those who lag behind at the expense of the front-runners are repudiated because they infringe the individual freedom that is central to 'the American way of life'. All American citizens are equal in the enjoyment of opportunity. If they eschew the policies that pass in Europe for egalitarian, that is because egalitarianism as they understand it is inscribed on their own banners. If socialism means aiming at greater equality, they do not need it, for they have equal opportunity already. If it means handicapping the more successful, they repudiate it, because it impairs the freedom to seize opportunity. This freedom they believe to be uniquely American.

In recent years this belief has been shown to be unfounded. International comparisons, of which some account will be given in Part II, have failed to reveal the differences in structure and function that would substantiate this general impression. Studies of the distribution of income have shown that this is very much alike in its inequality in most Western countries, despite all the differences in the political tendencies and social philosophy. The distribution of wealth does appear to be less concentrated in the United States than in the United Kingdom, because land is a more important component in the United States, and is held in many small parcels; but the difference is less than would be expected by Americans who contrast their own assurance of equality with the stratified societies of Europe. Most of all, studies of social mobility have shown that, at least on an overall measure of the extent of upward movement, there is no more of it in the United States than in a number of other Western countries.

We find a remarkable degree of similarity between a number of countries in recent years in the extents to which sons enter the same category of occupations as their father's, or move into categories adjacent or more distant in rank order, whether above their father's category or below it. Such evidence as we have for this sort of mobility in earlier years has revealed no course of change. We seem to be in the presence of a social process of much generality and persistence in Western countries. (Phelps Brown 1977: 199)

Such findings have come as a shock to American scholars. The confidently held belief that the United States had attained a social equality unknown in Europe, and has stood out in particular as the land of opportunity, was seen to be unfounded. But there is no question of the self-image of the American people.

How did it come to be formed? It is not hard to point to circumstances that could have shaped it. A country that is founded by immigrants and continues to be peopled in some measure by fresh waves of them brings to its national consciousness the immigrant's sense of escape from frustration to opportunity. Class structure apart, the immigrants were mostly escaping from population pressure to a land where abundance of natural resources set a premium on manpower. Although many of them went into the towns, these were part of an ever expanding economy; and beyond them lay the open frontier with land for the taking—the land so passionately desired, so impossible of attainment, by the children of the peasant households of Europe. The promise heard from afar was made good on arrival. Courage, vigour and enterprise did in fact reap their rewards. A standard of living far higher than in the old world confirmed the Americans' faith in their country as uniquely a land of opportunity for all.

That the factors noted here have been influential cannot be doubted, but comparison with other young countries shows that they cannot alone account for the American myth. Canada and Australia equally were founded by immigrants, and their populations continued to be built up by immigration as well as natural increase. In both, vast territories lay open to the pioneer. Both have attained high standards of living: in the 1860s the Australian standard was probably the highest in the world. But although each has its distinctive attitudes and way of life, neither has developed the egalitarian individualism that repudiates collectivism and the conscious intent to achieve a more just society by political means. Canada has been slow to develop a Labour Party, but it has never been hostile in principle to the intervention of government in economic and social affairs, and a substantial part of industry and communications is in the public sector. Its trade unionism, already in the 1920s more extensive than in the United States, has continued to grow in the last thirty years, during which time trade unionism in the United States has progressively declined, both as a proportion of the work-force and even absolutely. In Australia the Labour Party has been a political force throughout the twentieth century; it is supported not only by an extensive and often militant trade union movement, but also by a wide acceptance of the need for state intervention in pursuit of social justice. There have always been many people in both countries opposed to socialist tendencies, but they would not repudiate them with patriotic fervour as un-Canadian or un-Australian.

Where dissimilar outlooks arise out of seemingly similar origins, we have to look for what we have left out of account. One such element may well be a difference in the frontier. In the United States, that was pushed forward by pioneers fending for themselves, able to hold their own in what was often a lawless world. In Canada, where the prairies were separated by a thousand impassable miles from the accessible east, settlement depended on support by government, and from 1874 the Northwest had its own mounted police force:

In the United States it is the cowboy, a rugged individualist whose relation to the forces of law and order was at least ambiguous, who has come to symbolise the frontier, while in Canada the 'mountie', a policeman who clearly stands for law and order and traditional institutional authority, is the corresponding symbol of Canadian westward expansion. (Wrong 1955: 38; quoted in Lipset 1970: 45, n. 22)

In Australia, the strong arm of government preceded settlement from the day when Governor Philip first came ashore with his marines. When the gold rush came, the diggings were thoroughly policed (as they were to be in British Columbia). The area suitable for family farms was limited in any case: in the outback there were great acreages to be taken up only by those with capital to stock them with sheep by the thousand: the 'squatters', when drought did not ruin them, were wealthy.

But these differences are the outcome of a deeper-going divergence: the Americans' sense of their own nationhood arose out of a revolution that was social as well as political, and no such change of outlook was imprinted at their origins on the Canadians and the Australians. The distinctive Canadian outlook, indeed, began with the withdrawal north of the border of the Tories who repudiated not only the American revolt agains the Crown but the view of society that went with it. Both Canadians and Australians, at least down to the First World War, continued to feel themselves colonists, and to think of 'the Mother Country' as home. At least there was no conscious and explicit repudiation of their ties, social and intellectual as well as constitutional, with the United Kingdom. But the Declaration of Independence not merely threw off King George: by proclaiming the rights of man, it denounced the social structure that the monarch symbolized. The conscious adoption of the philosophy of eighteenth-century liberalism was followed by a conscious endeavour to inculcate it. The faith that all men were born free and equal became fused with the self-image of 'the first new nation' (Lipset 1979). It took on the quality of a religion, whose adherent reject other beliefs with the acrimony that attaches to heresy.

It is to this, above all, that we may trace the Americans' allergy to the egalitarian thought of Europe. They have their own egalitariansm already. It is realized in an equality of manners that proclaims the absence of class distinctions, and through a belief in equality of opportunity which, whatever the facts, encourages young people to set out with hope and vigour. This achieved equality, moreover, is seen to be linked with, and indeed dependent upon, the freedom of individual exertion and private enterprise that socialism would restrict. European egalitarianism not only seems to offer the American people nothing that they do not possess already; it threatens to sap the energies by which that possession is maintained.

This outlook is too firmly fixed in the national consciousness to be changed by the conflicting impact of adverse experience. At the end of the Second World War, it is true, it might have seemed otherwise, for the great depression of the 1930s might have been held to have brought about the same change of direction in American public policy as the Liberal government effected in the United Kingdom before 1914. A great upsurge of US trade unionism under fostering legislation in the 1930s, was carried forward by full employment reached during the war, and by the policy of the National War Labor Board. Public opinion polls in the 1930s showed substantial support for socialist principles. Comprehensive measures to help the poor and the disadvantaged minorities—even 'positive discrimination'—were enacted and enforced. But such measures, like trade unionism itself, were always unwelcome to those who felt that the unique American achievement depended on the spirit of self-help and the seizing of opportunity by the vigorous and enterprising. In the rising prosperity of the 1950s and 1960s, these attitudes regained their hold. Support for trade unionism in public opinion polls declined. There became evident a 'restoration of faith in traditional American values' (Lipset 1986: 447). The appeal of President Reagan lay in his embodying that faith. The reaction against fiscal egalitarianism and the welfare state occurred in some European democracies also, and here too it may be attributed to the persistance of other values among many people; but only in the United States were those values identified with nationhood.

8

Issues and Influences Reviewed

The differences between people are so conspicuous in all sorts of ways that one may well wonder that the notion of human equality has ever been entertained. The preceding chapters have shown how it has come to be so. The pupose of the present chapter is to review that account. We begin with the reasons for accepting or justifying inequality of treatment, status or condition. These reasons may be grouped under three heads; the next three sections deal with each of these in turn, setting out the influences in the realms of thought or material circumstance that have loosened the hold of inequality and strengthened that of egalitarianism, in principle and in practice.

8.1. The Justification of Inequality

The evident differences in capability between persons of each gender, and of function between men and women, have always been seen to call for differences of treatment, and in many respects continue to do so. To assign the same pay to workers of different ability seems as unnatural as to issue the same clothes to people of different size. In many matters besides clothes we look for what is fitting. This means treating people differently, in accordance with the differences between them. The very idea of justice, as it appeared in the Greek principle of suiting rewards and penalties to people's actions, involved differentiation. To make the punishment fit the crime seemed right because it would achieve a particular equality. In this way, an intuitive recognition of the rightness of equality in each case led to inequality between awards. The principle seen as self-evident in the law courts was extended to the arrangements of society at large, to the allocation of status, rights and resources. Slavery was the appropriate condition for those who were born with brutish natures. Those whose mechanical occupations cramped and warped their development could not be admitted to the rights of citizens. Although the extremes of wealth and poverty threatened to split the community, the remedy lay in the strengthening of the middle ranks, not in taking property away from those whose energies had acquired it and transferring it to those who had proved incapable of earning it. In all, the differences between people themselves were so unmistakable, that corresponding differences in their rights and assets and their relations with one another seemed inescapable. Because they were fitting, they were just.

But there were more grounds for acepting inequality of status, in particular, than this notion of what was fitting to each person: there was also the need for differentiation of status as a means to the welfare of society. Not all people were fit to govern: as the soul should rule over the body, the wise few should rule over the unenlightened many. This was in the interests of the many themselves, for only so would the state promote a good life for all its people. But before the state could make life good, it existed to make it possible: the primary necessity of keeping order called for authority, hierarchy and subordination. This was for long the main case for inequality of status. The alternative to ranking in a social order was anarchy and rapine. The medieval Schoolmen held that the sinful propensities of human nature after the Fall required restraint by the power divinely delegated to temporal authority. More than that, society must be structured by the assignment to each person of a station in life, with its rights and duties and its appropriate standard of life. Each of us might move within the structure, into 'that state of life unto which it shall please God to call me'; but those states themselves were fixed in the nature of things, or in the divine plan, and the Catechism taught each child 'to order myself lowly and reverently to all my betters'.

This view, in which each person was assigned a due place, high or low, was associated with another view of society, the organic. What the first view saw as ranks in a hierarchy, this other took to be organs of a body. The notion of inequality, which is essentially one of magnitude, does not apply to the differences between hand and foot. Instead of the differences between ranks or occupations or genders appearing anomalous, they are now seen as the natural accompaniment of differences of organic function. As a body has life, so we can speak of the life of a community. This life depends on its constituent organs, and they in their turn cannot live except within the community. They are complementary to one another in the performance of their functions. The posts that people fill must, if they are to play their part, be placed in certain relations to one another, relations that are often those of superior and inferior; they will, of their nature, carry with them certain duties and amenities; but the persons who fill them will be alike in fulfilling a common purpose, and on that account will be equally deserving of esteem.

This allocation of complementary functions suggests the division of labour; the division of function between individuals is harmonized through the market. This provides another view of the sources of human inequality, and another justification for it. People are free to work in whatever way they choose out of those accessible to them, and the market sets valuations on their work. Although this results in some receiving far more than others, it is in the interest even of those who receive least, for it provides incentives, and allocates resources, so as to make more available for all than any other system could yield. The institution of private property admits the accumulation of great wealth by some persons, and its transmission to heirs who have done nothing to deserve it, while many others have to make their way without inherited resources; but it is an essential condition of the enterprise and effort on which the livelihood of all depends. Only if each man can be secure of the produce of his labour will he make the most of it, and the community thrive; it was to protect property, it is held, that the state itself was set up. The wide differences of income and wealth that arise in a regime of private enterprise and property only reflect the differences that lie deep in human nature, as well as those of sheer luck. But such differences are inescapable; if we try to level them out, we shall only check activity, and the poor will be worse off still.

This belief that egalitarian measures do more harm than good has been supported by arguments to show that the free market is harmonious. Each agent can gain only by providing what others want. The sum of social welfare will be maximized when each person's work and property is priced in the market by transactions between a willing seller and a willing buyer, when competition presses firms towards the arrangement that will minimize cost and when consumers are free to spend and save so as to get the most out of their resources. The formal economic analysis that reached this conclusion was reinforced by the earlier observation that intervention did more to obstruct activity than to foster it. Governments disposed to protect particular forms of activity would be swayed by pressure groups, whom they would favour at the expense of the community at large; politics would be corrupted and the people impoverished; even well-meaning regulation, intended to promote the public interest, would clog the channels of trade. The simple rule of *laissez-faire* therefore was not merely negative, but prescribed the best way of promoting the social welfare.

The justification of inequality, as we have surveyed it here, has rested upon three considerations. First, there is the plain fact that people are unequal in all sorts of ways, not least in their ability to acquire wealth and income, the inequality of which appears as a natural counterpart to that of humanity itself. Second, the need for order in every society requires a structure of ranks and an allocation of functions accompanied by appropriately differentiated standards of living. Third, inequalities arise from the working of the market; but this if left unimpeded will do more to harmonize self-interest and raise the general level of welfare than can be achieved by intervention. In the course of time, each of these considerations has been counteracted by the rise of other ways of viewing man and society. We shall examine them in turn.

8.2. The Grounds of Belief in Personal Equality

From the earliest times, one notion of equality was present in the irresistible claim of justice: although different people must be treated differently, there must be an equivalence in each case between the award and its object. In that sense, it is the very nature of law that all people are equal before it. Some may be awarded damages and others be fined, but there should be no disproportion between the award and the facts on which it is based in different cases. The very idea of just or fair treatment requires us to treat people equally when they are in like case. The idea, moreover, is inescapable: even those who exalt the use of force feel the need to justify it; those who demand more for themselves say it is only fair. However it comes about that this application of equality imposes itself—we shall have more to say about this in Part III—it is present everywhere in the notion of law, and forms a central element in the notion of citizenship. Every citizen is entitled, as such, not to the same treatment, but to equality of treatment. If there is any justice in the world, it can only be justice for everyone. In this sense all human beings are alike. Wherever the Stoic or Roman conception of law extended, a principle of equality was instilled, and must have tended to spread from justiciable matters to other components of people's welfare.

This influence of positive law was the stronger, because underlying it was the notion of natural law. A number of ways of viewing humanity were derived from nature, or the state of nature. Central to these was the notion of design, whether the purposes of a creator conceived as a personal God or as a divine architect, setting up a system of forces that would operate impersonally according to principles that the genius of a Newton might discern. But these principles were not only Newtonian: it was assumed also that all things had a law of their own being. It was of their nature to bahave, and develop, in a certain way. It seemed only right and proper that they should do so. To find what was the right course for them to follow, therefore, we must discover their basic nature, that is, the propensities implanted in them so that they might fill their place in the great plan of the universe. The propensities of humankind would be revealed if we stripped off the accretions of custom and convention in society, and returned to the state of nature. If those propensities were found to be conflicting, that could be accounted for by the Fall, which had distorted the Creator's harmonious design; the Bible gave one account of this, and Rousseau, in his day, another. But for our present purpose the essential is that all humanity was held to be subject to nature law: everyone should live in accordance with the way that nature—or the Creator—intended. This was to view each person as a member of the species Man. As such, all were alike. The distinctive mark of the species was the faculty of Reason, the unique endowment that distinguished man from beast. The statement that all men were born equal, or created equal, meant that each human being was endowed as such with the attributes of humanity within the great scheme of things, and was the same in that respect as every other. It would then be asked why those who were equal in this basic respect should be unequal in so many others. The question applied especially to the distribution of wealth; for on any imaginative recovery of the state of nature, it appeared that nature had provided the resources of the earth equally for all her children. The fencing off of land into pieces of private property was a kind of Fall, a distortion of the original plan of creation.

The sense of common humanity was intensified by humanism. Instead of seeking the essential human being in the state of nature, humanism set men and women as they were in the centre of the earthly stage, and concerned itself with their experience of life, their powers of reasoning and artistic creation. Romanticism carried this further with its exaltation of the capacity for feeling, its delight in joy and compassion for sorrow. The aspects of human nature most valued here are those in which people differ least: it is them we think of when we appeal to 'common humanity'. They transcend in particular the most unmistakable difference of attributes and function, that between the genders: it is no accident that humanism brought with it in time a changed view of the status of womanhood. If all sorts of people are so alike in their capacity to enjoy and to suffer, how can we justify their being so unequally supplied with the amenities of life, so unequally exposed to its hardships? The question had special force to those whom humanism had sensitized to the sufferings of others, and who, instead of regarding them externally, entered into their experience with fellow feeling and compassion.

The same egalitarian effect appeared when the subjectivism of the Reformation paralleled that of humanism. The emphasis laid on the soul of man, and the direct access of each soul to God, concentrated attention on the individual, and on a respect in which all individuals were alike. As humanism was intensified in romanticism, so was the Reformation in evangelicalism. When all souls were equal in the sight of God, and all men and women were sinners for whose redemption Christ's blood had been shed, it was hard to attach importance to worldly differences of rank and wealth.

The concentration of attention on human nature opened up the study of psychology. In part this promoted a positive political science, directed to discover not the moral basis of authority, but the way in which the propensities of human nature lead to the formation of societies and government. It also affected thought about society by its assumption that the mind was furnished by the impact of sense impressions: what was at birth a *tabula rasa* was inscribed by the external world. This had two egalitarian implications. One was that at the core of each human being was a self which, although it bore impressions that then differentiated one person from another, was in itself undifferentiated. The essential ego was the same in all people. It could then be said that all were naturally equal—naturally, because the undifferentiated self was revealed as part of the original design of creation. But more than that: if this view of formation was extended from the storing of the mind to the shaping of adult personality and capability, then people could no longer be held responsible for what they were and did or failed to do. If the street porter was rough and ignorant only because he had not had the training, from boyhood up, that would have made a philosopher of him, it seemed unfair to assign him a scanty income on account of deficiencies that were no fault of his own. The fault lay rather with society, which had denied him education. Equally, the skilled and the cultivated could not claim that they deserved their higher incomes: their ability to command them was their good fortune and not their achievement. It followed that they might well feel guilt about receiving what in one sense they themselves had done nothing to deserve—for however hard they had worked, the very capacity to do so had been instilled in them. At least they could not feel justified in resisting taxes imposed on them to pay for social benefits. The 'lower orders' now appeared as 'the underprivileged' or 'the deprived'.

8.3. The Possibility of Changing Society

So long as most people were living in societies whose structure depended on landholding, they were seldom confronted with the necessity for change or even the possibility of it. The discontent of the poor and the landless might prompt them to rise up and dispossess the wealthy, but it was rare for them to consider, as the English Levellers did, the design of a different sort of community. However, with the growth of commerce and manufactures, and above all with the growth of towns, the new citizens were lifted out from an accustomed structure of property and power, and had to find a new basis for order and government. It is no accident that the very words 'civic' and 'citizen' derive from the word for a city, and that the positive study of political structure and the behaviour of man as a political animal took its rise in Athens and Florence. This study was comparative. Different forms of government were seen to have been tried at different times in one city and in different cities. The possibility of designing and changing institutions was evident.

But the townsman who had escaped the subordination of the countryside was still confronted with the need to keep order. The authority of government had to be established in practice and justified in principle. Where the Reformation prevailed, and government could no longer be founded upon divine decree, it had to be validated from other first principles. It was a mark of the detachment of the individual, and of the actual circumstances of life in the city, that the origins of government were found in an agreement between individuals previously existing in independence of one another. As the agreement was made out of self-interest, so it was intended to protect the person and property of each contracting party. The state thus appeared as instrumental to individual interests. There was no one mandatory form for the instrument. The test of its efficiency was its responsiveness to the wishes of those who fashioned it, and could change it if they thought fit.

It was a feature of this approach to social change by way of individualism that the state had no life of its own, and remained external to the lives of the individuals within it; 'the social welfare' could mean only the sum of the good and ill experienced by each of them. This understanding was the outcome of normative thinking. Positive studies had a different outcome. When modes of government and social customs were seen as objects to be described, compared and understood as if they were in the realm of natural history, they appeared as organisms. 'The state' receded as an object, in favour of 'society'. The appropriateness of institutions was assessed according to their adaptation to their environment. Already in the eighteenth century social structure was seen as adapting itself to methods of production, in successive stages. When in the next century the notion of evolution took hold, the analogy between societies and living organisms gained fresh significance. Societies would grow. Perhaps, like other organisms, they could also decay; but the more hopeful expectation of progress towards higher forms of life generally prevailed. Policy therefore became concerned with much more than the present. 'The good of society' might mean equally the current wellbeing of the community, or the interests of generations yet unborn. Measures should be judged by their power to promote healthy development. This outlook came naturally to a British people that had been increasingly urbanized since 1760 and had seen the towns and cities not only grow in size but improve in amenity as new institutions were developed.

On that view of society, inequality was no longer needed to keep order. Rather, there were good reasons for reducing it. It was divisive, when what was wanted was fraternity. The separation of classes was regrettable, not only because it gave rise to conflict, but also because the differences in living standards associated with it were invidious. The suffering of the poor must be a source of concern to the rich; the members of a society were 'members one of another', and one part of the body could not be healthy when another was sick. The ties between members of one family, and the responsibility of each for all, were felt to extend in some measure throughout society. A social conscience developed. When measures 'to elevate society' or 'advance social welfare' were proposed, something more was meant than benefiting a number of persons individually: it was felt that helping the less advantaged benefited those who were comfortably off but could not be at ease while their neighbours lacked so much of what they had themselves. The term 'socialism' has become familiar in so many contexts that we need to take fresh note of its message when newly minted—that people are to be seen and treated not as independent entities, but as constituted by a web of human relations. If then it was society that moulded individual lives, arrangements that fostered some and stunted others were indefensible.

Nationalism entered here, and interventionism with it. What mattered was the welfare of the whole people. As those who are proud of their village do not want to show some well kept houses and gardens to the world while others are squalid and neglected, so the social solidarity that went with nationalism wanted to see all the people well developed in mind and body. This sense of solidarity was heightened in wartime, when the weakness of any section of society was a national weakness, and those who were required to give their money could not protest, when others were giving their lives.

The influences that make for a change of social attitudes are not cumulative or irreversible. Each of us is moved both by self-interest and by fellow-feeling; the prevailing balance between the two shifts now this way, now that. There may even be a pendular movement, by which a period of predominance of either outlook and course makes their attendant disadvantages more apparent while their advantages come to be taken for granted, and the relative attraction of the other way becomes greater. The very course of events—notably, urbanization and war—may tilt the balance. In particular, the solidarity induced by the Second World War will have worn off simply by the lapse of time and the turnover of generations as the years have gone by. The outstanding and general advance in standards of living achieved in those years will have greatly reduced the hardships that the welfare state was designed to alleviate. It may be that the very success of social security measures appears to remove the need for them; certainly their abuses become more prominent. Those measures are applied in a field, as the national health service shows, where demand may be created by supply: they grow in response to the needs and opportunities they uncover. If, then, people generally are coming to feel freer to pursue their own ends than they did in times of danger and hardship, they become less willing to foot the bill for other people's welfare. Their wish to be unhampered in their self-seeking even gains approval as an engine of growth: the regime of high performance now rests on self-help more than on solidarity. These may be reasons why egalitarian tendencies have been checked or reversed in a number of Western countries in recent years.

8.4. The Promotion of Egalitarianism as a Practical Policy

The collectivist outlook just described led naturally to the practical expression of neighbourly compassion and hope for social betterment; but measures of the kind were opposed by the presumption that intervention would do more harm than good. This presumption was made to give ground, if it was not beaten back altogether, partly by the movement of events, partly by that of thought.

Urbanization threw up new evils that cried for control. Cholera made that cry loud and clear. But the shift of occupations as well as of residence also brought a new faculty of control, through the growth of the professional middle class. The administrators who came forward from it were armed with a new technique of investigation, and a compilation of statistics. In the light of that information, they designed measures that were adapted to the particular circumstances of the case, and practicable because they accepted propensities of human behaviour and aimed to canalize rather than dam them up. This 'social engineering' (to use a later term) was very different from the clumsy or biased intervention condemned by the eighteenth-century liberals. It was made possible on the national scale by two developments of the times: the great improvement in communications, whether for persons or for information; and the growth of taxable capacity, and the ability of government to draw on it. Experience of the first and tentative measures showed their promise: their weakness was only that they did not go far enough. Intervention by government was conspicuously effective, in its most enterprising form, of 'municipal socialism'. The middle-class politicians and administrators by whom this was promoted engaged in a kind of domestic colonialism: if they were authoritarians, it was plainly for the people's good.

But it was also that the people themselves began to make their demands for collectivist measures felt. They did not by any means always welcome the controls and requirements imposed on them by the expert, but they wanted protection and benefits to meet the needs they knew. It was the basic philosophy of trade unionists that human values should be protected from the unfeeling impact of market forces. The enfranchisement first of the urban artisan and then of a majority of working-class men transformed the social composition of the electorate. The attitudes of the new voters were various, but among them few would have resisted measures of social betterment because they disturbed the working of the market or impaired the freedom of enterprise.

At the same time, the development of economics worked to an effect very different from that of the old political economy. In one way, the new economics, with its integration of the analysis of demand with that of supply, validated the market: it showed that the allocation of resources would be optimal if it was governed by a plebiscite of consumers maximizing the utility they derived from their outlay, and by the actions of producers maximizing their profits. But this was on the assumptions that all concerned were rational, that competition in the market was perfect, and that the distribution of purchasing power between consumers was acceptable. The realistic and institutional studies of economists were hardly necessary to show that the first two of those assumptions were unwarranted. The third was called in question by economics itself: the line of thought known as the economics of welfare gave new force to the old observation that a redistribution of income would deprive the rich of less benefit than it conferred on the poor. Although economists would take account of more effects of egalitarian measures than this, the authority of political economy could no longer be claimed for resistance to them.

8.5. A Consideration of Causes

In the preceding pages we have watched a great change coming about, in outlook and in policy. How can we account for it? Search for the ultimate causes of any event in history is endless; the proximate causes, if sometimes evident, are commonly numerous and entangled. But something can be done to make our history more reasoned.

To watch changes taking place does in itself provide a first source of understanding. The narrative that shows us what once happened presents before our eyes a sequence of events that we interpret by applying our own everyday knowledge of natural laws and human nature. We gain an understanding of the past by an imaginative reconstruction which is really an extension of our own experience. A detailed account of the events leading up to the fall of a government or the rout of an army is then, as we say, 'readily intelligible'.

But this is only to provide explanation initially, at a first view of the affair. It applies to particular concentrated events, rather than to the broad movements that change the lives of whole peoples in the course of time. Nor does it partake of the ultimate nature of explanation. The core of this is causality. It must answer the question not how, but why.

That question seems hard if not impossible to answer, amid the confusion of forces in the drama of history. Short sequences there may well be, in which the direct effects of a particular action can be traced with some confidence; but in the larger scene, such as we are concerned with here, too many possible sources offer themselves for consideration beneath each change. There are general and pervasive influences, such as shifts in the climate, or in methods of production, or pressure of population on standards of living. Ideas respond in part to the changing environment, but they have their own spontaneity and impact. So do particular persons, such as teachers, politicians, soldiers. Sheer accident, and above all sheer force, have powerfully affected the course of events. Yet the mind still craves for understanding. The torrent thundering down the mountainside may long have stood for the primeval power of the gods, beyond the wit of man to fathom; but in time the scientists found the laws of nature under which the molecules of water rose to the clouds and came down again. There may be spontaneity in human action that will prevent us from discovering any like laws of human nature, but we still cannot help trying to understand history.

To that end we must rid our minds of the notion of causality as a knock-on—typified by billiard balls striking one another, or trucks being shunted on a railway track, hitting each other in succession. We have to think instead of a framework. This contains a large number of factors all bearing on the outcome of a process of change, some tending to move it in one direction, some in another. The presence of some, at least in minimal quantity, may be essential to a positive outcome; others may be helpful but dispensable; others again may be depressant but capable of being overpowered. We can if we like distinguish necessary and sufficient conditions, positive and negative influences, major and minor sources, mainstreams and catalysts; but one and the same factor may act in different ways according to the strength in which it is present and its conjunction with other factors.

The use of such a framework to make a course of change intelligible can be illustrated from a form of change which, at a certain level, is a great deal less complex than the changes in the outlook of Western man—the growth of a crop. At least a number of the principal factors that bear upon such growth can be visualized readily. The crop is dependent on supplies of water and of different kinds of nutrient and minerals, and on the circumambient warmth and light. In the open field, it is subject to accident, disease and depredation. In experimental conditions, variations in any one of the beneficial factors while the others are held constant are found to be associated with measurable variations in growth. There are also interactions between the factors, or joint effects: the response to a given dose of one fertilizer, for example, may be greater when another is being applied at the same time. Questions and answers about causality present themselves very differently here according to what changes they presuppose. If an increase in the input of one factor alone brings an increase in the crop, we may say that it caused it, although for the particular yield to be achieved all the other factors had to be present in their given amounts. If we take away altogether one of the factors such as water, some minimum input of which is a necessary condition for any crop at all, then certainly the drought is, of itself alone, the cause of the loss of the crop. But we shall not find any factor that is, of itself alone, a sufficient condition of growth: that is, any one that alone will give rise to output. Nor does history know any causality in that sense. What can be attempted in the judgement of the historian is what is carried out experimentally in agriculture: to establish the relative strength of the forces exerted by different factors—or, more accurately, since those forces sometimes converge, the forces flowing along different branches of the framework. Sometimes the relative strength of one such force seems so great and unmistakable that in common parlance it can pass for 'the cause' of a subsequent development. But the important task of explanation is to establish the framework.

Our particular task here is to make somewhat more intelligible the great reversal of attitudes towards egalitarianism, whose course we have been following in some of its varied aspects down the centuries. The subject matter has always been people's minds. The framework that we need will bring together such forces as affect our own minds and their outlook. It is through these forces that from time to time children come to see the world differently from their parents; judge right and wrong differently from them; and wish to order society differently. A simple framework with only three branches will serve initally, although each branch is broad. The outlook of everyone in society appears to be moulded by the forces exerted through branches that may be described as Information, Resources and Ideas. By reminding ourselves how these forces converged to promote the acceptance of egalitarianism, we shall not be tracing that development to its origins or reducing history to an orderly pattern, but we shall make the change of outlook more intelligible.

Information took its effect because people's attitude towards one another depended on what they knew or believed about their own ancestors and about other peoples of their own day. So long as they believed that human life began a finite number of generations ago, when their first parents were placed in the world by the Creator, mankind appeared as a family under the authority of the Heavenly Father; and the differences of age, sex and function within the family are so clear that claims for equality of treatment have usually been pressed only when some member was on the point of separation. So to those whose mental picture of society was as of a great family, descended from our first parents, placed by God on the earth to people it, its inequalities seemed natural. But the inhabitants of the Roman Empire, who saw its citizenship extended throughout its bounds, were acquainted with an axiom of unity amid the diversity of its peoples. The thought of that equality of status was an animating principle of Roman law, through which it returned to Western Europe. The discoveries made by the astronomers and navigators from the fifteenth century onwards, and the revolution they brought about in knowledge of the earth as a planet, dispelled the image of mankind as the children of God, uniquely created and sited by him at the centre of the universe, and threw men back upon themselves. They were more ready now, as the Greeks had been, to exalt human achievements; they had more regard for one another accordingly. The sense of the unity of mankind was deepened as the reports of travellers came in about primitive peoples in lands newly discovered. What was most striking was not their diversity but their common humanity. A human species was revealed. Its members shared a common fate, voyaging through space on a sphere. The historical and comparative methods also began to show that varieties of behaviour were not necessarily inherent but were adaptations to local conditions.

In sum, the effect of increasing information was to shift the prevailing view of humanity from that of a family with a naturally differentiated structure towards that of a species with a basic human nature in common. Between people who are basically so alike, there is a prima facie case for parity of treatment.

The extent of *Resources* available to households determines their ability to engage in activities beyond the drudgery of getting a living. When the greater part of the population is engaged in unremitting toil merely to keep alive, the case for redistribution might seem at its strongest; but there has been little pressure in practice, except, it may be, for riots at times of bad harvest. This is not because in such circumstances there is little surplus to share out: it is rather because such an economy is not accustomed to think of welfare. A rise in the standard of living is needed before those who have least enjoyment receive enough for the adjustment of their amenity, relatively to others, to be a matter of calculus and policy. The higher the general standard of living, the more alert will people be to the comparison of welfare. Twice during the periods surveyed here a rise in real income, sufficient to transform the way of life of a substantial section of society, has contributed to the rise of egalitarianism. In the fifteenth century the high standard of living attained widely in western Europe made possible leisure, and cultivation of the arts, as never before; it fostered individualism, and subjectivism, and a concern with feeling. The rise in the affluence of the British middle class in the mid-eighteenth century relieved its women of household chores, and promoted a notable advance in their education and status. More generally, as standards of living and education rose, the shape of the distribution of resources might show as wide a difference as before between the rich and the poor, but the poor were now at an absolute level that did not set them so far apart in their neighbours' eyes: they appeared as full but less fortunate members of the same society.

These are ways in which an increased availability of resources has strengthened the motives for the redistribution that it also made more feasible. But economic growth has contributed to egalitarianism in another way, because it has been associated with changes in the way people see themselves and each other. It has come about through the rise of methods of working that asked more of individuals than the traditional ways of life that they superseded had done. Instead of following custom in common with one's neighbours, those who engaged in trade and manufactures needed to think for themselves; they had scope for individual enterprise. The growth of output will have been associated with a rise of social mobility, a characteristic that distinguished the growing towns from the countryside. People were more likely to prosper or fail according to their own capacity, effort and luck. Individualism prevailed, not in the sense of unrestrained competition, but through an escape from old bonds and a heightened consciousness of each person's capacity to take a distinctive path through life.

This awareness of individuality directed attention to the ways in which people differ, yet it fostered egalitarianism through its subjectivism. As people became more conscious of themselves as independent individuals, and as personalities, the world of personal thought and feeling became the object of greater consideration; but that was a world of suffering and enjoyment in which all sentient beings shared. Individualism led to humanism.

Since we are not attempting to trace any influences back to their ultimate sources—if such there ever are—we need not try to meet the challenge of the materialists who hold that prevailing haibits of thought are always a response to the current methods of production. In naming *Ideas* as a main branch of the forces making for egalitarianism, we need only assume that once ideas are in the air they do impinge on individuals to affect their attitudes. It is a short step on from this to allow that ideas can acquire some of their power by the persuasive force of their own logic. There are some works, it is true, whose influence on minds and hearts has depended largely on their timing; but there are others that are in a sense timeless, because they deal percipiently with enduring issues. Their marshalling of the evidence and their cogent argument give them an influence over readers in varied circumstances. They do not merely amplify opinions that the course of events is promoting in any case, but can themselves form or deflect opinion. Trains of speculation or analysis may follow their own course of development. Although the reception of any argument depends on the current outlook of the audience, that outlook has itself been formed by received opinions. It seems right, then, to treat ideas as an independent source of influence.

It is largely with ideas that the discussion of the preceding sections has been concerned. A first idea noted as clearing the way for egalitarianism was the concept of natural law revealed to Reason: for this went with the belief that men were uniquely endowed with Reason—that this distinctive possession united and glorified men as a species. Here, it may be said, was the first discovery of the common humanity of all mankind. The Renaissance, by contrast, brought to western Europe a discovery of individuality, in the Greek way of life; yet this in its way also worked towards egalitarianism, because of the stress it laid on the inner life of individuals, their feelings, virtue, happiness and welfare. The philosophers intensified this stress when they assumed that fully habilitated individuals preceded the formation of society, or held that the human mind at birth was a *tabula rasa*, its development depending on the impressions made upon it, so that whether a child became lowly or eminent in later life depended solely upon his upbringing and training. This sensational psychology called in question the justice of rewarding attainments when these were due to neither nature nor effort but to circumstance. Individualism, or subjectivism, was also expressed in religion, in the concern of the Reformed churches for the salvation of the soul of the believer and his or her inner awareness of a relationship with God. As the subjectivism of the Renaissance was extended and intensified in the romanticism of the eighteenth century, so that of the Reformation was projected in evangelicalism. In these movements of thought and feeling, stress on the experience of the individual and his or her welfare, temporal and eternal, led to an equal consideration of all sentient men and women.

Such, in summary, is the answer that the materials assembled in the preceding pages suggest to the question why egalitarianism arose and attained its present hold. The summary is over-simple in one way and yet complex in another. Of all the threads in the tapestry of history, it draws out only a few, but these are still interwoven. There has been no question of reducing the course of history to the action of a single persistent underlying propellant. But if we have moved from the 'how' that we watched towards the 'why' that we want to grasp, it is because we have raised our viewpoint to a greater altitude, so that we now follow 'how' over a wider conspectus of time and place. This more comprehensive view enables us to hold together in the mind's eye the main changes which in the course of so much else promoted the rise of egalitarianism. We see this as an intelligible tendency within a society that has become aware of the common stock and mysterious endowment of *Homo sapiens* on the planet earth; has developed a relatively high standard of living, which liberates many people from the thraldom of toil and makes the fulness of welfare an object of concern; and whose thinkers have laid stress on the respects in which all persons share a common humanity.

PART II

Distributions of Income and Wealth
in the Living Economy

9

Distributions Displayed

9.1. The Method of Display

Distributions of income and wealth consist, by their nature, in masses of figures. The aim of this chapter is to see how they can best be displayed, for the purpose of comparison between different periods or countries.

The natural form of a distribution of income, which records the number of incomes found at each income level, is the familiar frequency distribution. Figure 9.1 shows how the distribution of personal income in the United Kingdom at two recent dates can be displayed. It also shows the limitations of this form of display. Apparently there were marked changes between the two dates: were these only the effect of a general inflation of monetary incomes, or were incomes at various levels affected differently? The later distribution is much less peaked: does this mean that it is more equal? Reflection suggests that some of the apparent change may be due only to the effect of a general inflation of the figures on an unchanged classification by £200 intervals. Between the two dates the mean income rose by nearly 70 per cent, from about £1000 to nearly £1700: the £200 interval of the earlier date is therefore effectively reduced by a divisor of 1.7, to provide the much narrower interval of about £120 at the later date. The effect is to flatten any peak. At the same time, the boundaries of the classes have been shifted, with uncertain effects on the profile. These complications apart, this kind of profile does not easily provide answers to such questions as whether the middle incomes have lagged behind the others or gained on them, let alone whether there has been any change in inequality overall.

To answer this last question, various measures have been proposed. One is readily visualized—the Gini coefficient, based on the Lorenz curve. Curves of this kind, for the two distributions of Figure 9.1, are shown in Figure 9.2. They are formed by cumulating the data. The incomes are arranged in ascending order, from lowest to highest. As we go along the array, and cover successively 5, 10, 15 per cent (and so on) of all income recipients, we ask at each point. What percentage of the total income has been covered so far? These pairs of percentages, of the cumulated number of recipients and the cumulated total of income, are then plotted in the coordinates of Figure 9.2. If everyone had the same income, the first 10 per

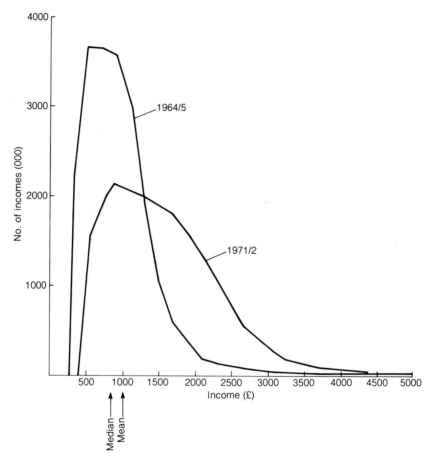

Fig. 9.1 Distribution of personal income before tax, United Kingdom, 1964/5 and 1971/2. *Source:* Royal Commission (1975: figs. 1 and 2).

cent of recipients would have 10 per cent of all income, the first 20 per cent, 20 per cent of income and so on; all these points would lie on the diagonal at 45 degrees, a gradient of one for one. If, at the other extreme, no income at all was received by all potential recipients save one, and this one had it all, then the points would lie along the base-line until, at all but 100 per cent of the recipients, the profile shot up the vertical axis. Actual distributions form curves lying somewhere between these two boundaries: the nearer is the curve to the second, rectangular, boundary, the more unequal is the distribution. The Gini coefficient reduces this position of the curve to a single figure, by measuring the area enclosed between the curve and the diagonal as a percentage of the whole triangular area. It varies, therefore, between zero, in the case of complete equality, and unity, at the extreme of inequality. (See the Statistical Appendix to this chapter.)

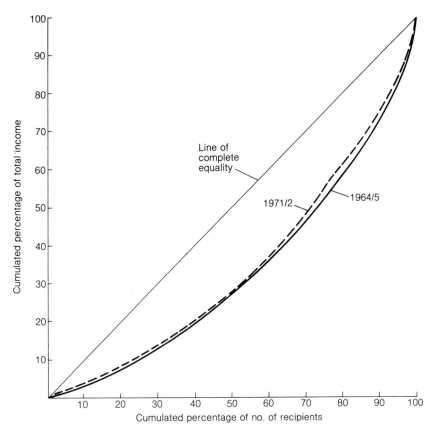

Fig. 9.2   Lorenz curves for the distribution of personal income before tax in the United Kingdom, 1964/5 and 1971/2. *Source:* Royal Commission (1975: table 1).

The Lorenz curves of Figure 9.2 make a very different impression from that of the frequency distributions of Figure 9.1. For most of their course up to the median, the two curves are indistinguishable. As we proceed beyond the median, incomes rise more in 1971/2 than in 1964/5; they therefore stand higher relatively to the top incomes. According to the convention adopted here, this is a movement towards equality; for part of its length the new curve lies nearer the diagonal than does the old one, and the Gini coefficient becomes 0.325 instead of 0.330. The clarification of the comparison is due in great part to the scale of income having been changed from original £s to cumulated percentages of total income: this avoids distortion of the scale by changes in the purchasing power of money. But cumulation also obscures the course of change within particular parts of the distribution; this has to be read from small changes of curvature.

Two other, more sophisticated, coefficients have been devised to express in a single number the degree of inequality in a distribution as a whole.

Some account of the indices formulated by Henri Theil and A. B. Atkinson is given in the Statistical Appendix to this chapter. In applying information theory to economics, Theil noted that it had taken over from thermo-dynamics the notion of entropy. This, he said, 'may be used for the degree of dispension in a distribution because it is "a measure of disorder" '. Accordingly, he used the formula for entropy as the basis of his own index of inequality. Atkinson (1970) has asked, in effect, what we mean when we say that a certain distribution is more unequal than another one, and has concluded it can only be that in that distribution there is more room for the raising of social welfare by equalization. Social welfare here means the sum of the utilities that the several income recipients derive from their incomes. Any measure of inequality must take account of this. Existing measures, such as the Gini coefficient, the mean difference or the standard deviation, are always liable to rank distributions differently because implicitly they give different weights to inequalities in different parts of the distribution. Atkinson has proposed that this weighting should be made explicit, and has devised an index whose value depends on the observer's own judgement of the relative benefit of a £ to income recipients at different levels. One term in the formula for the index is given a numerical value that expresses this judgement. According as the observer judges that a £ transferred from a rich to a poor man will bring a bigger or smaller increase in felt benefit, taking the two men together, the value assigned to that term will be higher or lower, and the index will show a given distribution as being more or less unequal.

These refinements are instructive as well as ingenious. But no one measure can convey all that interests us when we compare the distributions of income in two countries, or at different dates in the same country. We want to know at what levels the differences between them appear. If we are to trace the causes of those differences or changes, we must study them in their social contexts. This objection to reliance on any single measure applies equally to those measures that are sensitive to the form of the distribution, such as the range between the upper and the lower quartile, or the ratio of the top to the bottom decile. These leave out too much: they tell us nothing about the form of the distribution outside or between the points they rest upon.

More informative are the tables showing the shares of income received by successive quarters or fifths or tenths of the total number of recipients. An example appears in Table 9.1. Here we see the British distributions in the same two years as before, 1964/5 and 1971/2. It does not take long for inspection to bring out the main differences between them: there were next to none below the median, but the incomes immediately above it bulked larger in the later year, while those at the top had become smaller. The ability to display conformation in that way is a valuable property of this sort of tabulation. It has been used as a form well suited to international

TABLE 9.1   *Percentage components of total personal income, by quantile groups, United Kingdom, 1964–5 and 1971–2*

Quantile group	Percentage 1964–5	component (%) 1971–2
Top 1%	7.7	6.1
95–99%	10.6	10.3
90–94%	8.7	8.9
Top 10%	27.0	25.3
80–89%	13.9	14.5
70–79%	11.7	12.2
60–69%	10.1	10.7
50–59%	9.1	9.3
40–49%	7.9	8.1
30–39%	6.8	6.7
20–29%	5.6	5.6
10–19%	4.5	4.4
0–9%	3.4	3.2
	100.0	100.0

Source: Royal Commission (1975: table 3).

comparisons, and will be so used here. But it has its pitfalls. They lurk in the term 'share'. We speak of 'sharing' some good that has already come from somewhere and is there in front of us, only awaiting division: the cake has been baked, and the question now is the size of the slice to go to each avid applicant. This not merely neglects but distorts the relation between most of the income that people receive and their own productive contributions. The view of entitlement implicit in the use of the term 'share' will appear if we substitute that other term just used, and speak of the 'percentage contributions' of the quantile groups: if that seems to beg a question, so no less does speaking of 'shares'. But this is not all. The shares are percentage shares, and of their very nature, if the share of one group of persons goes up, that of one or more of the other groups must go down. It is natural then to speak of their 'fall', but we do not know how they have changed, if at all, in absolute terms. To take an example from the distribution of wealth, we are told that 'the considerable growth in the net stock of dwellings combined with the large increase in price had the effect of reducing the share of the top one per cent of wealth holders by 6.0 percentage points between 1960 and 1972' (Royal Commission 1979: para. 6.3). This was because so much of the increased quantity and higher price of dwellings went to swell the holdings of the middle ranks; but we might be tempted, on a view of the diminished share of the top wealth-holders, to suppose that the rich had got poorer. It would be easy, again, to speak of the middle groups having gained 'at the expense of' the top; and to fall into the habit of thinking that this is how gains are made. But if, say, the farmers, working hard and becoming more efficient, raise their output and their incomes with it, then—other things being equal—their share of all income will go up, and that of the rest of us will fall: but we shall in fact be better supplied with food. We therefore need a term that is free from the misleading associations of 'shares'. Unfortunately, both 'part' and 'portion' do have such associations: in common usage they indicate a sharing out, an allocation. 'Component' and 'proportion' seem the best alternatives, and although their use may jar at first by their unfamiliarity, they will be used henceforward in place of the 'shares' of which we have spoken hitherto. The term 'distribution', although it too may be used to describe the sharing out of a total that is fixed independently of the size of any allocation from it, is too deeply entrenched in general statistical usage to be abandoned.

There remains another difficulty. Taking the proportions of income accruing to quantile groups, as we do in Table 9.1, may suggest that the national income is divided between certain defined and unchanging bodies of persons; but many changes in distribution are actually due to changes in the size and boundaries of such bodies—for example, the extension and contraction of occupations.

Any table, moreover, has the limitation of not presenting a clear impression to the eye. A way to do this, and to reveal the changes that may take place in any part of the distribution, is offered by the 'Pen parade'. In his work on *Income Distribution* (1971), the Dutch economist Jan Pen invited the reader to consider the distribution of personal incomes as represented by a march-past of the recipients. They would be marshalled in order of the size of their incomes, the lowest coming first, the millionaires bringing up the rear. But more, they would be envisaged not in their own natural bodies, but endowed with heights proportional to their incomes. If those at the median were of the average actual height, most of those in front of them would appear stunted, and many of them tiny; while at the back a few millionaires would appear as giants with their heads in the clouds. If the procession took an hour to move past an observer, half the hour would have passed before people of normal height came by: until then, most of the time it would have been, in Pen's words, 'a parade of dwarfs' (1971): 48). Pen concluded his lively exposition by pointing out that a still photograph of the procession, from shortest to tallest, could be made in the form of a diagram.

This is the method of display that will be used here. Figure 9.3 presents the UK distributions for 1964/5 and 1971/2 in this form. The income levels of 1971/2 have been deflated by a price index to express them in £s of 1964/5 purchasing power.

In Figure 9.3 we are struck at once by the linearity of the 1964/5 profile for most of its course up to the 80th percentile. The constant slope, on a natural scale, means that the absolute difference in income as we move from one person to the next in the parade is constant. But this constancy

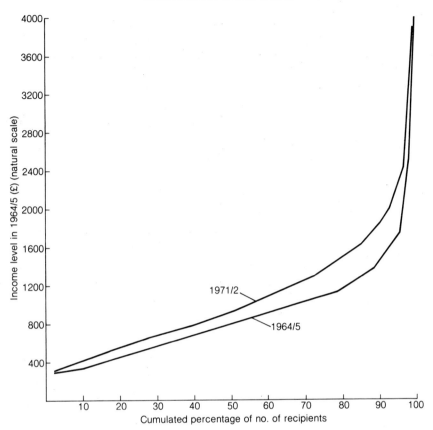

Fig. 9.3 Distribution of personal income before tax in the United Kingdom 1964/5 and 1971/2, displayed as Pen parades. *Source:* Royal Commission (1975: table 1).

implies a fall in the *proportionate* rise as we move into higher levels of income. For many purposes it is this proportionate difference that matters. We know, for instance, that when wage claims are made with reference to differentials, although it may be sufficient to cite the differential in pounds and pence when prices are fairly steady or when a general rise has not as yet gone far, after any pronounced change in the price level the differential will be reckoned, and contended for, as a percentage. It is clear that, if a differential of £20 a week were regarded as satisfactory between two grades of manual worker, it would be thought quite inadequate as between two grades of management: but the same *percentage* differential might be acceptable in the two cases.

It follows that where, as here, we find an approximately linear sector of the profile, we are actually confronted with a progressively falling rate of change as we move along the parade, from lower to higher incomes. This appears in Figure 9.4 which is drawn on a ratio scale, in which equal vertical distances denote equal proportionate differences. We see that the sector of the 1964/5 profile that was linear in Figure 9.3 now becomes concave downwards. The sector of the 1971/2 profile that was gently concave upwards on the natural scale now appears as more nearly linear.

These different impressions caution us against misinterpretation of the Pen profile, as that will usually be presented here, on a natural scale. There is an advantage in presenting incomes in their own usual form: the heights prevailing in different parts of the parade are those of incomes as they appear to us when we look around. It proves also that linear segments appear again in a number of distributions: they are a notable and intriguing characteristic. But we must always remember that a linear profile means a steady falling proportionate rate of rise as we move along the parade; and that a constant rate of rise (equal percentage differences) appears on a natural scale as a profile that is concave upwards throughout.

The ratio scale, moreover, has the advantage of enabling us to compare the dispersion or inequality of incomes in the two years by comparing the slopes of the profiles. In Figure 9.4 there is little difference over the first

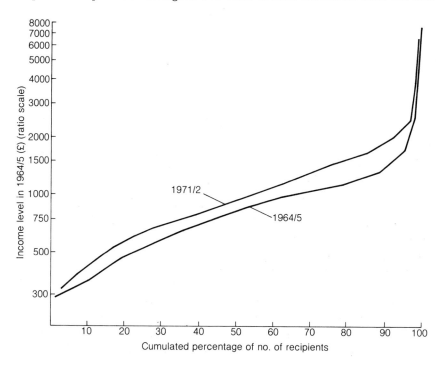

Fig. 9.4 Distribution of personal income before tax in the United Kingdom, 1964/5 and 1971/2, displayed as Pen parades on ratio scale. *Source:* Royal Commission (1975: table 1).

two-thirds of the income recipients. In both years the lowest incomes are more differentiated than those between the 30th and 60th percentile. Above that, a change has occurred: the upper middle-class incomes between the 60th and 85th percentiles have become higher in 1971/2 relatively to those on either side of them. At the upper quartile, incomes were 1.38 times the median in 1964/5, but 1.41 times in 1971/2. This change it is that makes the 1971/2 distribution yield a lower index of inequality as a whole—if we wish, for instance, to calculate the Gini. But the advantage of the Pen profile is that it shows just what and where the change has been.

At about the 85th percentile we enter on a quite different type of distribution. The differentiation, as marked by the slope even on the ratio scale, rises sharply, and the profiles soar out of the graphs. The formation of incomes seems to be governed here by principles very different from those that hold sway lower down.

To these advantages of the Pen parade in facilitating comparisons, and displaying the extent and location of differences throughout the distribution, may be added another property, although it is less valuable in practice. The total area under the profile represents total income, or wealth, and the relative size of the part enclosed between any two percentiles represents the proportion of the total that accrues to persons between those bounds in the array.

But there are also two disadvantages, which the figures illustrate. One, already mentioned, is the inability of this kind of diagram to contain and impress on the observer the very high incomes of the top 1 or 2 per cent of recipients. To do that, the vertical dimension of the diagram would have to be five times what it is now; or, alternatively, the scale would have to be so much smaller that the course of the profiles over all but the top 10 per cent of recipients would be flattened into insignificance.

The other difficulty brought out by Figure 9.3 is still more serious. How can we compare profiles at whose dates the purchasing power of money was different? In 1971/2 the British price level was some 44 per cent higher than in 1964/5; we are really dealing with different currencies in the two years. So are we, even more evidently, when we compare distributions in different countries.

In considering how to deal with this difficulty, we have to keep in mind two requirements. The first arises from an interest in inequality: we want to be able to read off the degree of inequality in any sector from the slope of the profile there and, on comparing two sectors of the same profile or of two different profiles, to be able to say that where the slope is steeper there the distribution is more unequal. But secondly, it is a great advantage of the Pen parade that it shows us the form of the distribution sector by sector; and when a change in the form comes about, we want to be able to tell how it has arisen, from what sort of shift and in which sector. If the lower incomes have risen, for example, relatively to those of middle rank, we want to see whether this is because both sorts of income have risen but the lower ones have risen more, or because the lower have risen while the others have stood still or fallen back; and so on. The aim will be the same in international comparisons: if one country's profile is steeper than another's up to the median, is that because the ratio of the lowest incomes in the first to those in the second country is lower than the corresponding ratio for incomes near the median, or for some other reason? We can bring out the source of difference in slope in this way only if the two profiles under comparison are both expressed in the same unit of income—say, in £s of specified purchasing power, such as the £ of 1964/5.

Unfortunately, it is hard to satisfy both these requirements at the same time. For the first, we must ensure that a given vertical distance signifies the same proportional change in income in both profiles. If the profiles are stated in absolute terms, this will not be so: if there were two distributions of exactly the same form, but in the first real incomes were double those in the second throughout, the slopes in the first profile would also be twice as steep. We can avoid this if we express the incomes in each distribution as relatives to their own mean or median. But then we fail to meet the second requirement, for we cannot see the changes in absolute levels of income sector by sector. This we can do only if the distributions under comparison are expressed in currency units of the same purchasing power. This raises the familiar difficulties of finding appropriate price indexes over any long span of time within one country, and coefficients of purchasing power parity between different currencies. But supposing those difficulties were overcome, we might still find ourselves comparing distributions at different average levels of real income, and the slopes of the profiles arising from the same form of distribution will vary with those levels. This is a consequence we can ignore only if the differences in average real income are small.

There remains a way of meeting both requirements at once—to state the profiles in a common unit of income, but plot them on a logarithmic or ratio scale. But this is possible only where we have trustworthy price indexes or measures of purchasing power parity; to compare distributions of different dates in two countries, we need both. Where they are lacking, we can fall back on the first expedient, and express the incomes in each distribution as relatives to their own central value, mean or median; or, which comes to the same, we can divide the incomes through by whatever constants serve to give their central values the same numerical value. Differences of slope will then signify different degrees of inequality, but we shall not be able to trace those differences to their source in absolute incomes. To do that—there is no escape from it—we have to solve the problems of price indexes and purchasing power parity. What we do in each particular case must be a matter of judgement.

There is one case in which we have no choice. Many of the available international comparisons of distributions take the form of tabulations of 'quantile shares'. The Statistical Appendix at the end of this chapter shows how a Pen profile can be derived from such a tabulation, for this readily yields income levels as relatives to the average income: but we cannot obtain any absolute levels.

In Figure 9.3, however, the two profiles were set out in income units of the same purchasing power: the income entries in the income scale of 1971/2 were all divided by 1.44, to convert them to £s of 1964/5 purchasing power. That the 1971/2 curve lies above that for 1964/5 throughout suggests that the real incomes of recipients at all levels had risen, but it may owe something to the inadequacy of the price index. The difference in levels was big enough to warrant setting the profiles out on the ratio scale of Figure 9.4.

9.2. The Definition of Income and the Choice of Unit

The questions of what income is, and who the recipients are, are complex. It might be thought that, since we are concerned with the form of distributions and not the absolute size of any income, the choice of definitions would not matter so long as we applied the chosen definition consistently throughout. But unfortunately, the choice is likely to affect income at different levels in different degree. A decision to include the imputed value of owner-occupied houses, for instance, will raise middle-class incomes in greater proportions than others. There is no basic principle from which to draw indisputable conclusions in these matters.

On one issue, however, a firm decision can be reached at the outset. The income measured in these statistics is seen as a flow of revenue to the recipient, irrespective of changes in that person's assets over the period studied. This definition differs from the concept of income generally adopted by economists, which is the amount available for consumption while keeping assets intact. It consists of the inflow of revenue, mostly by way of pay and profits, together with any accretion of assets coming about otherwise than by the recipient's own saving during the period. The 'accretion' may be negative, in which case part of the inflow of revenue must be set aside to offset it and maintain the total value of assets. This principle is recognized when we are dealing with any productive activity: the income generated is not given by the gross output, but is arrived at only when provision has been made for depreciation. The economists' definition of income goes farther, in that it brings into the reckoning changes in the assets held by the income recipient even when these play no part in his productive activity. But to apply this to personal income is unrealistic. Some application there certainly is to people's reactions to changes in their assets: a fall in the stock market may cause a holder of investments to spend less and save more out of his earned income.

But it goes against usage and common sense to say, if the market has fallen enough, that this person has received no income at all, despite a substantial salary. In any case, the statistics to fill out this definition of income simply do not exist. What we can collect are figures of income as the inflow of revenue.

Even with this guiding light, we face a numbr of doubtful questions, and there is no assurance that they will be answered in the same way in different countries. Should be include transfer incomes? Social benefits make up a large part of the lower incomes, but they may be seen as paid for by the taxpayer out of his or her income. If a parent gives a child an allowance we should not expect it to be added to the sum of incomes, and the transfer from the taxpayer to the recipient of social benefits is of the same kind, even though it is compulsory. But when we are recording personal income, we are concerned with something other than the composition of the national income. The fact is that many individual incomes do contain large elements of benefit; and at the other end of the transfer, we are concerned, at least in the first place, with incomes before tax. We need not mind if the sum of individual incomes exceeds the social income.

This judgement enables us to decide a similar question—Should we deduct superannuation contributions? It has been argued that, if we count both the income that is used to make the contributions and the subsequent pension, we are counting the same income twice, although in different years; the contributor has simply been pushing a slice of income forward in time. By actuarial reckoning, the later income will be paid partly out of the accumulated interest on investments purchased out of the contributions, and partly by drawing those investments down; in times of inflation, it may be supplemented by current contributions from the employer. The charge that in including the pension we are counting what has been counted already will lie only in respect of the drawing down of investments; the supplementation by employers raises the problem of fringe benefits, to be considered in a moment. But our concern is with the incomes of individuals, one with another, and there is no question but that pensions constitute a source of such incomes in the years when they are received, whatever their origin.

A third problem of definition is of a different kind—whether or how we should include elements of income not received or recorded in money. These are benefits in kind provided by employers, such as subsidized canteens; the 'perks' of executives, of which the provision of a car has become one of the most common and substantial; and the already mentioned imputed value of owner-occupied houses. There is no question but that benefits contractually or customarily treated as part of an employee's remuneration should be included: the difficulty is to evaluate and record them. There is also a problem of where to draw the line between remuneration and amenity. Conditions of work which may be provided at some cost to the employer may make a job more attractive and induce people to take it at lower pay in money, and in that case some valuation of the amenities might well be added to that pay; but they are hard to specify, and if we include them we ought equally to make some deduction from pay where that is high because the conditions of work are disagreeable. There is a strong case, however, for including the value of owner-occupied housing. If a couple sold investments in order to buy a house that they had been renting, they would lose income from the investments to the extent that they saved rent payments: they would have no reason to feel that their income had gone down. It is true that the same argument would apply to someone who bought a car instead of paying for public transport, or a washing machine instead of sending clothes to the laundry; indeed, every piece of household equipment locks up capital that might alternatively bring in some monetary income. The reason for including the annual value of housing and not that of other domestic assets is merely practical: this element is much larger than the others, and valuation is possible.

This last consideration is of a kind that proves weighty in deciding where to draw the line at a numbr of doubtful points: namely, what information is available? We have to make the most of the accessible sources. The product is unlikely to be the same in scope in different countries, or even at different times in the same country. We can only look for a fair degree of comparability, and be watchful for divergences that arise only from divergences of boundary. This is particularly important in international comparisons.

But the main sources of information[1] are much the same in kind, if not in detail, in most of the contemporary economies with which we shall be dealing. A major source is always found in the returns of direct taxation, although some income that should be assessed evades it, and many incomes lie below the exemption level. Light on these is thrown by employers' returns of wages, and by the figures of social benefits. In addition to these by-products of administration or officially required returns, there are in a number of country surveys of family or household income that proceed by sampling. In the United Kingdom, for example, the Family Expenditure Survey, set up in order to find the right weights for the index of Consumer Prices year by year, covers some 7000 households, which keep itemized records of their expenditure; because it is also desired to see how the pattern of expenditure varies at different levels of income, they are also asked to state their income. Among the annual sources of income data in the United States are the Current Population Survey and the Consumer Expenditure Survey.

These sources record the income accruing to several types of recipient

---

[1] Sources are listed for each of seven countries other than the UK in Thomas Stark (1977). The sources for the UK are described in Royal Commission (1975: Appendix F).

unit. The smallest unit is the individual man or woman, but this is found rarely. In the estimates in the UK Blue Book, the unit over most of the distribution was the taxpayer, the incomes of husband and wife being consolidated, but recipients below the income tax exemption limit appeared individually. In Australia, husband and wife are assessed to income tax separately, and have an inducement to divide property between them, so that a property income that would appear as £10 000 in the United Kingdom may well appear in Australia as two incomes each the equivalent of £5000. Because most of the inquiries that collect income data are designed to assist social policy, their concern is with social units, chiefly the family and the household. The merging of individual incomes in tax and consumer units reduces the dispersion of incomes; in particular, many of the relatively low earnings of women and young people are hidden within the family incomes that they supplement. British households and American consumer units typically contain 1.4 earners apiece. The definition of the recipient unit applied in different surveys is likely to vary. Evidently much care is needed if close comparability is to be achieved. Thomas Stark (1977: para. 482), in his international comparisons, reports that 'in most instances variations in the income recipient concept had a significant impact upon the distribution of income'. This must come about largely through the merging of small incomes in family or household income. The authors of an ILO survey of the distribution of income in 39 countries (Lecaillon *et al.* 1984) found that 'a distribution by economically active persons differs markedly from a distribution by households, and it is not possible to compare distributions by different receiving units'.

Thus the many differences of definition, both of income itself and of the income unit, perplex the attempt to compare distributions compiled from different sources. If our aim is to answer the question of whether one distribution is more unequal than another, and to answer it by reference to a single index such as the Gini, then much adjustment in detail is needed before an assured answer can be given; or, alternatively, the answer must be subject to qualifications of uncertain numerical effect. But our aim here is less exacting. We are concerned with the form of the distributions and its social significance. We are going on now to take up such questions as, Is there a typical form largely common to a number of different societies? If so, what sort of inequality does it reveal as an aspect of social structure? Has it changed in the course of time? For this purpose, we need not strain at the fine points of comparability. When we consider the factors that have caused changes in the form of distribution, we shall have to return to these sources of difference in the form reported at any one time; but for the most part we can take a broader view. Its justification will depend on the conviction that its observations carry, and their interest.

Statistical Appendix

1. The Gini coefficient, whose geometrical base has been described in the text, is equal to half the relative mean difference, that is, the average of the differences between each income and every other, divided by the average income. It is from this expression that the Gini is calculated.

2. H. Theil, in his *Economics and Information Theory* (Theil 1967: ch. 4), proposed an index of equality formulated as the difference between the expression for the entropy of the distribution and the maximum value of that expression. The entropy is the disorder or dispersion of the distribution of incomes, the income of each person or group being entered as a proportion of total income. The index assumes its maximum value in the extremity of inequality, when all income accrues to a sole recipient. Its value is then given by the logarithm of the total number of recipients—the greater the number of persons without income (over against the one millionaire), the greater the disorder of the system and its inequality are taken to be. If all incomes are equal, the index is zero. With a given form of distribution, that is a given profile, the index will be higher, the greater the total number of recipients.

3. If we say that one distribution is more unequal than another, we imply that we can measure the degree of inequality in each. A. B. Atkinson (1970) has pointed out that we cannot generally do this without making some judgement of value about the forms of distribution: what relative valuation do we set on a rich man's pound over against a pound for a poor man? Measures of inequality that purport to rest solely on the mathematical properties of the distribution—measures such as the coefficient of variation, the Gini index or the standard deviation of the logarithms—often give conflicting results when we ask them to tell us whether one distribution is more unequal than another. This is because they implicitly attach different weights to different forms of inequality within the distribution. 'The distribution of income in the developing countries is typically more equal at the bottom and less equal at the top than in the advanced countries' (Atkinson 1970: 261): one measure will be more sensitive than another to a scatter of very high incomes or, alternatively, to the differences among the incomes below the median. The difficulty appears clearly when two Lorenz curves intersect, because the lower incomes differ less among themselves in the one, the higher incomes in the other, yet the Gini index may be the same for both: if we are to say which is more unequal, we have to decide which branch of inequality we judge more important. Our criterion of importance is the effect on the total utility of all income recipients combined; or, putting this the other way round, the extent to which income yields utility to the recipient in different parts of the distribution. Any measure of the degree of inequality must be a

measure of the increase in total utility that would be effected by redistribution.

As soon as we accept this principle, we are in deep water. How the sum of utilities will be affected by a transfer of income from one person to another can only be a matter of personal judgement or taste—as Atkinson says, of one's aversion to inequality. But he has shown how this kind of judgement can be embodied in a neat index, capable of empirical application. He defines his index as

$$ 1 - \frac{-y_{EDE}}{\mu} $$

where $-y_{EDE}$ is 'the *equally distributed equivalent* level of income . . . or the level of income per head which if equally distributed would give the same level of social welfare as the present distribution', and μ is the mean of that distribution (Atkinson 1970: 250). Thus we might hold that the increase of utility through transferring income from the richer to the poorer so as to equalize incomes would be so great that the sum of utilities would be as big after such a redistribution as it is in the present unequal one, even though the total income was lower by 10 per cent. Or would it be 20 per cent, or 30? According as our aversion to inequality is strong or weak, we should accept a bigger or smaller reduction in total income as being offset by equalization.

Atkinson's formula for his index contains the coefficient ϵ, which expresses the observer's aversion to inequality. If he or she has no such aversion at all, and considers that any pound of income brings as much utility to the rich man as to the poor, then ϵ is zero. If the aversion is so powerful that nothing short of complete equalization will satisfy it, ϵ increases without limit. '$\epsilon = 1$ corresponds to our regarding it as ''fair'' to take £1.00 from the richer man and give £0.50 to the poorer; and $\epsilon = 2$ to it being regarded as fair to take £1.00 and give £0.25p to the poorer man' (Atkinson 1980; 42). The difference between the amounts taken and given may be ascribed to the administrative cost of the transfer, or to a loss of output through reduction of incentives; but the significance of the representation of the difference by ϵ lies in the judgement that the smaller amount brings as much utility to the poorer man as £1 does to the richer. Values of ϵ reckoned deserving of insertion in the index, presumably because they represent current attitudes, range from 1 to 3. With $\epsilon = 1.5$, the Atkinson index for a Western economy comes out at about 0.35, and this means that, if total income were lower by 35 per cent after equalization, it would still yield as much utility, on an aggregation of individual utilities, as the present unequally distributed income yields. The index may show one distribution to be more unequal than another if $\epsilon = 1$, but may reverse the ranking if $\epsilon = 3$.

4. We are concerned here with the procedures used in preparing the original data for presentation. The data of personal incomes in 1688, 1759,

1801–3 and 1867, which will be considered in Chapter 11, gave the average income received by the members of each of a large number of occupations or ranks. In Gregory King's estimates, for example, we find in part the particulars given in Table 9.2.

TABLE 9.2 *An extract from Gregory King's estimates, 1688*

No. of families	Ranks, degrees, titles and qualifications	Yearly income per family (£)	Total of the estate or income (£000)
150 000	Farmers	44	6600
16 000	Persons in sciences & liberal arts	60	960
40 000	Shopkeepers and tradesmen	45	1800
66 000	Artisans & handicrafts	40	2400
5 000	Naval officers	80	400

Source: Laslett (1973: 48–9).

The first step is to arrange these entries in ascending order of income per family, from the vagrants with £2 a year to the temporal lords with £6060 (in Lindert and Williamson's revision: see reference in Chapter 11). Each of the columns of 'Number of families', and 'Income per family', is then cumulated, and the cumulated series are expressed in percentage form, so that we have rows as in Table 9.3.

TABLE 9.3 *Cumulation of data extracted from Gregory King*

(1) Income per family (£s.)	(2) Cumulated no. of families (000)	(3) (2) as % of total (%)	(4) Cumulated income (£000)	(5) (4) as % of total (%)
20	721	51.8	8 062	14.8
25	794	57.1	9 887	18.2
38	957	68.8	16 076	29.6
42.5	1060	76.2	20 470	37.7

The problem of interpolation in data like these is presented in Figure 9.5. Although the sources give us only an average or typical income for each group, all that we know of individual incomes makes us believe that there

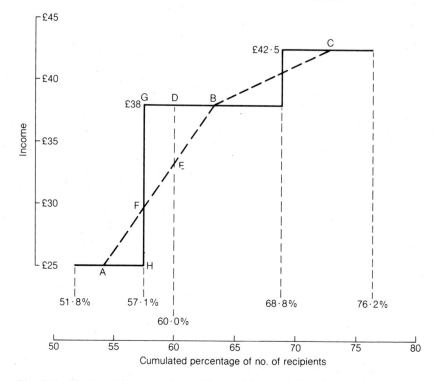

Fig. 9.5 Choice of Pen parade profile, and interpolation for percentiles. *Source:* data in Statistical Appendix, para. 2.

was actually a wide spread about the average. It seems better therefore to represent the Pen profile by a line such as *ABC* rather than by the steps formed by the tops of the rectangles that record each group. *A*, *B* and *C* are at the mid-points of those tops. The cumulated numbers corresponding to them are then found by splitting the difference between the abscissae of each group: thus, the coordinate of *B* is

$$57.1 + \tfrac{1}{2} (68.8 - 57.1) = 63.0\%.$$

The income at the 60th percentile is given by *E* and will be

$$£25 + (2.65 + 2.9) \text{ (slope of } AB = \frac{£13}{2.65 + 5.85}) = £33.5.$$

But we can find the whole component of income from the 60th percentile downwards to a sufficient approximation by simply adding to the component of income up to the end of the group with £25 average income a proportionate part of the component of the group with £38. Referring to column (5) in the data above, we find

$$18.2 + \frac{60.0 - 57.1}{68.8 - 57.1} (29.6 - 18.2) = 21.0\%.$$

In this approximation we are failing to include income under the profile such as the triangle *AHF*, but are adding the income represented by such areas as *FEDG*.

No problem of interpolation arises in the more recent distributions, in which incomes appear not as single figures for a certain number of recipients but as intervals, e.g. £2000–2499. We can take the (cumulated) frequency set against each interval as being attached to its upper limit.

5. In the matter of the order in which percentiles are numbered, practice varies—sometimes the quintile containing the lowest incomes is numbered 0–20 per cent, sometimes 81–100 per cent, and so on; there is no ambiguity about 'the top 10 per cent', but sometimes this is taken to comprise the percentiles 91–100, sometimes 0–10. Here it is the former convention that is adopted: in the Pen parades the scale of percentages of the cumulated total number of incomes is numbered normally from left to right, and the low incomes start over the low percentages.

6. The comparison of historically remote distributions is hampered by the lack of any index like the contemporary GNP deflator. Table 9.4 shows what indexes are available. Because prices of foodstuffs fluctuated more widely in earlier years, the average of five years centred on the relevant year has been taken rather than the index for that year alone. The Phelps Brown–Hopkins index was considered to record too exclusively the cost of living at what became a relatively low standard of living, and thereby to give too great a weight to foodstuffs, and especially breadstuffs, to be applicable to income at all levels; if we did apply it, we should find that average real income was 21 per cent *lower* in 1867 than in 1688, which is incredible. The decision taken was to adopt the Schumpeter–Gilboy index for 1688, 1759 and 1801–3, and splice it with the Rousseaux index to cover 1867. See Table 9.4, p. 282.

7. Where distributions are readily available only as tabulations of the 'shares of quantile groups', they can be converted to a Pen profile, although unfortunately there will be only a small number of points to mark out the profile. Take the tabulation of personal income in the United States in 1974 by Thomas Stark (1977: Table 132):

(Top 1%	7.0%)
(Top 5%	20.8%)
81–100%	51.5%
61–80%	25.0%
41–60%	14.4%
21–40%	7.1%
0–20%	2.0%
	100.0%

We can calculate the average income in each row in a relative form. Thus, if the top 5 in each 100 recipients get 20.8 per cent of all income, their

TABLE 9.4 *British price indexes for 1688–1863*

Ave. of 5 yrs centred on	Phelps Brown-Hopkins index		Composite Schumpeter-Gilboy index		Rousseaux index		Index adopted	Ave. income	
	Original	1688 = 100	Original	1688 = 100	Original	Spliced, 1688 = 100		In current money (£)	At 1688 prices (£)
1688	548	100	80	100			100	39	39
1759	679	124	83	104			104	46	44
1801–3	1449	264	171	214	167	214	214	91	43
1867	1283	234			115	147	147	72	49

Sources: Phelps Brown–Hopkins index: from Phelps Brown and Hopkins (1981: 54–8); *Schumpeter–Gilboy index:* from Mitchell and Deane (1962: 468–9). The series for consumers' goods and producers' goods are combined with weights 2,1. The series for producers' goods is lacking for 1802–4, and here a combined index has been estimated by reducing the entries for consumers' goods by the same factor as the formation of the combined index gave for 1800–1, 0.90; *Rousseaux index:* from Mitchell and Deane, (1962: 471–2). This index is spliced to Schumpeter–Gilboy at 1800–1; *Average incomes:* from Lindert and Williamson (1983: table 3).

average income per head will be $(20.8 \div 5) = 4.16$ times the average income per head of the whole 100. Similarly, the ratio in the top quintile will be $(51.5 \div 20) = 2.575$; and so on. Each such ratio can be taken to represent the income level at the midpoint of the group concerned. The ratio for the central quintile, 0.72, therefore represents the income level at the median; as usual, it is a good deal lower than the mean, represented here by unity.

10

The Form of Recent Distributions of Income

10.1. The Common Form Illustrated

The last chapter contained illustrations of the distribution of income displayed as a Pen parade. We shall now ask whether the form that appeared there is peculiar to a particular time and place, or is found in other countries, and in earlier as well as in later years.

Figure 10.1 shows the distribution in recent years in four Western countries. The income levels, originally given in the various currencies, have been brought into comparable form as relatives to the median income in each country. We know that the highest incomes in these countries run up to more than eight times the median, but all save the top 10 per cent are under a relative level of 2.5. To draw the profiles in this range distinctly, we have to devote the whole scale to it; we shall look at the top 10 per cent later. The data for the United States and West Germany record the income, before tax, of households. Over most of the range of the British data the income is that of the tax unit in which husband and wife are joined, but the estimates of income below the exemption level are almost certainly of individuals. The Swedish data are derived mainly from individual tax returns of assessed income from all sources, including social benefits, but they also, like the British, include estimates of income below the exemption level—they even record the number of persons with no income at all. Closer study would reveal more differences than these, but they are not likely to be so great as to deter us from drawing certain conclusions from the comparison presented in Figure 10.1

The first of these is that a common form exists. What is most striking about the four profiles is their resemblance. Should we be surprised? It might be said that all four countries are economically at a high level of industrial development, and politically they are all parliamentary democracies: that their income distributions are similar is therefore understandable, perhaps only to be expected. How much weight we should attach to this observation we cannot tell until we have gone on, as we shall do, to examine the income distributions in some countries of different type. But meanwhile we can note that there are also substantial differences in many respects between the four countries here—in standard of living, natural resources, ethnic composition, social attitudes and government

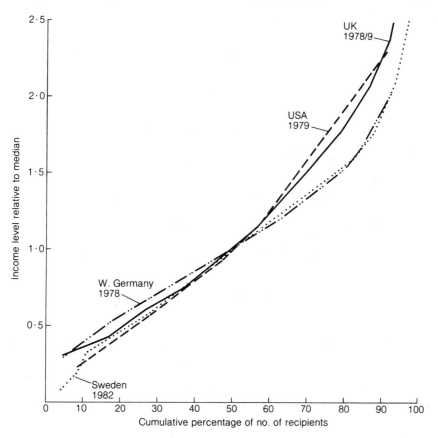

Fig. 10.1   Distribution of personal income in four Western countries, displayed as
Pen parades. *Sources:* as in Table 10.1.

policy over the last forty years, to name no more. These are large enough to
make marked differences in the form of the profiles intelligible, did we find
them: but we do not. We therefore carry forward the hypothesis that the
distribution of income is shaped by certain underlying processes and
human propensities that are common to a number of countries, and are so
powerful that they operate to much the same aggregate effect in very
various circumstances.

Next, we see that the common form is made up of at least two
distributions, and perhaps three. One of these, which contains the top 15
per cent of recipients, appears within Figure 10.1 only as its rapid rise takes
off. That distinct forces begin to take charge here is a possibility we have
already noticed. The further possibility, that the distribution of income
below the top 15 per cent is itself divided into two parts, in which incomes
are formed somewhat differently, is suggested by the contrasting course of

the profiles on either side of the median. Up to that point, there is no great divergence in the profiles. There are minor differences among them, it is true: the dispersion of incomes was lower in West Germany than in the other three countries, and among the bottom 35 per cent it was somewhat greater in the United States than in Sweden and the United Kingdom. But the similarity is more striking than any divergence. Above the median it is altogether different. Here the profiles divide. Incomes rose much more steeply in the United States and United Kingdom than in Sweden and West Germany. The profiles for these last two countries can hardly be distinguished. In them, incomes about the 85th percentile were 1.7 times the median; in the United States and United Kingdom, the corresponding ratio was 2.0 or more. This difference was brought about by a steadily greater rise between one person and the next in the array. This occurred in the ranks of the more skilled manual workers, the administrators and the professionals.

This survey of the profiles up to the 85th percentile must be supplemented by some separate notice of the remainder. What went on in the top 15 per cent is illustrated by Figure 10.2. This is drawn on a very different scale, with income levels entered as ratios to the level in each country at the 85th percentile. Only Sweden and the United Kingdom appear here, because they are the only countries in the preceding figure for which the needed detail is provided in this range. We note again the similarity—and here we may say the extraordinary similarity—of the two profiles, despite their divergence at lower levels. But what now also stands out is the concentration at the very end of the array of some incomes that are outstandingly high: within the last 4 per cent alone, incomes are raised by a factor of $3\frac{1}{2}$, to a level 20 times that at the 15th percentile in Sweden, 24 times in the United Kingdom—and that still does not include the highest incomes of all. The processes of income formation that assert themselves in this range must be of a kind that not only makes for big incomes in the first place, but readily makes them bigger still. It may well be that there are ways of making profits from enterprise and speculation that form incomes in a way very different from the formation of incomes from work and the rentier's capital.

The form of distribution that results is shown in another way by Figure 10.3. The two essential changes in presentation here are that we take the logarithms of the variables, and that the numbers of recipients are not, as in a Pen parade, those in receipt of an income at a given level, but the total having incomes at or above that level. These two changes between them give its unfamiliar appearance to the scale on the base-line. This should really be read from right to left. Thus, in moving back from 99 to 98 per cent of recipients, we are raising the proportion having incomes at or above the associated levels from 1 to 2 per cent; the same doubling occurs when we move from 98 to 96 per cent; and on a logarithmetic scale these equal

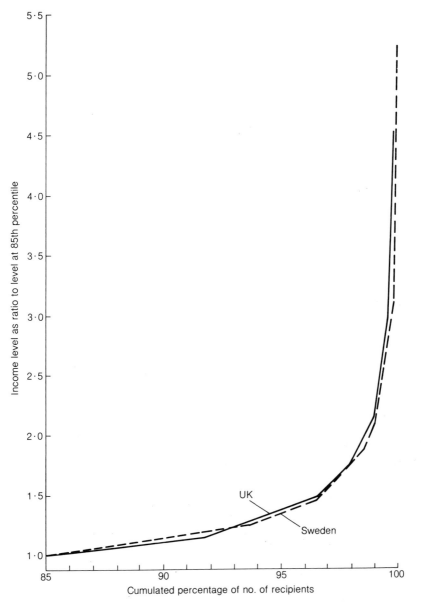

Fig. 10.2 Distribution of highest incomes in Sweden and the United Kingdom, as Pen parades. *Sources:* as in Table 10.1.

proportionate differences are marked by equal intervals. The impact of the figure is powerful: when the data are cast in this form, over most of this range they lie very closely on a straight line.

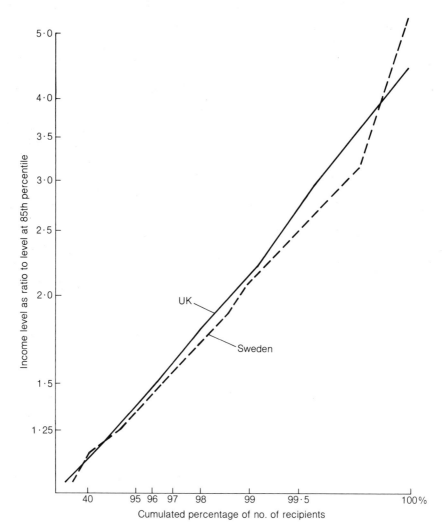

Fig. 10.3   Pareto lines of distribution of highest incomes in Sweden and the
United Kingdom. *Sources:* as in Table 10.1.

It was Pareto (1895, 1896, 1897) who discovered this. He examined the
number of incomes, N, above a level, y: the higher was y, the smaller was
N. What he observed, in a number of distributions, was that each
successive proportionate rise in y, by say 10 per cent, was associated with
one and the same proportionate fall in N, by say 35 per cent. If we express
the proportionate changes in the variables as differences in their
logarithms, Pareto's observation can be written as

$$\Delta \log N = -\alpha \, \Delta \log y$$

where α is a constant—in the numerical example we have just given, it is 3.5. This expression can be treated as derived from the standard form of a Pareto distribution

$$N = \frac{A}{y^\alpha}$$

where A is the total number of incomes above zero. If we write (10.2) in the form

$$\log N = \log A - \alpha \log y_9$$

we see the equation of a straight line. This is the famour Pareto line, such as appears in Figure 10.3. Let us take a numerical example from the Swedish line there. From Table 10.1 we can derive

y_1: 120 000 Kr N_1: 412 100
y_2: 140 000 Kr N_2: 230 600
y_3: 160 000 Kr N_3: 141 900

Then for the interval between the first two of those levels, we have

$$0 \cdot 35327 = \alpha(0 \cdot 06695)$$
$$\alpha = 3.78.$$

For the interval between the second and third levels we have

$$0 \cdot 20975 = \alpha(0 \cdot 05799)$$
$$\alpha = 3.68.$$

The value of α is not quite the same in this second interval as in the first: the line joining the points concerned in Figure 10.3. do not quite form one straight line, but the inflection is slight. If we calculate α for the whole span between Kr 100 000 and Kr 200 000, it comes out at 3.71: the divergences from this in the first two intervals are small.

Although the Pareto line gives so good an account of the top 15 per cent of incomes, it is wildly unsuited to the levels below. In particular, it crowds the frequency into the lowest levels. If, for instance, we carry the function we have fitted to the top Swedish incomes back to the interval Kr 5000-10 000—the lowest recorded interval but one—the number of recipients comes out at about 5 870 000, whereas the actually recorded number is only a little over 200 000. If we think that the form of the fitted function can throw light on the forces that shape the distribution, our earlier supposition that those forces are distinct in the top 15 per cent, or operate differently there, is strengthened.

There is another kind of linearity in the lower 85 per cent. It appears in Figure 10.4 because this is drawn on a natural scale, or, rather, separate natural scales for the four countries. These scales have been chosen so as to fit all four into the same frame, and this means that the slopes of all the profiles over the span from the 15th to the 85th percentile have been made very nearly the same on the paper, and we cannot compare them. There

TABLE 10.1 *Distribution of personal income in four countries, in years within 1978–1982*

Sweden 1982

Income level, upper limit (000)	No. of income recipients (000)	Cumulated percentage no. of recipients (%)
0	45.6	0.7
5	249.7	4.4
10	204.5	7.5
20	328.7	12.4
30	820.0	24.8
40	678.6	35.0
50	574.5	43.6
60	590.2	52.5
70	625.8	61.9
80	700.5	72.4
90	602.5	81.4
100	404.2	87.5
110	255.4	90.1
120	163.8	93.8
140	181.5	96.5
160	88.7	97.9
180	49.0	98.6
200	28.6	99.0
300	48.6	99.8
500	12.5	100.0
500 +	3.2	100.0
Total	6 655.8	

United Kingdom 1978/9

Income level, upper limit (£000)	No. of tax units (000)	Cumulated percentage no. of tax units (%)
1	1411	4.9
1.5	3670	17.5
2	2974	27.7
2.5	2701	37.0
3	2263	44.8
3.5	1975	51.6
4	1815	57.8
4.5	1698	63.6
5	1652	69.3
6	2855	79.1
7	2173	86.6
8	1460	91.6
10	1394	96.4
12	458	98.0
15	310	99.1
20	160	99.6
30	76	99.9
30 +	31	100.0
Total	2976	

United States 1979

Income level, upper limit ($000)	Cumulated percentage no. of households (%)
5	9.4
10	21.7
15	34.5
20	45.7
25	56.6
35	75.5
50	90.5
50 +	100

West Germany 1978

Income level, upper limits* (DM000)	No. of households (000)	Cumulated percentage no. of households (%)
8	1140	5.2
12	2169	15.0
14	1096	20.0
16	1175	25.3
18	1269	31.9
20	1217	36.6
22	1228	42.1
25	1822	50.4
30	2827	63.2
35	2453	74.4
40	1809	82.6
50	2100	92.1
200	1744	100
Total	22 050	

*Households with monthly incomes of DM20 000 or more not included.

Sources: Sweden: Statistisk Årsbok 1985, table 217, UK: National Income and Outlay (the Blue Book), 1982, table. 4.9; USA: Statistical Abstract of the US 1984, table 754; W. Germany: Statistisches Jahrbuch 1983, table 20.8.

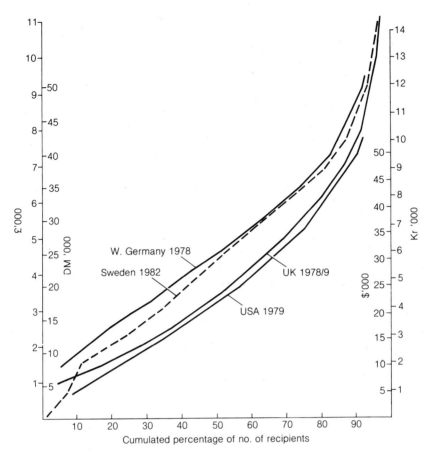

Fig. 10.4 Distributions of personal income in four countries, displayed as Pen parades. *Sources:* as in Table 10.1.

were in fact substantial differences in the extent of the rise of income overall: the ratio of income at the 85th percentile to that at the 15th is 3.6 in West Germany, 4.2 in Sweden, 4.8 in the United Kingdom and as much as 6.2 in the United States. These figures, it is true, depend to a considerable extent on divergences at the ends: if we take only the ratio of the upper to the lower quartile, the ratios are: West Germany 2.2, Sweden 2.7, United Kingdom 3.0, United States 3.2; but the differences remain substantial. We can learn something none the less from the form of these profiles, that is, the kind of course they take when they are drawn on a natural scale.

This course is marked by its linearity over wide ranges. The German profile is closely linear up to the median, with slight concavity upwards thereafter. The Swedish and US profiles are remarkably linear on either side of the median. Even in the modest UK curvature, there is a linear segment between the 30th and 50th percentiles. Evidently there is a strong tendency—it comes near 'a law'—for incomes up to the 85th percentile to be differentiated by the same absolute amount. This amount is somewhat higher above the median than below it; the rise comes later in the United States, a good deal earlier in Sweden. This rise is not big enough to prevent a fall in the proportion by which income increases as we move from any recipient unit to its neighbour in the array. In Germany, for instance, when we move from the 20th to the 25th recipient in an array of 100, income increases by 12 per cent, whereas the move from the 70th to the 75th recipient brings an increase of little more than 7 per cent. The curvature of the UK profile is sufficient to make the corresponding increases 15 and 10 per cent. The implications of this linearity, as distinct from those of constant proportional differences in the array, will be examined in Chapter 15.

But there is one aspect of linearity whose implications we may notice forthwith. This is the smoothness and steadiness of gradation. No doubt when we are dealing with very large numbers, as we are here, we should expect continuity; if there is a gap between one person's measurement and another's, some other people will always be found who will fill it. But this presumption cannot be applied to incomes without reflection. If society were divided into a limited number of classes, or groups of occupations, each with its characteristic and fairly narrow range of incomes, the profile would resemble a flight of steps. That it actually shows a continuous slope with no more than one change of gradient implies the absence of clotting in the underlying population. The higher incomes within the range may be six times or more the lower, but there is no group that will be conscious of itself as separated by its incomes from neighbours whose incomes are distinctly lower or higher; adjoining each person's income is another that is only a little lower or higher. This must affect social attitudes. The members of a class in the full social sense must be aware of each other as alike in some respects that mark them off sharply from others. If there are any such features of 'the working class' or 'the middle class' in the Western economies, income is not one of them. In economies dominated by the private ownership of land, or a sharp division between urban and rural populations, it may be otherwise. It has been otherwise in mining settlements: the high tension of industrial relations and the strength of left-wing politics in the South Wales valleys, or the mining towns and lumber camps of British Columbia before 1914, may be ascribed to the hard contrast between a mass of manual workers at much the same income level and a small but relatively well-to-do managerial class, a contrast that in neighbourhoods of longer settlement and greater diversity of occupations will be softened.

This is a question on which light may be thrown by the further international comparisons to which we proceed.

10.2. Further International Comparisons

A study carried out for the Diamond Commission by Thomas Stark (1977) enables us to extend our survey with data assembled with close regard to their comparability. From his report on *The Distribution of Income in Eight Countries* we select first the data on Australia and Canada, which, with the United Kingdom for comparison, are depicted in Figure 10.5. These present the money incomes of individuals. The Australian and Canadian data 'are derived from large-scale labour force surveys' (Stark 1977: (para 484), the British from the Family Expenditure Survey of some 7000 households, together with an inquiry into income in some 180 000 households made as a follow-up to the Census of 1971. The original tabulation allows us to calculate only six points through which to draw the profiles—with a seventh, the income of the top 1 per cent, away far beyond the top of the figure. But it is clear that the two-part form of the distribution

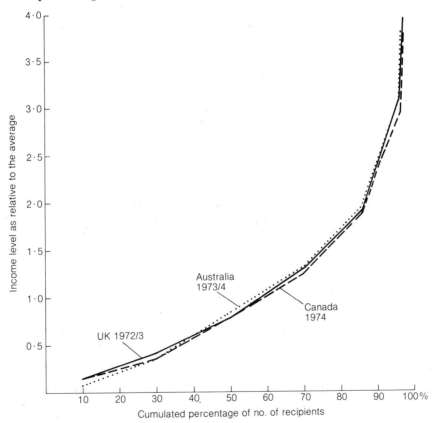

Fig. 10.5 Distribution of total personal income, by individuals, in Australia, Canada and the United Kingdom. *Source:* Stark (1977: table 132.)

appears again here, although the change of gear about the median, previously observed in the United Kingdom, and in some other countries in Figure 10.4, does not appear in Australia and Canada. Up to about the 85th percentile, the similarity of the three profiles is remarkable. If the Australian rises more than the others from start to finish of that span, this is because it starts exceptionally low: people with low incomes are relatively more numerous—or more fully recorded—in Australia than in the other two countries. The profiles as they take off into space can tell us little about the top 15 per cent; of the terminal points that we cannot see, the Canadian is actually highest, with an income for the top 1 per cent that is 7.7 times the average; the corresponding ratios for the other countries are smaller—6.4 for the United Kingdom and 6.1 for Australia. This is an offset to the somewhat greater differences of income in Australia lower down.

Figure 10.6 presents the distribution of personal income among households, and with this recipient unit we can bring in two more countries, France and Japan. A household consists of 'all persons sharing a dwelling and using common cooking facilities' (Royal Commission 1977: para. 277). Dr Stark warns us that 'the reliability and coverage of these distributions is very varied and comparability in many cases is highly

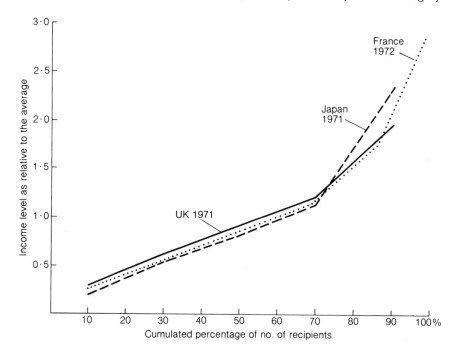

Fig. 10.6 Distribution of pre-tax total personal income, by households, in France, Japan and the United Kingdom. *Source:* Stark (1977: table 142).

tenuous' (Stark 1977: para. 503). There is the added difficulty that the tabulation gives even less information than before about the top 15 per cent; for two of the countries to be cited here we can derive only the average income of the top 20 per cent. The United Kingdom is cited again for comparison. A remarkable similarity up to the 70th percentile appears between all three countries; but probably the French slope should be steeper, because 'the French Household Income Survey data . . . largely exclude income below the tax thresholds and a wide range of transfer incomes' (Stark 1977: para. 504). The concavity that previously marked the British profile does not appear in these household incomes: the modest but persistent increase in the absolute difference between one income and the next highest as we go up the scale of income that prevailed for individuals is not found here. The importance of the distinction between the distributions above and below the 85th percentile is again apparent: so far as the limited observations allow us to tell, the top incomes stand higher, relatively to the average, in France than in Japan, and in Japan than in the United Kingdom.

These international comparisons have shown a predominant and significant similarity, albeit in part a similarity in divergence. Up to the region of the 85th percentile, the profiles are closely alike; after that, they differ. In their lower course they are mostly nearly linear, albeit with a hinge about the median. The slope in the middle part of this course varies somewhat, so that income at the upper quartile has been raised to a level ranging from less than two and a half to nearly five times that at the lower. On either side of those points there is more divergence, and the ratios of income at the 85th to that at the 15th percentile range more widely. But this is as nothing to the differences in the rate of rapid ascent among the last 15 per cent of recipients. It is mainly here that the differences in inequality found in any single measure are brought about.

The features we have just noted are all those of developed and industrialized economies: we have yet to see whether they appear in the Third World.

10.3. The Distribution of Income in Developing Countries

When statistics of the distribution of income have been assembled in highly developed countries with extensive and efficient administrative services, they are still regarded, not least by those who assemble them, as subject to a substantial margin of error. It might be thought that in countries still in early stages of development the margin would be very wide indeed. But the authors of a study of *Income Distribution and Economic Development* (Lecaillon *et al.* 1984) made for the International Labour Office have found it possible to present statistics that they regard as reasonably reliable for no less than 39 such countries. These estimates are based variously on 'household budget surveys, wage statistics, national accounts, censuses, etc.' (p. 24). We may remark on the importance of the census. The great aim must be to get the numbers of income recipients right. If one such unit is omitted, we make an error of 100 per cent in a unit of attributed income; if the unit is included, a bad mistake in the recording or estimating of its income may make an error of only 30 per cent. The authors further report that 'all estimates derived from incomplete sources, such as urban household budget surveys, have been rejected. Survey results have been corrected by reference to the national accounts and other available sources.' These surveys, it is noted, usually underestimate the high incomes. 'The results of the surveys have been adjusted wherever there might be a bias due, for example, to over-representation or under-representation of a particular category of households or to the exclusion of a particular income group' (Lecaillon *et al.* 1984: 24, 25).

Pen parades can be derived from the tabulation the authors provide of the proportions of total income accruing to quantile groups; the method has been described in the Statistical Appendix to chapter 9. Figures 10.7–10.9 show the profiles for a sample of three countries each from Africa, Asia and South America. In each figure a profile for the United Kingdom is included for comparison. The incomes are those of households in the three Asian countries, and of individuals, or economically active persons, in the others. To match this as far as possible, the British incomes are for households in the Asian figure (Figure 10.9) but for individuals in the other two. In comparing the profiles, we have to bear in mind that the income levels all had to be expressed here only as relatives to the average, and this means that the early part of the profile may be lower in one country than another, although the two levels of income were actually the same, just because the top incomes go higher in the first country, and raise the average there. This may well account for the low start to the profile for Turkey, where incomes around the 98th percentile stood at nearly six and a half times the average.

It is also to be noted that we have a limited number of observations—not more than seven—and when a change of course appears in the profile at one of these widely spaced points, we cannot tell whether it actually set in earlier.

The salient feature of the profiles in these graphs is that they reproduce the form with which we are now familiar in the developed countries, but only with substantial differences. For the most part, there is the same linear progression in the earlier stages, but the hinge at the median is more marked. The top incomes rise steeply, beyond the scope of the graphs, as they do in the developed countries, but the lift begins more often about the 70th percentile than the 85th, and in the last 10 per cent it goes farther. In comparison with the United Kingdom, this greater contrast between the later and earlier parts of the profile indicates greater inequality.

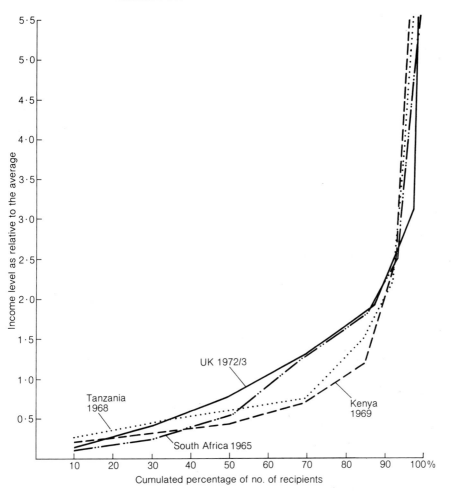

Fig. 10.7 Distribution of personal income to individuals in South Africa and Tanzania, and to economically active persons in Kenya, with distribution to individuals in the United Kingdom for comparison. *Sources: UK:* Stark (1977: table 132); *other countries:* Lecaillon *et al.* (1984: table 4).

These general observations are subject to some qualification in detail. The sharp upturn occurs at the median in South Africa, Brazil and Peru, but in Kenya, Tanzania and Korea it is deferred to the 70th percentile, and in India and Turkey there is a fairly steady transition in the Western manner all the way to the 85th percentile. But Kenya and Korea also show a hinge, if a less marked one, at the median.

Predominantly we get the impression that there are three distributions here: one forming the profile up to the median, the next made up of the incomes between the median and the 85th percentile, the third containing

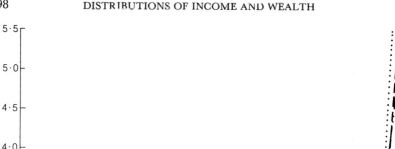

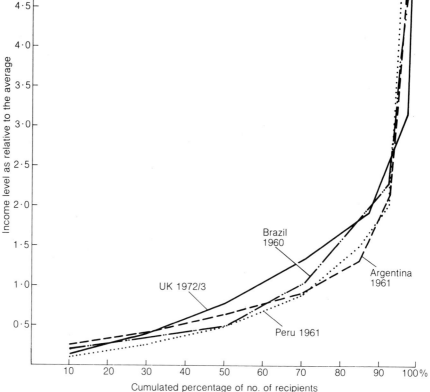

Fig. 10.8 Distribution of income of economically active persons in Argentina, Brazil and Peru, and of individuals in the United Kingdom for comparison. *Sources: UK:* Stark (1977: table 132): *other countries:* Lecaillon *et al.* (1984: table 4).

the steeply rising incomes of the top 15 per cent. The South African profile shows these divisions most clearly. It may well typify the social or ethnic divisions within the economy, from which the changing course of the profile arises. The slope of the first and linear phase of the profile is generally less than in the United Kingdom—that is, the people there are less differentiated among themselves. This is intelligible, for we might expect to find less specialization in the working population, less variety of skills and occupations, and hence of earnings, at lower stages of development. At the median we encounter 'the dual economy': the steeper rise that ensues marks the distribution of income, with its greater differentiation, in the

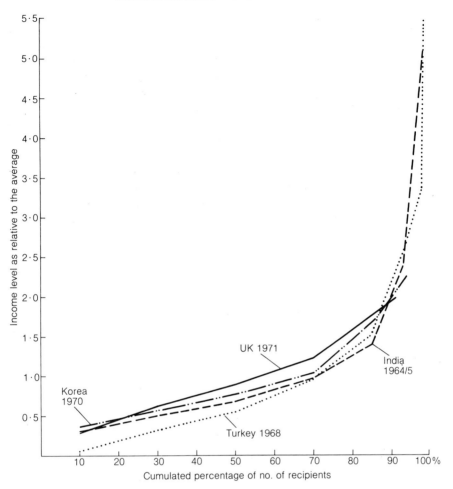

Fig. 10.9 Distribution of income to households in India, Korea and Turkey, and in the United Kingdom for comparison. *Sources: UK:* Stark (1977: table 142); *other countries:* Lecaillon *et al.* (1984: table 4).

urbanized and industrialized sector. What we have discerned as the third distribution may be only the long upper tail of the second, but the extent of the rise is outstanding. British incomes around the 98th percentile stood at about 4.25 times the average; in all of our nine countries save Korea the corresponding ratio was higher than this, and in some of them much higher—7.8 in Peru, 8.9 in Kenya. In his basic study of 'Economic Growth and Income Inequality', Simon Kuznets (1955) found that the greater inequality in the developing countries was due not so much to any shortfall in the relative incomes of their poorer people, as to the top incomes being higher. relative to the average, than in developed economies. The profiles selected for examination here bear out the finding of one of our ILO authors, Felix Paukert (1973), in an earlier study, that 'in general, the dispersion of the lower incomes is much slighter in the developing countries than in the developed; the greater degree of inequality prevailing in the developing countries is due primarily to the large share of total income accruing to the rich top 5 per cent of the population.'

In all, in this sample of nine developing countries we find more internal differentiation, marked by sharper changes in the form of the distribution over different ranges of income. This we may ascribe to greater ethnic or other social and regional divisions in the working population, and particularly to differences in the size of the industrializing part of a dual economy. There are further possibilities of acquiring incomes that are much larger, relatively to the average, than are most top incomes in the West.

10.4. The Distribution of Income in Soviet-type Economies

The difficulties that beset the study of the Soviet-type economies are particularly formidable in the case of income distribution. It is not the practice of these economies to publish statistics of this kind regularly, even if the administration compiles them. Western observers wishing to quantify the distribution of earnings in Russia have had to make the best use they could of the measurements of a small and ill-printed histogram, published without figures. We know more about earnings in the state sectors than we do about incomes as a whole, including cash benefits, and agricultural incomes. Where money income is reported it bears an uncertain relation to real income. There is the familiar problem of assessing benefits in kind, at all levels; much of the effective remuneration of the higher posts takes such forms as privileged access to housing and to particular sources of supply, with priority in the allocation of scarce and highly coveted commodities.

None the less, the three profiles in Figure 10.10 command some confidence through the extent to which they resemble one another and stand together in contrast to the West. These distributions for Czechoslovakia, Hungary and the USSR have been quite independently compiled: their sources are noted in Table 10.2. The sharp angles at either end of the Czechoslovakian profiles arouse some distrust, but these apart, the profiles are of the familiar form.

In their particular course, however, these profiles are distinctive. Two features mark it out, and distinguish it from the Western type: the much lower gradient, and the absence of a swift rise to great heights at the top end. The smaller dispersion of incomes that the lower gradient displays is striking: the ratio of the income level at the 85th percentile to that at the 15th, which in the British profile is 5 to 1, is only around 2.9 in the three of

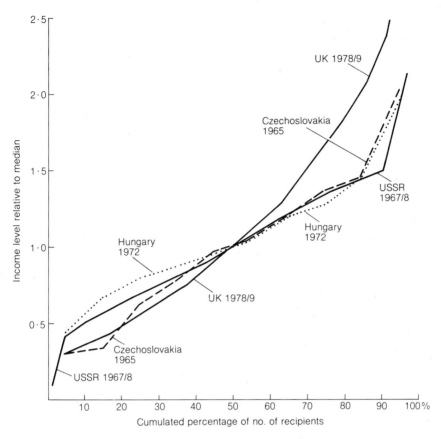

Fig. 10.10 Distribution of personal income in three Soviet-type economies, compared with the United Kingdom. *Sources: UK:* as in Table 10.1; *other countries:* as in Table 10.2.

Soviet type. Most of this divergence occurs above the median. Below it, the Hungarian and Russian gradients are gentler than the British throughout, though not the Czech; but the divergences are not wide. Above the median the paths divide. The British profile, continuing its concavity, turns upwards; the other three converge on an almost identical course, a little steeper than before for Hungary, and a downward inflexion for Czechoslovakia, with no change for Russia. We saw earlier (p. 269) that the British steepening was not enough to prevent differentials from falling in proportionate terms; it follows *a fortiori* that the differentials in the three Soviet-type economies contract in those terms, up to the 85th percentile.

Above that, the three show the same turn upward as we found in the West: indeed, it seems to be sharper, suggesting that we enter here on posts at a high level, where wide differentials are accepted as desirable. But the

TABLE 10.2   *Distribution of personal income in three Soviet-type economies (Income levels expressed as relative to the median)*

Cumulated percentage of nos.	Hungary (1972 income level)	Czechoslovakia (1965 income level)	USSR 1967/8	
			Cumulated percentage of nos.	Income level
5	0.44	0.29	1.10	0.19
15	0.66	0.34	4.78	0.42
25	0.79	0.63	10.46	0.51
35	0.87	0.77	17.45	0.61
45	0.94	0.91	25.50	0.70
55	1.06	1.06	34.73	0.80
65	1.20	1.20	44.01	0.89
75	1.27	1.36	61.89	1.03
85	1.45	1.42	75.99	1.22
95	1.97	2.02	90.09	1.50
			94.68	1.87
			96.88	2.25

Sources: *Hungary*: G. Szakolczai (1980: 209). The series cited here is for total personal income including benefits in kind. *Czechoslovakia*: Michal. (1972; see also 1973). The income recorded is believed to be 'money income of all persons, including transfers, before deduction of personal taxes'. *USSR*: McAuley (1977: 234, table 8). This series is formed on the assumption 'that the incomes of *sovkhozniki* were distributed . . . like those of *Kolkhozniki*'. The income reported is, for state sector employees, per capita money income, and in the collective farm sector 'total personal income per capita,' i.e. inclusive of income derived from private agricultural production.

movement seems not to go nearly as far. It is true that we cannot tell what level it reaches at its farthest—for Czechoslovakia and Hungary we have only average incomes of the top tenth, and the Russian series is open-ended. But our inference from the Western profiles, that at about the 85th percentile we enter upon a different sort of distribution, seems to hold of these Soviet-type economies too; only the distribution here is not seen to project any incomes as high as those in the top 2 percentiles in the West. This impression must be qualified, as we have seen, by an allowance for the extensive 'perks' that go with high-ranking jobs. But there are reasons to believe that there really is a contrast. Two major sources of vastly high incomes in the West are absent here—the inheritance of great wealth, and the profits of enterprise and speculation. The rewards of personal advancement take other forms.

The least differentiated structure of all three economies is the Hungarian. In displaying it to a British audience, Szakolczai (1980: 211) observed that it was 'strikingly egalitarian', and he was probably not going too far when he claimed that it was 'one of the most egalitarian of our time'.

Why are these Soviet-type structures less extended, more egalitarian, than the Western? It is not because of any doctrinal devotion to equality on the part of their rulers. The main lines of the distributions are laid down by the centralized wage and salary scales. In devising and modifying them, the administrators have regard to the need for incentives—incentives to workers to remain in particular industries or regions, or to move to them; to acquire qualifications, to work hard and to undertake heavier responsibilities. This means maintaining differentials; sometimes it means deliberately widening them.

There is nothing in this to conflict with Marx's teaching about what should be done at the present stage of development of the productive forces. In his *Critique of the Gotha Programme* (McLellan 1977: 569), he had expressed his objection to a policy that claimed 'a fair distribution of the produce of labour'. 'Fairness' in relative earnings was for him a bourgeois notion, resting upon the principles of private property which he repudiated as constricting and impoverishing the human spirit. But as we have seen (pp. 205–8), it remained applicable to a socialist society just emerging from capitalism—'which is thus in every respect, economically, morally, and intellectually, still stamped with the birthmarks of the old society from whose womb it emerges'. At this stage the rule must be 'From each according to his ability, to each according to his contribution'. The labour theory of value, moreover, involves the reduction of different qualities of labour to different amounts or intensities of 'simple labour', and if workers are to be paid at the same rate, those whose hour of work contains more 'simple labour' than others should be paid proportionately more. So the principle of equality 'tacitly recognizes unequal individual endowment and thus productive capacity as natural privileges'. Again, since men have different family responsibilities and other needs, even equal pay would make some better off than others. 'But these defects are inevitable in the first phase of communist society as it is when it has just emerged after prolonged birth pangs from capitalist society. Right can never be higher than the economic structure of society and its cultural development conditioned thereby' (McLellan 1977: 569).

The authority of Lenin has often been cited to the same effect. More difficult and responsible work, he declared, 'does not constitute its own reward'. A Soviet handbook of the 1970s repeats a statement that Lenin made in 1921: 'In determining the wage rates of workers with various skills, office staff, technical and higher administrative personnel, all thought of egalitarianism, *uravnitelost*, should be rejected' (McAuley, 1980: 242).

But we must not account for too much. The fact remains that the three Soviet-type distributions we have sampled are much more egalitarian than the Western type. The difference arises mainly from a slower rise of income above the median, that is, broadly: the more skilled manual occupations and still more the higher clerical, the professional and administrative, are paid less than in the West relatively to the bulk of manual workers. Allowance for 'perks' reduces the contrast, but is unlikely to remove it. The effect arises not from egalitarian conviction, nor from any intent to cut back the higher paid—on the contrary, there have at times been efforts to give them greater incentives—but from giving priority to raising the standard of living of the main guard of manual workers. It is noteworthy that the more than doubling of the real wages of state employees between 1950 and 1975 was associated with a reduction of inequality, through 'a substantial increase in the earnings of the low-paid, accompanied by a restriction on the growth of earnings among the highly-paid' (McAulay 1978: 9–10: 1977: 224).

11

The Historical Course of Change in the Distribution of Income

11.1. The Course of Change in the United Kingdom

The similarity of the distributions of income in some Western countries in recent years prompts the conjecture that this kind of distribution is governed throughout by laws that take much the same effect in countries otherwise set apart by many differences. But these countries do have this in common: they are at the same stage of economic development. May it not be, then, that in earlier stages of development their distributions were less alike? We can reach a first answer to that question by considering the evidence for the course of distribution over nearly three hundred years within the United Kingdom.

This evidence consists of four estimates, made at isolated dates. The first two were the by-product of political contention. We have seen already (pp. 126–30) how in 1696 Gregory King drew up his *Natural and Political Observations & Conclusions upon the State and Condition of England*, believing that a measure of the limited resources of the country would show the unwisdom of the warlike policy that was making such a drain upon them. Joseph Massie was a writer who collected some 1500 works on political economy. In 1760 he published *A Computation of the Money that hath been Exorbitantly Raised upon the People of Great Britain by the Sugar Planters, from January 1759 to January 1760*. For his attack on the planters' exploitation of their sheltered market, he made estimates of the income available, out of which to purchase tea, coffee and chocolate, in 51 classes. Like King, he estimated the number of families in each class, and his total of population was not far from the figure adopted by later demographers; but he had not as much evidence as King to draw on, and his estimates of the average income per family are often questionable. Patrick Colquhoun was a metropolitan magistrate, and later a merchant in Virginia and Glasgow, who published numerous pamphlets on social and economic issues of the early nineteenth century. With his Treatises on *Indigence* (1806) and on *The Wealth, Power and Resources of the British Empire* (1815) we enter the realm of modern statistics, for his estimates were based on the first Census, that of 1801, as well as on particulars of the income assessed to Pitt's income tax, and a parliamentary inquiry into poor relief. Dudley Baxter, again, addressed himself in 1868 to

The National Income in an objective inquiry by a political economist, even though his purpose was to display the progress made during the century. His classes were defined by income level—five classes down to the level of £100 a year; eight classes of wage-earners; and paupers. He had much more evidence to draw on than his predecessors, and his estimates are more acceptable accordingly. The first three have been regarded as having done no more than what was a notable achievement in its day, but as too slightly based to have much chance of being accurate.

Two American scholars, however, have now shown that all four estimates can be revised in the light of further evidence now available, so as to arrive at reasonably firm conclusions. In two papers in *Explorations in Economic History*, P. H. Lindert and J. G. Williamson (1982, 1983a) have subjected the original studies to detailed scrutiny, and with great patience and ingenuity have amended their figures so as to arrive at new and credible tables of the distribution of personal income. For instance, to amend King's estimates of the numbers in particular classes or occupations, Lindert (1980) used regression analysis to extend his own analysis of 26 local censuses, and the burial records of 41 parishes, to the whole of England and Wales. Or again, the authors raised the income that King assigned to the nobility and gentry, on the strength of the agreement of scholars who have reported in recent years their findings in documents of the time relating to family history. Massie's estimates of income the authors have generally raised, again on the basis of contemporary records of wage rates, salaries and the revenues of landlords. Colquhoun and Baxter called for much lighter revision. Only Colquhoun's numbers of soldiers and sailors disagreed substantially with independent evidence—they were too high. With all such emendations, the tables constructed by these authors command our confidence as an indication of the form of and change in the distribution of income in England and Wales, by observations at four dates—1688, 1759, 1801-3 and 1867.

A first question is, how much change has there been from end to end? Figure 11.1 compares the distribution of 1688 with that of 1978/9. (The comparison is imperfect, because the coverage is only of England and Wales in 1688, but of the whole United Kingdom in 1978-9.) The object here is to compare the forms of the distributions, not the prevailing levels of income; if we were concerned with the latter, we should need a graph with a very different vertical scale, and the two curves would be far apart, for the median income was only £20 a year in 1688, but about £3385 in 1978/9. We can reduce the disparity by taking account of the changed purchasing power of money: a chaining of inadequate index numbers of prices (see Table 9.4) indicates that the £ could buy about 29 times as much produce in 1688 as in 1978/9. But reducing the later incomes by this factor does not close the gap: against the £20 median income of 1688, we now have a median of about £117 in 1978/9—real income at the median seems to have

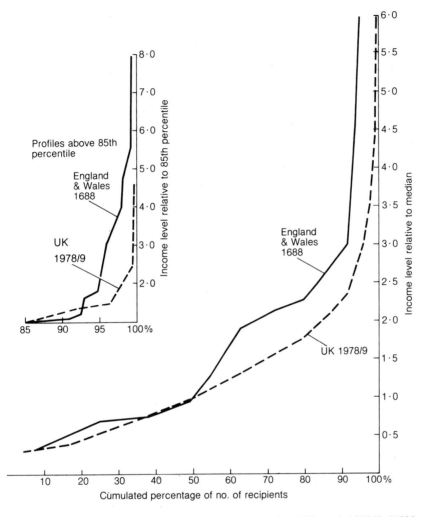

Fig. 11.1 Distribution of British personal income in 1688 and 1978/9 (1688: England and Wales; 1978/9: United Kingdom) *Source:* see Table 11.1.

been raised by a factor of nearly 6. There remains the course, adopted here, of bring the curves together for comparison by expressing income levels relatively to the median in each year.

What, then, does Figure 11.1 indicate? A first impression may well be that the change over nearly three hundred years has been remarkably small—three hundred years in which the population of England and Wales has been multiplied by a factor of 9 and the average real income, as we have just seen, by a (roughly estimated) factor of 6. Further consideration will strengthen this impression; that the form of the distribution has not

TABLE 11.1 *Distribution of personal income in England and Wales, 1688–1867, as Pen parades*

Estimates of the distribution of personal income in England and Wales in 1688, 1759, 1801–3, and 1867, set out in the form of a Pen parade showing the income levels, in current £ p.a. prevailing at various percentiles of the total number of recipients

King, 1688		Massie, 1759		Colquhoun, 1801–3		Baxter, 1867	
% of cumulated no. of recipients	Income level (£)	% of cumulated no. of recipients	Income level (£)	% of cumulated no. of recipients	Income level (£)	% of cumulated no. of recipients	Income level (£)
13.0	6.5						
		6.3	7				
				10.0	10		
25.5	14	13.1	14				
37.5	15						
		18.1	16				
		28.9	16.25				
50.0	20	38.0	20				
						4.1	22
		41.1	23				
54.5	25	49.6	25			10.7	25
						21.1	27
		58.3	27.5				
				20.0	30		
				27.8	31	30.9	31
				38.3	31.5		
						46.7	34
63.0	38	61.6	38				
		73.6	40	43.1	40		
		83.7	41.25				
72.5	42.5						
						64.7	44
79.9	45			46.4	45		
84.0	50	84.7	50				
						73.7	54
87.8	55			57.8	55		
91.8	60	86.1	60				
						78.9	65
		88.7	70				
92.5	72						
				69.4	75	86.4	75
		91.5	76				
92.8	80	93.0	80				
				73.5	90		
93.9	91						
		94.1	100				
95.1	120			81.3	120		
		95.1	150	89.4	150		
		95.9	152				
95.6	154						
				94.2	200	96.2	200
				96.3	350		
				96.7	500		

98.1	97.6	97.3	99.3
98.9	98.7	98.7	
99.5	99.1		
99.8			

Income in current £				
	240	200	700	881
	280	269	800	
	400	400		
	562.5			
Median	20.0	25.1	48.9	35.8
Mean	39.2	43.4	90.8	72.0

Sources: Lindert and Williamson (1982): tables 2, 3, 4; 1983a: table 1).

changed more than this when so much else in the economy has changed reinforces the belief that the distribution of income is governed by forces that operate in the same way in societies otherwise very different. This conclusion has already been suggested by a comparison of different countries at about the same time; we see now that it holds of different periods, even far removed, in one country. But there are also significant divergences here. Up to the median, it is true, the slopes of the two curves are the same, but two differences appear subsequently. The first is a much steeper rise in the earlier than in the later years among the incomes immediately above the median. The occupations that were thus relatively so much better off in 1688 were, in ascending order, the building and manufacturing trades, the farmers, the shopkeepers and the lesser clergymen and freeholders. The other difference appears in the top 10 per cent. Here incomes rose more steeply in 1688, and to much greater heights: those of the two hundred 'temporal lords' were reckoned to average, at £6060, some 300 times the median income of £20. In 1978/9 only about one in a thousand of the income recipients had income of £30 000 and over, at the peak, and £30 000 was only about 9 times the median income of £3385.

A suspicion that the incomes immediately above the median were overestimated in 1688 is aroused by the steepness of their rise, and the concavity downwards of the profile thereafter. The incomes in these levels have been left unrevised by Lindert and Williamson, for lack of evidence to set against King's estimates. Perhaps those estimates were indeed on the high side. But we cannot assume that the gradations of 1688 were as smooth as those that appear in later years. In any case, there can be no question of the great difference at the top. Not even the inset diagram in Figure 11.1 shows the full extent of this. It does show the 1688 profile mounting earlier and rising far higher by the time the 99th percentile is reached, but it stops at an income level eight times that reached at the 85th percentile, and fails to show that a few incomes remain, spread out over a range that extends to incomes not eight but 120 times as great as at the 85th. This is amazing by contemporary standards.

The finding, that those above the median were much better off in 1688 than in 1978/9, relatively to the largely unskilled manual workers below them, is borne out by comparison of the first and last columns of Table 11.2. In 1688 the bottom 40 per cent received less than 10 per cent of the total income; in 1978/9, more than 16 per cent. At the other end, the top 20 per cent received about 58 per cent in the earlier year, as against less than 43 per cent in the later. Within this, the difference in the proportion received by the top 10 per cent is even more striking: 45 per cent in 1688, as against less than 26 per cent three hundred years later.

Evidently, the greatest change has been the 'cutting down of the tallest poppies', but there has also been a marked raising of the income of the manual workers and the lowest paid generally, relatively to the middle class. This has not come about through any raising of the lowest relatively to the median: on the contrary, we are confronted with the near coincidence of the two profiles in the first half of their course. After nearly three hundred years, the dispersion of incomes among the lower half of recipients is unchanged. But what has changed is the rate of rise of incomes above the median and, still more, the level attained by the top 10 per cent.

How and when did these changes come about? Figure 11.2 tells us something about what was happening down to 1867. Here again, the series have been expressed as relative to the median. The jerkiness of the profile

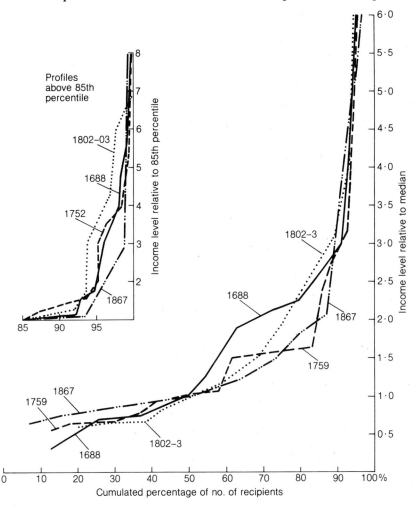

Fig. 11.2   Distribution of personal income in England and Wales, at dates from 1688 to 1867. *Source:* see Table 11.1.

TABLE 11.2   *Components of total income at dates from 1688 to 1978/9*

Quantile components of total income before tax, in England and Wales through
1867 and in the United Kingdom 1978/9, estimated by interpolation

Quantile group of recipients	King 1688 (%)	Massie 1759 (%)	Colquhoun 1801–3 (%)	Baxter 1867 (%)	Blue Book 1978/9 (%)
Top 10%	45.1	40.5	48.3	52.7	25.9
Top 20%	58.1	53.9	61.1	63.1	42.5
61–80%	20.9	21.7	18.9	14.1	26.9
41–60%	11.2	11.9	10.9	9.4	14.3
21–40%	6.7	7.9	6.9	8.5	10.3
0–20%	3.1	4.6	2.2	4.9	6.0

Sources: Estimates by King, Massie, Colquhoun and Baxter as revised by Lindert and
Williamson (1982, 1983a); data for 1978/9 from *National Income and Expenditure 1982* (1983):
table 4.9); quantile components obtained by interpolation in the original data when
arranged and cumulated.

for 1759 casts some doubt on its trustworthiness. One would have said in
advance that the sketchiness of all these estimates, made in times when so
little statistical information was collected, would prevent us from drawing
any reliable conclusions from them. But Figure 11.2 is its own justification:
we can hardly believe that four estimates, each hopelessly inaccurate,
would by chance agree as closely as for the most part these profiles do. It is
more plausible to suppose that they were fair if rough delineations of a
structure that retained its own form down the centuries. The margin of
dubiety in each of these profiles, taken singly, cannot be so great as to
prevent our drawing some credible conclusions from their agreement.

    One of these conclusions is that part of the change from end to end had
already come about by 1759. Only part of it—for at the very top, in the
small but conspicuous sector that held the highest incomes of all, those
incomes were higher still in 1759: whereas in 1688 the income of the
temporal lords had been about 300 times the median, in 1759 the ratio went
up to over 1000 times. But this was only at the peak: Table 11.2 shows that
the proportion of income received by the top 20 per cent, and even the top
10 per cent, was lower in 1759. The great change for most people, below
the 80th percentile, was the relative decline of the incomes above the
median: near the top of the middle class, at about the 80th percentile,
whereas in 1688 the income level was two and a half times the median, in
1759 it was little more than one and a half times. It is a disadvantage of the
device of expressing the different series as relatives to the median that in a
case like this we cannot tell whether those upper incomes were cut back
while the lower held their ground, or whether it was the upper that were
steady while the lower, including the median, went up. But reference to the

absolute figures of income shows that, while those of 1688 remain below £15 a year almost all the way to the median, those of 1759 passed £15 about the 20th percentile and reached £25 in the 40s, whereas the upper quartile was actually a little lower in the later than the earlier year. So the rise of the lower paid relatively to the middle class was brought about by an absolute improvement in their lot while that of the middle class hardly changed. Its likely cause is to be sought in the economic growth of the eighteenth century, and in the rising prosperity of which people became conscious about the middle of the century. This seems to have narrowed differentials within the range of the working and middle classes, and raised the incomes of the low paid more than those of the manufacturers, the tradesmen, the professionals and even the farmers; but it also raised the rent-rolls of the great landlords.

So much for the comparative levelling apparent in 1759. The profile for 1802–3 confirms the changed relative position of the income below and above the median—except perhaps for the impact of the war, for the lower incomes are held down by the presence of 120 000 'common soldiers', with incomes little greater than 'labouring people in husbandry'. But in the top third of the distribution incomes rise earlier and higher than before. Table 11.2 shows that the components formed by the top 20 per cent, and even more the top 10 per cent, of income recipients have increased substantially, until they now stand higher than in 1688. This suggests that we need to consider separately the movements of the highest incomes, and the relations one to another of the incomes at lower levels. In the Pen parades the slope of the profiles in the relevant region displays these relations, irrespective of what appears elsewhere. But there is no such transparency in Table 11.2, where the figure marking the proportions of income accruing to any sector below the top 20 per cent may rise or fall not only because the recipients in that sector are doing better or worse than their neighbours, but because the top 20 per cent are doing worse or better relatively to all those below them. Table 11.3 is therefore confined to the latter. It shows how the income they receive in the aggregate is distributed between them. We see at once the similarity in the distributions over this range between 1759 and 1801–3. That between 1801–3 and 1688 is yet closer. The substantial differences between these three years originate in and are largely confined to the top 20 per cent.

In 1867 the whole profile up to the 85th percentile has swung about the median as pivot; the rise in the lower incomes relatively to the upper middle class is much more marked, and the profile takes on the form of linearity or gentle concavity upwards with which we are familiar in recent years. This may be attributed to the great rise in the standard of living of the wage-earner achieved during the 1850s and 1860s. The labourers' incomes are higher relatively to those of the craftsmen, and what we may now call 'middle-class' incomes are lower relatively to those of manual workers

TABLE 11.3 *Stability and change in components of income below the top 20 per cent*

Division of total income accruing to recipients below the top 20 per cent, between four quintiles: England and Wales, 1688, 1759, 1801–3, 1867; UK, 1978/9

Quintile group of recipients	Gregory King 1688 (%)	Massie 1759 (%)	Colquhoun 1801–3 (%)	Baxter 1867 (%)	Blue Book 1978/9 (%)
Highest, 61–80%	50	47	49	38	47
41–60%	27	26	28	25	25
21–40%	16	17	18	23	18
Lowest, 0–20%	7	10	6	13	10

Sources: as for Table 11.2.

generally. Table 11.3 shows this in numbers: most strikingly, the proportion of the total income below the 80th percentile that goes to those in the highest of the four quintiles is now only 38 per cent, against 47–50 per cent at the three earlier dates. But at the top, the change was the other way about. The inset in Figure 11.2 shows the top incomes of 1867 beginning their upsurge later than in the earlier years, but even its enlarged scale cannot include the peak—more than 4000 incomes averaging nearly 600 times the median. This is not as high a peak as before, but Table 11.2 shows that the whole component of income accruing to the top 10 per cent was now greater than in the three preceding years. What peak we see depends on what type of recipient, such as the Temporal Lord, is separately reported. If we want to compare the summits in different years, we had better ask what proportionate part of income accrued to the top 5 per cent. This is a sensitive quantity, because even if it is small, those who receive it are conspicuous. But in fact, it was remarkably big, and was increasing: it was about 35 per cent in both 1688 and 1759, 40 per cent in 1801–3 and 44 per cent in 1867. Thus, it appears that a hundred years and more of industrial development raised the relative incomes of the lower paid, but at the same time gave scope at the other end for the amassing of great fortuness.

In sum, the structure of incomes had changed between 1688 and 1867 from a stack of three tiers to a smooth gradation. To characterize the structure of 1688 in that way is to simplify it overmuch; but in contrast with the later structure it does appear as formed of three groups—the cottagers and labourers, who made up half the whole number of income recipients; 'the aristocracy of labour'—the craftsmen, and with them the farmers and the professionals—a middle group with incomes substantially higher than the labourers' and rising fairly steeply within their own bounds; and at the top some very high incomes indeed. By 1867 this arrangement had been changed markedly. The lowest group had risen relatively to the others, and differed less among themselves. The middle group had ceased to differentiate itself so sharply from those below, both in the rate at which incomes rose and as a proportionate part of all income. So far, the movement had been towards greater equality. But the top group had become relatively richer than ever. The Pen parade serves to display and locate these varied changes, in whose presence any one measure of inequality means little.

There remain the changes between 1867 and 1978/9. These can be seen in Figure 11.3. Evidently, the changes were very different in the lower 70

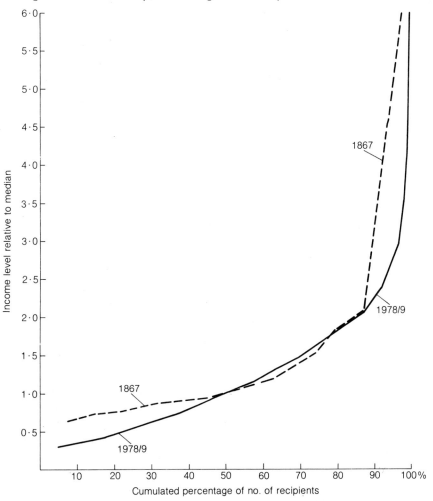

Fig. 11.3 Distribution of British incomes in 1867 and 1978/9.
Distribution of personal income before tax, in England and Wales in 1867; in the United Kingdom in 1978/9.
Sources: Tables 10.1, 11.1.

per cent of incomes and in the top 30 per cent. In the lower sector incomes had become much more unequal; in the upper, much more equal. There may be some illusion in the appearance of the first sort of change, in that the estimates of the later years were based on knowledge of individual incomes, whereas Baxter in 1867 could only assign average incomes to whole groups. But no such difference in reporting can explain the disparity overall: whereas income at the 70th percentile was nearly four times that at the 10th in 1978/9, the ratio had been only 2 to 1 in 1867 (Tables 10.1, 11.1). The change is unexpected, and hard to account for; it marks some return to the three-tier structure of the seventeenth century. But the opposite movement among the higher incomes is even more striking. The average income of the top 10 per cent was 5.3 times the mean of all incomes in 1867; in 1978/9 the ratio was just half that. The component of income in the top 5 per cent had been reduced even more, to a third of the 45 per cent of all income at which it had stood in the earlier year.

It seems that much of this relative fall in the highest incomes came about through the Second World War. The evidence is imperfect. Although we have a growing number of estimates of the national income over the intervening years, there are none that enable us to follow the distribution of income in comparable form until after the Second World War. The Survey of Personal Incomes carried out by the Inland Revenue does, it is true, provide particulars in the same form for 1938 as for the postwar years. But this is deceptive. The Survey covers only the incomes seen by the Inland Revenue, and it therefore omitted most wage-earners in 1938: in that year 56 per cent of total income lay below £250 a year, and accrued to a number of recipients that was not stated, but may well have been five times as many as the 3 million covered (Bowley 1944: 117). In 1947 the limit of £250 came much lower down the current scale of incomes, and the number covered was over 10 million. But these estimates are all we have to go on for whatever changes may have come about through the Second World War; and when they are cited in Table 11.4 they show changes so great as to be unmistakable, despite the lack of close comparability. That the lower quartile comes out so much higher before the war than after it must be ascribed, it is true, to the prewar inquiry having covered far fewer of the low incomes. But there can be no mistaking the relative reduction in the higher incomes. It is true, again, that if the income below £250 a year were added to the total income comprised before the war, the higher-income components would be reduced somewhat, but the effect would not be great enough to remove the drop now apparent by 1954/5. The component of the top 10 per cent, which was 45.5 per cent in 1867, still stood at 40.5 per cent in 1938/9. Even though this last figure should be lowered somewhat for the reason just given, we could hardly have come as much as half of the way towards the 28.3 per cent of 1954/5. Evidently, at least half of the relative reduction at the top came about through the Second World War.

TABLE 11.4   *Distribution of personal income in the United Kingdom before and after the Second World War*

Distribution of personal income before tax, within the scope of the Survey of Personal Incomes, UK, 1938-9, 1954-5, 1974-5

	1938/9 (%)	1954/5 (%)	1974/5 (%)
Quantiles as percentages of the median			
Highest percentile	1137	558	417
Highest decile	244	188	191
Upper quartile	143	140	142
Lower quartile	81	67	66
Average income of top 10 per cent as relative to mean income	4.0	2.8	3.2
Quantile components as percentages of total income			
Top 10%	40.5	28.3	24.8
Top 20%	52.4	42.1	39.4
61-80%	16.1	21.4	22.9
41-60%	12.3	16.6	17.5
21-40%	19.1	19.9	12.6
0-20%			7.6

Source: Royal Commission (1977): 240-1, tables D5, D6. The scope of the Survey of Personal Incomes is described in Appendix C of that Report.

The consequent rise in the other components was not spread over them evenly, but was concentrated on the two middle quintiles, and left out the poorest. Here we meet again that relative rise of the middle incomes that appeared on a comparison of the Pen parades for 1867 and 1978/9. But only in a banal arithmetic sense can we speak of 'a transfer' from the higher components: all we know is that over this span the middle incomes rose more rapidly than those above and below them.

To see whether there was much further change in the years after 1954/5, we turn to Tables 11.5 and 11.6. They may be taken together, despite some difference in coverage—the later one takes no account of incomes below the single man's tax allowance. They indicate some continued decline in the relative size of the highest incomes down to 1974/5, but not since; there may well have been some movement the other way since then. The consequent changes elsewhere have been spread fairly evenly, for the most part as modest rises. Thus, the change at the top that was so marked through the Second World War continued on a smaller scale afterwards, but was not now accompanied by a marked relative rise in the middle incomes. Figure 11.4, however, shows that in the depression of 1979-82,

TABLE 11.5 *Distribution of personal income in the United Kingdom after the Second World War*

Distribution of personal income before tax, as estimated in Blue Books, UK, 1954, 1964, 1974/5, 1978/9

Quantiles as percentages of the median	1954 (%)	1964 (%)	1974/5 (%)	1978/9 (%)
Highest percentile	592	535	449	437
Highest decile	212	209	214	227
Upper quartile	156	153	157	165
Lower quartile	42	51	54	55
Average income of top 10 per cent as relative to mean income	3.0	2.9	2.7	2.6
Quantile components				
Top 10%	30.1	29.1	26.6	25.9
Top 20%	45.2	44.6	42.4	42.5
61–80%	22.4	23.5	24.1	24.7
41–60%	16.3	16.6	16.9	16.5
21–40%	15.6	10.1	10.4	10.4
0–20%		5.2	6.2	6.0

Sources: 1954, 1964, 1974/5: Royal Commission (1977): 236, 237, tables D1, D2. *1978/9*: *National Income & Expenditure*, 1982 edn., table 4.9, from which the above entries have been estimated by interpolation.

although incomes below the median were virtually unchanged, those above it rose appreciably.

As we look back over the whole span of nearly three hundred years, one change is salient—the relative reduction of the highest incomes. So clear a movement entitles us to say with confidence that inequality has been reduced overall. But there has been no simple pattern of change. If the income component of the top 10 per cent declined in the eighteenth century, it rose in the nineteenth. When the great reduction occurred later, we knew that at least half of it came about through the Second World War, and have reason to expect that much of the remainder was affected by similar influences operating through the First World War. Below the top 20 per cent, again, the components followed no sustained course. They became more equal, one with another, in 1867, but the figures of 1978/9 reflect those of 1759 almost identically. The appearance at the outset of a middle group of incomes rising sharply above the incomes of labourers and cottagers in 1688 is replaced by a gentler rise and smoother gradation in the nineteenth century, but returns in 1978/9.

Simon Kuznets (1955) put forward the thesis that economic inequality increases in the early stages of development but decreases in the later ones.

TABLE 11.6   *Distribution of UK incomes, 1976-1984*

Distribution of incomes, before tax, as computed for tax purposes, above single person's allowance

1979/80		1982/3	
(1) Upper limit of income (current £)	(2) % of all incomes below given limit	(3) Upper limit of income (1979/80 £)	(4) % of all incomes below given limit
		1 500	3.8
		1 875	9.2
2 000	12.0	2 250	14.3
2 500	19.4	2 625	20.0
3 000	27.3	3 000	25.9
3 500	35.1	3 375	31.5
4 000	42.0	3 750	37.1
4 500	48.8	4 125	42.1
5 000	55.6	4 500	47.4
		5 250	56.7
6 000	67.1	6 000	65.4
7 000	76.5	7 500	78.4
8 000	83.9	9 000	86.4
10 000	92.2	11 250	93.1
12 000	95.8	15 000	97.1
15 000	98.0	37 500	99.8
20 000	99.2	75 000	100.0
50 000	99.9		

Note: The £ of 1982/3 taken to have 75% of the purchasing power of the £ of 1979/80.

Source: Board of Inland Revenue, *Annual Abstract of Statistics*, 1986 edn. Table 15.2.

Distribution of original household income by quintiles

Group of households, ranked by original income	Aggregate income of group, as % of all income			
	1976	1981	1983	1984
81-100%	44.4	46.4	48.0	48.6
61-80%	26.6	26.9	27.2	27.5
41-60%	18.8	18.0	17.7	17.5
21-40%	9.4	8.1	6.7	6.1
0-20%	0.8	0.6	0.3	0.3

Source: Central Statistical Office, Family Expenditure Survey; *Social Trends* 1987 edn., table A.8.

This has been endorsed by much subsequent study of distribution in economies passing through the earlier stages of development, and by the contrast between the greater inequality of income in the Third World and

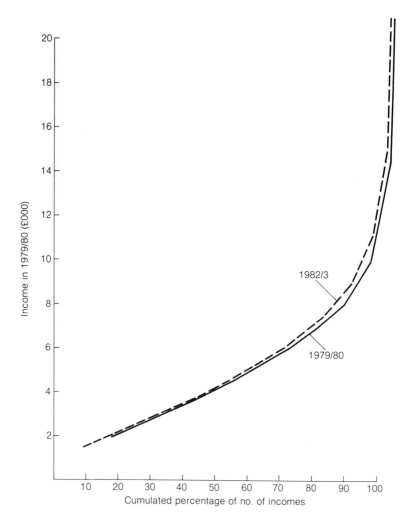

Fig. 11.4 Distribution of UK incomes in 1979/80 and 1982/3.
Pen parades showing distribution of incomes as computed for income tax
purposes, above level of single person's allowance, in the United Kingdom.
Source: Table 11.6.

the lesser inequality in the Western World. But we cannot say that the
thesis is sustained by the evidence we have examined here. It is true that the
most salient aspect of inequality, the relative size of the top incomes,
increased during the years containing the Industrial Revolution, between
1759 and 1867. But it seems to have been reduced substantially before that,
between 1688 and 1759; and when the eventual reduction came it was in a
period of slower development, and may be attributed to the two world wars

rather than to what development there was. Among the incomes below the top 20 per cent, moreover, there has been no systematic change at all.

11.2. The Course of Change in the United States

It may be instructive to see whether the sort of change through time that we have been observing within the United Kingdom appears in another country. Thanks to the thorough and penetrating study by Jeffery Williamson and Peter Lindert (1980), we can trace the probable course of change in the United States since early in the nineteenth century. Only for relatively recent years are distributions by income levels available, but movements towards or away from greater equality can be traced through earlier years by virtue of a subsequently observed correlation between extension and contraction of the pay structure, and increasing or decreasing inequality among incomes as a whole.

We have seen (p. 291 above) that in recent years incomes in the United States have been distributed rather more unequally than in the United Kingdom, and we can ask our authors whether this seems to have been always so. In the United Kingdom, we remember, the form of the distribution seems to have been very closely the same in 1759 as in a recent year, but in the nineteenth century it became more unequal, and then in the twentieth century it moved back again towards greater equality. There is much in the American record to agree with this. Our authors record two periods of extension of the pay structure in the nineteenth century, the one from 1816 to 1856, the other from 1896 to 1914; the intervening period, 1856-96, was one of 'stability, or modest levelling'. The first of these periods of extension was especially marked. 'The movements after 1856 pale by comparison. In four short decades, the American Northeast was transformed from the ''Jeffersonian ideal'' to a society more typical of the developing economies with very wide pay differentials and, presumably, marked inequality in the distribution of wage income' (Williamson and Lindert 1980: 131, 68). The renewed extension in the years down to the First World War carried inequality to its all-time maximum on the eve of the entry of the United States into the war. There followed, to 1929, another period of 'stability or modest levelling'. Strangely, the onset of the Great Depression in 1929 coincided with the opening of two decades of levelling. Between 1929 and the early 1950s, the proportion of family income received by the top 25 per cent fell from 55 to near 40 per cent (Verba and Orren 1985: Fig. 1.1). (Table 11.4 showed that in the United Kingdom the proportion of all personal income received by the top 20 per cent fell from 52 to 42 per cent between 1938-9 and 1954-5.) Since 1951 there has been little change in the United States; so much as there has been has brought more inequality, if anything.

The record, then, shows three periods of extension of the pay structure, with little reaction after them. Travelling this path in reverse, we conclude that the US distribution of pay—and probably with it that of incomes generally—had been much more equal about 1800 than it is now. There is a contrast here with the United Kingdom, which seems to have shared the movement towards inequality in the first half of the nineteenth century but reversed it later, very largely through the two world wars. The American entry into the first of those wars coincided with a check to the movement towards inequality, and in the years of the Second World War that movement went on rapidly. There is no simple relation between the direction of change and the level of activity or the trend of prices. We must look more deeply for the effective influences.

What these were are indicated by our authors. They name three in particular: 'technological process, labour supplies, and capital accumulation' (Williamson and Lindert 1980: 286). Technological progress affected the dispersion of pay when it went on at different rates in different sectors. This seems to have been the main source of the greater dispersion that came about in 1896–1914, when the rise of productivity in agriculture was checked or even reversed, and the fastest advances were made in the industries using high proportions of skilled labour. But this was also a period in which the second factor, labour supply, was also active, by reason of the high rate of immigration of unskilled labour. The levelling after 1929 was due to the withdrawal of both these first two factors: 'total factor productivity growth was more evenly balanced among sectors than in any other era since 1980', and immigration declined, as did the birth rate. The third factor, capital accumulation, favoured skilled workers because new equipment displaced the unskilled more than the skilled and, it is held, because the rising standard of living that it created brought with it a switch of demand from agricultural to industrial products, and so again released more unskilled than skilled labour. Williamson and Lindert attribute about half of 'the observed shift from sharply rising to relatively stable pay ratios in the nonfarm sector', after 1856, to slower capital accumulation, together with more even productivity growth (1980: 289, 287).

Two negative findings by Williamson and Lindert are also significant. One calls in question the accepted view that inflation promotes levelling. It is true that the onset of inflation, like the upward phase of the trade cycle, raises employment and pay more for the unskilled than for the skilled; but we have to account for the persistence of the levelling after the inflation has ceased. When we look at trends over longer periods, moreover, we find no reliable association between rising prices and narrowing dispersion. 'Pay ratios and income inequality drifted upward during the gentle 1900–1913 inflation, and they surged during the peacetime inflation from the 1840s to the 1850s'; there was no levelling during the inflation of the 1970s (Williamson and Lindert 1980: 137). It is changes in relative prices and different kinds of output that affect dispersion, not the fall in the purchasing power of money overall. The other negative finding concerns trade union power. Changes in this are associated with changes in dispersion in two instances—union weakness in the 1920s may be linked with the check to the levelling that had been going on up to 1916, and the revival and extension of unionism in the 1930s and 1940s played a part in the levelling of that period. The impact of unionism on differentials is clear in particular instances, but 'pay differentials have moved together in unionized and nonunionized industries' (Williamson and Lindert 1980: 139). In the aggregate, unionism cannot be credited, on any acceptable estimate of its differential effect, with anything like the full extent of actual levelling.

We should also notice one other significant consideration to which Williamson and Lindert call our attention: the effect of changes in the relative prices of foodstuffs and manufactures on the dispersion of real, as distinct from monetary, incomes. Because a higher proportion of the lower incomes is spent on foodstuffs, a rise in the price of these relatively to that of manufactures will increase the disparity between the lower incomes and the higher.

11.3. The Course of Change in Developing Countries

We have already referred (p. 299) to Simon Kuznetz's thesis of 1955. His view that inequality generally increases in the early stages of development and then decreases has been confirmed by a number of subsequent studies (Lecaillon et al. 1984: ch. 1). By statistical analysis of the movements of a large number of economies, these studies have fixed the level of average income at which the turning point is reached; or two such levels have been found, the component of income accruing to the poorest 20 per cent ceasing a fall and beginning to rise only later, that is, at a higher level of average income, than the component of the very rich, the top 5 per cent. That such inequality declines through the more advanced stages of development is more clearly established than that it rises in the early stages.

Models have been set up to account for this behaviour. They call our attention to what seems likely to be a main cause of it. Lydall (1977), for instance, took an economy made up of two sectors, in one of which income was twice as high as in the other: we may think of them as a modernized and industrialized sector, over against a traditional and agrarian sector. The distribution of income is lognormal in both sectors, and so is the degree of inequality as measured by the standard deviation of the logarithms, set at 0.65. As time goes on, the proportion of the working population in the modernized, high-income sector rises. On these assumptions, it follows that the degree of inequality in the incomes of the population as a whole rises until 30 per cent of the population is engaged in the modernized sector. It remains the same until the proportion reaches 50 per cent, then falls progressively as the proportion continues to rise. Something like this must have been happening in the real world. The agrarian sector has not generally advanced as rapidly as the industrial. In the nature of things, one cannot import the latest modern equipment, and the knowledge of how to operate it, so as to transform cultivation by peasants in the same way as a factory can be established. But we must not ascribe too much to this process. For one thing, it depends on the degree of inequality being no greater in the modern than in the traditional sector, but very likely it is in the modern sector that big new fortunes will be built up. The actual reduction of inequality has been brought about in great part by a fall in the relative size of the top incomes, and this suggests a change within the modern sector rather than a shift of the working population into it. It may be, again, that industrialization goes on without that kind of shift going far: highly capitalized processes embodying the latest techniques may be introduced to give high earnings to only a small number of workers.

We must therefore consider what other factors may contribute to the reduction of inequality. They are not far to seek. Prominent is the extension of education, carrying with it the possibility of developing a greater variety of capabilities and occupations than is found in a primitive community. This is associated with urbanization. The new activities may all be on the small scale. They are very different from the industrialization that is effected by setting up modern plants with imported techniques. But they provide a gradation of earnings—in the Pen parade, they raise the slope of the initial profile, and smooth out the angle that formerly occurred about the median or else around the 70th percentile. Inequality is reduced by greater occupational mobility. There is a greater choice of occupations. Entry is less obstructed in the growing towns than it was in a settled society by customary or institutional barriers. The very fact of spatial migration, quite apart from any shift into industry, promotes the smooth gradation of incomes. The actual cause of the reduction in the relative size of the top incomes may be the rise of many modest incomes out of the more nearly dead level of the poorest half of the population in former days.

12

The Redistribution of Income

The redistribution of income by way of taxes and benefits has proved itself a powerful instrument of social policy in the twentieth century. The transformation of the standard of living in Western countries has been made possible only by the advance of productivity; but the market forces that have distributed these gains among the working population have not of themselves helped those who, for whatever reason, are unable to work. These people have always depended for subsistence on transfers within the household and the community, but it is the national system of transfer developed in more recent years that has enabled them to share in the general advance. More widely, many households of lower income have gained from an excess of benefits received over tax paid. This chapter examines the evidence for the extent of redistribution.

12.1. Measuring Redistribution in Principle and Practice

In a system of redistribution, incomes are reduced by taxes, direct and indirect, and raised by benefits in cash and kind. Each income recipient contributes a certain sum in taxation, and receives a sum which is either remitted in cash or can be valued at cost when it is supplied in kind. The difference between contributions and receipts can be estimated as a sum of money for each recipient. For some—usually those who start with bigger incomes—it is negative; that is, contributions exceed receipts, and income is reduced. For others it is positive, and adds to income. The outcome in either case is a final income, as it is called. This consists of the command of resources that the recipient will use for consumption and saving. The total contributions of all recipients will exceed their receipts because a substantial part of the governmental expenditure that is financed out of taxation is applied to services like defence and police which cannot be allocated in given amounts as benefits to households. The British inquiry that we shall cite allocated less than half of all government expenditure to households.

All five elements—income itself, the two kinds of tax and the two of benefits—raise questions of coverage. The statistician attempting estimates must concern himself with many small matters, and must sometimes make arbitrary decisions to include or exclude. These questions need only be illustrated here. The income considered at the outset will naturally include all factor income—that is, pay, profits, interest and rent; but should it also include the annual value of a dwelling to the owner-occupier? In the British estimates, direct taxes include national insurance contributions by the employer, and indirect taxes, not only those laid on products bought by the income recipient, but those like value-added tax and custom duties that are laid on the producer, but assumed to be passed on. Benefits in kind consist of those public services for which there is a basis of allocation to the individual household. The national health service, for instance, is deemed to bring benefit to each type of household according to the number of children, persons of working age and retired persons it contains, weighted by knowledge of the average use of the service by the different types. Some benefits are included that are not directly supplied to recipients: housing and food subsidies are in effect negative indirect taxes, and will be allocated accordingly.

The changes from original to final income are usually seen as reducing the higher incomes and raising the lower. This is vertical redistribution. But there is also horizontal redistribution, between households whose original incomes are at the same level, but which contain different numbers of pensioners or children. The system transfers income from persons of working age to the young and the retired. This is only to be expected, when a large part of the benefits takes the form of services to children and old age pensioners—that is, of the provision of income to those who cannot obtain it by their own current activity. Indeed, the benefits to children may be seen as a loan which they will repay during their working lives by the taxes they pay, which also go to provide for the pensions they will draw later. There is no presumption that the accounts of each person, seen in this way, balance over his or her lifetime. We are in any case usually concerned only with the taxes and benefits of persons or households within any one year. But we are reminded that, if we could calculate those flows over the whole lifetime of each recipient, we should probably come out with quite different findings. This notion of redistribution between lifetime incomes is therefore to be noted, in addition to vertical redistribution between recipients at different levels of original income and horizontal redistribution between different types of person or household at the same level of original income.

Putting the figures on the five components—original income, direct and indirect taxes, benefits in cash and kind—requires in the first place a social survey, to record the incomes, direct taxes and cash benefits of particular types of individual or household, and the pattern of expenditure that goes with each type and income level. The recording of cash entries seems relatively straightforward, but it has been found that high incomes and investment incomes are generally understated; when the figures of the sample are grossed up to the national scale they fall well short of the totals in the national accounts. The same test shows that outlay on drink and tobacco is also understated. In the aggregate, moreover, total reported outlay usually exceeds total income. Beyond this margin of error in the data lies the dubiety of the assumptions that have to be made in allocating indirect taxes and a number of the forms of benefit. It is usual to assume that taxes on the products bought by income recipients are wholly passed on to them. Benefits in kind can be valued at cost, for example the cost of schooling, although we do not know that this is the value that consumers would put on these services if they had to buy them. In any case, the problem remains of how much to allocate to this recipient and that. For schooling it may have to be assumed that a child in any and every household attends the state school of the kind appropriate to its age, and receives a benefit valued at the average cost per pupil at that stage of education throughout the country. The national health service may be deemed to bring benefits to each household according to the number of children, men and women of working age and elderly persons it contains, and the average use made of the service by each of these types.

Such assumptions are bound to be bold, but they are also inescapable. The alternative course, which many inquiries have followed, is to take account of direct taxes and cash benefits, and stop there. But this will not do. The measure it offers of redistribution may be quite misleading. We shall see in the British estimates that indirect taxation is regressive throughout the scale of income: to leave it out is to overstate the equalizing effect of taxation as a whole by a long chalk. On the other hand, benefits in kind bring a consistently higher proportionate increase in command of resources the lower is original income. Where the outcome depends so much on these factors, there is much less risk of a bad error arising from mistakes in allocating them than from leaving them out altogether on the ground that allocation is hazardous.

But, it will be said, the boldest assumption of all is still to be mentioned. It is that the original income is independent of the taxes laid on it and the benefits added to it. This cannot be wholly so. There is a familiar uncertainty about the effect of an increase in income tax: will it induce people to work more, in order to keep their net earnings up, or less, because it offers them a smaller net reward for extra effort? An increase in tax has two opposite effects. If people do as much work and earn as much before tax as previously, the higher tax will leave them with less take-home pay and make them more anxious to earn more. But the addition to take-home pay obtained by working more is now smaller than before, by reason of the higher tax, and offers a smaller monetary compensation for the same extra effort and loss of leisure. Yet each unit of that money is now more highly valued. We do not know whether the resultant valuation by the worker of the return to extra work will be higher or lower. We also cannot tell how far the manual worker's appetite for overtime is reduced by the receipt of benefits to his family that are independent of his work. Taxes that raise costs of production may not simply be passed on to the purchaser of the product, but may result in lower pay for employees, or lower dividends for shareholders. Taxes that raise the employee's cost of living may make him or her press successfully for higher pay. If a high proportion of the expenditure of the rich goes on labour-intensive products such as personal services, reducing their incomes by progressive taxation will lower the demand for certain types of relatively low paid labour, and may reduce the rate of pay it commands. Advocates of self-help and incentives to individuals effort may contend that, under a regime of lower taxes and benefits, the general level of real income would be raised, so that many of those on lower incomes would gain more than they lost by the withdrawal of redistribution. On the other hand, if free schooling were not provided, how much production would be lost through the poorer quality of the labour force? In general, any purported measure of redistribution implies that we know the difference between the actual distribution of final income and what the original income would be if the system of redistribution were taken away. But we do not: we only know what original income is, in the presence of the system that has actually been set up.

Formally, this objection is nearly insuperable. We could overcome it only if our knowledge of the ultimate determinants of the actions of income recipients enabled us to predict with confidence how they would behave in the absence of the system; and we are far from that. There is a danger, when some economic measure is adopted, of accepting its impact as its full and ultimate effect: there are always some further reactions to take into account, even though they may be slow to come about, and hard to isolate from other changes occurring at the same time. On the other hand, we need a sense of proportion. It is unlikely that reactions such as those instanced above will be so big as to offset the substantial transfer of resources effected by the flows through the actual system of redistribution. What the kind of estimate we are now to consider does is to record those flows. If we must allow that we do not know just what would happen in their absence, and therefore cannot tell exactly what difference they make, we can at least measure the transfer of resources that is effected through them. We should not hesitate to measure the flows that are now running through the channels of an irrigation system, because we do not know just what course the waters would take in its absence, or what other resources the cultivators would then be stimulated to tap. There can be no doubt of the difference that the welfare state in the United Kingdom has made to the amenity of the elderly and of the children of the poorer homes.

All that has been said hitherto concerns redistribution between the incomes that people are receiving at any one time. A wider prospect opens when we take account of the ways in which today's redistribution can change the incomes of tomorrow. Education is the salient case in point.

The subsidization of education appears at any one time as part of the flow of benefits in kind that raises the real incomes of the lower-income households; but because education raises earning power, the children in those households will go on to earn higher incomes than they could have achieved if their actual education had been beyond their reach. A similar observation applies to all forms of benefit that give the children of the recipient households a better start in life. What the ultimate effect will be on the inequality of incomes cannot be decided readily. The incomes of a number of people who have all been held back by lack of opportunity are likely to be more alike than the incomes of the same people after the opening of opportunities, of which some of them will avail themselves more effectively than others. Their average income, however, will be higher, not only absolutely, but relatively to the incomes of those unaffected by benefits. Probably the main dynamic effect of redistribution is to promote the growth of the middle class.

Another way of viewing this dynamic effect is to regard it as changing the distribution of wealth. If the ability to earn that is acquired through education and training is treated as capital, no less than physical equipment, then human capital can be estimated to make up a large part of the total capital of society. The services and benefits that enable young people to acquire earning power they would otherwise have lacked can be regarded as endowing them with capital. The distribution of wealth, so defined, is made less unequal.

12.2. Redistribution of Income in the United Kingdom

The study of redistribution in the United Kingdom was opened up by J. L. Nicholson, and developed by him and his collaborators in the Central Statistical Office with great care and ingenuity. The present account is derived from the study based on and embodying his work in Report no. 7 of the (Diamond) Royal Commission on the Distribution of Income and Wealth (1979). This uses the findings of the sample of some 7000 households whose receipts and outlay were recorded by the Family Expenditure Survey in 1977.

The main findings are set out in Table 12.1. Let us first consider taxation. Row (3) shows what we expect, that direct taxes are highly progressive. They take over 24 per cent of the original income plus cash benefits of the top 10 per cent of income recipients, but the proportion falls at each stage as we move down the scale of income, especially through the lower half. In the lowest decile but one it reaches less than 1 per cent, and those in the poorest decile pay no direct tax at all. But they do pay indirect taxes (row (4)); in fact, 20 per cent of their income including cash benefits is taken up in this way. (The reason for including cash benefits in the base

TABLE 12.1 *Original income, direct and indirect taxation and benefits in cash and kind at different income levels of households in the United Kingdom, 1977*

	Top 10%	81–90%	71–80%	61–70%	51–60%	41–50%	31–40%	21–30%	11–20%	0–10%
(1) Ave. original income (£ per annum)	11 079	7392	6096	5194	4411	3607	2703	1442	392	20
(2) Original income + cash benefits (£ per annum)	11 298	7611	6334	5445	4696	3977	3256	2444	1578	1378
(3) Ave. direct taxes (as % of original income)	24.3	21.6	20.6	19.5	19.0	16.6	14.2	6.9	0.9	—
(4) Ave. indirect taxes (income and cash benefits)	13.8	16.3	16.7	17.7	18.2	19.0	20.7	21.0	20.8	20.1
(5) Ave. total taxes	38.1	37.8	37.3	37.2	37.2	35.6	34.9	27.9	21.7	20.1
(6) Total taxes (£ per annum)	4 305	2877	2363	2026	1749	1416	1134	683	342	277
(7) Ave. cash benefits (as % of original income)	2.0	3.0	3.9	4.8	6.5	10.3	20.5	69.5	302.6	6790.0
(8) Ave. direct and indirect benefits in kind	8.1	11.4	12.4	14.9	17.6	19.7	25.9	42.9	142.1	3065.8
(9) Ave. total benefits	10.3	14.4	16.3	19.7	24.0	29.9	46.3	112.4	444.6	9855.0
(10) Total benefits (£ per annum)	1 117	1062	994	1023	1053	1080	1254	1621	1742	1971
(11) Total benefits – total taxes (£ per annum)	– 3 188	– 1815	– 1369	– 1003	– 696	– 336	120	938	1400	1694
(12) Ave. final income (£ per annum)	7 891	5577	4727	4191	3715	3271	2823	2380	1792	1714

Source: Royal Commission (1979), table 3.4.

now appears: it would have been meaningless to express the nearly £280 of indirect taxes that the poorest pay, as a percentage of the £20 that is all their original income.) This indirect taxation is clearly regressive: as a percentage of income, it rises steadily as we move down through the income levels as far as the 20th percentile, and it falls hardly at all below that—the poor pay 20 per cent, the top tenth, less than 14 per cent. When the two forms of taxation are combined (row (5)) their opposing slants largely offset each other from the 30th percentile upwards. Below that, the percentage declines from near 35 to little more than 20 per cent: such is the extent of progression in the tax system as a whole.

Some salient features of the British system have now appeared. Taxes as a whole fall on households almost proportionately throughout the top 70 per cent: only the bottom 30 per cent are in some measure spared, but even the poorest tenth contribute a fifth of their receipts, and these consist mostly of cash benefits. Evidently, if the business of redistribution is to be done effectively, it is the provision of benefits that must do it. Again, just as in the original distribution of income the top 15 per cent formed a system in themselves, so here it appears that redistribution will be concentrated on the bottom 30 per cent.

It is noteworthy that the main finding about the channels of redistribution in the United Kingdom appears to hold for many other countries—taxation, when the direct and indirect forms are taken together, does little to change relative incomes, but a substantial redistribution emerges when benefits are added back. Pryor (1968) studied seven 'market economies' (which included Yugoslavia) and seven 'centralized econo-mies'—the USSR itself and six European satellites—in 1950–62. He warns of the danger of judging the incidence of taxes without regard to the local circumstance of their application; but subject to that, he reaches a significant conclusion:

From previous studies about the impact of public expenditure and taxes on the income distribution in a number of countries one easy generalisation is possible: public expenditures are considerably more progressive than taxes, at least in a short run sense (i.e. between people with different incomes at a single point in time); whether this represents a net lifetime redistribution between income classes is not known). (Pryor 1968: 304)

Transfer payments and government services accrue predominantly to the lower-income housholds.

On the other hand, the impact of taxes on the distribution of income (especially those taxes which are most easy to collect) is rarely progressive, as empirical studies of this phenomenon for various market economies have so frequently shown. (Pryor 1968: 305)

We see this form of redistribution at work in the United Kingdom in rows (7)–(9) of Table 12.1. Both cash benefits and benefit in kind rise as proportions of original income as we go down from the highest to the lowest incomes, throughout the scale, and their rise within the lowest 30 per cent is steep. Above the median, benefits in kind are at least three times as big as cash benefits, but that relation is entirely inverted among the poorest 30 per cent, where it is cash benefits that are much the most important. When the two kinds are put together, and their absolute amount is considered in row (10), it shows a remarkable constancy throughout the top 60 per cent, namely, about £1000 a year per household; among the lower incomes it rises, to reach nearly £2000 in the lowest tenth. The active agent of redistribution is thus the provision of benefits, and within these, benefits in cash much more than in kind.

In another sense, however, the system acts upon every level of income. What is given to the poorer households is taken from those who are better off. The boundary comes about the 40th percentile. Row (11) shows the balance of taxes paid and benefit received. Throughout the top 60 per cent this is negative—taxes exceed benefits; in the bottom 40 per cent it is the other way about, by a small margin at first, but by nearly £1700 in the poorest tenth.

This is illustrated in Figure 12.1. We see at the top a curve showing the positive contribution of benefits to households at each of ten levels of original income. Below the zero line the curve of total taxes extends from the £277 that was raised from the households in the lowest decile to the £4305 from the top decile. The curve in between marks the balance of taxes and benefits. In the lowest four deciles this is positive throughout, but it decreases rapidly as we go up the scale of income. In the region of the 40th decile taxes and benefits just offset each other, so that original income remains unchanged. At higher levels of income, taxes exceed benefits by an ever-increasing amount.

We have already seen that the curve recording this changing incidence of the balance lies so much below the zero line because the taxes are not all returned as benefits; that is, they do not simply serve to redistribute income, but also have to provide for the general purposes of government, the benefit of which to the community can hardly be allocated to particular households. But we might regard the excess of tax paid over benefits received by the top 60 per cent of households as made up of two parts, one a contribution to the general purposes of government, and the other destined for transfer to the poorer 40 per cent. It would be reasonable to fix the proportionate size of the second part as equal to the ratio of total benefit to total tax, and thus as constituting some 75 per cent of the whole excess of tax over benefit. On this assumption, it follows that the top 60 per cent gave up in all nearly 17 per cent of their original income to be transferred to their poorer neighbours. But they gave it up in very different proportions. The top decile gave up about 22 per cent; the proportions given up by the deciles below, in descending order of income level, were 18, 17, 14, 12 and

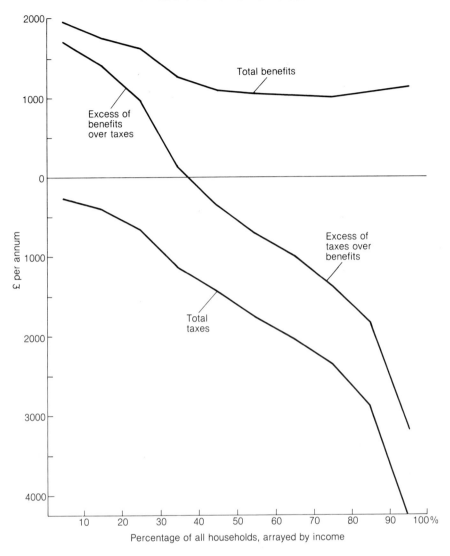

Fig. 12.1   Total benefit and taxes, and the balance of the two, for British
households at ten levels of income, 1977. *Source:* as for Table 12.1.

7 per cent. These proportions contrast with the steadiness over the same
range of the ratio of total tax paid to original income (Table 12.1, row (5).
On this hypothetical way of identifying the tax assigned to redistribution,
its incidence appears markedly progressive.

The most comprehensive view of redistribution as it was effected in the
United Kingdom in 1977 is afforded by the Pen parades in Figure 12.2.

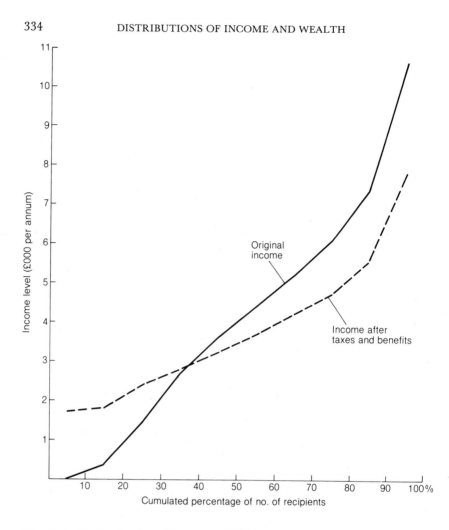

Fig. 12.2 Redistribution of incomes of UK households, 1977.
Pen parades showing original incomes, by deciles, and incomes (for an unchanged array) after taxes and benefits.
Source: Table 12.1.

The profile of income after taxes and benefits shows the final incomes of the same households as made up in each decile when arrayed by original income. The incidence of taxes and benefits varies between different types of household at the same income level: as we shall see, for example, households with children generally have smaller net outgoings than others which have similar incomes but no children. When households are arrayed in respect of final income, therefore, quite a number are found to have moved up or down from the places they occupied in the array by original income. But it is reasonable to retain that array for both profiles here, in order to display the effect of redistribution on given households. The figure shows this effect clearly. Final incomes are distributed much more equally than original incomes. The profile is swung round on a pivot near the 40th percentile. A smooth gradation remains; if anything, the final profile is more linear than the original, but the rate of rise is slower throughout. In this sense, equalization has come about at all levels. But it is specially marked in the lower ones. For income in the lower deciles is raised relatively to the median—instead of income in the decile 11–20 per cent being less than 10 per cent of income at the median, it has become fully 50 per cent.

The detail provided by the Diamond Commission gives us some glimpses of horizontal redistribution as well. Table 12.2 compares households containing two non-pensioners with those containing two adults and two

TABLE 12.2   *Horizontal redistribution*

Comparison of the net excess of tax paid out over benefits received, as a percentage of original income, by households of two non-pensioners and those of two adults and two children, at seven income levels, United Kingdom, 1977

	Decile of households (%)						
	90–100	81–90	71–80	61–70	51–60	41–50	31–40
Ave. original income (£ per annum)							
Two non-pensioners	10 525	7128	6033	5239	4538	3781	3052
Two adults, two children	10 580	7163	6199	5591	5056	4585	4183
Net outpayments as % of original income							
Two non-pensioners	34	34	33	32	28	19	14
Two adults, two children	26	22	26	15	15	13	9

Source: Royal Commission (1979: table 3.4).

children. We are dealing here, it must be noted, with comparatively small samples—about 2000 of the first type of household, less than 900 of the second. In the top four deciles, the average incomes of the two types are much the same, so that we can make a truly horizontal comparison. In the remaining three—those between the 60th and 30th percentiles—the average income is higher in the households with children; but so far as this goes, it should make any net outpayment a higher proportion of income. In fact, the table shows that this proportion is smaller at all levels for the households with children. This is the effect we may expect from the presence of allowances, and benefits in kind specially for children.

12.3. Redistribution in Sweden

Leaving indirect taxes and the receipt of benefits aside, we may look first at the effect of direct taxes on the relative earnings after tax offered by different occupations. How substantial this effect is in Sweden is illustrated by Figure 12.3 which is reproduced from a study by Assar Lindbeck (1983). This figure shows, first, the effect of taking lifetime instead of current pay for six occupations, relative to the pay of the welder. This reduces the range over which the pay for those occupations is spread, from about 2.7 times the welder's pay to 2.3 times. But this effect is small compared with that of pay after tax: the range now comes down to 1.4, and there is compression of all the differentials between. Taking the discounted present value of lifetime pay, instead of the simple total over time, proves to affect all the occupations except the carpenter's and welder's in much the same proportion, but the effect is not great.

The difficulty, already discussed, of knowing what change is really made, arises here acutely. Does the market, or custom and convention, set pay in its gross or its net form? Certainly when the international movement of executives, for example, is at issue, it is usual to consider the adequacy of what is left after tax. Where it is felt necessary to maintain a certain differential between posts in the same country, it might be thought equally obligatory to reckon it in terms of income after tax. So far as this is done, the distribution of earnings before tax lacks social significance. It is rather that different kinds of work bear different rates of tax which the employer must pay, just as consumers might pay different rates of purchase tax on various products. The ultimate incidence is often dubious in both cases. A tendency to 'charge tax forward' is implied by the belief that a reduction in the tax paid by manual workers will reduce their wage claims, and vice versa. On the other hand, pay before tax has an announcement effect. When the prospects in different posts are compared, it is commonly the pay before tax that is cited, if only because how much tax particular occupations actually pay varies with personal circumstances. Invidious comparisons, and protests against the absolute size of rises granted to those already highly paid, rest upon pay before tax. We can only conclude, as before, that we cannot tell how the allocation of resources under the present arrangement compares with what some alternative arrangement would bring about; but we can record the flows through present channels.

The same study by Assar Lindbeck shows the net effect of income tax and cash benefits in the country generally credited with the fullest extension of the welfare state. Figure 12.4 does for Sweden very much what Figure 12.1 does for the United Kingdom, but whereas the British data are simply flows of receipts and outgoings, the Swedish show the net flow, into or out of households, as a percentage of 'factor income', that is, of the household's receipts from the return on work and property. This net flow is termed the

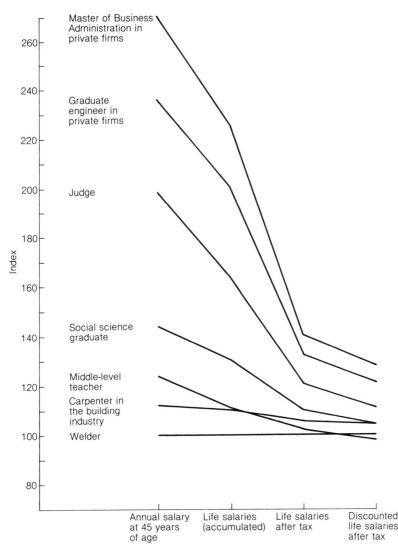

Fig. 12.3 Equalizing effects of progressive tax.
The effect of progressive taxation on the dispersion of lifetime incomes offered by
seven occupations in Sweden, 1981.
Source: Swedish Confederation of Professional Associations; reproduced here from
Lindbeck (1983: fig. 5B).

net income tax. No percentages can be quoted for the bottom decile of
factor incomes, most of which are zero or even negative. A more substantial difference is that the Swedish taxation is reckoned for income tax
alone, whereas the British include the estimated incidence of indirect taxes.

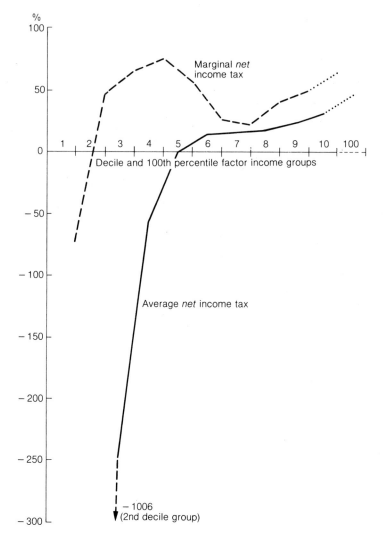

Fig. 12.4 Redistribution in Sweden.
The balance of income tax and cash benefits in Sweden in 1979, expressed as a percentage of household factor income, by deciles, together with the marginal form of that ratio, namely the change in the balance per unit increase in household factor income.
Source: Swedish National Central Bureau of Statistics, Income Distribution
          Survey, 1979; reproduced here from Lindbeck (1983: 247).

This may be one reason why the households that gain on balance are the poorest 45 per cent in Sweden, as against only the poorest 37.5 per cent in the United Kingdom. But a disparity that may work the other way is that the British benefits include those in kind, whereas the Swedish are of cash only.

The extent of redistribution in Sweden appears in a striking reduction in the contrast between the high and the low incomes when we move from the original factor incomes of households to their disposable incomes—that is, to what they have to spend or save after paying income tax and receiving cash benefits. Thus Lindbeck (1983: 232–3) observes that, 'while the ratio between the factor income of the tenth and the second decile groups is approximately 6.6 to 1, the ratio between the disposable incomes of the same factor decile groups is about 4.0 to 1. For disposable incomes per consumer unit it is approximately 2.2 to 1.' This last ratio is so small because, whereas the three lowest deciles consist mainly of pensioners and students, the higher deciles are made up of families, and 'the number of family members, and consumer units, rises broadly by factor incomes'. Because of this, transfers actually rise from the sixth decile to the eighth.

The behaviour of the marginal net income tax in Figure 12.4 is unexpected. This series shows the change in the balance of taxes and benefit, when we move from one decile of factor incomes to the next above it, as a percentage of the change in those incomes. Through the lowest four deciles pensions fall off rapidly, so that the initial excess of benefits over tax is reduced and reversed, and this change in the net tax goes on more rapidly than factor income rises. From the sixth decile to the eighth, marginal net tax falls, because pensions are no longer there to fall, families are growing bigger, and household income is increasingly divided among recipients who are taxed separately. We do not see what happens to a household of unchanged composition as its income rises.

Lindbeck calls attention to the extent of the inequality of income that is due simply to differences in hours worked. In 1979 nearly a fifth of Swedish employed men, and well over half of the women, were working part-time. 'Thus, whereas the Gini coefficient for factor incomes of all households is 0.50, of economically active households 0.33, and of individual employees 0.26, it is as low as 0.17 for the earnings of full-time employees' (Lindbeck 1983: 233). If those who work shorter hours do so voluntarily, because they prefer more leisure, the redistributive system can be seen as subsidizing them at the expense of those who prefer to work longer and earn more.

12.4. Redistribution in the United States

As with Sweden, we can take first the effect of taxes, leaving benefits aside, but the study by Pechman and Okner (1974) which we now cite includes indirect with direct taxation. 'It is assumed that the individual income tax is not shifted by the taxpayer and that the general sales and excise taxes are borne by consumers in proportion to their consumption of the taxed items'

(p. 37). For the rest, different assumptions about the incidence of the corporation, property and payroll taxes lead to different estimates of the equalizing effect. The two sets of assumptions applied in Table 12.3 are, respectively, the most and the least progressive in their effect of the eight

TABLE 12.3   *Combined incidence of federal and state–local taxes in the United States, by deciles of population arrayed by income, 1966*

	Total federal and state–local taxes as % of income	
Decile of population	On most progressive assumptions	On least progressive assumptions
1st	16.8	27.5
2nd	18.9	24.8
3rd	21.7	26.0
4th	22.6	25.9
5th	22.8	25.8
6th	22.7	25.6
7th	22.7	25.5
8th	23.1	25.5
9th	23.3	25.1
10th	30.1	25.9

Source: Pechman and Okner (1974: 64, tables 4–11).

sets of assumptions considered. The authors conclude that, 'regardless of the incidence assumptions, the tax system is virtually proportional for the vast majority of families in the United States. Under the most progressive set of assumptions . . . taxes reduce income inequality by less than 5 per cent; under the least progressive assumptions . . . income inequality is reduced by only about 0.25 per cent' (Pechman and Okner 1974: 64). The similarity in this respect with the findings for the United Kingdom in Table 12.1 is striking.

These estimates of the effect of taxation, without taking transfers into account, indicate little redistribution so far. Estimates of the inequality of income before tax, at various dates since the Second World War, have similarly concluded that there has been little change. These estimates of the Gini coefficient have been made in the usual way, by measuring the difference between the Lorenz curve of the actual distribution of incomes and the straight line at 45° that shows what the distribution would be if all households had the same income. But Paglin (1975) has pointed out that the basis of this comparison is unacceptable. For the 45° line supposes that every household has the same income, irrespective of the age of its head; whereas surveys have found a systematic relation between the income of the household and that age. This relation appears as an arched profile: income rises steadily with age until the mid-50s, and then as steadily declines. But the inequality arising from these changes in the course of the life-cycle of the household is hardly such as egalitarians object to. It is perfectly consistent with the lifetime incomes of all households being equal. It is in fact quite big: Paglin has estimated that, if all households of the same age had the same income, the poorest 20 per cent of households would still receive less than 13 per cent of all income. His suggestion is that this component should be subtracted if the real extent of inequality is to be measured.

This procedure throws fresh light on redistribution. It now appears that the constant inequality that appears on the usual way of reckoning, is due to a substantial redistribution towards the poorest 20 per cent having been offset by a greater arching of the age–income profile. This in turn has been ascribed to increased education, for the profiles of households with the more educated heads are more arched. When this effect is removed, a progressive reduction in inequality from 1947 to 1972 is revealed. 'The massive spending on education and training programmes, the more generous cash and merit good transfers, and the legislative and judicial actions directed at bringing minorities and under-privileged groups into the mainstream of the economy' (Pechman and Okner 1974: 603–4) did in fact raise the relative incomes of the poorest households substantially.

The estimates initially reported here include only benefits in cash. Paglin has estimated (1975: 606) that in 1973 benefits in kind added 1.6 percentage points to the proportion of all income received by the poorest 20 per cent of households, raising it from 5.4 to 7.0 per cent.

That even money transfers of themselves effected a substantial redistribution of family income is confirmed by a study of incomes in 1970 made by the President's Council of Economic Advisers. This measured inequality by the variance of the natural logarithm of income. The variance of family income excluding all transfer income was 1.57; when transfer income was taken into account the variance was only 0.74. The most influential components of that transfer income were social security and public assistance; some part was also played by unemployment benefits, workmen's compensation, government employee pensions and veteran benefits (Council of Economic Advisers 1974: 178, Table 49).

13

The Distribution of Wealth in Some Contemporary Economies

13.1. The Paradox of Prominence

To egalitarians, it is the sight of great wealth rather than high salaries that has caused concern. Holy writ denounced the man of property, not the labourer who was worthy of his hire, even if that were greater than another man's. When the stranger who came to Jesus asking for eternal life said that he had kept all the commandments, 'Jesus looked straight at him; his heart warmed to him, and he said,

One thing you lack: go, sell everything you have, and give to the poor, and you will have riches in heaven, and come, follow me.' At these words his face fell and he went away with a heavy heart; for he was a man of great wealth. Jesus looked round at his disciples and said to them, 'How hard it will be for the wealthy to enter the Kingdom of God!' They were amazed that he should say this, but Jesus insisted, 'Children, how hard it is for those who trust in riches to enter the Kingdom of God! It is easier for a camel to pass through the eye of a needle than for a rich man to enter the kingdom of God!' (Mark 10: 21-5)

In his influential work on *Equality* (1931), R. H. Tawney made a clear distinction between inequalities of earnings and of wealth. 'No one thinks it inequitable that, when a reasonable provision has been made for all, exceptional responsibilities should be compensated by exceptional rewards, as a recognition of the service performed and an inducement to perform it.' In a society unified by the liberal provision of social services and especially of education for all, 'these details of the counting-house are forgotten or ignored'. But such a society could be attained only by the abolition of inherited wealth. Given this, and the provision of ample communal amenities, the remaining differences of income would be unexceptionable. 'While diversities of income, corresponding to rarities of function and capacity, would survive, they would neither be heightened by capricious inequalities of circumstance and opportunity, nor perpetuated from generation to generation by the institution of inheritance.' Especially was it necessary to abolish 'the reverence for riches, which is the *lues Anglicana*, the hereditary disease of the English nation. And, human nature being what it is, in order to abolish the reverence for riches, they must make impossible the existence of a class which is important merely because it is rich' (Tawney 1931: 154, 212, 114). Tawney's eye was fixed on the division of society and the warping of human relations by the dominance of a class of great wealth largely acquired by inheritance. Especially he must have had in mind the great landowners of the United Kingdom in which he was growing up at about the turn of the century. It was from their estates that most of the highest incomes in the land were drawn. Their influence was powerful in government. At the apex of high society, they set the tone of a lord-loving people. Only the abolition of these private holdings of wealth could make possible a more egalitarian and humane society. The same belief, that it was the inequality of wealth, not of earnings, that the social reformer must attack, was affirmed in another influential work on socialist policy, C. A. R. Crosland's *The Future of Socialism* (1956). 'Some methods of redistributing work incomes', 'he wrote, would have a bad effect—notably, much higher taxation of marginal earnings. But this does not much weaken the socialist case. The largest inequalities stem not from the distribution of earned incomes, but from the ownership of inherited capital . . .' (p. 239).

This impression is understandable. Great wealth is not only conspicuous for the high incomes it brings; it is also invidious because the possessors enjoy income without labour, and quite often have done nothing to acquire it. Herein seems to lie the great source of social inequality. But when we come to facts and figures in Tawney's counting-house, we are confronted with a paradox: although the inequalities of wealth are much greater than those of earnings, they contribute only a small part of the inequality of incomes as a whole. If they were wholly removed, that inequality would not be much reduced. In the United Kingdom in 1977, rent, dividends and net interest amounted to little more than 6 per cent of all personal income, or, if we include the imputed rent of owner-occupied dwellings, about 10 per cent (Royal Commission 1979: table 2.2). They made up, it is true, a much greater part of the top incomes: investment income amounted to about a quarter of the incomes of the top 1 per cent of recipients, and a tenth of the incomes of the whole top decile, as against only about 3 per cent of incomes at lower levels (Table 2.12). Wealth is evidently responsible for much of incomes at the peak. But over most of the distribution, the removal of the income from wealth holdings would not reduce the dispersion of incomes very much. Jan Pen (1971: 64) reports an estimate that in the 1950s only a quarter of the variance of Dutch incomes was attributable to the inequality of wealth holdings. From Table 13.1 we can calculate that the exclusion of investment income from UK incomes in 1975-6 would reduce their variance by 17 per cent. Figure 13.1 shows how little the Pen profiles are affected by that exclusion, except in the top decile.

We need to carry this sense of proportion into our study of the inequality of wealth. At the same time, we have to bear in mind the possibility that it bulked larger in the past. In the balance sheets of British households in the

TABLE 13.1   *The effect of excluding investment income*

Personal incomes (net of deductions) in the UK, 1975/6, before and after exclusion of investment income

Quantile group	Ave. income net of deductions (£)	Investment income as % of (1) (%)	Ave. income after deduction of investment income (£)
0–10	719	1.7	707
11–20	1 004	2.5	979
21–30	1 288	3.0	1 249
31–40	1 649	3.7	1 588
41–50	2 126	3.3	2 055
51–60	2 591	3.2	2 508
61–70	3 188	2.7	3 102
71–80	3 664	2.9	3 558
81–90	4 444	2.9	4 315
91–100	7 143	10.2	6 414
91–95	5 404	4.1	5 182
96–99	7 251	8.7	6 620
100	15 444	23.5	11 815
Mean of deciles	2 782		2 648

Sources: Royal Commission (1979: tables 2.10, 2.12).

1970s, agricultural and other land made up less than $2\frac{1}{2}$ per cent of total net wealth (Royal Commission 1979: table 4.1), but that small proportion bears no relation to the significance of landowning in earlier years. Wealth is important in any case as a major source of those top incomes that we have already seen reason to regard as forming a distinct distribution. The possession of wealth, moreover, is regarded as conferring power and status as well as income. We have reason to proceed with our enquiry into its distribution, so much more unequal than that of income.

13.2. The Limited Sources of Knowledge of Wealth

It is another paradox that so few facts have been gathered about so prominent and contentious a subject as wealth. Call it capital, and violent controversy ensues—battles between those who uphold the personal ownership of the means of production and those who denounce it. One would have thought that a first step in clarifying the issue would be to find out who held what property, in what form. This did happen once in the United Kingdom: in the 1870s, when an unwillingly urbanized British people had taken up again its claim for access to the land, Parliament called for a new Domesday book, a *Return of Owners of Land* (Parliamentary Papers

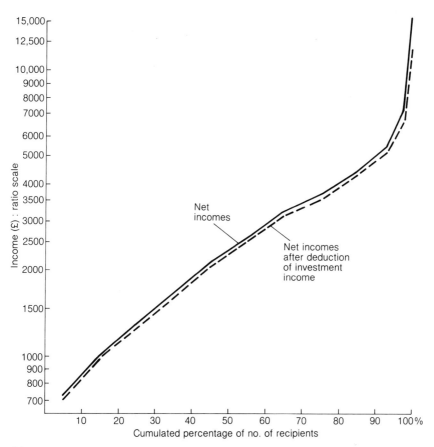

Fig. 13.1 The effect of deducting investment income from net personal income, United Kingdom, 1975/6. *Source:* Table 13.1.

1876). On this, John Bateman based his *Great Landowners of Great Britain and Ireland* (1878). The reason why statistics of wealth are so much scantier than those of income is that both sorts have become available not through purposeful inquiries, but as a by-product of administration, and it happens that this has thrown up much information about incomes and little about wealth. The collectors of income tax have long been assembling particulars of the sources and size of incomes; interest in the welfare of the working classes led in time to the compilation of wage statistics; the exigencies of war finance promoted the official production of estimates of the national income. There has been no counterpart for wealth; local taxation has been based on the assessed annual value of land and buildings, not on their capital value, or on the possessions of the occupant. If proposals for a capital levy had been adopted after the First World War, an assessment of at least the major forms of personal holdings must have been made then.

But the only British taxes on these as a whole have been laid on property passing at death, or otherwise transmitted.

Death duties go back a long way, but official records began with Sir William Harcourt's Estate Duty of 1894, and the setting up of the Estate Duty Office. This began to publish particulars of the net value of estates on which duty was paid, and of some others that had also been reported, though below the limit. Another annual series of the estates of persons who had died within the year went back to 1858, when the Central Probate Register began its calendar; but this included only personal property, not real estate, until 1898, and even then it did not cover settled real estate until 1926 (Rubinstein 1981: 59). The coverage of the estate duty returns raises issues of some consequence; even the relation between the date of valuation and the time of death needs consideration. It is a particular limitation that these returns, and the probate calendars likewise, can tell us nothing of the small estates that were all most people left. In 1873 it was estimated that only 8 per cent of all persons dying in England and Wales left estates large enough to require probate; by 1913–14 the proportion was higher, for it has been estimated that 'about 41 per cent of all adult men left estates' (Rubinstein 1981: 121–2)—estates, that is to say, that were big enough to need the authority of probate for the transmission of their assets. In the 1970s the method assigned wealth to about one-third of the population; but of the remainder, more than half were below the age of 25. Distributions relating to individuals may record a spouse as holding little or no wealth, when in fact he or she is a member of a wealthy family. Even among the estates reported, there are problems of the adequacy of valuation, and of kinds of property not included. But within their limits the probate calendar and the estate duty returns do provide an annual sample, in fairly consistent form, of personal wealth.

The task is then to expand this sample to a national aggregate. The method is to apply mortality rates. Suppose, for example, that on average 5 per cent of men in the age-group 65–74 die each year; then the estates of those who die are regarded as a 5 per cent sample of all the estates of those men, and the total values of their estates, in each category of size, will be 20 times those found in the sample. In the same way, the number of men in that age-group having estates of a given size will be estimated as 20 times the number who have died possessed of that size of estate. Mortality rates vary substantially with gender and age, evidently, but they vary also with region and with social status, which is indicated here by the size of estate. The samples are grouped accordingly, and a separate multiplier is applied to each group specified by gender, age, size of estate and region (Royal Commission 1975: tables J.1–J.8). More difficulties arise here, because in some groups the samples are very small, especially among young people and big estates. The multipliers in these groups are correspondingly larger. For women under 25 and with estates of £500 000 or more in England and

Wales in the early 1970s, the multiplier was in the region of 2500. This does not mean that fluctuations of mortality—in 1972, for example, there was an exceptional number of deaths of young millionaires—will result in greatly magnified and abrupt changes in the totals estimated, for the multiplier concerned is calculated afresh for each year, and will itself be varied in inverse proportion to the fluctuation. Nor would the effect be marked if there was no such compensatory adjustments of the multipliers: Atkinson (1974) has shown that, even if one general multiplier is applied throughout, the resultant distribution of wealth will not differ much from that yielded by multipliers differentiated by size of estate and age. But the smallness of the samples brings with it some uncertainty about the quantities inferred from them—the exact amount of wealth within a given category, and the composition of holdings. The method cannot give a reliable account of movements from year to year, but it can be trusted to trace the main proportions of the distribution of wealth at any one time.

Furthermore, its findings can be checked and adjusted by comparison with national totals of various forms of asset, estimated independently. The pioneering work of J. R. S. Revell (1967, 1971a, 1971b, 1974; with Royal Commission 1975: Table 27) has provided a balance sheet of the national aggregate of all personal assets and liabilities. The national aggregates found by the estate multiplier method are generally smaller, sometimes very much so, than the corresponding entries in the balance sheet. In 1972, for example, the aggregate value of dwellings on the estate multiplier method was 63 per cent of that in the balance sheet; the value of unit trusts was 53 per cent, and that of land and other buildings only 36 per cent, of the corresponding entries (Royal Commission 1975: Table 32). Such comparisons indicate that the value of the asset concerned should be raised in certain proportions wherever they occur in the estate multiplier estimates. When so adjusted, these estimates remain our essential source of knowledge of the distribution of personal wealth by size and composition.

But two other methods have been used. One of these begins with existing estimates of personal income from property—rent, dividends and interest—and applies appropriate rates of interest to calculate the capital values from which these flows arise (Atkinson and Harrison 1974). This way of estimating capital was developed by Josiah Stamp in his great study of *British Incomes and Property* (1916), and he showed there how different rates of interest, in the form of 'number of years' purchase', must be applied to the income drawn from different kinds of asset; but his concern was with national aggregates of capital, not personal holdings. The attraction of the method in its application to these is that it can link them with the holder's income from other sources. But the method has severe limitations. Particulars of investment income are available only for the larger incomes. Owner-occupied houses and other assets that do not yield taxable money income escape record, while interest on mortgages is deducted from the income that is reported. Worst of all, the capital values estimated depend directly on the rate of interest applied—a flow of £120 indicates a capital of £3000 with interest at 4 per cent but only £2000 at 6 per cent—and the choice of the appropriate rate for each type of asset year by year is hazardous.

The remaining method is to put questions about their holdings to the respondents to a social survey. There are some countries—notably Canada—in which this provides the only available information. Sampling by survey can often provide a reliable basis for estimating national aggregates, but there are difficulties about applying it to wealth holdings. The response rate is low, especially among the rich who between them hold so large a part of all wealth. Those who do reply may find it difficult, with the best of wills, to provide an inventory, with valuations, of all their assets. It is difficult to design a stratified sample when the possessors of holdings of given sizes cannot be designated with any precision by other characteristics.

It is the estate multiplier method, then, for all its limitations, that provides the most reliable and comprehensive estimates. But one of its limitations is the omission of certain assets from the valuations reported, and the question remains of what assets ought to be included. Everything subjected to probate or estate duty deserves to be included, and we have noted already that some forms of asset excluded from those requirements should if possible be added back. These are all marketable, and in principle valued at market. But there are also assets which the owner cannot transfer, and which therefore have no market. Life assurance policies are a leading case, but occupational pensions have become increasingly important. For purposes of estate duty, on the death of the holder a life assurance policy is valued at the sum assured, but during the holder's life it is worth only its surrender value. Annuities and occupational pensions represent an asset during the lifetime of the recipients, but at death it is extinguished. One expedient is to value these assets in the aggregate at the total value of the reserves of the companies providing them, and distribute this total to individuals on some intelligible if arbitrary basis; but some pensions—notably those in the civil service—are not funded, and in times of inflation some industrial pensions cease to be covered by reserves. Over and above those forms of assurance that individuals provide for themselves or under their employers' arrangements are the forms of state benefit. The entitlement to a pension that is vested in a person by virtue simply of citizenship can be valued as if the citizen, a man or woman of given age, had acquired it through a commercial policy; the value of accrued rights to widows' benefits can be assessed similarly. There are other rights to benefit that can in principle be equally considered to endow the citizen with capital: the right to free education for children can be regarded as comparable to an insurance policy for the payment of school fees, and the right to free medical care spares the cost of private insurance. There is also the value of the tenancy of subsidized housing. But the great objection to including such assets is the difficulty of allocating them to the holders of this or that amount of wealth of other descriptions. The annual value of benefits in kind can be allocated to households of various types on the basis of the knowledge of their composition and incomes that is provided by social surveys, and capital sums derived from these annual values could presumably be allocated in the same way. But the final aim is to allocate those capital sums between different levels of wealth holdings, and the social surveys have not provided sufficient knowledge of these.

The best treatment of those non-marketable assets that can be allocated to levels of wealth holding seems to be that adopted by the Royal Commission on the Distribution of Income and Wealth, namely to present separate estimates excluding and including them.

For those concerned with the distribution of the immediate command over resources, personal wealth may best be defined in terms of the ownership of marketable assets only; while for those concerned with the distribution of economic welfare in a more general sense, the definition may be extended to cover the value of a greater or lesser range of non-marketable assets as well. (Royal Commission 1975: para. 44)

It remains a limitation of our materials that they do not provide any linked distribution, showing both the income and the wealth of the same unit—person or household. We should like to be able to draw up a table in which, say, the columns showed income and the rows wealth. Each unit would then be assigned to the compartment whose coordinates contained that unit's particular combination of income and wealth. But this as yet we cannot do. The sampling of social survey that has asked householders to report both their incomes and their assets has not been extensive or reliable enough. In our distributions of wealth and income the units are therefore ordered differently: 'the top 10 per cent' of persons, for instance, will not be quite the same among wealth-holders and income recipients, for although very wealthy people generally have big incomes, there are some people with high earnings but no great wealth. When we are concerned with the composition of assets as an indication of how wealth is acquired, we can see how that composition varies at different levels of wealth, but not of income.

13.3. The distribution of Wealth in the United Kingdom contrasted with that of Income

In one respect, the distribution of wealth, like that of income, seems to be made up of two separate distributions: one for the main body and the other for the few at the top. But Figure 13.2 shows that both of these distributions

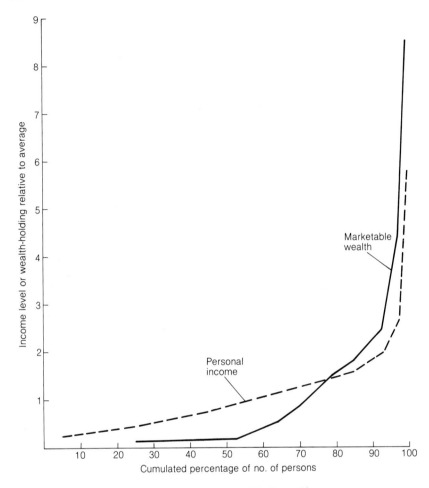

Fig. 13.2 Distribution of wealth compared with that of income.
The distribution of personal income before tax, 1975/6, and of holdings of
marketable wealth by the total adult population, 1975, United Kingdom. *Sources:*
as in Table 13.2.

are much more unequal than those of income. The wealth held by the
poorest half of the adult population does not exceed one-sixth of the average
holding, and even the lowest tenth of personal incomes stands higher than
that. As we rise above the median, people's wealth increases much more
rapidly than their incomes. But whereas we have noted that in incomes the
boundary between the main body and the top comes at about the 85th
percentile, in wealth holdings it seems to be deferred until well into the top
decile. Then, when the big rise does set in among the wealth-holders, it is
more rapid and goes farther—among the top 1 per cent, incomes are only
5½ times, but wealth holdings nearly 25 times, their respective means. One

TABLE 13.2 *Distributions of income and of wealth compared*

Distributions of personal income before tax, 1975/6, and of marketable wealth, all persons aged 18 and over, 1975, expressed as relatives to the mean, UK

(1) Quantile group of persons (%)	(2) Income level relative to mean	(3) Quantile group of persons (%)	(4) Level of net wealth relative to mean	(5) Cumulated percentage of persons (%)	(6) Level of net wealth relative to mean
100	5.7	100	28.5	99.6	16.52
96–99	2.67	99	7.0	98.9	8.3
		96–98	4.43		
91–95	1.96	91–95	2.84	92.6	2.48
81–90	1.61	81–90	1.82		
71–80	1.32	76–80	1.42		
61–70	1.15			69.4	0.83
		51–75	0.40	63.4	0.50
51–60	0.92			52.2	0.17
41–50	0.75				
31–40	0.58	1–50	0.134		
21–30	0.45				
11–20	0.35				
1–10	0.25				

Sources: Royal Commission (1979): tables 2.3, 4.2, 4.3. Cols.(3) and (4) are from table 4.2, cols. (5) and (6) are from table 4.3. Some apparent discrepancies may be attributed to the differences between the average wealth of groups and the level of wealth at a particular point.

expression of these various ways in which the distribution of wealth is more unequal is that more than 70 per cent of all holdings are smaller than the mean, whereas for incomes the corresponding proportion is well below 60 per cent.

These observations have been made on estimates for the United Kingdom in 1975. We need to say something about how the Central Statistical Office constructed those for wealth. These were made by the estate multiplier method. The mortality multipliers (the reciprocals of the death rate) were differentiated by age, sex, marital status and two broad groupings by social class. Insurance policies were valued according to the actuarial reserves held against them, and not the sums assured. Consumer durables were valued at their replacement cost less depreciation. When the aggregate values of each type of asset according to this method of estimate were compared with the total value of those assets in a personal sector balance sheet separately drawn up for the whole country, they were often found to be substantially lower. The estate multiplier method put the total wealth of persons at £190 billion in 1975, whereas the balance sheet made it £263 billion. The difference might be due to the limited coverage of probate and estate duty, or to under-reporting within that coverage. The differences item by item were used to raise the estate multiplier estimates. The adjustments included the allocation of £8.5 billion to estates of less than £1000, outside the coverage of probate and estate duty. Together with two other major adjustments, this allocation 'gave rise to an increase of approximately 20.5 million in the number of wealth-holders—roughly 18 millions of whom were owners of small estates—to extend the coverage of the estimates to the total UK adult population aged 18 and over' (Royal Commission 1979; Appendix C). How little we know about the wealth of half the population is apparent. We do know that it is small, but this is not to say that all those concerned have meagre resources or none at all: some of them at least will be members of families that are well endowed.

There is also an important form of property, widely spread, that has still to be taken into account. One of the benefits of holding wealth and the purposes of accumulating it is provision for old age. An alternative way of making that provision is to secure a pension. We have already noted the case for treating the capital value of pension rights as part of personal wealth—a compelling case for occupational pensions, an arguable one for state pensions. Figure 13.3 shows the effect of bringing in and allocating these amounts. The Pen parade that shows the distribution of wealth here runs over the same intervals as are used for pension rights by the Royal Commission (1979); there are fewer of these than were available for Figure 13.2. To make differences between the profiles clear, and keep their higher reaches in view, the present figure has been drawn on a ratio scale. It shows that the inclusion of occupational pensions has some effect in diminishing inequality, but a really marked effect appears only when state pensions are

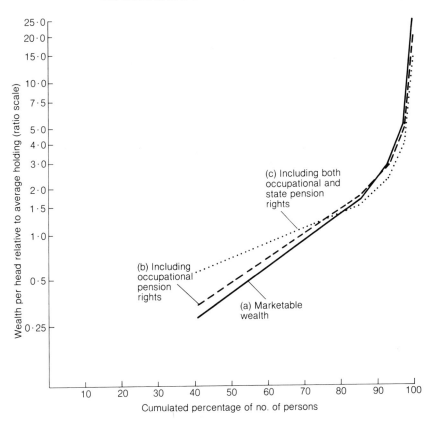

Fig. 13.3 Distribution of wealth in the United Kingdom in 1976, excluding and including rights to occupational and state pensions. *Sources.* as in Table 13.3.

brought in too. They are particularly important in raising the holdings that would otherwise be very small, and at these levels their proportionate effect is great. But they remain a limited form of wealth—an asset, certainly, but an inaccessible one. Having a state pension to look forward to is like having a sum in hand sufficient to buy an annuity on reaching pensionable age; but for the time being that sum is locked away, and if you die before you become pensionable there is nothing to pass on to your heirs. Rather than add state pensions to wealth holdings, it seems better to regard them, together with all other forms of social insurance and benefit, as providing some compensation and alternative support to those who possess little or no marketable wealth. It is the distribution of this that is the most significant.

We have seen how much more unequal the distribution of wealth is than that of income. Why the difference? One obvious reason is that people can exist while holding negligible wealth, but not with negligible income: those who are least well off will consequently stand higher relatively to the

TABLE 13.3   *The effect on the distribution of wealth of including rights to occupational and state pensions*

Wealth holdings per head within each quantile group as relatives to average of all holdings, all persons aged 18 and over, UK, 1976.

Quantile group (%)	Holdings as relative to average		
	(a) Marketable assets only	(b) (a) plus occupational pension rights	(c) (b) plus state pension rights
Top 1	24.9	21.1	14.1
96–99	5.32	5.02	3.75
91–95	2.88	2.80	2.24
81–90	1.70	1.74	1.50
1–80	0.28	0.34	0.56

Sources: Royal Commission (1979): tables 4.3, 4.13, 4.15; see also Dunn and Hoffman (1983).

median in the distribution of income than in that of wealth. Wealth, moreover, can be accumulated from year to year, but the ability to earn during each day ends with the day. There is no limit to accumulation, but earnings are limited by the inability of the worker, however valuable his services, to make them available to many buyers (although that limitation is transcended for those writers and performers whose products, as books, plays or recordings, are sold to a large public). Wealth, again, is acquired by saving, inheritance or other transmission, and by the profits of enterprise and speculation, and these are governed by processes different from those governing earnings: it is by these (other than saving) that the concentration of wealth in the top 10 per cent or so of holders is brought about. We shall discuss them when we consider the formation of distributions in Chapter 15. But here we have also to account for the distribution of wealth being more unequal than that of income within the middle ranks. We can understand this if the major source of acquisition here is saving. For there will be an age gradient. Suppose for the moment that there is no such gradient for income, but that all those in the middle ranks have earnings that remain the same in real terms despite increasing seniority, and that they save the same proportion of their incomes, that is, put aside the same absolute amounts, year after year. There will then be a marked age gradient for their wealth holdings, against no gradient for earnings. The same finding, that the age gradient for wealth is steeper, continues to hold when we adopt the realistic assumption of a positive age gradient for earnings too, if a constant proportion of these is saved—and it holds *a fortiori* if that proportion rises. A principal form of saving is house purchase, and houses form a particularly high proportion of net wealth in the middle ranks. In 1973 they formed more than a third of British holdings between £10 000 and £20 000 (Royal Commission 1975: Table 31); in 1976 they made up more than 40 per cent of the total wealth held by British households (Royal Commission 1979: table 4.1). The distribution of so important an asset must evidently affect strongly the distribution of wealth as a whole.

13.4. International Comparisons of the Distribution of Wealth

The possibilities of comparing the distribution of wealth in different countries are limited. In the survey on which the present section relies, Alan Harrison (1979) examined estimates for ten countries, and found their results 'often rather unreliable, and almost always impossible to compare at all precisely' (Harrison 1979: para. 130). Only three countries—the United States, Canada and the Republic of Ireland—yielded estimates judged capable of comparison with those available for the United Kingdom. The Canadian data came from a survey; the estimates for the United States and the Republic of Ireland, like those for the UK, rely mainly on estate duty records. Harrison warns us of many divergences, in method or range and kind of data, which differentiate the four sets of estimate and cannot all be removed by adjustments. But if we are content with something a good deal less than numerical exactitude, we shall find grounds for believing that the UK distribution of wealth which we have been examining is not exceptional, but is of a form common to a number of Western countries—although the numbers now arrived at indicate that in the 1970s it was more unequal than the Canadian, and still more than the US, distributions.

The closest comparison was with the United States. Here alone among the three countries were the totals yielded by the estate duty method compared with the national balance sheet of personal assets. The excess, it is true, was all assigned to the excluded population, but this allocation was not so arbitrary as it would have been in the United Kingdom, for the excluded population in the United States—those outside the scope of estate duties there—made up more than 90 per cent of all adults. Among a number of other points of difference, two took a noticeable effect on the findings. One of these was the US use of mortality multipliers drawn from life insurance experience rather than, as in the British estimates, the mortality of the population at large, which would have been higher. The UK multipliers were therefore lower than they would have been on the US basis; and as a general rule lower multipliers yield lower concentration (Atkinson and Harrison 1978: ch. 3). The other substantial difference lay in the valuation of life insurance policies, for which the US estimates rightly took the value of actuarial reserves and not, like the British, the surrender value, which was higher. By thus ascribing greater assets to many holders in the middle ranks, the British estimates showed a lower concentration at the top. In both respects, then, adjusting British estimates to bring them into line with those for the US would have raised the degree of concentration they showed. But with this in mind, we can make the comparison with confidence.

It is presented in Table 13.4, which also shows estimates by Wolff for the United States which have become available since Harrison drew his table up. In both countries we are concerned only with marketable wealth, without inclusion of pension rights. The two estimates for Great Britain differ mainly in the way they allocate the excess of balance sheet totals over those derived from estate duty: the Royal Commission applied part of this to raise items derived from estate duty, and allocated the remainder to the excluded population, but Atkinson and Harrison allocated so much of it as they thought reasonable to excluded population alone, and did not use any of it to raise items within the scope of estate duty. Their practice in this respect comes closer than that of the Royal Commission to the US method, and it is their estimate that provides the closer comparison.

TABLE 13.4   *Proportions of all personal wealth held by the most wealthy in the USA and Great Britain, 1972*

	Proportion held by top	
	1% (%)	5% (%)
USA (Natrella)	25.8	45.3
USA (Wolff)	30.8	49.2
Great Britain (Royal Commission)	28.1	53.9
Great Britain (Atkinson and Harrison)	32.0	57.2

Sources: *USA*: Natrella (1975): the figures given here 'are log-linear interpolations of percentages of adult population and total net worth', calculated from Table 4 in that paper; Wolff (1983). *GB*: Royal Commission (1975: table 34); Atkinson and Harrison (1978). The figures from all sources except Wolff are reproduced here from Harrison (1979: table 3).

This shows a distinctly higher degree of concentration in Great Britain. If Natrella's estimate were adjusted for the differences of procedure noted above, the disparity would be even greater. Wolff's estimate makes it smaller, but it is still marked. Can we account for it? Three factors may be put forward, although their quantitative effect cannot be established.

Harrison called attention first to the difference between the two countries in age distribution. In 1971, 13 per cent of the British population was aged 65 and over, and 37 per cent was aged 45–64; in the United States the corresponding proportions were only 10 and 20 per cent. If there is a marked age gradient in wealth holdings, a higher proportion of elderly people implies a higher proportion of the larger holdings.

The second factor brought forward by Harrison is house ownership. 'In Britain in the early 1970s,' he said, 'the proportion of the total stock which was owner-occupied had risen to over 50 per cent. In the USA the proportion of all occupied units which were owner-occupied in 1970 was 63 per cent' (Harrison 1979: para. 56). We have already called attention to the high proportion of the assets of the British middle ranks made up by dwellings. A greater home ownership in the United States would raise the relative volume of wealth held by those below the top 10 per cent. But we cannot treat it as a condition that is in a sense imposed from without, like age distribution: the question is, How do the owners acquire their property? The greater availability of rented houses in Great Britain reduces the pressure on householders there to make the savings required for—or after—house purchase. But savings are also likely to rise with income, and the lower concentration in the United States may also be an effect of the higher real incomes there.

The third factor is inheritance. The available evidence indicates a contrast between the part that this plays in the formation of big holdings in the two countries. An estimate prepared by Elfryn Jones for the Royal Commission (1977), and to be described in the next section, indicated that inheritances might amount to a fifth of all British wealth, or a quarter if assets transferred *inter vivos* were included. It may well be that the allowance for these transfers was inadequate. In that case, the contrast with the United States is even more pronounced; for the evidence suggests that the proportion of wealth acquired by transfer is much lower there. A sampling inquiry by the Brookings Institution into persons with incomes of $10 000 or more in 1961 indicated that only one-seventh of their aggregate wealth had been acquired by inheritance (Barlow *et al.* 1966). A later study cited by Harrison, by comparing this and other surveys with estate duty records, found reason to believe that the surveys had failed to uncover a large part of the assets actually held, but still concluded that 'inherited wealth amounted for only "about 12 per cent of 1959 household wealth" ' (Davies 1978; quoted here from Harrison 1979: para. 70).

But we have good reason to believe that at least the larger wealth holdings in the United Kingdom are closely linked with inheritance. Researches by C. D. Harbury into the estates of the fathers of persons who themselves left large estates in Great Britain found that in the 1970s 'approximately three-fifths of top male wealth-leavers (leaving over £200 000 in 1973 prices) were preceded by fathers who were at least moderately rich' (Harbury and Hichens 1977: 125). If this kind of linkage is also present in the United States, the smaller part played by inheritance there would make for a lower concentration of wealth. But the lower proportion of inheritances means a higher proportion of accumulation by other means; so it cannot account for the lower concentration of wealth in the United States, unless we can also explain why lifetime savings and profits should not have offset it. One reason may have been noticed already under the second of the present heads—a relatively greater amount of this form of accumulation in the middle ranks. We shall return to the relative parts of saving and inheritance when we discuss the formation of distributions of wealth in Section 15.5 below.

The main source for Canada was a Survey of Consumer Finances made in 1970. It obtained answers to all its questions from nearly 10 000 households, but as always the reporting of assets must have been incomplete, and Harrison directs us to a revision by J. B. Davies (1979). This corrects some of the understatements in the response to the survey, and adds estimates for consumer durables and life insurance. The effect is to raise the estimated degree of concentration considerably, but Table 13.5 shows that it was still lower than in Great Britain.

TABLE 13.5   *The concentration of wealth in Canada and Great Britain, 1970*

	Proportion held by top		
	1%	*5%*	*10%*
Canada, households (Davies)	21.6	45.7	59.8
Great Britain, individuals (Atkinson and Harrison)	30.1	54.3	69.4

Sources: Davies (1979: Table XII); Atkinson and Harrison (1978: Table 6.5). See also Harrison (1979: Table 6).

Two of the same circumstances as seemed possible reasons for the US degree of concentration being lower than the British were also present in Canada. We do not know about the part played by inheritance there, but in 1971 the proportion of elderly people in the population was even lower than in the United States, and the proportion of houses owned by their occupants was 60 per cent—somewhat lower than in the United States, but still higher than the 50 per cent in Great Britain.

'The estate data in Ireland', Harrison found (1979: para. 120), 'have allowed construction of estimates which, compared with others based on the same method, are probably matched or surpassed only by those in the UK and the USA.' The estimates of P. M. Lyons (1975) assume that the excluded population—three-fifths of the total—held no wealth: for fair comparison, we must take British estimates based on the same assumption. This is done in Table 13.6. The degree of concentration was evidently much the same in 1965 in the two countries; if anything, it was greater in Ireland. We shall see later that 1965 falls in a period when the British distribution was becoming less concentrated: we do not know if the similarity of 1965 marked only a momentary agreement, or whether the Irish distribution was following a parallel course.

TABLE 13.6   *The concentration of wealth in the Republic of Ireland and Great Britain**

	Proportion held by top:			
	1%	*5%*	*10%*	*20%*
Republic of Ireland, 1965–6 (Lyons)	33.7	63.0	78.1	93.2
Great Britain, 1966 (Royal Commission 1977, Series B)	31.8	56.7	71.8	87.3

* Estimates in both countries assume that excluded population holds no wealth.
Sources: Lyons (1975: table 3); Royal Commission (1977: table 33).

The comparisons hitherto have been based on the concentration at the top. Estimates for Canada and the United States becoming available since Harrison's report was drawn up enable us to compare the distributions of wealth in the middle ranks. Figure 13.4 shows that the two countries diverge from each other in that region quite widely, and both diverge again from the United Kingdom. In Canada the recipient unit comprises families and unattached individuals. From the 30th to the 70th percentile, wealth per unit rose more rapidly than in the other two countries. Whether this

TABLE 13.7   *Distribution of wealth in United States and Canada*

USA, 1969/70: all marketable wealth of households; Canada, 1977: marketable assets (excluding consumer durables other than cars) held by families and unattached individuals

	Cumulated percentage of no. of units	
Upper limit of wealth class, relative to mean	USA	Canada
0		10.8
0.02		20.0
0.11		30.9
0.21	29.0	
0.32		44.2
0.53	62.6	
0.65		57.2
1.06	81.7	
1.08		72.0
1.59	88.6	
2.12	92.2	
2.16		89.4
5.29	98.0	
10.59	99.3	

Sources: USA: Wolff (1983); *Canada:* Oja (1983).

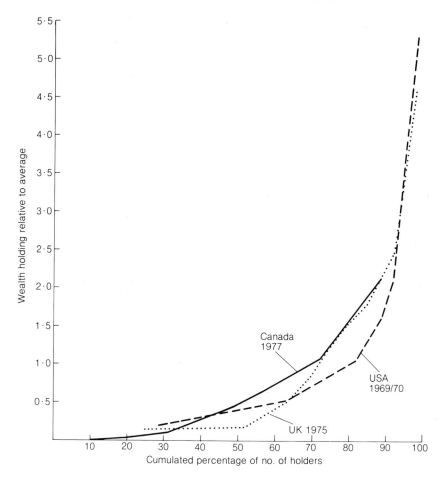

Fig. 13.4 Distribution of wealth in Canada and the United States, compared
with the United Kingdom.

Marketable wealth: Canada, 1977, families and unattached individuals; USA,
1969/70, households; UK, 1975, all adults.

Sources: Canada and USA: as in Table 13.7; *UK:* as in Table 13.2.

feature of the Canadian distribution makes it more or less unequal admits
of only an arbitrary answer, according to the measure of inequality that we
adopt; for there is greater disparity in this range than appears hereabouts in
countries where the middle holdings remain small, but in them the change
to the bigger holdings higher up is more marked. In the United States the
rise in holdings as we proceed from the 30th up to the 80th percentile is
more gradual, and the change to a steep rise thereafter correspondingly
more abrupt—here we see less inequality in the middle ranks, but more
overall. We have always to bear in mind that it is as relatives to the mean

that wealth holdings are measured here: and if the US holdings at the 80th percentile stood much lower relative to the mean than did those of Canadian and the UK, that may be only because the US average was raised by very big holdings at the top. The United Kingdom is conspicuous for the sharpness of the upturn about the median. There are indications of three distributions here, and three sets of formative processes, to which there is no counterpart in the other two countries.

After due allowance for inexact estimates and the pitfalls of relatives to the mean, there remain indications that the three countries differ appreciably in the distribution of wealth through the middle ranks. But the main finding is still that, in all of the three other countries examined, the distribution as a whole is of the same highly concentrated form as in Britain. The degree of concentration of wealth is everywhere far higher than that of income.

14

The Historical Course of Change in the Distribution of Wealth

14.1. A Dip into the Fifteenth Century

Continuous records from which to estimate the distribution of wealth are available only for recent years, but we have some glimpses of earlier times. They come from assessments of property for the purpose of taxation in the fifteenth century.

The Florentine *catasto* was a census of population, but also a fiscal instrument, which evaluated all assets liable to tax (Herlihy and Klapisch-Zuber 1978: 242–5). It distinguished the possessions regarded as essential to the householder and the producer, which were exempt from tax, from possessions over and above that, goods 'd'avanza alla vita', which formed the basis of personal taxation. The exempt possessions included the dwelling house with its furniture, however rich; the tools of the artisan; and the peasant's yoke of oxen and his ass. The value of agricultural holdings was estimated by capitalizing only half the yield, for this was all that the family who worked the holding retained for themselves, the other half going to the landlord. But the returns on funds engaged in business were capitalized in their entirety. Thus the inventory of assets evaluated was far from complete. It seems likely that a smaller proportionate reduction was made in the assets of the rich than in those of the smaller urban householders and producers and, even more, than in the value of agricultural holdings. If that was so, the effect would have been to increase the apparent degree of concentration. The total reported capital was made up of 53 per cent land, 30 per cent business funds and 17 per cent municipal loans. The other record comes from Basle in 1454. It appears to have been reported by Schmoller in 1905, and is taken here from Gibrat (1931).

The data are set out in Table 14.1. The two Tuscan series have been derived from the Lorenz curves presented by Herlihy and Klapisch-Zuber (1978). For both Tuscany and Basle, estimates of the level of wealth holding at a given percentile of the array of holders were derived in turn by applying the principle that, if a certain 10 per cent of the holders held 7 per cent of all wealth, then their average holding stood at 0.7 of the mean holding of the whole array. The extent of approximation involved makes the outcome far from exact—to say nothing of any failings of the original

TABLE 14.1 *Instances of the distribution of wealth in the fifteenth century*

Assets assessed to tax in the Florentine catasto of 1427, in Florence itself and in six towns of Tuscany (Arezzo, Cortona, Pisa, Pistoia, Prato and Volterra), and in Basle, 1454

Florence and Tuscany

(1) Cumulative no. of households (%)	(2) Proportion of wealth (%)	(3) Group of households (%)	(4) Wealth relative to mean
Florence			
40	2	40–50	0.1
50	3	50–60	0.3
60	6	60–70	0.4
70	10	70–80	1.0
80	20	80–90	1.4
90	34	90–95	3.2
95	50	95–100	10.0
100	100		
Six towns of Tuscany			
40	1	40–50	0.2
50	3	50–60	0.4
60	7	60–70	0.5
70	12	70–80	1.0
80	22	80–90	1.8
90	40	90–95	2.4
95	52	95–100	9.6
100	100		

Basle

(1) Fortune (fl.)	(2) No. of fortunes greater than (1)	(3) Cumulative frequency (%)	(4) Upper limit relative to mean
10	1403	44	0.11
50	788	60	0.23
100	560	64	0.34
150	502	78	0.68
300	309	90	2.25
1000	144	97	6.76
3000	48	98	11.26
5000	28		
Mean fortune 444			

Sources: Florence and the six towns of Tuscany: Herlihy and Klapisch-Zuber (1978: 250, fig. 5); *Basle:* Gibrat (1931: 139, table XXIII).

records. But the evidence receives some support from its own surprisingly familiar form when we see it in Figure 14.1.

Here the Pen parades for the six towns of Tuscany and for Basle are displayed together with that for the United Kingdom in 1975. What strikes the eye at once is the closeness of agreement up to the top decile between the Tuscan and UK distributions. We cannot trace the rate of rise at the top at all closely, or compare the heights reached at the peak. Possibly the very rich stood out more in the Tuscan towns than in the United Kingdom; but if we take the rough test of the proportion of all wealth held by the top

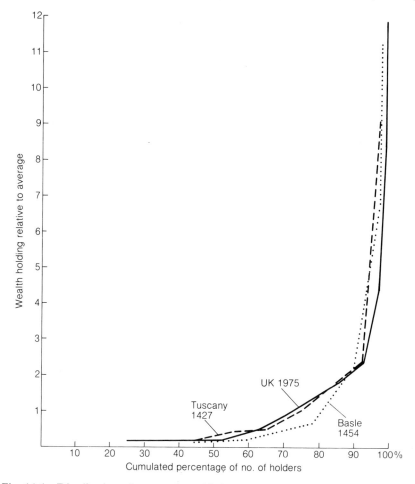

Fig. 14.1 Distribution of personal wealth in some towns of the fifteenth century. The distribution of assessed wealth in six towns of Tuscany in 1427, and in Basle in 1454, compared with the distribution of net worth in the United Kingdom in 1975.

Sources: Tuscany and Basle: as in Table 14.1; *UK:* as in Table 13.2.

10 per cent, that comes out as 60 per cent in the Tuscan towns and 66 per cent in Florence itself, as against 62 per cent for the United Kingdom in 1975 (Royal Commission 1977: table 35, series B). It is also true that the profile for Florence itself (not shown in the figure, to avoid clutter), although it agrees with the profile for the six towns in fixing the mean at about the 75th percentile, shows a somewhat lower course below it and continuing to the 85th percentile; after this it rises more steeply. The distribution thus appears to have been more unequal here than in the six towns: the wealth of the top 15 per cent was greater relatively to those below. This sort of difference is much more marked in the profile for Basle. Wealth holdings here appear to have risen much more slowly through the middling ranks nearly up to the 80th percentile, and above that to have risen more steeply; there was a more abrupt change from the lower and middling fortunes to the greatest, and more contrast between them. But these differences from the British profile are less striking than the resemblances. Across a span of more than five centuries, we might expect to find a radical change, but we do not. Agreement between the findings at two spot dates may be coincidental. But the similarity of the Tuscan and British profiles does at least establish the possibility that a society whose industry and commerce are highly developed and which is strongly urbanized may develop the same sort of distribution of wealth in widely separated times and places. Our records, however, as we go on to see, by no means indicate that the distribution is unchanging even in one locality.

14.2. English urban wealth in 1522–1525

The royal administration caused a survey to be made in 1522–3 of all adult males in respect of their fitness to bear arms and their taxable capacity. This was followed in 1524–5 by the 'great subsidy', a kind of income tax, for which each taxpayer's movable goods—or, if these amounted to very little, his wages—were assessed as an indication of his liability. Where the rolls have been preserved, they provide a source of information about the distribution of wealth in the localities concerned. We can draw upon it, thanks to the historians who have studied and summarized the documents (Cornwall 1962–3, 1970; Hoskins 1963; Schofield 1965; Pound 1966; MacCaffrey 1975; Phythian-Adams, 1979; Palliser 1979). The data are set out in Table 14.2, and displayed in Figures 14.2 and 14.3.

How reliable were the assessments? A check is provided by comparison with the survey that preceded them. In the 16 market towns studied by Cornwall (1962–3: 57–8), there were many names in the survey rolls that did not appear in the assessments, and vice versa. In these towns the assessments were less accurate than the survey, which 'commonly contains more names; its assessments are quite possibly genuine—they are usually

TABLE 14.2 *The distribution of English urban wealth about 1525*

	Norwich, 1525		Exeter 1524-5		16 Market Towns, 1524-5		Coventry, 1523		York, 1524	
Assessment group (£)	No. in group	Total wealth of group (£)	Assessment group (£)	No. in group	Assessment group (£)	No. in group	Total wealth of group (£)	Assessment group (£)	No. in group	Assessment group (£)	No. in group
under 2	570	570	wages 20s.	258	under 2	858	866	nil	268	wage-earners	330
2–4	416	1 037	1–1.9	199	2	556	1 112	0.2	218	1–2	177
5–9	141	870	2–4	202	3–5	309	1 188	3–5	120	2–10	176
10–19	124	1 485	5–9	85	6–9	150	946	6–10	72	10–19	83
20–39	80	2 016	10–19	68	10–19	170	2 089	11–19	32	20–100	59
40–99	52	2 850	20–39	45	20–39	86	2 226	20–49	65	100 +	3
100–299	25	3 585	40–99	33	40–99	29	1 518	50–99	25		
300–500	1	400	100–300	29	100–199	2	233	100 +	14		
500 +	3	2 067			200	5	1 000				
	1412	14 880		919		2165	11 178		814		828
Ave. holding	£10.5		£12.3		£5.2			£9.5		£5.4	

* The 16 towns are, in descending order of number of taxpayers (from Chichester with 322 to East Grinstead with 44): Chichester, Lewes, Aylesbury, High Wycombe, Petworth, Amersham, Buckingham, Horsham, Stony Stratford, Oakham, Midhurst, Beaconsfield, Arundel, Steyning, Uppingham, East Grinstead.

Sources: Norwich: Pound (1966); *Exeter:* MacCaffrey (1975); *16 market towns:* Cornwall (1962–3); *Coventry:* Phythian-Adams (1979); *York:* Palliser (1979).

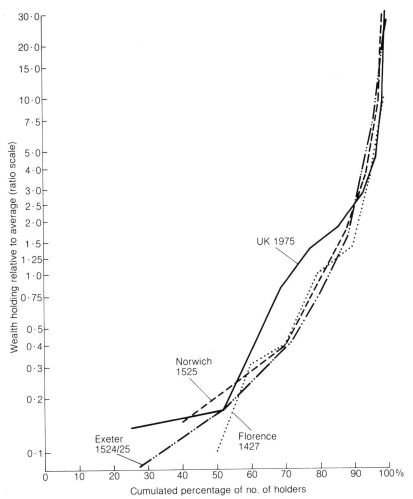

Fig. 14.2 Distribution of personal wealth in two English towns, 1525, compared. The distribution of assessed personal wealth in Exeter, 1524–5, and Norwich, 1525, compared with that in Florence, 1427, and with that of net worth in the United Kingdom, 1975.

Sources: Exeter and Norwich: as in Table 14.2; *Florence:* as in Table 14.1; *UK,* as in Table 13.2.

higher, and it draws a fairly clear line, as the subsidy fails to do—between those who had some goods and those who had none' (pp. 64–5). The indistinct boundary lay where goods might be valued at £2 or the taxpayer might be credited with £2 a year in wages—he or she would pay the same tax of fourpence in either case. But those clearly assessed on wages at Exeter 'amount to 47 per cent of the taxable population, at Salisbury to 48 per cent, at Lavenham to 50 per cent, and at Dorchester to 43 per cent'

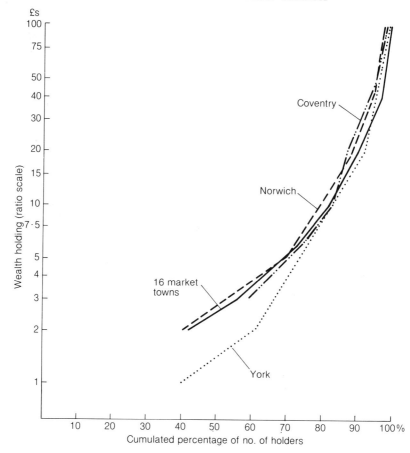

Fig. 14.3 Distribution of personal wealth in some English towns about 1525.
The distribution of personal wealth assessed in the survey of 1523 or for the
subsidy of 1524-5, in Coventry, Norwich, York and 16 market towns in
Buckinghamshire, Rutland and Sussex.
Sources: as in Table 14.2.

(Hoskins 1963: 83–4). Beyond these wage-earners, who were credited with
no property, were the poor, who were credited with neither property nor
wages. How many of these there were we cannot be sure; in Exeter,
Hoskins (1963: 83) puts them implicitly at a sixth of the adult population,
but MacCaffrey (1975: 249) speaks of 'a submerged 35 per cent'. What we
can and must bear in mind is that the number of persons in our
distributions is far from including all adults: beyond the 40 per cent shown
as holding goods valued at less than £2—and some of these may have had
so few goods that they were actually assessed on their wages—lay a wide
margin of the very poor and the destitute. If these were included in the total
number of persons, the coverage of say the top 10 per cent would be

widened, and the distribution would appear more unequal. There may also
have been substantial omissions among those deemed eligible for
assessment. Comparing the subsidy rolls of 1524 and 1525, Cornwall
(1970: 35-6) found that each contained only about two-thirds of all the
names in the two taken together. He inferred that each covered only two-
thirds of the potential taxpayers. But elsewhere he remarks (1962-3: 58)
that those missing were mainly poor. This affects the comparison of these
distributions with those of more recent date that cover all adults.

Any such comparison is also affected by the early assessments being
limited to movable goods. 'From 1515 debts owing to the taxpayer were to
be deducted. From 1524 personal apparel, other than jewellery, was
exempt' (Schofield 1965: 491). It is especially important that real estate was
not assessed. Possibly this does not matter very much for urban
assessments, because the values of dwellings may well be roughly
proportional to that of their contents, if disparity of site values does not
intrude. But we are reminded that our distributions come only from towns,
and do not show what the distribution of wealth was like in all its forms,
including land, and in the whole country. It is further possible, if these
assessments were made in the same way as those for the poor rate, that the
tools of the craftsman's trade and his stocks were exempt. These limitations
of the scope of assessment are important. They confined the reported
wealth to no more than in later years was entered for probate, perhaps even
somewhat less, and we are told that in the late seventeenth century
probated assets amounted to less than 40 per cent of all the wealth of
householders (Lindert 1985: 45).

We have also to ask if the valuation of so much as fell to be assessed was
fair. Certainly, the taxpayer had an inducement to secure an undervaluation. The rate of tax was sixpence in the pound or $2\frac{1}{2}$ per cent, where
goods were assessed at less than £20, but a shilling in the pound, or 5 per
cent, where the assessment was above that; in addition, those assessed at
£40 and more had to pay an 'anticipation' a year in advance, and those at
£50 and more had to pay at 10 per cent in the last of the four years over
which payments were spread. 'Assessments above £40', says MacCaffrey
(1975: 247) of Exeter, 'are conventional and do not represent anything like
real wealth. The rich were able to influence the assessors very effectively . .
. At the lower end of the scale, the assessment figures probably come pretty
close to financial reality.' In Norwich, says Pound (1966: 51-2), 'it seems
probable that more people were called upon to contribute to the subsidy in
1525 than in the previous year, but many taxpayers had their assessments
radically reduced'. In York, four of the six men who were given reductions
on their 1523 assessments were councillors. 'In 1498 the bishop of Carlisle
and the earl of Surrey had accused the city council of taxing themselves
lightly and the poor heavily, and it seems the council tacitly admitted the
charge' (Palliser 1979: 135). By Queen Elizabeth's time, at least, the

subsidy rolls had come to treat assessments as an acceptable basis of taxation, and not as a fair valuation of a complete inventory.

It is also possible that the personal wealth of the clothiers and merchants was lower in 1524-5 than it had been a few years before, for 1523 brought deep depression to the textile industry. The harvests of 1519-21 had been bad, all three of them. The dearth that set in, on the Continent as well as in England, drove up the price of food, and must have cut down spending on cloth. The export trade in clothes collapsed. 'At Bristol, probably one of Coventry's more important outlets, the worst year, 1522-23, represented the lowest point for cloth exports since the fourteenth century' (Phythian-Adams 1979: 61). It is possible, then, that at the time of assessment some of the personal wealth of the clothiers and merchants had been run down; and in any case, whatever possessions they held would probably have been assessed at lower values, according to the market prices of the day.

So we have various reasons to suspect that our distributions understate the actual inequality on an average of years. But they seem to do it to a remarkably similar extent in the different localities. Figure 14.2 shows the similarity of Norwich and Exeter, Figure 14.3 that of Norwich, Coventry and the 16 market towns of Sussex, Buckinghamshire and Rutland. (Exeter is not repeated here only because it would overlay Coventry for so much of their common course as to make the graph illegible.) York runs somewhat lower, especially up to the 80th percentile, but this may be only because wages and prices were lower in the North than in the Midlands and South (Palliser 1979: 137). It is noteworthy that the average assessment in York, £5.4s., was little more than half that in Coventry (£9.5s.) and much less than half that in Exeter (£12.3s.), although judging by the number of persons assessed these three cities were of much the same size. If, as it seems reasonable to conjecture, the monetary values in York should be raised by 20-25 per cent to express them in units of the same purchasing power as in the towns further south, then the York profile would not be so far away from theirs. York apart, we are confronted with the nearly common course of the profile for Norwich, Coventry, Exeter and the 16 market towns. Agreement of this kind, between the findings of four independent researchers, working on the records of four localities comprising 19 towns, is the strongest argument for accepting the assessments as realistic. It could not have been recorded if the actual distributions had differed greatly from one another, unless we suppose those differences offset by a remarkably appropriate set of errors in valuation. We have indeed allowed that the assessments might well be on the low side in the upper reaches; but again, if this possibility is to be invoked to show that the similarity of the distribution masks differences in actual inequality, we shall have to suppose that those differences were neatly offset by opposite differences in valuation—that when the actual distribution was most top-heavy, undervaluation was greatest, and so on. It is simpler to suppose that the assessments did record the actual state of affairs fairly well, if with some common bias towards understating the bigger holdings.

It seems, then, that we can approach with some confidence as well as with reservations the outcome that appears in Figures 14.2 and 14.3. These, unlike Figure 14.1 are drawn on a ratio scale, to give adequate space to the smaller holdings, for which we have information in some detail. One result of this choice of scale is that the profile for the United Kingdom in 1975, inserted for comparison in Figure 14.2, strikes us as being different from its appearance in Figure 14.1: what are minor inflexions in the natural scale appear as substantial variations in the ratio scale. We see how much greater the holdings of the upper middle ranks were in 1975 than in the towns of the fifteenth and sixteenth centuries. But the profiles for those towns themselves reveal a common form, not very different from that of Florence a hundred years before. In three of the localities the concentration of wealth seems to have been very similar, but in the 16 towns it was less.

That two of the leading manufacturing and trading cities of England in 1525 should resemble Florence at the height of its prosperity in 1427 is intelligible. Norwich was the second city of England, with a population probably between 12 000 and 13 000. Of the 700 or so freemen, 30 per cent were in the textile trades; next came 18 per cent in the distributive trades and 13 per cent in food and drink (Pound 1966). Exeter came fourth in size, with Bristol in between. Here too the textile industry had developed; there was much trade overseas, and the city served as an emporium and distributive centre for the region. In these cities, as in Florence, economic growth produced merchant princes. Pound (1966: 51), in his study of Norwich, instances the pre-eminence of the rich clothiers in the adjacent county of Suffolk. 'The widow and daughter of Thomas Spring of Lavenham, assessed on £1000 and £33.6.8 respectively, paid rather more than 30 per cent of the town's subsidy; Thomas Smyth of Long Melford, assessed on £600, contributed over 46 per cent.' Writing of Exeter in the 1670s—but his judgement can be carried back to earlier times—Hoskins (1935: 119) remarked on the emergence of the wealthy families at the top as an outcome of economic growth: 'the economically powerful minority who . . . provided all the members for the Chamber, filled the high Cathedral offices, and produced a not inconsiderable number of members of Parliament for the city, were twice as numerous as in the less economically-developed community of Leicester.' In the 16 market towns, again, less development went with a less top-heavy distribution; and perhaps it was the same condition that accounts for an equally lower concentration in York. If we consider the proportion of all assessed wealth held by the top 10 per cent, then it appears on rough interpolation that, whereas this was about 70 per cent in Norwich, 76 per cent in Exeter and 67 per cent in Coventry, in York it was only 56 per cent and in the market towns only 55 per cent. But whether the degree of concentration was higher or lower, the distribution of wealth in 1523–5, as in recent years, was made up of two parts, and the top part contained fortunes formed by processes different from those that governed the distribution below. This top part grew in relative mass in the course of economic development.

The proportions of personal wealth held by the top 10 per cent, just cited, compare with a figure of 60 per cent of net worth for the United Kingdom in 1975. But Figure 14.2 makes it plain that the greater equality of that later distribution is not due solely to the smaller relative mass at the top: it arises also from the much greater relative size of the middling estates. Here is the most striking difference. The proportion of all wealth that was held between the 60th and 90th percentiles was twice as great in the United Kingdom in 1975 as in Exeter in 1524–5. At that time the middle ranks were made up of masters in the handicrafts, shopkeepers and lesser merchants. The transition from their wealth and standing to the rich few at the top was relatively abrupt. A major change that has come over society is the substitution of a more even gradation, through the formation of more occupations for the middle and upper middle ranks, and the acquisition by those ranks of much more property, relatively to those both above and below them.

14.3. The Historical Course of Change in England and Wales

Until recently, we should have had to say that the distribution of wealth in this country remained unknown and unknowable until the eve of the First World War: the evidence on which to decide the controversy over what came about simply was not there. In particular, whether the industrial revolution made the rich richer while it degraded the middling ranks, or spread property more widely while it raised the level of all, could be argued only from instances one way and the other, and seemed incapable of decision by any comprehensive measure. But now, the outstanding work of an American scholar, Peter Lindert (1985), has shown how much can be achieved by sustained enterprise and energy in gathering evidence and a scrupulous ingenuity in using it. Thanks to his work, we have a very good idea of the composition and distribution of wealth in England and Wales over the two centuries between the Restoration and mid-Victorian times.

Something must be said first about Lindert's method, although a brief account can by no means describe all the steps in his working. Its main lines are those of the estate-multiplier method. The estates are evidenced here in the first place by the valuations of personality for probate. Of these, Lindert and his assistants have taken out more than 2500 on the average at each of five selected dates: 1670, 1700, 1740, 1810 and 1875. They come at each date from four regions, in different parts of the country and of various economic and social types—Cambridgeshire, London–Middlesex, the West Midlands, the East and West Ridings of Yorkshire. The valuations so obtained are then allocated to cells defined by the occupations, sex, age and region of the decedent. For men, 16 occupations are classified out of those recorded; women were usually described only by marital status. Special expedients are adopted to absorb the men whose occupations were not recorded, and to make good the lack of recorded ages at the four first dates. The valuations in each cell are then multiplied by the ratio of living persons to decedent prevailing within it at the time; here Lindert's own previous estimates of the occupational distribution of the population are drawn upon. But next, these mulitipliers are themselves multiplied by factors designed to extend the regional findings to all England and Wales, according to the believed affinity between each sampled region and other parts of the country. The outcome is a distribution of probated wealth, or personality, for the whole country, at each of the five dates.

Let us take, as a leading indication of concentration, the proportion of all personalty that was held by the top 10 per cent. From 1670 through 1700, 1740 and 1810, this lay between 57 and 61 per cent; in 1810 it was a little higher, but only a little, than it had been in 1670 (Lindert 1985: table 6). The personalty with which alone we are now concerned is fairly close in content to the personal property that was the basis of the Tudor assessments, so that the level trend here, rather below 60 per cent, may be compared with the 70–77 per cent we found in the three manufacturing towns of 1525, and the 55 per cent in the 16 market towns. Bearing in mind that we are comparing findings for the whole land, town and country together, with those for towns alone, we can hardly find reason here to believe there was any significant change from 1525 onwards. But a marked change there was after 1810. By 1875, and indeed earlier—by 1858—the proportion of personalty held by the top 10 per cent is found to stand at 77 per cent. 'The estimates for men imply that the ratio of the average estate of the top 5 per cent to the average estate of the rest jumped from 13 to over 35 between 1740 and 1858' (Lindert 1985: 44). We see a movement—the rich getting richer—that we readily connect with the industrial revolution, and the opportunities it offered to manufacturers, merchants and bankers to make their fortunes. Perhaps the tendency would have been marked as early as 1810, if that had not been a time of restricted trade because of the war.

That the increased concentration did come about in that way is indicated by the different movement of the personalty of men in different occupations. The rise in the value of personalty was outstanding in two of the occupations: 'titled persons', mostly landowners, and 'merchants', who included merchant bankers and some industrialists (Lindert 1985: Fig. 4). Between 1740 and 1810, also, the industrial trades acquired personalty faster than the shopkeepers and even than the farmers. That the land-owners' personalty rose can be accounted for by the increased profits of agriculture at a time of technical advance and restricted imports, and a falling trend of real interest rates, that is, a progressive rise in the 'number of years' purchase' by which the yield of land was capitalized.

So far we have been concerned only with personalty: Lindert takes two further steps to reach net worth. The first is to splice personalty with realty. He does this by capitalizing rents, and adding the land values so obtained in each occupational class to the personalty in that class, at each of the first four dates. Then he draws on the Parliamentary Domesday Book, or survey of all land holdings, of 1873 to identify the holdings of the decedents of 1875 individually. The concentration of the ownership of realty—land and buildings together—was very high, but not rising. Despite the general belief that it did rise, Lindert finds little change from 1688 to 1803, and that little the other way—he credits the top 10 per cent of families or households with 96 per cent of all realty in the former of those years, 93 per cent in the latter. The effect of combining realty with personalty depends upon two trends that offset each other. The rise in land values tended to raise the relative size of realty in the aggregate; but the growth of personalty from 1740 onwards tended to diminish it. As a result, the gross assets made up of personalty and realty together, although more concentrated than personalty alone, show little change in concentration over time from 1670 to 1875 (Lindert 1985: table 9).

The other step takes account of debts. This Lindert does by applying the ratios of debts to personalty found in certain classes of gross assets, for which he has some evidence, together with knowledge of the total amount of outstanding debt in its obverse form of financial assets. When debts so estimated are deducted from gross assets, we reach households' net worth.

The outcome is striking. From 1670 to 1875, and through the three dates in between, there was next to no change in concentration, as that is indicated by the proportion of all net worth held by the top 10 per cent, or top 5 per cent (although that held by the top 1 per cent does rise markedly from 1700 onwards) (Lindert 1985: table 10). In this last movement we may see the effect of those enlarged opportunities, already mentioned, brought by the industrial and agricultural revolutions for the accumulation of great fortunes. We have seen how this expansion raised the relative wealth of 'titled persons' and 'merchants', and increased the concentration of personalty. But it did not increase that of net worth as a whole. Independent courses of change happened to offset each other. From 1810 to 1875, when the concentration of personalty rose markedly, realty, especially land, was becoming a smaller part of the whole (Table 11); that is, a form of property whose ownership was very highly concentrated was contributing less to concentration in the aggregate. This fall in the relative mass of realty came about despite the rise in land values, because the mass of wealth in other forms rose even more, through the growth of industry and commerce.

This balancing of opposing trends we must regard as a matter of contingency. The stability of the concentration of wealth over two hundred years is indeed striking, but when we see how it arose from the combination of different sorts of change we cannot infer from it any inherent tendency to stability or equilibrium. In fact, a great shift was to ensue, as we shall now see.

14.4. Changes in the Distribution of British Wealth in the Twentieth Century

Hitherto we have dealt with estimates whose inescapable limitations simplified the handling of them. The similarities that emerged between them were so striking as to warrant more confidence in them than would have been inspired by any one of them by itself. But they were limited in their scope, and in handling them we had perforce to rely on some bold assumptions, or to dispense with some refinements altogether. They could serve only as indications—although as such they were clear—of the form and the course of change in the distribution of wealth in the country as a whole. But in the twentieth century we begin to have the fuller information that makes a more thorough treatment possible.

This opportunity has been taken by a number of statisticians, whose work has been summarized and carried forward by the Royal Commission on the Distribution of Income and Wealth, and notably by Atkinson and Harrison (1978). The work of these last authors in particular is distinguished by the professional refinement and the pertinacity with which they meet the strict requirements for comparability over time. Their observance of those requirements leads them to exclude the estimates that have been made for the years before the First World War, and their own measures of concentration begin only with 1923. We shall cite those measures here. But we shall also make bold to report some admittedly less reliable estimates, that should still be near enough to the mark to provide an answer within limits to the question whether there was any marked change in the distribution of wealth through the First World War—as there well might have been. We are encouraged to do this by the knowledge that the corrections that Atkinson and Harrison have made to the first workings on the data make no great difference to the measures of concentration arrived at in the end, for some of them work in opposite directions and offset one another. But it is fair to add that, as the authors point out, even modest changes in the measures at two dates, if in opposite directions, can make a considerable change in our estimate of the intervening trend.

To see first what change there was, if any, through the First World War, we turn to the estimates assembled by Revell (1965) and reported in the Royal Commission (1975: table 41), which are cited in Table 14.3. They use multipliers that are not varied by social class; since the death rate of the rich is lower than that of the poor, a multiplier based on an average death rate understates the wealth of the rich and the degree of concentration. In looking back from the 92 per cent of all personal wealth that is attributed to the top 10 per cent in 1911–13 to the proportions of 70–77 per cent that we found in some cities around 1525 and the 84 per cent found by Lindert in 1875, we have to remember the differences underlying them, especially in the coverage of the wealth they measure and of the people over whom it is distributed. The most we can say is that we have no reason to suspect that the concentration of wealth was any lower in 1911–13 than it had been in those earlier times. But when we look forward, and compare 1911–13 with 1924–30, we can make a closer comparison, even though we are rushing in where Atkinson and Harrison fear to tread. Their estimates for 1924–30 are included in Table 14.3. Their use of mortality multipliers varied by social class tends to raise the proportions of all wealth held at the top; their allocation of wealth to people exempt from estate duty tends to lower it. The net effect of these corrections is to attribute a smaller proportion to the top 1 per cent alone; for the rest of the top 10 per cent they come out with the same figures as Revell. Their estimates bear out the main finding from Revell—that through the First World War the relative size of the holdings of the top 1 per cent was reduced.

TABLE 14.3   *The distribution of personal wealth in England and Wales before and after the First World War*

Quantile group	% of all personal wealth held by given quantiles of population aged 25 and over		
	1911–13 (Revell) (1)	1924–30 (Revell) (2)	1924–30 (Atkinson & Harrison (3)
Top 1%	69	62	58
96–99%	18	22	22
91–95%	5	7	7
Top 10%	92	91	87

Sources: Cols. (1) and (2): Royal Commission (1975: table 41, citing Revell 1965); col. (3): Atkinson and Harrison (1978: table 6.5).

Some commentators have remarked that most of this came about only through a shift to those next below, and certainly, Table 14.3 shows the proportion held by the next 9 per cent rising from 23 to 29 per cent. But much of this is only the arithmetic consequence of the fall at the top. Suppose, to take convenient figures not far off those before us for 1911–13, the top 1 per cent hold 70 units of wealth, the next 9 per cent holds 21 units and the rest 9 units—in all, 100 units. Let the holdings at the top fall substantially, from 70 units to 45, while all the others remains unchanged, so that total holdings are now 75 units. The proportion held by the top 1 per cent falls to 45/75, or 60 per cent, while that held by the next 9 per cent rises to 21/75 or 28 per cent—and this without any rise in the absolute size of their holdings, or any transfer from the top 1 per cent. If it was solely by a transfer of that kind that a rise from 21 to 28 per cent in the proportion held by the next 9 per cent was to be effected, the top 1 per cent need lose only 7 units. The proportions recorded in Table 14.3 tell us only that in whatever changes have been going on—it may be that wealth has been growing in all sectors, if at different rates—the holdings at the top are now relatively smaller. The rises in the proportions held at lower levels do not allow us to infer any absolute growth there, or any transfer from the top.

The relative decline at the top is the most striking feature again of the course of change from the 1920s to a recent date. This is set out in numbers in Table 14.4, and displayed in Figure 14.4. If we allow that the Inland Revenue's Series C is reasonably continuous with the estimates of Atkinson and Harrison, we find the proportion held by the top 1 per cent coming down from around 60 per cent in the early 1920s to little more than 20 per cent by about 1980. The arithmetic effect would be to double the proportions held elsewhere, so that the proportion held by the next 9 per cent would have risen from the 28 or so at which it stood in the early 1920s to 56 by 1980. The actual proportion in 1980 is much less than this—30-35

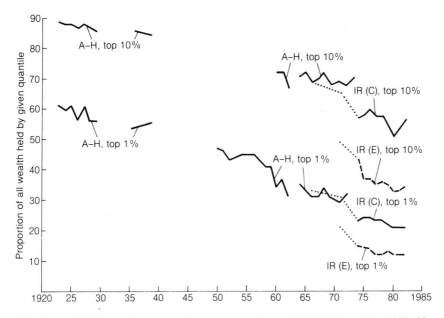

Fig. 14.4   Holdings of top quantiles as proportions of all British wealth, 1923–82. *Sources and description of series:* as in Table 14.4.

TABLE 14.4 *The concentration of British wealth, 1966–1982*

Proportions of total marketable personal wealth held by top 1 per cent and top 10 per cent of all persons aged 18 and over in England and Wales (Atkinson and Harrison) and United Kingdom (Inland Revenue)*

	A-H			A-H		Inland Revenue (IR)			
						Series C		Series E	
	Top 1%	Top 10%		Top 1%	Top 10%	Top 1%	Top 10%	Top 1%	Top 10%
1923	61	89	1960	34	73				
1924	60	88	1961	37	72				
1925	61	88	1962	31	67				
1926	57	87	1963	n.a.	n.a.				
1927	60	88	1964	35	71				
1928	57	87	1965	33	72	33	69		
1929	56	86	1966	31	69				
1930	58	87	1967	31	70				
1936	54	86	1968	34	72				
1938	55	85	1969	31	68				
1950	47		1970	30	69				
1951	46		1971	28	68	31	65	21	49
1952	43		1972	32	70				
1953	44		1973						
1954	45		1974			23	57	15	43
1955	45		1975			24	58	13	37
1956	45		1976			24	60	14	37
1957	43		1977			23	58	12	35
1958	41		1978			23	58	12	36
1959	41		1979			22	54	13	35

1980	21	51	12	33
1981	21	53	12	33
1982	21	56	12	34

A–H, estimates by Atkinson and Harrison, on assumption B3. Series C, wealth estimated from estate duty as a sample adjusted to agree with entries in national balance sheet. Series E, as in C but including the value of both occupational and state pension rights.

Sources: Atkinson and Harrison (1978: table 6.5); Inland Revenue, annual issues of *Inland Revenue Statistics*.

per cent. It follows that the great rise has been in the bottom 90 per cent: the proportion they hold has more than trebled, from about 12 to 45 per cent or more. Correspondingly, the outstanding feature is the relative decline of the whole top 10 per cent: their holdings, which used to be nearly nine-tenths of the whole, have come down to not much more than half.

That is to take the movement from end to end. If we come down only as far as the 1960s, we find the same sort of shift already prominent—indeed, even more marked than it was to become over the next two decades. Gaps in the estimates between 1938 and 1960 prevent us from seeing how far the shift was an abrupt effect of the Second World War, and how far a trend persisting through the war and postwar years. The later recorded course makes the latter possibility seem more probable.

It is natural to attribute this trend to the effect of estate duties, first imposed in place of a tangle of death duties in 1894, and progressively raised from the time of Lloyd George's budget of 1909 onwards. That fighting budget raised the rate of duty on estates of £1.1 million to 15 per cent; sixty years later, a Labour Government's budget raised it to 80 per cent. At the same time, the effective progression has been steepened by inflation shifting the scale downwards in real terms. The stages by which the incidence was raised are shown in Table 14.5. It would be remarkable if rates as heavy as these, from the end of the First World War onwards, had not bitten into the distribution of wealth.

TABLE 14.5   *Rates of estate duty, 1894–1969*

	Net capital value			Net capital value	
	£105 000 (%)	£1.1 m (%)		£115 000 (%)	£1.1 m (%)
1894–1907	6	8	1930–Apr. 1939	20	40
1907–09	6	11	Apr.–Sep. 1939	22	44
1909–14	9	15	Sep. 1939–40	24	48
1914–19	10	20	1940–46	26	52
1919–25	14	20	1946–49	35	70
1925–30	20	30	1949–Apr. 1969	50	80

Source: Sandford (1971: table 2.2).

But just what form the bite will have taken requires consideration. We can think of the larger personal holdings as being accumulated until they enter a certain category of size, being held for some time in that category and then being dispersed. There would be an exception to this where an estate was passed intact to a single heir, but this must have been exceptional even in the old days. Much more often, each holding of a certain size would have only a limited expectation of life at that size: the holder might draw it down in his lifetime, or at his or her death it would be divided among a number of heirs. The division might be very unequal, with the lion's share going to the oldest son; but the effect generally would be to substitute for the one big holding two or more smaller holdings. As holdings fell out in this way from a given category of size, others would be coming forward to take their place. If the exits and entrances were of equal size, the aggregate wealth in a given category would remain unchanged. A rise of the inflow would tend to raise that aggregate. It would be diminished, *pro tanto*, by any shortening of the 'length of life' within the category. If the number of heirs in the representative case was increased, so that holdings were more subdivided, the rate of inflow of assets further down the scale of holdings would be raised. Here we meet two effects of estate duty. If holders were moved to avoid it by transferring assets to their heirs during their own lifetime, they would in effect be shortening the 'length of life' of their own holdings. To the extent that estate duty was paid, the state was, so to speak, inserting itself as an heir in every will, so that holdings were more subdivided. But this is not all. An additional heir in the normal way would simply have part of the holding transferred to him in value or kind, and the transaction would end with the change of title; but when the heir is the state, then the value of the 'legacy' will be treated as current revenue, and turned back into consumption. (There is an exception, of not much quantitative importance, when the state accepts a work of art in lieu of duty, and retains it in a public collection.) It is true that the assets absorbed by the duty do generally themselves remain in the national inventory of personal wealth: when the executors of a landowner, for instance, sell off one of his farms in order to pay duty, the farm remains in someone's possession. But the sale will have absorbed new savings, either immediately or at the end of a chain of transactions. The flow of savings building up holdings, and the rate at which newly accumulated holdings cross the boundary into a certain category of size, will have been reduced.

There are, then, three effects of estate duties. So far as they have encouraged transfers *inter vivos*, they shorten the 'expectation of life' of holdings within any category of size. By inserting the state as an heir to every substantial property, they increase fragmentation. By diverting part of the current flow of savings back into consumption, they decrease the rate of accumulation. The first and third of these effects tend to decrease the aggregate of wealth held at any one time within any category of size. The second effect tends to increase the relative amount of wealth within the lower categories. Because the duty is graduated steeply, its effects in reducing the amount of wealth held within any category—reducing it absolutely under the first and third effects, and relatively under the second—are greater, the higher the category.

In this way, it becomes intelligible that the duties whose impact has been manifest in many conspicuous instances should have worked strongly towards the actual change in the distribution of wealth. But they are not alone. One other possibility, already mentioned, is the effect of high rates of taxation on income, and of inflation, in obliging the holders of some large fortunes to live in part on their capital. The previously unthinkable rates of tax imposed during the First World War bore hard on the customary way of life of many wealthy people, whose income did not in any case keep pace with the doubling of prices through those years. Similar pressures were exerted through the Second World War, and during the progressive inflation that followed. Everyday knowledge suggests that, even if there had been no estate duty, this incentive to dissave would have reduced the aggregate wealth of the rich.

It is natural to fix attention on the top 10 per cent in years when little wealth was held by the remainder. But as we enter recent years, we are confronted with a major change: the proportion of all wealth that the top 10 per cent hold has become much smaller. Remembering the pitfalls of proportions, we must ask what these numbers alone cannot tell us: how the change came about. Has there been an absolute fall in holdings at the top? Or a transfer of assets from above to below? Or, in a course of general accumulation, a greater rise in the lower than in the higher holdings? To help us decide between these and other possibilities, Figure 14.5 displays Pen parades for the extreme years of the period we have been considering, 1911–13 and 1980, and for two intermediate stages, 1924–30 and 1960.

    This mode of presentation gives us a new view of what has been most significant. We see at once that the greater part of the change came about between 1930 and 1960, with movement in the same direction continuing until 1980. These profiles are all drawn in currency units of the same purchasing power, as nearly as that can be reckoned over a span in which prices generally were multiplied by a factor of about 25. The index appears in Table 14.6, which shows that between the 1920s and 1980 the average holding of wealth in real terms was doubled. Presenting the data in these terms enables us to see how the change came about. Within the top 2 and 3 per cent the profiles overlie one another: we can see only an indication of an absolute reduction in wealth at the apex. This appears more clearly in the numbers of Table 14.7. If these show only a moderate limit as containing 100 per cent of all persons, that is because of the rounding up of the 99.9 per cent and more that actually appears there: some very much bigger holdings remain, but they are few. These top holdings are socially conspicuous, but it is not here that the great change has been made. The upward rotation of the profiles between the 50th and 95th percentile marks a process of growth and accumulation that has raised the holdings of these middling ranks far more than those above them. This is profoundly significant. The fanning out of these profiles marks 'a silent social revolution'. We may attribute it to the unprecedented growth achieved in the quarter-century after the Second World War; but this may have been

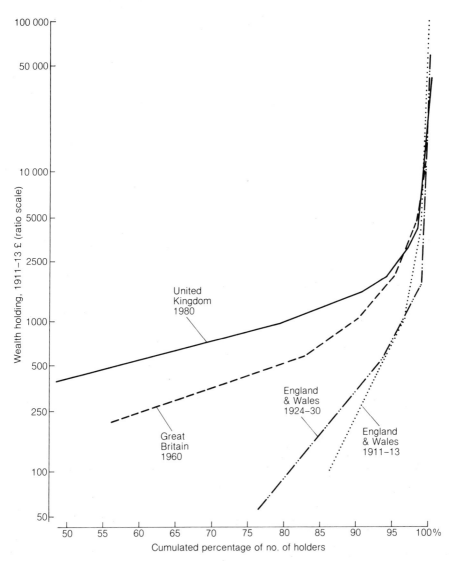

Fig. 14.5 British distribution of wealth, 1911–13, 1924–30, 1960 and 1980. *Sources:* as in Table 14.7.

only the quickening of a process that had been going on for a long time. In 1852, four years after the Communist Manifesto, G. R. Porter raised the question, at the British Association, 'whether the middle class, consisting of those who are possessed of property of limited extent, is or is not increasing, and whether it is probable that this part of our population . . . is likely once again to become absorbed by the other two, and society present the aspect which it wore in feudal times'. He showed that savings bank deposits,

TABLE 14.6   *Average wealth holdings corrected for changes in price level*

	England & Wales		GB	UK
	1911–13	1924–30	1960	1980
(1) Ave. holding (current £)	374	679	2878	18 884
(2) Index of prices	100	183	482	2 540
(3) Ave. holding (1911–13£)	374	371	597	743

Sources: *Row* (1): as for Table 14.4; *row* (2): *The British Economy. Key Statistics 1900–1964* (London & Cambridge Economic Service) Table E*) and Retail Price Index.

holdings of public debt and the returns of income tax and probate had all been showing greater increases for the less than the more wealthy; and concluded that, 'instead of growing poorer every day, and the wealthy growing richer . . . the middle class is as great, as powerful and as flourishing as ever' (Jones 1978: 163).

14.5. The Course of Change in America

The work of a number of scholars in recent years has revealed the characteristics of the distribution of wealth in many parts of the mainland colonies, some of them from the seventeenth century onwards, and more in the eighteenth. This work has been surveyed by Williamson and Lindert (1980), and much of the account that follows has been derived from their masterly study. The evidence consists of tax assessments and probate records. Both have their limitations. The tax assessments, although often maintained systematically, may be variously based, and provide an uncertain guide to changes over time. The probate records serve better in this last respect, but have their own deficiencies. 'As a rule the middle and southern colonies did not include real estate (land, improvements and buildings) in their records, but covered only personal estate. The New England colonies were more complete in asset coverage. In both cases, financial liabilities were rarely included' (p. 13). In any case, the figures of probate cannot be treated as samples of the wealth of persons of the same age as the decedent, because that age is not usually recorded, nor do we have age-specific rates of mortality. But the evidence, which is full and consistent enough to indicate the prevailing levels of concentration, leaves no doubt about differences in the degree of concentration in different places, and makes clear some changes in the course of time.

An indication of the level of inequality in one region is provided by the distribution of net worth in the Middle Colonies in 1774, as that has been estimated by Alice Hanson Jones (1971; Henretta, 1973: 106, table 3.2). It is illustrated in Figure 14.6. The comparison here with the profile for the United States in a recent year illustrates a simple but salient generalization

TABLE 14.7   *Cumulative distribution of wealth-holders over categories of wealth at constant prices*

1911–13, England & Wales

Upper limit of holding (£)	100	1000	5000	10 000	25 000	100 000
Cumulated percentage of no. of holders (%)	86.5	96.6	99.0	99.5	99.8	100.0

1924–30, England & Wales

Upper limit of holding (£)	55	546	2732	5464	13 661	54 644
Cumulated percentage of no. of holders (%)	76.3	93.6	98.3	99.1	99.7	100.0

1960, Great Britain

Upper limit of holding (£)	207	622	1037	2075	3112	4149	5187	10 373	20 747	41 494
Cumulated percentage of no. of holders (%)	56.2	82.7	90.2	95.5	97.2	98.1	98.5	99.5	99.8	100.0

1980, United Kingdom

Upper limit of holding (£)	394	984	1575	1969	2362	3150	3937	7874	11 812	19 685	39 370
Cumulated percentage of no. of holders (%)	48.3	79.8	90.9	94.0	95.6	97.3	98.2	99.5	99.7	99.9	100.0

Sources: 1911–13 and 1924–30: Daniels and Campion (1936: Tables 11, 21); *1960, 1980: Inland Revenue Statistics*, annual issues.

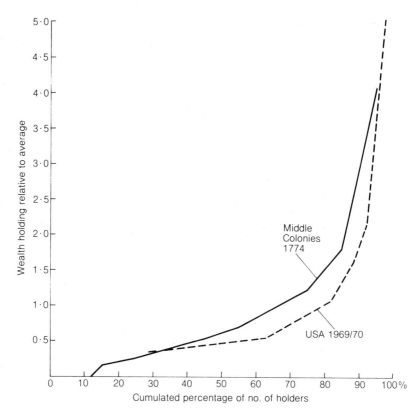

Fig. 14.6 The distribution of net worth in the Middle Colonies in 1774, compared with the distribution of marketable wealth of households in the USA in 1969/70.

Sources: Middle Colonies: Jones (1971:78; see Henretta 1973: table 3.2); *USA:* Table 14.7.

about the colonial distribution outside the South: by contemporary standards, it was remarkably equal. The earlier profile rises more rapidly and steadily through the middle range, so that the transition to the wealthier folk above the 80th percentile is less abrupt. At the top, whereas in 1969–70 the wealthiest 10 per cent of American households accounted for about 63 per cent of all marketable wealth, in 1774 the corresponding proportion was only 41 per cent. That is a figure that we can compare again with its counterpart among the contemporary households of England and Wales, which Lindert (1985: table 12) has put at about 54 per cent. In 1960 the proportion in the United Kingdom was 60 per cent.

To the North, wealth in the rural districts was even less concentrated. For more than a hundred years, from 1658 to 1769, the proportion held by the top 10 per cent in the Suffolk County of Massachusetts, excluding Boston, lay between 31 and 38 per cent. In Hartford, Connecticut, it was much the same from 1650 to 1774 (Williamson and Lindert 1980: Appendix A, series 17, 12). But in the towns wealth was more concentrated; for most of the eighteenth century, the proportion was around 44 per cent in New York and 54 per cent in Boston (Williamson and Lindert 1980: Appendix A, series 25, 8).

The South presents a very different prospect. Wealth was much more concentrated here. Calculations from the tax lists, mostly in the 1790s, show proportions ranging from 47 to 85 per cent in five counties of East Tennessee, and from 42 to 86 per cent in six counties of Kentucky. Of the eleven counties taken together, seven show proportions of over 60 per cent, and three are in the 80s (Prof. D. H. Fischer, personal communication).

There are evident reasons for these differences between localities and regions. That wealth was more concentrated in the towns may be ascribed to the very fact of their growth. These were centres that grew by immigration, partly from overseas but even more from the surrounding countryside; and the immigrants were mostly young people, on the make, but not yet in possession of capital. They were also trading centres, and the enterprising and fortunate merchant was able to expand his fortune more rapidly and widely than the enterprising farmer. We might therefore expect not only that wealth holding would be more concentrated in the towns than the country, but that this concentration would increase as the towns grew: however, the evidence is various. In Philadelphia concentration evidently did increase: the top 10 per cent there held only 36 per cent in 1684–99, but thereafter the proportion rose, to an outstandingly high 67 per cent over 1746–75. In Boston the course of change is not so clear. It is true that the low degree of concentration before 1700 appears here too, but it seems to have been the effect of the commercial depression of those years cutting into the capital of the leading merchants; after that, although concentration increased in times of prosperous trading and fell in depression, it changed little on balance down to the 1770s. In New York there is no evidence for any rise at all: in 1789 the proportion stood at the same 45 per cent as in 1695. These differences are consistent with the more rapid growth of Philadelphia.

It was economic growth also that accounts for differences among the rural communities. Working on the tax returns, J. T. Main (1965) has found that there were two sorts of frontier district. In one, speculators had taken up large holdings initially; here property was concentrated, and the degree of concentration was raised by the presence of landless labourers in some number. But in the other and more usual sort of district, the land was fairly equally distributed at first, in small family holdings, and 'the hired hand quickly obtained a farm of his own or left for better soils' (Main 1965:

278). In the course of time, however, a divergence appeared between those settlements that, being still remote, continued their subsistence farming and those with access to markets in which they could sell cash crops. The subsistence farmers maintained their substantial equality; among the marketing farmers, the more enterprising, industrious and fortunate expanded their holdings by taking over land from their neighbours. Thus Main (1965: 14, 29) contrasts Goshen and Groton, both in Connecticut. In 1741 Goshen was 'just emerging from the pioneer state'; of its 49 tax payers, the top five—'virtually the top 10 per cent'—paid 22 per cent of the tax, other than poll tax. 'Judging by the ownership of cows and oxen, about 40 of the men (including the top five) were landowners, but since none of the 35 owned more than 13 cattle, none was in a big way.' Ten years later the population had doubled, and the top 10 per cent were now paying 28 per cent of the tax. Groton, on the other hand, had more than 500 taxpayers by 1783; the large farmers who made up most of the top 10 per cent owned 29 per cent of the wealth; there was a middle class containing a lawyer, a physician, eight shopkeepers and numerous artisans; and a quarter of the men were landless labourers. Here, as in the Hudson River communities in New York and Chester County in Pennsylvania, where good soil went with access to markets, growth brought, besides an increased division of labour, some concentration of property in large farms employing landless labourers.

The greater concentration of wealth in the South confronts us with the outcome of a social structure and an economy that were contrasted with those of the North from the first. The southern immigrants brought with them the attitudes of a hierarchical society. Some of them were persons of substance in England, who were able to take up large holdings, and buy indentured servants and slaves with which to cultivate them. The frontier in such regions was not made up, as it was in many places in the North, of small holdings initially of much the same size, but contained large estates. Wealth per wealth-holder in 1774 was more than twice as great in the South as in New England (Jones 1980: 58, 98, 149–51). The kind of social relations, moreover, that the immigrants regarded as normal or desirable will have taken their pervasive effect, through the courts and on the government, and within the family, to foster inequality. The contrast between the democratic and in some sense egalitarian principles of the Puritans in the North and the more traditional, often royalist, origins of the southern colonists did not merely parallel the difference between the degree of inequality of wealth in the two regimes, but was a cause of it. Instead of the social structure being moulded by 'the relations of production', it shaped them in conformity with itself. But the kind of production did take its own effect. A plantation economy, with its crops of tobacco or cotton sold overseas, was subject to those pressures and rewards of the market that we have seen differentiating the market-related from the isolated rural communities in the north. Those planters who enjoyed better soil or communications profited more by good times. When the market fell they could take over the holdings of bankrupt neighbours. In her study of the tobacco plantations of Maryland, Gloria Main (1982: 92) has remarked that this 'was a highly stratified society from its beginnings, although economic expansion made possible a high degree of economic and social mobility. Economic depressions, however, severely retarded opportunity and transferred assets from debtors to creditors, exacerbating the degree of inequality and consolidating the position of the more fortunate.' Maryland in fact showed a rise in the proportion of gross personal wealth held by the top 10 per cent, from 43 per cent in 1656–83 to 64 per cent in 1713–19 (Main 1982: Table 11.3). It will be noted that, whereas in the towns inequality was increased by prosperity, through the more rapid growth of holdings that were already large, in the rural economy it was increased by depression, through the elimination of lesser holdings.

To view the colonial era as a whole, we can best follow Williamson and Lindert. 'In the aggregate,' they say,

'colonial inequality was stable at low levels. In some cities, inequality was on the rise. These were the fast growers, which attracted the young adult and/or the propertyless. In others, no rise in inequality can be observed. These were typically slow growers . . . Some settled agrarian regions exhibited inequality trends, others did not. Even frontier settlements exhibited some evidence of rising inequality. The colonial era exhibits a lack of consistent local behaviour . . . (Williamson and Lindert 1980: 10–11)

But this mixed behaviour resulted in stability on the whole, because population was shifting towards the communities which, though they might be becoming less equal as they grew, had been more equal initially.

The evidence for the first sixty years of the nineteenth century is conflicting. We can compare the estimate for 1774 by A. H. Jones, already cited, with Soltow's (1975) findings from a large sample of the real estate recorded in the census of population in 1860. This comparison indicates a marked increase in inequality: whereas the top 10 per cent held nearly half of all wealth in 1774, by 1860 they held nearly three-quarters. It is an arithmetical inference from this that the ratio of the average holding by the top 10 per cent to that by the remaining 90 per cent had about trebled. But in a more recent study, Soltow (1984) has compared his estimate for 1860 with figures of 'assets in land, buildings, houses, wharves, etc.—the real estate owned by individuals' recorded for the First Direct Tax in 1798. He has found that in both years the owners of real estate made up rather less than half of all adult white males. The distribution seems to have been more unequal in 1860, but not very much so. Taking account of the possible error of measurement, Soltow concludes that 'there was extensive inequality in wealthholding in the United States in 1798, and that this condition continued at a level almost as high two generations later'. It is unlikely that inequality rose sharply between 1774 and 1798 and little thereafter. But if the balance of evidence is in favour of at least some rise down to 1860, we may attribute this to the rapid economic growth of the period. Such growth brings with it—indeed, is largely created by—the innovative and constructive activity of the more energetic and enterprising as well as lucky people, who increase their fortunes more than the rest. Williamson and Lindert (1980: 287) contrast the 'rapid antebellum industrialization' with the 'slow growth and relative quiescence of the eighteenth century'. The connection between faster growth and accumulation is not invariable, for the rate of technical change intervenes. We must therefore look beyond econometrics to the particular circumstances of each period. It appears that the rapid growth down to the Civil War took the form of the physical expansion of productive capacity with existing techniques, rather than the technical transformation of that capacity.

It is not easy to trace the distribution of wealth in the United States through the years between 1860 and the 1920s. The needed estimates have not yet been made. The Federal Trade Commission studied large samples of estates probated in 1912 and 1923, but did not classify them by the age of the decedent and apply mortality multipliers; the reported distributions consequently show much more concentration than is likely to have been found if the estates had been treated as a sample of the holdings of the living, with due weight given to the smaller estates of younger decedents. But where distributions of probated estates are available both with and without the application of mortality multipliers, the changes in equality shown by the two sorts have been found to agree. We can therefore take the distinct reduction of inequality shown by the decedent distributions of 1912 and 1923 as good evidence for a similar reduction among the contemporary holdings of the living through the years containing the First World War. When we come to estimates of this latter kind for the 1920s, we find the change of the war period reversed, with the concentration of wealth increasing again down to 1929; during those years the proportion of wealth held by the top percentile of all adults lay within much the same range (31–36 per cent) as it had done (if we include slaves) in 1860 (Williamson and Lindert 1980: Tables 3.1, 3.8). 'The seven decades following the Civil War', Williamson and Lindert conclude, 'mark a period for which wealth inequality remained very high and exhibited no significant long-term trend (pp. 46–7, 51). The period 'is best described as a high uneven plateau of wealth inequality'.

A plateau calls for explanation, no less than an upward or downward slope. We can envisage each of the personal fortunes that make up, say, the top 10 per cent at any one time as having become big enough to find a place in the group at some time in the past, and being destined to be dispersed—as by the death of the holder—at some future date. For simplicity, let us rule out changes in the structure of population and in its total numbers. Then the concentration of wealth, as indicated by the proportion of all wealth that is held by the group, may be raised by a reduction in the size of holdings outside the group, and also by an increase in the size of holdings within it. In either case, what matters is the scope for accumulating relatively large fortunes. This scope would be widened by increased opportunities to accumulate them, at a time when the accumulation of middling and small fortunes remained no more easy or likely than before; but the same effect of increased concentration would follow from a reduced facility for accumulating middling and small fortunes, at a time when the very large fortunes remained no harder to accumulate than before. Each of these two kinds of change alters the differential scope for attaining relatively large fortunes. Suppose now that this scope shifts so that these fortunes become easier to attain than before. The effect on the aggregate wealth of the top group depends on how long, on the average, these big fortunes are retained until they are dispersed. If this were ten years, then the aggregate wealth of the group, and the concentration of wealth in the whole economy, would go on rising for ten years; after that, each year's entry of larger fortunes would be offset by the dispersal of those that entered ten years ago. Thus, the degree of concentration depends on two main factors: the size of the fortunes coming up to cross the line into the top group, and the length of time that, once in, they stay there. A change, once for all, in the first of these factors—the size of entrants—will be followed after a time by stability, so long as the second factor—'the expectation of life'—remains the same.

This framework enables us to say something about the possible reasons for the prevailing stability of the concentration of wealth between 1860 and 1929, which stands contrasted with the rise in concentration during the preceding period and, as we shall see, with the fall that came after it. Stability appears as the state of affairs we should expect, so long as there is no change in the differential opportunity to accumulate large fortunes, or in the relative expectation of life of their holders. It may well be that in the course of the nineteenth century the absolute expectation of life of the very rich lengthened, but a similar lengthening is likely to have been experienced by the less wealthy too, and so to have raised wealth at all levels. Constancy in the differential opportunity to accumulate seems less likely; but we may suppose that the earlier period, in which concentration rose, was one in which industrial expansion, both intensive and extensive, provided a scope for accumulations that were very big relatively to the general run of their time, in ways that were not afforded to the same extent by the growth that continued after 1860. These ways include the exploitation of great new technical developments, such as the railway in its day; the improvement of communications, widening the market accessible to any one trader; and urbanization with its enhancement of land values. Conceivably, there were wider openings of these kinds in the earlier phase of growth than in the later, when more of the sustained rise in productivity depended on the improvement of existing installations. But we lack the evidence that would show whether the rise of the largest fortunes actually behaved as this suggestion implies.

The estimates of concentration in the years from 1929 onwards are based on the estate tax now in force, with mortality multipliers, and on the Survey of Consumer Finances conducted by the Federal Reserve Board in 1962. These leave no doubt that a substantial reduction in concentration came about in the Great Depression that began in the autumn of 1929, and that it was carried farther in the Second World War, to reach a low point about 1949, from which it varied little in the two decades that followed (Smith and Franklin 1974). The profile of the distribution arrived at by 1969/70 is illustrated in Figure 13.4 and again in Figure 14.4. We have already noted that the top 10 per cent accounted for about 63 per cent of all wealth then; in 1860, the corresponding proportion had been between 74 and 79 per cent (Williamson and Lindert 1980: table 3.3)

Why was there this fall in the 1930s and 1940s? Williamson and Lindert have shown that it was not due to changes in the age composition of the population: what small effect can be attributed to these reduced it.

We may suggest the working of three other factors. One, which may be put forward with confidence, is the fall in the values of securities during the Great Depression. If wealthy Americans at that time resembled the wealthiest Britons in recent years, in keeping a higher proportion of their assets in the form of securities than did those with less wealth, their valuations will have been differentially depressed by the collapse of the stock market. Second, in no part of the 1930s and 1940s were the conditions propitious to the accumulation of great fortunes—certainly not in the deep and protracted depression and the years of the New Deal, nor under the wartime controls. Third, the economic recovery achieved during the war and sustained long afterwards, although it will have raised the wealth of the rich, will have done no less, and very likely more, to enable the middle ranks to accumulate.

We have seen that the greater equality of some modern distributions comes from the raising of the Pen profile between the 50th and 75th percentiles, and this displays the acquisition of assets, in the form of dwellings, consumer durables and life insurance, by the middle classes. These acquisitions rise with rising standards of living.

Williamson and Lindert (1980: 62–3) point out that the changes in the concentration of wealth since 1912 that have been noted above were accompanied, phase by phase, by changes in the same direction in the inequality of incomes. This becomes intelligible if we revert to our mental picture of the accumulation and dissolution of great fortunes, and the varying scope for accumulation. Times when this scope is wide will be times of innovation and, at least in some directions, of rapid expansion with high investment; but these developments also widen differentials in pay by a relative increase in the demand for skill. If we had only the eight-year business cycle to consider, the relation would have been inverse, for the depression that reduced the concentration of wealth widened differentials by lowering the pay of the unskilled more than that of the skilled. But other factors intervened to bring about the positive relation between the trends: unionization under the New Deal raised the relative pay of the unskilled and semi-skilled, and this effect was sustained by full employment in the Second World War. The stability of the concentration of wealth in the 1950s and 1960s has been attributed to the absence of change in the scope for accumulation, in times of fairly steady growth but no very rapid expansion in particular sectors; but these were also times in which there was no marked shift in the relative demand for different types of labour.

15

The Formation of Distributions of Income and Wealth

15.1. Three Approaches to Formation

The distributions of personal income and holdings of wealth that we have been examining have salient features in common. Wealth is much more unequally distributed than income, but the form of distribution is similar. There are three ways of asking how distributions came to take that form. These overlap, but there may be an expository advantage in following separate approaches initially, when a comprehensive understanding has to take account of so much.

In the first approach we look at the *components* of distributions. There are various distinct sources of inequality. Income and wealth typically vary with the age of the person concerned; income varies with occupation; both income and wealth are differently distributed in different places. A distribution on the national scale is made up of a number of such components. The immediate cause of a change in it may thus, for example, be a demographic movement.

But why should the assembly of these components result in a particular form of distribution? The second approach examines the *mathematical properties* of that form. It hopes to find in those properties a guide to the actual processes of formulation in everyday life. The generation of the mathematical expressions for typical forms of distribution may suggest actual counterparts and be treated as a simulation of the real world.

The third approach considers the formation of distributions as an *ongoing process*. In an earlier passage we treated the amount of wealth held in any category of size as depending on the rates at which growing fortunes become big enough to cross the threshold into it, and holdings leave it either upwards or downwards. Similarly, a person's income may grow for a time, passing over successive thresholds, and then fall off, until at death it ceases altogether. As particular holdings or incomes leave a category, their place may be taken by others; any distribution of income or wealth is the net outcome of exits and entrances, of attrition and renewal. We shall consider the ebb and flow of these currents in the course of history.

15.2. The Components of Distributions

The ultimate components of the distribution of income, or of wealth, are of course the millions of individual recipients of income or holders of wealth: the distribution in the country as a whole is formed when these individual receipts or holdings are assembled. But we can reduce the components to more manageable proportions if we think of the population as being distributed over a number of cells, each of which is defined by the factors determining the income or wealth of its occupants. Suppose there were only two such factors determining income—a person's occupation, and his or her age. We can envisage a table in which the cells were formed by the intersection of columns, each representing an occupation, with rows each representing an age. We could then regard the distribution of income in the whole country as formed by the distribution of the population over these cells, together with the differences of income in different occupations, and within any one occupation at different ages. As we ran our eyes down the columns we should be following the distribution of income by age; as we ran them along the rows, the distribution by occupation. What forms of distribution emerged in the aggregate would depend on how many persons were found cell by cell, and on the amounts of income in the several cells. We should then have three components to consider: the distribution of the population over the cells, and the differences of income between occupations, and between ages. But the cells in the actual world have more than two dimensions: besides the two just named, there are—among others—differences of industry, region, gender and trade union membership. The dimensions of the cells that underlie the distribution of wealth will include income, age, gender and the wealth of relatives.

How these last factors help to shape the distribution of wealth will be most conveniently described when we come to discuss the formation of distributions as an ongoing process, in Sections 15.4 and 15.5 below. Here we take up the components of the distribution of income.

A first step is to consider the spread of population over the cells. Evidently, changes in this will affect the whole distribution. But here we must be careful about causality. We must distinguish between those population movements that really initiate changes in the distribution of income or wealth, and those that are only the by-product of changes due to other causes. The question is whether we have to do with types of person who inherently carry a certain income or holding of wealth with them wherever they go, or whether people acquire the income or wealth by reason of moving into a certain cell. There is no doubt that a rise in the birth rate raises the number of young people, who inherently, by reasons of their youth, bring little wealth into their age bracket; or that a fall in the death rate, by increasing the number of old people, adds to the number of low incomes. At the other extreme, an increase in the number following some highly paid occupation will occur only when the demand for that kind of work has extended, and the entrants have qualified themselves for it. In between are the cases in which what people can earn is limited so closely by personal characteristics that when they move they can only take with them the ability to earn a certain amount and no more. It may be, for instance, that some people are so limited by their physique or mentality that they can never perform more than unskilled labour; then an increase in the number of such people would be the cause of a rise in the number of low incomes. But equally, the low-paid might increase in number if people were displaced from better-paid occupations. Generally, it is only when changes in the spread of population are demographic in origin, and affect the relative numbers of different ages and gender, that we can be sure of their originating changes in distribution, as distinct from those arising as the by-product of other changes.

An example of such demographic effect is provided by the 'shift–share analysis' of changes in the distribution of income in the United Kingdom in the 1950s and 1960s, carried out by Dinwiddy and Reed (1977). In the years that they studied, the proportions of both young and old people in the population increased; more young people continued to attend schools and colleges; and there was a marked rise in the proportion of women of all ages who worked outside the home. The changes in age distribution, increasing the weight of low-income recipients at both ends, would of themselves have made the distribution more unequal. So would the extension of full-time education, which increased the number of young people without earnings. But the higher proportion of earners among women worked the other way, by raising the middling incomes. None of these effects was large, but they were clear enough to remind us that the form of income distribution does not depend on the relative incomes of different types of person alone. What the net effect was of all the changes taken together we cannot say, for each was calculated on the assumption that the others did not occur. This limitation is avoided in the decomposition by Mookherjee and Shorrocks (1982) of the 'modest upward movement in the overall inequality' of UK household incomes over 1965–80. The main components of this movement were found to be changes in inequality within subgroups, in the relative numbers in those subgroups and in their mean incomes. Of these three components, it was the first that took most effect, through a change in the 'age–income profile, which has become progressively more arched'.

An example of the effect of demographic change is provided by the rise in the proportion of total wealth in the United Kingdom owned by women, from 33 per cent in 1927 to 42 per cent in 1960. The Royal Commission (1975: para. 239) attributes this with some confidence to the increases during that span of years in the extent to which women were outliving men. This will have raised the number of women relative to the number of men living at any time. The rise, moreover, would have been in the highest ages, and would have contained a high proportion of widows to whom their husbands had left substantial capital.

We turn to the sources of inequality that differentiate the cells. Here we shall draw at many points on *The Inequality of Pay* (Phelps Brown 1977).

Foremost among those sources is the difference of earnings by occupation. The structure of earnings is remarkably similar in many countries, both in the ranking order of the occupations and in the size of the differentials. Table 15.1 illustrates this for six European countries and the United States. There are no differences in the ranking order here, save for some variation in the relative earnings of the lower administrative occupations and the technicians. The one notable departure from similarity in the size of the differentials appears in the relative earnings of the two top groups, the higher administrative occupations and the professional engineers: these are much higher in France and Italy than in West Germany, and are lower in the United States than in any of the European countries. That the ranking order is the same in the Soviet-type economies is indicated by Table 15.2. Records of Leningrad engineering (Phelps Brown 1977: table 2.6) provide a similar indication for the USSR. But this sampling of engineering does not bring out one salient difference: whereas in the West the lower white-collar occupations are generally paid at least as much as the skilled manual workers, and sometimes more, in the Soviet-type economies it is the skilled manual workers who are paid the more highly. The table shows one other and even greater difference: managers in the Soviet-type economies are paid much less relatively to manual workers than managers in the West. Whereas a managing director in the West will commonly be paid five times as much as a skilled manual worker, in the Soviet-type economies it is more like three times. But this holds only of payment in money: in both types of economy managers receive some perquisites as well, and these probably raise the effective remuneration by a greater proportion in the Soviet type.

In the international comparisons we have made so far, a significant agreement appears between the structures, but this is only when they are formed of groups of occupations, such as 'engineers' or 'manual workers, semi-skilled'. When these groups are decomposed into particular occupations, such as 'civil engineer' or 'tool-setter', the similarity of ranking order disappears. On a survey of 20 occupations in 22 countries outside the Soviet zone (Phelps Brown 1977: table 2.17), every one of them is found to appear sometimes high and sometimes low within the manual class as a whole. Evidently, the forces that bring about so much agreement in the ranking order of grades of labour do not bear so closely on relativities within a grade, or else they operate very variously there in different countries.

TABLE 15.1 *The structure of earnings in European economies and the United States*

Average earnings of men in certain groups of occupations, expressed in each country as relative to a rough average of all earnings*

Group of occupation	Denmark 1965	France 1964	W. Germany 1965	Italy 1959	Norway 1964	UK 1960	USA 1958
(1) Higher administrative	2.6	2.9	1.45		1.9		1.4
(2) Engineers, professional	2.4	2.4	1.55	3.3	1.9	2.1	1.4
(3) Lower administrative	1.3	1.55	1.05	0.95	1.0		
(4) Technicians	0.9	1.2	1.2	1.4	1.15	0.95	
(5) Foremen	1.1	1.15				1.15	1.15
(6) Clerks, trade	0.7	0.85	0.8	0.7	0.8	1.15	1.0
(7) Clerks, office†	0.8	0.8	0.8			0.8	
(8) Manual workers, skilled	0.75	0.7	1.0	0.6	0.9	0.8	1.05
(9) Manual workers, semi-skilled		0.6	0.9	0.5	0.85	0.65	0.9
(10) Manual workers, unskilled	0.6	0.5	0.8	0.45	0.8	0.6	0.6

* Average of all earnings formed by combining groups (1) and (2), (6) and (7), (8), (9), with weights 3, 5, 9, 3 and set = 1.0.

† Including shop assistants, except in the UK, where they are included with semi-skilled manual workers.

Source: UN.ECE (1967: table 5.16); reproduced here from Phelps Brown (1977: table 2.1).

TABLE 15.2   *The pay structure of engineering in Soviet-type economies and in Great Britain*

Maximum salary rates of occupations in engineering in three Soviet-type economies, about 1962, compared with average pay in similar occupations (not confined to the engineering industry) in Great Britain, 1971*

	Czechoslovakia	Eastern Germany	Poland	Great Britain
Director	188	160	166	362 Managing director
				254 General manager
Chief engineer	167	159	149	138 Chief engineer
Production chief	151	131	142	208 Several works Works
				160 Single works Mgr.
Chief accountant	131	145	119	175 Chief accountant
Engineer	98.5	88	80	83 Engineer†
Foreman	64	84	89.5	69 Foreman‡
Technician	57.5	72	93	67 Technician
Highest-paid manual worker	60	53.5	70	68 Fitter toolroom, tool/die maker
Charwoman	30	—	—	23 Charwoman

* Relatives to unweighted mean of six included occupations = 100.
† Average, weighted by numbers in sample of: civil, structural; electronic; mechanical; planning and production. other.
‡ Average, weighted by numbers in sample, of: senior or higher level; other foreman or supervisor.

Sources: *Soviet-type economies*: UN.ECE (1967: Table 8.6); Great Britain: top six occupations, AIC Salary Research Unit, annual survey of UK executive salaries and fringe benefits at July 1971, as reported in *The Times* (London) 8 Nov. 1971; bottom five occupations, Dept. of Employment, *New Earnings Survey 1971* (HMSO, London), Table 57, median gross weekly earnings at April 1971. Reproduced here from Phelps Brown (1977: Table 2.7).

Is the degree of similarity between countries in recent years matched by similarity between past and present? We do find constancy in one differential that can be traced far back: it appears that for 500 years, from the early fifteenth century onwards, the rate for the building craftsman in southern England was persistently and continuously half as great again as that for the labourer (Phelps Brown and Hopkins 1981). This shows the force of custom, and the willingness of those who pay and earn wages to follow a rule of thumb. The same force of custom has been shown by British clerical workers maintaining a margin of pay and conditions over most manual workers depsite a great extension of the supply of people fitted for clerical work. It was shown also by the maintenance of traditional differentials between the trades in British engineering shops despite many changes in the tasks and equipment of those trades.

But the rule of custom can be shaken. Two world wars have done this in particular. When change in money terms is unavoidable and far-reaching, change in the structure can creep in. It is here that supply and demand come into their own.

The rise in the differential for skill in the British industrial revolution and its subsequent contraction was mirrored in Russian economic development from the First Five Year Plan to 1956. Similarly, that the differentials for skill are generally wide in the less developed economies, and become narrower as development proceeds, may be ascribed to the initial extension of demand for skills previously little used in the economy, and the subsequent increase in the number acquiring those skills. (Phelps Brown 1977: 98)

Supply and demand, it is true, may operate one-sidedly; an extension of demand for a particular skill may raise the relative rate for it fairly readily, but an extension of the supply of it will not so readily bring its relative rate down—as we saw for clerical skill, custom interposes a ratchet, which allows rates to rise, but checks them when they tend to fall back. Despite this, the effect of economic development has been generally to narrow differentials. The extension of education and the rise in the standard of living have reduced the differences of capability between one person and another. The improvements of equipment have increased the productivity of operators who bring no great skill to their work. Governments, and sometimes trade unions, have intervened to raise the lowest paid. But where a new requirement has appeared, such as the ability to design for the computer, a new and wide differential has been opened.

A survey of the past and present of the occupational pay structure thus suggests that it has been shaped mainly by supply and demand. But these market forces have not had the field to themselves. Their action has been checked by custom and other influences of social attitudes. Those influences have taken effect in various forms of discrimination, which we must go on to consider. But first we must examine another source of inequality within the occupational pay structure.

This other source of inequality is the variation of earnings within any one occupation according to the age of the earner. It is common knowledge that in most occupations earnings rise through the early years of working life, and in many continue to rise through the middle years; then they generally fall off somewhat, until at retirement or death they cease altogether. An approximation to the patterns traced in this way for four groups of British wage and salary-earners is shown in Figure 15.1. It can be treated only as an approximation, because it has been made by taking the earnings of people aged 20, 30, 40 and so on at one and the same time. We cannot infer from this cross-section how the earnings of the people aged 20 at that time will change over the years ahead of them. Those people form a cohort that will be subject to the peculiar influence of its own setting in history. People aged 50 in 1985 were born at a time when the means of many families were

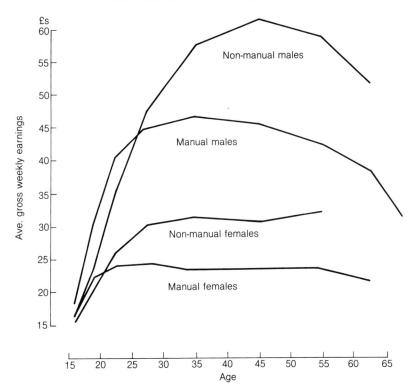

Fig. 15.1   Age–earnings profiles.
Average gross weekly earnings in different age brackets of four groups of
employees, United Kingdom, April 1974.
Source: New Earnings Survey 1974; *Department of Employment Gazette,* 82, 1003–4;
        reproduced here from Phelps Brown (1977: fig. 8.4).

straightened; their early schooling may have been upset by the war, and
they may have experienced the shock of evacuation, or of being bombed;
but some of them will have been able to seize opportunities provided by the
1944 Education Act that were not available to those born a few years earlier
than they. By contrast, those aged 30 in 1985 grew up in times of full
employment and rising standards of living in the home, and enjoyed
greater opportunities of tertiary education. The personal capacity of the
two cohorts is thus likely to have been developed differently. When we
straddle the two cohorts, and take the ratio of earnings at age 50 to those at
age 30 in 1985, we obtain only a rough guide to the rate at which those
30-year-olds will advance their earnings over their next twenty years. A
better guide than cross-sections can offer would be provided by the records
of cohorts followed through time; but these are scarce. We owe to Hart
(1975) the tracks of three cohorts over twenty years that are shown in

Figure 15.2. Marked differences appear here between the cross-sections and the cohort tracks—for example, we should take the typical rise in real earnings between ages 30 and 40 to be much lower if we were guided by cross-sections than if we followed the cohorts. The three cross-sections lie one above the other, because real wages were rising throughout, but they are not equally spaced at all three points: that is because, for example, the youngest cohort advanced much more than the other two in 1963–8. Such is the finding in one exploration, hardly wide in its coverage, but clear enough as a warning. Yet the findings of cross-sections of the broad-based

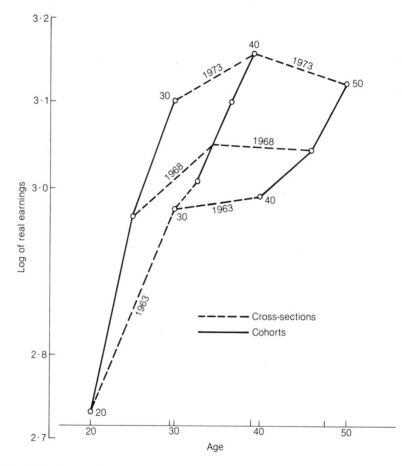

Fig. 15.2   Comparison of cross-section and cohort.

Annual earnings of sample of 687 persons in the UK who paid not less than 48 national insurance contributions in each of 1963, 1966, 1970 and 1973, made up of cohorts aged 20, 30 and 40 in 1963.

Source: Hart (1975); reproduced here from Phelps Brown (1977: fig. 8.5).

New Earnings Survey have been consistent enough to warrant acceptance as showing prevailing and persistent relationships between age and earnings.

Because these relationships are different for different occupations, earnings diverge more among older than among younger people. The variance is at its highest about the age 55; after that, as most individual earnings decline, so does the variance (Creedy and Hart 1979). It follows also from the divergences of the profiles for different occupations that the inequality of earnings among people of the same age is greater than that between the lifetime earnings of the same people. We cannot take these lifetime earnings out for comparison with one another, simply by adding up the real earnings year by year, for this would be to miss the effect of some people having to wait longer for their rises than others. A fair comparison will take prospective earnings discounted to the date of entry into the occupation (Creedy 1985: ch. 9). Much depends on the rate of discount taken: the higher it is, the smaller will be the differential advantage of the higher paid occupations, for these rise more slowly and reach their maximum later than the lower paid. In the United States, the current earnings of dentists in the 1950s were reckoned to be 2.6 times, and those of physicians 3.8 times, the average income of the occupied population (Scitovsky 1966: Tables 5, 9), but the corresponding ratios for lifetime earnings discounted at 5 per cent to age 14 were only 1.46 and 1.27 (Carol and Parry 1968: Table 1). Whereas the current earnings of labourers in the United States in 1958 were only 60 per cent of men's average earnings (UN, ECE, 1967, Table 5.16), the corresponding ratio for lifetime earnings, calculated as above, was 70 per cent. Thus, lifetime earnings give us a view of differentials quite other than that afforded by a snapshot of earnings in different jobs at any one time.

They also remind us that the inequalities experienced by individuals as they make their way through life may be very different from those that appear in a cross-section of society. There might be two societies with just the same distributions of individual earnings, but whereas in the one people's earnings were unchanged throughout their working lives, in the other many of the differences were between the earnings of younger and older people in the same occupation. In this second society we should expect less resentment of the higher earnings: the prospect and experience of advancement would reduce the sense of being held down at an inferior level in a stratified society. Differences between rates of pay might remain unchanged, but many people would experience change in their own lives. This is a consideration that measures of inequality derived from static distributions fail to express, but it must enter significantly into inequality as that is felt. The effect will be reinforced, as we shall see, if to advancement within a given occupation we add mobility, that is, movement between occupations of lower and higher pay.

A further source of inequality is of great social significance. This is discrimination, by which people of low status are prevented from earning as much as people of no greater potential but higher status can earn. The most prominent instances are the generally low earnings of women and of ethnically distinct types, often but not always minorities. These groups have all been assigned a lower social status by their dominant neighbours. There is a distinction to be made at the outset: discrimination may occur before the market or within the market. It occurs *before* the market if some people are denied the opportunities to acquire capability that are available to others who set out from similar starting points but do not bear the stigmata of the minority. There may for example be bars, explicit or conventional, to the entry of some types to schools and colleges that others with no better qualifications are free to enter. When these victims of discrimination enter employment, they may quite possibly be paid on the same terms as others, that is, according to their capability; but by this time the damage has been done, and their capability is lower. Discrimination *within* the market occurs when there is no such equality in the terms of payment, but some persons who bear the stigmata of a certain type are on that account paid less than is paid to others of greater personal acceptability, for work of no greater value.

The fact of discrimination *before* the market against women and people of inferior social status is unmistakable in many instances. 'Both types suffer from inferior education, training and instilled motivation in their preparation for employment; both are largely segregated and indeed crowded into certain employments; both tend to be denied entry into those avenues that provide considerable training on the job with prospects of subsequent progressive advancement' (Phelps Brown 1977: 177–8). Although in a number of countries an effective effort has been made to reduce these forms of discrimination, the unwillingness of one group of residents to regard others as fellow members of the community remains a source of the inequality of incomes. To the extent that this source is reduced, the supply of labour to better-paid occupations will extend, and that to the less desirable and lower-paid occupations will contract, with a consequent reduction in the differential between the pay of the skilled and the unskilled.

But this will be so only if workers of given capability are paid the same, whatever their status—that is, if there is no discrimination *within* the market. How far this kind of discrimination does in fact occur is hard to tell. It will occur only if the market forces of supply and demand are deflected by the prejudice or judgement of employers. If labour of given capability is available at a lower cost when it is provided by people of one social type than by another, employers concerned to keep their costs down might be expected to avail themselves of it, and their bidding for it would raise its price to parity. But in practice, there may be a bar to this in the employers' need to take account of the attitudes of the majority of their work-people, who feel their own status threatened by the raising up of those whom they are accustomed to regard as their inferiors. The employers may share this feeling themselves. They may also take a customary rather than a realistic view of the capability of the supposedly inferior type. This may be supported by instances of trouble experienced with some of the type, which leads to all applicants who bear its stigmata, be it gender or colour or accent, being suspect of the same propensities. Thus, blacks may be paid less for work of equal value because of 'a sense that lower pay is proper for those whose station in life is lower, the assumption that what costs less is worth less, and the apprehension that any black applicant for employment may prove to have shortcomings that are perceived as the objective characteristics of certain blacks' (Phelps Brown 1977: 173). The last reason provides a rational basis for differentiating pay. If many young women, for example, leave in order to raise a family, after they have been trained and gained experience, employers concerned to minimize the cost of labour will be unwilling to engage them at the same rate of pay as men who are alternatively available, even though while at work they are equally capable.

Discrimination, then—before the market certainly, and within it to some extent—forms a component of the distribution of incomes in any country whose working population contains groups separated in status, usually because they are distinguished by gender or ethnic origin.

The division of the working population into socially distinct groups has a counterpart in its division by region. That the same work should command different rates of pay in the possibly widely distanced parts of what is politically one country is as intelligible as the same sort of difference between one country and another. Distance is to be measured by ease and cost of transport, and when movement of goods and men between regions was much more difficult than it is now, the differences between the money incomes prevailing in them was also greater. In the United States, wages in manufacturing in the Far West were half as high again as those in the South in 1907; after the Second World War the differential had fallen to 35 per cent (Bloch 1948). In Great Britain, the labourer's pay in London and the Home Counties, which in Adam Smith's day was double the rate paid in the Lowlands of Scotland, in 1906 exceeded it by only 16 per cent. But wide differences remained: the hourly rate for a carpenter in London was still double that in the South-west (Hunt 1973; 60, 68). The extension of industry-wide collective bargaining during the First World War reduced these differences greatly. The aim was to establish a common basic rate throughout an industry, and after the Second World War this was often achieved, with the exception of a 'loading' for London and perhaps some other cities. But this extent of uniformity was attained only for basic rates: the actual earnings in a given occupation have continued to show differences between regions.

Part of these differences arise from some industries being concentrated regionally; for the pay of members of an occupation common to a number of industries tends to vary from one industry to another, according to the level of pay specific to each industry. Clerks or unskilled labourers tend to receive higher pay where they are working alongside highly paid skilled workers.

This is particularly the case where the rates that firms pay are not fixed for them by the going rates in an external labour market, but are set within the firm's own internal pay structure (Doeringer and Piore 1971). The rate of pay deemed appropriate for a given occupation will then depend upon the differentials that management wishes to maintain or that are yielded by job evaluation. Many surveys of wages in particular localities, in several countries, have shown remarkably big differences between what a given type of labour can earn even in plants quite close to one another. The US Bureau of Labor Statistics found that 'in all occupational wage surveys varying degrees of intraoccupational wage dispersion are found, no matter how narrowly the job or area is defined. The highest paid workers often exceed by 100 per cent or more the rate paid other workers in the same occupation, industry division, and area' (US Department of Labor 1969; 92). But trade unionism may break down the insulation of firms, by making differences between them known to all concerned, and basing claims on 'fair comparison', designed to bring the lower rates up to the level of the higher.

There are other ways, however, in which trade unions increase the inequality of earnings. Where they are strongly organized, they may push up rates of pay, or resist reductions, so as to obtain more for their members than is available to labour of the same grade elsewhere. In occupations and industries where both members and non-members are engaged, the members are commonly found to earn more. But how much of this is due to their unions? Two methods have been devised to find an answer. One has been used in the United States, where some sectors of an industry have been unionized and others not. Allowance must be made here for differences in the general level of pay prevailing in different regions. There is more unionization in cities than in rural areas, but the higher pay of unionists in the cities cannot be ascribed to their unions before account has been taken of the higher level of all wages there. When this has been done, it has still appeared that unionization makes a distinct difference, of 10–15 per cent (Lewis 1963) or even twice as much (studies surveyed by Ashenfelter and Johnson 1972). It remains possible that unions grow up where the soil and climate are most propitious—that they recruit well, and gain higher pay for their members, precisely in those firms and localities that are able to pay more in any case, and would pay more (but how much more?) even if they were not pressed by the unions. Some of the later studies have taken account of another possibility: that union membership is selective towards higher personal qualities, which equally would command higher pay, in some measure, in the absence of unionism.

Here is the starting point for the second method. This analyses the difference between the earnings of individual unionists and non-unionists in the same occupation, by comparing what each type actually earns with what its personal qualifications would be expected to secure for it in any case. A prevailing relationship can be established between such qualifications as the number of years of education received, length of experience at work, and health. The earnings predicted from such indications agree with the earnings of given types of labour generally but have been found to fall well short of those of unionists (Layard *et al.* 1977). The difficulty here again is that union membership may *follow* higher pay rather than cause it. What is nominally a common occupation may include jobs in higher-paying firms, or those held by persons with qualities not captured by the statistician; and the kind of person who gets and holds that job may also be more likely to maintain membership of a union.

But while measurement of the impact of the union remains a matter of doubt, it is highly probable that union pressure does raise pay in some cases. Because that pressure is not exerted evenly across the labour force, it forms a component of the distribution of incomes.

One further source of the inequality of incomes lies in the fluctuations of earnings in the short run. From the New Earnings Survey in the United Kingdom, we know that these fluctuations are large (Thatcher 1971; Department of Employment 1973); some of the highest earners in a given week earned as much as 25 per cent less a year later. At the same time, some of those whose earnings in the first week were low were found a year later with earnings nearer the average for their occupation. These fluctations arise mainly from the variation from week to week in bonus earned, earnings from piece-rates, overtime and shift premium. It is reasonable to suppose, although we lack statistical evidence, that the self-employed experience similar fluctuations in the net receipts from their trade. The effect of all these fluctuations is to make the dispersion of incomes wider when incomes are recorded for the short run than when they are aggregated over a longer period.

The components that have been noticed here are numerous, and the list is not exhaustive. They form dimensions of the cells that underlie the distribution of income as we have viewed it here. Each person is assigned to one of the cells according to his or her occupation, grade of skill, age, membership of a dominant or depressed group, region of work and residence, membership of a trade union, and current opportunity of earning where earnings are variable in the short run. We have seen in some instances how the extent of differentiation under these heads has changed over time, for example the reduction in the differential for skill and in the one wide regional differentials in Britain after the First World War. Meanwhile, the distribution of the working population over the cells has changed greatly. If we consider the likely effect on the distribution of manual workers, we shall expect much change. Table 15.3 shows that for 90 years, from 1886 to 1977, there was in fact extraordinarily little change in the dispersion from end to end. After that, in eight years, during which the median earnings were multiplied by a factor of 2.25, some widening of the spread appears; but in the upper half of the distribution this widening did not go further than had been observed in the Wage Census of 1906.

TABLE 15.3 *Distribution of earnings of manual men in Great Britain, 1886–1985, as a percentage of the median*

	Median earnings (£)	Lowest decile	Lower quartile	Median	Upper quartile	Highest decile
1886	1.21	68.6	82.8	100	121.7	143.1
1906	1.47	66.5	79.5	100	126.7	156.8
1938	3.40	67.7	82.1	100	118.5	139.9
1960	14.17	70.6	82.6	100	121.7	145.2
1977	68.2	70.6	83.1	100	120.3	144.4
1985	153.3	65.5	80.1	100	125.1	154.6

Sources: Thatcher (1968: 163–4; 1976: table 8.1); New Earnings Survey 1985 (pt. B, table 30).

The stability of dispersion over so many years is a remarkable finding that challenges explanation. Those years were full of changes. The time-span is long enough, Thatcher has reminded us (1968: 180), for the labour force to be replaced twice over. Average money earnings of manual men were multiplied nearly sixty-fold. Whatever explanation we find of the stability of the distribution about that changing mean is bound to throw light on the whole process by which incomes are determined.

A first inference from the recorded fact is that the view taken in this section, of the population being spread over many multi-dimensional cells, can only be regarded as provisional. Those cells, it will be remembered, are defined and distinguished by attributes of the occupants, such as occupation, grade of skill, age, high or low status, trade union membership, and current opportunity of earning where earnings are variable in the short run. At least some of these forms of differentiation changed greatly within the recorded period—the margin for skill in manual workers' rates, for example, and regional differences. Both of these changes made for a reduction in dispersion. If all the other changes had been in the same direction, dispersion must have been reduced. That it was not can only be ascribed to the changes having offset one another. But how extraordinary it would be if this had come about as a fact—one might say, as an accident—of history through all those years. No self-correcting mechanism has been suggested that would have ensured it. But some such mechanism there must have been. We must look for it elsewhere.

We may find it in the process by which people acquire their ability to work and earn. We should not think of a working population with given capabilities over against a changing array of opportunities for using them. The doubts expressed earlier about separating the spread of the population over the cells from the specifications of the cells themselves arise again here. We should not think of a colourless unit of the labour force getting a certain wage because he or she moves into a certain job: it is rather that the job puts a price on capabilities that the worker possesses already. Whether a given capability is great or small—indeed, whether it is a capability at all—depends on the demand for it. As that demand—in the short run, the demand for this or that type of person—changes, people respond by adapting their capabilities to the market. If they generally do this so as to get their capabilities priced to the full, whatever the channel through which this is achieved, the distribution of earnings will be based on that of capabilities as these are valued by the market; and if this distribution is governed by conditions of human nature that change little in the course of time, it will remain much the same even while the spread of labour over jobs and the jobs themselves change greatly.

This opens an approach that will be followed further in the next section.

15.3. The Mathematical Properties of the Form of Distribution

In the preceding pages the distributions of income and of wealth drawn from many different times and places have been displayed as Pen parades. These have shown a remarkable similarity of form. They have presented a profile that passes through two distinct phases, and perhaps three. Its course through the lower levels is often ill-defined. From about the 20th to the 80th percentile or thereabouts it is nearly linear or, more often, slightly concave upwards, the concavity being more marked for wealth than for income; here the absolute difference between each person's income or wealth and that of his or her neighbour in the parade varies little, or rises gently, as we go up the scale. But among the top 20 per cent or so, the differences behave quite otherwise: they rise rapidly, so much so that the profile finally shoots out of the graph.

We now have to ask how these various forms arise. The object of this section is to suggest what may be the conditions and processes in the real world that result in incomes and wealth being distributed as they are. We shall look for the counterparts in daily life of the ways in which the form may be generated mathematically. The explanation offered will rest upon life-paths and life-chances as the unit whose behaviour determines the forms of the aggregate. It will envisage a process in two stages; first, the formation of personal ability, and then, the transactions in the market by which given abilities are assigned certain earnings or acquire certain holdings of wealth.

In Chapter 9 we looked first at 'the familiar frequency distribution', but discarded it in favour of the Pen parade, because this displayed more clearly the respects in which one distribution might differ from another, segment by segment. Here, however, we need to return to the frequency distribution, because it is the mathematics of this that best shows the ways in which particular forms are generated.

There has long been agreement that the main and central segment of the distribution of income approximates to the lognormal. A lognormal distribution is one that assumes the normal, symmetrical and bell-shaped form when the variable—here, income or wealth—is represented by the logarithm of the original numbers. Figure 15.3 shows how a distribution of

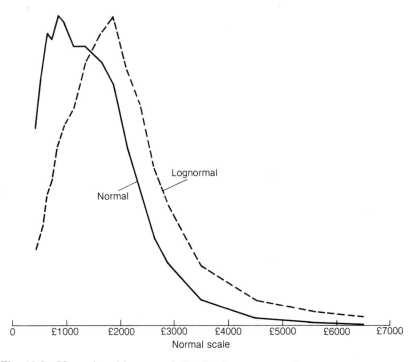

Fig. 15.3 Normal and lognormal distributions compared.
Distribution of personal income before tax in United Kingdom, 1971/2. *Source:* Royal Commission (1975: table 1).

income that is very lopsided on the normal scale becomes more symmetrical on the lognormal. The applicability of that form can be tested by a calculation such as is reported in Figure 15.4. To draw this graph it has been necessary to bring the incomes of different countries, each expressed in its own currency, on to a common scale. The obvious way of doing this, by expressing each country's income levels as relative to its own mean or median income, has the disadvantage in this case of imposing the curves indistinguishably on one another for much of their course. The alternative device has been adopted of dividing the income levels in their original

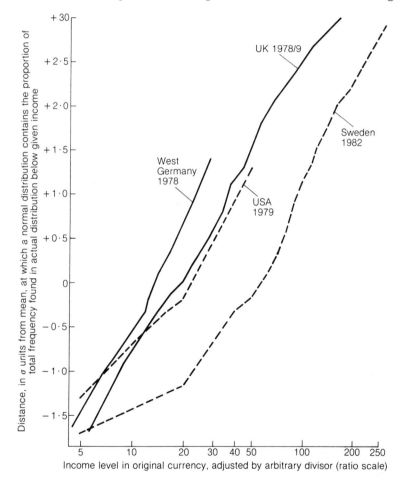

Fig. 15.4 Tests for applicability of lognormal form to distributions of personal income in Sweden, West Germany, United Kingdom and United States. *Sources:* Sweden: *Statistisk Arsbok,* 1985, table 217; W. Germany: *Statistisches Jahrbuch,* 1983, table 20.8; UK: *National Income and Outlay,* 1982, table 4.9; USA: *Statistical Abstract of the USA,* 1984, table 754.

currency units of pounds, dollars and the like by constants selected so as to yield quotients within the range 5–250. The abscissa of Figure 15.4 is therefore to be read as a scale in units of money which can be converted at constant rates of exchange into the four currencies concerned; for example, the UK income level of £4000 per annum corresponds to 22.9 in the scale, one of £8000 to 45.8, and so on. The original data record the percentage of the total number of incomes contained below a certain income level; thus 57.8 per cent of UK incomes in 1978/9 were below £4000 per annum. In a normal distribution, 57.8 per cent of the total distribution lies below a value of the variate that is 0.197 standard deviation units above the mean. In Figure 15.4 this value of 0.197 has been entered over against £4000, that is over 22.9 in the horizontal scale. If the original data were exactly lognormal, the points entered in this way would lie along a straight line, the one way of expressing the income level associated with a given frequency being simply a linear transformation of the other.

We look, then, at Figure 15.4 to see if the lines for the four countries are straight, or approximately so. Their relative positions are a matter of arbitrary arrangement, for the purpose of display: what matters is their form. In each of the four countries in the figure there are in fact indications of two straight lines, one in the lowest part of the range of income, the other in the remainder. The series for Sweden and the United Kingdom, which extend through most of the top decile of frequency as the other two do not, show a second change of slope as they approach the top. The indications are of the presence of segments of two lognormal distributions, and very likely a third; although in Sweden and the United States the departures from linearity in the middle segment are wide enough to show that the lognormal form does not fit closely there. Figure 15.5 shows a similar test of the applicability of that form to the distribution of wealth in Canada, the United Kingdom and the United States. The persistent concavity of the Canadian series indicates less applicability there; but the concavity of the other two series is not marked. We may conclude that the accepted view of the predominance of the lognormal form in the main and central segment of the distribution of income and wealth is not to be dismissed; the fit is not always close, but appears generally better, and often much better, than that of the normal distribution.

But there remain outstanding the tails at bottom and top. 'It has long been known', said Bowley (1933: 365), 'that at the lower end of the income scale, where weekly wages are the main constituent, the distribution has affinity to normality, and at the upper end of high salaries and large incomes from property, the Pareto form is appropriate.' But the lower end is not clearly defined. To quote Bowley again,

If . . . persons all had the same education, environment and opportunity, were paid by piece-rates, and worked with equal zeal, their earnings in a stated time would be normally distributed, with possible gaps at the extremities if the least

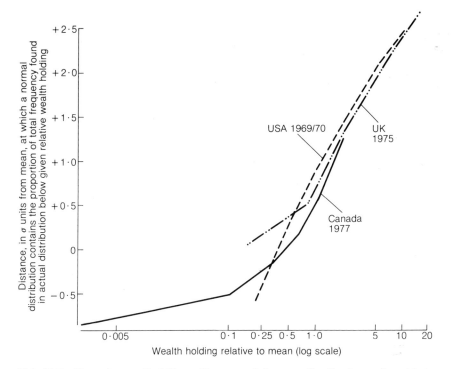

Fig. 15.5 Tests for applicability of lognormal form to distributions of wealth in Canada, United Kingdom and United States. *Sources: Canada:* Oja (1983); *UK:* Royal Commission (1979: tables 4.2, 4.3); *USA:* Wolff (1983).

efficient were not employed and the most efficient had passed on to a higher type of work. Such conditions are approximately illustrated in cotton-weaving in Lancashire, where tradition, environment, education and opportunity for work, are approximately homogeneous, and payment is by piece. In fact, records of earnings show at least a tendency to this normality. (Bowley 1933: 360)

On the other hand, Roy (1950a, 1950b) cited piecework earnings of workmen engaged on similar tasks that were lognormally distributed. It is the lognormal form again that predominates in broader groups of manual workers. Thus in Great Britain 'the earnings of manual men are lognormal, and have been so . . . since the first Wage Census in 1886 . . . Those of manual women are lognormal. (Thatcher, 1968)' (Phelps Brown 1977: 287). We may add that the difference between the normal and lognormal forms as approximations to the data may in any case be small at these lower levels.

It is otherwise with the top tail: here the form is well marked. For both income and wealth it is mostly Paretian. In a Pareto distribution the number of incomes on or above a certain level is related regularly to that level, in such a way, for instance, that the number of incomes decreases by

13 per cent for each 5 per cent rise in that level. Here the proportional change in the number of incomes is 2.6 times that in the income level; so far as the data conform with the Pareto relation, that ratio obtains throughout. Such a relation would imply far greater numbers at the lower levels of income than are ever found, but at the top of the distributions of both income and wealth there is often close agreement. Figure 15.6 gives examples. How widely the relation holds is hard to ascertain, because it

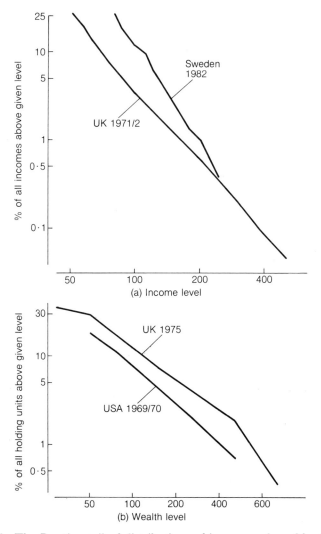

Fig. 15.6 The Paretian tail of distributions of income and wealth. *Sources:* (a) *Income level:* Sweden, *Statistisk Arsbok,* 1985, table 217; UK, Royal Commission (1975: table 1). (b) *Wealth level:* UK, Royal Commission (1979: table 4.2); USA, Wolff (1983: 125–46).

may well apply only within the top 4 per cent or less of the total frequency, and this is often insufficiently subdivided. Nor, where the data are available, is the fit of the Paretian form always so exact as to authenticate it unmistakably. 'If the lognormal "tail" is fitted only to the higher incomes, it often fits as well as (sometimes better than) Pareto' (J. Creedy, personal communication). None the less, the straight line between double logarithmic coordinates, where the lognormal would yield a parabola, has been observed sufficiently often to indicate that in the top tail the distribution generally changes towards the Paretian form.

The distributions of income and wealth can thus be regarded as typically taking a hydrid form, generated in three regimes. In its lowest part the distribution is approximately normal. The regime prevailing over the main body results in a lognormal distribution. As we approach the highest value a third regime intervenes, and the distribution comes closer to the Paretian form. In reaching this conclusion, we have relied on graphical inspection and have used no criteria of goodness of fit; nor have we taken account of the possibility that more complicated expressions would fit more closely. In any case, as Hart has pointed out (1981: 4), the conventional tests of goodness of fit cannot tell us, in an ever-changing world, whether it is that the actual distribution has not reached a theoretical form to which none the less it is tending, or whether we have the wrong form. 'It might even be argued,' Hart continues, 'that since statistical tests cannot help us to choose betwen an approximate generalisation and an invalid one, we should adopt a theoretical distribution if it is nearly true and if it simplifies our task.' The form that appears so widely, for both income and wealth, is in its elements so distinctive as to challenge explanation. If we take its main lines for granted while we busy ourselves with technical refinements, we avert our eyes from that challenge. At least, it seems permissible to take those main lines initially in the forms characterized here, in order to see whether they indicate the processes by which the actual distributions are generated.

We are interested, that is to say, in the observed regularities because we hope that their typical composition will indicate those conditions which, amid all the turmoil of the world, direct its workings to so uniform an outcome. It is true that this hope may be unfounded. Forms that are much alike over a certain range may behave very differently outside it, which is another way of saying that a number of different forms may fit the same segment tolerably well (Creedy 1985). Alternatively, 'the same form of distribution may result from different systems of causation, and it is not safe to argue from the form to the system' (Bowley 1933: 372). What appears to be a well-marked form may be created by the aggregation of dissimilar distributions; Edgeworth and Bowley (1902) showed how earnings of manual males, which we can see now approximated to the lognormal, were made up mainly of two distributions, for the unskilled and the skilled, each of which was normal. Particular groups within the main body, moreover, confront us with the further disturbing possibility that mathematical simulation is in any case no guide to the real processes whose outcome it describes, however closely; we might find expressions that would fit the different distribution of earnings in two industries, say mining and electronics, but we should hardly expect that the forms of these expressions would correspond to the evident sources of actual differences. But it is in the nature of statistical aggregates that they take their characteristic form only when a sufficient number of instances is assembled from disparate sources, and the form of the aggregate depends upon factors that are at work throughout, even though in particular instances they are overlaid by local pecularities. It seems likely that the hybrid distribution presents us with the outcome of such common factors. It is natural to ask whether the mathematical expressions of which the hybrid form may be taken to be composed will provide pointers to the processes that generate the distributions they describe.

We shall ask first how a distribution of *income* may be generated. Any distribution is made up of the attainments of individuals, and is generated by those individuals' behaviour. Each has his or her life-path, beset with life-chances. In following this path, he or she acquires means in certain amounts at each successive age. One cohort follows another, and the distribution recorded at any one time is a snapshot that catches each person at a certain stage along his or her life-path. The count of persons in a given range of income at any one time is a momentary record of an 'ensemble renouvelé', an aggregate constantly turned over as some persons move out to higher or lower levels, or leave the scene altogether, while others move in from above or below. Here we shall assume that entry into each range is only from below, and exit is only to a higher range, or out of the field altogether. In fact, many people do not move progressively upwards, but drop back after a time from the level once reached, or experience quite wide fluctuations of income from year to year. But the essentials of the process that generates the observed distribution will be displayed most clearly if we confine our attention to the main movement, which is upwards; or we can regard the upward movement as a net figure reached after deduction of those falling back. With this simplification we can regard the numbers at each level of income as made up of the members of a cohort who spend some time there before moving on or out, their place being taken by members of the succeeding cohort. In practice, successive cohorts differ from one another considerably (Hart 1975; Shorrocks 1975). But if we ignore those differences, we can use the way in which any one cohort advances from level to level in order to illuminate the process by which all income recipients are distributed over the different ranges at any one time. We can envisage the cohort as a party setting out to climb a hill of income on which the contours are drawn at equal intervals. In each such range some of the party will remain, while the rest continue to climb, until only a few extremely rich persons are left to occupy the highest range. If this movement is to deposit members of the cohort range by range in numbers forming a given type of distribution, the proportion of those attaining a certain range who advance beyond it must fall in a certain way as the attained level rises. We may call this relation the advancement function. It expresses the chance of rising further as a function of the income level attained.

Figure 15.7 illustrates the advancement functions implicit in those forms of distribution, the normal, the lognormal and the Paretian. All have been calculated on the assumption that we are dealing with the 99.4 per cent of the total frequency that in a normal distribution lies within $\pm 2.5\sigma$ of the mean. We assume that over this range income is multiplied tenfold, say from £100 to £1000, so that the standard deviation is 1/5 of £900, or £180. In the normal distribution we can then consider say 50 equal intervals within those limits, each being of 0.10σ or £18. A table showing the proportion of the total frequency lying below an ordinate at any point fixed in standard deviation units, in a normal distribution, will then give the numbers in a cohort that pass the lower and the upper boundaries of each interval. For example, if, following the table, we take a cohort of 99 379 as entering at the lower limit, then at the third interval, from £136 to £154, we find that 98 928 enter, of whom 98 610 go on to cross the upper boundary: so the proportion advancing is 98 610/98 928, or 99.60 per cent. Figure 15.7 shows that the proportion calculated in this way falls continuously as the level of income rises: the higher the level already attained, the smaller the chance of going farther up. The curve along which the chance declines has a particular form, which is that required to deposit members of the cohort, interval by interval, in the numbers constituting a normal distribution: why this requirement should ever be met, we shall inquire later.

If the resultant distribution is to be lognormal, the chance of advancement must vary very differently. In the calculation for a normal distribution above, we took the proportion going forward over an interval of £18. To compare what happens with other types of distribution, we must use the same intervals; but in a lognormal distribution we have equal logarithmic intervals, of continuously growing size, in £s. We have therefore to trace the lognormal distribution on its own base, and then interpolate to find the frequencies at the point in this base corresponding to the boundaries of the intervals in the natural scale. The advancement function obtained in this way for the lognormal distribution proves to fall at first from an initially high level, but then to flatten out, and even rise gently through its later course. If the distribution of income is lognormal, that is to say, those who attain the higher incomes have a somewhat greater chance of going still further up, the higher they go.

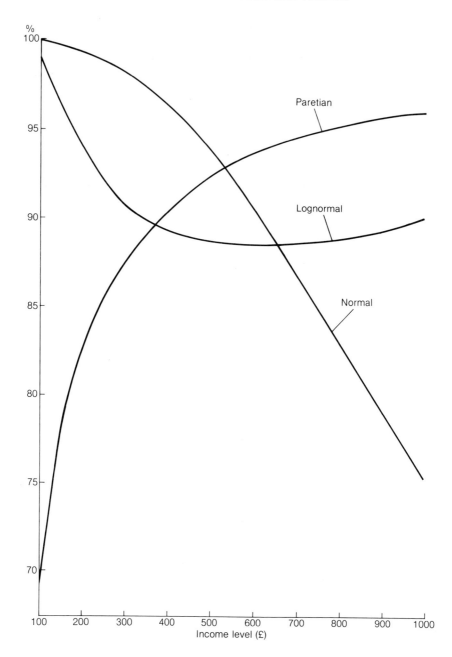

Fig. 15.7 Proportion of cohort who, after attaining given contour of income, go on above next contour, where contours are at intervals of 0.1σ = £18, in distribution whose range of $\pm 2.5\sigma$ is from £100 to £1000; according as the distribution between those limits is normal, lognormal or Paretian.

The calculations for a distribution that is Paretian throughout are made by similar interpolation. Figure 15.7 shows the resultant advancement function as starting at a comparatively low level but rising throughout, at a decreasing rate, but still faster than the lognormal at the higher levels of income. A Paretian distribution appears, that is to say, where 'success breeds success': the higher the income already attained, the greater the chance of going higher still.

So far we have followed the progress of a cohort that deposits a normal, lognormal or Paretian distribution of its members over levels of income. The inference we may draw at this stage is that the actual form of the distribution arises because the cohort's chances of advancement diminish at first, then are stabilized, and through the higher levels of income actually rise. But we have given no reason why the cohort should experience any such variation of its advance. The explanation now to be offered proceeds on a distinction between the process of acquiring the ability to work, and the rates at which successive levels of that ability are priced in the market. This distinction was made in one way when Rhodes (1942) posited a 'radix' that was not far off a normal distribution, and applied a transformation to obtain a Paretian distribution. He assumed that the distribution of capacity was described by the same function throughout the population, but that the mode of transformation differed in two arenas: in the one that contained most people, equal increments of capacity brought equal increments of income; but among the minority with the highest incomes, the equation relating income to capacity contained an exponential term. 'The higher up the scale the person is, the more a little extra [capacity] is worth in income. We may say that in the larger group the individuals line themselves up according to an arithmetic progression, while in the smaller group they are ranged according to a geometric progression' (Rhodes 1942: 256).

Our first step must be to account for a normal distribution of the ability to work. But the very notion of a numerical scale of ability needs justification at the outset. That an observer may rank people according to his assessment of their ability will be readily conceded. To this it may be added that a number of observers who have studied the subjects' performance in some detail can generally reach agreement on the ranking order. The objectivity of measurement depends on the availability of a procedure to achieve consensus; where a degree of consensus is present, assessments may claim a degree of objectivity even in the absence of a physical apparatus of measurement. If a ranking order of ability be then allowed, we can suppose so many persons included in it that the differences between any person and his or her next neighbour may be treated as a unit throughout: in this way the scale becomes numerical. We may reach the same conclusion if we consider the tests of ability that have actually been derived in order to measure it, for general tests of aptitude, and tests of intelligence in particular, certainly do usually yield normal distributions. It may well be objected that there is a risk of circularity here, because tests that do not do this will be discarded as biased; the fact remains that it is possible to devise many different tests, all of wide applicability, that do yield normal distributions. These various considerations warrant the heuristic assumption that ability can be measured in a numerical scale.

There is an evident likeness between the processes by which we acquire our ability to work, and those by which a normal distribution can be generated mathematically. In the latter, the cumulation of very many impacts, small in themselves and independent both of one another and of the size of the variate at the moment of impact, is shown to produce a normal distribution. This finds its counterpart in the innumerable successive chances by which people's ability to work is developed, or inhibited, as they proceed along their life-paths. Each of the events in this sequence can be regarded as the drawing of one out of a pack of possibilities (Meade 1974; Phelps Brown 1977: ch. 9). At conception there is the luck of the genetic draw. The child is born into a home that may be less or more propitious to physical, mental and emotional development. At school, and in training and early work experience, all manner of possibilities, helpful and harmful, arise at every stage. The original nucleus of the self can be regarded as subject to a 'molecular bombardment' of influences or chance happenings, each making a minute but cumulative difference to the ability to work that is being developed. Alternatively, we can think of the individual as he proceeds along his life-path being confronted with innumerable successive partings of the ways: one way leads towards greater, the other towards lesser, ability to work. Some people take a sufficient sequence of turnings in the helpful direction to develop their ability to work highly, so that they can proceed to the higher levels of the hill of income. Others have to stay lower down. The effect in the aggregate is that the typical cohort becomes spread over the different levels in numbers that form a normal distribution.

But this is a distribution according to the ability to work, and our concern is with the distribution of income. If our radix is a normal distribution of ability, we need a transformation equation to show how this ability gets priced in the market at its various levels. This equation must account for the transition from normal to lognormal in the middle ranges, and to the Paretian at the top. The pricing, that is to say, proceeds in three stages. At the lowest level, the ability to work is priced at a constant rate, and the distribution of earnings simply reproduces the normal distribution of that ability with a change of scale. As the level under consideration rises, an enhancement factor comes into play increasingly: the payments rise more than in proportion to the ability to work, and the distribution of earnings approximates to the lognormal. In the third phase, at the very top, the enhancement factor becomes so much stronger that the distribution becomes Paretian. We have now to make this process of transformation intelligible.

Whatever the course of change through the lowest levels, we know that, throughout the central segment and at the top, the rate of pay per unit of ability rises; and the rate of rise is faster, the higher the level already attained. If we consider the progress of a cohort, we have to explain why the chances of rising further cease to fall for those who attain the middle range of income, and for those who go beyond that actually rise progressively. Several factors may be suggested. One of these concerns not the rate at which ability is valued, but the degree of ability coming forward. As the cohort goes on, the average ability of the survivors rises, so that the pay that these command will rise without any rise in the rate of pay per unit of ability. But there are reasons to believe that this latter kind of rise will occur. One of these is the premium placed on eminence. The degree of superiority that puts a person ahead of others may be slight, but the fact of being out in front confers a special attraction and prestige. This applies especially to the earnings of the self-employed, in so far as those earnings depend on personal reputation. Again, 'success breeds success'; those who have attained an already high level will have acquired experience, resources and confidence that equip them for further advance. But most important of all is the disparity between the rate at which the potential contribution of posts rises as we move up the hierarchy, and the gradient of ability among those who fill them. Reder (1969: 221) analysed 'job sensitivity'. A job is insensitive 'if there is but a negligible marginal product to a higher degree of any aptitude beyond that commonly possessed by persons filling such jobs. Bank teller is a good example of a job having low sensitivity'; conversely, a sensitive job is one in which a small difference in the aptitude of the incumbent makes a substantial difference to effective operation. It is the extent of this effect, we may infer, and not the degree of aptitude of the ablest available incumbent, that sets a limit on what he or she will be paid. Phelps Brown (1977: 132) following Mayer (1960), noticed the 'scale of operations effect': 'the initial presumption here is that the amount a job is worth depends on the difference the holder of it can make to the product by doing it ably or not so ably'. Reder (1968: 590) gave reason to expect that 'the marginal product of an executive would have a strong positive association with the value of the resources under his control'. Lydall (1968: 132) cites 'surveys of chief executives' salaries in France, Germany, Great Britain, and the United States, which find a general tendency of these salaries to vary with the sales of the firm: as between one firm and another, the proportionate difference between the salaries of the chief executives was from a quarter to a third of the proportionate difference between the firms' sales' (Phelps Brown 1977: 132).

Grubb (1985) has distinguished between personal ability and the power over production inherent in jobs. People can be arrayed by ability, and jobs by power and production, and we may assume that generally the rank order of job-holders by ability will match that of the jobs they hold ranked by power over production; but there is no presumption that the two gradations will be the same. On the contrary, there is every reason to believe that the power over production of successively more advanced jobs rises more rapidly than the ability that suffices to gain access to them; and it is power over production that limits the pay the job will command. 'Ability differentials exceed power differentials at the bottom of the distribution and power differentials exceed ability differentials at the top; this makes earnings approximately proportional to the individual characteristic ability among low earners but approximately proportional to the job characteristic, power, among high earners (Grubb 1985: 194).

In all, these factors will account for the difference between a normal distribution and the lognormal and Paretian forms that more closely characterize the middle and higher parts of actual distributions As members of a cohort rise through the higher income levels, the chances of the survivors at each level having the ability to work that will carry them further up diminish; but because each increment of ability is now remunerated at a higher rate, those lower chances are offset, to maintain chances of a given advancement in terms of money, for most of the lognormal phase, or even to increase them in the Paretian.

The explanation just put forward has this great limitation: although it accounts for an increasing divergence between the actual distribution and a normal one, it does not show why the divergent path should come so close to the lognormal and the Paretian as in fact it does. Because of this deficiency, great interest attaches to the argument that derives a lognormal distribution of income directly from a first principle, the law of proportionate effect (Gibrat 1931; Aitchison and Brown 1957). This law states that, if in the 'molecular bombardment' the random impacts produce effects that are proportional to the size of the variate at the moment of impact, the variates thus moulded will form a lognormal distribution. To apply this in the present context, we must assume that each impact tends to raise or lower income by a small proportion of its momentary value. There are in fact reasons to expect that the successive chances encountered along the life-path will act in this way. It is proportionate and not absolute differentials that historically have maintained themselves in the labour market. We should expect an event that brought an increment of £100 to an income or capital of £5000 to bring one more like £400 to a base of £20 000. We might therefore regard the lognormal distribution as generated by the cumulation of random absolute changes in the logarithm of income; and Champernowne (1973) has given persuasive reasons for treating this 'income-power' as the effective unit of income, even though it does not figure in daily usage.

The 'law of proportionate effect' thus has some intuitive appeal as an explanation of the lognormal phase of the distribution of income. But it does not account for the transition from the lognormal to the Paretian form at the highest levels. The Paretian form itself has been derived from first principles by Champernowne (1953, 1973). Here the individual is regarded as placed initially at some point in a stack of discrete income levels whose intervals are equiproportionate; he or she is assigned equal chances of moving a given distance from starting points at all levels, but is somewhat more likely to move down than up. These assumptions do not find evident counterparts in the real world. The enhancement factor suggested here does at least commend itself as capable of treating the lognormal and Paretian phases continuously, and as resting intelligibly upon the actual workings of the market, despite the inability to account for the conformity of the data to two particular forms, rather than to any other equally consistent with its operation.

Most of the above considerations apply directly to the earnings of employed persons and the self-employed, whereas the distribution they are intended to account for is that of income, and incomes at all levels above the lowest generally contain an element of return on property. Only in the highest incomes, however, is this element considerable. In 1975-6, investment income did not make up as much as 3 per cent of British incomes averaged by quantile group up to the ninth decile. Nor was the proportion systematically related to the level of income: such differences as there were lay between some higher values appearing in the middle range, and some lower ones found above that range as well as below it. A much higher proportion obtained at the top—10 per cent among the top tenth as a whole, and 24 per cent in the top 1 per cent (Royal Commission 1979: table 2.12). If these findings are representative, we can regard an explanation of the distribution of earnings as applicable to that of all income through that part of the hybrid distribution that approximates to the lognormal; but when we come to the Paretian sector, we must bear the contribution of investment income in mind.

The discussion so far has concerned income, but our initial aim was to account for a form of distribution common to both income and *wealth*. Fewer distributions of wealth than of income have been recorded, and in those we have, the Pen profile is liable to show more concavity upwards through much of its course, and consequently to make a more gradual transition to the rapid rise at the top. We have seen that in the United Kingdom the distribution of wealth has changed far more than that of incomes in the course of the present century. But the distribution of wealth over the central segment of the population is likely to conform to that of income there, because so large a part of the wealth held there has been accumulated out of lifetime savings which vary with income. This effect appears to predominate even over that of bequests and transfers *inter vivos*, even though the importance of these, in the United Kingdom, is indicated by several observations. The wealth of younger people is distributed as unequally as that of older (Atkinson 1971; Royal Commission 1977: table 32); the estates of women rise more during the active years of life than do those of men (Inland Revenue statistics, annually); and women's estates have amounted in value to as much as four-fifths of men's (Royal Commission 1977: table J2). None the less, Atkinson (1971: 252) entertained the possibility that 'we can reasonably regard inherited wealth as explaining the share of the top 1 per cent or 5 per cent, but life-cycle factors as explaining the rest of the distribution'. These life-cycle factors work in the same way as those that we have seen shaping the distribution of income in the central sector. The ability to work may be highly correlated with the ability to accumulate wealth.

It is otherwise with the Paretian sector. There are reasons, it is true, for the rule, 'to him that hath shall be given', applying even more powerfully to wealth than to income. It should be possible, by spreading risks on a large portfolio, to obtain a higher average rate of return than the small investor can generally realize. Great wealth forms a mass of manoeuvre that confers power. The expansion of holdings is confined by no such limits as generally circumscribe the market for any one person's work. But such circumstances as these do not form a counterpart to what has been called here the 'enhancement factor'. That factor consisted in a progressive rise, with the income level, in the market valuation of the ability to work. The more rapid expansion of the greater fortunes rests on no such change in valuation: the circumstances conducive to it affect the holdings of wealth directly. We also have to recognize the large part played by inheritance in the greater fortunes. When to this we add the other sources—speculation, enterprise and the occasional big earnings of celebrities—we cannot but be amazed to find the resultant distribution so closely Paretian. That the rate of fall of the advancement function should be checked more strongly for wealth than for income we can well understand; but that the result should be a Paretian and no other form of stretched-out distribution remains mysterious.

15.4. The Formation of Distributions as an Ongoing Process: (i) Incomes

We have seen how the progress of any person through life can be regarded as a succession of decisions between alternative possibilities—decisions made, sometimes *by* that person, more often *for* him or her by external forces or even, it may seem, by chance. This is a way of envisaging the incessant ant-like activity by which the distribution of income and wealth is continually formed. Another way is provided by the study of social mobility. This records the kind of family in which a given person grew up, and what kind of occupation he or she has entered in adult life. The interest of this sort of inquiry lies in the extent to which occupations at a given social level are recruited from the children of those now following them, or from families above or below. The notion of a social level derives from the readiness of most people to say which of two occupations they consider preferable from the point of view of a prospective entrant, or deserving of more esteem from the community. Although there are naturally some differences among individual judgements, and some people find an occupation suits them that would generally be reckoned inferior to others open to them, sufficient consensus is found in practice to establish a ranking of occupations according to their 'general desirability' (Goldthorpe and Hope 1974). Inquiries into social mobility are then designed to find how far people move upwards or downwards from their origins in this hierarchy.

In the principal source of our knowledge of social mobility in England and Wales, namely the inquiry by the Oxford sociologists led by Goldthorpe (1980), seven classes were distinguished. They were formed by grouping occupations with similar rankings in a scale of 'general desirability' (Goldthorpe and Hope 1974). 'We combine occupational categories', says Goldthorpe (1980: 39), 'whose members would appear . . . to be typically comparable, on the one hand, in terms of their sources and levels of income, their degree of economic security and chances of economic advancement; and, on the other, in their location within the system of authority and control governing the process of production in which they are engaged, and hence in their degree of autonomy in performing their work-tasks and roles.' The scale of seven classes is as follows.

I   Higher-grade professionals, administrators and managers; proprietors of large businesses
II   Lower-grade professionals, administrators and managers; higher-grade technicians; supervisors of administrative and clerical employees
III   Routine clerical workers; shop assistants; other non-manual workers in subordinate positions
IV   Farmers; proprietors of small businesses; self-employed workers
V   Supervisors of manual workers; lower-grade technicians
VI   Skilled manual workers
VII   Semi-skilled and unskilled workers; agricultural workers.

These are better called classes than levels, although they do form a hierarchy of esteem. There are a number of salient exceptions to their ranking by income, and there is little in respect of either esteem or income to differentiate classes III, IV and V.

The Oxford inquiry, carried out in 1972, obtained particulars from

10 000 males selected so as to form a sample representative of all males aged 20–64. The kind of movement it found from the family of origin to the occupation being followed at the time of the inquiry appears in Table 15.4.

TABLE 15.4 *Intergenerational mobility in England and Wales: outflow*

The distribution over classes of occupation in 1972 of men aged 20–64 whose fathers were in a given occupational class when the son was aged 14; excluding agricultural occupations

| Class of father | Distribution of men having given class of father (%) | | | | | | | | |
	I	II	III	IV	V	VI	VII	Total	% of all fathers
I	45.7	19.1	11.6	6.8	4.9	5.4	6.5	100	7.9
II	29.4	23.3	12.1	6.0	9.7	10.8	8.6	100	6.4
III	18.6	15.9	13.0	7.4	13.0	15.7	16.4	100	8.0
IV	14.0	14.4	9.1	21.1	9.9	15.1	16.3	100	10.3
V	14.4	13.7	10.2	7.7	15.9	21.4	16.8	100	12.5
VI	7.8	8.8	8.4	6.4	12.4	30.6	25.6	100	30.0
VII	7.1	8.5	8.8	5.7	12.9	24.8	32.2	100	24.8
% of all sons	14.3	12.2	9.6	8.0	12.0	22.0	21.8		100

Source: Goldthorpe (1980: table 2.2).

A first and salient finding is that a great deal of movement, both upward and downward, is going on throughout the structure. Of the boys who began life in any one class of home, as classified by the father's occupation, some were found in adult life in each of the seven classes; some who began in the lowest class had gone to the top, some who began at the top had sunk to the bottom. But this movement was far from uniform. Those who began in each of the classes III, IV and V spread themselves fairly evenly over the other classes; those who began above and below that central bloc were much more concentrated in their class or origin and the adjacent classes. This tendency was most marked at the very top and bottom: nearly a half of the boys who began in class I has been able to stay in it, about a third of those who began in class VII remained there. The difference in those proportions calls our attention to a general preponderance of upward movement. This we can ascribe to the relative extension of the higher occupations: more than a quarter of the sons were in classes I and II, but only about an eighth of the fathers had been. At the same time, class VII contracted somewhat; but most of the upward movement came from outside the ranks of the manual workers—the proportion of the sons of classes III, IV and V who entered the top two classes was double that of the sons of classes VI and VII.

In respect of mobility, evidently we can divide the whole structure into three groups. The two classes at the top and the two at the bottom each form a group that is largely self-recruiting, and sends out relatively few of its sons into other classes. The middle three grades—mainly clerical and service workers, small businessmen and foremen—are transit camps, which receive many men coming down from above and up from below, and send many of their own sons out in each direction. The top and bottom blocs are also distinguished in that only in them does short-range mobility predominate; that is, only in them does the amount of movement diminish steadily with the distance moved. But although this emphasizes the distinctness of manual occupations, we have seen that nearly a sixth of the sons of manual fathers in classes VI and VII did make their way into the top two classes.

So far we have been starting with the sons' origins, and asking what classes of occupations the sons from a given class of home had reached by 1972: But we can also turn the question round, start with the sons already arrived in a given class of occupation, and ask from what classes of home they had set out. When we do this the extent of movement throughout the structure is made even clearer. This is shown in Table 15.5. The members

TABLE 15.5   *Intergenerational mobility in England and Wales: inflow*

The distribution over the class of occupation followed by the father when the son was aged 14, of men aged 20–64 in a given class in 1972

Class of son	Distribution of fathers of men in given class (%)								% of all sons
	I	II	III	IV	V	VI	VII	Total	
I	25.3	13.1	10.4	10.1	12.5	16.4	12.1	100	14.3
II	12.4	12.2	10.4	12.2	14.0	21.7	17.1	100	12.2
III	9.6	8.0	10.8	9.8	13.2	26.1	22.6	100	9.6
IV	6.7	4.8	7.4	27.2	12.1	24.0	17.8	100	8.0
V	3.2	5.2	8.7	8.6	16.6	31.1	26.7	100	12.0
VI	2.0	3.1	5.7	7.1	12.2	41.8	28.0	100	22.0
VII	2.4	2.5	6.0	7.7	9.6	35.2	36.6	100	21.8
% of all fathers	7.9	6.4	8.0	10.3	12.5	30.0	24.8		100

Source: Goldthorpe (1980: table 2.1).

of each class are drawn in some number from homes in every one of the other classes. It is not even true of them all that they come mostly from homes in their own and the immediately adjacent classes: the proportion who do so lies between 30 and 40 per cent in the top three classes, is rather more than a half in the next two, and is really high only in the two manual classes. The greater variety of origins near the top may be ascribed in part to the expansion of openings there, but it is evidence also for the effectiveness of the educational ladder. The outcome is that 70 per cent of the men in the two top classes had come from homes in classes below. This contrasts with the sons engaged in manual work, since among them it was 70 per cent who came from homes in the same class.

We lack evidence for the course of mobility in Great Britain in earlier years. The pioneer inquiry by David Glass (1954) in 1949 is not directly comparable with the Oxford inquiry that has just been drawn upon. But some indications are provided by a cohort analysis of the findings of these two inquiries—that is, by dividing all the respondents according to their decades of birth, and calculating the amount of movement among those born in each decade. The outcome is shown in Table 15.6. The main sources of changes in mobility in the course of time will be the rate of growth of the economy, which affects the rate at which higher-grade openings are being created, and the educational system, changes in which have increased the opportunities for children from homes of straitened means to advance their education. Both sorts of change will have contributed to the rise of upward mobility in the cohorts born after the First World War; these men were all able while still young to take advantage of the economic expansion after the Second World War. Little change appears earlier, unless we accept the strangely divergent figures for the cohort born before 1890. The apparent excess of downward over upward mobility among all those born before the end of the First World War may be due to the comparatively restricted growth of the economy during their early adult life, but it might arise from a tendency among respondents to elevate their fathers' status as they reported it. For earlier years we lack even these indications, although it has been argued that there were phases of high social mobility following the dissolution of the monasteries (Stone 1966) and in the industrial revolution (Pollard 1965).

A strong light is thrown on the sources of change by Harold Perkin's study of 'elites in British society since 1880' (1981): 151–67). The data abstracted from this and presented in Table 15.7 show how the effect of parental wealth has been decreasing, and that of educational opportunity increasing, as a means of advancement to high positions. It is likely that, if corresponding figures could be obtained for those who reached intermediate but substantial professional, administrative and executive positions, they would show no less forcibly this rise of education as a source of social mobility. But by 1970 education has taken much less effect in business than in the civil service.

Some inquiries that go further back in other countries indicate remarkably little change. Blau and Duncan (1967: 113), in a review of retrospective studies in the United States, found that 'what is most striking . . . is the essential invariance of the father–son correlation over a period of nearly 40 years'. One of those studies (Rogoff 1953), which compared the nexus between the occupations of father and son in Indianapolis in 1905–12 and 1938–41, found that, although that nexus changed in particular

TABLE 15.6   *Analysis of reported mobility by cohorts, pre-1890–1938–47*

Cohorts of those born pre-1890 to 1920–9: in Glass's sample in England, Wales and Scotland, 1949; from 1908–17 to 1938–47: in the Oxford sample in England and Wales in 1972

	Pre-1890	1890–9	1900–9	1910–19 1908–17	1920–9 1918–27	1928–37	1938–47
% upwardly mobile	16.5	23.3	23.2	21.2 19.9	20.9 24.5	30.5	30.5
% downwardly mobile	33.0	25.9	24.6	24.6 25.3	25.3 23.2	20.4	21.0
No.	679	540	751	772 1687	756 1498	2019	2191

Source: Heath (1981: table 3.2), drawing on Glass (1954: 186–7), and Goldthorpe (1980: ch. 3).

TABLE 15.7   *Sources of some élite in Great Britain, 1880–1970*

Proportion of persons attaining given positions from working-class origins, together with the average estates left by fathers of persons in given position. The 'working class' includes supervisory and white-collar occupations.

	1880–99	1900–19	1920–39	1949–50	1960–70
Conservative Cabinet					
working-class parents (%)	—	1.9	—	1.3	—
Father's estate (1913 £000)	80.4	52.4	58.6	31.4	7.3
Top civil servants, working-					
class parents (%)	1.8	4.0	10.7	11.2	19.0
Father's estate, (1913 £000)	14.8	11.7	3.9	1.7	1.3
Big company chairmen,					
working-class parents (%)	6.3	7.3	6.3	6.9	9.9
Father's estate, (1913 £000)	108.1	72.8	49.5	30.9	8.8

Source: Perkin (1981: 151–67, Appendix, tables 2, 5).

occupations, in both periods 'about 70 per cent of the men were in occupations different from those of their fathers' (p. 107). A study of the same nexus in Copenhagen was actually able to go back to 1838–42 by use of military enrolment lists: Rishøj (1971: 139) reported that 'in a preindustrial or early industrial community of Copenhagen we find the same rate of mobility as in the modern industrial Copenhagen'. These soundings indicate that social mobility is a process of marked generality in Western countries, and marked persistence through time.

But international comparisons in recent years indicate some differences. They lie, it is true, in a statistical minefield. It is not only that classifications differ, partly by the choice of the investigator, but also according to the various arrangements of occupations in different countries. The difficulty is also that, even when we are satisfied that a boundary is drawn in the same place in two countries, the amount of movement across it depends on the relative size of the classes above and below it, and on the rate at which they are growing or contracting. Our main interest in social mobility usually arises from the light it throws on society—on how far young people are held back or helped forward by the circumstances of their childhood, on what obstacles are set in the way of advancement by conventional attitudes, and on what education and training are accessible. It is these things that we think of when we ask whether a society is 'open'. But it is hard to separate propulsion from traction: how many people with a given background rise in the social scale, and how far, depends on the number of openings in the upper reaches. That the earlier cohorts in Table 15.6 show an excess of downward movement was attributed to the impact of economic depression on the number of higher-grade jobs. In assessing the significance of the upward movement into the two top classes in later years, we had to allow for their expansion between the fathers' time and the sons'. Similarly, in international comparisons we cannot conclude that in the society where more people rise careers are basically more open to talents, until we have allowed for any expansion in the number of higher-grade jobs: the greater movement may be only the reflex of a transient phase of economic growth.

A guide through the minefield is provided by Anthony Heath (1981: Appendix II). He concludes, in effect, that, whatever measure of movement we use, we have to keep an eye on the size of the receiving class. This is evidently so when we simply count the proportions that cross a boundary, such as that between the manual and the non-manual classes. But it is also so when we use the measure of mobility that is unaffected by changes in the relative size of classes between generations, namely the 'odds ratio'. This compares the chances of people originating, for example, in the homes of manual workers with those of people in the top class finding jobs in that top class: if 7 per cent of the sons of manual workers do this compared with 49 per cent of the sons of men in the top class, then the odds ratio is 7. Even here, in international comparisons we need to allow for differences in the size of the top class as that has been defined in different countries: the more widely it is defined, the more occupations will it include that are easier to enter.

With this caution in mind, we may consider the comparisons in Table 15.8. Here we have begun with data for 19 countries provided by Heath (1981): tables 7.1, 7.2) of the mobility between the manual and non-manual classes—that is, the total movement upwards and downwards across the boundary between them, expressed as a percentage of the total number in the two classes combined. Heath also provides for the same countries the size of the non-manual class as a proportion of all occupied men, and the proportionate change in the size of this class between the fathers' generation and the sons'. We expect that, where the non-manual class is relatively large, and has grown greatly, a greater number of manual workers will have moved into it, simply because there have been more openings in it; and the data confirm this expectation. If we find more mobility in one country than another, this may be simply because economic development has made more openings there, and not because its institutions and attitudes have been more propitious to movement. Mobility, for instance, was substantially lower in Finland than in Hungary, but, whereas the non-manual class had increased by less than a half in Finland, in Hungary it had more than trebled. To take this kind of effect out, we have calculated the relationship prevailing through the 19 countries between the size and growth of the non-manual class and the extent of mobility. For each country we have calculated the mobility that this relationship leads us to expect, and compared it with the mobility actually recorded.

TABLE 15.8 *International comparison of mobility between manual and non-manual classes*

Excess of actual mobility between manual and non-manual classes over the mobility that would be expected on the basis of the general relation between such mobility and (a) the relative size of the non-manual class, (b) the change in that size between the generations of the fathers and the sons

	Excess of actual over expected mobility (percentage points)
(1) Sweden (1974)	6.7
(2) USA (1973)	5.9
(3) USSR (1967–68)	5.2
(4) Australia (1965)	4.7
(5) England & Wales (1972)	4.4
(6) France (1970)	3.9
(7) Canada (1974)	3.3
(8) Norway (1972)	2.4
(9) Denmark (1972)	1.4
(10) Finland (1972)	0.4
(11) Bulgaria (1967)	0.2
(12) Poland (1972)	− 1.2
(13) Yugoslavia (1960)	− 2.2
(14) Italy (1963)	− 2.7
(15) Belgium (1968)	− 5.0
(16) Hungary (1973)	− 5.1
(17) Japan (1965)	− 5.5
(18) West Germany (1969)	− 6.1
(19) Spain (1974)	− 6.6

Source: Calculated by present author from data of mobility (M), size of non-manual class (S) and increase in size of that class (R), in Heath (1981: tables 7.1, 7.2). The regression equation is $M = 12.8 + 0.33S + 0.06R$

Whether, as so often, the differences apparent in Table 15.8 strike us as remarkably small, when found among countries distinguished from one another in so many other respects, or large enough to denote significant contrasts of institutions and attitudes between those countries, depends on the expectations with which we set out. But we can note some intelligible distinctions, and others that remain perplexing. The primacy of Sweden may well mark the effects of half a century of Social Democratic government there. In the high ranking of the United States and Australia, we may see the freedom of movement in a society formed by migrants who leave the stratification of the old countries behind them; yet two countries of the Old World—England and Wales and France—are close to Australia. The high ranking of the USSR marks it out from the three Soviet-type economies, Bulgaria, Poland and Hungary, and also from Yugoslavia: these other countries all experienced a much greater expansion of the non-manual class than did the USSR, and after allowance for this their societies appear to be less conducive to mobility than the Soviet Union. The countries in which mobility falls below expectation are strangely assorted—three Soviet-type, three Western democracies (Italy, Belgium and West Germany) and two with feudal traditions or a recent fascist government (Japan and Spain). What we can probably infer here is that rapid economic development—in Italy, Japan, West Germany and Spain—is no guarantee of heightened mobility; and this conflicts with the expectation noted above as seemingly borne out by some phases of rapid change in the British social and economic structure. Evidently, mobility depends on a complex of factors, and the presence of the same salient factor in two countries or periods does not warrant the expectation that mobility will have been similar there. The apparent lack of consistency in the findings may also arise from the limitations and divergencies of the original inquiries.

The caution thus inspired will be heightened when we go on to compare countries in respect of one particular but socially significant form of mobility—the openness of the élite. Heath (1981: table 7.3) has provided data of the élite/non-manual odds ratio in 11 countries. This ratio, it will be remembered, expresses the chance of the son of the élite father finding his way into an élite occupation, as a multiple of the chance of the son of a non-manual father doing so. This last chance will evidently tend to be greater, and the odds ratio consequently smaller, the larger the relative size of the élite.

The data provided by Heath show wide differences in this relative size. We can make some allowance for them by calculating the prevailing relation between this relative size and the odds ratio, and taking the difference between the actual ratio and the ratio that this relation would lead us to expect. If the actual falls short of the expected ratio, the relative chances of a non-manual worker's son entering the élite are higher than would generally be associated with the size of the élite in that case; and conversely. Our findings appear in Table 15.9. We see at once that the two countries that showed the most mobility across the line btween manual and non-manual, namely Sweden and the United States, are well down the array of the 11 countries now considered. On the other hand, Yugoslavia and Hungary, which were low in that array, now appear at the top. But there is some consistency in the showing of the remainder: Australia, England and Wales and France show relatively high mobility according to both tests; equally, Italy, Japan, West Germany and Spain remain low. Where differences appear between the arrays, we do not know how far they mark real differences in mobility at the two levels in the countries concerned and how far they arise only out of differences in the collection of data. The similarities we find, however, are sufficient to warrant belief in the influence of factors that are specific in kind or size to the countries concerned, and operate throughout them.

TABLE 15.9 *International comparison of chances of entering the élite*

Excess of the actual élite/manual odds ratio over the ratio expected on the basis of the proportionate size of the élite, in 11 countries. This ratio expresses the chance of the son of an élite father finding his way into an élite occupation, as a multiple of the chance of the son of a non-élite father doing so

	Odds ratio: excess of actual over expected (percentage pts.)
(1) Yugoslavia (1968)	− 3.1
(2) Hungary (1973)	− 2.1
(3) Australia (1965)	− 1.8
(4) England and Wales (1972)	− 1.3
(5),(6) France (1970) Sweden (1974)	− 0.5
(7) Japan (1965)	0.1
(8) W. Germany (1969)	0.6
(9) USA (1973)	1.2
(10) Spain (1974)	3.5
(11) Italy (1963)	3.9

Source: calculated by the present author from data provided by Heath (1981: table 7.3). The regression equation was: odds ratio = 6.17 − 0.175 (relative size of élite)

All the estimates considered so far have been for men. In all societies, women as earners and recipients of income have followed such distinctive paths that figures of the mobility of men and women in the aggregate would be confusing. But until comparatively recently, investigators have also had reason to believe that the mobility of women was quantitatively a much smaller object of study, simply because the great majority of women were married, and did not obtain monetary income from employment or self-employment. In more recent years, however, there has been a marked change in attitudes and practice: increasingly, women have come to regard the years of child-rearing as an interval in a career which they will continue to pursue; and the combination of work in the home and paid employment has been facilitated by the increase of part-time jobs.

It is therefore of growing interest to see how far women move upwards and downwards in the occupational scale through the jobs they take; and thanks to Heath (1981: ch. 4), we can use particulars of the family origins and present occupations of a sample of women collected in 1975 by the British General Household Survey. The findings prove to be dominated by what Heath terms 'the enormous concentration [of women] in "women's work"'—their employment as secretaries, shop assistants, clerks, telephone operators, waitresses, cooks and hardressers' (pp. 116–17). 'Class discrimination divides men, but sexual discrimination brings women together' (p. 135). This means that women as a whole have fewer chances of upward mobility than men: more girls than boys have to move downwards from the occupational class of their fathers, and the women who are potentially mobile upwards find fewer openings at the top. Even where a wife is earning at the same time as her husband, if he is the principal earner the choice of jobs is limited to the district in which his work anchors him, and she is not free to move on promotion. On the other hand, the jobs conventionally assigned to women provide openings for girls from manual workers' homes, and although the pay is lower than in some manual jobs, the conditions of work are generally regarded as making those openings more desirable.

If we are concerned with class not in the occupational but in a wider social sense, it is to be remembered that married women share their husband's status. But the figures of 'marital mobility' that Heath (1981: Table 4.1) has drawn from the Oxford survey show 'a great deal of "marrying up" that is balanced by other women "marrying down". . . The typical father from Class I is more likely . . . to have a son-in-law of lower social class than his son. Conversely, a girl from classes VI or VII is more likely to be upwardly mobile than her brother' (p. 113).

Single women do show much upward mobility, and little downward. But this can hardly be taken to show what openings there are for women provided they escape the restraints of marriage. The more probable explanation is that single women have remained such, whether deliberately or unconsciously, by reason of the same drive as carries them forward in their careers.

In sum, the conclusion stands that in Britain in the 1970s women's chances of upward mobility were much smaller than men's. On the evidence of the sample in the General Household Survey, it appears that, whereas the percentage of men who moved up was much greater than the percentage who moved down—32 as against 19—the corresponding percentage for women, 27 and 26, hardly differed from each other (Heath 1981: 116).

Social mobility is a powerful determinant of the degree of inequality as that is experienced by the members of any society. At one extreme we can envisage a society in which there is little difference between the incomes attached to the various posts, but where most people are confined to the kind of post occupied by their parents, and have no prospect of going up in the world. At the other extreme would be a society in which differences are wide but many people are upwardly mobile. Although this is offset by many other people moving down, the higher incomes will still seem less far removed from the lower when many people are seen to move between the two, and there is no denial of access to the higher ones. Snapshots of those two societies, recording their inequalities as they stood at any moment, would certainly show the second one as the more unequal; but when we took account of the changes occurring in the lifetime of the people there, we might doubt whether it was they who would feel the greater awareness or resentment of inequality. Their attitudes would be affected by the association of mobility with personal qualities, which would bring differences of income into more evident agreement with those of capability. This effect of mobility on perceptions of inequality is additional to that other effect, already noticed (p. 403), of considering incomes over lifetimes instead of at any one moment—namely, the rearrangement of differences between occupations.

How powerfully the extent of mobility affects the perception of inequality is brought out by an observation of de Tocqueville (1958). During his travels in England in 1833, he noted that what distinguished the English aristocracy

from all others is the ease with which it has opened its ranks . . . With great riches, anybody could hope to enter [it] . . . As everybody had the hope of being among the privileged, the privileges made the aristocracy, not more hated, but more valued. The reason why the French nobles were the butt of all hatreds, was not chiefly that only the nobles had a right to everything, but because nobody could become a noble . . . (de Tocqueville 1958: 59)

15.5. The Formation of Distributions as an Ongoing Process: (ii) Wealth

The evidence that we have examined for the distribution of wealth reveals it as the outcome of a persistent and pervasive process. It is one of growth and dispersal. We can apply to it the analogy that Marshall used for the structure of an industry containing firms of various sizes and ages, which he likened to the trees of a forest that itself remains much the same while particular trees grow and fall. No one tree grows until it has ousted all its neighbours; there are forces at work that check growth and ultimately reverse it. But these processes of reduction do not destroy the forest; while one tree is breaking up, another is growing. Here is an 'ensemble renouvelé', an enduring aggregation of transient components. So it is with wealth holdings. In some people's hands wealth is accumulated, and after a time growth may be promoted not only by the personal qualities of the holder but also by the power of manoeuvre provided by the resources already in hand. The individual fortune grows by the creation of new assets and by taking existing ones over from other people. But this process does not go on until one person or family becomes possessed of most of the wealth of the whole community. In various ways, the growth of holdings is checked; and then they are dispersed. We shall examine the forces at work in these processes of accumulation and dispersal, in turn.

We know that people accumulate wealth by saving out of their income and by gifts from other people, whether as bequests or transfers *inter vivos*.

What has been the relative size of these sources in recent years? Answers have been sought in two ways. One begins with the bequests and transfers, and estimates the part of present holdings that they have contributed. The other considers the building up of holdings, and their possible attrition, through the changing balance of income and consumption in the life-cycle of the individual.

The first path was followed when an estimate of the part played by bequests and transfers was made for the Royal Commission (1977: ch. 9; see Jones 1978). Here the 'perpetual inventory' method of measuring capital was adapted to the estimation of inheritances. The basic principle appears if we suppose that everyone dies at age 70, and makes bequests to children then aged 40: the total amount of the bequests received by people alive at any time would then be given by the sum of the bequests made in the preceding 30 years. The actual ages at death and inheritance are immaterial: the essential parameter is the interval between them, taken as 30 years in the example. The actual value of this span in England and Wales in 1973, as given by the average age of the father at the birth of a child, was 29 years. If we had only this to bear in mind, then all we should have to do to estimate the total value of bequests received by persons now living would be to sum all the estates left during the past 29 years—after reducing them to currency units of constant purchasing power, by applying an index number of asset prices.

But of course, the world is not so simple as that. Testators do not simply leave their estates to their children, but make bequests to other relatives and friends of various ages, as well as to charity. To find out what they actually do, Elfryn Jones drew upon a survey of wills made for the Royal Commission. This provided the prevailing pattern of bequests by each of four types of testator—married and unmarried men, widows and single women. (He did not have to consider the wills of married women because, as we shall see, he assumed that these all survived their husbands, and would therefore make bequests only as widows.) But all that the wills show is that a certain proportion of the estate was left to a surviving wife, or to the second or sometimes the third generation, or to friends. To obtain the needed spans between the date of bequests and the recipient's own death, Jones applied some demographic assumptions. He assumed that the experiences of all persons were those found as the average of the whole population of England and Wales in 1972–4. Thus, in his model all men would die at age 71 and women at 77. Of the men, 90 per cent were married to wives three years younger than themselves, so that after the husband's death at age 71 the wife lived for nine years as a widow. The numbers of men and women were taken to be the same at all ages; it followed that 10 per cent of the women were single. The second generation was assumed to be 29 years younger than the testator, so that they inherited at age 42 from their fathers dying aged 71, and nine years later, at age 51, from their mothers, dying nine years after their husbands. The third generation, taking off 29 years again, was assumed to inherit when aged 22.

On these assumptions, we can trace the flows of inheritance, both the bequests that reach recipients directly from the father and those that are, so to speak, passed on by the mother at her death later. These flows are given as percentages of the estate typically left by men, or again by women, but we do not know how big the typical woman's estate is relatively to the man's. This relative size can be calculated, however, because the model forms a closed system in which a given amount of assets is being circulated, and the relative size of women's estates must be such that the flows of bequests provide the recipients with that amount of assets in all. The ratio proves to be 2.4. This seems strangely large at first, when in recent years the value of estates left by women has been only four-fifths that of men's (Royal Commission 1977: table J2). But that proportion applies to the sum of assets acquired by men and women alike from all sources, whereas here we are dealing only with the transfer of an existing stock: 'in a closed system in which there is no saving out of income and in which bequests remain intact from the remaining lifetime of the recipient' (Royal Commission, 1977: para. 410), far more of that part of the circulation which is channelled through men flows to women than to men, while women in addition receive a substantial part of the estates of other women.

The next step is to turn these flows, expressed in units of a notional stock, into money values. The flow to men aged 42 is 12 per cent of men's estates (or more strictly, 12×0.97 per cent, to allow for the share of charities). At any one time there will be some men who have just reached the age of 42; others who were 42 last year, and are presumed to carry forward the bequests they received then; others again, now aged 44, who received their bequests two years ago; and so on—for 29 years, that is, until we reach men now aged 71, the age of death. To find the sum of bequests received at age 42 by men now living, we have therefore to take about 12 per cent of the total estates left by men over the past 29 years. The required amounts are available from the returns of estate duty; they need to be deflated by an index number of the price of assets (Royal Commission 1977: Tables J2, J1).

This procedure leads to the estimates shown in Table 15.10. In the aggregate, it appears, the bequests that decedents have themselves received have amounted to only about a fifth of the value of the estates they leave. These estates provide a sample of the size and composition of the wealth of all persons at the time. It thus appears that only a fifth of this wealth has been acquired by inheritance; the rest has come from lifetime saving and from profits.

But this conclusion requires two qualifications. One is that, at best, this

TABLE 15.10   *Inheritances relatively to total wealth*

The estimated value of inheritances that have been received by the present holders
of wealth in England and Wales in 1973, as a percentage of the total of that wealth
estimated by the estate duty method

Type of holder	(1) Inheritances (£b)	(2) Total wealth (£b)	(3) (1) as % of (2)	
Men	10.6	99.3	10.7	
Married women	8.5	31.7	26.8	34.8
Unmarried women	14.0	32.9	42.6	
TOTAL	33.1	163.9	20.2	

Source: Royal Commission (1977: table 90).

estimate only aggregates the (deflated) values of bequests as they stood
when received. We do not know how they have changed by the time of the
recipient's death. The form of estimate supposes that they have been kept
intact, but they may actually have been dissipated, or developed and
expanded. The other qualification is that the estimate so far has taken no
account of transfers before death. The estate duty returns do not include
the value of gifts *inter vivos* made more than seven years before death, or
that of settled property which is exempt from duty. The Royal Commission
estimated that these would add 15–20 per cent and 5 per cent respectively
to the reported amounts (1977: Appendix 1). Taking them together, it
appears from this model that the value of transmissions received by present
wealth-holders in England and Wales in 1973 may have amounted to about
a quarter of the total value of their present holdings. The remainder will
have been accumulated by savings out of earnings and the yield of assets
already acquired, and by making profits through enterprise and
speculation.

The second basis for estimating the relative contributions of savings and
inheritance to personal holdings has been found in the life-cycle. A great
part of the existing inequality of wealth can be accounted for simply on the
assumption that most people enter adult life with little wealth, but build
their holdings up progressively until retirement. Consider even a society so
egalitarian in some respects that there were no bequests or transfers, and all
the people in each age group earned exactly the same: then, it has been
held, if earnings rose with age as they generally do now, and people saved a
given proportion of their current incomes, the resultant inequality of
holdings between older and younger people would approach the actual
inequality of holdings amassed from all sources.

Several estimates have been made of the amount of distribution of wealth that would result from lifetime savings alone. They suggest that those savings, in Great Britain and the United States, can account for not more than half of all wealth: the rest must have been acquired by bequest and transfer, and through the profits of enterprise and speculation. White (1978) made a model to simulate the savings being made in the United States, in 1953, 1959 and 1964. The structure was provided by assumptions of the life-cycle theory concerning 'a lifetime income stream [and] a lifetime optional consumption path' for the people in each age group (p. 549, n. 6). The model 'in its original form' proved to account for 'at best, 42 per cent of observed personal saving'; 'the inclusion of families and upward sloping lifetime income streams *reduces* the simulated value of aggregate saving' (p. 559). Kotlikoff and Summers (1981) worked from records of income and consumption to calculate by difference the net worth that would have been accumulated in the United States in 1974 according to the life-cycle hypothesis. Their estimate was that such accumulation would have accounted for rather less than 20 per cent of the total net wealth—a much lower proportion than White arrived at.

The staff of the Royal Commission (1977: Appendix K) made a model of lifetime savings that was painstaking in its representation of actual circumtances. We expect the amount of savings to vary with the sex, age and occupation of the person concerned, and the aim of the model-builders was to construct a population subdivided by those characteristics and with the appropriate relative numbers in each subdivision. The population taken was not the actual one but a steady-state population—that is, one in which the number in each subdivision was what would appear if a constant number of births sufficed to hold the total population constant, given the actual recent mortality rates. To each age group of men and of women was applied a representative activity rate, to give the number 'economically active'; and earnings were assigned to each such number according to the levels recently prevailing in each group defined by age, sex and social class. It was then assumed that saving out of those earnings went on at 7 per cent of earnings before tax throughout, although other possibilities, including accumulation at compound interest, were investigated. Allowance was made for dissaving in old age and during periods of unemployment; in particular, it was assumed that from retirement onwards capital would be drawn down at the rate of 2 per cent per annum, so that someone retiring at 65 would still have 80 per cent of his capital left at the age of 80.

The outcome was that, as long as compound interest was not brought in, the accumulated total savings appeared likely to make up half the total assets held by persons; with compound interest reckoned, they would account for very nearly all of it. The actual figures are, for total net wealth of the United Kingdom in 1973, £215b (Royal Commission 1977: Table 36); total accumulated savings, on the assumption of a 7 per cent saving ratio throughout, £105–108b, or, if compound interest was brought in,

£212.5b (Table K14). This last figure goes beyond belief; it leaves no room for transfers or for accumulation out of capital gains as distinct from income. But the proportion of one-half for lifetime savings can be accepted as the order of magnitude arising from a careful and well-founded estimate. It compares fairly closely with White's estimate for the United States.

One significant finding from the Royal Commission model was that savings would form a much lower proportion of the big holdings than of the small; how much so appears in Table 15.11. Savings, it appears here, make

TABLE 15.11   *Savings as a proportion of all assets at different levels of wealth*

Estimated accumulated savings as a proportion of all assets held by quantile groups of holders (as adjusted by personal sector balance sheet), United Kingdom, *c.* 1974

Quantile group	Savings as ratio of all assets (%)
Top 1 %	25
96–99%	48
91–95%	63
81–90%	75
Bottom 80%	100

Source: Royal Commission (1977: Appendix K, para. 17).

up only a quarter of the top 1 per cent of holdings, but provide the whole of those of the bottom 80 per cent; although all these last are credited with no assets other than their savings, only because of inability to subdivide this range. It must have been the same variation with size of holding that Atkinson (1971: 252) had in mind when he entertained the possibility that 'we can reasonably regard inherited wealth as explaining the share of the top 1 per cent or 5 per cent, but life-cycle factors as explaining the rest of the distribution'. Working with the Inland Revenue statistics of British estates in 1963–7, he concluded that the distribution of holdings below the top 5 per cent was 'not too different from some of the more unequal distributions generated in the hypothetical egalitarian society' in which wealth was acquired by the life-cycle of savings alone. When we remove the big holdings to which savings have contributed comparatively little, we find that those savings might conceivably account for most of the rest.

We thus have two estimates which, to say the least, are some way apart from each other: the one suggests that savings may be responsible for half, the other for three-quarters, of all accumulation. When we think of the importance that has been attached to inheritance, even the lower of these proportions seems high. But in the United States, at least, it is the higher proportion that seems to be nearer the mark. We have seen (p. 357) that a sampling inquiry by the Brookings Institution into persons with incomes of $10 000 or more in 1961 indicated that only one-seventh of their aggregate wealth had been acquired by inheritance (Barlow *et al.* 1966); but, whereas Elfryn Jones corrected the value of gifts and bequests at the time of their transmission by an index of the prices of assets down to the year in which current holdings were valued, in this Brookings study it was the original value of legacies that was compared with current holdings. A later study, on comparing this and other studies with estate duty records, found reason to believe that the surveys had failed to uncover a large part of the assets actually held, but still concluded 'that inherited wealth amounted for only "about 12 per cent of 1959 household wealth" ' (Davies 1978; quoted here from Harrison 1979: para. 70).

These proportions apply to wealth in the aggregate. A study of the United States in 1969–70 by Wolff (1983) reminds us that the proportion is likely to be very different at different levels. Wolff divides all 'household disposable wealth' not into lifetime savings and transfers, but into 'life-cycle wealth' and 'capital wealth'. 'Life-cycle wealth' is made up of 'equity in owner-occupied housing, durables, household inventory, demand deposits and currency, and the cash value of life insurance and pensions less consumer debt'. 'Capital wealth' contains 'time and savings deposits, bonds and securities, corporate stock, business equity, net equity in investment real estate, and trust fund equity'. Most items under each head might be acquired either by saving or by inheritance and making profits, but the main source of 'life-cycle wealth' for most people will be saving, while inheritance and profits will be a very considerable source of 'capital wealth'. Wolff found that 'life-cycle wealth' was much the more evenly distributed of the two: its concentration was nearer that of income. 'Only 58 per cent of households owned some form of "capital wealth" ' (Wolff 1983: 142), whereas 'among the top wealth groups' some 80 per cent of all wealth took that form (p. 125); in the group holding $500 000 or more the proportion was 97 per cent (p. 145). So Wolff concluded that 'households that do accumulate wealth over the life-cycle do so mainly for own use (housing, durables, inventory), liquidity (currency and demand deposits), and retirement (pensions and life insurance cash value). Capital wealth, on the other hand, is accumulated by another class and very likely for other reasons such as power and control' (p. 142).

In so far as present holdings of wealth have been formed by savings during the holder's lifetime, the inequality of holdings will be linked with differences of age, between those who have begun to earn and save only recently and those who have been saving for some time. Does this link between age and wealth actually appear? Answering this question will provide a check on the estimates that have approached savings directly.

The ready way to see how wealth varies with age is to take the estates of those dying in each decade of life as a sample of all the holdings of people of that age. There is always this difficulty, that those who die young in any one year form a small and erratic sample; but Table 15.12 shows the

TABLE 15.12   *Variation of wealth with age*

Average net capital of estates left by men and by women in given age group at death, in Great Britain, on the average of the ten years 1972/3–1981/82 (current £s); 'houshold disposable wealth' classified by age of head of household, USA, economic data of 1969, demographic of 1970 (current $)

GB, 1972/3–1981/2			USA, 1969/70	
Age group	Men (£)	Women (£)	Age group	Heads of household ($)
Under 25	4 349	2 837	Under 25	17 745
25–34	11 292	8 763	25–34	27 404
35–44	14 325	11 564	35–44	36 688
45–54	14 909	12 270	45–54	48 637
55–64	15 092	14 937	55–64	63 668
65–74	16 643	15 223	65 & over	64 798
75–84	17 525	14 795		
85 +	19 237	15 068		

Sources, GB, *Inland Revenue Statistics*, annual issues 1974–83; USA; Wolff (1983: table 5).

average of ten years in Great Britain, 1972/3–1981/2. It also offers for comparison the corresponding figures for one year, within the same period, in the United States. At first sight the British data are surprising. If indeed half or as much as three-quarters of all wealth has been saved out of income or the profits of enterprise and speculation, then people's wealth will rise with their age, at least until retirement. Women, again, with their limited opportunities for saving, will accumulate much less than men. But this is not what we find in Great Britain. A rise there was in men's estates: it amounts to fully a third over the thirty years of life from age 30 onwards; but this is less than we should look for, if people generally start with next to no accumulated savings in their twenties, but by the end of their working lives amass those savings to make up three-quarters of their holdings. On that assumption, their total holdings should have been multiplied meanwhile by a factor of nearly four. The factor recorded for the United States is well over two. Again, why did men's estates rise nearly as much in the thirty years or so of old age from age 60 onwards as in the thirty years before? And if estates were increased mainly by savings out of income, why was the rise in women's estates, over the active years of life, much greater than that in men's (it was a rise of nearly three-quarters)? What we know, moreover, about prevailing ages at death, and the age gap between decedents and heirs, makes us expect a noticeable rise in estates as legacies accrue to people in their forties; but no such rise appears. The fall in women's estates in old age, again, was negligible: those estates were virtually constant from age 60 onwards.

One consideration about the source of this evidence makes it less surprising. It consists, namely, of estates as valued for estate duty: savings in the form of pension rights or annuities disappear at death. Estates below the exemption limit, moreover, are mostly not reported at all, so that the reported estates of those who die young do not include those who start with little but would have gone on, if they had lived, to accumulate substantial holdings. Both these gaps in the record lead to understatement of the actual rise in savings.

This reminds us of the difference between the kind of cross-section we are looking at in Table 15.12 and the lifetime experience of the various cohorts that the cross-section intersects—a difference already mentioned in the discussion of the relation between age and income. Anyone who died at age 50 in 1980 passed the active years of life between ages 25 and 40 in 1955–70, a period of rising prosperity; one who died in 1980 aged 75 passed those years in 1930–45, a period of depression followed by six years of war. A comparison of these two persons' estates, in a cross-section at 1980, is likely to underestimate the rate at which people generally add to their estates between the ages of 50 and 75.

To see how much this amounts to in practice we must trace a cohort. Shorrocks (1975) has done this for the British cohort of age 75–84 in 1961. These people were the survivors of those aged 65–74 in 1951; and so on backwards, to those aged 25–34 in 1911. Shorrocks took the reported estates in each of these cells, raised them by the appropriate multipliers and expressed them all at the prices of 1961. Thereby he was able to trace the growth of the wealth of this cohort (born in the ten years centred on 1880) from the age of 25 onwards, and to compare it with the cross-section at 1961 purporting to show the same relation between wealth and age. This comparison is presented here in Figure 15.8. The indication is clear and strong, that the cross-section overestimates holdings in the earlier years. The track of the cohort agrees much better with the hypothesis of lifetime savings than does the cross-section.

But the holdings of the cohort still go on rising after the age of retirement. Shorrocks, it is true, introduced a correction at this point, with a consequent reversal of direction. He noted that 'the rich live longer'—or, we might conjecture, 'those whose vitality enables them to accumulate riches are longer lived, by the same token'—and this actually to a marked extent. The members of the cohort who die in the later years therefore provide a sample that, compared with the original contribution of the

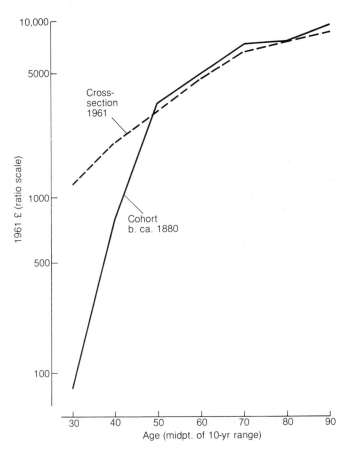

Fig. 15.8 Cross-section in 1961 of wealth holdings by age, compared with holdings of wealth at successive ages of cohort born 1875–84 in Great Britain. *Source:* Shorrocks (1975: fig. 2 and table 1).

cohort, is increasingly biased towards wealth. Shorrocks corrected for this bias by changing the mortality multiplier. His aim was to estimate 'the wealth of the ideal cohort' in which there is no correlation between wealth and mortality; in 'the theoretical ideal', 'mortality has been at random' (Shorrocks 1975: 160). In effect, the correction restores to the cohort those poorer members who have not in fact survived. The outcome is a cohort track with a pronounced hump, 'with maximum wealth attained approximately at the normal age of retirement' (p. 161): the continued rise through the declining years of life, so unexpected on the life-cycle hypothesis, has disappeared. But whether this raising of the dead is legitimate or not is a nice point. Its aim is to show the effect of living on through the declining years, irrespective of whether those who do it are rich or poor. But one gets older while one is doing anything, and we are concerned here with the effects not of the ageing of the body but of what one does as the body ages. It is hard to conceive of these actions apart from the type of person who is acting. Do people run down their holdings in their seventies? That depends on what sort of people they are; and if in fact it is the richer people who live longer, we must take old people as we find them. The constitution of the cohort changes as it goes on through life; the resultant change in behaviour is what we are out to record.

The upshot is that we have good reason to believe that wealth holdings in the earlier years of adult life are lower, and the part played by lifetime savings is higher, than cross-sections would give us to believe. That the US cross-section, moreover, does show accumulation rising with age may be connected with the evidence already cited of the smaller part played by intergenerational transfers in that country. That the British cross-section shows bigger holdings in the earlier years may have two explanations: it may be the effect of differences between cohorts, which happen to have run that way in the approach to the date of the cross-section; or it may mean what it says, that younger people have acquired wealth by bequest and transfer.

The latter explanation is support by two observations. One, already noticed, is that women's wealth is not much less than men's. In the absence of a commensurate ability to save out of personal income, this can be explained only by the receipt of capital by bequest and transfer. The other observation is the minor extent of differences in the distribution of wealth at different ages. If saving played the predominant part, holdings would not be very different from one another in the earlier years when all holdings were small; but as saving went on, by different amounts according to increasing differences of income, the distribution of wealth would become increasingly unequal. It seems not to do so. Table 15.13 shows that in Great Britain in 1975 the share of the top 10 per cent did rise from age 35 to 75 among men, whereas among women it was actually at its highest in the younger years; taking the two together, there was little change from beginning to end, although a low peak was reached around age 70. This again is most easily explained if a great part of the wealth in question was acquired by bequest and transfer. Most of this part, again, will have consisted of transfers made in the donor's lifetime; for inquiries conducted by the Royal Commission (1977: para. 387) have indicated that 'most inheritances are received by persons who are already in middle or old age.'

None the less, we have reason to treat cross-sections cautiously. We should like to have more estimates of cohorts, but they are lacking. In their absence, we can only see what we can learn from the cross-sections, of which we have a number. It is hard to weigh evidence from different times and places in the same scales, but we may be able to reach some conclusions. These will concern both the supposed drawing down of wealth

TABLE 15.13 *Distribution of British personal wealth within age groups*

Proportions of total wealth within given age groups, held by top 1 per cent and top 10 per cent of the group, in Great Britain, 1963–7 and 1972 (percentages)

Age group	1963–7 Men Top 1%	1963–7 Men Top 10%	1963–7 Women Top 1%	1963–7 Women Top 10%	1975 Men Top 1%	1975 Men Top 10%	1975 Women Top 1%	1975 Women Top 10%	1975 Men & Women Top 1%	1975 Men & Women Top 10%
25–34	31	64	55	93	20	50	29	73	23	59
35–44	27	63	44	88	16	48	39	78	23	59
45–54	28	67	38	81	21	54	24	66	22	59
55–64	27	66	29	71	26	61	23	68	25	64
65–74	27	68	27	69	30	70	21	63	25	66
75–84	29	72	26	69	24	63	17	57	20	59
85 & over	30	75	27	72	23	59	17	57	19	58

Sources: 1963–67: Atkinson (1971); 1975: Royal Commission (1977: table 32).

in order to maintain consumption after retirement, and the relative parts of savings and of bequests and transfers in building up holdings in earlier years.

On the question of whether people draw down their wealth in their declining years, we are at least less troubled, within a limited span of years, by possible differences between cohorts. Some studies have found a distinct fall in holdings. Atack and Bateman (1981), in a study of the northern agricultural community in the United States in 1860, found that the wealth–age curves peaked in people's fifties and then fell almost as rapidly as they had climbed before—holdings by those aged 80 and over were as much as 30 per cent down on holdings at the peak. 'In the nineteenth century,' the authors observe, 'most persons were employed by age 15 and could expect to live to 60. Those wishing to enjoy a few years of leisure before death would presumably retire sometime after their half-century, and begin to draw down their wealth balances. This is exactly what the distributions reveal.' King and Dicks-Mireaux (1982) found a marked drawing down, after age 64, of the net worth of a large sample of Canadian families in 1977—or, rather, a marked fall in the ratio of net worth to permanent income. Because of the greater longevity, already noticed, of the rich, the greater the age of decedents, the higher will be the proportion of the rich among them, so that the average net worth of decedents is kept up as their age at death rises, even though each individual among them has drawn his or her own net worth down. To correct this bias, the authors expressed the net worth of each family as a proportion of its permanent income, 'defined as normal age-adjusted annual earnings' (p. 254). It is the proportion that falls—by more than a quarter—between those aged 60–64 at death and those over 75. None the less, the authors conclude, 'the rate at which wealth declines after retirement is less than would be predicted by a life-cycle model with neither bequests nor uncertainty about date of death' (p. 265). When, moreover, Mirer (1979) made a correction with the same object to data drawn from a Survey of the Economic Characteristics of the Aged made in 1968 in the United States, the effect was to raise holdings after retirement. 'The raw cross-section data show that wealth . . . declines modestly, or perhaps not at all, with age among the aged . . . at all levels of wealth. When adjustments are made to correct for intercohort differences in wealth at retirement, it is found that wealth clearly increases with age' (p. 442). Here is a case in which correcting the bias towards the rich in old age signally fails to discover capital consumption.

The findings of cross-sections, moreover, seem too strongly marked to be put down wholly to that bias. Menchik and David (1983), in a study of the decedents in Wisconsin in 1946–64, found that the mean estate declined only slightly after the cohort whose ages at death were around 50, and rose sharply for those aged 67 or more at death. The rise in the value of estates shown in Table 15.12 throughout the advancing years of the decedents in both Great Britain and the United States is emphatic.

We conclude that, although there are differences between even neighbouring families, and still more between different times and places, the tendency of holdings to grow with the age of the holder is not reversed in old age. It may even be strengthened. To anyone who has himself entered on those years, this is entirely intelligible. Whatever the life tables say, one cannot predict the date of one's own death, but must retain resources, not only to provide income for an indefinite period, but to meet the costs of medical and other care which may multiply in later years. Husbands wish to ensure that if they die first their wives will be well provided for. Some transfers to children will have been made at earlier stages of the childrens' lives, and the rest can wait. Meanwhile the ebbing of animal spirits reduces the activity that involves spending. As Alfred Marshall (1890. IV, VII, 6) remarked long ago, 'That men labour and save chiefly for the sake of their families and not for themselves, is shown by the fact that they seldom spend, after they have retired from work, more than the income that comes in from their savings, preferring to leave their stored-up wealth intact for their families.' We may conclude that the retention, perhaps even the increase, of wealth through the later years of life can be accepted as a component of the inequality of wealth.

But what of the years up to retirement? Is not a great part of the inequality of wealth brought about then through the difference between the holdings of those who have only begun to save and those who have been saving for much of their working lives? This will certainly be so if savings account for a large part of holdings. If on the other hand a large part comes by way of bequest and transfer, and a substantial amount of these accrues early in the holders' adult lives, then holdings will not grow so much with the age of the holder. Preponderantly, the evidence does show that holdings grow with age. Whatever their findings about the later years, three of the studies recently cited agree in finding a persistent rise through the years of adult life up to retirement. The age–wealth curves drawn by Atack and Bateman for the rural community of the northern states in 1860 rise steeply to a peak between the ages 50 and 60. The ratio of net worth to permanent income calculated by King and Dicks-Mireaux from Canadian family returns in 1977 rises from 0.7 at ages 25–29 to 4.4 at ages 50–54. Both the British series for men and the American series for heads of households in Table 15.12 rise progressively throughout, the American far more than the British, which in the age group 55–64 stands at only about a third above 25–34. These are all cross-sections, but the cohort track found in Great Britain by Shorrocks rose even more strongly through the earlier years.

There is thus evidence for a progressive rise from a low start in early years. But is the rise as great as we should expect if the part played by savings were really as big as estimates we have quoted for it indicate (as much as three-quarters, on Elfryn Jones's estimate, and he is not alone)? King and Dicks-Mireaux (1982), in their study of Canadian families, found that 'the behaviour of the ''average'' household . . . appears to fit well with the life-cycle model of saving allowing for an uncertain date of death. There is, however, a great deal of variation in household behaviour'—quite a high proportion save less than the model supposes' (p. 263); 'the estimated ''life-cycle'' model accounts for only 50 per cent of the variance of the ratio of wealth to permanent income' (p. 265). The British figures in Table 15.12 are particularly hard to fit into any such model: men's holdings grow slowly, and although women's grow faster, they are higher relatively to men's than we should expect if they were acquired mainly by saving. There is also the observation, in Table 15.13, that the concentration of wealth was much the same at all ages.

These findings are all explicable if in fact substantial transfers accrued to both men and women in their early adult years, and assets continued to be transferred to married women within the family. There are two possible explanations for the failure of British men's holdings to rise more: that lifetime accumulation is offset by some process of attrition, and that transfers, especially to the young, bulk larger than has been supposed. These two possibilities are one if the attrition takes the form of transfers *inter vivos*. Elfryn Jones assumed, on the strength of estimates by Whalley (1975) and Horsman (1975), that those transfers, together with settlements on spouses and certain discretionary trusts, would add $22\frac{1}{2}$ per cent to the total flow of bequests. But this is a matter of great uncertainty. What estimates we have are based on the stamp duty paid on transfers, or on gifts made close enough to death to be liable for estate duty. But there are some forms of transfer that incur no stamp duty, and others—perhaps many others—that may be made informally: those reported are likely to be a poor guide to the actual total. Suppose that this is actually much larger than $22\frac{1}{2}$ per cent. Then we may follow the Royal Commission (1977: Appendix I, para 11) in expecting that the transfers of which we now take account will have been made earlier in the life of the recipients than legacies received on the death of the testator. The effect will be to raise holdings at lower ages relatively to those at higher.

This is most obviously the case where the division of property among different classes of beneficiary is the same for transfers among the living as for transfers at death; but in addition other considerations may serve to reinforce the age-reducing effect, e.g. if sizeable transfers are commonly made by wealthy parents when their children marry. (Royal Commission 1977: Appendix I, para 11)

The hypothesis that transfers to young people bulk quite large is the most likely explanation of the relatively big—and concentrated—holdings of wealth found in the earlier years of adult life. But what of the very different relation between age and wealth in the United States? The continuous rise in average wealth with the age of the householder is consistent with lifetime savings playing a large part in the accumulation of wealth. In fact, Wolff tells us that the 'life-cycle wealth' that is formed out of savings does predominate in the more modest holdings. 'Among the lower wealth groups, over 80 per cent of household wealth takes the [life-cycle form], whereas among the top wealth groups the proportion is under 20 per cent' (Wolff 1983: 125). The distribution of wealth has been somewhat less concentrated in the United States than in Great Britain; the middling fortunes have bulked larger there, and lifetime savings have played a larger part in consequence. There is thus reason to believe that they have contributed more to the accumulation of US householders' wealth as a whole.

The question of how much of people's wealth has been accumulated out of their savings and how much has come from bequests and transfers is important for policy. Inequality of savings and of inheritance stand very differently before the bar of public opinion. The evidence we have reviewed does not enable us to divide present holdings according to origin at all exactly, but it does allow some general statements. It indicates that lifetime savings contribute a substantial component to the inequality of wealth. They are formed by a twofold inequality of income—between the younger and the older people in any one occupation, and between different occupations, a divergence that widens with age. But the actual distribution of wealth is also much affected by bequests and transfers. We have some knowledge of bequests, and a fifth of holdings in Great Britain has been estimated to have been derived from them. How great the transfers are we really do not know, although we may infer that they are substantial from the distribution of British wealth between age groups and between men and women, as also from the comparative absence of differentiation between younger and older age groups in the concentration of holdings. What is perhaps the 80 per cent of holdings not acquired by bequest has been formed by lifetime savings and transfers from other people during their lifetime. The relative size of these elements is conjectural. All that the evidence allows us to say is that the lifetime savings have not been so big in Great Britain as to shape the distribution, whose observed form owes much to bequests and transfers.

So far we have been considering accumulation, but the distribution of wealth depends also on attrition and dispersion. At the same time as some holdings are being built up, others are being run down, handed over in part or divided up at death altogether. There are in fact four ways in which this process of reduction is carried on. One, which occurs only occasionally or sporadically, is a fall in the value of holdings. Particular investments may collapse, a fall in farm prices may depress land values, or a depression may lower the valuation of all manner of assets. Since the proportion of assets held in the form of stocks and shares rises with the size of the holding, the wealth of the top 1 per cent of holders is particularly vulnerable to a fall in the stock market. The number of probated British estates of £100 000 and over, which had been rising steeply since the 1850s, hardly rose at all in 1875-9 and 1885-9, the two troughs of the great Victorian depression (Rubinstein 1981: table 2.5); that the fall in another severe depression, that of 1930-4, was small may be explained by the rise in gilt-edged at that time. A second form of reduction is the drawing down of savings to maintain consumption after retirement. The evidence cited above indicated that, although this occurs in some cases, it is far from being a general practice. But the possibility of capital consumption is present at all stages of the holder's life; where wealth in the aggregate is found to grow with age, it is net growth that is recorded. We have also surveyed the third form, namely transfers in the donor's lifetime, and have seen reason to infer that these play a substantial part in forming the British distribution; but we lack direct observations.

For the remaining way—dispersion at death—we have at least some sampling inquiries into the pattern of bequests. Rubinstein (1981: 134) studied the wills of 66 millionaires and 123 half-millionaires, all of them non-landed, who died in England and Wales in 1858-99. He found the principles of concentration and dispersal mingled: 59 of the 66 millionaires left their property 'to a principal heir of a succeeding generation', but only 14 of them left more than 80 per cent to that heir. Of the 123 half-millionaires, 102 had a principal heir of a succeeding generation, but of these heirs only 24 received 60 per cent or more. 'In a substantial number of cases, the principal heir received less than one-third of the total inheritance.' A study made for the Royal Commission (1977: ch. 8) shows the same mixture of tendencies. It examined the wills of 238 estates of £15 000 and more that received probate in England and Wales in 1973. Some of the findings are shown in Table 15.14. Here again, we find a high proportion of principal heirs (rows (4) and (5)); in the two higher ranges there was one in over half of all wills, and in the two lower ranges the proportion was nearly three quarters. But we now see also that the proportion left to spouses (row (6)) was smaller, the bigger the estate. The proportion left to children was also lowest among the biggest estates (row (7)). Correspondingly, the proportion bequeathed to 'other relatives' was higher in the top than in the bottom ranges. As a whole, what was kept within the family formed a smaller proportion of the estate, the bigger the estate; but the variation was not wide. Settlements on the surviving spouse for his or her life were not included in the estates, and if more of these were made by the wealthier, the apparent tendency of these testators to leave more outside the family would have to be modified. But there is no doubt that division *within* the family does vary with the size of the estate: the smaller, it seems, was this, the less was left over for others after the testator had provided adequately for his or her surviving spouse (row (6)). Thus,

TABLE 15.14   *The pattern of British bequests*

Dispositions in the wills of 238 disposable estates of £15 000 or more admitted to probate in England and Wales in 1973

	Estate class			
	I	II	III	IV
(1) Range of total estate before duty (£000)	500 +	100–500	50–100	15–50
(2) Average value after duty (£000)	525	114	53	26
(3) No. of estates	62	69	53	54
No. of bequests that each amounted to the following proportion of the whole disposable estate:				
(4) 75% or more	12	14	17	28
(5) 50–74%	11	24	22	9
Percentages of disposable estate bequeathed to:				
(6) spouses	14	21	28	38
(7) children and their issue	23	34	36	28
(8) other relatives	39	31	21	25
Percentages of disposable estate bequeathed (incl. life interest) by married persons to				
(9) spouses	31	45	59	77
(10) children and their issue	30	41	29	14
by widowed persons to				
(11) children and their issue	26	45	62	61

Sources: Royal Commission (1977: tables 79, 82, 83, 85).

the 'large estates tend to be both more widely and more equally distributed than small ones'—'the average number of bequests per estate increases from five in estates of £15 000—£50 000 to 24 in estates of £500 000 and over'; and 'the average size of the largest single bequest is proportionately much smaller in the largest estates than in the small ones' (Royal Commission 1977: para. 396). We must remember, however, that an estate that is largely left to a spouse is likely to be passed on again to the children of the marriage (row (11)), so that within a few years the dispersal of the smaller estates will have become much greater than at first. On the other hand, we do not know how much was transferred to the principal heir during the lifetime of the testator.

This division among the children is an important part of the process of dispersion. In half of the estates where there were two or more children, the bequests to the children were equal. In the other half, 'it can be calculated that on average the most favoured child received 74 per cent of the property bequeathed' to two children, and about 51 per cent where there were three or four children (Royal Commission 1977: para. 372). The extent of inequality did not vary with size of estate. Thus there was no dominance of promogeniture; and in the half of the cases where one child received more than an equal share, the others still had substantial portions. There were also significant bequests to grandchildren. These were found mainly in the biggest estates, in which 'bequests to members of the third generation averaged around £50 000 per estate' (para. 389). This helps to explain the unexpected observation, already remarked upon, that the distribution of wealth among the youngest adults is very unequal.

There is one important element still to be included in our account of dispersion. The estates whose allocation we have been considering are only the disposable estates that are left after estate duty (as it was in 1973) has been deducted. This duty formed an additional claimant to be provided for out of each estate—a very exacting claimant if the estate were large. 'The average rate of duty paid on estates in our sample increased from 8.8 per cent among estates valued at £15 000–£50 000 to 53.4 per cent among estates valued at £500 000 or more' (Royal Commission 1977: para. 375). But in so far as people save more—very likely through life insurance—in order to pay the duty, what it claims does not make the portions into which the estate is divided smaller than they would be if there were no duty.

Against the tendencies of dispersion must be set those that concentrate or enlarge the holdings of the recipients. There is always the possibility that a recipient will receive bequests or transfers from more than one source. There is also the observed tendency of money to marry money: one person who has inherited a portion of a parental estate may marry another who equally has received a parental bequest, so that two of the streams that drained the original estates unite to make a river, and the extent of subdivision of the parental properties is reduced. It is another common observation that money breeds money. What may be a small part of a big estate brings the recipient a substantial advantage, which can be used to build up a much greater fortune than could ever have been acquired without it. The researches of Harbury (Harbury 1962; Harbury and McMahon 1973; Harbury and Hichens 1976, 1977) have shown that a high proportion of those who died rich in Great Britain in recent years were themselves the children of wealthy men. Harbury took all estates over £100 000 in 1956–7, together with a sample of those between £50 000 and £100 000; in addition, of the estates left in 1965, he took about half of those over £100 000. In each case he succeeded in tracing most of the estates of the testators' fathers, or sometimes their fathers-in-law. He found a strong link between the wealth of the two generations—those who died rich were predominantly the sons, or sons-in-law, of the well-to-do. The link, as he himself makes clear, is far from affording a measure of inheritance: we do not know, for instance, how much the sons actually received out of their fathers' estates, or how much had been transferred to them during the father's lifetime, or had reached them from other sources. We also do not know how much was inherited by those sons who themselves left estates too small to be included in the sample. But there is no mistaking the significance of the findings.

Of men dying in 1956–57 and 1965 leaving £100 000 or more, nearly 60 per cent had fathers whose estates were valued at £50 000 or more (in 1956-7 prices). If there were no connection between fathers and sons, less than 1 per cent of the population of sons would be expected to have had fathers with this size of fortune. If we define as self-made men those whose fathers had left less than £10 000, they account for only about a quarter of those leaving estates of £100 000 or more. (Royal Commission 1975: para 269)

An inquiry of the same kind had been carried out by Josiah Wedgwood (1929) for the years 1924–6: his findings (Royal Commission 1975: table 53) were remarkably similar to Harbury's. This was unexpected in a period that had seen such great economic and social changes, not least a big rise in the rates of estate duty; but the fact remains.

Brittain (1978: 83) showed how close was the agreement between the inquiries by Wedgwood and Harbury when he calculated the prevailing relation between the holdings of father and son in each. Formally, in the regression of the logarithm of the father's holding on that of the son, he obtained from the data of each inquiry exactly the same coefficient: 0.61. This means, for instance, that if the estate of one man was 6 per cent greater than another's, a son of the first man would himself leave an estate than was 10 per cent bigger than that of the other man's son. This is hard to interpret. It may mark a general tendency for richer men to transfer more assets to their sons during their own lifetimes. It may also come about because the benefits that a father can give his son at his start in life increase more than in proportion to the father's resources.

The processes of growth and dispersion of holdings result in a certain stock of wealth lying at a given time within any range of size. Holdings are always entering that range as people acquire more, through lifetime savings or transfer and bequests, or by reaping the profits of enterprise and speculation. Meanwhile, other holdings are leaving the range—upwards as acquisition goes on, downwards as holdings fall in market value, are drawn down by dissaving and parcelled out by transfer during the holder's lifetime or by bequests at death. As long as inflow exceeds outflow, the stock within the range will rise. But the slowness of change in the distribution of wealth tells us that this sort of building up—or its opposite, running down—has never gone far, let alone indefinitely. The reason is to be found not in any equilibrating mechanism, but in the simple fact that all holders are mortal—all personal holders, that is; wealth may be held in perpetuity by institutions like colleges, which have shown their ability to retain it for many centuries. Of personal holdings, some leave a given range because they become too big for it. The others, having entered it, remain in it until they are devalued, drawn down, given away, or disposed of on the death of the holder. What is certain is that were every other form of exit to cease, this last one would remain. We hardly need find room for the possibility that the death of the holder brings a mere change of name, with no dispersion of the holding and no duty to pay. Generally, what follows death is the breakup of a holding into a number of smaller portions, so that the density of the distribution is shifted downwards; in many cases the original holding will disappear from the range. So far as this is so, every holding that enters the range is sure to leave it after a span of time terminated by the death of the holder. If the rate of entrance begins to exceed that of exit, from whatever cause, the consequent building up of the stock within the range can continue only during that span, whose length is set by the average lapse of time between a person's acquiring enough wealth to bring it within the range, and his or her own death. Similarly, any running down of the stock, due to an excess of the current rate of exits over that of entrances, will continue only so long as there are holdings to be eliminated that were within the range before the excess of exits arose. The size of the stock will always tend towards the rate of entrance multiplied by the entrants' average length of stay, and can never be permanently greater or less than this.

Thus while young trees grow up, and old trees decay and fall, the forest remains. Each tree is programmed to grow at a certain rate and then to decline and die. As long as the rate of growth and the length of life remain the same, an increase in the number of trees beginning to grow will result for many years in an increase in the stock of trees at each stage of growth. But those years will be limited by the life of the tree: at the end of that period, one additional tree will die for every addition to the number beginning to grow, and the stock will be stabilized. It will also be raised by an increase in the length of life of the tree, but if that increase is once for all, the stock will be stabilized again at the new higher level. A change in the growth curve will affect the relative amount of timber at different stages of growth. We may transpose these observations to the economy. The number of holdings entering any range of wealth depends on the number of persons who begin to accumulate and the rate at which their holdings grow. Holdings leave the range by becoming too big for it or too small. The rate at which they become too big is given by the growth curve. They become too small occasionally by the loss or devaluation of assets, but mainly by dissolution—during the lifetime of the holder by transfers, and at his or her death. Any change in the number of starters, the rate of growth, the rate of lifetime transfer or the length of life that raises the rate of entry to a range or lowers the rate of exit from it will increase the amount of wealth within the range; but the increase will continue for a period set by the prevailing growth curve, that is by the time it takes a holding to reach the upper bound of the range, or else by the length of life before the death of the holder brings the dissolution of the holding. At the end of that period the amount of wealth within the range will cease to grow.

Thus, the governor of the distribution of wealth is found in the stability of three parameters of individual behaviour: the rate of accumulation, the rate of dispersal by lifetime transfer, and the length of life. So long as these remain unchanged, the distribution of wealth will attain a certain form and will not depart from it. If one of them changes—if, for example, in a period of more rapid expansion of the economy the rate of accumulation rises—then the stock of wealth will increase throughout; but the increase will continue in each range only for the time it takes the representative holding to leave it, either by outgrowing it or by dissolution. We must fix our eye on the life-cycle of the individual. It is because the form of this has remained much the same over long periods, save for a lengthening of life in more recent times, that the distribution of wealth has changed so little in comparison with the economy around it.

15.6. The Great Fortunes

In all our studies, it has been very clear that the biggest incomes and holdings of wealth form a distinct system. The Pen profiles of income generally turn sharply upwards about the 85th percentile, and continue to rise far more steeply than before, to reach heights often too great to be shown in the graph. 'Within the last 4 per cent alone,' we noted above (p. 286), 'incomes are raised by a factor of $3\frac{1}{2}$, to a level 20 times that of the 15th percentile in Sweden, 24 times in the United Kingdom—and that still does not include the highest incomes of all.' Equally, in the distribution of wealth there is a change of slope near the top, although, because lower down the distribution is more unequal than that of income, the change of slope is not so marked. But there is no doubt that, in wealth no less than in income, inequality within at least the top 10 per cent is altogether greater than below. The distinct form of the distribution at the top is made clear by the Pareto line, which generally fits the data of this sector closely, but makes nonsense if it is projected far below.

We also know that income and wealth are both very differently composed near the top and lower down. In British personal incomes as a whole in 1975-6 investment income made up only 5 per cent, but the proportion was twice that in the top 10 per cent, and about five times as great in the top 1 per cent (Royal Commission 1979: table 2.12). In British personal wealth as a whole in 1976, land made up less than 4 per cent, but in the holdings of £200 000 and over it made up 20 per cent; stocks and shares formed 12 per cent of all holdings, but 42 per cent of the biggest; on the other hand, the corresponding figures for dwellings were the other way about—41 and 13 per cent (Royal Commission 1979: table 4.6). The model of lifetime savings built for the Royal Commission (1977: Appendix K) indicated that these savings contributed only a minor part of the biggest holdings—only a third of the holdings of the top 5 per cent in 1974—the remainder being made up of transmitted wealth together with 'entrepreneurial fortunes, financial windfalls and wealth accumulated from investment income derived from inheritances'. But savings are shown as contributing four-fifths of the holdings of the remaining 95 per cent (Royal Commission 1979: para. 17). In the United States, equally, savings seem to contribute only a small part of the biggest holdings: we have seen (p. 451) how the kind of asset generally accumulated in households by saving out of income made up no more than a fifth of the holdings of the top group as a whole; it made up 3 per cent of the biggest holdings, those of $500 000 or more, the remainder being made up financial assets such as are commonly acquired, in large quantities, by transmission and out of profits.

Evidently, the top incomes and holdings of wealth are formed under distinct influences. Here, very likely, we have to do with both a different mode of acquisition and a special type of person. The mode of acquisition includes two linked arrangements which require separate consideration—the transmission of wealth by gift and bequest, and the ownership of land. One source of very high incomes—the earnings of celebrities—stands by itself. There remain, as sources of both high incomes and great fortunes, the activities of entrepreneurs and speculators.

The transmission of wealth as we have studied it here has been a process of dispersion of existing fortunes rather than the formation of new ones. But we have seen how Harbury found that the great majority of his sample of men who died rich were the sons of men of substance; a fraction of a great fortune may still be a large sum in itself, and the receipt of even a modest legacy early in life may reinforce the recipient's own efforts to accumulate. In his study of the estates at death of the British wealthy from early in the nineteenth century onwards, Rubinstein (1981: 125) found that up to a third of all millionaires had had wealthy fathers, 'and moreover the tendency for the very wealthy to have themselves sprung from very wealthy backgrounds became increasingly common between 1880 and 1939 . . . Nearly a majority of non-landed millionaires had had wealthy fathers' valuations are known were the sons of men who left £100 000 or more.' We saw reason to infer, moreover, that transfers during the donor's own lifetime were substantial in amount, relatively to bequests at death; and these transfers are particularly likely to be made at a time when they will be most useful to the recipient. One common occasion for such transfers is the marriage of a child, and the effect is enhanced when 'money marries money'.

There is, then, a phoenix-like propensity in great wealth. Although big fortunes are constantly being dispersed, new fortunes grow up out of their fragments. The effect is to reduce what may be called the rate of social turnover of the wealthy. Some existing fortunes become fragmented without succession. On the other side, some new fortunes are always being accumulated by people without wealthy parentage. But in between are the fortunes which themselves owed much to transmission, and will themselves be transmitted in part to form fortunes in a succeeding generation. Although the personal wealth of the population as a whole is largely the product of lifetime saving, the fortunes of the very wealthy are distinguished by what they owe, directly and indirectly, to transmission. A high proportion of the very wealthy, unlike their neighbours of more modest means, have wealthy origins.

In the United Kingdom the power of transmission has been specially manifest among landed estates. There are reasons why these are more likely than other forms of wealth to be handed down intact. The possession of broad acres has traditionally conferred a social status and political influence not afforded by the ownership of equal wealth in other forms: here was 'the acre-ocracy of England' (Bateman 1876). To sell off part of the estate is a conspicuous sign of the family coming down in the world, whereas securities can be sold without publicity. The concept of the family is important here: there is a sense in which the present proprietor is felt to be holding the estate in trust. Even when it is not formally entailed or settled, it is not his own to dispose of as he thinks fit: if in financial straits, he will sell his Gainsborough rather than part with a farm. Where great fortunes consist largely of financial assets, although there may well be a principal heir in the next generation, a substantial part remains for others; but where a landed estate supports an ancient lineage, primogeniture seems to be in the nature of things.

Throughout the nineteenth century—indeed, down to the end of the First World War—a great part of the land of Great Britain was held in this way. Until about 1880, moreover, the holders made up the great majority of the most wealthy people in the country. About 1790 the landed aristocracy had consisted of rather more than 300 families, each the holder of not less than 10 000 acres, with an annual rental of not less than £10 000 (Thompson 1963: 25). When the New Domesday Survey was made in 1873, it 'showed that four-fifths of the land of the United Kingdom was owned by less than 7000 persons' (p. 27). This is counting all acres as equal, be they ploughland or moorland. Valuing property according to its rental, Lindert (1973: Appendix table A3) found that just 685 persons in a total population approaching 8 million held nearly a quarter of all real estate in England and Wales outside London; and that the top 10 per cent of potential owners held a proportion of all rental income in England and Wales that lay between 86 and 99 per cent. At this time, moreover, it was the landowners who owned most of the great fortunes: there were some millionaires who owned little or no land, but they were in a minority. A contemporary account of landholders, compiled from the survey of 1873, found 161 of them with annual rentals of £30 000 or more, which Rubinstein reckons put the value of their estates at not less than £1m; and probably there were more, because this account only assembled the holdings of each landlord within one county, and some whose property was more widely spread would have appeared as wealthier if all their holdings had been counted together. The number of non-landed millionaires whose wills were probated in 1860–79 is given by Rubinstein (1981: table 3.3) as 27, and on the assumption that one-thirtieth of such millionaires died each year, we might put the number extant at about 40. Thus, the non-landed millionaires amounted in the 1870s to at most a quarter, and probably less than a quarter, of the landed. The probate figures indicate that earlier in the century the proportion had been much lower; by the first two decades of the twentieth century, the non-landed millionaires seem to have become nearly as numerous as the landed. They had been increasing while the number of landed millionaires remained much the same. There was some turnover among these, it is true. Some estates were reduced as land was sold to pay off debts incurred by extravagance. On the other hand, some great new estates were formed as money came in from the city, and holdings were amalgamated by marriages with heiresses. The owners of arable acres suffered from the halving of the price of wheat after 1873, but livestock and dairy farming did well through those years. Landholders up and down the country gained from the rise of site values as the towns grew. It is a fair estimate that half of the great fortunes of the country were still landed in 1914.

A few years later, the scene had changed dramatically. During and after the war estate duties were raised to unheard-of heights. Where, within a few years, a landowner died and his heir was killed at the front, the effect was crippling. The high casualty rate of the sons of the great houses, in families where there were fewer sons then than there used to be, broke that strong tie of lineage that had formerly made it a matter of pride, and even duty, to hand an estate down intact from father to son. Not only estate duty, but income tax was raised. This, 'which took barely 4 per cent of gross rents at Wilton and Savernake before 1914, was taking over a quarter in 1919, and the burden of all direct taxes taken together (land tax, rates and income tax) had risen from 9 to 30 per cent of the rental' (Thompson 1963: 328). Meanwhile prices doubled in five years, and the costs of upkeep with them; but landlords did not raise their rents—it would have seemed indecent to make money out of the war in which so many in the rural community were giving their lives. In 1919, therefore, many landlords found themselves constrained to sell, at the same time as much of the former inhibitions had been removed. The land was now worth more to the tenant than the capitalization of the current rent. A pressure was redoubled that had appeared already before the war. Agriculture as a way of making money had by no means expanded as industry and commerce had done; if farms were valued at the prices tenants were prepared to pay for the freehold, the return on capital in the form of land was lower than could be obtained elsewhere. As a consequence of the same relative expansion of business, as well as of the extension of the franchise, the ownership of land no longer conveyed such social pre-eminence and political influence.

So it came about that

> precisely a quarter of England and Wales passed from being tenanted land into the possession of its farmer in the thirteen years after 1914 . . . Such an enormous and rapid transfer of land had not been seen since the confiscations and sequestrations of the Civil War, such a permanent transfer not since the dissolution of the monasteries in the sixteenth century. (Thompson 1963: 332)

When we turn from transmitted wealth to the fortunes that are built up by the exertions of their holders, we find ourselves in a sector of the field of activity in which opportunities are rare but exceptionally rewarding. Throughout most of the field, the steady application of good personal qualities generally secures advancement; and although sheer chance has its disturbing impact, on the whole, a greater effort and ability will secure a higher return. There is a sufficient array and variety of opportunities, spread widely enough, for most people to find one within reach. These opportunities are well defined, widely known and reliable in the returns they offer, but the returns are only modest. In the sector of fortune-making, on the other hand, the opportunities are differently disposed. They are relatively few, and not evident at first, and they offer no certain return; but they hold rich rewards. Whereas the modest opportunities are present at most times, these rich ones tend to offer themselves in particular surges: a new product, or new method of production, becomes available, and those who are the first to exploit it vigorously find their own enterprise borne on by a strong-flowing tide. To change the metaphor, we can envisage the structure of opportunities as a goldfield with two parts. In the one, alluvial gold is thinly but widely spread, near the surface; in the other, deep shafts must be sunk to reach veins of rich ore, and these are elusive. We should expect the distributions of miners' gains in the two parts of the field to be shaped very differently.

We should also expect the two parts of the field to attract different types of prospector. The combination of uncertainty with the possibility of outstanding advancement attracts the type who do not fear to lose, but are excited and energized by the prospect of winning. But although the speculator may be a gambler, the successful speculator has more than luck on his side: he is restlessly energetic in searching out openings, and he exploits them with a compulsive boldness and a feeling for the movement of the market. The entrepreneur has elements of the speculator in his boldness, but finds his satisfaction in more constructive achievement. As the mountaineer is inwardly driven to conquer a rockface, so the entrepreneur to maintain his self-respect must overcome the obstacles to the expansion of his business. He initiates, and is fertile in expedients, because he does not merely respond to external stimuli, but is inner-directed. He works extremely hard because he is endowed by nature with an exceptional fund of energy, and needs the continued reassurance of achievement. Schumpeter has characterized him:

First of all, there is the dream and the will to found a private kingdom, usually, though not necessarily, also a dynasty . . . What may be attained by industrial or commercial success is still the nearest approach to mediaeval lordship possible to modern man. . . .

Then there is the will to conquer: the impulse to fight, to prove oneself superior to others, to succeed for the sake, not of the fruits of success, but of success itself. . . The financial result is a secondary consideration, or, at all events, mainly valued as an index of success and as a symptom of victory. . . .

Finally, there is the joy of creating, of getting things done, or simply of exercising one's energy and ingenuity . . . Our type seeks out difficulties, changes in order to change, delights in ventures. (Schumpeter 1936: 93–4)

The distinctive qualities of entrepreneurs are those of personality, not of intellect. A good intelligence of course they must have; their performance has to be sustained by a fund of unflagging energy. But they are distinguished from others who have those qualities by their motivation. They are driven ever onwards by an inner demand for achievement, and for the demonstration of their power to master difficulties. There may be a hereditary element in this disposition, but we know also how it may be formed by experience in the earliest years of life. What sort of parents a child has, how it is treated by them, the view it forms of life by extension of the way it is lived in the home—these imprint lasting traits.

Those who make fortunes are not all of one type, and those who do resemble one another may have had very different origins; but in the biographies of leading businessmen one syndrome of the childhood home recurs. It is that of the weak or unreliable father and the strong, supportive and directing mother. In their study of 8000 US business leaders, Warner and Abegglen found that

without exception the mother is singled out as the person who has trained them, who provides them with a sense of a larger and different world from that in which they live, and who is the close and stable figure in the family. She is at the same time a controlling figure. . . . It is the mothers of these men who initially provide them with the notion that by dint of hard work and personal effort they can achieve goals they set themselves. (Warner and Abegglen 1955: 103–4)

No less influential, but in a different way, is the contrasting character of the father:

in most cases . . . distant from the sons, and not at all supporting or reinforcing. The father is an unreliable figure. At the same time, there is this feeling of loss or deprivation, that the father is withholding something from the son that he might provide, and some of the process of mobility may be seen as an effort to gain this withheld support, and to prove oneself a worthy and able figure in the eyes of the father. (Warner and Abegglen 1955: 77–8)

The son's reaction has been interpreted by Everett Hagen:

If his father is weak, the son may come to feel instead a rather melancholy warmth and closeness to him, coupled always with an awareness of a lack of strength which ought to be made good. Especially, he may resent his father's inadequate care of his mother and may feel always a restless need to erase this unsatisfying model he carries in his mind by doing better himself. As a child he was never able to do enough to keep his mother from discomfort and anxiety. The guilt that this inadequacy instils will never wholly leave him. It is perhaps the largest element in the insatiable need for success that such an individual manifests. (Hagen 1962: 222)

Insatiable indeed—those characters can never sit down to rest at the cairn on the summit: for them there is always a higher peak to be climbed; their need for reassurance can never be stilled by the achievements to which it drives them.

Some great fortunes are made by speculation, and the temperament of the speculator is different from that of the businessman as director. Some willingness to take risks there must be in all entrepreneurs, but this is a matter of willingness to back one's own judgement in an uncertain world, and not a liking for a gamble. It is the gamble that excites the speculator: what is a deterrent to some investors is an attraction to him. The need to take risks is a trait that takes various forms, such as fast driving. It has been ascribed to anxiety, to a fear of succumbing to external forces beyond one's power to control, and to the wish, which may become a compulsion, to put those forces to the test and show that one can keep the upper hand. In that case it is the chance of losing that is the lure because it must be overcome; but the speculator may also be attracted by the chance of winning, and the positive assurance this will give that he is after all the master of his fate. He can deserve his luck by his good judgement and choice of the right horse to back. The speculator is thus something more than a gambler at the tables. He may take a good deal of trouble in choosing his point of entry. His activity shades into that of the entrepreneur who needs nerve because his constructive project is attended by risk. His success depends not simply on the luck of the draw, but on the exercise of an objective judgement unswayed by hopefulness or haste.

Whatever the ability and drive of the entrepreneur or speculator, the possibility of making a fortune depends on the field of activity. The manufacturer of a particular product is limited by the market for that product. Even if the firm beats down all competition at home until it supplies the whole market, this will only support a business of limited turnover, and advances in export markets may be subject to hazards and restraints. It is comparatively recently that the development of methods of management that combine central control with delegated executive discretion has enabled one person to create and lead conglomerate organizations containing a variety of activities and spread over a number of countries. But the obstacles that impeded the manufacturer never constrained the merchant and banker. The merchant could deal with a variety of commodities, the banker with a variety of clients, and it was in the nature of their dealings that they could readily extend them internationally. It was by these types, and not by manufacturers, that most of the Victorian fortunes were made. But industrial entrepreneurs have also made fortunes, when they took up and developed a new process or product, capable of wide use, at an early stage of a world-wide development: such were the great railway contractors, and the makers of motor cars by mass production. Rubinstein (1981: 61) found that, 'although there were indeed a substantial number of wealthy fortunes in certain manufacturing and industrial trades like cotton manufacturing and engineering, the wealthy in Britain have disproportionately earned their fortunes in commerce and finance—that is, as merchants, bankers, shipowners, merchant bankers and stock and insurance agents and bankers'. The number of industrial fortunes increased from the last decade of the nineteenth century onwards, but remained a minority. Rubinstein (1977) has recorded that, of the 40 biggest fortunes left by men and recorded for probate or estate duty between 1809 and 1914, half were Londoners, 16 of them from the City. Of the other half, 4 were landowners, and only among the remaining 16 were industrialists found—5 of these others were Clydesiders, and 4 came from Bristol. 'Apart from Brassey and the ironmasters Wm. Baird and Wm. Crawshay, all of the non-landed millionaires . . . deceased prior to 1888 were Londoners, and it is only in the late Victorian period that provincial fortunes appear of a size sufficient to rival the largest among Londoners' (p. 613). The ascendancy of commerce over industry is shown by Liverpool providing more fortunes than Manchester.

There is one field in which the limitations that a localized market imposes on the manufacturer have been transcended by recent developments in communications. We noted earlier that the earnings of celebrities deserve separate consideration. The market for artists, writers and performers generally used to be limited by their inability to muster a large audience at any one time. The invention of printing enabled writers to reach a large number of readers, and in the nineteenth century some authors made high incomes. But other artists and entertainers remained limited by the capacity of an auditorium. The coming first of the film and then of broadcasting and television has swept this limitation away. One performance may be seen by millions of viewers, and the fees that the performer can command have risen correspondingly. So it has come about that some of the highest incomes of recent years have accrued to international celebrities in the visual arts and in sport.

16

The Significance of the Statistical Record

Reasons were given in the Introduction for approaching an assessment of egalitarianism by way of a study of actual distributions. Information about the actual state of affairs evidently affects our choice of practical policy, but it will influence our judgement about the ends no less than the means. That judgement is formed not by contemplating a Platonic essence of equality, the same beneath all its manifestations, but in reaction to particular circumstances, or in the light of our view of them. The present chapter accordingly is meant to bring out some of the ways in which that view is affected by knowledge of the facts as those have just been surveyed.

16.1. The Form and Extent of Inequality

A first feature to stand out in the distributions of income and wealth is that, up to about the 85th percentile, the differences of income and wealth between one person and another present themselves as a steady and gentle gradation. In none of the countries noticed is there a block of persons with similar incomes or holdings of wealth, separated from others by a gap. On the contrary, each person rubs elbows with others who are a little better or worse off than he or she is. The gradation is generally steeper for wealth than for income, but it is still a gradation and not a flight of steps or a division into blocs. This smoothness and continuity, it is true, is what we commonly find in large aggregates, and there is no implication that each person, take him or her where you will, has actual neighbours with incomes or wealth close to his or her own. We can readily envisage communities in which that is far from the case, where for instance a majority with very similar low incomes is set over against a prosperous minority. A mining valley might hold such a community. One may appear (or have appeared) in an Asian village, where a rich landowner is surrounded by poor peasants. The medieval manor seems to offer much the same prospect. But probably even in such instances as these, the incomes of the supposedly uniform group would prove to show a wide variation from one household to another. We may note how the earnings of male manual workers in Great Britain are known to have been disposed in the same lognormal form since 1886; and how the Soviet planners use the lognormal to plot the wages in their economy. Employees themselves watch differentials closely, and those on the upper side of them are much concerned to maintain them. There is reason to see the smoothness of gradation not as a statistical artefact but as a social reality.

So far as it enters into our own experience, we may take it for granted; but it is a fact of great significance for the structure and working of society. The circumstances it records do not foster class consciousness. A class, in the full sense of the term, consists of people who are keenly aware of a characteristic or condition that they all share and that marks them off from others. This common badge may be found, as the term 'working class' implies, in the level of education and training, and the kind of job held. People are indeed conscious of these things, in many countries; in the light of them they will readily classify themselves, and rank themselves as superior or inferior to those in other classes. In the matter of income and wealth, they are aware of big differences between themselves and those at some distance above or below them. But they are more directly aware of many smaller differences among those around them; and if they and their neighbours are marked off as 'in a different class' from others, it is not that they are separated by any gap in the gradation of income and wealth. There is a reason here for the stability of societies, Western or less developed, and their ability to experience political revolutions with little change in the social structure. There is no gulf to separate two classes or two nations, any more than short people form a tribe opposed to a tribe of the tall.

It is true that, even within the first 85 per cent of income recipients, the span from lowest to highest is wide. Income at the 85th percentile is typically five times that at the 15th. For wealth the lower limit must be put at the 30th percentile, below which holdings are negligible: the ratio is then more like 9 to 1. But the impact of this contrast is cushioned because it is reached only over many small intervals of a size that varies little or increases only gently with the level attained. When people view income or wealth much greater than their own, it is generally over a foreground and middle distance that are filled with folk not very differeent from themselves.

The differences in one's own neighbourhood, moreover, are generally intelligible, and acceptable. At least there are criteria for them, criteria whose acceptance makes job evaluation practicable. Differentials may be found anomalous according to those criteria, but that is quite often because they are too small and not because they exist at all. If higher income appears right and proper when close at hand, it is not likely to seem an outrage when it appears at a distance, even though it stands so much higher. Differences of wealth have no such justification as job evaluation provides for differences of income, but even here the very fact that our everyday experience is of many small differences lessens the impact of the larger ones that we see too; for the larger possessions, like the larger incomes, are arrived at only by extension of a gradation that within most people's experience is continous. In both income and wealth, a salient fact, so familiar that it escapes notice, is the absence of gaps across which groups of very differently circumstanced people view each other at a wide remove.

But this holds only over a range that is bounded by about the 85th percentile. The people above it are indeed separated by no gap or barrier from those below, but their income and still more their wealth are outstanding in size and distinctive in formation. They differ much more one from another; whereas Swedish incomes, for instance, took from the 40th percentile up to the 85th to double, they doubled again in the short span between the 85th and the peak. Their rapid rise in this segment carries the top incomes to great heights. It follows that, when they are given their due place in the national whole, our conception of the extent of inequality is transformed. In income, if we look only at the lower 85 per cent, the upper limit has been found at about double the median of that truncated distribution in Sweden and West Germany, and at 2.4 times the median in the United Kingdom and the United States; but the peak of the whole distribution was more like eight times the appropriate median in West Germany, and ten times in Sweden and the United Kingdom—the estimates we have quoted do not allow us to fix the peak in the United States (Table 10.1). In wealth, such estimates as we have show an even greater contrast. In the truncated distribution, the corresponding ratio might be put at rather less than 4 in the United States, at about 6 in Canada and as much as 12 in the United Kingdom; but in the whole distribution the ratios were about 27 or 28 in both the United Kingdom and the United States—we could not fix the peak in Canada (Tables 13.2, 13.7). There is of course a margin of dubiety in the underlying estimates, a margin that can displace the calculated ratios widely if it lies on opposite sides of the terms compared; but there can be no doubt that a striking contrast is revealed. In the regime that prevails up to about the 85th percentile, the incomes and—except in the United Kingdom—the wealth of those who are the best off are not so far removed from the main body; when we consider the national distribution as a whole, the peak rises far above it. This relative heightening of the peak is even greater in wealth than in income.

Evidently, the form that inequality takes in the community as a whole depends greatly on this regime at the top. How it works will be considered in the next section.

16.2 How Distributions are Generated

The account given earlier in these pages of the generation of distributions of income and wealth was based on the propensities of individual behaviour. The outcome of a myriad random happenings was shown to be predictable, and to take such a form as is commonly found in practice. This was bound to cast doubt on the practicability of egalitarianism. There seems to be an inevitability in the impersonal working out of countless life-chances in countless life-histories. The generative process is guided by the decisions of no one authority: its innumerable currents cut their own channels. It is natural to infer that 'things will be what they will be': although changes might come about spoantaneously, they could not be imposed. What no authority has designed, none can control. The justification of this inference is now to be examined here. At the outset we should note some distinctive features of the account from which the inference is made.

One of these is the way in which distribution is envisaged in the first place. If distributions of income and wealth really were formed by cutting up a national cake into slices of various sizes, we should be hard put to it to account for the generality and persistence of the actual forms of distribution. That simile of the cake is as misleading as it is familiar. The income and wealth of a country do not arise as a whole before being shared out. They exist only as statistical compilations of individual incomes and wealth. It is the process by which those personal acquisitions are made that determines the distributions of income and wealth among persons as those are subsequently observed.

This is a first distinctive feature of the account that has been put forward here. Another is that it views the reported distributions, which describe a momentary state of affairs, as only a snapshot of an ongoing movement. As people travel along their life-paths, the life-chances they encounter bring them a certain personal potential, and certain acquisitions—or losses—of income and wealth. The account given above shows how what in any one person's history appears only as contingent, to be recorded in a biography that can have little that is systematic about it, is in fact subject to systematic influences that appear when many persons' records are aggregated. These influences bring it about that successive cohorts become distributed over different levels of income and wealth in such a way as to produce a persistent common form. The sources of that form are to be found in the impact day by day of life-chances.

A third feature of our explanation is its dependence on human propensities. It is because these are persistent that the resultant distribution is so stable, and because they are common to people in different countries that it is so general. They appear, evidently, on the side of supply. There is an initial genetic endowment of physical, intellectual and temperamental potential. Qualities of application, enterprise and foresight—or the lack of them—are distributed among the working population. But human propensities also govern demand. The valuation that is set upon the ability to work in all its forms, with their products, plays a vital part in determining each person's acquisitions. Skill commands a premium, outstanding performance brings high rewards, only because people very generally will pay more for them. Human nature, moreover, appears sufficiently uniform in the relevant respects for these valuations to be made in much the same way in different times and places. The persistance and generality of the form of distribution of income and wealth rests upon persistent and general traits of humanity.

On this view we have to discard the belief of egalitarians that, whatever may be the inescapable requirements of production, we can modify distribution at will. It is a belief that comes down from the most influential work on political economy of the nineteenth century, John Stuart Mill's *Principles*. 'Its main theme', said Gertrude Himmelfarb (1974: 227–8), 'was the separation of production and distribution, production being governed by scientific, deterministic laws of nature, and distribution by social arrangements that were the product of human will and effort. This distinction, Mill admitted, he had originally learned from the Saint-Simonians. But it was Harriet Taylor who made it the animating principle of the book.' It now seems wholly mistaken. Distribution occurs simultaneously with production. The same human propensities activate both processes. The proven possibility of redistribution through taxation and benefits does not show that the inequality of original incomes could be reduced likewise.

So far, the account we have given suggests a Tolstoyan view of the outcome. What emerges from the actions of countless people cannot be ordained by authority. You cannot legislate for an ant-heap: the ants have ways of their own. But this conclusion would follow only if our account covered all that has to be explained, and were completely convincing. In fact, it raises some difficulties.

One of these concerns the top 15 per cent. We have noted that we are dealing with a different regime: is it really amenable to the same treatment as the main body? If the top incomes were made up only of the high salaries of top executives and the big earnings of outstanding performers in the professions and the arts, no difficulty would arise: these earnings are formed by the same process of valuation as governs lesser ones, save only that the productivity or prestige of the post held rises so steeply. It is also relevant that modern methods of communication enable some of those concerned to widen the market for their talents very greatly. But they differ from lower earners in degree, not in kind. A distinctive feature does appear among them, however, in that a substantial part of some of these top incomes is drawn from property. Whereas, if British figures are typical, income from property is a small part of the lower incomes, and does not vary systematically with the level of income below the top 15 per cent, it does form a substantial part of those top incomes. When we turn to the top holdings of wealth, moreover, we meet other difficulites. Whereas a large part of the holdings by the less wealthy consists of their lifetime savings, a large part of the top holdings is inherited. The inheritance of land has special social significance. Landed estates tend to be kept intact, more than other forms of property; they may attract increments of value with no effort on the part of their proprietors; in some countries, where most employment depends on access to the land, the possession of large estates puts certain families in a position to exploit the peasants. The kind of distribution that we have been surveying here, by contrast, is the product of an urbanized and industrialized economy.

This is only the extreme case of the problem presented by all wealth, a problem that raises a further difficulty in drawing inferences from a supposedly general form of distribution. In so far as wealth is acquired by the savings of its owners, out of their earnings or the profits of enterprise, it is formed like income as people proceed along their life-paths; but a substantial part is acquired by transfer, during the lifetime of the donor or at his or her death. We have seen how a process of formation and dispersal of holdings goes on continually. Some large holdings are simply inherited. Other blocks of capital, transferred or bequeathed, provide the recipients with resources that they use to increase their holdings by their own exertions. Some people who start with next to no resources accumulate fortunes out of their profits or their exceptional earnings in self-employment. But at the same time, existing accumulations are being broken up, by transfer and bequest, with taxation taking its share, although until quite recently many landed estates have been kept intact, away from the general tendency to dispersal.

This account of the distribution of wealth is intelligible, but it contains elements that cannot be attributed to that play of life-chances to which we have ascribed the prevailing form of distributions. So far as wealth is accumulated by saving out of income, we can treat it as an appendage whose distribution depends on that of income, even though it is more unequal. So far as fortunes are made by enterprise, speculation and celebrity, the combination of opportunity with the power to seize it is likely to occur with a frequency that obeys some law of probability. But the receipt of property by transfer or bequest, and still more the holding of landed estates intact, are intrusive and recalcitrant elements.

Were it not for them, we could regard the top 15 per cent as subject to the same explanation in principle as the main body of the distribution. They may be said to come under a separate regime, but this by reason of quantitative rather than qualitative differences. The members of a cohort who survive to high levels of income will have more of the ability to advance that most members have shown in some degree. The earnings and the profits that can be acquired in this upper region are more expansible of their nature than those accessible below. But advancement, and the valuation of ability, work in the same way at all levels, even if within the top regime they are higher-geared. What does stand outside the common process, most conspicuously at the top but in some measure at most levels, is the transmission of property. It is significant that property is the element that has changed most in recent years.

Another difficulty is raised by the absence of any reference to class. The life-path is formally the same, whether it leads to great income and accumulation or stops short lower down; but there is all the difference in the world, it will be said, between setting out from a poor home and setting out from one that is well endowed. Not only are people grouped by origin, moreover, but the levels that they can ever attain are limited from the outset—limited both by the qualifications they are able to acquire and by the posts that are open to them. The inequality of income and wealth, in other words, is simply one expression of class structure.

The facts on which this view rests are indisputable, but they are not all the facts. It is true that society is stratified, that a gradation of ability as that is commonly measured stands in fairly close agreement, on the average, with the stratification, and that young people who set out from homes at a given level are more likely to move into an adjacent level, above or below, than to one far removed. But the studies of mobility reported above show that many people do move, both up and down. The stability of Western democracies, and the sense of personal freedom that pervades them, are inexplicable unless we take account of the extent of vertical mobility. It is remarkable that measures of that extent indicate no salient differences between countries whose political structures differ, and whose class structures expressed in people's customary attitudes to one another may even be contrasted sharply. In the Soviet-type economies, it may be the high degree of mobility that makes a party dictatorship seem tolerable. We have to note also the continuous gradation illustrated by the Pen parades. We spoke just now of stratification, but in income and wealth at least there are no clear dividing lines between the strata. It is essential to the notion of classes that they are marked off from one another: no such blocs appear in personal incomes and wealth.

This is not to say that the distribution of income and wealth is independent of social structure. On the contrary, there is a causal relation between them, in both directions. The American Mainland Colonies, north and south, gave us examples of different social structures and attitudes brought by the settlers, resulting in very different degrees of inequality in the economies they established. The rulers of the Soviet-type economies, whether from doctrinal conviction or political strategy, improved the standing of manual urban workers and raised their incomes relatively to those of the white-collar workers. The profile of incomes in Hungary was the most egalitarian of all that we surveyed. Most obviously, again, a structure that excludes the personal ownership of any substantial amount of capital removes a principal source of income of the top 15 per cent in other countries; while on the other hand a country dominated by a caste of landowners, in the absence of much industry, will show great inequality of income and even more of wealth.

Our survey of the distributions generated in various times and places has stressed the persistence of a certain form, but within this there have been many changes. A review of these will throw more light on the process of generation

16.3 The Sources of Past Change

The changes indicated by the records we have surveyed are of three kinds. Some of them are contingent: they belong to that class of happenings that cannot readily be associated with any systematic process. But a second type of change does bear a systematic relation to economic growth. A third type, again, if not always brought about deliberately, does occur as the outcome of acts of policy.

The contingent changes include those in the numbers of the population and their distribution by age. A rise in the relative number of young people increases the proportion of people with low incomes and little property. We have seen how much of the inequality of wealth arises simply from the course of lifetime saving, and the extent of it is influenced by the relative numbers at different stages of the life-cycle. Because earnings commonly rise with age, at least up to a point, the same observation applies to them. An increased relative number of elderly people will contain more pensioners with little or no original income, but also more people holding their completed lifetime savings. To the extent that wage rates are responsive to changes in the number of job-seekers, movements of the birth rate, and more especially the balance of migration outwards and inwards, have in practice impinged upon the relative size of the lower incomes. These demographic changes have not worked in any one direction, but they have been significant as accounting for changes whose emergence in the short run would otherwise cause concern.

Another source of short-run change lies in the fluctuations of the stock market and property values. These may produce marked changes in the concentration of wealth when holdings are valued at the prices of the day. The associated movements of the trade cycle work in opposite directions. On the one hand, a depression commonly throws out of work a higher proportion of the lower than of the higher paid; but its effect on the substantial part of the highest incomes that is drawn from investments is also marked. Some ratchet effect may be observed here. The squeezing of profits relatively to earnings in the depression may not be reversed when activity rises again; a lower rate of profit becomes implicitly accepted as normal. A tendency since 1914 towards greater equality may be attributed to this, among other factors. Depressions also reduce the concentration of wealth, in so far as they check the formation of new fortunes. At any level of wealth there is a constant turnover: existing holdings are being dispersed, and—if the stock of wealth at that level is to be maintained—their place is taken by new accumulations. If the times have become unpropitious to accumulation by enterprise and speculation, the stock will fall.

Prominent among the contingencies impinging on distribution in the short run have been wars and the accompanying inflations. In the atmosphere of the war effort, returns on property are more restrained than the earnings of labour; there is, for example, a feeling that rents should not be raised, and this has been enforced by legislation.War expenditure, like other expansions of monetary demand, begins by raising profits; wages and salaries get adjusted with various lags, and some contractual payments may not be changed at all. It seems highly probable that the variance of employees' incomes will be raised, but whether average income per employee will rise or fall relatively to the average return per unit of capital is uncertain. In the reaction to wartime inflation, as in 1921, the unions resisting cuts are the anvil on which profit margins are beaten thin by the blows of falling demand.When inflation comes, as it has done in recent years, through pressure by trade unionists, that is through cost-push, the effect again is to squeeze profit margins. Since profits generally enter in greater proportion into big incomes than smaller ones, the effect will be to decrease inequality. Under cost-push, also, the lower dividends are likely to be accompanied by higher nominal rates of interest, and both depress capital values, with consequent reduction in the relative size of the larger holdings. Changes in distribution effected in these ways are not always and wholly reversible: if they persist for some time, notions of the normal may shift towards the current state of affairs.

On the whole, the contingent changes have worked to reduce inequality of income, and even more that of wealth. Among them, the effects of war and inflation have been outstanding.

Later studies of the systematic relation between economic growth and the inequality of income have generally supported the proposition of Kuznets (1955): as activity grows from a low initial level, inequality increases; but as the growth continues, it is reduced. If we look farther back, indeed, we can say that the very form of distribution that is typical of contemporary economies was made possible only by the growth of commerce and industry with their accompanying urbanization. These bypassed the bottleneck of land, the means of production whose supply was virtually fixed by nature once and for all, so that those who owned it could exact a toll from the rest of the community. As forms of equipment were developed that could be increased without limit, and gave increasing openings to labour, a market developed in which there was less possibility of the owners of the means of production holding wages down below the worker's contribution of production. The towns of the Middle Ages must have provided a far less unequal distribution of income than a feudal and rural economy of lord and peasant. But as growth went on, and as it has proceeded in the less developed countries of our own time, inequality increased. It has done so because some sectors have advanced in productivity more rapidly than others; and because the openings now afforded to enterprise have been taken by the more enterprising, who have advanced more than their neighbours. We have seen how, in the American Mainland Colonies, inequality increased in some rural communities that had access to urban markets, and how it increased generally in the American economy during the three decades of technical innovation and capital construction down to the Civil War. The recorded changes are mostly those in the distributions of income: that similar changes occur in the distribution of wealth we may conjecture, but the data are fragmentary.

That further growth has reduced inequality may be attributed to the accumulation of capital outrunning the rise in the working population, and to the rise in the standard of living, and in the level of education, raising the productivity especially of the less qualified part of the labour force. Property income, always more concentrated than income from work, has become smaller relatively to earnings. The reduction in inequality has taken the form especially of an increase in the relative numbers and affluence of the middle class. Technical advances have worked in the opposite direction, in so far as they have released an additional supply of industrially unskilled labour from agriculture; but on the other hand they have extended the demand for the improved qualifications provided by extended education. Part of the conspicuous reduction in the inequality of wealth in recent years has been due not to contraction at the top, although that has occurred, but to 'the middle-class bulge'—the acquisition of more property of various kinds, not least houses and consumers' durable goods, raising the profile in the central three or four deciles of the distribution. The capacity to accumulate in this way is clearly a product of a rising standard of living.

It is also a product of public policy, in two ways. One is that the provision of secondary education for all, and the subsidization of tertiary education, have increased the number of persons with qualifications that command rates of pay above those of manual workers. The other is that pressure to save for the purchase of a house has been increased indirectly by rent control and associated legislation, which have largely eliminated the private landlord with houses to let; while tax concessions have subsidized house ownership.

On the other side, taxation has reduced the concentration of wealth at the top. It has done so directly, through taxes on estates at death, which by inserting another claimant increase the fragmentation of the holding. If transfers to heirs are made during the lifetime of the holder—and there is indirect evidence that they have in fact been made in the United Kingdom on a considerable scale—the process of dispersal is accelerated. Graduated taxation, running up to high rates on the top tranches of big incomes, also tends to reduce the top holdings, by cutting down the spare income that might go into further investment, and by reducing the advantages of holding an asset in comparison with those of realizing it.

This application of taxation is a leading instance of the use of public policy to change social structure. The distributions of income and wealth depend upon that structure in a number of ways. The structure in turn depends on custom and prevailing attitudes as well as on law. Whether convention, or law, provides equal employment opportunities for women; whether parents commonly leave a lion's share to their eldest son, or are expected to divide their property equally among their children, sons and daughters alike; whether the government is concerned to gain support for itself by strengthening a certain part of the structure, as in earlier days it was to reward some notables, and in the Soviet-type economies it has favoured the manual industrial workers; what sort of stratification by education and type of upbringing today inherits from yesterday—in all such issues as these, the social structure, broadly conceived, enters as a circumstance that is formed independently of the current distributions of income and wealth, and acts upon them.

Acts of governmental policy towards the structure, and campaigns to change attitudes towards it, are therefore likely to change the distributions, whether or not that is their aim. The connection is seen most clearly in the Soviet-type economies, where the whole ostensible purpose of the regime is to establish a certain type of structure. But here the limitations of government in this sphere are also evident; the ruling party, for all its dictatorial power, cannot fix relative incomes at will, but must remain within limits of tolerance set by the propensities of individual behaviour in both the supply of effort and the demand for particular products. Generally, public policy towards social structure has taken most effect on distribution in two ways: by checking the growth and promoting the dispersal of the biggest acquisitions, and, most widely, by removing obstacles in the life-path of the individual, and smoothing the road of advancement.

16.4 The Possibilities of Deliberate Change

One major conclusion emerges from this survey: the distributions of income and wealth are resistant to great imposed changes. The play of individual choices, directing the exertion of individual energies, asserts itself every day in a myriad places. The countless rivulets come plashing down: their flow may be diverted here or there, but it cannot all be dammed up. If intervention extends to equalization by edict—a fixing of the same pay for all, or a distribution of property in equal shares—then we have reason to believe that human propensities will assert themselves, through innumerable transactions day by day, to restore much of the original state of affairs. Even less drastic changes, such as a reduction of the differential for skill, will encounter sustained resistance: the authorities may be able to repress organized opposition, but not the pressures exerted individually by people in their millions, at a myriad points, continually. If the state becomes the sole employer, it is not free to set what rates of pay it chooses, unless it makes slaves of all its people. David Hume made this point in his essay *Of Justice*, originally published in 1741–2:

'Render possessions ever so equal, men's different degrees of art, care and industry will immediately break that equality. Or if you check these virtues, you reduce society to the most extreme indigence, and, instead of preventing want and beggary in a few, render it unavoidable to the whole community. The most rigorous inquisition too is requisite to watch every inequality at its first appearance; and the most severe jurisdiction, to punish and redress it.' (Hume 1875: II, 188–9)

As much as any private employer, the state cannot exceed the tolerances set by the reactions of its employees. If all possibility of inequality of holdings outside the household is removed by taking all land and equipment into national possession, the great wealth at the top of Western distributions disappears, but the difference made to inequality among the great majority, the lower 85 per cent or so of income recipients, will not be great, for receipts from property compose only a small part of their incomes. Such a measure, moreover, cannot be applied without transferring to a central administration functions otherwise performed by private enterprise and the market; and hitherto a centralized and bureaucratic administration has not done well for the material well-being of the people. To the extent that individual men and women remain free to choose their jobs and lay their money out within some effective range of choice, their actions in the aggregate generate a certain form of the distribution of income and of what property they are allowed to possess. In varying degrees this form will embody the kind of inequality found in contemporary societies.

But if this is the main answer to our question, it is at the same time a partial one. It considers men and women as they are, and in their present setting of constraints and opportunities; but human nature can be changed, and life-paths can be smoothed. People change, in their personality and capability, with the conditions of their upbringing, education and training. The limitations and openings along their life-paths depend in part on institutions and attitudes that can be refashioned. Here are many possibilities for intervention. If sweeping measures are ineffective or inefficient, there are influences that can be exerted and obstacles that can be removed. But we need to consider where intervention promises to be most effective in raising life-chances.

This may appear if we look back over the origins of inequality, and ask how far they are amenable to imposed change. They are generally recognized; although some theorists have rested their argument on one or other of them and disregarded the others, and opinions about their comparative importance differ, it is rare to find the contribution of any denied outright (Sahota 1978). There is first the genetic programming, by which a person is born with a certain physical, mental and emotional constitution and potential for development. Children are then further differentiated by their nurture in the home (Phelps Brown 1977: ch. 7). The personality they form depends greatly on the way they are treated in the first five years of life, and on a variety of circumstances and happenings, such as hospitalization, that may impinge upon them then. Their ability to learn also depends on their interactions with other people in those years, and on their 'cultural inheritance' in the home. Bloom (1964) studied the development of five characteristics—height, general intelligence, aggressiveness in males, dependence in females, intellectuality in males and females, general school achievement—and concluded that for these characteristics 'there is a negatively accelerated curve of development which reaches its midpoint before age 5'. In proportionate terms, half the difference in height, for example, between a newborn baby and the adult is reached by that age. It is reasonable to suppose, Bloom continues, that 'the environment would have its greatest effect on a characteristic during the period of its most rapid development' (p. 214). Any teacher meeting a class of entrants to a first school at five years of age can have no doubt of the wide range of character, and of ability to learn, already present there. The schooling that follows, both formal and vocational, is an evident source of further differentiation of the ability to work, the more so because it interacts with and magnifies the influence of the home: the children from the better homes go to the better schools, and are able to profit more from education. At the entry into work, the diffferences between homes asserts itself again, in the entrants' varied knowledge of possible openings, and connections with people who can advise and help them. Here something too depends on the variety of temperament; there are choices to be made between occupations that offer different combinations of money income and satisfaction in work, or free time away from it. A taste for risk-taking, again, or aversion to it, affects the supply of labour to different forms of activity. After entry into work there is further differentiation through the extent of opportunities for training on the job, and gaining efficiency with experience. This may take more effect than the previous schooling—it is noteworthy that the variance of the earnings of a cohort rises with age.

What stands out here, when we consider the possibilities of intervention, is the relative importance of the home. Outside it, the openings for public policy are evident. The provision of general and vocational education, both by maintaining schools and by supporting students; guidance in choice of careeer and help in job-finding; stimulus to training within industry—all these are taking marked effect, and can take more. Legislation also has reduced discrimination. Wherever a person with given potential is kept back by obstacles to economic and social mobility, or lack of facilities for further development, the possibility of effective intervention arises. But it is harder to see how to raise the potential that is formed in early childhood. The way may be shown by the health services, which do not merely provide remedial treatment, but spread information about children's needs, and principles of hygiene and diet. Not so long ago, in the lifetime of people now living, how many parents in Britain knew that they should teach their children to clean their teeth? There is a counterpart in parents' understanding of how the child is attached to them, how vulnerable it is and how its capacity to learn depends upon its relations with them. The growth of playgroups in recent years has done much on these lines to change the attitude of parents as well as to develop their children. On traditional ways of thinking, such matters lie outside the purview of economists; but they are in fact basic to the issue of how to enable each person to develop his or her full economic potential.

The improvement of life-chances will not reduce inequalities in every case. On the contrary, the removal of a constraint that has held back two people of unequal potential behind the same barrier will allow them to diverge. But the general effect will be, as we see it to have been already, to raise the relative supply of the greater proficiencies, and so to compress the hierarchy of earnings. Another aspect of the same process is the extension of what is conventionally termed 'the middle class'. There is an essential link between the degree of inequality and the extent of social mobility. All the provision that improves the life-chances of the individual raises the relative supply of higher qualifications, and shifts the weighting of income upwards. The process is limited by the genetic distribution of potential.

In the foregoing discussion, income and wealth have been considered only before tax: the possibilities of reducing inequality extend widely when we bring tax in. We have seen how effective redistribution through taxation and social benefits has been in some Western countries. The extent to which inequality is felt and resented depends greatly on the condition of the poorest, and redistribution of income has transformed this. At the same time, wealth has been spread more widely, on one intelligible way of reckoning, in that the provision of state pensions has endowed every potential beneficiary with an asset that is valuable for the holder even though it is not marketable. If public policy can act on incomes and wealth before tax only indirectly but gradually, it can redistribute income, and make some provision in lieu of personal savings, effectively and directly. But there are limits to this process too. They are set on the one side by the resistance of the taxpayer, a resistance that is strengthened when, on the other side, the disbursements are believed to be going beyond the relief of need and in some cases to act as a disincentive to effort and encouragement to irresponsibility. These limits, however, have been wide enough to allow redistribution in the present century to transform the face of society.

PART III

Egalitarianism Analysed and Assessed

17

The Basis of Egalitarianism

The two preceding parts, concerned with the history of ideas and the formation of actual distributions, have prepared the way for a final assessment of egalitarianism in principle and in practice. At the outset, we distinguished various applications of egalitarianism to the distributions of income and wealth, according as it called for equality of treatment, of opportunity or of consideration. Underlying all these is the same judgement of what is morally right in human relations: transactions and dispositions that are in some sense equal are only fair, only just. So stated, the judgement is inescapable: no one can be in favour of injustice. The principle of equality admits of debate only in application to particular circumstances. But it is also only here that its content becomes manifest. The present chapter takes up the linked questions of what the principle of equality calls for in particular applications, and what claim it makes, so understood, upon us. To what sorts of transactions or relations do we apply it? And what is there in it that commands assent?

17.1 Applications of Equality

Fair prices and the just wage

A first appeal to our acceptance of equality as fairness is made by the notion of the fair price or the just wage. We saw that the medieval doctor's doctrine of the just wage meant in practice that the wage paid must be no less, and need be no more, than what the labour in question commanded in the market as a rule: the employer must not take advantage of the weak position of particular workmen to pay them less, nor must he cut the pay at times when trade is slack. What the labour was worth was decided by the willingness of others to pay for it, generally and normally. Given this valuation of what the worker provided, the principle of equality required that it should be offset and balanced by what the employer paid. In the same way, prices are deemed fair if they are equal to the value of the product as that value is determined by the general and persistent working of the market, fluctuations and local deviations apart. Questions might be raised about the validity of this form of valuation, but what concerns us here is the reason, given any valuation, for applying the principle of equaltity to the payment.

We may see the reason if we ask why we feel it unfair to pay less than the principle calls for, even when the seller is willing to accept it. Suppose, for instance, that a collector finds in a cottage a piece of china that he knows would fetch £100 in the market: why should he not buy it for £10 when that would be acceptable, even gratifying, to the cottager? The answer is that he would be using his superior knowledge to rob the cottager of £90. The case for the fair price or just wage is the case against theft. We allow everyone a right of property in his or her labour or possessions. This right imposes on other people the duty of taking no action that will impair the property: we must not damage it or steal it, and if some of it is transferred to us we must hand back as much as we get. The requirement of equality between the two sides of such transactions is thus a corollary of the basic principle of the sanctity of property.

On this basis we may proceed to *equality of treatment*, or at least to the application of it that forbids discrimination. The rule against discrimination says that people must be treated alike except as they differ in respects that are relevant to the purpose of the treatment. If women workers in engineering require adjuncts that men doing the same work do not require, it is not unfair to pay the women at a rate that is reduced by the cost of the adjuncts; but where women in teaching or administration are doing the same work as men in the same conditions, it is discriminatory and unfair to pay them less because the comparative lack of alternative employment makes them available for less. The dubious validity of valuation by the market appears here again; for the lower supply price of women's work might be held to be as much a part of the market as the higher price put upon the same work when supplied by men. But it is also possible to hold that if employers are willing to pay at a certain rate for work done by men they would be willing to pay no less, if they had to, for the same work done by women. In that case, the amount of property that the women have in their own labour is measured by the men's rate, and for the employers to pay less is an infringement of property rights. A similar argument, with a similar reservation, applies to other instances of discrimination, as between ethnic groups, or between those for whom a monopoly fixes different charges according to its estimate of 'what the traffic will bear' in each case.

The notion of deserts

The principle of equality is invoked when we fix an amount to be paid or awarded to the deserts of the recipient. When we speak of a wage as being well earned, or a punishment as richly deserved, we are assuming that, it is right and proper to make awards 'on the merits of the case'. This assumption may be accounted for in more than one way.

One of these takes us back to the notion of property. If we consider what the deserts are that should be recompensed, we find that, whatever actions or traits may constitute them, they are always such as benefit other people.

If they deserve to be compensated, rewarded or requited, it must be because 'the labourer is worthy of his hire'. True, admirable qualities may sometimes seem to deserve recognition when they have not made any contribution to the welfare of other people; but what makes them admirable is precisely that they are the kind of quality that commonly does make such a contribution. A wholly self-regarding life deserves no reward or penalty at the hands of its neighbours, of whom indeed it cannot really have any. To say that we should get what we deserve can therefore be taken to imply that what we have done for or to other people, for good or ill, should be reciprocated, in an amount equal to the goodness or badness of our deed. This is another form of the sanctity of property.

But the notion of deserts can lead us to a different destination. It does so when we consider it as correlative with responsibility: if I am not responsible for an action, I do not deserve reward or punishment for it. But when we ask for how much of my actions I really am responsible, we run into familiar difficulties. It is not only that my abilities have been formed by heredity, upbringing and circumstance, so that in a sense they are mine only in the same way as I might have acquired a box of tools; but all the temperament that stamps one as lazy or hardworking, mean or good-natured, shifty or honest has certainly been strongly influenced, if not wholly determined, by the same origins and environment. When we learn of the appalling childhood of a criminal, we say 'There but for the grace of God go I'—or but for my better luck in the draw for parentage and home: why should he be punished for having been already damaged so much? By the same token, I cannot claim credit for any good deeds I may perform. People are no more deserving of award for having been born with a good brain than with big ears.

One way that we sometimes take out of this difficulty is to distinguish between abilities and will, between powers at our disposal and the use we choose to make of them. We impose handicaps on contestants to offset differences in their bodily strength and skill, so that the prize shall go to the one who makes best use of his or her endowment. One practical purpose of this is to provide a contest with the sporting interest of an unpredictable outcome, rather than let the same contestants win every time. But the device also implies a belief about who deserves to win—the one who tries hardest. People are not responsible for their mental and physical abilities, but they do retain responsibility, it is held, for how they exert them. The will is free, not in the sense that I can do whatever I choose, but in the sense that I can make more use or less use of what powers I have. Certainly this assumption, for all the difficulties it raises, does underlie the way in which we very commonly treat one another.

Indeed, it forms one basis for demanding *equality of opportunity*. The inequalities of ability imposed by family origins should not, it is felt, be increased by giving better access to education, and avenues of advancement generally, to the children of some families than those of others. All people, however different their abilities, are held to be alike in their freedom to decide how hard they will try. Those who have the will to get on should not be denied any opportunity to do so that is open to others and can be extended to them. The notion of handicapping enters again here, for it indicates the belief that deserts lie not in the ability to achieve but in the determination with which achievement is sought; and the purpose of the handicap is to make the contest one between degrees of determination and not lengths of leg. The purpose of equality of opportunity is in any case to give equal scope to energies that all can exert, not to enable them all to exert them to the same effect. Even where it prevails, there will remain many differences in achievement, but these will be due only to differences of natural endowment which cannot be altered, and not to the differences of determination that it is right to reward differentially.

But although the distinction between abilities and will is one on which we often act, it is difficult to sustain, and this difficulty too is recognized in our everday acquaintance with human nature. It lies in this: that the self, which is taken to be free to choose, is seen to use that freedom consistently—it possesses characteristics, that is to say, which differentiate one person from another. These characteristics form persistent traits of personality. How then shall we distinguish them from those abilities that the self has acquired but for which it is not responsible? The behaviour of adopted children offers an opportunity of distinguishing between heredity and environment which appears to show that a tendency to delinquency can be hereditary (Mednick *et al.* 1984). The power to control the use I make of my abilities, although I am conscious of exerting it, may itself be outside my power to control. What constitutes myself, as that is known to other people, has been made 'for and not by me'. The 'me' there refers to a centre of consciousness and feeling that might have come to be linked with other characteristics than those with which it is linked at present, just as it might have been sited in another body. We arrive at the notion of the indistinguishable self, or soul.

This again is a notion present in our everyday thinking. We find it intelligible to say such things as 'If I had been born a Frenchman', or 'If I had been musically gifted'. The belief held by some Asian people in successive incarnations of the same self, some of which may be in the bodies of animals, is intelligible even to those who are far from sharing it. The same belief appears in the sense of oneself as having existed in 'the cave of the unborn' before entry into a particular foetus; so that when one sees the misery of some poor wretch one thinks, 'It might have been me'—if I had a drawn a different number in the lottery of birth. 'Put youself in his place'. Religion again has proclaimed the immortality of the soul, which leaves behind the body in which for a time it has been lodged. The self or soul so conceived, moreover, is recognized as having no distinguishing characteristics. 'A man's a man for a' that'; 'All men are equal in the sight of God'; 'There is no such thing as Jew and Greek, slave and freeman, male and female; for you are all one person in Christ Jesus' (Galatians 3: 28; also Colossians 3: 11).

Here we reach the ultimate source of egalitarianism. If the core of the individual lacks all individuality, and what I refer to essentially when I say 'I' is no different from what you refer to when you use that same pronoun, what grounds are there for giving one any preference over another? People—taking them as they come—differ in all manner of respects, which call for differences of treatment; but the self that is the bearer of identity and the centre of consciousness in each of us is not so differentiated. Every person, then, it appears, considered as a person, is entitled to *equality of consideration*.

Needs

Egalitarians distinguish needs from wants, in that needs are those wants that lay other people under an obligation to meet them. There are many things I want that no one else feels under any obligation to supply me with; but if I have needs, the community must take notice. Needs are seen as conferring an entitlement: 'Where there's a need there's a right'. It might seem that the line between needs and wants could be drawn by distinguishing the basic requirements of life from mere amenities, but how much is basic is a matter of judgement that has varied widely in different stages of society, Nowadays it will be generally agreed that every child has a need for education which society must meet; but it was not so agreed in any country until comparatively recently, and even now there is no agreement on how much education should be provided at the public expense. Similarly for the support and care that folk of all ages may need: how much medical care, for instance, or relief in old age or unemployment, can they reasonably expect other people to provide for them? Evidently, what makes a want a need is the judgement of the community.

That judgement is guided by benevolence, compassion or altruism, the fellow feeling by which we identify ourselves with others who may include animals as well as human beings—so that we suffer with them and are ourselves gladdened by their happiness. The clearest example is a mother's loving care for her child. Generally, members of a family feel an obligation to meet one another's needs, at least to the extent of not indulging themselves when relatives are suffering want alongside them. Socio-biology has shown how altruistic behaviour may be selected for by the evolutionary test of survival, because although being programmed to behave altruistically will reduce the chances of survival of any one individual, it improves those of the bearers of that set of genes generally. But although our being genetically programmed to help one another will account for a sense of obligation within a certain range of kinship and affinity, it provides no guidance on how far we should go in extending help to any one person, or in accepting other people of all sorts as having any claim on us at all. Nor does it establish any cause for meeting people's needs equally.

Such a case, however, was put forward by the Utilitarians, as far back as Archdeacon Paley. If transferring £1 from A to B causes less loss of welfare to A than B gains, it will increase the sum of welfare taking the two together. If A and B have equal capacities for suffering and enjoyment, transfers will be of that kind so long as A's income exceeds B's. Generalizing, then, we can see that the welfare of the whole community will be maximized when all incomes are equal. Allowing that people may be so circumstanced that their needs differ although their capacity for feeling is the same, we can amend the conclusion to state that the proportion of income to needs should be equalized—that is, the extent to which needs were met should be the same for all throughout the community.

As a guide to action, this argument encounters a difficulty that goes deeper than any doubts we may have about the assumption of equal capacity for feeling. Even supposing that the aggregate welfare could certainly be maximized by equaliziing incomes, or improved by reducing their inequality, why should I trouble myself with the welfare of everybody else? why should I not be concerned to maximize my own welfare, even at their expense? Rainborow's answer was that 'the poorest he that is in England hath a life to live as the greatest he'. This is the principle of equality of consideration again. This principle, we have seen, itself rests on the notion of the 'he' as an indistinguishable self. This case for meeting needs equally rests on the concept of the interchangeability, so to speak, of the centres of consciousness by which needs are felt.

Justice

Egalitarians commonly stigmatize the existing distributions of income and wealth as unjust: their aim in reducing differences is to achieve 'a more just society'. They find it unjust that people's means are not proportioned at all dependably to their deserts or their needs. People who devote their lives to the service of the community are often paid little, while some speculators in property make fortunes; there are wealthy people who hardly know what to do with their money, while the incomes of many households hardly provide the bare necessities of life. These inequalities are reckoned not merely undesirable, but specifically unjust, because justice is bound up with equality.

So it is indeed, and that in two ways. One is that 'all are equal before the law': there should be no 'benefit of clergy', or 'one law for the rich and another for the poor'. In the second way, justice is bound up with equality in that its awards should match the claims, entitlement or culpability of the subject: people should get what they deserve, and the punishment should fit the crime. These two requirements are connected. The first will be met if the second one is, for if every claim is matched by the award, all awards will have been made in conformity with the same rule. But the reverse does not hold; we should hold it unjust, for example, to inflict the death penalty on a number of motorists guilty of the same parking offence, even though they were all being treated alike.

Evidently, the first requirement is another statement of non-discrimination. The rules of law, whether substantive or procedural, may of course make different provision for persons differently circumtanced, but it is unjust to provide differently for persons in like case on the grounds of some attribute of theirs—such as gender or race—that forms no part of their claim or their wrong doing. We saw that the case against discrimination rested on the principle that whatever was supplied by other people should be fully compensated to them, and this principle in turn rested ultimately on the sanctity of property.

The second requirement rests on the same principle: the very idea of matching, that is of compensation and retribution, implies the obligation to keep property intact. But in applying the principle a distinction must be made between claims and needs. Justice, it is said, requires awards to match both. But the two are not on the same footing. When we discussed needs, we held that they could make a claim on other people's pockets only in so far as those people were moved by fellow feeling to meet them. If that is so, it would be better to speak of needs as appealing to benevolence, rather than liken them to claims. When we see the disproportion in which different people's needs are met, we may well wish to reduce it, but justice does not require us to do so. We are free to do it by our own actions to whatever extent we choose, and in practice we generally do more to help the needy who are close to us in one way or another, and with whom we can identify ourselves, than those whose need may be greater but who are remote. But although we speak of someone 'claiming our sympathy', and of claiming it in the name of our common humanity, that is only to say that we are invited to put ourselves in that poor person's place: if we do not choose to do so, we have disregarded no obligation that justice imposes. For justice is concerned with claims only in the sense of entitlements, to neglect which is to do wrong to the claimant. The basic principle of justice, of matching the award to entitlement or culpability, implies that it is applicable only where there is an entitlement of ascertainable magnitude.

This means that we cannot properly speak of a distribution of income or wealth as being just or unjust. 'Justice', as Anthony Flew has said, 'is essentially concerned with deserts or entitlements', and these 'have to be grounded in some sort of fact or facts about the persons who deserve and are entitled' (Flew 1981: 81, 85). If a cake has been divided, we cannot say whether justice has been done among the recipients unless we know facts about them that show whether one is entitled to more than than another—facts such as that one has done more than others to make the cake. We cannot tell whether a distribution is just or unjust until we know the claim of each recipient. But no one has a claim to a *share* in the national product, that is, in the aggregate of individual products. What people are entitled to is to keep and enjoy what they have lawfully acquired, and to be compensated for what they transfer to others. Justice upholds those entitlements. It does not require me to make an unrequited transfer, that is to be benevolent or charitable, although I may well feel in a particular case that it is the 'right thing to do'.

Those who feel that the existing distribution is unjust may well be unconvinced by this. Agreed, they may say, that justice consists in matching awards to deserts: can you really say that someone who lives in luxurious idleness because he has inherited a fortune deserves to do so? The question is really the same as whether the surgeon deserves to earn more than the labourer. In each case we imply that a person's economic resources should match his or her deserts, that those resources are the subject of an award, and that the present award is in excess of the accepted deserts, and therefore unjust. But there are difficulties here. Present incomes and wealth holdings have not mostly been fixed by any discretionary award, but have been formed by the activity and position of individuals within a certain social and economic structure. The deserts that are compensated within that structure are not those that we impute according to our own judgement of the deserving, but those that are assigned by the judgement, in the aggregate, of the market, and by the rules—of inheritance, for example—adopted by society. What those who find the outcome unjust are really saying is that they wish deserts were assigned differently; a society in which income and wealth were more evenly distributed would in their view be a more just society because economic resources would more nearly match what they deem to be people's deserts. But in the present state of affairs, the deserts that it is just to compensate are determined otherwise.

What the egalitarians really object to, the real source of the injustice that they resent, is the way in which deserts are determined. The market may be willing to pay vastly more for the services of the surgeon than for those of the labourer, but the labourer works to the best of his ability, and the surgeon cannot do more than that. Society has upheld the family by allowing the transmission of wealth from parent to child, but this gives the children of wealthy parents an unfair start in life, and no one should be able to live without working. What egalitarians claim, then, in the name of justice, is the formation of a society and economy in which justice would make different awards because entitlements that it is its tasks to meet and match would be different. If the disparity between the surgeon's income and the labourer's is held to be unjust, that is because the valuation put upon their services by the willingness of people to pay for them is rejected as the measure of their entitlement. If the inheritance of wealth is held to be unjust, that is not because entitlements under the present law are disregarded, but because that law is rejected for creating an entitlement where there should be none. 'A more just society' would be one designed according to the designer's judgement of deserts.

Two basic principles

We have been examining the demands that equality makes on us in our own conduct and in the arrangements of society. These demands are presented in various forms, but are found to rest on two principles which, it seems, we are bound to think right if we think at all. One of these is *the sanctity of property*, with its implication of due compensation and retribution. The other is *the interchangeability of the self*, which forms the centre of consciousness in each of us but itself has none of the characteristics that distinguish individuals as we know them; while each self acquires a particular set of such characteristics, it could quite well have acquired a very different one. Each of us, then, can put himself in another person's place. The doctrine of the fair price and the just wage rested on the sanctity of property. The sense of obligation to meet needs comes from the fellow feeling of the indistinguishable self. The belief that the receipts of each of us should match our deserts flows from the sanctity of property when it invokes compensation, and from the indistinguishable self when we make deserts conterminous with personal responsibility. Justice, whether as the common rule without distinction of persons or as the matching of awards to entitlements, rests throughout on the sanctity of property.

If someone askes why transfers out of property, whether voluntary or involuntary, should be reciprocated, it is hard to give any reason that rests on a more basic or cogent principle: the judgement seems ultimate as it stands. But the notion of the indistinguishable self does not impose itself immediately as a basis of obligation. To realize that the ultimate sentient core is the same in all of us may inspire mutual respect, but why does it require equality of consideration? If I have two indistinguishable day-old chicks, why should I not give one more food than another if I so choose? There must be some superior principle from which we infer the obligation to match the common property of selfhood in living human beings with equal status and, it may be, equal well-being.

In recent years one philosopher has taken this challenge up. John Rawls, in his *Theory of Justice* (1972), has advanced an argument to show that anyone who accepts the distinction between the indistinguishable core of selfhood and the attributes or abilities that become attached to particular instances of it must, if rational , choose a society that will allot equal incomes to all—or, if differences are allowed as incentives that will result in the production of more for all, the society in which those who have least have the most they can possibly have. This argument deserves separate consideration.

17.2 Egalitarianism of the Indistinguishable Self: *Rawls's Theory of Justice*

Rawls approaches his problem, and conception of the self, by way of an observation about our moral judgments already noticed above—the difficulty we feel about giving people credit for a superior performance when their ability to achieve it is the product of heredity and upbringing. It is a difficulty that arises from contemporary sensibility. We are no longer as sure as we used to be that the boy at the top of the form deserves a prize. His brains have come to him as a matter of genetics; even his ability to work hard is due to his good fortunes in early upbringing. He has only drawn a lucky number in a lottery. Rawls is very clear about this: it is where his inquiry begins. Commenting on 'the liberal conception' of equality of opportunity, he remarks that

> it still permits the distribution of wealth and income to be determined by the natural distribution of abilities and talents...distributive shares are decided by the outcome of the natural lottery; and this outcome is arbitrary from a moral perspective. There is no more reason to permit the distribution of income and wealth to be settled by the distribution of natural assets than by historical and social fortune. Furthermore, the principle of fair opportunity can only be imperfectly carried out, at least as long as the institution of the family exists. The extent to which natural capacities develop and reach fruition is affected by all kinds of social conditions and class attitudes. Even the willingness to make an effort, to try, and so to be deserving in the ordinary sense is itself dependent upon happy family and social circumstances. (Rawls 1972: 73-4)

Thus, Rawls finds in modern genetics and child psychology reasons for rejecting at the outset all those principles of justice that would base each person's receipts on his or her attributes or performance. For a person is clever or stupid, vigorous or lazy, only because of the chances of being endowed at conception with a certain genotype, being born into a particular family in a particular locality, and encountering various contingencies in the course of growth. We have learned much more in recent years about the genetic factor in intelligence and the influence of a child's relationship during its first four or five years on its capacity for subsequent development. Those who have fared well in these respects cannot but doubt their entitlement to higher rewards than those who have chanced worse in 'nature's lottery'. They will respond to Rawls when he declares that 'no one deserves his greater natural capacity nor merits a more favourable starting place in society' (p. 102), and sets out to find a principle of justice that disregards the lottery.

His object is 'to look for a conception of justice that nullifies the accidents of natural endowment and the contingencies of social circumstances as counters in quest for political and economic advantage', and thereby to find principles that 'express the result of leaving aside those aspects of the social world that seem arbitrary from a moral point of view' (p. 15). These are also aspects of men and women as we know them individually in daily life. We have seen that what is left in each person when we leave those aspects aside is a nucleus only, a self that is a bearer of characteristics, but itself has none that distinguish it from other such centres of consciousness. Rawls does in fact build his theory upon just such indistinguishable selves.

The theory postulates a form of social contract. It leads Rawls to principles for the basic institution of a just society, which fall under this 'General Conception': 'All social primary goods—liberty and opportunity, income and wealth, and the bases of self-respect—are to be distributed equally unless an unequal distribution of any or all of these goods is to the advantage of the least favoured' (p.303).We shall now ask how he reaches this conclusion, as it concerns income and wealth.

Rawls begins by rejecting capability as a basis of entitlement. This rejection is ultimately an intuitive judgement, but one of some subtlety. When he holds that we deserve no credit for qualities that have been implanted in us, he might be thought to allow that we do deserve credit for what we really do ourselves, and then the question arises of what the selves are that have none of those qualities that make up capability. But Rawls is really rejecting the whole notion of entitlement. For him, those qualities are not undeserving but 'irrelevant'. They are irrelevant to the conception of justice which he brings to bear from the first, and whose essential is indicated by the title of his first chapter, 'Justice as Fairness'. Fairness implies the conduct of a procedure according to its rules, without any intervention or omission or departure that could affect the prospects of the parties concerned.Justice always expresses 'a kind of equality' (p. 58). If we put those two concepts together, we can interpret Rawls's purpose as that of developing principles of justice that will treat all persons equally without disturbance of the outcome by factors that differentiate people arbitrarily. He will have the race run fairly, and not upset by nature's capricious handicapping.

But what differentiation is arbitrary depends on what the rules are. The rules postulated by Rawls must show that the imprint of heredity and circumstance on the capabilities of individual is left out of account if justice is to be done between them. There was a Greek view that justice consisted in treating different people differently. Why does Rawls hold that all the differences between people constituted by their genotype and imposed by their social environment are irrelevant to justice? The answer, it seems, is that he does simply so affirm, by an initial intuitive judgement. We may put it negatively, as we have done so far here, and say that he rejects the very notion of entitlement from the outset in so far as it attaches to personal capability and performance. We can also put his case positively, and follow him as he develops his own contract theory of justice: this we shall do next. We shall first state the gist of the theory without comment, and then take up points of difficulty.

This theory is to be developed by asking what principles of justice will be accepted by persons who are unbiased by knowledge of any advantages they enjoy from the natural endowment or social position with which they have actually been favoured. Rawls therefore asks us to consider hypothetical persons whose view of the actual world is limited by a 'veil of ignorance'. They know the general facts about society and how it works, but what they do not know is what particular life-patterns exist there, and which actual person with his or her life-pattern each of them is identified with. Any one of them may find, on lifting the 'veil of ignorance', that 'he' is actually an able woman, socially well established, or a half-starved illiterate man in a slum, and so on: 'he' simply does not know, and it is in the absence of all such knowledge that 'he' has to decide how 'he' wants to see the income and wealth of society distributed. It is understandable that, since the veil of ignorance hides their life-patterns from these hypothetical persons, they do not know what ends, or aims in life, they entertain in the actual world; but they remain motivated by a desire for what Rawls calls the 'primary social goods'. These are the instrumental goods that 'a rational man wants, whatever else he wants'. They consist of 'rights and liberties, opportunities and powers, income and wealth'. The hypothetical persons all 'prefer more of these goods rather than less' (Rawls 1972: 92). They desire this, each for 'himself': they feel neither envy nor sympathy, and reach their decisions as inviduals, 'mutually disinterested' (p.13). But Rawls asks us to consider a number of them as coming together with a view to reaching agreement on principles of justice that shall govern the basic institutions of a society in which they will co-operate. With an echo of earlier social contract theories, he speaks of this meeting as taking place in 'the original position'. The hypothetical persons are fully rational, 'in the sense of taking the most effective means to given ends'.

The end that each person pursues, of acquiring the greatest possible amount of primary goods, is to be assured by the institutions of the society, under the principles now to be adopted. What principles will recommend themselves to this end, and will it be possible to secure agreement? Rawls is clear that his hypothetical persons will adopt the rule set out above as his 'General Conception': income and wealth should be distributed equally, unless inequality results in higher receipts for the least advantaged members of society. He is also satisfied that complete agreement will be reached on this.

For the adoption of the rule, he gives two main reasons. The first is simply that its reasonableness stares one in the face. There is no way, he says, for any one person

'to win special advantage for himself. Nor, on the other hand, are there grounds for his acquiescing in special disadvantages. Since it is not reasonable for him to expect more than an equal share in the division of social goods, and since it is not rational for him to agree to less, the sensible thing for him to do is to acknowledge as the first principle of justice one requiring an equal distribution. Indeed, this principle is so obvious that we could expect it to occur to anyone immediately. (Rawls 1972: 150-1)

The mental picture here is of each hypothetical person bargaining with the others about the size of each person's slice of given cake.

An alternative picture is of a great variety of individual life-patterns, ranging potentially from poverty to riches, in the actual world: each hypothetical person knows that 'he' coincides with one of these, but 'he' does not know which. Moreover, 'he' does not know the probability of turning out to be poor or rich or in between: so he will follow the principle of *maximin*, which says, Adopt the course that offers the least bad among the worst outcomes. Here this means that he will choose the distribution of resources which will make his lot as tolerable as possible if he turns out to belong to the least favoured group in the society: he will try to arrange that there should be no least favoured group at all—that no one should be left with less than anyone else. Maximin thus becomes a route to equality.

There will be no difficuty in reaching agreement on the adoption of principles to which these considerations lead. 'It is clear', says Rawls, 'that since the differences among the parties are unknown to them, and everyone is equally rational and similarly situated, each is convinced by the same arguments ... If anyone after due reflection prefers a conception of justice to another, then they all do, and a unanimous agreement can be reached' (p. 139).

But the rule cannot be simply that everyone has the same absolute amount of the primary goods: we have to take account of the possibility that giving some people more than others provides so effective an incentive that a greater product is available for all, and the least favoured, though they now have less than some people, do have more than they would otherwise. '*The difference principle*' is a strongly egalitarian conception in the sense that unless there is a distribution that makes both persons better off (limiting ourselves to the two-person case for simplicity), an equal distribution is to be preferred' (p, 76). This principle may be seen, just as we have approached it here, as an outcome of the original approach, in which each person chooses the arrangement that will give him or her the most should he or she prove to be least advantaged: maximin will allow a departure from equality if that will benefit the least favoured. But Rawls also puts the relationship the other way round, deriving justice from the difference principle: '... the general conception [of justice] is simply the difference principle applied to all primary goods including liberty and opportunity' (p. 73). It is not that the concept of justice, independently formulated, leads to the difference principle, but that our intuitive acceptance of the difference principle provides our concept of justice.

The basic argument for equality, which has now been set out, is open to a number of objections. These may be stated under four heads, according as they concern (1) 'the original position', (2) the motivation of the hypothetical persons, (3) maximin and (4) the ambiguity of equality.

1. Rawls places his hypothetical persons in *'the original position'*, behind a 'veil of ignorance' which denies them knowledge of the life-patterns of the actual world and the actual identification of each with one such pattern; but in this position they agree upon principles that are to govern the relations of those actual persons.

(a) It is hard to see why an engagement that appears rational, and binding, to a person of one kind, allowed very limited information, should continue to be acceptable to or binding upon that person when he and all others like him have been greatly changed and are altogether better informed (Joseph and Sumption 1979: 91). At one point Rawls does speak as if the principles adopted by the hypothetical persons would commend themselves to the actual persons of ordinary life. Those principles, he says, seem to be a fair agreement on the basis of which those better endowed, or more fortunate in their social position ... could expect the willing co-operation of others when some workable scheme is a necessary condition of the welfare of all' (Rawls 1972: 15). But the whole point of his describing 'the original position' and the hypothetical persons in it was that principles should be adopted by persons who did not know whether they were actually better or worse endowed, more fortunate or less so in their social position, in real life.

(b) Rawls's account of how agreement is reached in the 'original position' is only a statement of identity. The hypothetical persons who meet there have been stripped of all the personal particularities of their actual selves, until only identical units remain.

'No one knows his place in society, his class position or social status; nor does he know his fortune in the distribution of natural assets and abilities, his intelligence and strength, and the like. Nor, again, does anyone know his conception of the good, the particulars of his rational plan of life, or even the special feature of his psychology such as his aversion to risk or liability to optimisim or pessimism... I assume that the parties do not know the particular circumstances of their own society. That is, they do not know its economic or political situation, or the level of civilization or culture it has been able to achieve. The persons in the original position have no information as to which generation they belong [sic]. (Rawls 1972: 137)

So these hypothetical persons stand outside all countries and centuries. It is a minor matter after this that they do not know if they are male or female (Flew 1981: 73, citing Bedeau 1969: 242). The hypothetical persons having been made indistinguishable, not surprisingly behave identically.

(c) It is hard to see in what sense the hypothetical persons are persons at all. They are simply nuclei. They have none of the characteristics borne by genes, none of those implanted by upbringing in the home and by the social environment. They are blank units. The man in real life who feels most keenly that his talents and strengths are only the luck of the draw must still identify himself with those characteristics: it is they that give him his sense of identity. They are not appendages, like articles of dress that can be discarded: they are part of his essential self, through which he conceives his pesonal ends, and knows himself for what he is. He may allow that he has been moulded by 'the accident of natural endowment and the contingencies of social circumstances', but these factors have moulded *him*, the whole man; they have not simply attached faculties to him that can be removed, leaving the elemental person freestanding.

2. *The motivation ascribed to the hypothetical persons* is questionable in various ways.

(a) The hypothetical persons are appetitive. However much they have, or think they have, of primary social goods already, they would still like to have more. This is the implication of the proposition, already quoted in part, that these are goods that 'a rational man wants whatever else he wants ... Regardless of what an individual's rational plans are in detail, it is assumed that there are various things which he would prefer more of rather than less'(Rawls 1972: 92). But Rawls himself calls this account of motivation into question when he says later,

'It is a mistake to believe that a just and good society must wait upon a high material standard of life. What men want is meaningful work in free association with others, these associations regulating their relations to one another within a framework of just basic institutions. To achieve this state of things great wealth is not required. In fact, beyond some point it is more likely to be a positive hindrance, a meaningless distraction at best if not a temptation to indulgence and emptiness'. (Rawls 1972: 290)

(b) The desire for 'more [income and wealth] rather than less' is placed in the breast of persons who are allowed to feel no sympathy for one another; for Rawls impose on them the condition of mutual disinterestedness—'the parties take no interest in one another's interests'(p.127). Sir Keith Joseph and Jonathan Sumption remark that they are allowed no moral preferences:

'Experience suggests that men ...do frequently have moral preferences in politics which have little or nothing to do with their personal interests. If this were not so, the history of political theory would be shorter than it is, for authority has certainly been more often justified by its intrinsic moral rightness than by any consideration of utilitarian and personal advantage'. (Joseph and Sumption 1979: 90)

Rawls's determination of the range of feeling of the hypothetical persons seems arbitrary.

(c) It is hard to see how the primary goods as defined can be kept apart, as merely means, from the ends of the life-plans that they will serve. For some people the amassing of income and wealth becomes an end; and, conversely,

Rawls himself considers the possiblity of the ascetic rejecting worldly goods (1972: 142). In constructive and satisfying activities, it is hard to separate means and end.

(d) The purpose of excluding 'ends' is presumably to avoid interpersonal conflict arising from diversity of interest, and no such diversity arises from primary social goods, because they are what 'all men want': but do they all want them in the same proportions? They are of many different kinds. So Rawls proposes to form an index of them: this must be weighted, he says, according to the preferences of the group 'with the least authority and the lowest income', because, according to the difference principle, this is the group whose expectations of primary social goods are to be raised as much as possible. The representative member of that group is asked which combination of primary goods it is 'rational for him to prefer'. 'Rational' must mean 'arranged as the most efficient means to a given end', but this hypothetical person does not know what his ends are. Even if he did, it is still hard to see how he could decide on the 'most efficient' combination of the goods in question. For these goods are 'the powers and preogatives of authority, and income and wealth' (pp. 93–4), and it is hard to see how these can all be treated simply as means: some of them will be valued for their own sake. There is the further difficulty that the member of the least advantaged group who is asked to formulate the index number cannot tell what the weights will be unless he knows in advance the standard of living that he is to enjoy.

3. We saw that one of Rawls's arguments for a social contract that gives priority to equality of income and wealth, and affirms the difference principle, was that his hypothetical persons in the original position were bound to adopt *the maximin course*. This is the course that provides the least bad of the worst foreseeable outcomes.

(a) Such a course does not commend itself to everyone. It appeals to those who are apprehensive of loss, and are not greatly attracted by the chances of gains that risky courses may offer. It caters for aversion to risk. But no hypothetical person knows 'the special features of his psychology such as his aversion to risk ...' (p. 137). Is there not a contradiction here? No, says Rawls: certainly, the parties choose *as if* they had such an aversion, but their choice is strictly rational (p. 172). A rational choice is one that selects the most effective course to attain a given object. In 'the original position' the one object that each hypothetical person is allowed by Rawls to entertain is to obtain 'more primary social goods rather than less' (p. 142). But why does he see maximin as the way to do this? Why is it rational to play for safety, and not have a go for a big win? The decision for maximin implicitly rates the deterrence of loss above the attraction of gain.

(b) Rawls does indeed impute a lack of interest in big gains to his hypothetical persons. 'The person choosing has a conception of the good such that he cares very little, if anything, for what he might gain above the minimum stipend that he can, in fact, be sure of by following the maximin rule' (p. 154). But R.M.Hare (1973: 250) points out that on the very next page Rawls reminds us that 'the parties do not know their conception of the good'.

(c) It is natural to think at this point about the probability of each type of outcome: but Rawls is clear that the parties have no knowledge of these probabilities. Such ignorance seems hard to reconcile with all that they do know about actual societies. 'They know the general facts about human society. They understand human affairs and the principles of economic theory; they know the basis of social organization and the laws of human psychology. Indeed, the parties are presumed to know whatever general facts affect the choice of the principles of justice' (Rawls 1972: 137). These 'general facts', so described, might well be taken to include the form of the distribution of income that is so very widely found: the main body approximates to the log-normal, with the highest incomes forming a Pareto tail. If the hypothetical persons knew this as one of 'the general facts about human society', they could estimate the probability of becoming identified with any one level of actual income.

(d) But if we give up this objection, and accept Rawls's stipulation that they should know nothing about the probabilities of different outcomes, the question arises why they apply to those outcomes the maximin principle and not that of insufficient reason. This latter principle states that, when we have no reason to assign different probabilities to different outcomes, we should assign equal probabilities; Rawls insists that his hypothetical persons will not use this principle, 'in view of the fundamental importance of the original agreement and the desire to have one's decision appear responsible to one's descendents who will be affected by it. We are more reluctant to take great risks for them than for ourselves ...' (p. 169). (Here is aversion to risks openly admitted.) But Hare (1973: 151–2) points out that, had Rawls allowed reliance on the principle of insufficient reason, the argument would have 'led direct to a kind of utilitarianism'. Each hypothetical person would have reckoned it equally probable that he would prove to be identified with a poor, a moderately well off or a well-to-do actual person; the principle he would choose in his own interests would therfore be one that made the average income as high as possible.

(e) Maximin justifies the removal of a sum, however great, from a larger income if that brings an increase of a penny to the least advantaged. Rawls is conscious of this sort of difficulty, and answers that 'the problem of social justice is not that of allocating *ad libitum* various amounts of something ... among given individuals...The possibitities which the objection envisages cannot arise in real cases ...' There is 'one conception of justice which applies to the basic structure of society as a whole. The operation of the principles of equal liberty and open positions prevents these contingencies from occuring' (Rawls 1972: 157–8). This is far from convincing.

4. *Equality arrived at by way of maximin* is a strange principle. Rawls holds it to be, above all, a principle of justice, which it is the whole purpose of his inquiry to define. The claims of justice moreover, are absolute and uncompromising: there cannot be any trade-off between justice and other considerations. Yet the difference principle allows departures from equality if these benefit the least advantaged: if equality is prescribed by a principle that admits of no compromise, how can this be? It can very well be, if equality has in fact been arrived at only as a safety ploy under maximin. The aim here is not to secure some aim of parity, associated perhaps with mutual respect and fraternity, but to ensure that one person, concerned only to protect 'himself', will fare as least badly as possible in the worst possible event. There is an analogy in another contrived case that Rawls himself describes. One man is to cut up a cake into slices for a number of recipients, and himself to get the one slice that will be left after thay have all helped themselves: he will assure himself of the biggest slice possible if he makes the slices all exactly equal. This he does out of self-interest, and so it is with the hypothetical person who chooses maximin. It is intelligible that the equality of this sort should be compromised, if occasion arises, in the continuing interest of those whose interest it was to develop the principle in the first place. But this is not the justice that is uncompromising.

What a limited principle of equality it is that comes out of maximin appears when we consider its expression in the difference principle. We have seen how this states that, unless there is a distribution that makes both of two parties better off, an equal distribution is to be preferred. The intended practical application is that the profits that raise the incomes of entrepreneurs above those of workers shall be regarded as justified if they stimulate developments that cause the incomes of the least advantaged workers to be higher than they would be otherwise. The test is always whether the inequality raises the absolute level of the least advantaged. The difference principle in this form follow logically from maximin. For the object of any hypothetical person in adopting maximin is to secure the best form of the worst outcome, that is, the largest amount of primary social goods in the event of 'his' proving actually to be a member of the least advantaged group. So the principle that 'he' and all others like 'him' adopt assigns as much as possible to that group. In the first place, this is achieved by equality with all other groups, on the cake-cutting principle, to ensure that no one can be left with less than any one else. But then, equality is waived in favour of prosperity; if giving another group more will raise the absolute receipts of the least advantaged, well and good: they will get a smaller share, but more cake. Equality, it appears, was only a means, never an end in itself—there was no intention to maintain that you would confer a benefit on society by cutting down the standard of living of all the comfortable classes, so that all enjoyed parity, albeit in penury. The end was always to limit one's possible loss.

The trouble lies in the ambiguity of 'equality' in this context. It is hard to see what equality, in this role of a maximin safety ploy, has to do with justice. But equality as generally understood is inherently linked with justice in most people's minds (Rawls 1972:58). The confusion of the two uses of the term thus hallows the difference principle that comes from maximin with the sanctity of the principles of justice that concern equality in a quite different sense. The difference principle warrants transferring income and wealth from other groups to the least advantaged, at least until the point is reached at which the withdrawal of incentive would mean that the least advantaged would lose as much from the fall of total output as they would gain from the increment of transfer. This equalizing transfer, then, by association of ideas, appears to be warranted by justice. 'Whether the principles of justice are satisfied, then, turns on whether the total income of the least advantaged (wages plus transfers) is such as to maximize their long-run expectations ...' (p. 277). But such transfers are actually only a cushioning of the risk aversion of Rawls's hypothetical persons.

The numerous difficulties thus raised by Rawls's arguments may be traced to the way in which he casts his problem initially. He asks, what is the just way to distribute a given product among a number of people, when justice requires that the share of each shall be such as all concerned will agree to? This formulation contains certain assumptions.

A first assumption concerns the nature of distribution. This is seen as the slicing of the cake, which somehow is already there to be eaten. Income and wealth are 'at the disposition of society': we are to consider the distribution of manna (p. 62): But that is not how they are created. The actual process is one in which a myriad persons are working each to contribute his or her product to 'the national heap', and each amassing or decumulating wealth. In this process there is a twofold link between what each contributes and each receives: on the side of demand, the payment made depends on the product, and on the side of supply, how much will be produced depends on the prospective payment. Rawls begins by disregarding this link: his problem of distribution is one only of shares, in effect of percentages. But when his argument reaches the receipts of the least advantaged, he becomes concerned with their absolute amount, and allows that giving a larger share to some people might raise their productivity and so enable the least advantaged to get more absolutely.

The initial neglect of the link between individual product and receipts may arise from another assumption about distribution, namely that the principle of justice is applicable to the payments made through it. That principle says, To each his due. If it applies to the resources accruing to each individual, it means that he or she must deserve them, must have a valid claim on them. It then rules out payments proportioned to the ability to work, for that ability depends on heredity, upbringing and circumstance, all beyond the choice and control of the worker. But this is to misunderstand the function of the market. If the principle of justice is applicable to the earnings of performers—and we are entitled to ask whether an excellent performance *deserves* to be paid more than a second-rate one—then we should equally ask whether a pound of strawberries *deserves* to be priced more highly than a pound of potatoes. What the principle of justice really does, in its application to the valuation and recompense of labour, is to forbid discrimination. This says that the treatment of different persons shall not be differentiated in respect of any characteristic that is not relevant to the purpose of the treatment. There is nothing discriminatory or unjust in paying more for greater skill, experience and talent: these are all relevant to the purpose of making payment for their exertion—viz., to match the quality and quantity of the product, and to stimulate activity.

There remains the view of human nature that informs Rawls's approach. He assumes that people are actuated solely by self-interest. On that limiting assumption, he sets out to show how it is rational for them none the less to be egalitarian. The demonstration involves hypothesizing the 'original position'—'we want to define the original position', he says (1972: 141), 'so that we get the desired solution.' That position in turn requires the appearance of undifferentiated selves as the dramatis personae. It is between these indistinguishable souls that the just allocation of resources to beings of flesh and blood in all their actual variety is decided. These artificialities can be spared if we set out with a more realistic picture of human nature, and allow that people want to make the distribution of income and wealth less unequal simply because they feel sorry for the poor.

The justification of accepting ourselves as we are, with all the characteristics by which we live and others know us, is the final outcome of the argument. It began with the misgivings that some of us have about being well paid for abilities that are our good fortune and not our achievement. It proceeded to examine the arrangements that would be chosen by a self that was divorced from all its abilities and simply did not know what they were. The difficulties which that train of thought ran into indicate the falsity of its starting point. The case for egalitarianism must be applicable and acceptable to people as they are. We go on to consider it in that light.

18

An Assessment of Egalitarianism

The preceding discussion has shown that egalitarians have two major faults to find in contemporary society—and for that matter in most developed societies at all times and places: they hold that the distribution of this world's goods is unjust, and they are shocked by the contrast between the equal dignity of all human beings and their unequal resources. Corresponding to these two faults are two remedies; for the first equality of treatment and of opportunity; and for the second, equality of consideration. The issue of justice arises in cases of requited transfers; that of equal consideration, where transfers are unrequited. A requited transfer occurs when a person supplies a service or a product to someone else, or to the community at large, and receives a payment or reward in exchange. It also occurs when it is a loss or hurt that is inflicted on other people, and this is requited by a penalty. Justice concerns the right form and amount of such compensation or retribution. Unrequited transfers occur when the traffic, so to speak, flows one way only: something is remitted to a person who (currently at least) gives nothing in exchange for it. Gifts, charitable donations and various social welfare payments are of this kind. We may well feel it right that they be made, but the principle of equality that constitutes justice cannot tell us how big they should be. Those who make them are moved by fellow feeling , by compassion, which makes inequality in the lot of any two human beings painful, at least if they are close to one another; but the equality desired here is not the equality between award and entitlement in which justice consists.

The first issue, that leading to equality of treatment and opportunity, will be discussed in Sections 18.1–18.3 below; the second, leading to equality of consideration, in Section 18.4. A final section sets out the egalitarian measures that emerge from this discussion as constructive. It is difficult to talk about one issue at a time, and to develop the argument consecutively, where some of the same considerations converge on one ganglion after another, and it seems impossible to establish a logical order of priority among them; yet exposition has to be linear, and we must accept that considerations raised at one point in the line recur later.

18.1 'A More Just Society'

One reason why egalitarians hold the distribution of income and wealth to be unjust is that it does not match the claims and deserts of the recipients. High pay is unjust not because it is much greater than the pay of many others, but because it is out of all proportion to what is judged to be the contribution of the recipient. Low pay is unjust not because the recipient has so little to live on, but because it does not match the true value of his or her work. Some people serve the community devotedly for a lifetime without ever earning much; others make big profits by a lucky speculation, or simply inherit a fortune that brings them a high income for which society demands no return.

There can be no dispute with the principle of justice invoked here, but there are difficulties in its application . The principle governs awards: it says that they should match the entitlement—or the offence—of the recipient. The producer, and the worker, are entitled to a price equal to the value of their product. In exchanges we must give like for like. This is just; but the principle can be applied to fix a payment only when we know the value of what has been supplied. It is here that egalitarians pause. In the payments made for labour and its products, they call in question the way in which their value is commonly determined—that is, through valuation by the market. This they hold to be biased in more than one way, so that the outcome is unjust.

18.2. Valuation by the Market

The allegation of bias has to be made good against an initial presumption in favour of the buyers' verdict. The case for taking the willingness of consumers as a body to pay for this or that article as fixing its true value is a strong one. Each of us, it is true, can point to instances of other people 'throwing their money away'. Their taste is not ours—nor, we may think, it is as good as ours. In particular, there seems to be a general willingness to spend more on what has immediate appeal and provides quick gratification, than on what will add more to the quality of life in the long run. But the days of sumptuary legislation are over, except in wartime. People are free to spend as they will, and their spending constitutes an ongoing plebiscite to decide what things are really worth. As with other democratic votes, any one of us may differ from the verdict of the majority without refusing to accept it.

But egalitarians still feel that valuation by the market is unsatisfactory. For one thing, the market does not work perfectly; various dealers in it are denied the prices they could get for their work or products if they had access to all potential buyers. In practice, that access is denied partly by the inherent obstacles of distance and deficiency of information, but also by monopolies and monopsonies in all their various forms. But even if the market were perfect, the verdict of the buyers' plebiscite would still be rejected, because the ballot is rigged—or at least there is a card vote instead of 'one person-one vote'. Since the rich have more to spend than the poor, any argument that tries to justify the present state of affairs by appealing to the valuations that come out of it is obviously circular. This applies in another way too, for the whole structure of supply—what products are forthcoming in what amounts, and how much labour of each kind is on offer affects valuation just as much as demand does. Unskilled labour is low paid, and professionals command high salaries, because many people have been unable to qualify for professional callings, whereas unskilled work is open to all; and this difference arises from the class structure and its tendency to perpetuate itself. It is further held that the valuation of labour is in any case liable to follow customary notions about the relative values of different kinds of labour. The product of the self-employed worker using only simple tools is distinct and apparent, but most employees work alongside many others, and depend on all manner of equipment: how can the manager determine what each contributes to the product? It seems more likely that managers can only take the existing and customary wage structure as given, and hire such numbers of each kind as are required to operate their plants.

Here are three objections to valuation by the market: the imperfection of the market, the weighting of votes by the means of the voter and the difficulty of isolating the products of persons employed by firms. We will consider them in turn.

1. Imperfections are so pervasive that observations of the working of a model of perfect competition have to be handled with caution. Generally, the effect of imperfections is two-fold: because resources are not allocated so effectively as they might be, the total product is smaller; and some people gain a larger part of that product, at the expense of others. The effect on inequality depends on who are the gainers and who are the losers. Monopoly is associated with higher profits than could be made under competition, and an approach to monopsony in the local labour market makes it possible to raise profits at the expense of pay; but these tendencies are often restrained by the threat of competition from new entrants, especially from foreign suppliers, and by the bargaining power of organized labour. Restrictions on entry into particular employments, imposed by trade unions, professional bodies or sheer custom, keep some rates of pay up at the expense of others. The net effect of imperfections upon inequality in the whole community is hard even to conjecture; no case has been made out for it being clearly in one direction or the other. The consequences for efficiency, both in the internal organization of firms and in the allocation of resources throughout the economy, seem more important.

But there is one form of imperfection that stands out as a source of inequality, namely discrimination. We have seen (pp. 404–5) how it may occur, *within* the market or *before* the market. In any one instance its effect is to widen the difference between the groups concerned—such as whites and blacks, or men and women. But this effect has to be reconciled with the observation that when the groups are combined, the distribution of the incomes of all persons in the economy shows a smooth gradation and not two or more segments. The reason may be that discrimination acts only as one of the innumerable factors bearing upon each person's ability to earn. None the less, it is a cause of needless inequality. The question arises how it can persist.

Discrimination *before* the market may be accounted for by attitudes and practices traditional in society and endorsed by the self-esteem and self-interest of the better treated part of the community; but how can discrimination *within* the market have survived the market's normal workings? If, for example, women's labour is available at a lower price than men's in the same occupation, why have not employers competed to hire it and substitute more of it for men's labour, until its price has been raised to parity? Several reasons can be put forward. In some cases the substitution has been effectively resisted by the men: there have been well understood quotas for women, or arbitrary lines between 'men's work' and 'women's work'. The employers themselves, being almost always male, may have accepted this as in the nature of things, and may have supposed that women's rates had always been lower because their labour was less productive. Where sheer physical strength was needed (as in farm labour), less productive it was, and differentials set there may have carried over into other occupations where they had no such justification. There is also a possiblity of mistaken signalling. If some members of an ethnic group, say, have been found troublesome, employers may be wary of engaging any one of that appearance. There are thus many reasons why a distinctive type of labour that is in a minority should continue to be paid less than the same labour when supplied by the majority. But this is certainly unjust: justice requires 'equal pay for equal work'.

Discrimination *before* the market will be felt by most people to be no less wrong, but it is not unjust. We are dealing here with unrequited transfers. The claim of girls to as good an education as their brothers get, or of ethnic minorities to equal access to professional training, is not the sort of claim that justice must meet, but is based on our fellow feeling, and the principle of equality of consideration for every human being. This is an issue that we shall take up later.

2. Valuation by the market depends upon the existing distribution of resources and opportunities, and is therefore not acceptable unless that distribution is accepted first: so runs this objection. Those who do not accept the existing state of affairs deplore all the manifestations of inequality that it engenders. Their basic objection is not to the injustice of particular transactions, although they may notice these as well, but to the way in which

the system of its very nature offends their feelings of fraternity and compassion for their fellow men. They condemn it, that is to say, in the light of the principle of equal consideration, and this is to be considered in a later section.

3. The difficulty of measuring the contribution of any one of a number of employees of various grades and qualifications, working with elaborate equipment, is not one for the economist alone, but confronts the managers with a very pratical problem. At any one time, it is true, they must take the going rates for each kind of labour as given, within limits that are seldom wide. These rates will have been handed down by past practice, with some adjustment. The question is, how is this adjustment made? What managers are free to do is to adjust the quantity of each kind of labour that they employ at the going rate. At any one time, it is true, they may have little discretion to vary those quantities; the relative amount of any one kind is fixed by the current method of production, and the absolute amount depends upon the order book. But in the course of time opportunitites to change methods do arise, and must be used by efficient management to reduce cost per unit of output. It will do this, formally, in so far as it succeeds in adjusting the intake of each factor of production so that its marginal product, or contribution to value added, will be proportional to that factor's price. In considering any one type of labour, management has to estimate whether the cost of employing one more unit of that type will be warranted by the consequent addition to value added, or whether the same outlay would not produce a higher return if made elsewhere. Management seldom commands objective data with which to measure marginal contributions; it may seldom make estimates of the kind explicitly; but it is efficient only to the extent that it arrives at arrangements that do make them implicitly, for only those arrangements will minimize cost per unit of output. Competition, we may suppose, works at least to check any substantial divergence from them. The adjustments required to realize them then being made, the demand for some types of labour will be extended, and for others contracted; and with more or less delay or obstruction by force of custom and the conservatism of the bargaining system, those shifts in demand take effect on relative rates of pay.

These considerations encourage us to believe that the basic reason for relative rates of pay being what they are is that they are proportional to relative contributions to value added, whether those contributions are assessed directly by the consumer to whom the services are rendered or by the management of firms. Skilled labour is paid more highly than unskilled, not just because that is customary, or because people agree that higher qualifications inherently deserve higher pay, but because managers generally find that an hour of the skilled labour contributes more to value added than an hour of the unskilled. Nor, if relative pay were the outcome only of historical contingency, or of the varied incidence of bargaining power, could we explain why the hierarchy of rates is so similar in many countries that are very different in some other respects.

But this international similarity might be used to support another explanation. The hierarchy of rates, it is said, that is so similar in different countries corresponds throughout to an also similar ranking of occupations by status. People everywhere, it is found, find questions about the relative social standing of different occupations intelligible. They judge by the life-style of the occupants and the general desirability of the work. Not only the willingness, but also the propensity to rank occupations and those who follow them in this way, is so pronounced that mankind has been termed *Homo hierarchicus*. The typical earnings of an occupation enter into the judgement of its place in the rank order, if only because they are a condition of the life-style that goes with it. But instances of high status accorded to low-paid occupations, and conversely, indicate that judgements of status are formed on many considerations other than pay, and may stand while pay changes. When, therefore, we find as we do that in a number of countries the rank order of occupations by pay agrees closely for the most part with that by status, the hypothesis suggests itself that society assigns relative pay to match a prior status. There is a good deal in daily practice to support this; people do claim rises in pay to match what they hold to be the status inherent in their occupation, or call for the recognition of a higher status for it as the necessary condition for adequate pay. Certainly, the long-continued agreement between the two ranking orders has come to seem part of the nature of things, so that when well educated clerical and administrative workers are found to be earning less than some navvies, it is felt to be unnatural.

But it is hard to believe that consumers and employers are willing to pay more for skilled than for unskilled labour simply because everyone accords higher social standing to the skilled. Are they all deceived about what each type is really worth to them? Even if they had been at one time, surely someone would have torn the veil of convention apart, and done well for himself by using more of the labour that was better value at the price.

That the two ranking orders do so largely agree can be better explained by their both depending on the ability to meet the same job requirements:

Where there is an effective market for labour, in that the workers concerned have effective access to alternative employers or customers, who for their part can bid up the pay of the workers in short supply, the relative pay of occupations varies with (among other factors) the natural ability, the education and training, and the experience they call for, and the responsibility they impose. These are the factors that determine the productivity of the labour concerned. But it is upon these factors that the status attributed to an occupation mainly depends. Generally, then, the rank order of occupations by status will be much the same as that by pay. The similarity in this respect of societies that differ widely in respect of culture and of political and economic organization indicates a general agreement about which qualities are worth paying more for and which attract the attribution of higher status. (Phelps Brown 1977: 141–2)

The upshot of this discussion of valuation by the market is that valuations, as the outcome of the interplay of supply and demand, are generally the aggregate effect of a great many individual decisions—about what an article is worth or how much a certain type of labour will contribute to value added; and about what qualifications to acquire and which job to take. There is therefore no sanctity to be claimed for these valuations: they are made upon no normal principle. The process of exchange from which they emerge is circular in logic as well as in its actual flow, for the incomes whose outlay helps form them depend upon them. They cannot be upheld in principle against those who would make arrangements in conformity with their own moral or cultural standards. But our discussion has shown the condition on which alone such a new order can be brought in: individual freedom to choose and change must be curtailed. The market works as it does because people are largely free to spend and save out of their incomes as they will, and to choose and change their jobs within the range accessible to them. Prices and rates of pay are adjusted in the main so as to make these dispositions compatible with one another. If the relative pay of a certain occupation is deemed too high, and reduced by ukase, what will prevent a shortfall in the number who acquire qualifications for it and are willing to work in it? If people are not to be allocated to jobs by their own decisions guided by the signals of the market, the decisions must be taken for them by higher authority—there must be 'direction of labour'. Each of us, thinking of the values that he or she would like to see realized in society, may well reject the valuations that the market makes, but they are the outcome of freedom.

The difference is apparent between the view of distribution taken here and that implicit in the common analogy of shares in a cake. In this, the national product is taken to be like a cake that someone has already made. There it is, waiting to be cut up and shared among those around the table; if one of them gets a bigger share, there will be so much the less left for the others. But the national product is not like that at all: it is simply an aggregate, compiled by statisticians, of a host of individual products. There is no national cake: each of us makes his or her own bun. We can and do reckon how much we have if all individual products are put together, but that is not an amount that is arrived at before it is divided: the process of 'distribution' goes on simultaneously with production. The country's output of wheat is not grown as a whole and then distributed among farms, but the several outputs farm by farm can, if we will, be added up on paper; how much each farm is credited with is decided *before* we know the total. If one farm, moreover, raises its output and, as a matter of arithmetic, gains 'a bigger share' in the national total, it does not thereby reduce the crops on other farms. It is true that, wherever there is trading, it is always possible for the terms of trade to move in favour of one party and against the other, so that the value of the one party's product rises as the other's falls. But it is also possible for one party, by working harder or with better methods and equipment, to raise his product without detriment to anyone else's; and this is the way in which the sum of all products is raised.

We began by taking up the contention that the distribution of income and wealth is unjust because it does not match the claims and deserts of the recipients. In this contention the principle of equality that constitutes justice was seen as calling for equality between the two sides of a transaction: pay is just, for example, when it matches the worker's contribution to production. But the question arises of how that contribution is to be measured. The only alternative to valuation by the decision of this or that person appears to be the valuation by the market, which arises out of the decisions of very many people, both buying and selling. If that form of valuation is accepted as arising necessarily out of a state of society that we wish to retain, the distribution of resources that results from it cannot be condemned as unjust so long as the payments made match the valuations formed by the free working of the market. But we noticed some ways in which the working was not free, and injustice arose. The need here was to establish equality of treatment, get rid of discrimination and advance towards greater equality of opportunity.

But so far, the discussion has been mainly concerned with pay, and with the relation between this and the worker's contribution. We have now to turn to that part of the distribution of resources where often there is no current contribution to match the resources allocated, namely the acquisition and transmission of capital.

18.3. The Acquisition and Transmission of Wealth

To most egalitarians, the inequality of wealth is far more objectionable than that of income. Not only is it much greater, but it is much harder to justify. If justice requires that awards should match entitlements, high earned incomes can claim to be justified by the activity of the recipients; but what contribution to the community can be set against the fortune that is made by speculation, or is simply inherited?

It is not the possession of wealth but the way in which it has been acquired that is under attack. The savings that many families make, to buy a house and to make provision for retirement, are defensible as a reasonable way of applying an earned income, even though the incomes of many other families are never big enough to enable them to do the same. In point of fact, as we have seen, much the greater part of all the wealth of Western countries—if the United Kingdom and the United States are typical—is acquired and held in this way. It has been shown that, because under this life-style of accumulation holdings rise with age, a very unequal distribution of wealth would appear in a cross-section at any one time, even though all incomes were equal and the holdings built up by each family over time were equal too. One part of the cycle is the transmission of capital to widows, and this helps to account for the high proportion of British wealth held by women. Another outcome is that the stock of wealth at any one time is an aggregate of holdings that are constantly being turned over, as they accumulate in the working life of the holders and are dispersed in old age and at death. All in all, there is no suggestion that wealth acquired and disposed of in this way is obtained at other people's expense, or is used to perpetuate a class of idle rich.

But if the other forms of accumulation and transmision are in the aggregate a minor part of the whole, they result in individual fortunes whose size is outstanding and to many people disturbing. Whatever their size, they raise a major issue of principle: whether obtained by speculation or inheritance, they are seen as conferring the power of drawing on other people's produce without making any compensating contribution at the time—or having done so in the past.

The major objection to successful speculation is probably not the luck of the speculator—for the winner, say, of a fortune in a football pool is not grudged his good fortune. The objection is rather that, whereas the pool is open to all, the speculator operates 'on the inside', in the property or stock markets to which most people do not in practice have access. To this is added the feeling that those who make a profit by buying an asset and selling it in unchanged form at a higher price are inherently parasitic, for they are acquiring claims on a national product to which they have added nothing. It may be pointed out that in many cases a speculative venture is linked with development and enterprise, and that part at least of the rise in the value of the assets dealt in may be due to improvements made in them. But this apart, the question stands out of where the gains come from when someone sells in unchanged form an asset that has risen in value since he acquired it.

To find the answer, we must look at the setting in which the gain is made. This is a market in which not only the current output of products and services is offered for sale, but also such portions of pre-existing assets as their ownners choose to dispose of, assets that are not products of current activity but can be exchanged for such products. Whoever holds a durable asset holds a store of exchange value. If the asset that someone holds rises in value, for whatever reason, the total value of resources that can be currently traded rises just as it does if a producer raises his current output; the difference is only that the producer can point to his own activity as entitling him to the increase of value in exchange, whereas the holder of the asset has received a windfall gain. (He may think it a reward for his good judgement in selecting an asset that was likely to rise, but foresight is not productivity.)

The gain of the speculator, then, is not made at the expense of anyone else. What has happened is that the total value of tradable resources has been raised by an increment all of which falls into the lap of the speculator. The necessary conditions of the 'unearned increment' are that private property is allowed in durable assets, that they can therefore be traded against the products of current activity, and that any rise or fall in the market's valuation of them accrues to the owner. The gains of the speculator cannot be condemned as unjust, save in so far as the opportunity to speculate is unequally distributed, or unless the political structure that allows private property in durable assets is held to be inherently inequitable from the first.

These considerations have their bearing on inheritance. Property rights are delimited by law: no one can claim to do what he will with his own. In particular, the right of testamentary disposition—the right to direct how one's property shall be allocated after one's death, and to make the allocation in whatever way one chooses—is commonly restricted. Testators may not be allowed to deprive dependants of all support, however much they may wish to penalize them: the Code Napoleon prescribes a certain pattern of bequest. But it would be hard for the law to prohibit bequests altogether, even though they may bring the recipients resources that they have not earned. The case for such a prohibition rests on their bringing advantages, sometimes great and conspicuous advantages, to some people who have done nothing to earn them, while others who are no less deserving of consideration by the community get nothing. But testamentary provision for dependants and descendants is often an extension of what the testator was doing for them during his lifetime. The widow for whom a wealty husband leaves a large legacy will have shared in his standard of living during his lifetime. The parents who make substantial bequests to their children will have had large resources to apply during their own lifetime to the children's upbringing. If bequests are limited, or heavily taxed, assets that might have passed at death will be transferred during the owner's lifetime. It is hard to distinguish in principle between transfers at death and *inter vivos*.

Here as elsewhere, the institution of the family presents itself as an obstacle to egalitarian measures. It is the essence of it that loyalties and obligations are far stronger between its members than between them and other people. Those members who command resources will apply them much more readily to help close relatives than unrelated persons, however needy or deserving. So far as economic resources can improve a child's upbringing, the children in well-to-do homes will be given a better start in life than the children of poorer parents. The family is an irremovable obstacle to equality of opportunity. Inequality of inheritance is only one part of this.

There is a clear case for restricting both speculative gains and inheritance, on the ground that both bring the recipient an increment of resources not earned by current activity. According to the formal distinction adopted here, they are unrequited transfers, and these not of a kind approved by the community's judgement of the need of the recipient. Inheritance alone tends to perpetuate differences which would be reduced if people had only their own exertions to rely upon. There are two possible forms of restriction. One is fiscal, by way of capital gains tax and capital transfer tax. The other is radical: the personal ownership of durable assets is forbidden altogether, save for household equipment and consumer goods.

The taxation of capital gains, gifts and bequests has evident attractions for governments that have to raise revenue in some way or other; they do not affect the cost of living, and because they are remote from current activity, any adverse effect they have on the incentive to work and on enterprise and accumulation is probably minor. Their potential effect on the distribution of wealth is substantial. We have seen that, in so far as the taxation of transfers *inter vivos* is less stringent than death duties, children will be endowed earlier, and wealth will be spread more evenly over members of the family. If we compare the consolidated wealth of families as a whole, there will be no reduction in inequality, but if we take the holdings of individuals, there will be some. In particular, the inequality of holdings by age will be diminished by an increase in the holdings of young people. We have also seen that death duties, by introducing an additional beneficiary (the state), widen the dispersal of holdings that is always going on at the same time as accumulation. This process of dispersal would be further stimulated by a progressive scale in which the rate of duty varied with the size not of the whole estate but of individual legacies.

The radical solution, by which all durable assets except some consumer durable goods are retained in public ownership, does away with the great individual fortunes that egalitarians find most offensive. By nationalizing land, moreover, it removes from private hands the form of capital that gives the owner most power over other people. The owner of an industrial plant seldom has a captive labour force at his gates, isolated from other employment, and the total supply of capital in industry and commerce can be and constantly is being increased; but the people of a rural district may have access to few avenues of employment beyond those commanded by the local landowner, and the supply of land, in its ultimate source as a gift of nature, is fixed. These considerations have led some egalitarians to regard the inequality of wealth as their prime target. But in fact, the contribution of the return on property to the inequality of incomes as a whole is minor; and property seems to be fairly evenly distributed over the central sector of British incomes. Public ownership of property thus does relatively little to reduce inequality; but it it does bring in a totally different society. The Soviet-type economies show us central planning and bureaucratic administration substituted for private enterprise. It is on the merits of that change rather than on the reduction of inequality that the case for public ownership depends.

18.4 The Equality of Humanity

The basic drive of egalitarianism springs from the contrast between the claim of every human being to an equal status, in respect simply of our common humanity, and the inequality of income and wealth. That equality of status is expressed in our notion of rights inherent in every human being, by reason only of his or her sentient existence. We speak of 'human rights', and expect them to be recognized in every land, whatever the structure of its society or the policy of its government, simply because the inhabitants are human beings as are we. Every person who shares with us the experience of voyaging on this planet between birth and death is in like case with us, and in some respects is entitled to an equal consideration. Those respects appear in civic rights, such as free speech, access to justice, the vote, and protection of property. They appear also where duties are imposed, such as conscription, or jury service; even taxation is required to lay an equal burden on households' ability to pay. In all these and other respects, we feel it wrong to accord or deny rights to people according to their parentage, their abilities, their attainments and even (except in extreme cases) their conduct. Increasingly in recent years it has been held that we should make no distinction by gender. We rate the standing of a country in the scale of civilization by the extent to which it observes these rights. Yet even where they are observed most fully, and the people pride themselves on their civic equality, they are divided from one another by great differences in their income and wealth, with all the consequent differences in their way of life. The spirit of humanity works in one way , the market economy in quite another.To many people who look for no revolutionary change, this disparity is shocking.

What prompts this sense of incongruity amounting to injustice? It is accepted without demur that people who are equal in their civic rights are unequal in a hundred other respects—their age and gender, their bodily strength and mental abilities, their usefulness to other people or dependence on them: why then should anyone be surprised and pained to find that they are unequal in their income and wealth too? There is an evident reason. Our belief in human rights stems from our sense that every human being is like ourselves in having a life to live, and we must wish it to be as full for him or her as we wish our own to be.As Sir Thomas More said, in a passage already quoted from his *Utopia*, 'Nature also wants us to help one another to enjoy life, for the very good reason that no human being has a monopoly of her affections. She's equally anxious for the welfare of every member of the species' (More 1965; 92). Fellow feeling sees human rights as a charter for fulness of life. Their function is to prevent our common humanity from being cabin'd, cribb'd, confin'd, and to leave each person free to enter into life to the full. But evidently poverty does confine us; and ample means, although no guarantee of richness of experience, can help greatly to achieve it if requisites of other kinds are there. The US trade union leader Samuel Gompers is famous for his answer to the question, what did trade unionists want? 'More.' But he also made it clear what more dollars meant for him. 'I do not value the labour movement', he said 'only for its ability to give better wages, better clothes, and better homes. Its ultimate goal is to be found in the progressively evolving life possibilities in the life of each man and woman. My inspiration comes in opening opportunities that all alike may be free to live life to the fullest' (cited by Raskin 1986; 11). The inequalities of income and wealth seem anomalous because they differentiate the opportunity to live life to the fullest that egalitarians believe every human being should enjoy by virtue of his or her humanity.

Various reasons for that belief have been proposed. One has been examined here in the work of John Rawls. It sets out from the assumption that acquisitions of income and wealth must be justified by an entitlement on the part of the person who acquires them: they must be deserved. But the ability to acquire them is implanted in me by heredity, upbringing and circumstance, and so is not something for which I am responsible. This 'I', this characterless nucleus, is necessarily undifferentiated: conciousness of self is the same in every human being. Likeness of the core of life calls for equal opportunity of living. We found difficulties enough in this approach—in its initial separation of distribution from production; its assumption that acquisitions of income and wealth must be justified by entitlement; and its attribution of entitlement to the undifferentiated self.

Another reason has been found in moral law. Egalitarianism, it is said, only applies Kant's maxim, 'Act in such a way that you always treat humanity, whether in your own person or the person of any other, never simply as a means, but always at the same time as an end.' The conception of 'humanity as an end in itself' is a philosophic counterpart of what has been treated here as a sense of identity with, or fellow-feeling for, each and every human being, simply because he or she is such, as we ourselves are. Kant derived the conception from the nature of rational action, and from the ends given us by reason—the ultimate and inescapable conviction of our obligation to do what is right. He inferred an obligation to altruism.

As regards meritorious duties to others, the natural end which all men seek is their own happiness. Now humanity could no doubt subsist if everybody contributed nothing to the happiness of others but at the same time refrained from deliberately impairing their happiness. This is, however, merely to agree negatively and not positively with *humanity as an end in itself* unless everyone endeavours also, so far as in him lies, to further the ends of others. (Paton 1948; 91, 12)

But the difficulty arises here that our actual sense of identity does not extend nearly so widely as this obligation discerned by Kant, 'to further the needs of others'. The intuition of interchangeability, with its consequent impulse towards equal apportionment, varies in strength with the distance between those concerned. It is at its strongest within the family: it would be monstrous to enjoy a good dinner while one's own child sat beside one before an empty plate. We feel an obligation to help distressed people whom we know in our own neighbourhood. But most of us go on enjoying our dinners while children are starving, to our knowledge, but far away. There seems to be a kind of Newtonian principle, by which the strength of the moral law varies inversely with the distance (or the square of the distance?) between the persons concerned.

If we turn away from introspection to look at men and women as they are, rounded or angular in all their individuality, and each acquiring his or her income and wealth in the course of daily life, we open another avenue of explanation. We see human nature as endowed with the impulse 'to share and share alike' where that promotes survival. The strongest case of altruism is the devotion of a mother to her child; the strength of this throughout most of the animal kingdom shows how mankind has been selected towards the genetic transmisssion of the propensity. In recent years socio-biologists have shown the same process of selection at work to promote altruism of wider scope: animals that by giving warning of predation increase the chances of their own destruction but improve the chances of escape for other members of their group are increasing the chances of survival of the genes they carry in common with those other members. It seems that human beings are programmed to find self-interest in protecting and fostering some other beings. But who these beings are to whom we are tied depends upon the extent of our identification with them. Can we put ourselves in their place? We have remarked how our ability and propensity to do that vary with distance. The plight of the destitute far away moves us to action when television brings them as human beings into our own homes. Generally, the sense of obligation is compelling within the family, strong within neighbourhoods, and acknowledged within one's own country, where the taxpayer is willing to meet the costs of a social minimum. But this limitation by remoteness among human beings is sometimes accompanied by a sense of what it is like to be some animal, and a consequent obligation to advance its welfare at one's own expense. 'I believe all living things to be of equal value,' wrote Jan Morris; 'a human soul is no more precious, and no less, than the soul of a beetle or a bear. It follows that the rights of animals should be precisely the same as the rights of man' (*The Times*, 2 January 86). Shakespeare too felt for beetles:–

> And the poor beetle, that we tread upon,
> In corporal sufferance finds a pang as great
> As when a giant dies.
>
> (Measure for Measure, III, i, 75.)

What animals we feel for in this way is a matter of predilection. It seems to depend on the extent to which we identify ourselves with the animal: the owner of a terrier who incurs veterinary charges to restore it after an injury may look on with pleasure and approval when it savages a rat. The thoroughgoing vegetarian is as unwilling to kill any animal as a human being. What distinguishes the animal, after all, is its anima, its living core of feeling. The romantic form of humanism does not stop at the animal kingdom: Wordsworth proclaimed his

> faith that every flower
> Enjoys the air it breathes.

It is our capacity to realize what we should feel if we were in the place of other people, and thereby to identify ourselves with them, that accounts for the egalitarian's rejection of the inequality of the resources of indistinguishably sentient beings.

This identity is assumed in the very idea of social welfare, for this involves the adding together of some measure of the welfares of different people. The familiar argument for redistribution, that a pound taken from a rich person deprives him or her of less benefit than it brings to the poor person to whom it is transferred, implies that there is a sum of utilty that is raised thereby, and that this raising is a good thing. For whom? It can be only for the amalgam of the two persons. But personal attributes cannot always be added together: if Jack and Jill are walking arm in arm, it makes no sense to add the numbers of their limbs, and their ages, and say 'There goes a quadruped aged 42.' Then why add their utilities? It makes sense only if those two selves, Jack and Jill, are identical units of the common stuff of humanity.

On the view that has been put forward in these last paragraphs, the sense of identity that calls for fulness of life for all alike is a product of evolution, our forbears down the ages have been selected towards the propensity to protect others of their kind. The propensity asserts itself most strongly towards those who are most clearly and closely of one's own kind, the members of one's family and, next to them, the members of one's clan or tribe. It is experienced as natural affection, as philanthropy, patriotism, benevolence; the common element is fellow-feeling, the identification of oneself with other people and what they suffer. The strength of fellow-feeling usually diminishes with distance: there is felt to be something unnatural about a Mrs Jellaby who is greatly concerned with Borrioboola-Gha and neglects her own children. But humanism, and romanticism with its stress on the feelings of love and hate, joy and pain that are common to all humanity, lengthen the radius of identification to embrace all mankind.

If the corresponding sympathy extends to human beings everywhere, must it not also embrace posterity? A parent may well think that he or she ought not to lavish so many resources on an existing child that there will be little left for a child yet to be born. We are using up the planet's stock of fossil fuels at a rate that makes us comfortable but may confront our grandchildren with appalling difficulties. Why do we do it? Again, the factor of distance comes into play. We identify ourselves with others only within a certain radius.

Even within that radius, our sympathy is patchy in the areas it covers, and variable in the extent of beneficence that is held due. Not only is the nomination of beneficiaries a matter of personal choice, but how much those who are helped shall receive is decided variously in different times and places. The British people decided a hundred years ago that every child should receive free schooling, but the age at which that benefit ceases has been changed from time to time. The same electorate has decided to provide free hospital services for everyone—but not free medicine, or free dental service; free libraries—but not free television, or a free postal service; legal aid to people of modest means—but not grants to help them take a holiday. Non-contributory old age pensions were introduced in the United Kingdom in 1909, in the United States in 1966. The amount of aid that the West gives to the Third World varies from country to country as a proportion of the national product. Whether it is a question of who shall be aided or what aid shall be given, where we draw the line is at our discretion.

These considerations show that, in considering redistribution of income and wealth, we are dealing with the benevolence of those who give, and not with the rights of those who receive. To describe the claim that other people make on our sympathetic consideration as 'human rights' is a misnomer. A right is essentially justiciable. If I have a right to a certain payment for my work, I can at need go to court to have it enforced. 'Human rights' are not of that sort. It is true that when they are laid down by statute they become justiciable. If an Education Act lays on local authorities the duty to provide schooling for all the children in its area, then a parent who finds his children's school unnecessarily closed can seek an order against the authority. But before the Act was passed, the proposition that 'every child has a right to free schooling' was not a rule known to the courts. The provision of free schooling is an unrequited transfer, to which the basic priciple of 'like for like' in justice does not apply. The public may well believe, for a variety of reasons, that they are well advised to pay rates and taxes in order to make free schooling available to every child, but the child has no right to it in the sense that a worker has a right to his or her pay. The child has done nothing to deserve it. The mere fact of coming into existence, the community may hold, gives the child a claim on it; but this is a decision by the community to make a gift to the child, and not a return for some service that the child has rendered to the community. The rights that seem to be conferred by our common humanaity are actually conferred by the community at its discretion.

In fact, the term 'rights' is used in two quite different senses. There are rights to deny which is to inflict an injustice on the person concerned; the notion of what is due is then extended to what the community decides someone should be allowed. The extension is made the more readily because the decision of the community is often embodied in a statute, which confers rights of the first sort. To implement the first sort is an act of recompense; to implement the second is one of benevolence. The first sort is created by some antecedent action on the part of the holder, the second by the judgement of the community. The first sort is transferable, but the second is not. It is ultimately on the sanctity of property that the first sort rests; the second springs from fellow-feeling, and goes no farther than that feeling extends.

We have been considering the argument that our common humanity gives every human being an equal entitlement to a free and full life, and that the unequal distribution of income and wealth is consequently anomalous. We have found no entitlement; the claims of those who have less on those who have more arise, rather, from our own capacity to identify ourselves with others within a certain range and accept an obligation to help them, which has been implanted in us by the course of evolution.

18.5 The Advancement of the Less Advantaged

The preceding discussion has questioned the claim of egalitarianism to be a dominant precept of policy, but at the same time it has pointed the way to the reduction of inequalities. It has thrown light on how these inequalities arise, and why it is that many people—not only those who expect to gain from redistribution—have come to regard greater equality as a major object. The upshot has been that inequalities are a necessary outcome of freedom, and that the case for reducing them rests not upon justice, rightly understood, but upon the impulses of fellow-feeling. But this leaves a wide scope for action. Freedom is exercised through the market, but the market is imperfect; reducing the obstacles it imposes on disadvantaged people will reduce some inequalities. If the public wishes to redistribute a greater proportion of its incomes—and the removal of obstacles in itself often involves redistribution—the means of effecting it are available and practicable. The object of this section is to describe action along those lines.

The section might accordingly have been headed 'The reduction of needless inequality'. This would have been a fair description of the outcome of the action described, but in one way it would have been misleading. For the object of the action is not to diminish inequality for its own sake, but to improve the life-chances and enrich the lives of those whose lives as yet are most impoverished. The respects in which equality is good in itself are limited, and they do not include equality of income and wealth. The object of a national health campaign is to make unhealthy people well, not to equalize health—that could be done by making healthy people ill. Although the kind of action now to be considered sets out from the contrast between the life-chances of the prosperous and the needy, the thriving and the poorly, its object is the advancement of the disadvantaged, and not directly the reduction of contrast. The measures it requires are often possible only if the prosperous contribute to them, but the consequent reduction in inequality is a by-product which itself makes no one better off. Not many people would see virtue in an equality attained by making everyone equally poor.

The measures to be considered fall under two main heads: improvement of the market, and redistribution. Under the first head we shall consider the removal of discrimination and the advancement of equality of opportunity, together with the effect of both of these on social mobility.

Discrimination , we saw, may take place within or before the market. *Within* the market, it can be reduced by legal requirements; reducing discrimination *before* the market calls for deepgoing changes in social custom and practice. The effectiveness of anti-discriminatory legislation has been demonstrated by laws designed to eliminate discrimination within the market, against women in the United Kingdom and against non-whites in the United States.

The British Equal Pay Act of 1970 and the Sex Discrimination Act of 1975 both came into force at the end of 1975. The Equal Pay Act required employers to provide equal pay for 'like work': this was defined as the same work as a man was doing, or work 'broadly similar'. The comparison of a women's work with a man's was limited to men employed by the same firm. The possibility that discrimination might be maintained by separate agreements, or compartments of a job structure, covering men only or women only, was met by the provision that such arrangements might be referred to a Central Arbitration Committee. Individual women could enter their claims to Industrial Tribunals or the courts, and parties to collective agreements could take cases to the Central Arbitration Committee. There is no doubt that these provisions of the law have brought about marked changes in the position of employed women, changes in consideration as well as in pay. It is true that a good many employers conformed with the law outwardly without changing relative pay. A study of 26 organizations through 1974–77 by a team from the London School of Economics found that 'in over half the organizations, action was taken which reduced employers' obligations under the Equal Pay Act and resulted in women receiving less benefit than they otherwise would have done'—action such as 'the introduction or restructuring of grading systems such that women ended up on lower rates or grades regardless of their skill level'. None the less, the same investigators concluded that 'the implementation of equal pay resulted in considerable and sometimes dramatic narrowing of differentials between the basic rates of main groups of manual workers and non-manual women and those of men' (Snell et al. 1981: Summary).

The effect of the law was limited by the prevalence of job segregation—the traditional assignment of certain types of work exclusively to men, and other types to women. This made it hard if not impossible for women to cite 'like work' being done by men. One way out is to substitute for 'Equal pay for equal work' the principle, 'Equal pay for work of equal value'. This makes it possible to compare the work of a canteen cook with that of a fitter in the shops of the same firm, both jobs being assessed within a common system of job evaluation. As early as 1951, the basis of 'equal value' had been adopted in a Convention of the ILO, and it has since been endorsed by a directive of the EEC.

Another counter to segregation was provided by the Sex Discrimination Act. This outlaws discrimination both direct and indirect. Direct discrimination occurs when a woman is given less opportunity to take up certain work, or to gain promotion, than would be given to a man no better qualified. Indirect discrimination occurs when requirements are imposed on a job that are not needed for its adequate performance, and that women cannot meet as readily as men; it has been held, for instance, that to require applicants for a post to be not more than 28 years of age discriminates against women, who may be seeking to return to employment at a later age after raising a family. Further legislation has removed restrictions on the employment of women formerly imposed in order to protect them—the prohibition of night work, for example, or employment on certain supposedly dangerous or overtaxing work. The banning of non-essential reservations of occupations to one gender has had the effect of changing the wording when jobs are advertised; unless the nature of the work clearly requires that only one gender or the other can do it, the announcement can no longer call for male—or female—applicants. How much difference this has made to the way in which the place is filled in the event is another matter. If women can now apply where formerly they were not invited to, they may still be found less suitable than some male applicant. Much depends on customary attitudes, and these are tenacious. But the law may have done something to change them. In most of the organisations studied by the investigators just cited, job segregation continued, but there were some instances of a few women moving into what hitherto had been only men's jobs; there were also two instances of men moving into women's jobs.

Evidently, the raising of the relative pay of women continues to depend upon the opening of more sorts of jobs to them. A vicious circle obtains, whereby the closure of many avenues to women has discouraged girls from qualifying for them. The preparation of boys and girls for adult life has been adapted to existing job opportunities. Discrimination *within* the market is maintained by the crowding of women into certain occupations, by reason of discrimination *before* the market.

The latter sort of discrimination can be reduced only in so far as those customary practices are changed that deny girls the education and training that are provided for their brothers. This goes deep into the attitudes, the unexamined premises of actions, that are a main part of the social fabric. In particular, it depends upon the change in the generally held conception of the role of women, from which the disparate upbringing of girls followed naturally. That conception has been changing in Western societies . Whatever it is that IQ tests measure, women have been found to have as much of it as men, and that lays to rest an old presumption of masculine superiority. The strictures of St Paul carry less authority than they did. In two world wars women showed their ability to perform tasks that it was once thought only men could do. Pioneering women who made their mark in the professions and in business, as well as in public life, have demonstrated the capacity of their gender and dissipated some myths about the troublesomeness of its temperament. The career pattern in which a woman returns to paid employment after raising a family is ceasing to appear anomalous. But the change that is being brought about in these ways in the accepted role of women depends upon complementary changes in the accepted role of men. They have to take a much greater share in the household chores and the care of children. A man who is no longer the sole breadwinner cannot regard his own work and avocations as enjoying a natural priority over the claims of a home: if a child is ill, it will not always be the mother who must stay away from work; when both husband and wife return home in the evening, the husband will take his turn in getting the supper.

As attitudes and practice change in these ways, parents will come to see their daughters as needing as full a preparation for their working lives as do their sons. It is hard to see what measures there can be that will promote the change and so go to the heart of the problem of discrimination *before* the market. The Sex Discrimination Act takes the horse to the water but cannot make it drink: what selection boards or personnel managers decide still depends on their judgement of the suitability of individual applicants. This judgement is likely to be influenced by experience of the number of well qualified women applicants; the demand may be stimulated by the supply, and this in turn may be raised by financial and other encouragements to girls to follow courses of training for occupations into which few as yet have found their way. But again, this requires a change in the attitudes of the men, who will have to accept the unfamiliar presence of women as colleagues—and not seldom superiors , too.

Although we have been concerned here only with the reduction in the United Kingdom of discrimination against women, there has of course been a British programme of action also to reduce discrimination against ethnic minorities. How much can be effected in this way by legislation has been shown in the United States.

That the average income of non-white Americans has risen markedly relatively to that of whites since the 1950s is in part a matter of trend. The shift of non-whites from South to North has been associated with a progressive improvement in the education of nonwhite children, and a movement of nonwhite adults into higher paid occupations. But a rise in the rate of change in the 1960s suggests the impact of some new factor. Whereas the relative incomes of male non-whites had risen only modestly on the whole between 1949 and 1959, over the next ten years they rose markedly at all ages—for those aged 25–34, from 61 per cent of white incomes to 70 per cent. The relative incomes of non-white women had been rising more rapidly than the men's in the first period, but in the second they rose more rapidly still, and those in the 25–34 age group reached 95 per cent of white incomes by 1969 (Freeman 1973: Table 3). These rises cannot be accounted for by trend factors such as better education, or by the current cyclical movement of the economy. It is reasonable to attribute them in great part to the Civil Rights Act of 1964, which set up the Equal Opportunities Commission. These brought anti-discrimination into the South for the first time. In addition,

Executive Order 11246, which required federal contractors (who employ a significant proportion of the work force) to take 'affirmative action' in minority employment, and several voluntary programmes such as the Plans for Progress and the Natinal Alliance of Businessmen, were also initiated in the late sixties. Using boycotts, court cases and political pressure, civil rights groups, whose attention had shifted from school issues to the job market, further operated to raise the cost of discrimination. (Freeman 1973: 94)

Evidently, the legislative and administrative measures were effective because they were supported by a movement of public opinion, out of which indeed they arose. Not only did a body of white activists arise to denounce discrimination, but the predominant attitudes of the public had moved against it. The National Opinion Research Center reported the proportion believing 'that Negroes should have as good a chance as white people to get any kind of job' as 45 per cent in 1944 and 80 per cent in 1963 (Freeman 1973: 94, n. 19). Legislation was necessary to make the change of attitudes effective, and may well have carried it further, but without it could have done little. The sources of changes in attitude are complex; to discover them analytically would be a triumph of reasoned history. But we may note here how a movement, once begun, can stimulate itself; as the education of the lowly minority improves, and the gap between their way of life and that of the majority is narrowed, the discrimination that keeps them at a distance appears increasingly unreasonable.

The removal of discrimination provides greater opportunities for those whose advancement was obstructed; there are also positive measures that promote equality of opportunity. The principal source of the existing inequality lies in the preparation for their working life that children receive and young people can attain. Part of their capacity is determined genetically, but how far that inherited potential is developed depends upon their upbringing in the home, their schooling and their subsequent training.

The change made in the British people by compulsory and free elementary education has been described as a 'silent social revolution'. Since 1902 the opportunity to enter secondary education has been extended, by free places and the extension of the school-leaving age; and in more recent years a more limited number of subsidized or wholly free places has been provided in colleges and universities. But comparison with other countries, notably the United States and Germany, shows how inadequate is the British provision for education and training beyond the school-leaving age. Too few of the young people who could benefit from courses adapted to their interests and potential in those years are able to follow them. The barrier is partly the limited number of such courses, partly the lack of maintenance for the student in the absence of parental support. It is in these years that the greatest inequality of opportunity for the young arises from the inequality of their parents' ability or willingness to support them. But opportunity depends also on the availability of training on the job. What firms can afford to provide in this way depends on their ability to fund such training as a form of investment, and on the prospect of their retaining employees after trainiing. In both respects, Japanese firms have an advantage: they are not under such pressure to keep up their current distribution of profits in order to maintain a stock exchange quotation, and they can expect to retain a substantial core of their employees throughout their working lives. Elsewhere public support of education and training after the age of 16 may be supplemented by loans and cadetships. The local banker in an American town is able to make loans on the security of his personal knowledge of the young person. Indentured labour is outlawed, but firms able to support students in return for an undertaking, albeit unenforceable, to enter their service subsequently provide an alternative very much in the interest of young people as well as themselves. The American example shows the importance of the willingness of young people to 'work their way through college': the effective extent of opportunity depends in part on the sense of young people that they are expected to seize it. Once again, prevailing attitudes are decisive. Where there is a general belief that opportunities to qualify for advancement exist, and an expectation that young people will show their mettle by seizing them, the public will be more ready to support the needed courses, and a higher proportion of young people will pass through them.

But there are limits to what can be achieved to help the less advantaged children by the public provision of educational opportunity. The commonly cited contrast between privileged and under-privileged children implies that the difference between them stems from their parents' incomes; moneyed parents can buy educational advantages for their children that constitute a privilege because they cannot be afforded by the majority. There is force in this, even if private schools are not always better than state schools, especially at the primary level. But the proposal of some egalitarians to put an end to privilege by prohibiting the private purchase of education elevates a notion of 'fair competition' between members of the rising generation over the strong desire of parents, at every social level, to do the best they can for their own children. Once again, the family appears as an obstacle to equality. It is also because of the powerful influence of the family that the transfer of resources to provide an educational ladder accessible to every child does not achieve equality of opportunity. The formative influences on the child's development can only partly be provided outside the home. Within the home itself, moreover, they depend only partly on household income. This is illustrated by the contrast between the traditional 'son of the manse', brought up in a home where every penny must be watched but he is assured of his parents' devoted care and feels their expectations of him, and the 'poor litle rich girl', on whom luxuries are lavished but who sees little of her parents and is emotionally bewildered by the instability of her milieu. It is she who is deprived. The qualities that determine what use a child with given genetic endowment will make of its education depend upon the way in which it is treated by adults in the early years—how they play and talk with it and guide it, what assurance of affection they afford, what example they set.

It seems clear that a child's capacity to develop has been largely formed by its fifth year. Teachers meeting the intake into primary school are confronted with a range of potential, from the 'mentally dull and backward' to those who will learn readily and achieve distinction. Part of that difference is of genetic origin, but much is also due to upbringing in the home. How far the child's interests have been stimulated by the activtties provided for it, and its parents' own attention to it; the practice and encouragement they have given it by playing and talking with it; the emotional security and capacity for the development of personality that are instilled by stable and loving relationships—these are dominant influences not only in youth, but throughout life. The studies that have made these things clear are recent. That their significance has not been appreciated long since may be due to the adult proclivity to forget the experiences of early years, not least some of those that hurt most at the time. Little can be learned in this respect from the biographies of outstanding people, when so little is commonly recorded of the formative influences that in those first years did so much to shape their later way of life. Economists concerned with the calculus of welfare may regard an interest in those years as unprofessional; the notion that the quality of life in later years depends more on the moulding of personality in childhood than on the subsequent acquisition of marketable assets may seem eccentric. But the evidence stands. Once we lay aside our traditional notions of what is important, we see how much misery arises not from poverty but neurosis, how much illness is psychogenic, how much inability to associate and co-operate and how many outright disorders of conduct spring from the warping of emotions in those vulnerable years. Let us consider, on the other hand, how much of the quiet confidence of balanced characters, the ability to love and accept love, the capacity to work and enjoy it, is imparted by steady, active and affectionate relations with parents. It is now apparent that the extension of good practice in the upbringing of the 'under-fives' would greatly widen the possibilities of personal development and reduce a major present source of inequality.

Such an extension depends on a growth of understanding and the spread of information. The process is already at work, but the work is uphill. There seems to be a fatal propensity whereby, whether consciously or not, we treat our children as we were treated ourselves. In particular, 'cycles of deprivation' appear in which harmful practices of child upbringing, or neglect, are transmitted from generation to generation—whether or not this is associated with the genetic transmission of weaknesses. Good practice also tends to maintain itself by repetition in successive generations. There is one respect in which recent changes make it harder to maintain and extend that practice. The widening opportunities for the development of women's lives in work outside the home have stimulated a demand for a reduction of the claims that the care of children makes on the time and attention of the mother—for greater participation by the father, but also for the provision of creches, all-day nurseries and baby minding generally, such as has been publicly provided on a large scale in Sweden. It seems clear that children of two and three years of age cannot be treated in this latter way without emotional deprivation and disturbance. In the changing roles of parents and pattern of the family, it is hard but vital to work out a way of combining the enlargement of the lifechances of women with the contribution to the life-chances of the child that it lies in a mother to make.

In a discussion of equality of opportunity among professionals, there is a natural reluctance to consider matters of the nursery as deserving more than conversational mention. Certainly, they cannot be put through the professional machinery. But there is reason to believe that more can be done to reduce the sufferings and enrich the experience of grown men and women by improvements here than by the public provision for their welfare or further rises in their standards of living.

> How small, of all that human hearts endure
> That part which laws or kings can cause or cure!
> Still to ourselves in every place consigned,
> Our own felicity we make or find ...

That felicity, as Dr Johnson knew, depends on freedom from internal conflict, and on the unhampered flow of energies, interest and affection. The experiences of our earlier years profoundly affect our ability to attain it.

They are bound to be prominant in the discussion of the inequality of life-chances.

More equal opportunity will bring higher social mobility. This is by no means certain to bring greater equality of income and wealth; but people's feelings about inequality in their society depend very much upon the extent of social mobility within it. In the earlier discussion of the statistics of it, we noted that a society in which differences of income were wide but mobility was high might feel less unequal than one where differences of income were smaller but a larger proportion of young people had no prospect of rising about the level of their parents. In discussing the reasons for the comparative absence of socialism in the United States, we saw the importance of the American people's belief that theirs was peculiarly a land of opportunity, that is of high social mobility. The extent of this mobility is a factor of the first importance in the social structure of any country. It has been too little isolated and discussed. Its presence helps to explain why societies in which there are both rich and poor are not on that account always liable to disruption, as the Greeks thought they must be. One reason, we saw, is that Western societies are not made up of classes whose members have in common an amount of resources clearly differentiated from that held by other classes: instead, the Pen parade shows a continuous gradation, in both income and wealth. But over and above that, the economic stratification of society is effectively less rigid where social mobility is high. The life history of cohorts makes a different picture from a snapshot of the strata at any one time.

The fellow-feeling that we have also called altruism, benevolence and compassion operates widely and effectively to help the needy and thereby reduce inequality, in two ways: through private and voluntary action, and through public and statutory administration.

The biological function of altruism is clearest, and the impulse to help the needy strongest, within the family, which itself may be regarded in part as an arrangement developed for the support of the young, the aged and the unfortunate. As the radius of identification of self with others extends, the impulse weakens. The field of compassion is patchy: we feel more obligation to help those who resemble ourselves in some respects—as adherents, for example, of the same faith—than those who are no less needy and no more remote, but wholly strangers to us. None the less, private charity is extensive. If we could estimate the total flow of resources through it and within the family, it would surely reveal a great redistribution.

But private charity, and even to some extent the obligations of the family, are limited by the donors' sense of how much can be fairly expected of them, in comparison with other people. There is an old warning against making the willing horse bear all the burden. Those who feel the duty to contribute strongly often fix a certain percentage of their income as a reasonable limit. This can hardly be based on an assessment of one's own needs relatively to other people's, which are oceanic in their extent in comparison with one's own thimbleful. There must rather be a sense underlying it of what might be acceptable as a general rule, so that the donor gives as much as can be given without relieving other people of their obligation. This leads naturally to the organization of relief by government, which lays the obligation to fund it fairly on all taxpayers. This has been the practice since early times in local communities, even where local action has relied on nominally voluntary contributions; whether in the old collections at the church door or in more recent 'community drives', there has been a presumption that all should contribute in proportion to their means. But there have been other motives for substituting public for private action. Private charity may be inefficient, with its overlapping, its lack of consistency and its patchiness. The sense of solidarity, of fellowship throughout the occupants of a region, has been heightened by the biological view of society and, for a time at least, by war. As soon, moreover, as the interests of the community come to be considered as something distinct from those of the individuals who compose it at any one time, various forms of aid present themselves as an investment in maintaining and developing the community's health and strength. These factors have given rise to the welfare state throughout the Western world. Though countries differ in their attitudes towards it, and in the extent of the provision they make, they agree in devoting a substantial part of their budgets to maintaining a social minimum.

The case for the welfare state is overwhelming to those who remember some of the city streets, or the cottages in the villages, as they were before the First World War; or who today visit countries of the Third World where no such provision has been made. But there are limits to the extension of welfare, and reactions against it. It presupposes that the people of the country will accept the reasonableness of contributing; but fellow-feeling does not extend universally, and in any case the contributions are merged in a sum of taxation whose burden is resented. This resentment has mounted as the visible expenditure on welfare has grown. It has had an inherent tendency to grow, partly through the propensity of all administrative systems to become more cumbrous, partly through the response of the demand for social services to the supply. Public administration, it has been held, has its inefficiencies no less than private charity; rules of nationwide application are necessarily inflexible, and those who administer them cannot distinguish between the extent of need and desert case by case as, say the overseers of the poor in the old days could do at their best—using their personal knowledge and discretion. There is a danger, it has been alleged, of people looking too much to the system rather than to their own efforts for support, and of a weakening of the alternative support system provided by the customary ties of the family. There has followed a political reaction against the public provision of welfare.

Despite this check, that provision remains a staple function of the nation-state in the developed economies. Indeed, it is almost a definition of the nation-state that it is a form of government based on the fellow-feeling that constitutes a people or nation. The relief of want and the provision of benefits to the poorer households, together with the progressive taxation of the rich, have proved themselves effective in redistributing income and changing the face of inequality.

REFERENCES

AITCHISON, J., and BROWN, J. A. C. (1957), *The Lognormal Distribution*. Cambridge.

ARISTOTLE (1981), *Politics*, trans. T. A. Sinclair. London.

ARNOLD, E. V. (1911), *Roman Stoicism*. Cambridge.

ARNOLD, M. (1879), *Mixed Essays*. London.

ARNOLD T. (1832), *Thirteen Letters on our Social Condition* (place not stated).

ASHBY, M. K. (1961), *Joseph Ashby of Tysoe, 1859–1919*. Cambridge.

ASHENFELTER, O., and JOHNSON, G. E. (1972), 'Unionism, Relative Wages, and Labor Quality in US, Manufacturing Industries', *International Economic Review*, 13, 488–508.

ASTON, M. E. (1960), 'Lollardy and Sedition', *Past and Present*, 17, 11.

ATACK, J., and BATEMAN, F. (1981), 'The "Egalitarian Ideal" and the Distribution of Wealth in the Northern Agricultural Community: A Backward Look', *Review of Economics and Statistics*, 63, 124–9.

ATKINSON, A. B. (1970), 'On the Measurement of Inequality', *Journal of Economic Theory*, 2, 244–63; reprinted, with a non-mathematical summary, in Atkinson (1980), 23–43; reprinted, with a bibliography of related studies, 1970–82, in A. B. Atkinson, *Social Justice and Public Policy*, Brighton, 1983.

(1971), 'The Distribution of Wealth and the Individual Life-cycle', *Oxford Economic Papers*, 23, 239–54.

(1974), 'The Distribution of Wealth in Great Britain in the 1960s—the Estate Duty Method Re-examined', in Smith (1974).

—— (ed.) (1980), *Wealth, Income and Inequality* (2nd edn.). Oxford: University Press.

—— and HARRISON, A. J. (1974) 'Wealth, Distribution and Investment Income in Britain', *Review of Income and Wealth*, 20, 125–42.

—— (1978), *The Distribution of Personal Wealth in Britain*. Cambridge: University Press.

AVES, E. (1908), *Report on the Wage Boards and Industrial Conciliation and Arbitration Acts of Australia and New Zealand*, Cd. 4167. London: HMSO.

BAGEHOT, W. (1872), *The English Constitution* (2nd edn). London.

BAILYN, B. (1967), *The Ideological Origins of the American Revolution*. Cambridge, Mass. Harvard University Press.

BARLOW, R., BRAZER, H. E., and MORGAN, J. N. (1966) *Economic Behaviour of the Affluent*. Washington, DC.

BATEMAN, J. (1879), *The Great Landowners of Great Britain and Ireland*. London.

BECKER, C. (1922), *The Declaration of Independence*. New York.

BEDEAU, H. A. (1969), *Civil Disobedience*. New York.

BLACKSTONE, W. (1765–9), *Commentaries on the Laws of England*. Oxford.

BLAND, A. E., BROWN P. A., and TAWNEY, R. H. (1914), *English Economic History: Select Documents*. London.

BLAU, P. M., and DUNCAN, O. D. (1967), *The American Occupational Structure*. New York.

BLOCH, J. W. (1948), 'Regional Wage Differentials, 1907–46', *Monthly Labor Review*, 71, 371–7.

BLOOM, B. S. (1964), *Stability and Change in Human Characteristics*. New York.

BOURDEN, H. L., GABRIEL, R. H., and WILLIAMS, S. T. (1925), *Sketches of Eighteenth-Century America*. New Haven, Conn.

BOWLEY, A. L. (1933), 'The Actions of Economic Forces in Producing Frequency Distributions of Income, Prices and Other Phenomena: A Suggestion for Study.' *Econometrica*, 1 358–82.

—— (1944), *Studies in the National Income 1924–1938*. Cambridge.

BOWLEY, M. (1937), *Nassau Senior and Classical Economics* London.

BOWRING, J. (ed.) (1843), *Works of Jeremy Bentham*, Vol. 1. Edinburgh.

BOYD, C. W. (ed.) (1914), *Mr. Chamberlain's Speeches*. London.

BRAILSFORD, H. N. (1961), *The Levellers and the English Revolution,* ed. Christopher Hill. London.

BRITTAIN, J. A. (1978), *Inheritance and the Inequality of Material Wealth*. Washington, DC.

BRUCE, M. (1968), *The Coming of the Welfare State* (4th edn.) London.

BURCKHARDT, J. (1898), *The Civilisation of the Renaissance in Italy*, trans. S. G. C. Middlemore. London.

BURROW, J. W. (1966), *Evolution and Society: A Study in Victorian Social Theory*. Cambridge.

CANNAN, E. (1896), *The History of Local Rates in England*. London.

CARLYLE, A. J. (1903), *A History of Mediaeval Political Theory in the West*. Edinburgh and London.

CARLYLE, T. (1915), *English and Other Critical Miscellanies*. London and New York.

CAROL, A., and PARRY, S. (1968), 'The Economic Rationale of Occupational Choice', *Industrial and Labor Relations Review*, 21, 183–96.

CARRITHERS, D. W. (ed.) (1977), *The Spirit of Laws* (Thomas Nugent's translation of *De l'esprit des lois*). Berkeley, Cal.

Central Statistical Office (1983), *National Income and Expenditure, 1982*. London.

CHAMBERS, A. W. (1935), *Thomas More*, London.

CHAMPERNOWNE, D. G. (1953), 'A Model of Income Distribution', *Economic Journal*, 63, 318–51.

—— (1973), *The Distribution of Incomes between Persons*.

CLARK, C. (1937) *National Income and Outlay*. London.

COLE, M. (1945), *Beatrice Webb*. London.

COLLARD, D., LECOMBER, R., and SLATER, M. (1980) *Income Distribution: The Limits of Redistribution*. Bristol.

CONDORCET, M. J. A. N. C. (1970), *Esquisse d'un tableau historique des progrès d l' esprit humain*, ed. O. H. Prior. Paris.

CORNWALL, J. (1962–3), 'English Country Towns in the 1520s', *Economic History Review*, 15, 54–69.

—— (1970), 'English Population in the Early Sixteenth Century', *Economic History Review*, 23, 32–44.

COUNCIL OF ECONOMIC ADVISERS (1974), Annual Report, in *Economic Report of the President*. Washington, DC.

CREEDY, J. (1972), 'Economic Cycles in the Life of Individuals and Families', B. Phil. thesis, Oxford University.

_____ (1985), *Dynamics of Income Distribution*. Oxford.

and HART, P. E. (1979), 'Age and the Distribution of Earnings', *Economic Journal*, 89, 280-93.

CROSLAND, C. A. R. (1956), *The Future of Socialism*. London.

DANIELS, G. W. and CAMPION, H. (1936), *The Distribution of National Capital*. Manchester.

DAVENANT, C. (1771), *Political Arithmetick*, in Sir Charles Whitworth (ed.), *The Political & Commercial Works of the Celebrated Writer, Charles d'Avenant LL.D.* London.

DAVIES, J. B. (1978), 'The Impact of Inheritance on Lifetime Income Inequality in the United States', manuscript.

_____ (1979), 'On the Size Distribution of Wealth in Canada', *Review of Income and Wealth* 25, 237-59.

D'ENTRÈVES, A. P. (1948), *Aquinas: Selected Political Writings*. Oxford.

DE ROOVER, R. (1958), 'The Concept of Just Price: Theory and Economic Policy', *Journal of Economic History*, 18, 418-34.

DE STE CROIX, G. E. M. (1981), *The Class Struggle in the Ancient Greek World*. London.

DE TOCQUEVILLE, A. (1958), *Journeys to England and Ireland*, trans. G. Lawrence and K. P. Mayer. London.

DEPARTMENT OF EMPLOYMENT (1973), 'Low Pay and Changes in Earnings', *Department of Employment Gazette*, April, 335-48.

DINWIDDY, R., and REED, D. (1977), *The Effects of Certain Social and Demographic Changes on Income Distribution*. Royal Commission on the Distribution of Income and Wealth, Background Paper no. 3. London.

DOBSON, R. B. (1970), *The Peasants' Revolt of 1381*. London.

DOERINGER, P. B., and PIORE, M. J. (1971), *Internal Labor Markets and Manpower Analysis*. Lexington, Mass.

DOVER, K. J. (1974) *Greek Popular Morality in the Time of Plato and Aristotle*. Oxford.

DOWELL, S. (1884). *A History of Taxation and Taxes in England*. London.

DUNN, A. T., and HOFFMAN, P. D. R. B. (1983), 'Distribution of Wealth in the United Kingdom: Effect of Including Pension Rights and Analysis by Age-group' *Review of Income and Wealth*, 29, 243-82.

DURBIN, E. (1985), *New Jerusalems: The Labour Party and the Economics of Democratic Socialism*. London.

EARLE, P. (1977), *Monmouth's Rebels: The Road to Sedgemoor 1685*. London.

EDEN, F. M. (1797), *The State of the Poor*. London.

EDGEWORTH, F. Y. (1925), *Papers Relating to Political Economy*, Vol. 2. London.

_____ and BOWLEY, A. L. (1902), 'Methods of Representing Statistics of Wages and Other Groups not Fulfilling the Normal Law of Error', *Journal of the Royal Statistical Society*, 65, Pt. II, 325-54.

EHRMAN, J. (1983), *The Younger Pitt: The Reluctant Transition*, Vol. 2. London.

EMY, H. V. (1973) *Liberals, Radicals and Social Politics, 1892-1914*. Cambridge.

ENGELS, F. (1878), *Anti-Dühring: Herr Eugen Dühring's Revolution in Science*, trans. from 3rd German edn., 1894. Moscow.

FERGUSON, A. (1767). *An Essay on the History of Civil Society*. Edinburgh.

_____ (1773), *Institutes of Moral Philosophy* (2nd edn.). Edinburgh.

FINER, S. E. (1952), *The Life and Times of Sir Edwin Chadwick*. London and New York.

FITZMAURICE, E. (1895), *The Life of Sir William Petty 1623-87*. London.

FLETCHER, R. (1966), *Auguste Comte and the Making of Sociology*. London.

FLEW, A. (1981), *The Politics of Procrustes*. London.

FOGARTY, M. (1961), *The Just Wage*. London.

FONER, E. (1976), *Tom Paine and Revolutionary America*. New York.

FOSTER, M. B. (1942), *Masters of Political Thought*, Vol. I. London.

FREEDEN, M. (1978), *The New Liberalism*. Oxford.

FREEMAN, R. B. (1973), 'Changes in the Labor Market for Black Americans, 1948-72' *Brookings Papers on Economic Activity*, 1, 67-120.

GALSWORTHY, J. (1923), *A Commentary* (1st ed. 1908). London.

GARVIN, J. L. (1932), *The Life of Joseph Chamberlain*, Vol. I. London.

GEORGE, H. (1880), *Progress and Poverty*. New York.

GIBRAT, R. (1931), *Les Inégalités économiques*. Paris.

GIERKE, O. (1900), *Political Theories of the Middle Age*. Cambridge.

GLASS, D. V. (1954), *Social Mobility in Britain*. London.

GOLDTHORPE, J. H. (1980), *Social Mobility and Class Structure in Modern Britain*. Oxford.

_____ and HOPE, K. (1974), *The Social Grading of Occupations: A New Approach and Scale*. Oxford.

GOODWIN, A. (1970), *The French Revolution* (5th edn.). London.

GOTTSCHALK, L. R. (1927), *Jean-Paul Marat: a Study in Radicalism*. London.

GRAY, A. (1946), *The Socialist Tradition: Moses to Lenin*. London.

GREEN, F. C. (1955), *J. J. Rousseau: A Critical Study of his Life and Writings*. Cambridge.

GREENE, J. P. (1976), *All Men Are Created Equal: Some Reflections on the Character of the American Revolution*. Oxford.

GROSART, A. B. (ed.) (1876), *Prose Works of William Wordsworth*, Vol. I. London.

GRUBB, D. (1985), 'Ability and Power over Production in the Distribution of Earnings', *Review of Economics and Statistics*, 67, 188-94.

HAGEN, E. E. (1962), *On the Theory of Social Change*. Cambridge, Mass.

HALÉVY, É. (1928), *The Growth of Philosophic Radicalism*, trans. Mary Morris. London; reprinted 1962.

_____ (1948), *Histoire du socialisme Européen*. Paris.

HAMILTON, A., JAY, J. and MADISON, J. (1941), *The Federalist* (First Modern Library edn.) New York.

HAMICHE, D. (ed.) (1974), *J-P. Marat, Plan de Législation Criminelle*. Paris.

HARBURY, C. D. (1962), 'Inheritance and the Distribution of Personal Wealth in Britain', *Economic Journal*, 72, 845-68.

_____ and HICHENS, D. M. (1976), 'The Inheritances of Top Wealth Leavers: Some Further Evidence', *Economic Journal*, 86, 321-6.

_____ and HICHENS, D. M. (1977) 'Women, Wealth and Inheritance', *Economic Journal*, 87, 124-31.

_____ and McMAHON, P. C. (1973), 'Inheritance and the Characteristics of Top Wealth Leavers in Britain', *Economic Journal*, 83, 810-33.

HARDMAN, J. (1973), *French Revolution Documents*. Oxford.

HARE, R. M. (1973), 'A Critical Study of J. Rawls' *A Theory of Justice*', *Philosophical Quarterly*, 23, Pt. I, 144-55; Pt. II, 241-52.

HARRIS, J. (1757) *Essay upon Money and Coins*. London.

HARRISON, A. (1979), *The Distribution of Wealth in Ten Countries*. Royal Commission on the Distribution of Income and Wealth, Background Paper no. 7. London.

HART, P. E. (1975), 'A Cohort Analysis of Changes in the Distribution of Incomes, United Kingdom, 1963–73'. University of Reading Discussion Paper in Economics, Series A, no. 74.

——— (1981) 'The statics and dynamics of income distributions: a survey', in N. A. Klevmarken and J. A. Lybeck (eds.) *The Statics and Dynamics of Income*. Clevedon, Somerset.

HARVIE, C. (1984), 'Revolution and the Rule of Law (1789–1851)', in K. O. Morgan (ed.), *The Oxford Illustrated History of Britain*. Oxford.

HEATH, A. (1981), *Social Mobility*. London.

HENRETTA, J. A. (1973), *The Evolution of American Society, 1700–1815*. Lexington, Mass.

HERLIHY, D. and KLAPISCH-ZUBER, C. (1978), *Les Toscans et leurs familles*. Paris.

HEXTER, J. H. (1952), *More's Utopia: The Biography of an Idea*. Princeton, NJ.

HILL, C. (1972), *The World Turned Upside Down*. London.

——— (1974), *Change and Continuity in Seventeenth Century England*. London.

HILTON, R. (1973), *Bond Men Made Free: Mediaeval Peasant Movements and the English Rising of 1381*. London.

HIMMELFARB, G. (1952), *Lord Acton: A Study in Conscience and Politics*. London.

——— (1968), *Victorian Minds*. London.

——— (1974), *On Liberty and Liberalism: the Case of John Stuart Mill*. New York.

——— (1984), *The Idea of Poverty*. New York and London.

HOBBES, (1651). *Leviathan*.

HOBHOUSE, L. T. (1893), *The Labour Movement*. London.

HOLMES, G. S. (1977), 'Gregory King and the Social Structure of Pre-industrial England', *Transactions of the Royal Historical Society* Fifth Series, 27, 41–65.

HONORÉ, T. (1978), *Tribonian*. London.

HORSMAN, E. G. (1975), 'The Avoidance of Estate Duty by Gifts *inter vivos*: Some Quantitative Evidence', *Economic Journal*, 85, 516–30.

HOSKINS, W. G. (1935), *Industry, Trade and People in Exeter, 1688–1800*. University College of the South-West of England, History of Exeter Research Group, Monograph no. 6. Manchester.

——— (1963), *Provincial England*. London.

HUME, D. (1875), *Essays Moral, Political and Literary*, ed. T. H. Green and T. H. Grose (2 vols.). London.

——— (1955) 'Of Refinement in the Arts', in Eugene Rotwein (ed.), *Writings on Economics*. Edinburgh and London.

HUNT, E. H. (1973), *Regional Wage Variations in Britain, 1850–1914*. Oxford.

JANET, P. (1883), *Les Origines du socialisme contemporain*. Paris.

JEBB, R. (1904), *The Tragedies of Sophocles Translated into English Prose*. Cambridge.

JENYNS, S. (1767), *Thoughts on the Causes and Consequences of the Present High Price of Provisions*. London.

JONES, A. H. (1971), 'Wealth Distribution in the American Middle Colonies', OAH Conference Paper, New Orleans.

——— (1978), *American Colonial Wealth: Documents and Methods*, Vol. III. New York.

——— (1980), *Wealth of a Nation to Be*. New York.

JONES, E. (1978), 'Estimation of the Magnitude of Accumulated and Inherited Wealth', *Journal of the Institute of Actuaries*, 105, 131–75.

JOSEPH, K., and SUMPTION, J. (1979), *Equality*. London.

KAY, J. (later Sir James Kay-Shuttleworth) (1862), *Four Periods of Public Education*. London; reprinted 1973, Brighton.

KAY-SHUTTLEWORTH, J. (1964), *Autobiography*, ed. B. C. Bloomsfield. Education Libraries Bulletin, Supplement 7. London.

KING, M. A., and DICKS-MIREAUX, L-D. L. (1982), 'Asset Holdings and the Life-cycle', *Economic Journal*, 92, 247–67.

KINGSLEY, C. (1848), *Yeast: a Problem*. London.

KOTLIKOFF, L. J. and SUMMERS, L. H. (1981), 'The Role of Intergenerational Transfers in Aggregate Capital Accumulation', *Journal of Political Economy*, 89, 706–32.

KRIEGER, L. (1965), *The Politics of Discretion: Pufendorf and the acceptance of Natural Law*. Chicago.

KUZNETS, Simon (1955), 'Economic Growth and Income Inequality', *American Economic Review*, 45, 1–28; reprinted in his *Economic Growth and Structure*, London, 1966, 257–87.

LAKOFF, S. A. (1964), *Equality in Political Philosophy*. Cambridge, Mass.

—— (1967), 'Christianity and Equality', in J. R. Pennock and J. W. Chapman (eds.), *Equality*. New York.

LASLETT, P. (ed.) (1973), *The Earliest Classics: John Graunt and Gregory King*. London.

LAVISSE, E. (1920), Histoire de la France Contemporaine, vol. 1 by P. Sagnac Paris.

LAYARD, R., METCALF D., and NICKELL, S. (1977), 'The Effect of Collective Bargaining on Wages,' paper presented to IEA Conference on Personal Income Distribution, 18–23 April.

LECAILLON, J., PAUKERT, F., MORRISON, C., and GERMIDIS, D. (1984), *Income Distribution and Economic Development*. Geneva.

LEONARD, E. M. (1900), *The Early History of English Poor Relief*. Cambridge.

LEWIS, H. G. (1963), *Unionism and Relative Wages in the United States*. Chicago.

LINDBECK, A. (1983), 'Interpreting Income Distributions in a Welfare State: The Case of Sweden', *European Economic Review*, 21, 227–56.

LINDERT, P. H. (1973), 'Who Owned Victorian England?' Agricultural History Center, University of California at Davis, Working Paper no. 12.

—— and WILLIAMSON, J. G. (1982), 'Revising England's Social Tables 1688–1812', *Explorations in Economic History*, 19, 385–408.

—— (1980), 'English Occupations, 1670–1811', *Journal of Economic History*, 40, 685–712.

—— (1983a), 'Reinterpreting Britain's Social Tables, 1688–1913', *Explorations in Economic History*, 20, 94–109.

—— (1983b), 'English Workers' Living Standards during the Industrial Revolution: A New Look', *Economic History Review*, 2, 1–25.

—— (1985), 'Lucrens Angliae: The Distribution of English Private Wealth since 1670', Agricultural History Center, University of California at Davis, Working Paper no. 18.

LINDGREN, J. R. (ed.) (1967), *Early Writings of Adam Smith*. New York.

LIPSET, S. M. (1970), *Revolution and Counter-Revolution* (rev. edn.). New York.

—— (1979), *The First New Nation*. New York and Toronto.

—— (1986), 'North American Labor Movements: A Comparative Perspective', ch. 17 in S. M. Lipset (ed.), *Unions in Transition*. San Francisco.

LOCKE, J. (1690), *(First and Second) Treatise on Government: an Essay concerning the True Original, Extent and End of Civil Government*, in P. Laslett (ed.) (1967), *John Locke, Two Treatises of Government* (2nd edn.). Cambridge.

LYDALL, H. (1968), *The Structure of Earnings*. Oxford.

—— (1977), *Income Distribution during the Process of Development*. Research Working Paper WEP 2-33/WP 52. Geneva.

LYND, H. M. (1945), *England in the Eighteen-Eighties*. Oxford.

LYONS, P. M. (1945), 'Estate Duty Estimates and the Mortality Multiplier', *Economic and Social Review*, 6, 337-53.

MACAULAY, G. C. (1895), *Lord Berners's Translation of Froissart*. London.

MACAULAY, T. B. (1848), *History of England from the Accession of James the Second to the Death of William the Third*, Vols. I and II. London.

MACCAFFREY, W. T. (1975), *Exeter, 1540-1640: The Growth of an English County Town* (2nd edn.) Cambridge, Mass.

MACHIAVELLI, N. (1961), *The Prince*, trans. George Bull. Harmondsworth.

—— (1970), *The Discourses*, ed. Bernard Crick. Harmondsworth.

MACKENZIE, N., and MACKENZIE, J. (1977), *The First Fabians*. London.

MAIN, G. (1982) *Tobacco Colony*. Princeton, NJ.

MAIN, J. T. (1965), *The Social Structure of Revolutionary America*. Princeton, NJ.

MALONE, D. (1933), 'Thomas Jefferson', *Dictionary of American Biography*, Vol. X. Oxford.

MALTHUS, T. R. (1803), *Essay on Population* (2nd edn.) London.

—— (1960), *On Population*, ed. G. Himmelfarb. New York.

MARQUAND, D. (1977), *Ramsay Macdonald*. London.

MARSHALL, A. (1890) *Principles of Economics*. London.

—— (1897), 'The Old Generation of Economists and the New', *Quarterly Journal of Economics*, 11, 115-35.

MARTIN, W. J. (1949), *The Physique of Young Adult Males*, Memo. no. 20. London.

MATTHEW, H. C. G. (1973), *The Liberal Imperialists*. Oxford.

MAYER, T. (1960), 'The Distribution of Ability and Earnings', *Review of Economics and Statistics*, 42, 189-95.

McAULEY, A. (1977), 'The Distribution of Earnings and Incomes in the Soviet Union', *Soviet Studies*, 29, 214-37.

—— (1978), *Economic Welfare in the Soviet Union*. Madison, Wisconsin.

—— (1980), 'Social Welfare under Socialism: A Study of Soviet Attitudes towards Redistribution', in Collard *et al.* (1980).

McBRIAR, A. M. (1966), *Fabian Socialism and English Politics 1884-1918*. Cambridge.

McILWAIN, C. H. (1932), *The Growth of Political Thought in the West*. London.

McLELLAN, D. (1977), *Karl Marx, Selected Writings*. Oxford.

MEADE, J. E. (1964), *Efficiency, Equality and the Ownership of Property*. London.

—— (1973), 'The Inheritance of Inequalities: Some Biological, Social, and Economic Factors', *Proceedings of the British Academy*, 1973, 355-81; reprinted in Atkinson (1980, 239-53).

MEDNICK, S. A., GABRIELLI, W. F. Jun., and HUTCHINGS, B. (1984), 'Genetic Influences in Criminal Convictions: Evidence from an Adoption Cohort', *Science*, 224, 4651, 891-3.

MENCHIK, P. L., and DAVID, M. (1983), 'Income Distribution, Lifetime Earnings, and Bequests', *American Economic Review*, 73, 672-90.

MICHAL, J. M. (1972), 'Size Distribution of Earnings and Income in Czechoslovakia, Hungary and Yugoslavia', paper presented at the joint AEA-ACES meeting, Toronto, December.

_____ (1973), 'Size Distribution of Earnings and Household Income in Small Socialist Countries', *Review of Income and Wealth*, 19, 407-27.

MILL, J. S. (1848), *Principles of Political Economy*. London.

MILLAR, J. (1771), *The Origin of the Distinction of Ranks*. London.

MINEKA, F. E., and LINDLEY, D. N. (eds.) (1972), *The Later Letters of John Stuart Mill, 1849-73*, Vol. II. Toronto.

MIRER, T. W. (1979), 'The Wealth-Age Relation among the Aged', *American Economic Review*, 69, 435-43.

MITCHELL, B. R., and DEANE, P. (1962), *Abstract of British Historical Statistics*. Cambridge.

MONRO, C. H. (trans.) (1904), *Digest of Justinian*. Cambridge.

MOOKHERJEE, D., and SHORROCKS, A. F. (1982), 'A Decomposition Analysis of the Trend in United Kingdom Income Inequality', *Economic Journal*, 92, 886-902.

MORE, T. (1965), *Utopia*, trans. Paul Turner. Harmondsworth.

MORLEY, E. J. (ed.) (1927), *The Correspondence of Henry Crabb Robinson with the Wordsworth Circle*, Vol. I. Oxford.

MUSGRAVE, R. A., and PEACOCK, A. T. (1967), *Classics in the Theory of Public Finance*. London.

NASH, G. B. (1979), *The Urban Crucible*. Cambridge, Mass.

NATIONAL CONFERENCE OF CATHOLIC BISHOPS (1984), 'Catholic Social Teaching and the US Economy' (first draft) *Origins*, 14, 22/23.

_____ (1986), *Economic Justice for All*. Washington, DC.

NATRELLA, V. (1975), 'Wealth of Top Wealth Holders', paper presented to the 135th Annual Meeting of the American Statistical Association.

NEUMAN, M. (1972), 'Speenhamland in Berkshire', in E. W. Martin (ed.) *Comparative Development in Social Welfare*. London.

NICHOLLS, G. (1854), *History of the English Poor Law*. London.

OJA, G. (1983), 'The Distribution of Wealth in Canada', *Review of Income and Wealth*, 29, 161-73.

OKUN, A. M. (1975), *Equality and Efficiency: The Big Trade Off*. Washington, DC.

OWEN, R. (1920), *The Life of Robert Owen, by Himself*. London.

PAGLIN, M. (1975), 'The Measurement and Trend of Inequality: A Basic Revision', *American Economic Review*, 65, 598-609.

PAINE, T. (1796), *Agrarian Justice*. Philadelphia.

_____ (1937), *The Rights of Man*, ed. H. B. Bonner (first published 1792). London.

PALEY, W. (1785), *The Principles of Moral and Political Philosophy*. London.

PALLISER, D. M. (1979), *Tudor York*. Oxford.

PARETO, V. (1895), 'La Legge della demanda', *Giornale degli Economisti*, 10,2.

_____ (1896), *La Courbe de la Répartition de la Richesse*. Lausanne.

—— (1897), *Cours d'économie Politique*, ed. G. H. Bousquet and G. Busino. Geneva, 1964.

Parliamentary Papers (1834), Poor Law Commissioners' *First Report* (Vol. IX of *Reports from Commissioners*). Parliamentary Papers, Vol. XXVII. London.

—— (1841), *Handloom Weavers Report*. Parliamentary Papers (296), Vol. X. London.

—— (1876), Parliamentary Papers (335), Vol. LXXX. London.

—— (1920), *Enquiry into Wages and Conditions of Dock and Waterside Labourers*. Vol. I, *Report and Evidence*. Parliamentary Papers (179), Vol. XXIV. London.

PATON, H. J. (1948), *The Moral Law*, including Kant's *Groundwork of the Metaphysics of Morals*. London.

PAUKERT, F. (1973), 'Income Distribution at Different Levels of Development', *International Labour Review*, Aug.–Sept., 97–125.

PECHMAN, J. A. and OKNER, B. A. (1974), *Who Bears the Tax Burden?* Washington, DC.

PELLING, H. (1968), *Popular Politics and Society in Late Victorian Britain*. London.

PEN, J. (1971), *Income Distribution*, trans. T. S. Preston. London. The passage describing the parade is reproduced in Atkinson (1980: 23–43).

PERKIN, H. (1981), 'Who Runs Britain? elites in British Society since 1860', in *The Structured Crowd*, pp. 151–67. Brighton.

PHELPS BROWN, H. (1977), *The Inequality of Pay*. Oxford.

—— and HOPKINS, S. V. (1981), *A Perspective of Wages and Prices*. London.

PHYTHIAN-ADAMS, C. (1979), *Desolation of a City: Coventry and the Urban Crisis of the Later Middle Ages*. Cambridge.

PLATO (1941), THE REPUBLIC, trans. F. M. Cornford. Oxford.

—— (1970), *The Laws*, trans. T. J. Saunders. Harmondsworth.

POLE, J. R. (1978), *The Pursuit of Equality in American History*. Berkeley, Cal.

POLLARD, S. (1965), *The Genesis of Modern Management*. London.

POOR LAW COMMISSIONERS (1834), *First Report*. Parliamentary Papers, (Vol. IX of *Reports from Commissioners*). London.

POUND, J. F. (1966), 'The Social and Trade Structure of Norwich 1525–1575', *Past and Present*, 34, 49–69.

PRATT, J. (ed.) (1877), *The Acts and Monuments of John Foxe* (4th edn.). London.

PRIESTLEY, J. (1768), *An Essay on the First Principles of Government* (2nd edn. 1771). London.

PRIOR, G. H. (ed.) (1970), Condorcet's *Esquisse d'un Tableau Historique des Progrès de l'Esprit Humain*. Paris.

PRYOR, F. L. (1968), *Public Expenditure in Communist and Capitalist Nations*. London.

RAMSAY, J. H. (1892), *Lancaster and York, 1399–1485*. Oxford.

RASHDALL, H. (1909), 'John Wycliffe', entry in *Dictionary of National Biography*, Vol. XXI. London.

RASKIN, A. H. (1986), 'Labor: A Movement in Search of a Mission', in S. M. Lipset (ed.), *Unions in Transition*. San Francisco.

RAWLS, J. (1972), *A Theory of Justice*. Oxford.

REDER, M. W. (1968), 'The Size Distribution of Earnings', in J. Marchal and B. Ducros (eds.), *The Distribution of National Income*. London and New York.

—— (1969), 'A Partial Survey of the Theory of Income Size Distribution', in Lee Soltow (ed.), *Six Papers on the Size Distribution of Wealth and Income*, pp. 205–53. New York.

REVELL, J. R. S. (1965), 'Changes in the Social Distribution of Property in Britain during the 20th Century', 3rd International Conference of Economic History, Munich.

_____ (1967), *The Wealth of the Nation*. Cambridge.

_____ with ROE, A. (1971a), 'National Balance Sheets and National Accounting—A Progress Report', *Economic Trends*, 211, vii—xix.

_____ with ROE, A. (1971b), *The Financial Interdependence of the Economy*. Cambridge.

_____ with TOMKINS C. (1974), *Personal Wealth and Finance in Wales*. Cardiff.

RHODES, E. C. (1942), 'The Distribution of Incomes', *Economica*, 9, 245-56.

RICARDO, D. (1817), *Principles of Political Economy and Taxation*. London.

RISHØJ, T. (1971), 'Metropolitan Social Mobility, 1850-1950—The Case of Copenhagen', *Quality and Quantity*, 5, 131-41.

RITCHIE, D. G. (1887), *The Moral Function of the State*. London.

ROBBINS, L. C. (1952), *The Theory of Economic Policy*. London.

ROBERT, A., BOURLOTON, J., and COUGNY, G. (eds.) (1891), *Dictionnaire des Parlementaires Français (1er Mai 1789-1er May 1880)*. Paris.

ROBERTS, D. (1979), *Paternalism in Early Victorian England*. London.

ROGOFF, N. (1953), *Recent Trends in Occupational Mobility*. Glencoe, Ill.

ROSE, R. B.(1958), *Socialism and the French Revolution: the Cercle Social and the Enragés*. Manchester.

_____ (1978), *Gracchus Baboeuf, the First Revolutionary Communist*. Stanford, Cal.

ROUSSEAU, J-J. (1755), 'Économie politique', in the *Encyclopédie*. Paris.

_____ (1947), *Du contrat social*, ed. C. E. Vaughan. Manchester.

_____ (1959), *Oeuvres complètes*, Vol. I, ed. B. Gagnabin and M. Raymond. Paris.

_____ (1964), *Oeuvres complètes*, Vol. III, ed. B. Gagnabin and M. Raymond. Paris.

ROY, A. D. (1950a), 'The Distribution of Earnings and of Individual Output', *Economic Journal*, 60, 489-505.

_____ (1950b), 'A Further Statistical Note on the Distribution of Individual Output', *Economic Journal*, 60, 831.

ROYAL COMMISSION ON THE DISTRIBUTION OF INCOME AND WEALTH (1975), *Report No. 1, Cmnd. 6171*. London.

_____ (1977), *Report No. 5*, Cmnd. 6999. London.

_____ (1979), *Report No. 7*, Cmnd. 7595. London. HMSO.

RUBINSTEIN, W. D. (1977), 'The Victorian Middle Classes: Wealth, Occupation and Geography', *Economic History Review*, 30, 602-23.

_____ (1981), *Men of Property*. London.

RUSSELL, F. W. (1859), *Kett's Rebellion in Norfolk*. London.

SAHOTA, G. S. (1978), 'Theories of Personal Income Distribution: A Survey', *Journal of Economic Literature*, 16, 1-55.

SAMSON, L. (1974), 'Americanism as Surrogate Socialism', ch. 10 of J. H. M. Laslett and S. M. Lipset, *Failure of a Dream: Essays in the History of American Socialism*. New York. (First published in 1935.)

SANDFORD, C. T. (1971), *Taxing Personal Wealth*. London.

SCHENK, W. (1948), *The Concern for Social Justice in the Puritan Revolution*. London.

SCHOFIELD, R. S. (1965), 'The Geographical Distribution of Wealth in England, 1334-1649', *Economic History Review*, 18, 483-510.

SCHUMPETER, J. A. (1936), *The History of Economic Development*. Cambridge, Mass.

SCITOVSKY, T. (1966), 'An International Comparison of the Trend of Professional Earnings', *American Economic Review*, 66, 25–42. 'Les tendances des revenus des professions libérales: une comparaison internationale', *Analyse et Prévision*, 1, 177–206.

SELIGMAN, E. R. A. (1908), *Progressive Taxation in Theory and Practice* (2nd edn.). Princeton, NJ.

SHAW, G. B. (ed.) (1920), *Fabian Essays*. London.

SHEHAB, F. (1953), *Progressive Taxation*. Oxford.

SHORROCKS, A. F. (1975), 'The Age–Wealth Relationship: A Cross-section and Cohort Analysis', *Review of Economics and Statistics*, 57, 155–63.

SKINNER, A. S. (1979), *A System of Social Science: Papers relating to Adam Smith*. Oxford.

SMITH, A. (1759), *Theory of Moral Sentiments*. London.

———— (1776), *An Inquiry into the Nature and Causes of the Wealth of Nations*. London.

———— (1896), *Lectures on Justice, Police, Revenue and Arms*, ed. E. Cannan. Oxford.

———— (1963), *Lectures on Rhetoric and Belles Lettres*, ed. J. M. Lothian. Edinburgh and London.

———— (1978) *Lectures on Jurisprudence*, ed. R. L. Meek, D. D. Raphael and P. G. Stein. Oxford.

SMITH, F. (1923), *The Life and Work of Sir James Kay-Shuttleworth*. London.

SMITH, J. B. (ed.) (1974), *Personal Distribution of Income and Wealth*. New York.

SMITH, J. D., and FRANKLIN, S. D. (1974), 'The Concentration of Personal Wealth, 1922–1969', *American Economic Review*, 64, 162–7.

SMITH, T. V. (1927), *The American Philosophy of Equality*. Chicago.

SNELL, M. W., GLUCKLICH, P., and POVALL M. (1981), *Equal Pay and Opportunities*, Research Paper no. 20. London.

SOLTOW, L. (1975), *Men and Wealth in the United States, 1850–1870*. New Haven, Conn.

———— (1984), 'Wealth Inequality in the United States in 1798 and 1860', *Review of Economics and Statistics*, 66, 444–51.

SOUTHERN, R. W. (1970), *Medieval Humanism*. Oxford.

STAMP, J. (1916), *British Incomes and Property*. London.

STARK, T. (1977), *The Distribution of Income in Eight Countries*, Royal Commission on the Distribution of Income and Wealth, Background paper no. 4. London.

STEINDL, J. (1965), *Random Processes and the Growth of Firms*. London.

STEPHEN, L. (1909), *William Paley*. Dictionary of National Biography, Vol. XV. London.

STONE, L. (1966), 'Social Mobility in England, 1500–1700', *Past and Present*, 33, 16–55.

———— (1977), *The Family, Sex and Marriage in England 1500–1800*. London.

SURTZ, E. L. (1957), *The Praise of Pleasure: Philosophy, Education and Communism in More's Utopia*. Cambridge, Mass.

SZAKOLCZAI, G. (1980), 'Limits to Redistribution: The Hungarian Experience', in Collard *et al.* (1980).

TAWNEY, R. H. (1926), *Religion and the Rise of Capitalism*. London.

———— (1931), *Equality*. London.

THATCHER, A. R. (1968), 'The Distribution of Earnings of Employees in Great Britain', *Journal of the Royal Statistical Society* (A), 131, 133–80.

_____ (1971), 'Year to Year Variations in the Earnings of Individuals', *Journal of the Royal Statistical Society* (A), 134, Pt. 3, 374–82.

THEIL, H. (1967), *Economics and Information Theory*. Amsterdam.

THOMPSON, F. M. L. (1963). *English Landed Society in the 19th Century*. London and Toronto.

TOYNBEE, A. (1894), 'Progress and Poverty: A Criticism of Mr Henry George', in an appendix, separately published, to his *Lectures on the Industrial Revolution in Eighteenth Century England*. London.

TRENCHARD, J. and GORDON, T. (1754), *Cato's Letters* (4 vols). London.

UN, ECE (1967), *Incomes in Post-War Europe: Economic Survey of Europe in 1965*, Part 2. Geneva.

US Department of Labor (1969), *Wages and Related Benefits*. Part II: Metropolitan Areas, United States and Regional Summaries, 1967–68, *Bureau of Labour Statistics Bulletin*, no. 1575–87. Washington DC.

VAUBAN, Le Prêtre de (1933), *Projet d'une Dixme Royale*, ed. E. Coornaet. Paris.

VAUGHAN, C. E. (1962), *The Political Writings of J. J. Rousseau*. Oxford. (1st edn., Cambridge, 1915.)

VERBA, S. and ORREN, G. R. (1985), *Equality in America: the View from the Top*. Cambridge, Mass.

VERMES, G. (1981), *The Gospel of Jesus the Jew*. University of Newcastle-upon-Tyne; reprinted in his *Jesus and the World of Judaism*, London, 1983.

VLASTOS, G. (1981), *Platonic Studies*. Princeton, NJ.

WARNER, W. L. and ABEGGLEN, J. C. (1955), *Big Business Leaders in America*. New York.

WEARMOUTH, R. F. (1937), *Methodism and the Working Class Movements of England, 1800–50*. London.

WEBB, B. (1926), *My Apprenticeship*. London.

WEDGWOOD, J. (1929), *The Economics of Inheritance*. London.

WHALLEY, J. (1975), 'Estate Duty as a "Voluntary" Tax: Evidence from Stamp Duty Statistics', *Economic Journal*, 84, 638–44.

WHITE, B. B. (1978), 'Empirical Tests of the Life-cycle Hypothesis', *American Economic Review*, 68, 547–60.

WILLIAMSON, J. G., and LINDERT, P. H. (1980), *American Inequality, a Macroeconomic History*. New York and London.

WINTER, J. M. (1985), *The Great War and the British People*. London.

WOLFF, E. N. (1983), 'The Size Distribution of Household Disposable Wealth in the United States', *Review of Income and Wealth*, 29, 125–46.

WOODWARD, E. L. (1962), *The Age of Reform 1815–1870* (2nd edn.). Oxford.

WRIGLEY, E. A., and SCHOFIELD, R. S. (1981), *The Population History of England 1541–1871*. London.

WRONG, D. (1955), *American and Canadian Viewpoints*. Washington, DC.

YOUNG, G. M. (1936), *Victorian England: Portrait of an Age*. Oxford.

_____ (1962), *Victorian Essays*. Oxford.

YULE, G. U. and KENDALL, M. G. (1946), *An Introduction to the Theory of Statistics*. London.

INDEX